APPLETONS'

GENERAL GUIDE

TO THE

UNITED STATES

AND

CANADA.

WITH RAILWAY MAPS, PLANS OF CITIES, AND ILLUSTRATIONS.

**SIMON &
SCHUSTER**

London · New York · Sydney · Toronto · New Delhi

A CBS COMPANY

This edition first published in Great Britain by Simon & Schuster UK Ltd, 2016
A CBS COMPANY

Originally published in the United States of America in 1879

1 3 5 7 9 10 8 6 4 2

Simon & Schuster UK Ltd
1st Floor
222 Gray's Inn Road
London WC1X 8HB

www.simonandschuster.co.uk

Simon & Schuster Australia, Sydney
Simon & Schuster India, New Delhi

The author and publishers have made all reasonable efforts to contact
copyright-holders for permission, and apologise for any omissions or errors
in the form of credits given. Corrections may be made to future printings.

A CIP catalogue record for this book is available
from the British Library

Hardback ISBN: 978-1-4711-5994-7

Printed and bound in Germany by CPI Books GmbH, Leck

MIX
Paper from
responsible sources
FSC® C020471

Simon & Schuster UK Ltd are committed to sourcing paper that is made
from wood grown in sustainable forests and support the Forest Stewardship Council,
the leading international forest certification organisation. Our books displaying
the FSC logo are printed on FSC certified paper.

APPLETONS'

GENERAL GUIDE

TO THE

UNITED STATES

AND

CANADA.

WITH RAILWAY MAPS, PLANS OF CITIES, AND ILLUSTRATIONS.

PART I.

𝕹𝖊𝖜 𝕰𝖓𝖌𝖑𝖆𝖓𝖉 𝖆𝖓𝖉 𝕸𝖎𝖉𝖉𝖑𝖊 𝕾𝖙𝖆𝖙𝖊𝖘 𝖆𝖓𝖉 𝕮𝖆𝖓𝖆𝖉𝖆.

NEW YORK:

D. APPLETON AND COMPANY,

549 & 551 BROADWAY.

1879.

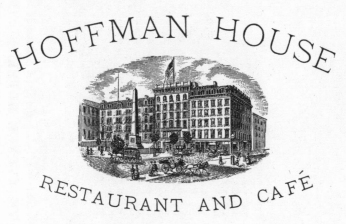

HITCHCOCK, DARLING & CO.   FIFTH AVENUE HOTEL.   MADISON SQUARE, NEW YORK.

THE FINEST HOTEL IN THE UNITED STATES.

LAKE GEORGE, NEW YORK.

FORT WILLIAM HENRY HOTEL,

T. ROESSLE & SON, Proprietors,

Also of "THE ARLINGTON," Washington, D. C.

Terms, $3.00 per day

ST. LOUIS HOTEL,

ST. LOUIS STREET, QUEBEC.

THIS HOTEL, WHICH IS

UNRIVALED FOR SIZE, STYLE, AND LOCALITY,

IN QUEBEC,

Is open throughout the Year, for Pleasure and Business Travel.

It is eligibly situated near to, and surrounded by, the most delightful and fashionable promenades—the Governor's Garden, the Citadel, the Esp'anade, the Place d'Armes, and Durham Terrace—which furnish the splendid views and magnificent scenery for which Quebec is so justly celebrated, and which is un-surpassed in any part of the world.

To Durham Terrace has been added what *will be* called Dufferin Terrace, an extension of *fourteen hundred feet*, with an average width of *eighty feet*, to a point directly under the flag-staff of the Citadel, with steps leading from the Terrace up to the inclosure of the Citadel, thus forming one of the finest prome-nades in the world, and being two hundred and fifty feet above the river.

The Proprietors, in returning thanks for the very liberal patronage they have hitherto enjoyed, inform the public that this Hotel has been *thoroughly reno-vated and embellished*, and can now accommodate about five hundred visitors; and assure them that nothing will be wanting on their part that will conduce to the comfort and enjoyment of their guests.

THE RUSSELL HOTEL COMPANY,

PROPRIETORS.

WILLIS RUSSELL, President.

Through the Highlands of the Hudson River by Daylight !

AFTERNOON BOAT

FOR

West Point, Cornwall, Newburgh, Poughkeepsie, Rondout, and Kingston,

LANDING AT

Cozzens's (Highland Falls), Milton, New Hamburgh, and Marlboro', by Ferry.

THE FAST STEAMBOAT

MARY POWELL,

Captain ANDERSON,

Will leave every Afternoon (Sundays excepted), from

VESTRY ST., PIER 39, NORTH RIVER, NEW YORK, at 3.30 P. M.,

(Adjoining Pennsylvania R. R. Ferry),

AFFORDING AN OPPORTUNITY FOR VIEWING

Cro' Nest, Storm King, and other Points of Historic Interest and Beauty.

The tourist by this line sees the Hudson Highlands "at the gloaming," the finest hour for Mountain and River Scenery.

CONNECTIONS.—*With Elevated Railways at Canal St. and Grand St. With* "*Brooklyn Annex*" *Boats. With* **Evening Trains on Hudson River R. R. at Poughkeepsie for the North.** *With Walkill Valley R. R. at Kingston. With Pennsylvania R. R. to and from Philadelphia.*

☞ Tickets sold and Baggage checked to all points on the *Ulster & Delaware Railway.*

NORTH.		SOUTH.	
Leave Brooklyn, foot Fulton St............	3 00 P. M.	Leave Rendout and Kingston............	5 30 A. M.
Leave New York, Vestry St...............	3 30 "	" Hyde Park.........................	6 00 "
" Cozzens's Hotel Dock...............	6 00 "	" Poughkeepsie....................	6 30 "
" West Point.......................	6 10 "	" Milton..........................	6 45 "
" Cornwall........................	6 30 "	" Marlboro' and New Hamburgh..	7 00 "
" Newburgh	6 45 "	" Newburgh.......................	7 30 "
" New Hamburgh and Marlboro'.....	7 15 "	" Cornwall........................	7 45 "
" Milton	7 30 "	" West Point.......................	8 05 "
" Poughkeepsie....................	7 45 "	" Cozzens's Hotel Dock.............	8 10 "
" Hyde Park.......................	8 00 "	Arriving in New York.................	10 45 "
Arriving at Rondout and Kingston........	8 30 "	Arriving in Brooklyn.................	11 00 "

Tickets sold and Baggage checked to all Points on the Route of the "Mary Powell," at Offices of Pennsylvania R. R. and North Penn. R. R. in Philadelphia.

Refreshments served at all hours, on the European Plan.

CARDS OF LEADING HOTELS.

By referring to the advertising pages of these Guides, the traveler will find advertisements giving full information of many of the leading Hotels, as also Bankers and others.

ALBANY, N. Y.

THE KENMORE,
Cor. West Pearl and Columbia Sts., is a fine hotel, on the European plan; *cuisine* not excelled in the city.
A. BLAKE, Proprietor.

BALTIMORE, MD.

MALTBY HOUSE,
Conducted on both American and European plans. Located in the commercial center of the city.
C. R. HOGAN, Proprietor.

BOSTON, MASS.

AMERICAN HOUSE,
Hanover Street. Prices reduced to $3.00 and $3.50 per day.
LEWIS RICE & SON, Proprietors.

CATSKILL N. Y.

PROSPECT PARK HOTEL.
First-class new Summer Hotel. A well-situated, well arranged, and well-conducted place of resort, of easy access, on the banks of the Hudson River, with all the latest improvements.
PROSPECT PARK HOTEL COMPANY.

CATSKILL MOUNTAIN HOUSE.
56th Season. 1824—1879. This famous Summer Hotel is situated on the Catskill Mountains, *eight miles west of the Hudson River*, and *twelve miles* from the village of Catskill, N.Y. Open June 1st to October 1st. *Great reduction in rates.* Send for circular.
C. L. BEACH, Proprietor, Catskill, N. Y.

LAKE GEORGE, N. Y.

FORT WILLIAM HENRY HOTEL.
This magnificent hotel has accommodations for 900 guests. $3 per day.
T. ROESSLE & SON, Proprietors.

NEW HAVEN, CONN.

MOSELEY'S NEW HAVEN HOUSE
Is by far the best hotel in the city, and one of the best in the country. Terms, $3.50 per day.
Mr. S. H. MOSELEY.

NEW YORK.

WINDSOR HOTEL.
Fifth Avenue, 46th and 47th Streets. A new and magnificent hotel; its location is delightful, being near the famous Central Park, and within three minutes' walk of the Grand Central Railway Station.
HAWK, WAITE & WETHERBEE,
Proprietors.

FIFTH AVENUE.
An imposing marble structure in Fifth Avenue, fronting Madison Square.
HITCHCOCK, DARLING & Co., Proprietors.

HOFFMAN HOUSE AND RESTAURANT, Madison Square—said by all travelers to be the best hotel in the world; its restaurant can not be surpassed.
C. H. READ, Proprietor.

OLD POINT COMFORT, VA.

THE HYGEIA HOTEL,
Situated within one hundred yards of Fort Monroe, with ample capacity for 600 guests. Open all the year.
HARRISON PHŒBUS, Proprietor.

PHILADELPHIA, PA.

SAINT GEORGE HOTEL,
Broad and Walnut Sts. Location the best; appointments and *cuisine* first class.
JNO. D. WARD, Proprietor.

LA PIERRE HOUSE,
Broad and Chestnut Streets, recently changed hands, remodeled and refurnished, with its superior location, is now the leading up-town hotel.
EDWARD A. GILLETT, Manager.

COLONNADE HOTEL,
Chestnut Street, cor. 15th, Philadelphia. Most desirably located, and adapted in all respects to the requirements of the best class of the traveling public.
H. J. & G. R. CRUMP.

GIRARD HOUSE,
Corner of Chestnut and 9th Streets, Philadelphia. J. M. KIBBIN.
Accessible by street-cars from all the depots.

GUION LINE.

United States Mail Steamers.

WYOMING	3,716 Tons.	MONTANA	4,320 Tons.
NEVADA	3,125 "	ARIZONA	5,300 "
WISCONSIN	3,720 "	UTAH (building)	5,300 "

☞ These Steamers are built of iron, in water-tight compartments, and are furnished with every requisite to make the passage across the Atlantic both safe and agreeable, having Bath-room, Smoking-room, Drawing-room, Piano, and Library; also, experienced Surgeon, Stewardess, and Caterer, on each Steamer.

The State-rooms are all on Deck, thus insuring those greatest of all luxuries at sea, perfect Ventilation and Light.

SAILING FROM

NEW YORK EVERY TUESDAY.

LIVERPOOL EVERY SATURDAY.

For Cabin, Intermediate, or Steerage Passage at Lowest Rates, apply to GUION & CO., 25 Water Street, Liverpool, or 7 Garrick Street, Covent Garden, London; J. M. CURRIE, Paris and Havre; WM. LANGTRY, Belfast; D. R. DAWSON, Dundee; JAS. SCOTT & Co., Queenstown; J. S. BAGSHAW, Manchester; WILLIAMS & GUION, New York; also to authorized agents in all the principal cities in the United States.

PREFACE.

THE leading idea which has governed the preparation of the following work has been to combine fullness and precision of information with the utmost attainable economy of space ; to present the information in such a manner as to be most easy of use ; to furnish such a Handbook for the traveler as will supply the place of a guide in a land where *couriers* or professional guides are unknown. All the important cities and great routes of travel in the United States and Canada are carefully and minutely described in it, and also every locality which is sufficiently visited for its own sake to entitle it to a place in such a work. At the same time it is believed that the book will be not less useful for what it excludes than for what it includes. Most previous guides have been either too sketchy and incomplete to be of any practical use, or have usurped the functions of a gazetteer—obtruding upon the traveler's attention multitudes of places and facts which can not possibly be either useful or interesting to him, and furnishing him with no test by which to discriminate between the noteworthy and the unimportant. In the present work the gazetteer plan has been deliberately discarded, and mention is made only of those places, facts, and items which are considered in some way interesting and worthy of attention.

The Editor desires particularly that his method in this respect shall be clearly understood. Small stations *en route* are often mentioned in order to indicate distances and rate of progress—in itself, frequently, a highly interesting item of information ; but, as a general rule, not only are merely local lines of travel and off-route places (unless attractive for special reasons) omitted entirely, but the tourist's attention is invited only to such things as are really worth attention, and the Editor has been much more anxious in describing a route to indicate the characteristic features of the

country traversed, and where fine views may be obtained, than to enumerate and describe all the little
stations at which the train may happen to pause. Nor
has he scrupled to devote more space to a famous mountain-view, to a bit of grand or exquisite scenery, to a
great achievement of nature or art, than to many cities which are important as regards population, commerce, and industry, but which possess no special interest for the traveler. In short, the standpoint is not
that of a gazetteer, but of the tourist, who cares little
for statistical or geographical data, but wishes to see
and learn about whatever is novel, picturesque, beautiful, memorable, striking, or curious.

The plan of the book, its arrangement and classification of matter, and the system of treatment, are
based on the famous Baedeker Handbooks, which are
conceded to possess in a preëminent degree the grand
desiderata of compactness, portability, and facility of
consultation. As much aid as possible is afforded to
the eye by printing the names of places and objects either
in italics, or, where they are of sufficient importance, in
bold-faced **black type.** Objects worthy of special attention are further distinguished by asterisks (*).

The Plans of Cities also follow the excellent Baedeker system of numbered and lettered squares, with
figures corresponding to similar figures prefixed to lists
of the principal public buildings, hotels, churches, and
objects of interest. This system will be found to add
very materially to the usefulness of the maps. The
Illustrations afford a trustworthy idea of American
architecture, and in a less degree of American scenery.

Great care has been taken to make the GUIDE accurate and fully up to date in its information ; in most
cases the descriptions of important places have been
submitted to the revision of a resident. Nevertheless,
in dealing with so many and diverse facts it is probable
that some errors have crept in and that there are some
omissions. The book will be subjected to a thorough
annual revision, and the Editor will be grateful for any
corrections and suggestions.

CONTENTS.

NEW ENGLAND AND MIDDLE STATES AND CANADA.

MAPS.

PLANS OF CITIES.

⁎ The present volume is the first half (but complete in itself) of "Appletons' General Guide to the United States and Canada," of which the second part, making a similar volume, is devoted to the Western and Southern States. Both parts are also published together in one compact and handy volume of about 520 pages.

THEODORE B. STARR,

(Of late firm STARR & MARCUS,)

206 Fifth Avenue, Madison Square,
NEW YORK,

*Importer of Diamonds, Pearls, and other Precious Stones, and Manu-
facturer of Rich Jewelry.   Entire originality and artistic beauty of
design, with the most skillful workmanship in the production of every
article, is one of the leading aims of this establishment.   Visitors,
whether with or without intention to purchase, are always welcomed
to an inspection of a stock which is one of the largest to be found in the
United States, and at moderate prices.*

WINDSOR HOTEL,

Fifth Avenue, 46th & 47th Sts., New York.

HAWK, WAITE & WETHERBEE, - - - Proprietors.

The Windsor is more magnificent and commodious, and contains more real comforts, than any other Hotel in America.

Its location is delightful, being surrounded by the most fashionable residences in New York; it is also near the famous Central Park and within three minutes' walk of the Grand Central Railway Station. The rooms, with all the modern improvements, are especially adapted for travelers; this Hotel also has elegant apartments, *en suite* for families, permanent or transient. The light, ventilation, and sanitary qualities, are perfect, and are not excelled by any Hotel on either continent. Its table is of unexceptionable excellence.

SAMUEL HAWK.   **CHARLES C. WAITE.**   **GARDNER WETHERBEE.**

INTRODUCTION.

I. Passports, Customs Duties, etc.

PASSPORTS are not required in the United States. The examinations of baggage at the ocean ports and the Canadian frontier are usually conducted in a courteous manner, but are at times very rigid; and the visitor from abroad will do well to include in his luggage only such articles as can be strictly regarded as of necessary personal use. The articles most watched for and guarded against by the customs authorities are clothing (new and in undue quantity), silks, linens, laces, cigars, watches, jewelry, and precious stones. In case of any portion of the luggage being found "dutiable," it is best to pay the charges promptly (under protest), and forward complaint to the Treasury Department at Washington.

II. Currency.

The present currency of the United States consists of gold and silver coin, and of U. S. Treasury notes (called "greenbacks") and national-bank bills redeemable in coin at par. In California gold alone is the standard of value, and silver is taken only at a discount. The fractional currency (which includes all sums below a dollar) is of silver, with nickel five-cent pieces, and copper pieces of the value of one and two cents. In Canada the currency is coin, or the notes of the local banks, which are at par. Foreign money is not current in the United States, but may be exchanged for the usual currency at the brokers' offices at fixed rates. For practical purposes, a pound sterling may be rated as equivalent to five dollars of American money, and a shilling as equivalent to twenty-five cents, or a "quarter." A franc is equivalent to about twenty cents of American money; five francs to a dollar.

III. Hotels.

The hotels of the United States have the reputation of being among the largest, finest, and best conducted in the world. In the larger cities there are two kinds: those conducted on what is called the American plan, by which a fixed charge includes lodgings and the usual meals at *table d'hôte;* and those conducted on the European plan, where the charge is made for lodgings alone, and the meals are taken *à la carte* in the hotel or elsewhere. At a few hotels the two plans are combined, and the traveler has his choice between them. The charge at first-class hotels (on the American plan) is from $3 to $5 a day; but good accommodations may be had at houses of the second class for $2 to $3 a day. A considerable reduction is usually made on board by the week. The charge for rooms at hotels on the European plan ranges from $1 to $3 a day. The "extras" and "sundries" which make European hotel-bills so exasperating are unknown in America; and the practice of feeing servants, though it has some slight and irregular observance, has never attained the force of custom. The best hotels at the various points are designated at their proper places in the body of the GUIDE; they are named in what the Editor believes to be the order of their reputation. At the larger hotels, besides a reading-room for the use of guests, there will nearly always be found a letter-box, a telegraph-office, and an office for the sale of railroad tickets.

IV. Conveyances.

The average cost of travel by *Railroad* is two to three cents per mile in the Middle States and New England, and from three to five cents in the Western and Southern States. Children between the ages of five and twelve are generally charged half price ; those under five are passed free. Between distant places which may be reached by competing lines there are usually what are called "through tickets," costing much less than regular mileage rates. These tickets are good only for the day and train for which they were purchased, and, if the traveler wishes to stop at any intermediate point, he must notify the conductor and get a "stop-over check." Attached to all "through trains" on the longer routes are Palace or Parlor cars, which are richly finished and furnished, provided with easy-chairs, tables, mirrors, etc., and, being mounted on twelve wheels, run much easier than the ordinary coaches. Those attached to the night-trains are so arranged as to be ingeniously converted into sleeping-berths, and are provided with lavatories in addition to the usual conveniences. From $2 to $3 a day in addition to the regular fare is charged for a seat or berth in these palace-cars, or a whole "section" may be secured at double rates. On a few of the more important lines have been placed what are called "restaurant and kitchen cars" (on the same plan as the palace-cars), where meals are served *en route* in first-class restaurant style. The average speed on express-trains is 30 miles an hour.

Travel by *Steamboats* is somewhat less expensive and less expeditious than by rail. The ticket (in case of a night-passage) gives the right to a sleeping-berth in the lower saloon; but the extra cost of a state-room (usually $2 per night) is more than compensated by the greater comfort and privacy. On the much-traveled lines, state-rooms should be secured a day or two in advance, and, if possible, in the outside tier. Meals are usually an extra on steamboats, and will cost about $1 each when the service is not *à la carte*.

The vast extension of the railway system has nearly superseded the old *Stages* and *Coaches*, but a few lines still run among the mountains and in remote rural districts. Where the object is not merely to get quickly from point to point, this is perhaps the most enjoyable mode of travel, and, in pleasant weather, the traveler should try to get an outside seat. The charges for stage-travel are relatively high—often as much as 10c. or 15c. a mile.

In all the cities and larger towns there are *Omnibuses* at the station on the arrival of every train, which connect directly with the principal hotels; a small charge (usually 50c.) is made for this conveyance.

V. Baggage—The Check System.

It is the custom in America to deliver baggage to a person known as the baggage-master, who will in return give a small numbered brass plate (called a " check ") for each piece, on presentation of which the baggage is delivered. Baggage may be " checked " over long routes in this way, and the traveler, no matter how many times he changes cars or vehicles, has no concern about it. The railroad company are responsible if the baggage should be injured or lost, the " check " being evidence of delivery into their hands. The traveler, arrived at the station or depot, should first procure his ticket at the ticket-office, and then, proceeding to the baggage-car or proper station of the baggage-master, have his trunks checked to the point to which he wishes them sent. (The baggage-master usually requires the traveler to exhibit his ticket before he will check the trunks.) Arriving at his destination, the checks may be handed to the hotel-porter, always in waiting, who will procure the various articles and have them sent to the hotel. Should the owner be delayed on the route, the baggage is stored safely at its destined station until he calls or sends for it (of course presenting the check). Beyond a certain weight (usually 80 or 100 lbs.) for each ticket bought, baggage is charged for extra; and this may become a serious item where the distances are great. Before arriving at the principal cities a baggage- or express-man generally passes through the cars and gives receipts (in exchange for checks) for delivering baggage at any point desired.

VI. Round-trip Excursions.

Every summer the leading railway companies issue excursion-tickets at greatly reduced prices. These excursions embrace the principal places of interest throughout the country, and are arranged in a graded series, so that the tourist may have choice of a number of round trips of a day or two to popular resorts near by, or may make one of the grand tours to distant points affording thousands of miles of travel. As the tickets are good for thirty, sixty, and ninety days, the traveler can consult his convenience *en route*, lingering or hastening on as he may happen to choose. Lists of these excursions and such information about them as may be required can be obtained at the central offices of the various companies in the larger cities, either by personal application or by letter.—Messrs. Cook, Son & Jenkins (with central office in New York) also issue excursion-tickets, the difference between their plan and that of the railway companies being that they arrange the tour to suit the wishes of the individual traveler. There is no affinity between this plan and the "personally conducted tours" which have made "Cook's Tourists" a-by-word throughout the world; it is, in fact, little more than an arrangement for enabling the economically minded traveler to save money on his railway-tickets and hotel-bills.

VII. Climate and Dress.

Of course in a country so extensive as the United States the differences of climate are very great, New England and the Middle States being frequently buried in snow at the very moment when the Southern States are enjoying their most genial season, while California has but two seasons (the wet and the dry) instead of the four seasons of the temperate zone. It is true of the country as a whole, however, that the summers are hotter and the winters colder than those of Europe; and that there is greater liability to sudden changes from heat to cold, or from cold to heat. For this reason it is highly important that the traveler should be dressed with sufficient warmth; it will be better for him to suffer at noonday from too much clothing than to expose himself at night, in storms, or to sudden changes of temperature, with too little. Woolen underclothing should be worn both summer and winter, and a shawl or extra wrap should always be on hand. At the same time, exposure to the vertical rays of the sun in summer must be carefully avoided; sunstroke being by no means unusual even in the Northern cities.

CORRECTIONS AND ADDENDA.

Since the GUIDE was sent to press the following changes and desirable additions have come to the knowledge of the editor :

Page XIV. (Introduction).—The firm of Cook, Son & Jenkins has ceased to exist. The business is now carried on at the same address (see advertisement) by *Thomas Cook & Son*, the original firm.

Page 1.—The *Hoffman House* is not at the cor. of 24th St., but on Madison Square, between 24th and 25th Sts.

Page 3.—The *New York Aquarium* is at the cor. of Broadway and 35th St. (*not* 45th St.).

Page 20 (Long Branch).—The name of the *Pavilion Hotel* has been changed to *Atlantic*. The *Central Hotel* is a new brick hotel near the railroad depot, open all the year round.

Page 27 (Philadelphia).—The *West End Hotel* has been closed.

Page 38 (Cape May).—A revised list of the hotels is as follows : The *Stockton House* and *Congress Hall* (each $4 a day), and the *Arlington House, Sawyer's Chalfonte, Windsor, Merchant's, West End, Arctic*, and *National* (each $3 a day).

Page 40 (Baltimore).—The *St. Clair Hotel* is closed. The *Maltby House* and the *Howard* charge a uniform rate of $2.50 a day.

Page 65.—The fare from Catskill to the *Mountain House* has been reduced to $2, and the charges at the *Mountain House* to $2.50 and $3 a day.

Page 68.—The *New Haven House* charges $3.50 instead of $4 per day.

Page 82.—The new *Providence Line* to Boston (leaving Pier 29, North River, at 5 P. M.) runs fine steamers, with excellent accommodations, and is one of the most popular routes between New York and Boston.

Page 178 (Lake George).—The *Fort William Henry Hotel* charges this season a uniform rate of $3 a day.

Page 239 (St. Lawrence River).—The Royal Mail Steamers leave Kingston daily at 5 A. M. (*not* 5.30 A. M.)

Page 291 (Chicago).—The *Grand Pacific Hotel* has reduced its prices to $3 and $3.50 a day.

Page 385 (Kansas Pacific R. R).—The Kansas Pacific R. R. has two termini on the Missouri River, one at Kansas City, and one at Leavenworth. The Leavenworth Branch joins the main line at Lawrence. At Kansas City 12 railroads converge, instead of 9.

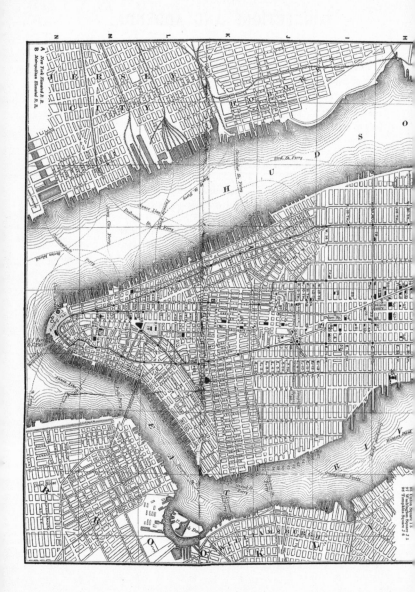

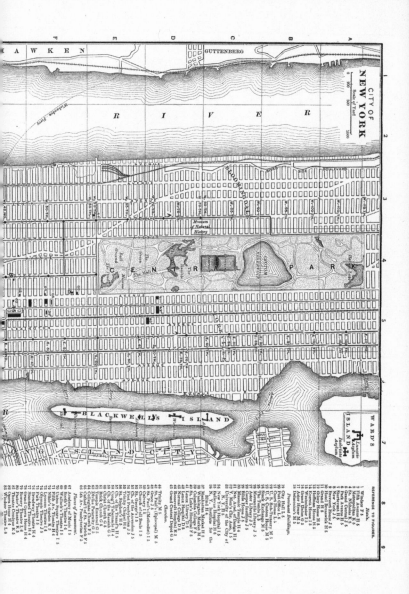

NEW ENGLAND AND MIDDLE STATES AND CANADA.

1. New York City.

Hotels.—Of the hotels conducted on the regular or American plan, the best are: the *Windsor* ($4 a day), a large and handsomely appointed house, cor. 5th Ave. and 46th St.; the *Fifth Avenue* ($4 a day), an imposing marble structure in 5th Ave., fronting Madison Square; the *Metropolitan* ($3 a day), a capacious brown-stone building, cor. Broadway and Prince St.; the *St. Nicholas* ($3 a day), a lofty marble edifice in Broadway, between Spring and Prince Sts.; the *Grand Central* ($3 a day), another towering marble building in Broadway, opposite Bond St.; the *Park Avenue Hotel* ($3 to $4 a day), a vast iron structure, cor. 4th Ave. and 32d St.; the *Sturtevant* ($2.50 to $3.50 a day), occupying the block on Broadway between 28th and 29th Sts.; the *St. Cloud*, cor. Broadway and 42d St.; and the *New York* ($3 a day), in Broadway, between Washington Place and Waverley Place. Of the hotels conducted on the European plan, among the best are the *Brevoort House*, cor. 5th Ave. and 8th St.; the *Hotel Brunswick*, cor. 5th Ave. and 26th St.; the *Grand Hotel*, cor. Broadway and 31st St.; the *Gilsey House*, cor. Broadway and 29th St.; the *Hoffman House*, cor. Broadway and 24th St.; the *Everett House*, cor. 4th Ave. and 17th St.; the *Westminster*, cor. Irving Place and 16th St.; the *Clarendon*, 4th Ave. and 18th St.; the *Grand Union*, opposite the Grand Central Depot; and the famous old *Astor House*, in Broadway, opposite the Post-Office. The charges for rooms range from $1 to $3 a day, with meals *à la carte* in the house or elsewhere. The *Buckingham* (cor. 5th Ave. and 50th St.), the *Rossmore* (cor. Broadway and 42d St.), and the *Gramercy Park House* (between 20th and 21st Sts., facing the beautiful Gramercy Park), are excellent family hotels. Among the cheaper hotels, frequented by business men, the most desirable are the *Merchants'*, *Western*, *Cosmopolitan*, *French's*, *Leggett's*, *Earle's*, the *Brandreth House*, and the *United States*, all situated in the lower portion of the city. There are upward of 150 other hotels of all grades; and board and lodging may be obtained at boarding-houses in all parts of the city at from $7 to $15 per week—for which consult advertisements in the *New York Herald*.

Restaurants.—*Delmonico's*, cor. 5th Ave. and 26th St., is one of the best restaurants in the world, and is famous for its elaborate dinners. The *Café Brunswick*, also at the cor. of 5th Ave. and 26th St., is admirably appointed and has an excellent *cuisine*. *Clark's*, at the S. W. cor. of Broadway and 18th St.; *Parker's*, in Broadway near 34th St.; *Bigot's*, 14th St., Union Square; *St. Denis*, cor. Broadway and 11th St.; *Purssell's*, 910 Broadway; and the *Metropolitan*, cor. Broadway and Prince St., are all of excellent repute, and places where ladies or families may dine. The *cafés* and restaurants attached to the large hotels on the European plan are generally well kept, and are much visited by ladies; among the best of these are the *Hoffman House* (cor. 24th St. and Broadway), the *St. James* (cor. Broadway and 26th), and the *Astor House* (in Broadway near the Post-Office). *Delmonico's*, at 112 and 114 Broadway; *Rudolph's*, at 162 Broadway; *Mouquin's*, Ann St. near Nassau St.; *Nash's*, in Park Row opposite the City Hall Park; and *Sieghortner's*, 32 Lafayette Place, are first-class restaurants for gentlemen. There are a number of restaurants where excellent *table-d'hôte* dinners may be got from 5 to 6 P. M., for from 75c. to $1, the latter price usually including wine; of these may be mentioned *Philippe's*, 19 University Place; *Jacques's*, 54 W. 11th St.; *University Hotel*, University Place—all near Broadway. There are also English chop-houses,

1

so called, where a first-rate grill may be obtained; of these "*Old Tom's*" (near rear
of Trinity Church), *Farrish's* (64 John St.), and *Black's* (Manhattan Lunch), 493
Broadway, are noted. Oysters in every variety may be found in the small saloons
in Fulton Market; and an oyster supper at *Dorlon's* used to be one of the characteristic New York experiences, and is still popular. *Martinelli's* (35 E. 17th St.,
Union Square) has the Italian *cuisine*, and is visited by many artists.

Modes of Conveyance.—Wherever they run in the city the favorite mode
of transit is by the new *Elevated Railways.* The Metropolitan (or Gilbert) Elevated Railway runs cars from Rector St. (in rear of Trinity Church) to Central
Park, with stations at Rector St., Cortlandt, Park Place, Chambers, Franklin,
Grand, Bleecker, 8th, 14th, 23d, 33d, 42d, 50th, and 58th Sts. Other cars of the
same road run down 53d St. to 9th Ave., and pass up town on the tracks of the N.
Y. Elevated Railway; and the East Side Div. to Harlem is in process of construction. The cars are luxurious, and drawn by small locomotives. The N. Y. Elevated Railway (West Side Branch) runs from South Ferry *via* Greenwich St.
and 9th Ave. to 83d St., with numerous stoppages. The East Side Branch runs
from South Ferry to Harlem Bridge, with branches to the Grand Central Depot,
the City Hall, and 34th St. Ferry. (Fare on either line, 10c.; between the hours
of 5 and 7 morning and evening, 5c.) The principal lines of *Horse-cars* start from
the vicinity of the Astor House, and traverse the city from end to end on both the
east and west sides. Besides these there are several cross-town lines, running from
river to river. Fare on most of the lines, 5c. The *Omnibuses* (called "stages")
start from South, Wall St., and Fulton Ferries, and run up Broadway as far as 23d
St., whence one line diverges west to Hudson River R. R. Depot at 30th St. and
9th Ave.; another up Madison Ave. to Grand Central Depot; another up 5th Ave.
from 14th St. Fare, 5c. The *Hackney-coaches* have stands in different parts of
the city, and attend the arrival of every train and steamboat. A tariff of fares is or
ought to be hung in each carriage, but the drivers frequently try to practice extor-
tion. In such cases, appeal should be made to a policeman. Disputed questions
as to time, distance, or price, must be settled at the Mayor's office (City Hall).
The legal rates are, for 1 or more passengers for a distance of 1 m. or less, $1; for
more than 1 m. and not more than 2 m., $1.50; for more than 2 m. and not exceed-
ing 3 m., $2; for more than 3 m. and not exceeding 4 m., $2.50; for more than 4 m.,
75c. a mile; by the hour, stopping as often as may be required, $1. The principal
hotels have carriages in waiting for the use of guests; they may be engaged at
the clerk's desk.

Railroad Depots.—The *Grand Central Depot*, in 42d St. between 4th and
Madison Avenues, is used by most of the passenger trains of the New York Central
& Hudson River R. R., and also by the New York & Harlem and New York
& New Haven Railroads. Some trains of the Hudson River R. R. leave the old
depot at Tenth Ave. and 30th St. The depot of the *Pennsylvania R. R.* (in Jersey
City) is reached by ferries from foot of Desbrosses and Cortlandt Sts.; the *Erie*
(also in Jersey City) from foot of Chambers and W. 23d Sts.; the *Jersey Central*
from foot of Liberty St.; the *Delaware, Lackawanna & Western* (Morris &
Essex), from foot of Barclay and Christopher Sts.; the *Midland R. R.*, same as the
Pennsylvania; the *New Jersey Southern* from foot of Liberty St.; the *Long Island
R. R.* and the *Flushing R. R.* from James Slip and foot of E. 34th St.

Ferries.—There are ferries to *Brooklyn* from foot of Broadway, Wall St., Fulton St., and Catherine St.; to the Eastern District of Brooklyn (Williamsburg) from
foot of Roosevelt St., Grand St., and E. Houston St.; to *Greenpoint* from foot of
10th and E. 23d Sts.; to *Hunter's Point* from James Slip and foot of E. 34th St.
To *Harlem* from Piers 22 and 24 East River, near Fulton Ferry. To *Jersey City*
from foot of Liberty St., Cortlandt St., Desbrosses St., Chambers St., and W. 23d
St. To *Hoboken* from foot of Barclay and Christopher Sts. To *Staten Island*
from foot of Whitehall St (two lines). To *Weehawken* from foot of W. 42d St.
To *Mott Haven* from Peck Slip. To *Astoria* from Pier 22 East River. To *Blackwell's Island* from foot of E. 26th St.

Churches.—There are nearly 500 churches of all denominations in the city, and
at any of them the visitor is sure of a polite reception. The following are the principal of those whose Sunday services are most attended by strangers: Trinity
Church (Episcopal), in Broadway, opposite Wall St., with cathedral choral service;
Trinity Chapel (Episcopal), 25th St., near Broadway; St. George's (Episcopal), in
Stuyvesant Square, E. 16th St.; Grace Church (Episcopal), Broadway, near 10th St.,
fine music; and St. Alban's (Ritualistic), cor. Lexington Ave. and 42d St. Of the

Roman Catholic churches the Cathedral of St. Patrick (cor. Mott and Prince Sts.), and St. Stephen's (149 E. 28th St., famed for its impressive musical services) are most attended. The Presbyterian churches of Dr. John Hall (cor. 5th Ave. and 55th St.) and the Brick Church (5th Ave. and 37th St.) are very popular; also the Methodist Church of St. Paul's (cor. 4th Ave. and 22d St.—very fine); the Unitarian Church of All Souls (Dr. Bellows, cor. 4th Ave. and 20th St.), and of the Messiah (cor. Park Ave. and 34th St.); the Universalist Church of the Divine Paternity (Dr. Chapin, cor. 5th Ave. and 45th St.); the Congregational Tabernacle (cor. Broadway and 34th St.); the Reformed Dutch Collegiate Church (cor. 5th Ave. and 29th St.); the Church of the Disciples (Rev. W. R. Davis, cor. Madison Ave. and 45th St.); the Swedenborgian Church (Rev. Chauncey Giles, 114 E. 35th St.); the Moravian (cor. Lexington Ave. and 30th St.); and the Church of the Strangers (Dr. Deems, Neilson Place, near 8th St.). The Sabbath (Saturday) services of the Jewish Temple Emanuel (5th Ave., cor. 43d St.) are very impressive, and the interior decorations of the building remarkably rich. The newspapers on Saturdays usually give lists of the place and time of the most important services of the ensuing Sunday.

Theatres and Amusements.—The *Academy of Music,* in 14th St., cor. Irving Place, a short distance E. of Broadway, is the home of Italian Opera in New York, and is also used for balls and large public gatherings; the auditorium is richly decorated in crimson and gold. *Booth's Theatre,* perhaps the finest in America, is at the corner of 23d St. and 6th Ave. *Wallack's Theatre,* home of the legitimate comedy, is at the corner of Broadway and 13th St.; its company is always good, and the plays are mounted with great care. The *Union Square Theatre* (S. side Union Square, between Broadway and 4th Ave.), and the *Fifth Avenue Theatre* (in W. 28th St., a few doors from Broadway) are small but fashionable theatres at which light comedy or melodrama is usually exhibited. Other theatres devoted to no special class of entertainments are : *Niblo's Garden,* Broadway, near Prince St.; *Lyceum Theatre,* 14th St., a few doors W. of 6th Ave.; *Olympic Theatre,* 622 Broadway; *Park Theatre,* Broadway, between 21st and 22d Sts.; the *Broadway Theatre,* cor. Broadway and 30th St.; the *Standard Theatre,* cor. Broadway and 33d St.; and the *Grand Opera House,* cor. 23d St. and 8th Ave. The latter is one of the finest theatres in the city, but being "too far west" is more seldom used than those nearer Broadway. The *Bowery Theatre* (in the Bowery, near Canal St.), presents popular melodrama of the most pronounced type; and *Tony Pastor's Theatre* (587 Broadway) and the *Théâtre Comique* (514 Broadway) are devoted to varieties. Negro minstrelsy is usually found at the *Opera House,* cor. Broadway and 29th St. The *Windsor Theatre,* in the Bowery, near Canal St., is devoted to variety entertainments. *Steinway Hall,* in 14th St., near Broadway, and *Chickering Hall,* cor. 5th Ave. and 18th St., are the principal concert and music halls. The favorite lecture-hall is *Association Hall,* cor. 4th Ave. and 23d St. *Gilmore's Garden* (also called the Hippodrome), cor. 4th Ave. and 26th St., is used for summer concerts, circuses, shows, sports, etc. The *New York Aquarium,* cor. Broadway and 45th St., has an interesting collection of rare animals and fishes, and occasionally offers dramatic performances.

Still another class of places of amusement is that known as "Gardens," of which the *Atlantic Garden,* adjoining the Bowery Theatre, is the best known. It is a great hall where, in the evening, several thousand Germans come with their families to listen to well-executed vocal and instrumental music. As a rule, however, the Gardens are located in the upper part of the city, near the rivers; or in Hoboken and Jersey City. The cellar concert-saloons in the Bowery and elsewhere should be carefully avoided, as they are both disreputable and dangerous. *Horse-races* at Jerome Park, the most aristocratic race-course in America (see page 152); at Fleetwood Park, half a mile beyond Macomb's Dam Bridge, on the Harlem River; and at the Prospect Park and Deerfoot tracks, near Brooklyn (reached by horse-cars from Fulton Ferry).

Reading-Rooms.—In all the chief hotels there are reading-rooms for the use of guests, supplied with newspapers from all parts of the country. The *Astor Library* (in Lafayette Place near 8th St.) contains 180,000 volumes, and is open to visitors from 9 A. M. to 5 P. M. The *Cooper Institute* (cor. 4th Ave. and 8th St.) has a fine reading-room, open to all from 8 A. M. to 10 P. M. The *City Library* (in the City Hall) is free to all from 10 A. M. to 4 P. M. The *Young Men's Christian Association* has free reading-rooms at 4th Ave. cor. 23d St.; at 161 5th Ave.; at cor. 3d Ave. and 122d St.; at 285 Hudson, 69 Ludlow, and 97 Wooster St.—all open from 8 A. M. to 10 P. M. The *Mercantile Library* (Astor Place near Broad-way) has an excellent reading-room to which strangers are admitted on introduction by a member.

Art Collections.—At the *National Academy of Design* (cor. 4th Ave. and 23d St.) there are annual exhibitions of recent works of American artists (entrance, 25c.). The *Metropolitan Museum of Art* (5th Ave. and 82d St.) has a fine collection of paintings by the old masters, and usually has on exhibition other collections loaned by the wealthy *virtuosi* of the city, including pictures by American artists, statuary, pottery and porcelain-ware, arms and armor, coins and medals, antique and mediæval curiosities, and various articles of *vertu*. It also contains the famous Cesnola Collection of Cypriote Antiquities. On Mondays, admission to the museum is free; on other days, 25c. At the rooms of the *Historical Society* (cor. 11th St. and 2d Ave.) is a fine gallery of paintings with many old portraits, the Abbott Collection of Egyptian Antiquities, the Lenox Collection of Nineveh Sculptures, etc. There are usually pictures on exhibition (free) at the sales-galleries of *Goupil*, cor. 5th Ave. and 22d St.; *Schaus*, 744 Broadway; and *Avery*, 88 Fifth Ave. Many artists' studios may be found in the Young Men's Christian Association Building, cor. 4th Ave. and 23d St.; the Kurtz Art Building, Madison Square and 23d St.; the University, Washington Square; and the Studio Building, 51 W. 10th St. The best private collections in the city are those of Mrs. A. T. Stewart, Marshall O. Roberts, James Lenox, August Belmont, Lucius Tuckerman, John Hoey, John Wolfe, R. L. Stuart, Robert Hoe, and R. L. Cutting. Admission to these may generally be obtained by sending a letter (inclosing card) to their owners.

Clubs.—The most prominent city clubs are the *Century*, 109 E. 15th St.; the *Knickerbocker*, 5th Ave. cor. 28th St.; the *Manhattan*, 5th Ave. cor. 15th St.; the *Union*, cor. 5th Ave. and 21st St.; the *Union League*, cor. Madison Ave. and 26th St.; the *Lotos*, 149 5th Ave.; and the *Army and Navy Club*, 28 W. 30th St. Admission to these is obtained only by introduction by a member.

Post-Office.—The General Post-Office, at the southern end of City Hall Park, is open continuously, except Sundays, when it is open only from 9 to 11 A. M. There are also 13 sub-post-offices in the city, called "Stations," and alphabetically named; these are open from 6.30 A. M. to 8 P. M.; on Sundays, from 8 to 10 A. M. Letters may also be mailed in the lamp-post boxes (of which there are 700), whence they are collected many times daily by the letter-carriers.

NEW YORK CITY, the commercial metropolis of the United States, and largest city of the Western Hemisphere, is situated at the mouth of the Hudson River on New York Bay, in latitude about 41° N. and longitude 71° W. from Greenwich (3° 1' 13″ E. from Washington). It occupies the entire surface of Manhattan Island; Randall's, Ward's, and Blackwell's Islands in the East River; Bedloe's, Ellis's, and Governor's Islands in the Bay, used by the United States Government; and a portion of the mainland north of Manhattan Island and separated from it by Harlem River and Spuyten Duyvel Creek. The extreme length north from the Battery is 16 miles; greatest width from the Hudson to the mouth of Bronx River, 4¼ miles; area, nearly 41½ square miles, or 26,500 acres, of which 12,100 acres are on the mainland. Manhattan Island, on which the city proper stands, is 13½ miles long, and varies in breadth from a few hundred yards to 2¼ miles, having an area of nearly 22 square miles. The older portion of the city below 14th St. is somewhat irregularly laid out. The plan of the upper part includes avenues running N. to the boundary of the island, and streets running across them at right angles from river to river. The avenues are numbered from the east to 12th Ave.; east of 1st Ave. in the widest part of the city are Aves. A, B, C, and D. Above 21st, between 3d and 4th Aves., is Lexington Ave., and above 23d St., between 4th and 5th Aves., is Madison Ave.; 6th and

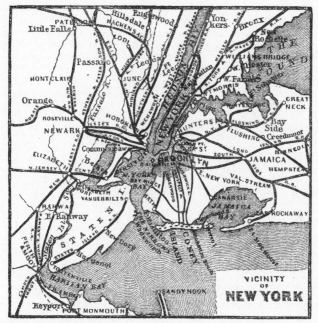

VICINITY
OF
NEW YORK

7th Aves. are intersected by Central Park. The streets are numbered consecutively N. to 225th St., at the end of the island ; 21 blocks,
including streets, average a mile. The house-numbers on the avenues
run N. ; those on the streets E. and W. from 5th Ave. The city is
compactly built to Central Park, about 5 miles from the Battery, and
on the E. side for the most part to Harlem, $3\frac{1}{2}$ miles farther. Manhattanville (8 m.) and Carmansville (10 m.) on the W. side are populous
villages. Distances are calculated from the City Hall. At Fort Washington and above are many handsome country residences.

The harbor of New York is one of the finest and most picturesque
in the world. The outer bar is at Sandy Hook, 18 miles from the Battery, and is crossed by two ship-channels, either of which admits vessels of the heaviest draught. On the steamers from Europe the American coast is usually first sighted at the line of the Navesink Highlands,
or off Fire Island Light, and the bar is crossed soon after. As the
steamer enters the Bay and sails through the Narrows, between the
villa-crowned shores of Staten and Long Islands, on the left are seen
the massive battlements of *Fort Richmond* and *Fort Tompkins ;* while
opposite, on the Long Island shore, are *Fort Hamilton* and old *Fort
Lafayette,* the latter more famous as a political prison than as a fort-

ress. Passing amid these imposing fortifications, the panorama of city
and harbor rapidly unfolds itself. To the left is Bedloe's Island, the
proposed site of the colossal statue of Liberty which France is to present to New York ; Ellis's Island, with a fort, stands still farther toward
the Jersey shore ; and to the right is Governor's Island with *Castle William* and old *Fort Columbus.* Directly ahead, the city opens majestically to the view, with Brooklyn on the right and Jersey City on the left.

The site of New York is said to have been discovered by Verrazzani, a Floren-
tine mariner, in 1524 ; but authentic history begins with the visit of Henry Hudson,
an Englishman in the service of the Dutch East India Company, who arrived there
Sept. 3, 1609. Hudson afterward ascended the river as far as the site of Albany,
and claimed the land by right of discovery as an appanage of Holland. In 1614 a
Dutch colony came over and began a settlement. At the close of that year the future metropolis consisted of a small fort (on the site of the present Bowling Green)
and four houses, and was known as New Amsterdam. As late as 1648 it contained
but 1,000 inhabitants. In 1644 it was surrendered to the British, and, passing into
the hands of the Duke of York, was thenceforward called New York. In 1667 the
city contained 384 houses. In 1700 the population had increased to about 6,000. In
1696 Trinity Church was founded. In 1711 a slave-market was established in Wall
Street ; and in 1725 the *New York Gazette* was started. The American army
under Washington occupied the city in 1776 ; but after the battles of Long Island
and Harlem Heights, it was captured by the British forces, and remained their
headquarters for 7 years. The British troops evacuated the city Nov. 25, 1783.
Within ten years after the War of Independence, New York had doubled its population. In 1807 the first steamboat was put on the Hudson ; the completion of the
Erie Canal followed in 1825 ; and since that time the growth of the city has been
rapid. Its population in 1800 was 60,489 ; it was 123,706 in 1820, 515,847 in 1850,
812,869 in 1860, 942,377 in 1870, and 1,041,886 in 1875. It is estimated that there are
1,500,000 persons in New York at noon on every secular day. Commerce and industry have kept pace with the population. In 1870 there arrived at this port 14,587
vessels from the American coast, and 4,688 from foreign ports. In 1876 the imports
were $199,025,371, and the exports $279,097,186. More than half the foreign commerce of the United States is carried on through the customs district of which this
is the port, and about two thirds of the duties are here collected, the whole amount
for the year ending June 30, 1874, being $160,522,284.63, of which $109,549,790.79
was collected in the New York district. The manufactures of New York, though
secondary in importance to its commercial and mercantile interests, are varied and
extensive. In the value of products, according to the census of 1870, it is the first
city in the Union, though surpassed by Philadelphia in the value of materials used,
amount of capital invested, and number of establishments. The whole number of
manufacturing establishments in 1870 was 7,624, employing 129,577 hands, and
producing goods valued at $332,951,520.

The * **Battery** is a pretty little park at the southern extremity of
the city, looking out upon the Bay, adorned with fine trees and verdant lawns, and protected by a massive granite sea-wall. It was the
site of a fort in the early years of the city, and later was surrounded
by the residences of the wealthy, being then the fashionable quarter.
The round brick structure at the S. W. end is *Castle Garden*, the depot
for immigrants, who are received here from their ships and given such
aid and information as they require. Just E. of the Battery is *Whitehall St.*, at the foot of which are the South and Hamilton Ferries to
Brooklyn, and the ferries to Staten Island. Here converge the two
branches of the N. Y. Elevated Railway, and several omnibus and
horse-car lines. *South St.*, beginning here, follows the East River
shore for over 2 miles, passing the East River piers and the Long
Island ferries, while *West St.* skirts the shore of the Hudson (or North)

River for 2 miles, passing the North River piers and the ferries to the Jersey shore. The large building at the corner of Whitehall and Pearl Sts. is the *Produce Exchange.* Just N. of the Battery, at the foot of Broadway, is **Bowling Green,** the cradle of New York ; in the times of the Dutch it was the court end of the town, and was surrounded by the best houses. The row of six buildings facing the Green on the S. side covers the site of the old Dutch and English fort. The *Washington House*, No. 1 Broadway, built in 1760 by the Hon. Archibald Kennedy, then collector of the port, is one of the most interesting antiquarian relics now left standing in New York. In colonial times it was the heart of the highest fashion of the colony, having been successively the residence and headquarters of Lords Cornwallis and Howe, General (Sir Henry) Clinton, and General Washington. Talleyrand also lived there during his stay in America. Benedict Arnold occupied No. 5 Broadway, and in Clinton's headquarters his treasonable projects were concerted. Fulton (inventor of the steamboat) died in a room in the present No. 1 Marketfield St. ; it was then (1815) used as a boarding-house.

Passing up **Broadway** from the Green, between continuous rows of large warehouses and offices, in a short time * **Trinity Church** towers up on the left, with its beautiful spire 284 ft. high. It is in the Gothic style, of solid brownstone, and is 192 ft. long, 80 wide, and 60 high. It has rich stained-glass windows and the finest chime of bells in America. The *Astor Memorial Reredos*, in the chancel, is one of the richest and costliest in the world ; it is 33 ft. wide and nearly 20 high, its materials being marble, glass, and precious stones, with statuary, the most delicate and elaborate carving, and the richest mosaics. It was erected in 1878 at a cost of upward of $100,000. The Trinity Parish is the oldest in the city ; its first church was built in 1696 and destroyed by fire in 1776 ; its present edifice was begun in 1839 and consecrated in 1846. The church is open all day ; there are prayers twice daily (at 9 A. M. and 3 P. M.), and imposing choral services on Sunday. The graveyard surrounding the church is one of the most picturesque spots in the city. It occupies nearly two acres of ground, is embowered in trees, and contains many venerated tombs—among them those of Alexander Hamilton, Captain Lawrence (the hero of the "Chesapeake"), Robert Fulton, and the unfortunate Charlotte Temple. In the N. E. corner is a stately Gothic monument erected to the memory of the patriots who died in British prisons at New York during the Revolution. The * view from the lookout in the spire is exceedingly fine, and is accessible at any hour of the day (308 steps ; small fee).

Beginning directly opposite Trinity Church, **Wall St.,** the monetary center of the country and resort of bankers and brokers, runs to the East River. One block down (at the corner of Nassau St.) is the * **U. S. Sub-Treasury,** a stately white marble building in the Doric style, 200 ft. long, 80 wide, and 80 high. The main entrance on Wall St. is reached by a flight of 18 marble steps, and in the interior is a lofty Rotunda 60 ft. in diameter and supported by 16 Corinthian columns (visitors admitted from 10 to 3 o'clock). The old Federal Hall used to stand on this site, and the spot is classic as that whereon Washington delivered his first inaugural address as President. On the opposite corner is the handsome *Drexel Building*, of white marble in the Renaissance style; and a little farther S. on Broad St. are the *Gold Room* and * *Stock Exchange*. A visit to the Strangers' Gallery of the Stock Exchange during business hours (10 to 3 o'clock) is well worth making. On Wall St. below the Treasury (at the cor. of William St.) is the * **U. S. Custom-House,** built in 1835 as the Merchants' Exchange and famous for the great granite plinths of the columns that support the pediment of the front elevation. It is of massive Quincy granite, with a depth of 200 ft., a frontage of 144 ft., and a rear breadth of 171 ft. Its height to the top of the central dome is 124 ft. Beneath this dome, in the interior of the building, is the Rotunda, around which are eight lofty columns of Italian marble, the superb Corinthian capitals of which were carved in Italy. They support the base of the dome and are probably the largest and noblest marble columns in the country (open to visitors from 10 to 3 o'clock). Below the Custom-House on either side are a number of fine buildings; and from the foot of Wall St. a ferry runs to Montague St., Brooklyn. *Pearl St.*, crossing Wall just beyond the Custom-House, is the seat of a heavy wholesale trade in cotton and other staples. *Nassau St.*, one of the busiest in the city, extends from Wall St. (past the old Post-Office) to Printing-House Square.

Continuing from Wall St. our saunter up Broadway, the massive granite building of the *Equitable Life Ins. Co.* (cor. Cedar St.) first attracts attention. It is mingled Doric and Renaissance in style, and is one of the most solid and substantial structures in the city. Just above, at the corner of Liberty St., is the six-story building of the *American Bank-Note Co.*, surmounted by a tower containing a clock; and on the other side of Broadway, at the cor. of Dey St., is the building of the *Western Union Telegraph Co.*, ten stories high (including three in the roof), with a clock-tower 230 ft. high. The junction of Broadway and Fulton St. is the place of all others to see what Dr. Johnson calls "the full tide of human life"; from morning to night it presents a struggling throng of vehicles and pedestrians. To the E. *Fulton St.* runs through an active business quarter to *Fulton Ferry ;* to the W. it leads to the *Washington Market*, which is well worth visiting, especially on Saturday morning. Externally it is a collection of unsightly sheds, but within it presents an unequaled display of fruits, vegetables, meats, fish, etc. At the S. E. corner of Fulton St. is the lofty *Evening Post* building, and on the next block (adjoining each other on the same side of Broadway) are the *Park Bank* and *New York Herald* buildings, both of white marble. **St. Paul's Church** (Episcopal), on the other side of the way, is a venerable structure, built in 1776, and standing in the midst of a graveyard in which are monuments of great interest. The pediment of the façade contains a white marble statue of St. Paul, and below is a monument (mural tablet) of General Montgomery. Immediately above (on the left) is the long and severely simple front of the historic *Astor House*, opposite and on each side of which most of the

horse-car lines have their termini. Opposite the Astor House, at the S.
end of the City Hall Park, is the new * **Post-Office,** an imposing
granite building of Doric and Renaissance architecture, 4 stories high,
besides a Mansard roof, with a front of 279 ft. toward the Park, and
of 144 ft. toward the south, and two equal façades of 262½ ft. on Broad-

Post-Office.

way and Park Row. It is fire-proof, and cost $7,000,000. The upper
floors are for U. S. Courts. The *City Hall*, in the Park, N. of the
Post-Office, is a pleasing structure in the Italian style, 3 stories high,
with front and ends of white marble and rear of brownstone. It is
216 ft. long by 105 ft. deep, with Ionic, Corinthian, and composite
pilasters lining its front, and surmounted by a cupola containing a
four-dial clock which is illuminated at night by gas. It was erected
from 1803 to 1812, at a cost of $500,000, and is occupied by the
Mayor, Common Council, and other public officers. The Governor's

Room, in the second story, contains the writing-desk on which Washington wrote his first message to Congress, the chairs used by the first Congress, the chair in which Washington was inaugurated first President, and a number of portraits of American worthies, mostly by eminent artists. It has also a very fine portrait of Columbus. N. of the City Hall is the new * **Court-House,** which was commenced in 1861, and has been occupied since 1867, but it is not yet completed. It is a massive edifice in the Corinthian style, three stories high, 250 ft. long and 150 wide, and the crown of the dome is to be 210 ft. above the sidewalk; the walls are of white marble; the beams, staircases, etc., are of iron; while black walnut and pine are employed in the interior decoration. The main entrance on Chambers St. is reached by a flight of 30 broad steps, which are flanked by massive marble columns. The cost of the building and furniture was over $12,000,000, the result of the notorious "Ring frauds," of which it was the instrument.

On the E. side of the City Hall Park is *Printing-House Square*, where are the offices of most of the daily and many of the weekly newspapers. Fronting the Square on the E. is the * **Tribune Building,** the loftiest on the island. It is built of red pressed brick, granite, and iron, is absolutely fire-proof, and has a clock-tower 285 ft. high, with four dials. On the N. is the stately granite building of the **Staats-Zeitung,** with statues of Gutenberg and Franklin above the portal; and on the S. are the more modest quarters of the *N. Y. Times.* In front of the *Times* office stands a bronze statue of Franklin, of heroic size. A few squares E., on Franklin Square, is the extensive publishing-house of the *Harpers.* Leading northward from Printing-House Square are *Centre St.*, which 4 squares above passes the city prison called *The Tombs*, a vast granite building in the gloomy Egyptian style, covering an entire block; and *Chatham St.*, the habitat of Jew tradesmen, old-clothes dealers, and low concert-saloons. At the end of Chatham St. is *Chatham Square*, running N. from which about a mile is the **Bowery,** a broad and crowded thoroughfare, which offers a striking contrast to Broadway. It is the avenue of the lower classes, and is lined with cheap retail-shops, beer and concert saloons, and the like. The City Hall branch of the N. Y. Elevated Railway begins at Printing-House Square, and runs up Chatham St. to the main line in the Bowery.

Above City Hall Park on Broadway (cor. Chambers St.) is the vast marble building formerly used for the wholesale trade of A. T. Stewart & Co.; it stands on the site of one of the forts erected by the British for the defense of the city during the Revolution. Farther up (on the corner of Leonard St.) is the beautiful building of the * **N. Y. Life Insurance Co.,** of pure white marble, in the Ionic style; and opposite is the fine building of the Globe Mutual Life Insurance Co. *Canal St.*, once the bed of a rivulet, is one of the chief thoroughfares running across the city from E. to W. Above Canal a succession of fine buildings present themselves, among them the *St. Nicholas Hotel* (white marble, on the left), the *Metropolitan Hotel* (brownstone, on the right), and the publishing-house of *D. Appleton*

& Co. (549 and 551 Broadway). At the cor. of Bond St. is the hand-some building of Brooks Bros., of red brick trimmed with light-colored stone; and opposite is the lofty marble façade of the *Grand Central Hotel.* A few blocks above (on the right) Astor Place leads off to the *Mercantile Library,* containing 180,000 volumes and an excellent reading-room, to which strangers are admitted on introduction by a member. Half a block S., on Lafayette Place, is the **Astor Library,** occupying a plain but spacious brick building in the Romanesque style. It was founded by John Jacob Astor, who endowed it with $400,000, to which additions were made by his son William B. Astor. It contains 180,000 volumes, and is complete in many special departments of study (open to the public from 9 A. M. to 5 P. M.). At the end of Astor Place (2 blocks from Broadway) is the *****Cooper Institute,** a large brownstone building, occupying the entire square bounded by 3d and 4th Avenues and 7th and 8th Sts. It was founded and endowed by Peter Cooper, a wealthy and philanthropic merchant; and contains a free library, a free reading-room, free schools of art and telegraphy for women, a free night-school of art for men, a free night-school of science for both sexes, and free lectures. The reading-room is open to all from 8 A. M. to 10 P. M. Opposite the Cooper Institute is the *Bible House,* an immense brick structure, covering an entire block, and 6 stories high. It is the headquarters of the American Bible Society, next to the British the largest in the world.

Returning to Broadway and passing N., *A. T. Stewart & Co.'s Store* is seen on the right; a spacious iron building, painted white, 5 stories high, and occupying the entire block between 9th and 10th Sts. and Broadway and 4th Ave. At 10th St. Broadway turns slightly toward the left, and *****Grace Church** (Episcopal), with its rich marble façade and graceful spire, seems to project into the middle of the highway. The interior of Grace Church is extremely rich and ornate, and the music is generally very fine. Passing the *Methodist Book Concern* (publishing-house), *Wallack's Theatre* (near 13th St.), and the lofty and florid building of the *Domestic Sewing-Machine Co.* (cor. 14th St.), we enter *****Union Square,** a pretty little park, oval in shape, 3¼ acres in extent, and filled with trees, shrubbery, and green lawns. At its southern end, on the E., is the *****bronze equestrian statue of Washington by H. K. Browne, and Bartholdi's bronze statue of Lafayette; and on the W. is a bronze statue of Lincoln. The Square, formerly the most fashionable residence quarter, is now surrounded by fine hotels and shops, chief among which is the palatial jewelry store of Tiffany & Co. (cor. W. 15th St.). On the S. side of the Square, between Broadway and 4th Ave., is the *Union Square Theatre,* one of the most popular in the city. *Fourteenth St.,* a leading cross-town thoroughfare, runs E. from Union Square past *Steinway Hall,* the *Academy of Music,* and *Tammany Hall* (the headquarters of the Democratic party), all within 2 blocks of Broadway; and to the W. it passes for several blocks through a line of handsome stores and offices. Just W. of 6th Ave. is the *Lyceum Theatre,* and beyond are private residences.

Above Union Square, Broadway, now contracted to a narrow street, leads past the great dry-goods stores of Arnold, Constable & Co. (cor. 19th St.), and Lord & Taylor (cor. 20th St.), to *Madison Square, another beautiful little park, 6½ acres in extent, tastefully laid out in lawns and shrubbery, and bordered on every side by fine buildings. Opposite the N. W. angle, at the junction of Broadway and 5th Ave., is a monument to General Worth; and near the S. W. corner is Ball's fine bronze statue of Seward. Overlooking the Square, on the W. side, is the spacious white marble edifice of the *Fifth Avenue Hotel*, past which 23d St. runs west to *Booth's Theatre (cor. 23d St. and 6th Ave.). This is a remarkably handsome building of Concord granite, in the Renaissance style, with rich interior decorations. Opposite is the *Masonic Temple, also of granite, 100 by 140 ft., 5 stories high, and with a dome 50 feet square, rising 155 ft. above the pavement. It contains several fine rooms, and the Grand Lodge Hall, 84 by 90 ft. and 30 ft. high, will seat 1,200 persons. Two blocks farther W. along 23d St. (at the cor. of 8th Ave.) is the *Grand Opera House, one of the handsomest buildings in the city, with a specially rich interior, but seldom used on account of its remoteness. One block *east* of Madison Square on 23d St. (cor. 4th Ave.) is the *National Academy of Design,* built of gray and white marbles and bluestone in the Gothic forms of the 12th cen-

National Academy of Design.

tury, with certain features copied from a famous palace in Venice. It has an imposing entrance and stairway leading to extensive galleries,

where every spring and summer are held exhibitions of recent works
of American artists (admission, 25c.). Opposite is the elegant building of the *Young Men's Christian Association*, constructed chiefly of
freestone and brownstone in the Renaissance style, with a central
and three angular towers. Besides a library, free reading-room (open
from 8 A. M. to 10 P. M.), gymnasium, etc., it contains a lecture-hall
capable of seating 1,500 persons.

A walk down *Fourth Avenue* to Union Square will carry the
stranger past several of the finest churches in the city. At the corner of 22d St. is * **St. Paul's** (Methodist), a beautiful white marble
edifice in the Romanesque style ; and at the cor. of 21st St. is the
Calvary Church (Episcopal), a brownstone Gothic building. At the
cor. of 20th St. is the *Church of All Souls* (Unitarian, Dr. Bellows), a
rious structure in the Italian style, with alternate layers of brick
and light-colored stone. A short distance to the E. on 20th St. is the
aristocratic *Gramercy Park*. Taking 16th St. to the E. from 4th
Ave., Stuyvesant Square is soon reached, in which stands * **St.
George's** (Episcopal), one of the largest churches in the city. It is
of brownstone, in the Byzantine style, with double spires, and the
interior is magnificent.

Broadway runs from Madison Square two miles N. to Central Park,
passing a number of theatres and hotels, among which the most noteworthy are the lofty and picturesque *Stevens House* (cor. 27th St.),
the *St. Cloud* and the *Rossmore* (cor. 42d St.), and the three spacious and ornate French-flat houses known as the Hotels Newport,
Saratoga, and Albany. The continuation of Broadway above 59th
St. is known as the * **Boulevard,** a grand avenue 150 ft. wide, divided in the center by a series of little parks, and extending N. to Harlem River. It follows, for the most part, the line of the old Bloomingdale Road, and is the favorite drive above Central Park. By it
may be reached the villages of *Manhattanville* (125th–132d St.) and
Carmansville (1 mile beyond); still N. of which is * **Fort Washington** (or Washington Heights), the chief summit on Manhattan Island
(238 ft. high), and commanding a noble view of the city, the Hudson,
and the opposite Jersey shore. It is now occupied by elegant villa
residences. (Fort Washington is most easily reached from the lower
part of the city by taking the Elevated Railway to the Hudson River
R. R. depot at 30th St., whence frequent trains run to Manhattanville,
Fort Washington, etc.)

Fifth Avenue begins at *Washington Square* (a pleasant park of
9½ acres laid out on the site of the old Potter's Field, where over
100,000 bodies were buried) and runs N. for 6 miles to Harlem River.
As far as Central Park it is lined with compact rows of houses; between 59th and 110th Sts. it has the Park on the left, and houses at
greater or less intervals on the right; and from Mt. Morris to Harlem
River (118th to 135th Sts.) it is lined with villas. Hotels and shops
are invading the portion below Madison Square, but above that the
avenue is devoted almost exclusively to those elegant private residences
which have made it famous.

Washington Square has fine residences on all sides, and on the E. side is the *University of the City of New York*, a beautiful marble building in the Gothic style, 200 by 100 ft. The Chapel, with its spacious window 50 ft. high and 24 ft. wide, is a noble room. The University was founded in 1831, and has about 50 instructors and 500 students. Adjoining it is a handsome church (Methodist) of granite in the Gothic style. Passing up Fifth Ave. from Washington Square, the *Church of the Ascension* (Episcopal) is seen at the cor. of 10th St., and the *First Presbyterian* at the cor. of 11th. On the cor. of 15th St. is the building of the *Manhattan Club*, the social headquarters of the Democratic politicians; and a short distance to the left (on 15th St.) are the Italian-Gothic buildings and church of the *College of St. Francis Xavier*, the headquarters of the Order of Jesus in North America. Near by is the spacious building of the *New York Hospital*. To the E. on 15th St. (No. 109) are the rooms of the *Century Club*, the most noted literary and artistic club in America. At the cor. of 18th St. *Chickering Hall* lifts its ornate and tasteful front, and at the cor. of 20th St. is the house of the wealthy *Union Club*. At the cor. of 21st St. is the S. Dutch Reformed Church, and at the cor. of 22d St. * *Goupil's* art gallery; beyond which the avenue leads past Madison Square on the right and a line of superb hotels (including the Fifth Avenue) on the left. From Madison Square to Central Park, Fifth Ave. is the most aristocratic street in America, lined with splendid residences, and presenting a brilliant spectacle, especially on Sunday afternoons. At all times it is thronged with the equipages of the wealthy and richly dressed pedestrians, and a succession of costly churches challenge the attention of the passer-by. Just off the avenue in W. 25th St. is the elegant *Trinity Chapel* (Episcopal), with its richly decorated interior and impressive choral services; and on opposite corners of 26th St. are *Delmonico's* (a world-famous restaurant) and the *Café Brunswick*, whose reputation is scarcely inferior. To the E. on 28th St. No. 149 is * *St. Stephen's Church* (Roman Catholic), unattractive as a building, but containing some excellent paintings and the most expensive and elegant altar-piece in the country. Its music is famous and attracts many visitors. At the foot of E. 28th St. is **Bellevue Hospital,** the largest in the city, with accommodations for 1,200 patients. At the cor. of 5th Ave. and 29th St. is the *Collegiate Church* (Dutch Reformed), a stately granite edifice; and on 29th St. just E. of the avenue is the picturesque *Church of the Transfiguration* (Episcopal), known familiarly as "the little church round the corner." At the cor. of 34th St. is * **Stewart's Palace,** as it is called, a showy white marble structure, 3 stories high with a Mansard roof, and splendidly decorated and furnished. It is the finest private residence in America, and cost $3,000,000. Passing west along 34th St. the spacious *Congregational Tabernacle* (Dr. Taylor) is seen at the cor. of 6th Ave.; the vast marble buildings of the *N. Y. Institution for the Blind*, with turrets and battlements, at 9th Ave.; and on the river at the foot of the street, the great * **Manhattan Market,** one of the largest structures of the kind in the world (800 by 200 ft.), completed in 1871 at a cost of $1,250,000. The view from its tower (228 ft. high) is very fine. Two blocks E. of 5th Ave., 34th St. emerges into * **Park Avenue,** a beautiful street 140 ft. wide, bordered by handsome private residences, and divided in the center by a row of beautiful little parks, surrounding openings in the railroad-tunnel which runs underneath. On Park Ave., at the cor. of 34th St., is the elegant *Church of the Messiah* (Unitarian), and at the cor. of 35th St. is the spacious *Church of the Covenant* (Presbyterian), of graystone in the Lombardo-Gothic style. Just below (cor. 4th Ave. and 32nd St.) is the vast iron building erected by A. T. Stewart as a Working-women's Home, but now used as a hotel. Its interior courtyard is a unique and striking feature. On 5th Ave., at the cor. of 35th St., is the ritualistic *Grace Church* (Episcopal), renowned for its frescoes and its music ; and on the 37th St. corner is the *Brick Church* (Presbyterian). Occupying the left side from 40th to 42d St. is the *Distributing Reservoir* of the Croton Aqueduct, massively built in the Egyptian style, and covering 4 acres. It is no longer in use, and it is proposed to convert it into an armory or to remove it altogether. West of it is the pretty little Reservoir Square, and opposite are the quaint buildings of *Rutgers Female College.* Two squares E. on 42d St. is the * **Grand Central Depot,** the largest and finest in the country, built of brick, stone, and iron, at a cost of $2,250,000, 692 ft. long and 240 ft. wide, and surmounted by several Louvre domes. At the cor. of 5th Ave. and 43d St. is the Jewish * **Temple Emanuel,** the chief synagogue of the city, and the finest specimen of Saracenic architecture in America. The interior is gorgeously decorated in the Oriental style. At the cor. of 45th St. is the Universalist Church of the *Divine Paternity* (Dr. Chapin); at 46th St. the imposing front of the **Windsor Hotel** towers up; and at the cor. of 48th St. is the costly and ornate *Collegiate Church* (Dutch Reformed). Passing E. along 50th St. to Madison Ave., we reach *Columbia College,* standing in the midst of picturesque grounds. It is the oldest college in the State, having been chartered by George II. in 1754, is richly endowed, and has a library of 23,000 volumes, with a museum. Occupying the square on 5th Ave. between 51st and 52d Sts. is the * **Cathedral of St. Patrick** (Roman Catholic), the largest church in the city and one of the largest and finest on the continent. It is of white marble in the decorated Gothic style, and is 332 ft. long, with a general breadth of 132 ft., and at the transept of 174 ft. At the front (not yet completed) are two spires, each 328 ft. high, flanking a central gable 156 ft. high. The interior is extremely rich. At the cor. of 53d St. is the handsome church of *St. Thomas* (Episcopal); and at 54th St. is **St. Luke's Hospital,** one of the most notable objects on the avenue. It is in charge of the Episcopal Sisters of the Holy Communion, and is a refuge for the sick without regard to sect or nationality. At 55th St. is the **Fifth Avenue Presbyterian Church** (Dr. Hall's), the largest of that sect in the world; and at 59th St. Central Park is reached.

The portion of Fifth Ave. bordering Central Park is sparsely built, and the only building worth attention is the * **Lenox Li-**

brary, a stately edifice of Lockport limestone, extending from 70th to 71st St. It was founded and erected by James Lenox, and is designed as a free gift to the city on Mr. Lenox's death (a card of admission can be obtained by written application to Mr. Lenox). It possesses, besides other valuable donations, " the collection of MSS., printed books, engravings and maps, statuary, paintings, drawings, and other works of art," made by the founder, and is particularly rich in early American history, Biblical bibliography, and Elizabethan literature. Close by it is the *Lenox Hospital* (also founded by Mr. Lenox), a pleasing brick and stone structure with graceful spires. A short distance E. (cor. 4th Ave. and 69th St.) is the **Normal College,* a beautiful building in the secular Gothic style, 300 ft. long, 125 ft. wide, and 70 ft. high, with a lofty and massive Victoria tower. It is part of the common-school system, and is free. Between 120th and 124th Sts. is *Mount Morris Square,* a park of 20 acres, with a rocky hill in the center 101 ft. high, commanding picturesque views. Beyond this the avenue passes amid tasteful villas to Harlem at the end of the island. (As far up as the Windsor Hotel, Fifth Ave. may be advantageously seen by taking a 5th Ave. stage. Above this, the visitor must either walk or take a private conveyance.)

Among the institutions and buildings not yet mentioned but worthy of notice are the following : The *Five Points House of Industry* (155 Worth St.) and the *Five Points Mission,* facing each other on what was once the vilest and most dangerous part of the city. The *Howard Mission,* near by, supports day and Sunday schools and a home for needy children, and distributes food, clothing, and fuel to the deserving poor. The *Roosevelt Hospital* is a vast and imposing edifice on 59th St. near 10th Ave. The **Deaf and Dumb Institution* is located on Washington Heights (see p. 13); the buildings, which are the largest and finest of the kind in the world, cover 2 acres and stand in a park of 28 acres (visitors admitted from 1.30 to 4 daily). The *Convent of the Sacred Heart,* in Manhattanville (see p. 13), is beautifully situated on a hill surrounded by park-like grounds. The **Bloomingdale Asylum for the Insane* occupies a commanding site on 117th St. near 10th Ave. ; the buildings, 3 in number, can accommodate 170 patients and are always full. At Manhattanville is *Manhattan College* (Roman Catholic), with stately buildings and 700 students.

**Central Park is reached from the lower part of the city by either of the Elevated Railways ; by the horse-cars of the 3d, 6th, 7th, and 8th Ave. lines ; or by drive through 5th Ave. It is one of the largest and finest parks in the world, embracing a rectangular area of 843 acres, extending from 59th to 110th St. and from 5th to 8th Ave. It has 18 entrances (4 at each end and 5 at each side), and four streets (65th, 79th, 85th, and 97th) cross it, to afford opportunity for traffic, passing under the park walks and drives. The original surface was exceedingly rough and unattractive, consisting chiefly of rock and marsh ; but by engineering skill the very defects that once seemed fatal have been converted into its most attractive features. Between

79th and 96th streets a large portion of the Park is occupied by the
two Croton reservoirs, the smaller one comprising 35 and the larger
107 acres. The Lakes, five in number, occupy 43½ acres more.
There are 10 miles of carriage-roads, 6 miles of bridle-paths, and 30
miles of footpaths, with numerous bridges, arches, and other architectural monuments, together with many statues. The *Mall*, near
the 5th Avenue entrance, is the principal promenade; it is a magnificent esplanade, nearly a quarter of a mile long and bordered by double
rows of stately elms. At various points are fine bronze statues of
Shakespeare, Scott, Burns, Goethe, Halleck, and * Daniel Webster;
and also a number of groups. Particularly worthy of notice are the
bronze groups of " The Indian Hunter and his Dog " (near the S. end
of the Mall) and " The Falconer " (near the upper end). In the Music
Pavilion, in the upper part of the Mall, concerts are given on Saturday
afternoons in the summer. The Mall is terminated on the N. by * *The
Terrace*, a sumptuous pile of masonry, richly carved and decorated.
Descending the Terrace by a flight of broad stone stairs, *Central Lake*
is reached, the prettiest piece of water in the Park. Between the Terrace and the Lake is a costly fountain with immense granite basins
and a colossal statue of the Angel of Bethesda. The *Ramble*, covering 36 acres of sloping hills, and abounding in pleasant shady paths,
lies N. of Central Lake. On the highest point of the Ramble stands
the * *Belvedere*, a massive piece of architecture in the Norman style.
The tower commands attractive views in all directions. Just above
the Belvedere is the Old Croton Reservoir (holding 150,000,000 gallons), and above this the New Reservoir (holding 1,000,000,000 gallons). Still above this is the Upper Park, less embellished by art than
the lower portion, but richer in natural beauties. On *Mount St. Vincent*, in the N. E. corner, a large restaurant is located in the building
formerly occupied by a Convent of the Sisters of Charity; and the
chapel contains 87 casts from the statuary of Crawford. In and about
the Old State Arsenal, at the S. E. end, are the * *Zoölogical Gardens*,
with an interesting collection of animals, birds, reptiles, etc.; and at
82d St. on the 5th Ave. side (near the Lenox Library) is the spacious
building of the * *Metropolitan Museum of Art* (see " Art Collections "
on p. 4). In Manhattan Square, which adjoins Central Park on the W.
between 77th and 81st Sts., is the *American Museum of Natural
History*, in a large brick building containing Indian antiquities, minerals, shells, and stuffed and mounted specimens of birds, fishes, quadru-
peds, insects, etc. Admission is free except on Mondays and Tuesdays, which are reserved for special students and the teachers and
pupils of the public schools.—Park carriages, so constructed as to
afford every passenger a good view, run from 5th and 8th Ave. entrances to the principal points of interest (fare 25c.). Hackney-coaches
may be hired at the entrances for $2 per hour, and the circuit can be
made in an hour.

One suburban excursion which no visitor should fail to make is
that to * **High Bridge** (reached by small steamer from Harlem, by

Harlem River R. R. from Grand Central Depot, or by carriage-drive through Central Park). This magnificent structure, by which the Croton Aqueduct is carried across Harlem River, is of granite throughout, and spans the entire width of valley and river, from cliff to cliff. It is 1,450 ft. long, 114 ft. high, and supported on 14 massive piers, and has been well called "a structure worthy of the Roman Empire." On the lofty bank at its S. end is a capacious reservoir for the supply of the higher portions of the city, the water being pumped into it by powerful machinery. From this point a comprehensive view of the city and surroundings may be had. A little below High Bridge, picturesquely situated on the Hudson River, is the old *Morris Mansion*, once the headquarters of Washington and later the property of Madame Jumel.

The **East River Islands** may be seen in connection with the trip to High Bridge (or independently) by taking one of the small Harlem steamers from Pier 22 or Pier 24 East River (fare 10c.). The river offers a most animated spectacle, with the teeming Brooklyn and New York shores on either hand. Opposite the foot of E. 46th St. is *Blackwell's Island*, 120 acres in extent; upon it are located the Almshouse, Lunatic Asylum (for females), Penitentiary, Workhouse, Blind Asylum, Charity, Small-pox, and Typhus Fever Hospitals, Hospital for Incurables, and Convalescent Hospital, all built of granite, quarried on the island by the convicts. The boat now passes the picturesque village of *Astoria* on the right, and then skirts the W. verge of *Hell-Gate*, long the terror of all vessels entering or leaving the harbor by way of Long Island Sound. It was a collection of rocks in the channel, which offered so much resistance to the tides as to cause a succession of whirlpools and rapids. Of late years the Gate has been shorn of most of its terrors, and the U. S. Engineers are engaged in removing the few remaining rocks. *Ward's Island* (200 acres) divides the Harlem from the East River; upon it are the Lunatic Asylum (for males), the Emigrant Hospital, and the Inebriate Asylum, the latter a large and imposing building. *Randall's Island*, the last of the group, separated from Ward's Island by a narrow channel, is the site of the Idiot Asylum, the House of Refuge, the Infant Hospital, Nurseries, and other charities provided by the city for destitute children. (Permits for visiting any of these islands must be procured at the office of the Commissioners of Public Charities, cor. 3d Ave. and 11th St.) Beyond Randall's Island the steamer follows the Harlem River and stops near Harlem Bridge.

* **Staten Island** is reached by ferry-boats (hourly) from foot of Whitehall St. to New Brighton, Port Richmond, Snug Harbor, and Elm Park ; and by another line from adjoining pier (running hourly) to Tompkinsville, Stapleton, Clifton, and Vanderbilt's Landing (fare 10c.). The sail down the bay is extremely pleasant, and the island offers beautiful scenery. Staten Island is the largest in the harbor, having an area of 58½ square miles; it is separated from New Jersey by Staten Island Sound and the Kill van Kull, and from Long Island by the Narrows. The drives about the upper part are very attractive, especially those on Vanderbilt Ave., Richmond Terrace, the Serpentine, and the Clove Road. From the heights there are broad views over harbor and ocean. *New Brighton* is the largest village on the island, and contains several fine summer hotels, a number of churches, and many handsome villas. Horse-cars traverse the North Shore, and the Staten Island R. R. runs from Vanderbilt's Landing to Tottenville (13 miles). One mile S. E. of Clifton is *Fort Wadsworth*, the most powerful series of fortifications in the harbor, and commanding a fine view of the others.— *Governor's Island* (reached by ferry from pier adjoining Staten Island ferry) is a national military station, with two powerful forts (Fort Columbus and Castle William) and some attractive officers' quarters.

Coney Island.

This most popular of all the resorts near New York lies just outside the entrance of New York Bay, about 10 miles from the city (by water), and consists of a very narrow island 4½ miles long, with a hard, gently sloping beach, affording unsurpassed facilities for sea-bathing. Prior to 1875 it offered only the rudest accommodations to visitors, and was given over to the rowdy classes of New York and Brooklyn; but since that year, upward of $6,000,000 has been invested in improvements, and the island is now not only the most frequented but the most attractive sea-side resort in America. The name **Coney Island,** which was formerly applied to the entire island, is now restricted to the western half. The best part of this section (*Cable's Hotel*) is reached by crossing the Fulton Ferry to Brooklyn, and taking horse-cars thence to the depot of the Prospect Park & Coney Island R. R. (cor. 20th St. and 9th Ave.), whence large, open steam-cars convey passengers to the beach in 10 minutes (fare for the round trip, 25c.). Time from Fulton Ferry, 40 minutes. Cable's Hotel and Restaurant is one of the best on the island, has excellent bath-houses, pavilions, etc., attached, and is at the end of the noble Ocean Parkway drive from Brooklyn. Near by are a lofty Observatory, an Aquarium, a Camera Obscura, the Concourse (a fine esplanade fronting the beach), and several smaller hotels and restaurants. There is a concert each day and evening on the plaza in front of Cable's. The portion of the island W. of Cable's is now comparatively little frequented, and contains only a few inferior lodging-houses, of which *Norton's* is the best. It is reached from New York by a small steamer starting from foot of W. 24th St., and touching at W. 10th, Canal St., Franklin St., and Pier 2, North River. It lands back of Norton's. Another steamer line runs from foot of W. 22d St., Leroy St., Franklin St., and Pier 13, North River, to Locust Grove, where transfer is made to steam-cars running to *Ryan's Hotel* on the beach. From Brooklyn this portion of the island is reached by steam-cars from the main entrance of Greenwood Cemetery. * **Brighton Beach** lies about ½ mile east of Cable's, and has a vast and splendid hotel, with accommodations for 200 guests, dining-rooms seating 1,500 people at a time, and beautifully arranged grounds. The bathing facilities here are excellent, and there is a con-

cert every day and evening. It is reached from New York by 34th
St. Ferry to Hunter's Point, or 23d St. Ferry to Greenpoint, whence a
double-track railroad runs to the hotel; from Brooklyn by a ride of
15 minutes from the depot cor. Flatbush and Atlantic Aves. (fare for
round trip, 40c.). The E. end of the island is called * **Manhattan
Beach,** and here is another spacious hotel, with first-class restaurant
attached, famous for its fish and clam-chowder. The bathing establishment here is the best on the island, having separate sections for
men and women, a vast amphitheatre with 3,500 seats for those who
prefer to look on, and an inclosed beach for the bathers. Here also
are daily concerts. There are 3 routes by which Manhattan Beach
may be reached from New York : (1) by steamer from 22d, Leroy, and
Rector Sts., North River, to Bay Ridge, and thence by rail (time, 1
hour); (2) by 23d St. Ferry to Greenpoint, and thence by rail (time,
45 minutes); and (3) by horse-cars from Fulton Ferry, Brooklyn, to
Prospect Park near Washington Ave., and thence by rail in 18 minutes
(round-trip ticket by either route, 40c.). The Marine Railway, running
along the beach, extends from the Manhattan Beach Hotel to the extreme E. end of the island (fare, round trip, 10c.).

Rockaway Beach has within a few years improved in the same
way as Coney Island, and is only less popular with excursionists. New
hotels, eating-houses, and pavilions have been erected all along the
beach (which is about 4 miles long), and the old ones have been enlarged. The bathing is superb—surf-bathing on one side and still-
water bathing on the other. Fish and clams are abundant; and Jamaica Bay affords fine opportunities for boating. The beach is reached
from Hunter's Point (34th St. Ferry), *via* Long Island R. R. (round-
trip ticket, 50c.); and from Brooklyn by same line (depot cor. Flatbush and Atlantic Aves.). The favorite way of reaching it, however,
is by the large steamers which, with several landing-places in New
York and Brooklyn, ply to and fro at frequent intervals. By this
route a delightful sail of 25 miles each way is obtained (round-trip
ticket, 50c.).

Long Branch.

There are two routes from New York to Long Branch. (1.) An all-rail route
via Long Branch Division of New Jersey Central R. R. (fare, $1; round trip, $1.50).
(2.) By steamer leaving Pier 8 North River, 4 times daily in summer, to Sandy
Hook (20 miles), and thence *via* New Jersey Southern R. R. (11 miles). Time,
2 hrs.; fare, $1. The sail to Sandy Hook is extremely pleasant, affording fine views
of the harbor and bay. From Philadelphia Long Branch is reached *via* Camden
& Burlington and New Jersey Southern R. R. (distance, 79 miles; fare, $2.25).

Hotels.—The *West End*, located at the W. end of the beach, has a capacity of
nearly 1,200 guests, and is very popular ($4.50 a day). *Howland's Hotel*, N. of the
West End, accommodates 500 guests ($3 to $5 a day). The *Ocean House* is a
vast hotel near the R. R. depot, 700 ft. long by 250 deep, with accommodations
for 800 guests ($3 to $5 a day). The *Hotel Brighton* is a new hotel on the site of
the old "Metropolitan" ($3 to $4 a day). The *Mansion House*, adjoining the
Ocean House on the S., has a capacity of 600 guests ($3 to $4 a day). These are the
principal hotels, and are provided with ball-rooms, billiard-rooms, brass and string
bands, bowling-alleys, shooting-galleries, and the like. Other good hotels on a
smaller scale are the *Clarendon, Pavilion, United States, Jackson's, Iauch's,* and
others. Boarding-houses are numerous, in which good board may be had from $10
to $18 per week.

Long Branch, the other great summer resort in the vicinity of New York, is situated on the Jersey shore of the Atlantic, where a long beach affords admirable facilities for bathing. The old village of Long Branch lies back from the shore about a mile, but the great summer hotels and cottages occupy a broad plateau 20 ft. above the sea, and commanding fine views. The Beach Drive, on which are the leading hotels and handsomest villas, runs directly along the bluff, beneath which is the beach. The regular time for bathing is near high tide, when white flags are displayed over the hotels, and boats are stationed outside the surf-line to aid persons who get into too deep water. The scene then is one of extraordinary animation and brilliancy. Gentlemen are allowed to bathe without costume before 6 o'clock A. M. The *Monmouth Park Race-Course* is 4 miles from Long Branch, near the line of the New Jersey Southern R. R. ; it cost $250,000, and is one of the finest in America. The drives in the vicinity of Long Branch are very attractive. One excellent road extends S. to old Long Branch, Oceanport, and Red Bank (10 miles), and another leads to Atlanticville, Seabright, and the Highlands (8 miles). **Deal** is a quaint old village on the shore, 5 miles S. of Long Branch, with several hotels; and near by are the great Methodist camp-meeting grounds of *Ocean Grove* and *Asbury Park*, containing several hundred cottages. *Shark River*, just S. of Deal, is a favorite resort for picnickers from Long Branch, and is noted for its oysters and crabs. **Pleasure Bay,** on the Shrewsbury River, about a mile N. of the Branch, is another favorite picnic resort, also famous for its oysters. Here are several hotels, and yachts and boats may be hired. Other resorts on the Shrewsbury River are Branch Port, Tinton Falls, and Rumson Neck.

The **Highlands of Navesink** are a series of bold and picturesque bluffs on the Shrewsbury River, extending S. E. from Sandy Hook Bay, which are passed on the way to Long Branch. The highest point, Mt. Mitchell, is 282 ft. above the sea-level, and from its summit extensive views may be obtained. These highlands are usually the first land seen on approaching New York from the ocean, and the last to sink below the horizon on leaving. There are two lighthouses about 100 ft. apart on Beacon Hill, at the mouth of the Shrewsbury; the southern one, a revolving "Fresnel," 248 ft. above the water, being the most powerful one on the Atlantic coast. On the river, a short distance from Beacon Hill, is the little village of *Highlands*, an attractive resort, with fine bathing and fishing, and pleasing scenery. The Red Bank boat from New York touches at Highlands daily, and it is also reached *via* New Jersey Central R. R. **Red Bank** is a remarkably pretty town of 2,000 inhabitants, at the head of navigation on Shrewsbury River. It possesses among other attractions sailing, fishing, and bathing, and being only 8 miles from Long Branch by an excellent driveway (9 by railway), many summer visitors, who wish to be within easy reach of that fashionable resort yet away from its excitement, pass the season here. Red Bank is reached from New York by either the New Jersey Southern or the New Jersey Central R. R. ; also by steamer from Pier 35 North River (fare, 50c.).

2. Brooklyn.

Ferries.—The principal ferries between New York and Brooklyn are the Fulton Ferry, the Wall St. Ferry (from Wall St., New York, to Montague St., Brooklyn), and the South Ferry (from Atlantic Ave., Brooklyn, to Whitehall St., New York). Fulton Ferry is the best for visitors to take, as it is the converging point of all the Brooklyn horse-car lines. Other ferries to New York are from foot of Hamilton Ave., Main St., So. 7th St., and Grand St. (E. D.). The "Annex" boats run from foot of Fulton St. to Jersey City, connecting with all the trains of the Pennsylvania R. R., and with the Albany and Fall River steamers.

Hotels and Restaurants.—The *Pierrepont House* ($4 a day), at the cor. of Montague and Hicks Sts., is the only hotel of the first class. The *Mansion House*, 117 Hicks St., is a quiet family hotel. The leading restaurants are *Dieter's*, 373 Fulton St., and *Taylor & Co.'s*, 365 Fulton St.

Modes of Conveyance.—*Horse-cars* afford easy access to all parts of the city (fare 5c.). All the lines either start from or connect with Fulton Ferry. *Steam-cars* running on Atlantic Ave. afford "rapid transit" between the depot, cor. Flatbush and Atlantic Aves., and East New York, with stations every few blocks (fare 5c.). *Hackney-coaches* are usually in waiting at the principal ferries; the charge must be agreed upon with the driver.

BROOKLYN, the third largest city in the United States, lies just across East River from New York, at the W. end of Long Island. Its extreme length from N. to S. is 7¾ miles, and its average breadth 3½, embracing an area of 20.84 square miles. The surface is elevated and diversified. Brooklyn was settled in 1625, near Wallabout Bay, by a band of Walloons, and during the Revolutionary War was the scene of events that give great interest to some of its localities. On the Heights back of the city the battle of Long Island was fought (Aug. 26, 1776), and the Americans defeated with a loss of 2,000 out of 5,000 men. The population of Brooklyn, which was 3,298 in 1800, had increased by 1875 to 482,493. The main business thoroughfare is **Fulton Street**, extending from Fulton Ferry to East New York (5 miles). *Atlantic Ave.* runs nearly parallel with Fulton St. from South Ferry to East New York; it is an active business street in its lower part, and from Flatbush Ave. to East New York is occupied by the tracks of the "rapid transit" railroad. * **Clinton Ave.** is the handsomest street in the city, being embowered with trees and lined with fine residences surrounded by ornamental grounds. *St. Mark's Place* is scarcely less attractive. Remsen and Montague Sts., on the Heights, contain many fine residences; and from *Montague Terrace, on the latter, is obtained a magnificent view of New York city and harbor. The favorite drive is through Prospect Park and along the * **Ocean Parkway,** a splendid boulevard 200 ft. wide, extending from the S. W. corner of the Park to the seashore at Coney Island (6 miles). The *Eastern Parkway*, also a popular drive, extends from the Park entrance to East New York (2¼ miles). Still another attractive drive is to Bay Ridge and Fort Hamilton.

The *City Hall* (reached from Fulton Ferry *via* Fulton St. in ½ mile) is within easy walking distance of nearly all the public buildings in Brooklyn that are worth attention. It is of white marble in the Ionic style, surmounted by a belfry with a four-dial clock, and stands in an open square. Just E. of the Hall, fronting toward Fulton St., is the

*County Court-House, a large building with white marble front in the Corinthian style, with a very fine portico, and an iron dome 104 ft. high. Alongside the Court-House stands the *Municipal Building*, of marble, 4 stories high, with a Mansard roof, and a tower at each of the 4 corners. Across Court St. from the City Hall, at the corner of Joralemon St., are the rooms of the *Long Island Historical Society*, containing a valuable library and many curious relics (admission free). On the cor. of Remsen St. is *Court Square Theatre* (varieties). On Fulton St., opposite the City Hall, is the *New Park Theatre*. The *Post-Office* is in Washington St. just N. of the City Hall. On Montague St., immediately W. of the City Hall, is the *Academy of Music*, a large brick building of no special architectural merit, but with fine interior decorations. Adjoining it is the **Academy of Design**, with highly ornate front tastefully carved. Opposite is the **Mercantile Library**, a handsome structure in the Gothic style, containing a library of 58,000 volumes and two fine reading-rooms. Just beyond, at the corner of Clinton St., is the beautiful ***Church of the Holy Trinity** (Episcopal), in the decorated Gothic style, with rich stained windows and a graceful spire 275 ft. high. To the left down Clinton St. (corner Livingston) is the church of *St. Ann* (Episcopal), in the pointed Gothic style with exceedingly ornate interior. To the right, in Pierrepont St., is the *Dutch Reformed Church*, of brownstone in the Roman Corinthian style, with a Corinthian portico, and a very rich interior. Near by (corner Pierrepont St. and Monroe Place) is the Unitarian *Church of the Saviour*, an elaborate structure in the pointed Gothic style. Other noteworthy churches in this vicinity are *Grace* (Episcopal), cor. Grace Court and Hicks St.; *Christ* (Episcopal), cor. Clinton and Harrison Sts.; and the *Church of the Pilgrims* (Congregational; R. S. Storrs, Pastor), cor. Remsen and Henry Sts. *Plymouth Church* (Henry Ward Beecher's) is a large but plain building in Orange St. near Hicks. Other churches visited by strangers are the *Lafayette Ave. Presbyterian* (Dr. Cuyler), the *Clinton Ave. Congregational*, and Talmage's *Tabernacle*, in Schermerhorn St., said to be the largest Protestant church in America. The church of **St. Charles Borromeo* (Roman Catholic), in Sidney Place, is famous for its music. The *Long Island College Hospital* has a large and imposing building, in extensive grounds, on Henry St. near Pacific. The *County Jail*, in Raymond St., is a castellated Gothic edifice of red sandstone; the *Penitentiary* is an immense stone pile in Nostrand Ave. near the city limits. The *Young Men's Christian Association* has a fine building on Fulton St. cor. Gallatin Place, with library and reading-room (free).

In crossing Fulton Ferry to or from New York the massive towers and ponderous cables of the ***East River Bridge** are conspicuous objects. The towers are 268 ft. in height, and the distance across the river between them is 1,595 ft. The total length of the bridge will be 6,000 ft. and its width 85 ft., affording space for 2 railroad-tracks, 4 wagon-ways, and 2 footpaths. From high-water mark to the floor of the bridge in the center the distance is to be 135 ft. The bridge was begun in 1871, and has already cost nearly $10,000,-

000. The *United States Navy Yard* (reached by horse-cars from
Fulton Ferry), on the S. shore of Wallabout Bay, is the chief naval
station of the Republic. It contains 45 acres, inclosed by a high
brick wall, within which are numerous foundries, workshops, and
storehouses. Representative vessels of every kind used in our navy
may usually be seen at the Yard, and the trophies and relics preserved
here are of great interest. The ***Atlantic Dock,** at the other end
of the city, a mile below South Ferry, is a very extensive work, and
merits the attention of strangers. The basin covers an area of $42\frac{1}{2}$
acres, and surrounding it are piers of solid granite, on which are spacious warehouses.

* Prospect Park (reached by several lines of cars from Fulton
Ferry) is one of the most beautiful in America. It contains 550 acres,
is situated on an elevated ridge, and commands magnificent views of
the two cities, of the inner and outer harbor, Long Island, the Jersey
shore, and the Atlantic. It is beautifully shaded in many parts by old
woods which have been skillfully improved, and its combination of
broad meadows, grassy slopes, and wooded hills, is unequaled elsewhere. It contains 8 miles of drives, 4 miles of bridle-paths, and 11
miles of walks. The main entrance on Flatbush Ave., known as the
Plaza, is paved with stone and bordered by grassy mounds; in the
center are a fine fountain and a bronze statue of President Lincoln.
Park carriages, starting from the entrance, make the circuit of the
leading points of interest (fare 25c.). *Washington Park* (30 acres) is
an elevated plateau E. of the City Hall, between Myrtle and De Kalb
Aves., commanding extensive views. During the Revolutionary War
it was the site of extensive fortifications, of which Fort Greene was
the principal.

* Greenwood Cemetery (reached by cars from Fulton Ferry),
the most beautiful in the world, is situated on Gowanus Heights in the
S. portion of the city. It contains upward of 500 acres, skillfully
laid out, and nearly 200,000 interments have been made in it since
its opening in 1842. The main entrance, near 5th Ave. and 23d St.,
is an elegant monumental structure in the pointed Gothic style, ornamented with sculptures representing scenes from the Gospels; and
the new entrance on the E. side is of scarcely inferior beauty. The
grounds have a varied surface of hill, valley, and plain, and are traversed by 17 miles of carriage-roads and 15 miles of footpaths. The
elevations afford extensive views. There are many beautiful monuments, chief among which are the Pilots' and Firemen's, Charlotte
Canda's, and that to the "mad poet" McDonald Clark. By keeping
in the main avenue called *The Tour*, as indicated by finger-posts,
visitors will obtain the best general view of the cemetery, and will be
able to regain the entrance without difficulty. About 4 miles E. of
Greenwood are the cemeteries of *The Evergreens* and *Cypress Hills*.

Coney Island and *Rockaway Beach* have already been described
(see pp. 19 and 20).

3. New York to Philadelphia.

a. Via Pennsylvania R. R., 90 *miles. Time,* 2¼ *to* 2¾ *hours. Fare,* $2.50.

FERRY-BOATS convey passengers from foot of Desbrosses and Cortlandt Sts. to the depot in Jersey City. **Jersey City** is on the Hudson River opposite New York, of which it is practically a portion. It is a place of much commercial and industrial activity, is agreeably situated and well built, and has a population of about 85,000; but except for the fact that it contains the depots of several of the most important railways leading south and west from New York, and the docks of leading transatlantic steamers, it possesses no interest for the tourist. The route after leaving Jersey City is across broad meadows to **Newark** (9 miles), a large manufacturing city of nearly 120,-000 inhabitants, but, like its rival Jersey City, offering little of interest to the tourist. The city is built on an elevated plain upon the right bank of the Passaic River, 4 miles from Newark Bay, and is regularly laid out in wide streets crossing each other at right angles. Broad St. is the main business thoroughfare, and runs N. and S. through the heart of the city. The principal E. and W. street is Market St., on which are some of the finest buildings, including the *Court-House*, an imposing stone edifice in the Egyptian style. Other noteworthy public buildings are the *City Hall* (cor. Broad and William Sts.), the *Custom-House and Post-Office* (cor. Broad and Academy), and many handsome churches. The building of the Mutual Benefit Life Ins. Co. is said to be the finest in the State. Of the literary institutions the most noteworthy are the *Library Association* (20,000 volumes), the *State Historical Society,* and the *Newark Academy.* From the grounds of the latter (on High St.) an extensive view of the Passaic Valley is had. Newark is distinguished for its manufactures of jewelry, carriages, paper, and leather; and its lager-bier is excellent. (*Hotels:* Continental, Park, and Newark.)

Six miles beyond Newark is **Elizabeth** (*Sheridan House*), the handsomest city in New Jersey, with 25,000 inhabitants, and many fine residences, a few of which are visible from the cars. **New Brunswick** (*City Hotel ; New Brunswick*) stands at the head of navigation on Raritan River (32 miles from New York), and has a population of about 20,000, with extensive manufactures of india-rubber, harness, and hosiery. There are fine residences in the upper part of the city, but the "institution" of New Brunswick is *Rutgers College,* an old, richly-endowed, and flourishing establishment. *Princeton Junction* (48 miles) is 2½ miles from Princeton, noted as the seat of **Princeton College,** one of the most famous institutions of learning in America. The college buildings (especially the Library, Nassau Hall, and Dickinson Hall) are remarkably fine, and stand in a green and shady campus. Dummy engines convey passengers from the junction to the town. (*Hotel:* Mansion House.) **Trenton** (58 miles) is the capital of New Jersey, and is pleasantly situated at the head of navigation on

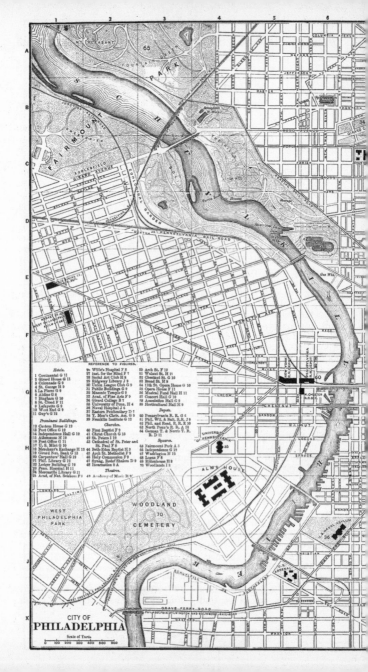

the Delaware. It has a population of about 25,000, with important manufacturing interests (chief among which are the Potteries), and is a remarkably well-built, cleanly, and attractive town. State St. is the principal thoroughfare, and next to this is Main St., which crosses State at right angles. The leading event in the past history of Trenton is the famous victory over the Hessians won by Washington, Dec. 26, 1776; and its chief present attractions are the public buildings. The *State House* (in State St.) is a stone structure, beautifully situated on the Delaware, and overlooking the river and vicinity. The *Post-Office*, also in State St., is a massive stone building in the Renaissance style; and the vast *State Penitentiary* (in Federal St.), the *State Arsenal* (near the Penitentiary), and the *State Lunatic Asylum* (1½ mile N. of the city) are all worth visiting. (HOTELS: *Trenton House; American; United States.*) The only place between Trenton and Philadelphia requiring mention is *Bristol* (67 miles), a pretty town of 3,500 inhabitants, on the Delaware nearly opposite Burlington.

b. Via "Bound Brook Route," 88 miles. Time, 2¼ to 2¾ hours. Fare, $2.50.

The depot in Jersey City is reached by ferry from foot of Liberty St. The country along this route is very similar in character to that along the preceding route, but there are fewer large towns and a scantier population. Highly cultivated farms and smiling orchards stretch away on every side, and the prospect in summer is very pleasing. Besides *Newark* (9 miles) and *Elizabeth* (13 miles), both of which have been described above, the only important town on the route is **Plainfield** (24 miles), containing about 6,000 inhabitants, and pleasantly situated near the foot of Orange Mountain. Washington's Rock (seen from the train on the right) is on the mountain 2 miles W. of Plainfield, and is noted as the place whence Washington watched the movements of the enemy during the campaign in this vicinity. At *Bound Brook* (31 miles) the Americans were defeated in 1777 by Lord Cornwallis. There is a Princeton Station on this route also, and a short branch road runs to Trenton.

c. Via Amboy Division of the Pennsylvania R. R., 92 miles. Time, 5 hours. Fare, $2.50.

From pier 1 North River to South Amboy (30 miles) this is a steamer route, and the sail down the Bay, past the villa-lined shores of Staten Island, and up the Raritan River, is very pleasant, particularly in summer. *South Amboy* is situated on Raritan Bay at the mouth of Raritan River, across which is **Perth Amboy,** a port of entry, and one of the oldest cities in New Jersey, much frequented in summer (*Eagleswood Park Hotel*). At South Amboy the cars are taken, and the route leads through a barren and uninteresting country to the Delaware River at Bordentown (64 miles). **Bordentown** (*Bordentown House*) is a flourishing town of 6,000 inhabitants, situated on the E. bank of the Delaware, with extensive founderies and machine-shops, and the terminal basins of the Delaware and Raritan Canal.

It is a favorite resort of Philadelphians during the summer season. The principal object of interest is the mansion and park occupied for 26 years by Joseph Bonaparte, ex-king of Spain. **Burlington** (73 miles) is another city of 6,000 inhabitants on the Delaware, 19 miles above Philadelphia, whence it is much visited in summer by steamboat. *Burlington College* (Episcopal) is located here, and there are handsome churches and school-buildings. **Camden** (92 miles) is a flourishing city of 25,000 inhabitants on the Delaware opposite Philadelphia, with which it is connected by 4 ferries. It is the terminus also of the *West Jersey* and *Camden & Atlantic Railways ;* and there are extensive ship-yards, besides manufactures of iron, glass, chemicals, etc. The vicinity abounds in fruit orchards and vegetable gardens. (*West Jersey Hotel.*)

4. Philadelphia.

Hotels.—The leading hotels on the American plan are the *Continental* ($3 to $4.50 a day), cor. Chestnut and 9th Sts.; the *Girard House* ($3 a day), on Chestnut St. opposite the Continental; the *Colonnade* ($3 to $4 a day), cor. Chestnut and 15th Sts.; the *St. George* ($4 to $5 a day), cor. Broad and Walnut Sts.; and the *La Pierre* ($2.50 to $3.50 a day), on Broad and Chestnut Sts. The two latter are up town, and more quiet than the others. The *Aldine* ($5 a day), in Chestnut St. above 20th, is elegant and aristocratic. The *Bingham* ($2.50 to $3.50), cor. 11th and Market, and the *St. Cloud* ($2.50), in Arch St. between 7th and 8th, are much patronized by merchants. The *Hotel Lafayette*, cor. Broad and Sansom Sts., is conducted on both the American and European plans. Of hotels on the European plan the best are the *West End*, in Chestnut St. above 15th; and *Guy's Hotel*, cor. Chestnut and 7th Sts. The charges at these are $1 to $3 a day for rooms, and both have excellent restaurants attached. Good board may be had in private houses at $6 to $12 per week.

Restaurants.—*Finelli's*, in Chestnut St. near Broad, is the Delmonico's of Philadelphia, and is handsomely appointed. *Green's*, cor. Chestnut and 8th Sts., is first class; and *Brewster's*, near the cor. of 8th and Arch Sts., is much frequented by ladies. Other first-class restaurants are those attached to the hotels on the European plan, as given above. The *Continental Restaurant*, on the first floor of the hotel, is much frequented by business men. Good lunch-rooms and chop-houses may be found in the lower part of the city, in the neighborhood of Third St.

Modes of Conveyance.—The *Horse-cars* traverse the city in every direction, rendering all parts easily accessible. The fare is 6c., and points on any connecting line may be reached by "transfer-tickets" (costing 3c. additional) which should be called for on paying the fare. *Carriages* are found at all the depots, and at stands in various parts of the city. The fares are regulated by law, and a card containing them should be in every carriage. They are as follows: for 1 passenger, a distance of one mile or less, 75c.; 2 passengers, $1.25; each additional one, 25c. For 1 passenger, 2 m. or less, $1.25; 2 passengers, $1.75; each additional mile, 50c.; by the hour, $1.50. Children between 5 and 14 years of age, half price. In case of dispute, call a policeman, or apply at the Mayor's office.

Railroad Depots.—The depot of the *Pennsylvania R. R.* is at 32d and Market Sts.; of the *Amboy Division* (for New York) by ferry from foot of Market St. to station in Camden. Of the *Philadelphia, Wilmington & Baltimore R. R.*, cor. Broad and Washington Ave.; of the *Philadelphia & Reading R. R.*, 13th and Callowhill Sts.; of the *North Pennsylvania*, cor. Berks and American Sts.; of the *West Chester & Philadelphia*, cor. 31st and Walnut; of the *Germantown & Norristown*, cor. 9th and Green; of the *Camden & Atlantic*, by ferry from foot of Vine St. to station in Camden; of the *West Jersey*, by ferry from foot of Market St. to station in Camden; of the *Philadelphia & Atlantic City*, at foot of Walnut St.

Ferries.—To *Camden* (fare, 5c.) from foot of Market St., Vine St., South St. in the lower part of the city, and from Shackamaxon St. in Kensington. To *Gloucester, N. J.*, from foot of South St. (fare 10c.).

Churches.—Among the 424 churches of all denominations in Philadelphia the following are those most visited by strangers: The *Cathedral of St. Peter and St. Paul* (Roman Catholic), on Logan Square, 18th St., noted for its impressive services and fine music ; *St. Peter's* (Episcopal), a venerable relic of the early days of the city ; *St. Mark's* (Episcopal), cor. 16th and Locust Sts. ; the *Holy Trinity* (Episcopal), cor. 19th and Walnut ; *St. Stephen's* (Episcopal), in 10th St. near Market ; *St. Andrew's* (Episcopal), in 8th St. near Spruce ; the *Church of the Incarnation* (Episcopal), cor. Broad and Jefferson ; the *Beth-Eden Baptist Church*, cor. Broad and Spruce ; the *First Baptist*, cor. Broad and Arch Sts. ; the *West Arch St. Presbyterian*, in Arch St. ; the *Second Presbyterian*, cor. 21st and Walnut ; the *Washington Square Presbyterian;* the *Central Congregational*, cor. 18th and Green ; the *Arch St. Methodist*, cor. Broad and Arch Sts. ; and the *Lutheran Church*, cor. Broad and Arch. The Jewish *Synagogue*, on Broad St. near Green, has Sabbath (Saturday) services. Among the Friends' meeting-houses those at the cor. of Arch and 4th and Race and 15th Sts. are best worth a visit.

Theatres and Amusements.—The *Academy of Music*, cor. of Broad and Locust Sts., is the largest opera-house in America, being 268 by 140 ft., with sittings for 3,000 persons. It is used for operas, concerts, lectures, balls, etc. The *Arch St. Theatre* (Mrs. John Drew's), in Arch St., near 6th, has a good company. The *Walnut St. Theatre* is at the cor. of Walnut and 9th Sts. ; the *Chestnut St. Theatre* is in Chestnut St. above 12th; and the *Broad St. Theatre* is in Broad St. near Locust. Negro minstrelsy is found at the *Eleventh St. Opera-House* (11th St., above Chestnut) and at the *Opera-House* (in Arch St. above 10th). *Wood's Museum* is at the cor. of 9th and Arch. Musical entertainments are given at the Academy of Music, at *Musical Fund Hall* (seating 2,500 people), in Locust St. below 9th; at *Concert Hall*, in Chestnut St. above 12th; at *Association Hall*, cor. Chestnut and 15th, and at *St. George's Hall*, cor. Arch and 13th Sts. The *Horticultural Hall*, cor. Broad and Locust Sts., is the scene of the annual floral displays of the Horticultural Society.

Reading-Rooms.—At all the leading hotels there are reading-rooms for the use of guests, provided with newspapers. The *Mercantile Library*, in 10th St. near Chestnut, contains 135,000 volumes and a well-supplied reading-room (open from 9 A. M. to 10 P. M.). The *Philadelphia Library*, in 5th St. near Chestnut, with 100,000 volumes, is free from 10 o'clock till sunset ; the "Ridgway Branch," with two reading-rooms, is at the cor. of Broad and Christian. The *Athenæum*, cor. 6th and Adelphi Sts., has a library of 20,000 volumes, a reading-room, and a chess-room (introduction by a member). The *Young Men's Christian Association*, cor. 15th and Chestnut Sts., has a free reading-room (open from 9 A. M. to 10 P. M.). The *Historical Society of Pennsylvania*, 820 Spruce St., has a rich library (open from 10 A. M. to 5 P. M.). The *Franklin Institute*, in 7th St. above Chestnut, has a free library and reading-room.

Art Collections.—At the *Academy of Fine Arts*, cor. Broad and Cherry Sts., in one of the best collections of paintings, statuary, casts, and prints in America (entrance 25 c.). Fine pictures may usually be seen (free) at the sales galleries of *Earle*, 816 Chestnut St., and *Haseltine*, 1,516 Chestnut St. Among the richest private collections in the country are those of Henry C. Gibson (1612 Walnut St.), James L. Claghorn (on W. Logan Square), the late Joseph Harrison, Jr. (in Rittenhouse Square), and A. E. Borie. Admission to these may usually be obtained by application to the proprietors, personally or by letter.

Clubs.—The Union League Club has a handsome building cor. Broad and Sansom Sts. ; it is of brick in the Renaissance style, with façades of granite, brick, and brown-stone. It contains the best refectory in the city, a reading-room, paintings, statuary, etc. A member's introduction will secure the visitor the privileges of the Club for one month. The *Reform Club* has a fine brown-stone building in Chestnut St. near 19th (introduction by a member). The *Penn* and the *Philadelphia* are prominent social clubs. The *Social Art Club* occupies a fine marble building in Walnut St. near 18th.

Post-Office.—The general Post-Office is a plain white marble building in Chestnut St. below 5th, open all the time except on Sundays, when it is open from 9 to 11 A. M. A large new building for this purpose is being constructed at the cor. of Chestnut and 9th Sts. Letters may be mailed in the lamp-post boxes in all parts of the city, whence they are collected at frequent intervals by the carriers.

PHILADELPHIA, the largest city as to area in the United States, and the second in population, lies between the Delaware and Schuylkill

Rivers, 6 miles above their junction and 96 from the Atlantic Ocean.
Its latitude is 39° 57′ N. and longitude 75° 10′ W. from Greenwich.
It is 22 miles long from N. to S., with a breadth of 5 to 8 miles, and
an area of 1,294 square miles.　The city, as originally incorporated,
was bounded by the rivers Delaware and Schuylkill and Vine and South

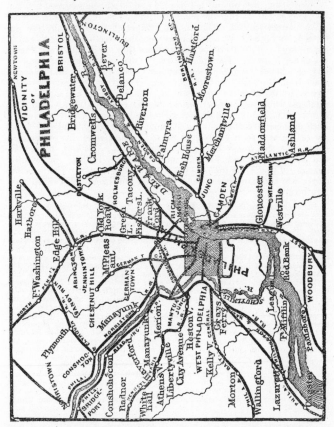

Streets, and this area was not enlarged until 1854, when the corporation was extended over the entire county.　Within its present area
there are over 350 miles of paved streets, and more buildings than in
any other city in the country.　The city is regularly laid out, the streets
running N. and S. being numbered in succession from the Delaware to

the Schuylkill, which is reached at 23d St., the first street above that
being 30th. These are crossed at right angles by named streets. A
few irregular avenues, formerly country-roads, stretch away from the
original town-plot. The houses on the streets running E. and W. are
numbered toward the W., all between 1st and 2d streets being between 100 and 200, and all between 2d and 3d streets between 200 and
300, and so on; so that the number of the house indicates the number
of the street as well. Thus if the number of the house be 836, 8th
St. is E. and 9th St. W. In like manner, the streets running N. and S.
are allowed 100 numbers for every square they are distant from Market
St., either N. or S. This plan is very convenient in going about the
city, as whenever one can see a number he can calculate his exact distance from Market St. or the Delaware. The great business thoroughfare is *Market St. ;* it runs E. and W., is 100 ft. wide, and contains the
principal wholesale stores. *Broad St.*, the central street N. and S., is
113 ft. wide, and is lined with churches and elegant private residences.
Each of these streets is built up continuously for about 4 miles. *Chestnut St.*, parallel with Market on the S., is the fashionable promenade,
containing the finest hotels and retail stores. Walnut, farther S.,
and Arch, Race, and Vine, N. of Market, are leading and wealthy
streets. *Third St.* is the banking and financial center. The principal
drives are through Fairmount Park, and out Broad St. toward Germantown.

Philadelphia was founded by William Penn, who came over from England in
1682, accompanied by a colony of Quakers, and purchased the site from the Indians.
The emigration thither was very rapid, and in 1684 the population was estimated at
2,500. Penn presented the city with a charter in 1701. It prospered greatly, and
was the most important city in the country during the colonial period and for more
than a quarter of a century after the Revolution. The first Continental Congress
assembled here (in 1774), as did also the subsequent Congresses during the war.
The Declaration of Independence was made and issued here, July 4, 1776. The
convention which formed the Constitution of the Republic assembled here in May,
1787. Here resided the first President of the United States, and here Congress
continued to meet until 1797. Until 1799 it was the capital of the colony and state
of Pennsylvania, and from 1790 to 1800 was the seat of the government of the
United States. The city was in possession of the British from September, 1777, to
June, 1778, a result of the unfortunate battles of Brandywine and Germantown.
Since the Revolution the city has grown steadily and rapidly. The population,
which in 1800 was 41,220, had increased to 121,376 in 1850, to 565,529 in 1860, and
to 817,448 in 1876. The commerce of Philadelphia is large and increasing, but
manufactures are its chief source of wealth, and in these, according to the census
of 1870, it is the first city of the Union, surpassing New York in the number of
establishments (8,184), in the number of hands employed (137,496), and in the
amount of capital invested ($174,016,674). The products of the year 1870 were val-
ued at $322,004,517. The leading industries are the manufacture of locomotives
and all kinds of iron-ware, ships, woolen and cotton goods, shoes, umbrellas, and
books. In commerce Philadelphia ranks fourth among the cities of the United
States.

Chestnut St. is the fashionable promenade of the city, and contains the finest hotels, retail stores, etc. It begins at the Delaware
River and runs W. to the city limits, crossing the Schuylkill at 23d
St. The first two or three squares are occupied by spacious stone
warehouses and offices, but offer nothing noteworthy. On 2d St. N.
of Chestnut is the *Commercial Exchange*, a large brown-stone build-

ing standing on the site of the old "Slate-roof House," once the
residence of William Penn, and later the home of John Adams, John
Hancock, Baron De Kalb, and Benedict Arnold.　On 2d St. near Market St. is **Christ Church** (Episcopal), one of the most venerable of
the antiquarian relics of the city, begun in 1727, and still a fine building.　Its steeple is 196 ft. high, and contains the oldest chime of
bells in America.　(Two services are held in the church on Sunday,
and it is open for prayers on Wednesdays and Fridays at 11 A. M., at
which times it may be visited.)　At the cor. of Market and Front
Sts. is a small brick house, now used as a tobacco-shop; it was built
in 1702, and a hundred years ago was the famous *London Coffee-*

Public Buildings, cor. Broad and Market Sts.

House, frequented by the magnates of the city.　A few steps from
this (in Letitia St., S. of Market) is *Penn's Cottage*, built for William Penn before his arrival in the settlement, and the first brick
building erected in Philadelphia.

　　Third St. is the banking and financial center, especially the first
few blocks S. of Chestnut St.　Here (at the cor. of Walnut St.) is the
*** Merchants' Exchange,** a fine marble building, with an ornamented front on Dock St., a semicircular colonnade of 8 pillars, and a
spacious rotunda within on that side.　The Reading-room in the rotunda of the second story is handsomely frescoed.　Near by is the
Girard National Bank, a stately edifice with handsome portico, origi-

nally built for the first United States Bank, and occupied by Stephen
Girard until his death.   It was copied from the Dublin Exchange.
Opposite (fronting on S. 2d St.) are the massive *U. S. Appraiser's
Stores.*   To the S. (cor. 3d and Pine Sts.) is the church of *St. Peter's*
(Episcopal), one of the oldest in the city, begun in 1758 and finished in
1761.   In the steeple is a chime of bells, and in the yard a monument
to Commodore Decatur.

Above 3d St., on Chestnut, is the brown-stone *Bank of North America,* and near by the massive marble edifice of the *Fidelity Safe Deposit
Co.*   On the S. side of Chestnut St. between 3d and 4th a narrow court
leads to **Carpenters' Hall,** where assembled (in 1774) the first Congress of the United Colonies.   It is a plain two-story brick building,
surmounted by a cupola, and carefully preserved.   Between 4th and
5th Sts. (on the left) is the * **U. S. Custom-House,** built in 1824 for
the United States Bank, a chaste specimen of the Doric architecture,
with imposing fronts on Chestnut and Library Sts., each having 8 massive fluted columns, supporting a heavy entablature.   Just above, on the
same side, is the plain marble *Post-Office ;* and opposite are the costly
buildings of the *Farmers' and Mechanics' Bank* (marble), the *Philadelphia Bank* (granite), and the *Pennsylvania Life Ins. Co.* (Quincy granite).   Between 5th and 6th Sts. stands * **Independence Hall,**
the most interesting object in Philadelphia.   It was begun in 1729 and
completed in 1735, at a cost of £5,600.   In the E. room (Independence
Hall proper) the Continental Congress met, and here on July 4, 1776,
the Declaration of Independence was adopted, and publicly proclaimed
from the steps on the same day.   The room presents the same appearance now as it did at that time ; the furniture is that used by Congress ;
there are a statue of Washington and numerous portraits and pictures.
The W. room is a depository of many curious Revolutionary relics.   In
it is preserved the old "Liberty Bell," the first bell rung in the United
States after the passage of the Declaration.   In Congress Hall, in the 2d
story, Washington delivered his farewell address.   Visitors are admitted
from 9 A. M. to 4 P. M. daily.   The Superintendent will, on application,
furnish tickets admitting the bearer to the belfry, from which a fine panoramic view of the city may be had.   On the sidewalk in front of the
Hall stands Bailey's statue of Washington ; and in the rear is *Independence Square,* an inclosure of 4 acres containing some fine old trees.
Diagonally opposite Independence Square (on the S. W.) is **Washington Square,** inclosed with an ornate iron fence, and celebrated for containing nearly every variety of tree that will grow in this climate, whether indigenous or not.   There is a map of the Square showing the position of each tree.   Fronting on the Square is the *Athenæum,* with a
library of 25,000 volumes, a reading-room, and a chess-room.   On 5th
St. near Chestnut, in a plain old building, is the * **Philadelphia Library,** founded in 1731 through the influence of Benjamin Franklin
and the members of the "Junto."   It contains about 100,000 volumes,
and is rich in early printed books, and works on American history (free
admission from 10 A. M. till sunset).   Further along 5th St. (at the
S. E. cor. of Arch St.) is *Franklin's Grave,* which may be seen from

the sidewalk through iron railings that have been inserted in the brick wall of the cemetery.

At the cor. of Chestnut and 6th Sts. is the stately * *Ledger Building*, of brown stone, 5 stories high, with Mansard roof; and near by are the offices of nearly all the leading morning and evening journals. The office of the *Press* is at the cor. of 7th St., and to the right along 7th is the *Franklin Institute*, designed to promote the mechanic and useful arts, and provided with a library (7,500 volumes), a reading-room, and free courses of scientific lectures. At the S. W. corner of 7th and Market Sts. stands the * house in which Jefferson wrote the Declaration of Independence, the identical room being still shown. Just above 7th on Market St. is the spacious six-story publishing-house of *J. B. Lippincott & Co.* To the S. from Chestnut, 8th St. leads past the long and rambling buildings of the **Pennsylvania Hospital,** standing in ample grounds shaded by venerable trees, and containing a medical library and anatomical museum (visitors admitted on Monday and Thursday afternoons). Close by (at 820 Spruce St.) is the building of the *Pennsylvania Historical Society*, containing a large library, particularly rich in local and family histories, and many interesting historical relics (open from 10 A. M. to 5 P. M.). At the corner of Chestnut and 8th is the new and handsome *Times Building.*

At the cor. of 9th St. is the lofty **Continental Hotel,** built of Pictou sandstone, 200 ft. long and 6 stories high; and opposite is the handsome building of the *Girard House.* At the N. W. corner is the splendid but yet unfinished new * **Post-Office,** a spacious granite structure in the Renaissance style, 4 stories high, with an iron dome, and costing $4,000,000. At the cor. of 10th St. is the imposing building of the *N. Y. Mutual Life Ins. Co.;* and to the right, on 10th St., is the * **Mercantile Library,** with 135,000 volumes and a spacious reading-room (open from 9 A. M. to 10 P. M.). In *St. Stephen's Church* (Episcopal), opposite the library, are some fine monuments. At the cor. of 12th St. is the elegant white marble jewelry-store of *Bailey & Co.*, and near by are a number of handsome shops. Just above (cor. Juniper St.) is the * **U. S. Mint,** a white marble building in the Ionic style, with a graceful portico. The processes of coining are very interesting, and the collection of coins preserved here is the largest and most valuable in America. Visitors are admitted from 9 to 12 o'clock, and the processes pointed out by an attendant.

Crossing Broad St. (same as 14th St.), with its imposing hotels and churches, Chestnut St. passes the *La Pierre House* (cor. Broad and Chestnut), the *Colonnade Hotel* (cor. 15th and Chestnut), and the massive and spacious * building of the *Young Men's Christian Association* (cor. 15th and Chestnut). The latter is of sandstone trimmed with marble, 230 by 72 ft., 4 stories high, with a tower, and containing a library, reading-room, etc. (open from 9 A. M. to 10 P. M.). Near 16th St. is the new and handsome *West End Hotel.* We have now entered the residence quarter, and there is little to challenge the attention. Up 18th St., to the right, is **Logan Square,** a pretty little park of 7 acres, neatly laid out and delightfully shaded. Fronting the square on the E. side is the

Roman Catholic * **Cathedral of St. Peter and St. Paul,** the largest church edifice in the city. It is of red sandstone in the Roman-
Corinthian style, 136 by 216 ft., with a dome 210 ft. high. The façade
consists of a classic pediment, upheld by 4 lofty Corinthian columns,
flanked by pilastered wings. The interior is cruciform and adorned
with frescoes; the altar-piece, by Brumidi, is conspicuous for its fine
coloring. Also fronting on the square (at the cor. of 19th and Race
Sts.) is the handsome building of the * **Academy of Natural Sciences,** of serpentine stone trimmed with Ohio sandstone, in the Collegiate Gothic style. Its library contains 26,000 volumes, and there
are extensive collections in zoölogy, ornithology, geology, mineralogy,
conchology, ethnology, archæology, and botany. The museum contains
upward of 250,000 specimens; and Agassiz pronounced it one of the
finest natural science collections in the world (open Tuesday and Fri-
day afternoons; admission, 10c.). Facing the square on the S. is
Wills's Hospital for the treatment of diseases of the eye; and at the
cor. of Race and 20th Sts. is the *Institution for the Blind*, where the
unfortunate persons for whose benefit it was founded are instructed in
useful trades, in music, and in the usual branches taught in schools.
Farther along 20th (at the cor. of Spring Garden St.) is the *Preston
Retreat* for poor children. To the left (S.) from Chestnut St., 18th St.
leads in one block to the aristocratic * **Rittenhouse Square,** surrounded by costly private residences. Near 19th St. the *Reform Club*
has a fine brown-stone building, and in Walnut St., W. of 18th, stands
the chaste and elegant marble building of the *Social Art Club*. Above
23d St., Chestnut St. crosses the Schuylkill on a massive iron bridge
(completed in 1866 at a cost of $500,000), and leads for a mile or so
amid the beautiful residences of West Philadelphia. (Horse-cars traverse Chestnut Street almost from end to end, but the points we have
described are not beyond the limits of a morning or afternoon stroll.)

Broad St. is a noble thoroughfare, 113 ft. wide, extending from
the Delaware for 15 miles through the heart of the city. At the foot
of Broad St. is **League Island** (600 acres), on which is located the
U. S. Navy Yard, and which is being converted into a great naval
depot. In the " Back Channel," which separates the island from the
mainland, a fleet of monitors and iron-clads is usually anchored. For
3 miles after leaving the river, Broad St. passes across dreary flats
occupied by truck-farms. The first building requiring notice is the
Baltimore Depot, cor. Washington Ave. At the cor. of Christian St.
is the splendid * **Ridgway Library** (a branch of the Philadelphia
Library), an elegant granite structure 220 × 105 ft., standing in beautiful grounds, and admirably arranged. It was a bequest of the late Dr.
Rush, and cost $1,500,000 (open from 9 A. M., to 10 P. M.). At the
cor. of Pine St. is the long granite building of the *Deaf and Dumb
Asylum* (tickets at *Ledger* office); and one square above (cor. Spruce
St.) is the superb **Beth-Eden Baptist Church,** one of the finest
on the street. Just beyond is *Horticultural Hall*, where are held the
annual floral displays of the Horticultural Society; and next door is
the * **Academy of Music,** the largest opera-house in America, with

seats for 3,000 persons. Opposite the Academy is the *Broad Street Theatre ;* and above, on the same side, are the *St. George Hotel* and the handsome brick and stone building of the **Union League Club** (*see* p. 28). At the cor. of Sansom St. is the lofty and ornate *Hotel Lafayette,* and still beyond, near the crossing of Chestnut St., is the *La Pierre House.* On *Penn Square,* at the intersection of Broad and Market Sts., are being erected the vast ***Public Buildings** (for law-courts and public offices), of white marble, 486½ ft. long by 470 wide, 4 stories high, and covering an area of nearly 4½ acres, not including a court-yard in the centre 200 ft. square. The central tower will be 450 ft. high, and the total cost of the building over $10,000,000. Near the N. W. cor. of these buildings is the *School of Design for Women ;* and beyond, at the cor. of Filbert St., the massive ***Masonic Temple** lifts its imposing front ; a solid granite structure in the Norman style, 250 ft. long by 150 wide, with a tower 230 ft. high. The Porch is especially fine ; and within there are large halls finished in the Corinthian, Doric, Egyptian, Ionic, Saracenic, Norman, and Gothic styles of architecture. At the intersection of Broad and Arch Sts. is a cluster of fine churches : **Arch St. Methodist,* of white marble ; the **Holy Communion* (Lutheran), of green serpentine, in the Gothic style ; and the *First Baptist,* of brown stone. Beyond, at the cor. of Cherry St., is the profusely ornamented ***Academy of Fine Arts,** in the Byzantine style, 260 by 100 ft., and containing an excellent collection of pictures, statuary, casts, etc. (entrance, 25c.). Passing now through a shabby quarter, we reach, at the cor. of Callowhill St., the depot of the Philadelphia and Reading R. R., just above which, on the opposite side, are the extensive *Baldwin Locomotive Works,* the largest of the kind in the world. N. of the Baldwin Works Broad is crossed by **Spring Garden St.,* lined with fine residences, and leading toward Fairmount Park. At the cor. of 17th St. is the new *Girls' Normal School,* a spacious brown-stone building. At the cor. of Green St. are a handsome Presbyterian church, in the Norman style, and the plain building of the *Central High School ;* beside which stands the ***Synagogue Rodef Shalom,** in the Saracenic style, with rich interior decorations. Broad St. now traverses for about a mile an elegant residence quarter, forming a popular drive and promenade (with the splendid Episcopal *Church of the Incarnation* at the cor. of Jefferson St.), and then enters a rural district, passing the *Monument Cemetery,* and running straight N. to **Germantown** (6 miles from Chestnut St.), a pretty town, with fine villas and churches, inhabited chiefly by the business men of Philadelphia. Here was fought the Battle of Germantown (Oct. 4, 1777), in which Washington was defeated by the British under Lord Howe. (Germantown may be reached from Philadelphia by horse-cars or by railroad from cor. 9th and Green Sts.)

Other places of interest are as follows : ***Girard College** (2 miles N. W. of the State House by Ridge Ave. cars) was founded by Stephen Girard, a native of France, who died in Philadelphia in 1831, leaving an immense fortune. He bequeathed $2,000,000 to erect suitable buildings " for the gratuitous instruction and support of destitute orphans," and the institution is supported by the income of the residue of the estate after the payment of certain legacies. The estate now amounts to about $7,000,000. The site of the college grounds (42 acres) is on the summit of a slope commanding a fine view. The central or college building is a noble marble structure of the Corinthian order, 218 ft. long, 160 wide, and 97 high. The roof commands a wide * view over the city. In the building are interesting relics of Girard, and in the grounds is a monument to the graduates of the col-

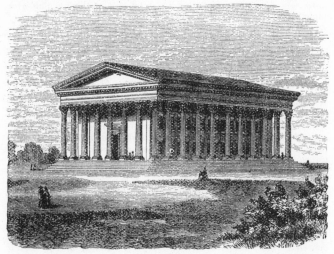

Girard College.

lege who fell in the civil war. (Permits to visit the college may be obtained at the principal hotels, of the Secretary, or of the Directors; clergymen are not admitted.) The *University of Pennsylvania* occupies a group of spacious and substantial stone buildings at 36th and Locust Sts. (reached by Darby cars). It has a library of 18,000 volumes, a fine museum and cabinets, and a hospital and medical college (students in 1874–'75, 800). Near by (on 36th St.) is the *Blockley Almshouse*, with four handsome buildings 500 ft. long, and grounds of 187 acres (tickets of admission at 42 N. 7th St.). The **Penn. Hospital for the Insane,** Haverford Road, West Phila. (take Market St. cars; tickets at *Ledger* office), has two spacious buildings in ample grounds, and is worth a visit, if for nothing else, to see Benjamin West's picture of " Christ Healing the Sick." (Admittance every day except Saturday and Sunday.) The *Episcopal Hospital* has magnifi-

cent buildings in the Norman-Gothic style at 2649 N. Front St. The
* **U. S. Naval Asylum** (on Gray's Ferry Road near South St.) is an
immense marble building, standing in the midst of spacious and highly-
cultivated grounds. The Ionic portico, with 8 graceful columns, the
trophy cannon, and the official residences, are worthy of notice. There
are two *U. S. Arsenals*, one a short distance S. E. of the Naval Asylum,
and the other near Frankford (reached by the red cars of the 2d and
3d St. line). The former is devoted to the manufacture of shoes, equipments, and clothing for the army; the latter is devoted to the manufacture of fixed ammunition, and contains one of the largest powder-
magazines in the United States. The * **Eastern Penitentiary,** in
Fairmount Ave. above 22d St., covers about 10 acres of ground, and in
architecture resembles a baronial castle of the middle ages. The separate (*not* solitary) system is adopted here. Each prisoner is furnished
with work enough to keep him moderately busy, and is allowed to see
and converse with the chaplain, prison-inspectors, and other officials,
but not with any of his fellow prisoners. (Tickets of admission are
obtained at the *Ledger* office.) The *Moyamensing Prison*, 10th St. and
Passyunk Road, is a vast granite building in the Indo-Gothic style,
appropriated to the confinement of persons awaiting trial, or who are
sentenced for short periods (tickets at *Ledger* office).

*Fairmount Park, the largest city park in the world, extends along
both banks of the Schuylkill River for more than 7 miles, and along
both banks of Wissahickon Creek for more than 6 miles, commencing
at Fairmount, an elevation on the Schuylkill from which the park derives its name, and extending to Chestnut Hill on the Wissahickon, a
total distance of nearly 14 miles, embracing a total area of 2,740 acres.
It possesses much natural beauty, being well wooded and having a
great variety of surface; but art, other than that of landscape-garden-
ing, has as yet done little for it. The main entrance to the Park is at
its lower end, and is reached by horse-cars from all parts of the city.
Just inside, on the right, is Fairmount Hill, on the summit of which
are 4 reservoirs of the Schuylkill Water-Works, covering 6 acres, and
surrounded by a graveled walk, from which may be had a fine view
of the city. The buildings containing the water-works machinery lie
just in front of the visitor as he enters the Park; and in the grounds
adjoining them are several fountains and statues. Beyond the buildings is an open plaza, surrounded by flower-beds and shrubbery, and
containing Randolph Rogers's colossal bronze statue of Abraham Lincoln; and beyond this still is *Lemon Hill*, on the summit of which
is the mansion (now used as a restaurant) in which Robert Morris lived
during the Revolutionary War. The principal points of interest in the
park, besides those we have mentioned, are *Sedgeley Hill*, a little above
Lemon Hill on the carriage-road; the *Solitude*, a villa built in 1785 by
John Penn, grandson of William Penn; the * *Zoölogical Gardens*, containing a fine assortment of American and European animals (admission 25c. for adults and 10c. for children); *George's Hill*, and the *Belmont Mansion* (now a restaurant), from both of which there are noble
views; *Belmont Glen*, a picturesque ravine; the various bridges across

the Schuylkill River; and the romantic drive up the *Wissahickon.*
Park-carriages, starting from the Fairmount entrance, traverse the
most interesting portions of the Park (50c. for the round trip). Carriages may also be hired for $1.50 per hour. The grounds on which
the Centennial Exhibition of 1876 was held are located in the Park at
the head of Girard Ave., and may be reached by several lines of horse-
cars. Many of the buildings which then crowded the space have been
removed; but enough are still standing to make the spot worth a visit.
The *Main Exhibition Building* (1,876 ft. long and 464 ft. wide, covering an area of 21¼ acres) is used for a permanent exhibition of art and
industry (entrance, 15c.). *Memorial Hall*, erected by the state and
city at a cost of $1,500,000, stands on an elevated terrace just N. of
the Main Building, and is a splendid stone edifice 365 ft. long, 210
wide, and 150 high. It was used during the Exhibition as an art gallery, and is designed for a permanent art and industrial collection similar to the famous South Kensington Museum in London. Just N. of
Memorial Hall stands the *Horticultural Building*, a charming structure
in the Moresque style, with polychromatic frescoes and arabesques.
It is a conservatory, filled with tropical and other plants, and around
it are 35 acres of ground devoted to horticultural purposes.

   Laurel Hill adjoins the upper part of Fairmount Park, and is
one of the most beautiful cemeteries in the country. It embraces
nearly 200 acres and is divided into North, South, and Central Laurel
Hill. Many fine monuments adorn it; but the distinctive feature of
the cemetery is its unique garden landscape, and the profusion of beautiful trees, shrubs, and flowers. (Admission every day except Sunday
from 9 o'clock till sunset.) *Mount Vernon Cemetery* is nearly opposite
Laurel Hill; *Glenwood* is prettily situated on a ridge between the Delaware and the Schuylkill (reached by Ridge Ave. cars); and *Woodlands*
is in West Philadelphia (reached by Darby cars). The latter contains
the Drexel Mausoleum, the costliest in America.

Cape May.

   From Philadelphia Cape May is reached *via* West Jersey R. R. (ferry from foot
of Market St.), in 2¼ hrs.; fare, $2.50 (distance 81 miles). The road traverses an unin-
teresting and thinly-populated section of New Jersey, the only important station
being *Vineland* (34 miles). There are also daily steamers in summer to and from
Philadelphia (fare, $1 to $2). From New York *via* New Jersey Southern R. R. (141
m.; fare $4.50).
   Hotels.—The leading hotels are the *Stockton House* ($4 a day), with accommo-
dation for 1,200 guests, and *Congress Hall* ($4 a day) with a capacity of 1,000 guests.
Other good houses charging $3 to $4 a day are the *Chalfonte, Sawyer's*, and the
National, besides many smaller ones. The "cottage system" is growing in favor,
and there are boarding-houses where board may be had at $10 to $18 a week.
[Congress Hall and several other leading hotels were burned down late in 1878.
Congress Hall is expected to be rebuilt at once.]

   Cape May, the Long Branch of Philadelphia, is the extreme southern point of New Jersey, fronting the Atlantic at the entrance of Delaware Bay. Its beach is over 5 miles long, and, being hard and
smooth, affords a splendid drive, which has been artificially improved.
The bathing is unsurpassed, the surf being especially fine, and the

water (so it is claimed) less chilling than elsewhere on the coast. The fashionable hours for bathing are from 11 A. M. to 1 P. M., and the spectacle is then very brilliant. Gentlemen are allowed to bathe without costume at sunrise. A long promenade extends along the water-front, and is generally thronged in the forenoon and late afternoon. Cape May is a favorite resort of Southern and Western people, besides being the place of all places for Philadelphians, who give a distinctive tone to its society—more sedate than Long Branch and Saratoga, and less formal and exclusive than Newport. The hotels and cottages are built on a small piece of land, about 250 acres in extent, known as Cape Island, having formerly been separated from the mainland by a small creek. The village contains 6 churches, about 1,500 permanent residents, and many fine villas.

The most popular resort in the vicinity of Cape May is *Schellinger's Landing ;* it is on the Atlantic, and is reached by horse-cars from Cape May. *Cold Spring* is on the line of the railroad about 2 miles N. of the beach. The steamboat-landing is on Delaware Bay, about 2 miles from the village, and a light-house, with powerful revolving light, is down the beach to the W. Between the steamboat-landing and the village is *Sea Grove*, with 3 hotels and a number of private residences. The favorite drive is on the ·beach, which may be traversed from Poverty Beach to Diamond Beach, a distance of 10 miles ; but the roads inland have lately been much improved.

Atlantic City.

From Philadelphia Atlantic City is reached in 1¾ hr. *via* Camden & Atlantic R. R. (distance, 60 miles ; fare, $1), and by Philadelphia & Atlantic City Narrow Gauge R. R. From New York *via* N. J. Southern R. R. to *Winslow*, and thence *via* Camden & Atlantic (distance, 126 miles ; fare, $3). The route thither from Philadelphia traverses a barren, sparsely-settled, and uninteresting region.

Hotels.—The principal are the *United States* ($2.50 to $4 a day), *Congress Hall* ($2.50 to $4 a day), the *Surf House* ($2.50 to $3.50), the *Brighton*, and the *Chalfonte* ($3 a day). Smaller and less expensive houses are the *Fothergill*, the *Clarendon*, the *Tremont*, the *St. Charles*, and *Dennis Cottage* ; the charges at these are $2 to $3 a day. At the boarding-houses the charges are $10 to $18 a week.

Like Cape May, Atlantic City is a favorite resort of the citizens of Philadelphia, but during the season it draws thousands of visitors from .ll parts of the country. The hotels and larger cottages are located on an island, just off the mainland, and the beach is one of the best and safest on the coast. The regular bathing-hour is 11 o'clock A. M., but gentlemen are allowed to bathe without costume before 6 A. M. The city proper contains about 1,200 inhabitants, and is laid out in broad and pleasant avenues. The surrounding country is flat and uninteresting, consisting for the most part of wide-stretching salt-marshes ; but the boating and fishing in the vicinity are excellent, and game can generally be found by the persistent sportsman. The Vineland and New Jersey Southern Railways (connecting with the Camden and Atlantic) place Atlantic City in easy connection with the famous hunting-grounds of *Barnegat, Waretown, West Creek,* and *Tuckertown.* A short distance N. of Atlantic City is the beautiful but ill-omened *Brigantine*

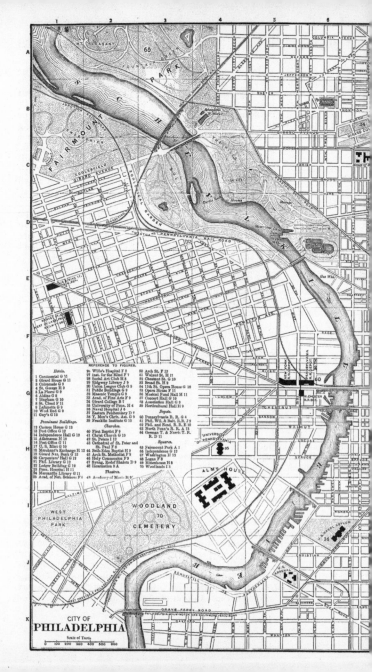

CITY OF PHILADELPHIA

Scale of Yards
0   100   200   300   400   500   600

REFERENCE TO FIGURES.

Hotels.
1 Continental G 11
2 Girard House G 11
3 Colonnade G 9
4 St. George H 9
5 La Pierre G 9
6 Aldine G 9
7 Bingham G 10
8 St. Cloud F 11
9 Lafayette G 9
10 West End G 9
11 Guy's G 12

Prominent Buildings.
12 Custom House G 12
13 Post Office G 12
14 Independence Hall G 12
15 Athenæum H 12
16 Post Office G 11
17 U. S. Mint G 10
18 Merchant's Exchange H 12
19 Girard Nat. Bank G 12
20 Carpenters' Hall G 12
21 Phil. Library G 12
22 Ledger Building G 12
23 Penn. Hospital H 11
24 Mercantile Library G 11
25 Acad. of Nat. Science F 8

30 Wills's Hospital F 8
31 Inst. for the Blind F 7
32 Social Art Club H 8
33 Ridgway Library J 8
34 Union League Club G 9
35 Public Buildings G 9
36 Masonic Temple G 9
37 Acad. of Fine Arts F 9
38 University of Penn. H 4
39 Naval Hospital J 6
37 Eastern Penitentiary D 7
Y. Men's Chris. Ass. G 9
38 Franklin Institute G 12

Churches.
40 First Baptist F 9
41 Christ Church G 13
42 St. Peters I 13
43 Cathedral of St. Peter and St. Paul F 9
44 Beth-Eden Baptist H 9
45 Arch St. Methodist F 9
46 Holy Communion F 9
47 Synag. Rodef Shalom D 9
48 Incarnation I 9

Theatres.
48 Academy of Music H 9

50 Arch St. F 12
51 Walnut St. H 11
52 Chestnut St. G 10
53 Broad St. H 9
54 11th St. Open House G 10
55 Opera House F 11
56 Musical Fund Hall H 11
57 Concert Hall G 10
58 Association Hall G 9
59 Horticulteral Hall H 9

Depots.
60 Pennsylvania R. R. G 4
62 Phil. Wil. & Balt. R.R. J 9
61 Phil. and Read. R. R. E 10
62 North Penn's R. R. A 13
62 German T. & North T. R. R. D 11

Squares.
65 Fairmount Park A 1
66 Independence G 12
67 Washington F 13
68 Logan F 8
69 Rittenhouse H 8
70 Woodlands I 3

Beach, called by the sailors " the graveyard," on account of the number
of fatal wrecks that have occurred there. Also near by is the famous
Long Beach, favorite of fishermen and hunters.

5. Philadelphia to Baltimore.

Via Philadelphia, Wilmington & Baltimore R. R. Distance, 98 m. ; time 3¼ to
5 hrs. ; fare, $3.20. The through-trains from New York to Baltimore pass through
West Philadelphia, and make the entire distance (188 m.) in 5 to 7 hrs. ; fare, $6.20.

THE country traversed on this route has few scenic attractions,
though the highly-cultivated farms and clustering towns indicate a
populous and long-settled region. *Chester* (14 miles) is the oldest town
in Pennsylvania, having been settled by the Swedes in 1643. It now
has 12,000 inhabitants, and here are the vast ship-yards of John Roach.
The *Brandywine* (crossed 4 miles beyond Chester) is famous for the battle
fought on its banks in September, 1777. **Wilmington** (28 miles) is
the chief city of the State of Delaware. It has 42,500 inhabitants, and
its manufactures are very extensive and various, embracing ship-building, car manufactories, cotton and woolen factories, flour mills, powder
mills, and shoe and leather factories. The city is regularly laid out,
with streets at right angles, the principal ones paved with stone, and
all lined with brick sidewalks. The buildings are uniformly of brick,
of which an excellent quality is made in the vicinity. The public buildings are the *City Hall,* the county *Almshouse,* the *Custom-House and
Post-Office* (cor. King and 6th Sts.), the *Wilmington Institute and Public
Library,* and the *Opera-House.* There are several handsome churches,
including the Central and West Presbyterian, the Grace (Methodist),
and the Church of the Sacred Heart (Roman Catholic). The **Old
Swedes' Church,* of stone, erected in 1698, is still in good condition.
The *Clayton House* ($3 a day), cor. Market and 5th Sts., is a fine build-
ing. There is a restaurant in the depot, and the. trains usually stop
from 5 to 10 minutes.

Newark (40 miles) is an academic town, seat of several excellent
educational institutions, and 4 miles beyond the train crosses the celebrated *Mason & Dixon's Line* (long the boundary between the Northern and Southern States), and enters Maryland. At *Havre de Grace* (62
miles), the Susquehanna River is crossed on a lofty wooden bridge
nearly a mile long. In entering Baltimore a pleasing view of the Patapsco River and Fort McHenry may be obtained from the car-window
on the left.

6. Baltimore.

Hotels.—The *Carrollton House* ($2.50 to $4 a day), cor. Baltimore and Light
Sts., is handsome and exclusive ; *Barnum's Hotel* ($3 to $4 a day), cor. Calvert
and Fayette Sts., is the largest in the city ; the *Eutaw House* ($3 a day) is a fa-
mous old hotel, cor. Baltimore and Eutaw Sts. Smaller but good houses are the
Maltby ($2.50 to $3 a day), in Pratt St. near Light, the *St. Clair,* on Monument
Square, and the *Howard* ($3 a day), in Howard St. near Baltimore St. On the
European plan are the *Mount Vernon* (small but elegant), in Monument St. near
Mount Vernon Place, and *Guy's,* on Monument Square. Board may be had in pri-
vate houses at $6 to $12 per week.
Restaurants.—*Painter's,* in Lexington St., between Charles and Liberty, is

the fashionable resort for ladies; *Rennert's,* in Fayette St. near Calvert, is also favored by ladies; and *Pepper's,* on Holliday St. near Fayette, is good. *Guy's Hotel,* on Monument Square, has an excellent restaurant attached; also the *Maltby House.*

Modes of Conveyance.—*Horse-cars* (fare 6c.) afford easy access to all parts of the city. *Public carriages* wait at the depots and at stands in various parts of the city. Tariffs of fares are placed inside the carriages; in case of disagreement with the driver, apply to a policeman. The rates are, for carrying 1 passenger from any railroad station or steamboat to any house or hotel in the city, 75c.; each additional passenger, 25c.; each trunk or box, 15c. For 1 hour $1.50, and $1 for each additional hour. Children over 10 half price. *Stages* run daily to Long Green and Harford Road, to Franklin and Powhatan, and to Pikesville; to Bellair three times a week (Tuesday, Thursday, and Saturday); and to Kingsville, Kellville, and Franklinville, on Mondays, Wednesdays, and Fridays.

Railroad Depots.—The depot of the *Philadelphia, Wilmington & Baltimore R. R.* is in President St. near Central Ave.; of the *Baltimore & Ohio R. R.,* in Camden St., near Howard; of the *Northern Central R.R.,* cor. Calvert and Franklin Sts.; same depot used by the *Baltimore & Potomac R. R.;* of the *Western Maryland,* cor. Hillen and Exeter Sts.

Theatres and Amusements.—*Ford's Grand Opera-House* (in Fayette St. near Eutaw) has an ornate interior, with seats for 2,000 persons. The *Academy of Music,* in Howard St., seats 1,500 persons; and the *Holliday St. Theatre* (opp. the City Hall) is a favorite resort. The *Front St. Theatre* (Front St. near Gay) is devoted to varieties and spectacles. At the *Concordia Opera House* (cor. Eutaw and German Sts.) German opera and drama are usually given. The *Central Theatre* (varieties) is near the bridge on Baltimore St. Concerts and lectures are given in the hall of the *Masonic Temple,* at the *Peabody Institute,* in the hall of the *Maryland Institute,* and at the *New Assembly Rooms,* cor. Hanover and Lombard Sts. The *race-course* of the Maryland Jockey Club is at Pimlico, 2 m. from the N. W. boundary of the city.

Reading-Rooms.—At the *Peabody Institute,* cor. Charles and Monument Sts. (open from 9 A. M. to 10 P. M.); the *Mercantile Library,* cor. Saratoga and St. Paul Sts. (open from 10 A. M. to 10 P. M.); the *Maryland Institute,* cor. Baltimore and Harrison Sts.; the *Baltimore Library,* cor. Saratoga and St. Paul Sts.; and the *Young Men's Christian Association,* cor. Charles and Saratoga Sts.

Art Collections.—The *Maryland Academy of Art* (in Mulberry St. opp. Cathedral) has a collection of paintings, engravings, casts, etc. (introduction by a member). A Department of Art, in connection with the Peabody Institute, is in process of organization. Annual exhibitions of American paintings are held at the *Athenæum,* cor. Saratoga and St. Paul Sts. Good pictures are usually on exhibition (free) at the sales-galleries of *Myers & Hedian,* 46 N. Charles St., and of *Butler & Perigo,* cor. Charles and Fayette Sts. The private gallery of Mr. W. T. Walters, No. 65 Mount Vernon Place, is one of the richest in America (admission may usually be obtained by sending a letter, inclosing card, to the owner).

Post-Office.—The Post-Office is in the Exchange building, on Gay St. between 2d and Lombard. Open from 7 A. M. to 9 P. M.

BALTIMORE, the chief city of Maryland, and in population and commerce one of the most important in the United States, is picturesquely situated on the N. branch of the Patapsco River, 14 miles from its entrance into Chesapeake Bay, and about 200 miles from the Atlantic. It embraces an area of about 12 square miles, nearly half of which is thickly built upon. Jones's Falls, a small stream running N. and S., spanned by numerous bridges, divides the city into two nearly equal parts known as East and West Baltimore. The harbor is capacious and safe, consisting of an inner basin into which small vessels can enter, and an outer harbor accessible to the largest ships. The entrance is defended by Fort McHenry, which was unsuccessfully bombarded by the British fleet in the war of 1812. **Baltimore St.,** running E. and W., is the main business thoroughfare, and on it are located the principal retail stores, hotels, restaurants, etc. *North Charles St.* is the most

attractive and fashionable promenade, though *Mount Vernon Place*, the
vicinity of the monument, and *Broadway*, are also frequented. The
favorite drives are through Druid Hill Park, out Charles St. to Lake
Roland (6 m.), on the old York Road to Govanstown (4 m.), and over
a well-shaded, well-paved turnpike to Franklin (5 m.).

 The present site of Baltimore was chosen in 1729, and its name was given it (in
1745) in honor of Lord Baltimore, the proprietary of Maryland. In 1780 it became a
port of entry. In 1782 the first pavements were laid in Baltimore St., and in the
same year the first regular communication with Philadelphia was established through
a line of stage-coaches. The charter of the city dates from 1797. The population,
which at that time was 26,000, had increased by 1850 to nearly 200,000; in 1860 it
was 212,418, in 1870, 267,354, and in 1876 was estimated at 325,000. The commerce
of the city is very active. Two lines of European steamers now start from her harbor; and through her two great arteries of traffic (the Baltimore & Ohio and the
Northern Central Railroads) she is successfully competing for the trade of the North
and Northwest. Large shipments of grain are made to Europe, and tobacco, cotton,
petroleum, bacon, butter, cheese, and lard, are also exported. Baltimore is the chief
point for working the rich copper-ores of Lake Superior, and produces nearly 4,000
tons of refined copper yearly; the smelting-works are in Canton, and employ 1,000
men.   There are also iron-works, rolling-mills, nail-factories, locomotive-works,
cotton-factories, and other industrial establishments (2,261 in all). The canning of
oysters, fruits, and vegetables, is estimated to reach the annual value of $5,000,000;
and 500,000 hides are annually made into leather and sent to New England.

From the number of its monuments, Baltimore is often called "the Monumental City," and its chief glory in this line is the ***Washington Monument,** standing 100 feet above tide-water, in the heart of the city, at the intersection of Mount Vernon and Washington Places. The base of the Monument is 50 ft. square and 20 ft. high, supporting a Doric shaft 176½ ft. in height, which is surmounted by a colossal statue of Washington, 16 ft. high. The total height is thus 312½ ft. above the river. It is built of brick with an outer casing of white marble, and cost $200,000. From the balcony of the monument a magnificent *view of the city, harbor, and surrounding country is obtained (access by a circular staircase within; fee, 15c.). The ***Battle Monument** stands in Monument Square, at the intersection of Fayette and Calvert Sts., and was erected in 1815 to the memory of those who fell defending the city from the British in Sept., 1814. The square sub-base on which

Washington Monument.

the monument rests is 20 ft. high, with an Egyptian door at each front, on which are appropriate inscriptions, and representations (in *basso-rilievo*) of some of the incidents of the battle. The column rises 18 ft. above the base, is encircled by bands on which are inscribed the names of those who fell, and is surmounted by a female figure in marble, emblematic of the city of Baltimore. The *Wildey Monument* (on Broadway near Baltimore St.) is a plain marble pediment and shaft surmounted by a group representing Charity protecting orphans; it is dedicated to Thomas Wildey, founder of the order of Odd Fellows in the United States. The *Wells and McComas Monument* (cor. Gay and Monument Sts.) commemorates two boys who shot Gen. Ross, the British commander, Sept. 12, 1812. The *Poe Monument* stands in the churchyard of the Westminster Presbyterian Church, cor. Greene and Fayette Sts.

Facing the Washington Monument on the S. is the stately white marble building of the ***Peabody Institute,** founded and endowed by George Peabody, the eminent London banker, and designed for the diffusion of knowledge among the masses. It contains a free library of 58,000 volumes, a lecture-hall, and a conservatory of music. A new building for the Gallery of Art is being erected adjoining the present

structure. Also fronting the Monument (cor. Charles and Monument
Sts.) is the costly *Mount Vernon Church (Methodist), built of green
serpentine stone, with outside facings of buff Ohio and red Connecticut
sandstone, and 18 polished columns of Aberdeen granite. This is the
most aristocratic residence-quarter of Baltimore, and surrounding the
Place and on the adjacent streets are some of the finest private houses
in the city. One block off (at the cor. of Park and Madison Sts.) is the
*First Presbyterian Church, the most elaborate specimen of the
Lancet-Gothic architecture in the country. Its spire is 268 ft. high,
with side towers 78 and 128 ft. high, and the interior is richly decorated.

The *City Hall, completed in 1875, is one of the finest municipal
buildings in America. It fills the entire square enclosed by Holliday,
Lexington, North, and Fayette Sts., is 225 by 140 ft., and cost $2,271,-
135. It is of marble, in the Renaissance style, 4 stories high, with
French roof and an iron dome 260 ft. high. A balcony 250 ft. above
the street affords a magnificent view of the city (visitors may ascend
on Mondays from 10 A. M. to 3 P. M.). Near by (cor. Fayette and
North Sts.) is the U. S. Court-House, a massive granite structure. The
*Exchange, in Gay St. between 2d and Lombard, is a large and ele-
gant structure, with a façade of 240 ft. It has colonnades of 6 Ionic
columns on the E. and W. sides, the shafts of which are single blocks
of fine Italian marble, of admirable workmanship. The whole is surmounted by an immense dome, 115 ft. high and 53 ft. in diameter,
which is brilliantly frescoed and overarches a spacious rotunda. The
Post-Office, the U. S. Custom-House, and the Merchants' Bank are all
located in this building; which also contains a fine Reading-Room 50
ft. square. The Corn and Flour Exchange, cor. Wood and South Sts.,
is a solid and handsome building; and the Rialto Building, cor. 2d and
Holliday Sts., is a fine specimen of Renaissance architecture. The
Masonic Temple, in Charles St. near Saratoga, is a stately stone
edifice, completed in 1870 at a cost of $400,000. The Main Hall is
used for concerts and lectures. The Odd Fellows' Hall, in Gay St. near
Fayette, is a handsome Gothic building, containing a large library.
The new building of the Y. M. C. A., cor. Charles and Saratoga Sts.,
is one of the finest in the city, and contains a library, reading-room,
gymnasium, etc. Among business structures the offices of the American
(S. W. cor. Baltimore and South Sts.) and the Sun (S. E. cor. same
streets) are noteworthy. The Merchants' Shot Tower (cor. Front and
Fayette Sts.) is one of the landmarks of the city; it is 216 ft. high and
60 to 20 ft. in diameter, and contains 1,100,000 bricks.

Two of the finest churches in the city have already been mentioned
(see above). The most celebrated is the *Cathedral, cor. Mulberry
and Cathedral Sts. It is of granite, in the form of a cross, 190 ft. long,
177 broad at the arms of the cross, and 127 high from the floor to the
top of the cross which surmounts the dome. At the W. end rise 2 tall
towers, crowned with Saracenic cupolas resembling the minarets of a
Mohammedan mosque. It contains one of the largest organs in America, and 2 excellent paintings: "The Descent from the Cross," pre-

sented by Louis XVI., and "St. Louis burying his Officers and Soldiers slain before Tunis," the gift of Charles X. of France. The Roman Catholic churches of *St. Alphonsus* (cor. Saratoga and Park Sts.), of *St. Vincent de Paul* (in N. Front St.), and of *St. Ignatius Loyola* (cor. Calvert and Read Sts.), are rich in architecture and decorations. *Grace Church* (Episcopal), cor. Monument and Park Sts., is a fine specimen of Gothic architecture, in red sandstone. Close by, at the cor. of Read and Cathedral Sts., is *Emanuel Church* (Episcopal), also Gothic, built of gray sandstone. *Christ Church* (Episcopal), is a beautiful marble structure, cor. St. Paul and Chase Sts. *St. Paul's* (Episcopal), cor. Charles and Saratoga Sts., is a pleasing example of the Norman style; this is the Bishop's church. Other fine Episcopal churches are *St. Peter's*, of marble, cor. Druid Hill Ave. and Lanvale St., and *St. Luke's* (Ritualistic), near Franklin Square. The **Unitarian Church,** cor. N. Charles and Franklin Sts., is an imposing structure, with a colonnade in front composed of 4 Tuscan columns and 2 pilasters which form the arcades. From the portico the entrance is by 5 bronze doors. The *Eutaw Place Baptist Church,* cor. Eutaw and Dolphin Sts., is noted for its beautifully proportioned marble spire, 186 ft. high. The *Brown Memorial Church* (Presbyterian), cor. Park and Townsend Sts., is a spacious marble edifice in the Gothic style; and the *Westminster,* cor. Green and Fayette, is noteworthy for containing the grave and monument of Edgar Allan Poe. The Hebrew *Synagogue,* in Loyd near Baltimore St., is large and handsome.

The * **Athenæum,** cor. Saratoga and St. Paul Sts., is a spacious building in the Italian style: it contains the *Mercantile Library* (26,-000 vols.; open from 10 A. M. to 10 P. M.), the *Baltimore Library* (15,000 vols.), and the collections of the * *Maryland Historical Society,* comprising a library of 10,000 vols., numerous historical relics, and some fine pictures and statuary (admission free). In the picture-gallery are held annual exhibitions of American paintings. The **Maryland Institute,** designed for the promotion of the mechanic arts, is a vast brick structure, cor. Baltimore and Harrison Sts. The first floor is used as a market (*Central Market*), and in the main hall, 260 ft. long, is held an annual exhibition of the products of American mechanical industry. It also contains a library (14,000 vols.), lecture-rooms, a school of design, etc. The *Academy of Sciences* (in Mulberry St., opposite Cathedral St.) has a fine museum of natural history, including rich collections of birds and minerals, and a complete representation of the flora and fauna of Maryland (admission free). The **Johns Hopkins University** (endowed with over $3,000,000 by Johns Hopkins, a wealthy citizen who died in 1873, bequeathing an immense property to educational and charitable objects) is temporarily located at the cor. of Howard St. and Druid Hill Ave. Its permanent site will probably be at Clifton, 2 miles from the center of the city on the Harford road. The **Johns Hopkins Hospital** (endowed with over $2,000,000) is building on Broadway cor. Monument St., and will be the finest in America. It will be connected with the Medical Department of the Johns Hopkins University. The *State Normal School,* cor.

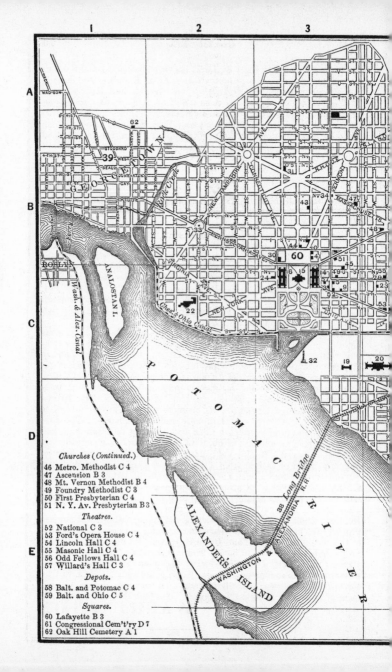

Churches (Continued.)

46 Metro. Methodist C 4
47 Ascension B 3
48 Mt. Vernon Methodist B 4
49 Foundry Methodist C 3
50 First Presbyterian C 4
51 N. Y. Av. Presbyterian B 3

Theatres.

52 National C 3
53 Ford's Opera House C 4
54 Lincoln Hall C 4
55 Masonic Hall C 4
56 Odd Fellows Hall C 4
57 Willard's Hall C 3

Depots.

58 Balt. and Potomac C 4
59 Balt. and Ohio C 5

Squares.

60 Lafayette B 3
61 Congressional Cem't'ry D 7
62 Oak Hill Cemetery A 1

REFERENCE TO FIGURES.

Hotels.

1 Arlington B 3
2 Riggs House D 6
3 Willard's C 3
4 Congressional C 5
5 Ebbitt House C 3

6 National C 4
7 Metropolitan C 4
8 Washington C 4
9 Imperial C 3
10 Wormley's B 3
11 St. Marc C 4
12 St. James C 4

Prominent Buildings.

13 Capitol C 5
14 U. S. Treasury C 3
15 Executive Mansion C 3
16 State, War and Navy Departments C 3

17 Patent Office C 4
18 General Post Office C 4
19 Dept. of Agriculture C 3
20 Smithsonian Institute C 4
21 Botanical Gardens C 4
22 U. S. Naval Obser. C 2
23 Army Medical Mus. C 4
24 Ordnance Museum C 3
25 U. S. Arsenal E 4
26 Navy Yard E 6
27 Marine Barracks D 6
28 City Hall C 4
29 Masonic Temple C 4
30 Corcoran Art Gallery B 3
31 Louise Home B 3
32 Washington Mon um't C 3
33 Stat. of Washington B 2
34 Statue of Gen. Scott B 3
35 Statue of Lincoln C 4
36 Naval Monument C 5
37 Howard University A 4
38 Long Bridge E 3
39 Georgetown B 1

Churches.

40 Cath. of St. Aloysius B 5
41 St. Matthew's B 3
42 St. Dominic's C 4
43 St. Augustine B 3
44 St. John's B 3
45 Ch. of the Epiphany C 3

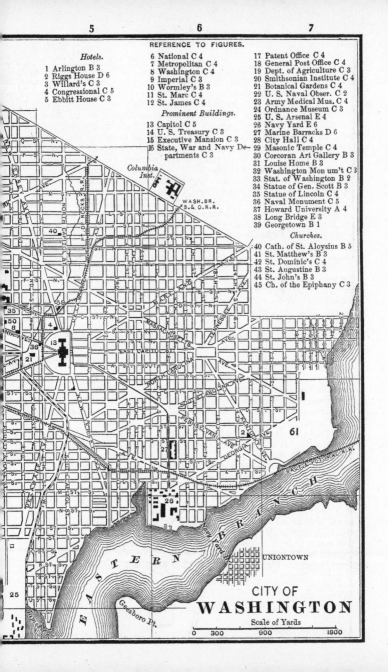

CITY OF
WASHINGTON

Scale of Yards

0   300   900   1800

Carrollton Ave. and Townsend St., is one of the finest buildings in
the city. The *City College*, in N. Howard St., is a graceful edifice in
the Collegiate-Gothic style.

Prominent charitable institutions are the *Maryland Hospital for the
Insane*, in E. Monument St.; the *Maryland Institution for the Instruction of the Blind*, a large marble building in North Ave. near Charles
St.; the *Mount Hope Hospital*, conducted by the Sisters of Charity, on
North Ave. cor. Bolton St.; and the *Episcopal Church Home*, for the
relief of the afflicted and destitute, in Broadway near Baltimore St.
The * **State Insane Asylum** is a massive pile of granite buildings
near Catonsville (6 miles from the city). The *Sheppard Asylum for
the Insane*, founded by Moses Sheppard, a wealthy Quaker, occupies a
commanding site near Towsontown, 7 miles from the city; and the
Mount Hope Retreat for the insane and sick is 4 miles from the city
on the Reistertown Road. The * **Bay View Asylum** (Almshouse)
is a vast brick building, superbly situated on a commanding eminence
near the outskirts of the city on the Philadelphia road, whence noble
views are had (reached by Madison Ave. cars).

* **Druid Hill Park** (reached by Madison Ave. cars) is a beautiful pleasure-ground of 680 acres, situated in the northern suburbs of
the city. The architectural decorations of the park are few; its charms
lying chiefly in its rural beauty, its secluded walks, drives, and bridle-
paths. The surface is undulating and well wooded, the trees being
among the oldest and finest in any public park in America. Several
of the eminences overlook the surrounding country, and from the
* tower at the head of Druid Hill Lake there is a superb view of the
city and harbor. *Patterson Park*, at the E. end of Baltimore St., embraces 70 acres, pleasantly laid out, and commands extensive views
in every direction. The principal cemeteries are **Greenmont Cemetery,** in the N. part of the city (reached by York Road horse-cars), and
Loudon Park Cemetery, 2 miles from the city *via* Franklin Square
and Ellicott City horse-cars. Both have imposing entrances, contain
many handsome monuments, and are picturesquely laid out.

* **Federal Hill** (reached by horse-cars from cor. of Baltimore and
Hanover Sts.) is a commanding eminence on the S. side of the inner
basin, and affords fine views of the city, river, and bay. It has been
purchased by the city for a park, and contains a U. S. Signal Station.
Fort McHenry, at the entrance of the harbor, is worth a visit: it
is situated at the end of Whetstone Point, 3 miles from the City Hall,
and is reached by S. Baltimore horse-cars and also by ferry from foot
of Broadway. The sentinels will usually admit strangers. The **Railroad Tunnels,** by which all the railroads on the N. side of the city
are connected with tide-water at Canton, are among the wonders of
Baltimore. The Baltimore and Potomac Tunnel is, next to the Hoosac
Tunnel, the longest in America (6,969 ft.) and the Union Tunnel is
3,410 ft. long. They were completed in 1873, at a cost of $4,500,000.

7. Baltimore to Washington.

THE traveler has a choice of two routes in going from Baltimore to Washington: the Washington branch of the *Baltimore & Ohio R. R.* and the *Baltimore & Potomac R. R.* The distance by the former is 40 miles and by the latter 43 miles; time, 1½ to 2 hrs.: fare, $1.20. The country traversed is flat, with few picturesque and no very striking features. On leaving the Baltimore depot, the trains of the Baltimo & Potomac line pass through the great tunnels beneath the city, mentioned above; and just before entering Washington through another tunnel 1,500 ft. long. By the Baltimore & Ohio line the splendid * *Washington Viaduct* is crossed (9 miles out). The first view of the Capitol in approaching Washington is very fine and should not be lost.

New York to Washington.—The regular Express trains run through in 8 to 9 hrs. (fare, $7.50). The *Limited Express*, composed exclusively of Pullman palace-cars, accomplishes the distance in 6 hrs. 40 minutes, stopping only at Newark, Elizabeth, New Brunswick, Philadelphia, Wilmington, and Baltimore (fare, $10).

8. Washington City.

Hotels.—The best on the American plan are the *Arlington* ($3 to $4 a day), in Vermont Ave., between H and I Sts.; the *Riggs House* ($3 to $4 a day), cor. 15th and G Sts.; *Willard's* ($4 a day), cor. Pennsylvania Ave. and 14th St.; and the *Congressional* ($4 a day), cor. New Jersey Ave. and B St. The *Ebbitt House* (cor. F and 14th Sts.) is a favorite with army and navy officers ($2.50 to $4 a day). Other good hotels on the American plan are the *National* ($2.50 to $4 a day), cor. Pennsylvania Ave. and 6th St.; the *Metropolitan* ($3 to $4 a day), in Pennsylvania Ave. near 6th St.; the *Washington*, cor. Pennsylvania Ave. and 3d St.; the *Imperial*, in E St., between 13th and 14th; *Wormley's*, cor. 15th and H Sts.; the *Globe*, cor. F and 12th Sts.; the *Continental* ($3 a day), Pennsylvania Ave., between 3d and 4½ Sts. ($3 a day). The best on the European plan are the *St. Marc*, cor. Pennsylvania Ave. and 7th St.; and the *St. James*, cor. Pennsylvania Ave. and 6th St. Board in private houses may be had at $8 to $20 a week.

Restaurants.—*Welcker's* (in 15th St. near H) is the best in the city, famous for its *cuisine* and wines. *Wormley's* (cor. 15th and H) is a fashionable resort. The *St. George* (in F St. near 9th) is much frequented by ladies. *Russell & Leonard's* (cor. Pennsylvania Ave. and 9th St.) is excellent, and *Harvey's* (cor. Pennsylvania Ave. and 11th St.) is noted for its oysters. The hotels on the European plan have good restaurants attached. In the basement of the Capitol, under each House, is an excellent restaurant.

Modes of Conveyance.—*Horse-cars* (fare 5c.) afford easy access to all points of interest in the city. *Hackney Carriages* are found at the depots and at numerous stands. The legal rates of fare are: for 1-2 passengers 1 m. or less, $1; for each additional passenger, 50c.; per hour, $1.50. One-horse coaches are allowed to charge 75c. per hour or per course; if less than 1 m., half rates. In case of disagreement, call a policeman or drive to a police-station. For excursions beyond the city limits it is better to hire carriages at the livery-stables or hotels. A *steamboat* for Mount Vernon leaves the 7th St. wharf daily at 10 A. M. *Ferry-boats* run to Alexandria hourly during the day from 7th St. wharf (fare, 15c.: round trip, 25c.).

Railroad Depots.—The depot of the *Baltimore & Potomac R. R.* is a spacious and highly ornate building, cor. B and 6th Sts. That of the *Baltimore & Ohio R. R.* is at the cor. of New Jersey Ave. and C St.

Churches.—Those most visited by strangers are the *Cathedral of St. Aloysius* (Roman Catholic), cor. N. Capitol and I Sts., noted for its rich interior and fine choral music; *St. Matthew's*, E. of Lafayette Square, usually attended by Catholic members of the Diplomatic Corps; *St. Dominic's* (Roman Catholic), an imposing granite structure, cor. 6th and F Sts.; *St. Augustine* (Roman Catholic), in 15th,

between L and M Sts., noted for its music; *St. John's* (Episcopal), fronting Lafayette Square on the N., a famous old church, attended by Presidents Madison and
Monroe; the *Church of the Epiphany* (Episcopal), in G St., between 13th and 14th;
the *Metropolitan Methodist*, a splendid brown-stone edifice, cor. 4½ and D Sts.;
the *Ascension* (Episcopal), of light stone, the finest church in the city, cor. Massachusetts Ave. and 12th St. N. W.; the *Mount Vernon Methodist*, cor. 9th and K
Sts.; the *Foundry Methodist*, in F St. near 14th (attended by President Hayes);
the *First Presbyterian*, in 4½ St. near C St.; and the *N. Y. Avenue Presbyterian*,
in N. Y. Ave. near 14th St.

Theatres and Amusements.—The *National Theatre*, on E St. near 14th,
is the principal in the city, and usually has a good stock company. *Ford's Opera-
House*, on 9th St. near Pennsylvania Ave., seats 1,500 persons. *Lincoln Hall* (cor.
9th and D Sts.) is the finest in the city, and is used for concerts, lectures, readings,
etc. In *Masonic Hall* (cor. F and 9th Sts.) public parties and balls are often given.
Odd-Fellows' Hall, in 7th St., between D and E, and *Willard's Hall*, in F St.
near 14th, are also used for lectures and concerts. *Schuetzen Park* is a popular
German resort on 7th St., beyond the Howard University.

Reading-Rooms.—At all the leading hotels are reading-rooms well supplied
with newspapers. The *Library of Congress*, in the Capitol, is open to visitors
from 10 A. M. to 4 P. M. The excellent library and reading-rooms of the *Young
Men's Christian Association* (cor. 9th and D Sts.) are open (free) from 9 A. M. to
10 P. M. The *Patent-Office Library* is rich in scientific and mechanical works. At
the offices of the Washington correspondents of leading American newspapers (on
Newspaper Row, near the cor. of 14th and F Sts.) files of newspapers are usually
accessible to the visitor.

Art Collections.—The *Corcoran Gallery of Art* (cor. Pennsylvania Ave.
and 17th St.) has one of the richest collections in America (see p. 56). Admission
free on Tuesdays, Thursdays, and Saturdays; on other days, 25c. Mr. J. C. Mc-
Guire, 614 E St. N. W., has a fine private gallery of pictures.

Post-Office.—The *City Post-Office* is on F St. near 7th. Open from 6 A. M. to
11 P. M.; on Sundays from 8 to 10 A. M. and 6 to 7 P. M.

WASHINGTON CITY, the political capital of the United States, is situated on the N. bank of the Potomac River, at its confluence with the
Eastern Branch. Its site is an admirable one, consisting of an extensive undulating plain surrounded by rolling hills and diversified by
irregular elevations which furnish advantageous positions for the various public buildings. The plan of the city is unique ("the city of
Philadelphia griddled across the city of Versailles"), and is on a scale
which shows that it was expected that a vast metropolis would grow
up there. It covers an area 4½ miles long by 2½ broad, embracing
nearly 9½ square miles. A very small portion of this, however, is as yet
built upon. **Pennsylvania Avenue,** in that part of its course between the Capitol and the White House (1⅓ mile) is the busiest and
most fashionable street in the city; it is 160 feet wide, and on it or near
it are the leading hotels, theatres, stores, etc. **Seventh St.,** which
intersects Pennsylvania Ave. about midway between the Capitol and
the Treasury, is the next most important thoroughfare, and contains
many handsome retail stores. *Massachusetts Ave.* extends entirely
across the city (4½ m.), parallel with Pennsylvania Ave., and on portions of its course is lined with fine residences. *Maryland Ave.* leads
S. W. from the Capitol to the Long Bridge, and N. E. to the Toll-gate.
Vermont Ave. contains many handsome residences. *Fourteenth St.* is
one of the most important of the cross-streets. The favorite drives
are to the Old Soldiers' Home; to the Heights of Georgetown; to the
Little Falls of the Potomac (3 miles above Georgetown); to the Great
Falls of the Potomac (17 miles from Washington); and across the

river to Arlington, Alexandria, and the embattled heights along the Virginia shore of the Potomac.

The best time to visit Washington, if one wishes to see its most characteristic aspect, is during the sessions of Congress. These begin on the first Monday in December, and last until March 4, in the odd-numbered years, and until June or July in the even-numbered years. During this period the galleries of the Senate and House of Representatives are open to visitors. The sessions of both Houses begin at noon and usually close before sunset, but sometimes they are prolonged far into the night. A flag displayed over the N. wing of the Capitol indicates that the Senate is in session; over the S. wing that the House is in session. When the sittings are prolonged into the night, the great lantern over the dome is illuminated, affording a brilliant light which is visible for many miles. The best times for seeing the natural beauties of Washington are May, or early June, and October.

The site of Washington City, if not chosen by Washington himself, seems to have been selected through his agency, and it was he who laid the corner-stone of the Capitol. This was on Sep. 18, 1793, seven years before the seat of government was removed thither from Philadelphia. Under Washington's direction the city was planned and laid out by Andrew Ellicott. It appears to have been Washington's desire that it should be called the "Federal City," but the name of "the city of Washington" was conferred upon it on Sept. 9, 1791. Its ancient name was Cono-cocheague, derived from a rapid stream of that name which ran near the city, and which, in the Indian tongue, means the Roaring Brook. The city was incorporated May 3, 1802. Its population in 1860 was 60,000; in 1870, 109,189; and in 1875, 133,000. This is increased during the sessions of Congress by a floating population amounting to many thousands. The commerce and manufactures of Washington are unimportant.

The Public Buildings [1] are the chief attraction of Washington, and the ** **Capitol** is not only the finest of these, but is probably the most magnificent public edifice in the world. It crowns the summit of Capitol Hill (90 ft. high), and consists of a main building 352 ft. long and 121 ft. deep, and two wings, or extensions, each 238 by 140 ft. Its whole length is 751 ft. 4 in., and the area covered rather more than $3\frac{1}{2}$ acres. The material of the central building is a light-yellow free-stone (painted white), but the extensions are pure white marble. The surrounding grounds, which are beautifully cultivated, and embellished with fountains and statuary, embrace about 50 acres and are known as East and West Grounds. The main front is toward the E. and is adorned with three grand porticoes of Corinthian columns. On the steps of the central portico are groups of statuary by Persico and Greenough; and on the grounds in front of it is *Greenough's colossal statue of Washington. Colossal marble statues of Peace and War are on the r. and l. of the entrance; and over the doorway is a bass-relief of Fame and Peace crowning Washington with laurel. The W. front projects 83 ft., and is embellished with a recessed portico of 10 columns. This front, though not so imposing architecturally as the eastern, commands a fine view of the central and western portions of

---

[1] All public buildings, including the Capitol and the several Departments, are open to the public every day (except Sundays) from 9 A. M. to 3 P. M., and closed at most other times. No fees are asked or expected for showing them.

The Capitol at Washington.

the city and of all the principal public buildings. The *Bronze Door*, which forms the entrance to the Rotunda from the E. portico, is worth attention. It was designed by Randolph Rogers, cast by Von Müller at Munich, is 17 ft. high and 9 ft. wide, weighs 20,000 lbs., and cost $30,000. The work is in *alto-rilievo*, and commemorates the history of Columbus and the discovery of America. There are also bronze doors at the entrance to the Senate wing, designed by Crawford, and completed (after his death) by Rinehart, of Baltimore. The *Rotunda* is 96 ft. in diameter and 180 ft. high. In the panels surrounding it are 8 large pictures, illustrating scenes in American history, painted for the Government by native artists; and over the 4 doors or entrances are *alti-rilievi* in stone. At a height of 107 ft. from the floor, Brumidi is now painting a series of illustrations of American history, on a space 9 ft. high encircling the spacious wall. The floor is of freestone, supported by arches of brick, resting upon two concentric peristyles of Doric columns in the crypt below. The **Dome* rises over the Rotunda in the center of the Capitol, and is the most imposing feature of the vast pile. The interior measures 96 ft. in diameter, and 220 ft. from the floor to the ceiling. Externally it is 135½ ft. in diameter, and rises 241 ft. above the roof of the main building, 307½ ft. above the base-line of the building, and 377 ft. above low tide. Visitors should not fail to make the ascent of the Dome. A spiral stairway between the outer and inner shells (diverging to the l. from the corridor outside the N. door of the Rotunda) affords easy access, and gives a favorable opportunity for inspecting from different points of view the fresco-painting on the canopy overhead. This is the work of Brumidi; it covers 6,000 ft. of space and cost $40,000. All the figures (63 in number) are of colossal proportions, so as to appear life-size when seen from the floor beneath. From the balustrade at the base of the canopy is obtained a magnificent* view of the city and the surrounding country. From the gallery immediately underneath the fresco gallery another spiral stairway leads up to the lantern (17 ft. in diameter and 52 ft. high). This is surmounted by the tholus, or ball, and this in turn by Crawford's fine bronze statue of Liberty, 19½ ft. high.—Leaving the Rotunda by the S. doorway, the visitor finds himself in the *Old Hall of Representatives* (now used as a "National Statuary Hall"). This room, the noblest in the Capitol, is semicircular in form, 96 ft. long and 57 ft. high to the apex of the ceiling. The 24 columns which support the entablature are of variegated green *breccia*, or pudding-stone, from the Potomac Valley; and the ceiling is painted in panel, in imitation of that of the Pantheon at Rome. Light is admitted through a cupola in the centre of the ceiling. Over the S. door is a statue of Liberty, by Causici, and an eagle by Valaperti. Over the N. door is a statue by Franzoni representing History standing in a winged car, the wheel of which, by an ingenious device, forms the dial of a clock. In 1864 the room was set apart as a National Statuary Hall, each State being requested to send statues of two of its most eminent men. A number of States have responded, and the Hall is slowly filling up, containing already a numerous array of statues and busts, of which those of Hamilton, Jef

ferson, Washington (Houdon's), and Roger Williams are most noteworthy. Moran's great painting of the "Grand Cañon of the Yellowstone" further adorns the hall.—The corridor to the S. leads to the
present *Hall of Representatives*, the finest legislative chamber in the
world, 139 ft. long, 93 ft. wide, and 36 ft. high. The ceiling is of iron-
work, with 45 stained glass panels on which are painted the arms of
the States. To the l. of the marble desk of the Speaker is a full-
length portrait of Lafayette, and to the r. a full-length portrait of
Washington, copied from Stuart's, by Vanderlyn. Two landscapes by
Bierstadt, "The Discovery of the Hudson," and "Settlement of California," and a fresco by Brumidi, of Washington parting with his officers, fill panels on the S. wall. The Stranger's Gallery (reached by two
grand marble stairways) extends entirely round the hall; the space not
specially appropriated for the use of the diplomatic corps and the re-
porters for the press is open to visitors. The *Speaker's Desk*, of white
marble, is very fine, and the *Speaker's Room*, immediately in rear of his
desk, is a richly-decorated apartment. From the S. lobby of the Hall
two stairways descend to the basement, where are located the Refectory and committee-rooms. The room of the *Committee of Agriculture*
will repay a visit; the walls and ceiling are painted in fresco by Brumidi.—The *Senate Chamber*, reached by the corridor leading N. from
the Rotunda, is somewhat smaller than the Hall of Representatives,
being 113¼ ft. long, 80¼ ft. wide, and 36 ft. high. It is very tastefully fitted up. The visitors' galleries are reached by * marble stairways, which are among the most striking architectural features of the
Capitol. The President's and Vice-President's Rooms, the Senators'
Retiring-Room, the Reception-Room, and the Senate Post-Office, are
beautiful chambers. In the Vice-President's Room hangs Rembrandt
Peale's great portrait of Washington. The *Marble Room* is particularly chaste and rich in its decorations; senators alone have the privi-
lege of allowing visitors to enter it. In the basement of the Senate
Extension are committee-rooms, richly frescoed and furnished, and
the corridors are exquisitely painted.—The *Supreme-Court Room* (formerly the Senate-Chamber) is reached by the corridor leading N. from
the Rotunda. It is a semicircular apartment, 75 ft. long and 45 ft.
high, decorated with rich Ionic columns of Potomac marble, and with
busts of the former Chief Justices. Visitors are admitted during the
sessions of the Court (October to May, 12 to 4 P. M.). Underneath the
room is the apartment formerly occupied by the Court and now devoted
to the Law Library (30,000 volumes).—The *Library of Congress* is
reached by the corridor from the W. door of the Rotunda. It occupies the entire W. projection of the Capitol; the main room is 91 ft.
long and 34 ft. wide, ceiled with iron, and fitted up with fire-proof
cases. The Library was founded in 1800; was burned by the British
in 1814; was again partially burned in 1851; and went into its present
rooms in 1853. The collection, which is the largest in the United
States, now numbers over 330,000 volumes, exclusive of pamphlets,
and is increasing at the rate of 10,000 or 15,000 volumes a year. All
copyright books are, by law, required to be deposited in this library,

and the representation of American publications is by far the most complete in the country. It is also rich in foreign books in every department of literature. Books may be read in the library by visitors, but not taken away (open from 10 A. M. to 4 P. M.).—The lighting, heating, and ventilating apparatus of the House and Senate Chambers are worthy of notice. The total cost of the Capitol was $13,000,000.

The site of the Capitol was located in 1791; the corner-stone was laid in Sept., 1793, by Washington. The wings were burnt by the British in 1814. The building was finished in 1827. Mr. Walters's design for its extension was commenced in 1851, and the entire building as it now stands was finished in 1865, with the completion of the new Dome.

From the W. entrance of the Capitol Grounds, Pennsylvania Av⌐ leads in 1¼ mile to the * U. S. Treasury (cor. 15th St.), a magni⌐ cent building in the Ionic style, 468 ft. long and 264 ft. wide, 3 stories high above the basement, erected at a cost of $6,000,000. The E. front has an Ionic colonnade 342 ft. long, modeled after that of the Temple of Minerva at Athens. This front is of Virginia freestone; the rest of the building is of Dix Island granite. The W. front has side porticoes, and a grand central entrance with 8 monolithic columns of enormous size. The N. and S. fronts are alike and are adorned with stately porticoes. The building contains about 200 rooms, of which the finest is the *Cash Room*, extending through 2 stories, and lined throughout with rich marbles. The *Gold Room*, in which there is usually about $10,000,000 in gold coin, may be seen by permit from the Treasurer. The building is open to visitors from 9 A. M. to 2 P. M.

Just W. of the Treasury is the * **Executive Mansion** (usually called the "White House"). It is of freestone, painted white, 170 ft. long and 86 ft. deep, two stories high, with a portico on the N. side (main entrance) supported by 8 Ionic columns, and a semicircular colonnade on the S. side of 6 Ionic columns. It was built in 1792; first occupied by President Adams in 1800; burned by the British in 1814; and restored and reoccupied in 1818. The grounds lie between 15th and 17th Sts., and extend to the Potomac, comprising about 75 acres, of which 20 are enclosed as the President's private grounds, are handsomely laid out, and contain a fountain and extensive conservatories. The *East Room* (open daily from 9 A. M. to 2 P. M.) is the grand parlor of the President; it is a fine chamber 80 ft. long, 40 wide, and 20 high, richly decorated and furnished. The Blue, Red, and Green Rooms are on the same floor, and are elegant in their appointments. The *Executive Office* and the *Cabinet Room* are on the 2d floor, as are also the private apartments of the family. N. of the White House is **Lafayette Square**, the finest public park in the city, laid out in winding paths and filled with trees and shrubbery. In the centre is Clark Mills's * bronze equestrian statue of Gen. Jackson, remarkable for its delicate balancing, which was accomplished by making the flanks and tail of the horse of solid metal.

Just W. of the White House (fronting on Executive Ave. between 17th and 18th Sts.) is the vast and ornate building of the * **State, War, and Navy Departments,** of granite, in the Roman Doric style, 567 ft. long and 342 ft. wide, 4 stories high, with lofty Mansard roof. It has 4 façades, those on the N. and S. and those on the E. and W. respectively being counterparts. The State Department occupies the S. portion of the building; and the Hall of the Secretary of State, the Ambassadors' Saloon, and the Library (30,000 volumes) are splendid rooms. The War and Navy Departments occupy plain brick structures in 17th St. which are to be taken down to give place to the new building.

The office of the *Department of the Interior*, better known as the * **Patent Office**, is a grand Doric building of marble, freestone, and granite, occupying 2 blocks in the central portion of the city (between 7th and 9th and F and G Sts.), 453 ft. long and 331 ft. wide, including porticoes, and 75 ft. high. The F St. portico (main entrance) is reached by broad granite steps, and consists of 16 Doric columns of immense size, upholding a classic pediment. The interior contains many noble rooms. The *Model-Room* (open from 9 A. M. to 3 P. M.) occupies the entire upper floor of the edifice, forming 4 large halls or chambers unequaled for extent and beauty on the continent. The total length of this floor is 1,350 ft., or rather more than a quarter of a mile; and it is filled with cases containing immense numbers of models representing every department of mechanical art. The frescoes on the ceiling of the S. Hall are much admired. In this room are cases containing a collection of Revolutionary curiosities and relics, among which are the printing-press of Benjamin Franklin, and many of the personal effects of Washington, including the uniform worn by him when he resigned his commission as Commander-in-Chief.—On the second or main floor are the offices of the Secretary of the Interior, of the Indian Bureau, of the General Land Office, of the Pension Bureau, and of the Commissioner of Patents.

The * **General Post-Office**, on F St. opposite the Patent Office, is an imposing edifice of white marble in the Italian or modified Corinthian style, 300 ft. long, 204 ft. wide, and 3 stories high, erected at a cost of $1,700,000. The *City Post-Office* occupies the lower story of the F St. front ; and the rest of the building is devoted to the use of the U. S. Post-Office. The *Dead-Letter Office* (2d story) contains some curious objects.

The * **Department of Agriculture** (open from 9 A. M. to 3 P. M.) occupies a spacious brick and brown-stone building in the Renaissance style, situated on the Mall at the foot of 13th St. It contains a library, a museum, an herbarium (with 25,000 varieties of plants), and extensive greenhouses. The grounds are tastefully laid out, and contain a great variety of trees and plants. The *Flower-Gardens* (in front of the main building) are adorned with statuary, and when in bloom present a memorable sight.—A short distance E. on the Mall is the * **Smithsonian Institution**, a beautiful red sandstone building in the Romanesque style, 447 by 150 ft., with 9 towers ranging from 75 to 150 ft. in height (reached from Penn. Ave. *via* 7th St.). This noble institution was founded by James Smithson, an Englishman, "for the increase and diffusion of knowledge among men." The building was

commenced in 1847 and completed soon after. It contains a museum
of natural history with numerous and valuable specimens, arranged in
a series of spacious halls; and metallurgical, mineralogical, and eth-
nological collections, with many curiosities. The grounds attached to
the Institution (52½ acres) were laid out by Downing, the eminent land-
scape-gardener, to whose memory a rich vase of Italian marble has
been erected by the Pomological Society. Visitors are admitted to the
Institution from 9 A. M. to 4 P. M.—Also on the Mall, just E. of the
Smithsonian and W. of the Capitol grounds, are the * **Botanical
Gardens** (entrance on 1st St.). They are under the control of the
Library Committee of Congress, and consist chiefly of a series of vast
conservatories filled with rare and curious plants, flowers, and fruits
(free to visitors from 9 A. M. to 6 P. M.).

The * **U. S. Naval Observatory** (lat. 38° 53′ 38·8″, lon. 77° 3′
1·8″ W. from Greenwich) occupies a commanding site on the bank of the
Potomac at the foot of 24th St., with handsome grounds embracing 19
acres. It was founded in 1842, and is now one of the foremost institutions of the kind in the world. It possesses many fine instruments (including a 26-inch equatorial telescope), and a good library of astronomical works. Visitors are admitted at all hours, and are allowed to
inspect the telescope and other instruments when they are not in use.

The *Signal Office*, the headquarters of the Weather Bureau, is on
G St., near the War Department. The instruments used here are extremely delicate. The * *Army Medical Museum* is on 10th St., between E and F Sts. (open from 9 to 3). It contains 16,000 specimens,
illustrating every species of wound and disease. The * *Ordnance
Museum* (on the 2d floor of Winder's Building, cor. F and 17th Sts.)
has an interesting collection of flags and trophies, specimens of all
kinds of arms and ammunition, uniforms and military equipments, and
models of field and fortress artillery in position, and fortifications.
The *U. S. Arsenal* is located amid pleasant grounds on Greenleaf's
Point, at the confluence of the Potomac and the Eastern Branch
(reached by 4½ St.). The buildings contain vast stores of arms and
ammunition, and near the center of the grounds is an immense park
of artillery, containing nearly 1,000 cannon of all kinds. The * **Navy
Yard** is situated on the Eastern Branch, about 1¼ mile S. E. of the
Capitol (reached by 8th St. horse-cars). It has an area of 27 acres,
enclosed by a substantial brick wall, within which, besides officers'
quarters, are vast foundries and shops, 2 ship-houses, and an armory.
The *Naval Museum* (open from 9 to 4) contains an interesting collection of arms, ammunitions, and relics; and in the yard are cannon and
trophies. Other interesting features are the Experimental Battery and
the fleet. Two blocks N. of the Navy Yard are the *Marine Barracks*,
the headquarters of the U. S. Marine Corps; and near by is the *Marine Hospital*, for sick and disabled sailors.

Noteworthy buildings not belonging to the Government are the
City Hall (on 4½ St. near Louisiana Ave.), the *Masonic Temple* (cor.
F and 9th Sts.), *Odd Fellows' Hall* (in 7th St. between D and E Sts.),
Lincoln Hall (cor. 9th and D Sts.), containing the library and read-

ing-room of the Y. M. C. A., and the churches and hotels already enumerated under their respective heads.

The *Corcoran Art Gallery* is a large brick and brown-stone building in the Renaissance style near the White House (cor. Pennsylvania Ave. and 17th St.). It was founded by W. W. Corcoran, the banker, who deeded it to the people, and presented it with his superb private art collection and an Endowment Fund of $900,000. It contains upward of 148 paintings, most of them masterpieces; the finest collection of casts in the country, and among the marble statuary "The Greek Slave," by Powers, and "The Dying Napoleon," by Vela; the richest bronzes in America; and specimens of *bric-à-brac*, porcelain, and majolica-ware. (Admission free on Tuesdays, Thursdays, and Saturdays; on other days, 25c.). Another noble institution, founded and liberally endowed by Mr. Corcoran, is the *Louise Home* (cor. 17th St. and Massachusetts Ave.), a handsome building erected at a cost of $200,000, designed to furnish a home to impoverished elderly ladies of education and good family.

The **Washington Monument,** which was to have been the loftiest and finest in the world, stands on the Mall near 14th St., and in its present unfinished state is rather a blemish than an ornament to the city. Its design contemplated, besides a spacious "Temple" or base, a shaft 600 ft. high; but after $230,000 had been expended in building it to a height of 174 ft., funds gave out, and the work was suspended. In 1876 Congress made an appropriation for the completion of the monument on a new plan to be chosen by experts. Clark Mills's colossal equestrian *Statue of Washington* stands in Washington Circle, at the intersection of Pennsylvania and New Hampshire Aves. H. K. Brown's colossal equestrian *Statue of General Scott* stands in Massachusetts Ave. near 14th St.; it is a noble work. The same artist's bronze equestrian statue of General Brown stands on Maryland Ave., ¼ of a mile N. E. of the Capitol. Ball's colossal bronze *Statue of Lincoln* stands in Lincoln Park (in the E. part of the city); it was erected by contributions of colored people. Another statue of Lincoln, by Lot Flannery, stands in Judiciary Square, on 4½ St., N. of the City Hall. In Rawlins Square (New York Ave. near 18th St.) is a bronze statue of General Rawlins, by J. Bailey. A statue of Admiral Farragut is soon to be erected in Farragut Square (cor. Connecticut Ave. and I St.), and one of General Thomas in a circle at the intersection of 14th St. with Massachusetts and Vermont Aves. The *Naval Monument*, erected to the memory of the officers and seamen and marines who fell in the civil war, stands in the middle of Pennsylvania Ave., near the W. entrance to the Capitol Grounds.

The *Soldiers' Home* (for disabled soldiers of the regular army) occupies an elevated plateau 3 miles N. of the Capitol (reached by 7th St. horse-cars or by a charming drive). It consists of several spacious marble buildings in the Norman style, surrounded by a beautiful park of 500 acres. It has been the custom of several Presidents to occupy one of the smaller buildings of the Home as a summer-retreat, and here President Lincoln passed some of the last hours of his eventful term. N. of the Home is a *National Cemetery*, in which 5,424 soldiers are buried. On the 7th St. Road just beyond the city limits is the **Howard University,** founded in 1864 for the education of youth " without regard to sex or color," but patronized almost exclusively by negroes (700 students). The University building is a vast brick structure, painted white, situated on elevated ground, and surmounted by a tower, from which there is a fine view of the city and its environs. The **Government Asylum for the Insane** (of the Army, Navy, and District of Columbia) occupies a lofty eminence on the S. bank of the Anacostia (reached by crossing the Navy Yard bridge and ascending the heights beyond Uniontown). The building is in the Collegiate-Gothic style, 711 ft. long, and is surrounded by a park of 419 acres, from which there are noble views. (Admittance on Wednesday from 2 to 6 P. M.). In the * **Congressional Cemetery** (1 mile E. of the Capitol near the Eastern Branch) are the graves of Congressmen who have died during their term of service. Its situation is high, and it contains some noteworthy monuments. *Glenwood* is a pleasant rural cemetery about a mile N. of the Capitol. The celebrated **Long Bridge** crosses the Potomac into Virginia from foot of 14th St. It is a shabby structure about a mile long.

  * **Georgetown** (*Union Hotel*) is an old and picturesque town, distant but 2 m. from the Capitol, and divided only by Rock Creek from Washington City, with which it is connected by 4 bridges and 2 lines of horse-cars. The town is beautifully situated on a range of hills which command a view unsurpassed in the Potomac Valley. It is the port of entry of the District, and a line of steamships plies between it and New York. One of the chief points of interest is *Georgetown College*, at the W. end of the town. This is an old institution of learning (founded in 1789, and incorporated as a university in 1815), and the most famous belonging to the Roman Catholic Church in the United States. It is under the control of the Jesuits. The buildings are spacious, and contain a library of 30,000 volumes, among which are some extremely rare and curious books, some beautifully illuminated missals, and some rare old MSS.: an astronomical observatory, and a museum of natural history. In the rear of the college is a picturesque rural serpentine walk, commanding fine views. The *Convent of the Visitation* (in Fayette St. near the College) was founded in 1799, and is the oldest house of the order in America. It consists of several fine buildings in a park of 40 acres. Visitors admitted between 11 A. M. and 2 P. M. The *Aqueduct*, by which the waters of the Chesapeake & Ohio Canal are carried across the Potomac, will repay inspection. It is 1,446 ft. long and 36 ft. high, with 9 granite piers, and cost $2,000,000. There is a carriage-way above the water-course. * **Oak Hill Cemetery,** on the N. E. slopes of the Heights, though containing but 30 acres, is one of the most beautiful in the country. It contains an elegant Gothic chapel with stained-glass windows and completely overgrown with ivy, the massive marble mausoleum of W. W. Corcoran, and several notable monuments. Many eminent men are buried here, among them Secretary Stanton and Chief Justice Chase.

Arlington House, once the residence of George Washington Parke Custis, the last survivor but one of the Washington family, and later of Gen. Robert E. Lee, occupies a commanding position on the Virginia side of the Potomac, nearly opposite Georgetown (reached from Georgetown *via* Aqueduct Bridge, or *via* Long Bridge). It stands more than 200 ft. above tide-water, and the view from the portico is among the best this part of the river affords. The lower rooms of the mansion are open to the public, but contain nothing of interest, the collection of pictures and relics having been removed. In the office of the Superintendent a register is kept for visitors, and a record of all who are buried in the *National Cemeteries* now located on the place. The graves of the white soldiers are W. of the house; those of the colored troops and refugees about ½ m. N. There are about 15,000 in all.

Alexandria is situated on the S. side of the Potomac 7 m. below Washington (reached by railroad, or by ferry-boats hourly from 7th St. wharf). It is a quaint old town, dating from 1748, and is intimately associated with the life and name of Washington. In *Christ Church* (cor. Washington and Cameron Sts.) the pew in which he sat (No. 59) is an object of much interest. Pew No. 46 was occupied by General Robert E. Lee when he resided at Arlington before the war. The Museum, Court-House, Odd Fellows' Hall, and Theological Seminary are among the prominent buildings. On the outskirts of the city is a *National Cemetery*, in which nearly 4,000 soldiers are buried.

* **Mount Vernon** is 15 m. below Washington, on the Virginia side of the Potomac, and is reached by steamers which leave the 7th St. wharf daily at 10 A. M. (fare for the round trip, including admission to the grounds, $1.50). The sail down the river is delightful, and affords excellent views of the country around Washington. Mount Vernon, then known as the "Hunting Creek estate," was bequeathed by Augustine Washington, who died in 1743, to Lawrence Washington. The latter named it after Admiral Vernon, under whom he had served in the Spanish wars. George Washington inherited the estate in 1752. The central part of the mansion, which is of wood, was built by Lawrence, and the wings by George Washington. It contains many interesting historical relics, among which are the key of the Bastile, presented by Lafayette, portions of the military and personal furniture of Washington, portraits, and Miss Peale's painting of "Washington before Yorktown." The *Tomb of Washington* stands in a retired situation near the mansion. It is a plain but solid brick structure, with an iron gate, through the bars of which may be seen the marble sarcophagi containing the remains of George and Martha Washington. The Mount Vernon domain (including the mansion and 6 acres), which had remained since the death of Washington in the possession of his descendants, was purchased in 1856 for the sum of $200,000, raised by subscription, under the auspices of the "Ladies' Mount Vernon Association," aided by the efforts of Edward Everett. It is, therefore, and will continue to be, the property of the nation.

9. The Hudson River.

The trip up the Hudson may be made either by railroad or steamboat, the latter affording the better opportunity for viewing the scenery. The **day boats** leave the pier at the foot of Vestry St. at 8.45 A. M., and from W. 34th St. 15 minutes later, reaching Albany at 6 P. M. The **night boats** start from the foot of Canal St. at 6 P. M., reaching Albany at 6 o'clock the next morning. The steamer "*Mary Powell*" leaves the pier foot of Vestry St. daily at 3.30 P. M., and runs to Rondout and Kingston, passing through the Highlands just at the hour when, as the sun sinks behind them, they put on their most impressive aspect. A delightful excursion may be made by taking the morning boat to West Point, Cornwall, or Newburg, and returning on the afternoon boat (fare for the round trip, $1). The **Hudson River R. R.** runs along the E. bank of the river all the way to Albany (143 miles), and though the view from the cars is restricted for the most part to the other and least attractive side of the river, the journey is nevertheless a most attractive one. The time to Albany is 4½ to 5 hours; fare, $3.10. The traveler should secure a seat on the left-hand side of the cars going north, and on the right-hand going south.

THE trip up the Hudson River (especially by steamer) will afford the traveler advantageous views of some of the most picturesque scenery in America. The Hudson has been compared to the Rhine, and what it lacks in crumbling ruin and castle-crowned steep it more than makes up by its greater variety and superior breadth. George William Curtis says of it: "The Danube has in part glimpses of such grandeur, the Elbe has sometimes such delicately penciled effects, but no European river is so lordly in its bearing, none flows in such state to the sea."

The first few miles of the steamer's course afford fine views of the harbor and city, of the Jersey shore, and the northern suburbs, including *Fort Washington*. Before the city is fairly left behind, the **Palisades** loom up on the left—a series of grand precipices rising in many places to the height of 300 ft., and stretching in unbroken line along the river-bank for more than 20 miles. The rock is trap, columnar in formation, and the summit is thickly wooded. In striking contrast with the desolate and lonely appearance of these cliffs, the right bank presents a continuous succession of beautiful villas standing in the midst of picturesque and exquisitely kept grounds, with a frequent sprinkling of villages and hamlets. *Mount St. Vincent* (15 miles from New York on the E. side) is the seat of the Convent of St. Vincent, under the charge of the "Ladies of the Sacred Heart." The buildings present a striking appearance from the river, and among them is the castellated structure known as "Fonthill," formerly the residence of Edwin Forrest, the tragedian. **Yonkers** (17 miles on the E. side) is a populous suburban town, beautifully situated on villa-crowned slopes at the mouth of the Neperan or Saw-Mill River. It is an ancient settlement, and was the home of the once famous Phillipse family, of which was Mary Phillipse, Washington's first love. The Manor House, a spacious stone edifice built in 1682, is still to be seen; and near by is Locust Hill, where the American troops were encamped in 1781. *Piermont* (22 miles on the W. side) is at the end of the Palisades; it takes its name from a mile-long pier which runs out from the shore to deep water. A branch of the Erie R. R. terminates here; and 3 miles S.

W. is the old town of *Tappan*, interesting as one of Washington's headquarters during the Revolution, and as the place where the unfortunate Major André was imprisoned and executed. The house occupied by Washington is still shown, and near by is the spot where André was executed (Oct. 2, 1780). At Piermont begins the widening out of the river into the broad and beautiful * **Tappan Zee,** which is nearly 10 miles long and 4 miles wide at the widest part. On the E. bank, 26 miles from New York, is the village of *Irvington*, named in honor of Washington Irving, whose unique little cottage of **Sunnyside** is close by, upon the margin of the river, but hidden from the traveler's view by the dense growth of the surrounding trees and shrubbery. The cottage is a quaint and picturesque structure, and the E. front is embowered in ivy, the earlier slips of which were given to Irving by Sir Walter Scott, at Abbotsford, and planted by Irving himself. In the vicinity of Irvington are many fine residences, the most conspicuous of which is the *Paulding Manor*, situated on a high promontory, and said to be the finest specimen of the Tudor architecture in the United States. Just above is * **Tarrytown,** which has many attractions, historic as well as scenic. It was at a spot now in the heart of the village that André was arrested, and Tarrytown witnessed many stormy fights between guerrillas on both sides during the Revolution. It takes its chief interest, however, from its association with Irving's life and writings. Here is the church which he attended, and of which he was warden at the time of his death (Christ Church); here he is buried (in the graveyard of the old Dutch Church, the oldest religious edifice in the State), and near by are the scenes of some of his happiest fancies, including the immortal Sleepy Hollow and the bridge rendered classic by the legend of Ichabod Crane. Opposite Tarrytown, at the foot of a beautifully wooded range of hills, is the pretty town of **Nyack,** a popular summer resort, with several large hotels and many handsome villa residences.

Sing Sing (33 miles) is on the E. bank, occupying an elevated slope, and makes a fine appearance from the river. The State Prison is located here, and its vast stone buildings are conspicuous objects from the steamer (the railway passes beneath them). Many fine villas crown the heights above and around the village, looking down upon the Hudson, which at this point attains its greatest breadth. Four miles above, on the E. side, is *Croton Point*, a prominent headland projecting into the river, and covered with rich vineyards and orchards. At this point the Croton River enters the Hudson, and 6 miles up this stream is Croton Lake, which supplies the metropolis with water. The lake is formed by a dam 250 ft. long, 40 ft. high, and 70 ft. thick; and the water is conveyed to New York by the famous **Croton Aqueduct,** which is over 40 miles long, with 16 tunnels and 24 bridges (the lake may be reached by carriages from Sing Sing, from Croton, or from Croton Falls station on the Harlem R. R.). Above Croton Point is *Haverstraw Bay*, another lake-like widening of the river, and as the boat enters it the Highlands begin to loom up in the distance. At the head of Haverstraw Bay are *Stony Point* (on the W.), a rocky peninsula on which are a lighthouse and the ruins of a famous Revolutionary fort, and *Verplanck's Point* (on the E.), notable as the spot where Henry Hudson's ship, the "Half Moon," first came to anchor after leaving Yonkers. Here also are remains of a small Revolutionary fort. Above, on the E. bank, is **Peekskill** (43 miles from New York), one of the prettiest towns on the Hudson, situated at the mouth of the Peek's Kill or Annsville Creek; opposite which (reached by ferry) is *Caldwel. s Landing*, memorable for the costly but futile search after the treasure which the famous pirate, Captain Kidd, was supposed to have secreted at the bottom of the river here. At this point the river makes a sudden turn toward the W., which is called "The Race."

We have now reached the **Highlands,* and for the next 16 miles the scenery is unsurpassed in the world. On the left is * *Dunderberg* (Thunder Mountain), and at its base a broad deep stream which, a short distance above its mouth, descends to the river in a beautiful cascade. On the right is *Anthony's Nose* (1,128 ft. high), a rocky promontory whose base is penetrated by a railway tunnel 200 ft. long. Lying in the river near this point is the picturesque *Iona Island,* a favorite picnic resort, 300 acres in extent, and containing extensive vineyards. Just above (on the right) is *Sugar-loaf Mountain* (865 ft. high), and near by, reaching far out into the river, is a sandy bluff on which Fort Independence once stood. At the foot of Sugar-loaf is *Beverly House,* where Benedict Arnold was breakfasting when news came to him of André's arrest, and whence he fled to the British vessel (the "Vulture") anchored in the stream below. Passing swiftly on, the *Buttermilk Falls* soon come into view (on the left), descending over inclined ledges a distance of 100 ft. On the lofty bluff above is the spacious and handsome *Cozzens's Hotel,* one of the favorite summer haunts of pleasure-seeking New Yorkers. There is a special landing for passengers who wish to reach the hotel, and on the opposite river-bank is *Garrison's,* another popular summer resort, with fine hotels and picturesque surroundings.

*West Point (just above Cozzens's, 51 miles from New York) is one of the most attractive places on the river, and should be visited. It is the seat of the National Military Academy, the buildings for which occupy a broad plateau, 175 ft. above the river, reached from the landing by a steep and costly road cut out of the solid cliff-side. The most noteworthy of the buildings are the Cadets' Barracks, the Academic Building, the Mess Hall, and the Library (26,000 volumes), in w' :ch is the Observatory. The Chapel and the Museum of Ordnance and Trophies are interesting. The buildings front the spacious Parade-Ground, smooth as a lawn and level as a floor; and the grounds are tastefully laid out, containing several fine monuments, and commanding a variety of pleasing views. The Cemetery is reached by a winding road; and from the crumbling walls of **Fort Putnam* (on Mt. Independence, 600 ft. above the river) a view is obtained which will abundantly repay the labor of reaching it. The best time to visit West Point is during June, July, and August; the scenery being then at its best, and the military exercises of the Academy offering additional

attractions. The "Commencement," or graduating exercises, occurs about the 3d week in June, and about June 20th the cadets go into camp for the summer.

Above West Point, on the same side, is *Cro' Nest*, one of the loftiest of the Highland group (1,428 ft.), and still above is *Storm King* (or "Butter Hill"), which is 1,529 ft. high and the last of the Highland range upon the W. Between Storm King and Cro' Nest lies the lovely vale of *Tempe ;* and opposite is the pretty little village of *Cold Spring*, behind which rises the massive granite crown of *Mount Taurus* ("Bull Hill"). Beyond, still on the E. side, the Highlands are continued in the jagged precipices of *Breakneck* and *Beacon Hill*, respectively 1,187 and 1,685 ft. in height. These mountains are among the most commanding features of the river scenery, and from the summit of the latter New York City may be seen. **Cornwall Landing,** a rambling and picturesque village on the W. bank, is the most frequented summer resort on the river, and contains a number of hotels and boarding-houses, adjacent to which are fine drives. Here the Highlands come to an end, and the steamer enters the broad expanse of Newburg Bay, on the W. shore of which is **Newburg,** a thriving and handsomely built city of 18,000 inhabitants. Newburg was the theatre of many interesting events during the Revolution, and *Washington's Headquarters, an old gray stone mansion S. of the city, is still preserved as a museum of historical relics (admission free). Opposite Newburg is *Fishkill Landing*, a small but pretty village; and 15 miles above, on the E. bank (75 miles from New York), is *Poughkeepsie* (*Morgan House*, $3 a day), the largest city between New York and Albany, built on an elevated plain, nearly 200 ft. above the river, and backed by high hills. There are several fine churches, numerous handsome residences, and no less than 8 important educational institutions, including *Vassar College*, one of the leading female colleges of the world. The buildings of Vassar College occupy a commanding site 2 miles E. of the city, the main building (500 ft. long) being modeled after the Tuileries. N. of the city, on an eminence overlooking the river, are the vast and stately buildings of the Hudson River State Hospital for the Insane. Across the river from Poughkeepsie (ferry) is *New Paltz Landing*, from which stages run 14 miles to *Lake Mohonk* (*Mountain House*), a delightful summer resort situated near the summit of Sky Top, one of the loftiest of the Shawangunk Mountains, 1,243 ft. above the river. The lake and its vicinity are extremely picturesque, and the views from neighboring summits surprisingly fine. (Lake Mohonk is also reached from New York *via* Wallkill Valley branch of the Erie R. R. to New Paltz, and thence by stage, in 6 miles. Fare from New York, $3.50.)

Five miles above Poughkeepsie, on the E. bank, is *Hyde Park*, a handsome town built on a terrace, ½ mile back from the river, containing several summer boarding-houses, with fine country-seats in the vicinity. *Rondout*, on the W. side, and *Kingston*, 2 miles above, are populous cities, with a large trade, but present nothing of special interest to the tourist. At *Rhinebeck Landing*, opposite Kingston, is the ancient Beekman House, nearly 200 years old, and the best specimen of an old Dutch homestead to be found in the valley of the Hudson. A short distance above is *Rokeby*, the estate of the late Wm. B. Astor, and still farther on, above the little hamlet of Barrytown, are *Montgomery Place*, the handsome residence of Edward Livingston, and *Annandale,* the villa of John Bard.   Along this portion of the river voyage the Catskill Mountains loom up grandly on the left, presenting a succession of noble views.   **Catskill Landing** (111 miles) is the point of departure for the mountains (*see* Route 10).   Four miles above (on the E. side) is the flourishing city of **Hudson** (*Worth House*, $3 a day), finely situated upon a bold promontory, at the head of ship-navigation on the river.   From Prospect Hill (500 ft. high) there is an incomparably fine view of the Catskills.   Five miles from Hudson, in the Claverack Valley, are the **Columbia Springs,** a quiet rural resort much frequented by invalids and others.   From Hudson to Albany the scenery, though pleasing, is somewhat monotonous, and offers nothing calling for special notice.

Albany.

Hotels, etc.—*Delavan House* ($3 to $4 a day), in Broadway, near the R. R. depot; *Stanwix Hall* ($3 a day); *American; City.*   The *Kenmore* (cor. N. Pearl and Columbia Sts.) is a fine hotel, on the European plan.   *Reading-rooms* at the State Library, back of the old Capitol; at the Young Men's Association, 38 State St.; and at the Y. M. C. A. in S. Pearl St.   *Horse-cars* to different parts of the city and to Troy.   *Ferry* to Greenbush.

Albany, the capital of New York State, is finely situated on the W. bank of the Hudson, at the head of sloop-navigation and near the head of tide-water.   It was founded by the Dutch as a trading-post in 1614, and, next to Jamestown in Virginia, was the earliest European settlement in the original 13 States.   Its present name was given it in 1664 in honor of the Duke of York and Albany (afterward James II.).   It was chartered in 1686, and made the State capital in 1798, since which time its population has increased from 5,349 (in 1800) to 86,541 in 1875.   Albany has a large commerce from its position at the head of navigation on the river, as the *entrepot* of the great Erie Canal from the W. and the Champlain Canal from the N., and as the center to which several important railways converge.

Broadway is an important business thoroughfare near the river. *State St.* leads by a steep ascent from Broadway to Capitol Square, in which are the public buildings.   The *Old Capitol,* a plain brown-stone structure, built in 1807, is still occupied, but will be demolished as soon as the costly new Capitol is finished.   The * **New Capitol,** to the W. of the old, was begun in 1871, and its exterior is nearly finished.   It is of Maine granite, in the Renaissance style, and when completed will be the largest and most splendid edifice in America except the Federal Capitol at Washington.   It stands on the most elevated ground in the city, and its tower, 320 ft. high, will be visible for many miles around.   The * **State Library,** a handsome fire-proof building fronting on State St., in rear of the old Capitol, contains 86,000 volumes, and an interesting collection of curiosities and historical relics.   *State Hall*, in Eagle St., built of white marble in 1843, contains several of the principal offices of State. The *City Hall,* in Eagle St., foot of Washington Ave., is a beautiful white marble edifice, 100 by 80 ft., 3 stories high, with a rich Ionic portico in front. The *City Building*, in S. Pearl St., is another handsome structure, containing various offices of the city government. The *State Arsenal*, cor. Eagle and Hudson Sts., is a large, gloomy, castellated structure; and the *Merchants' Exchange*, at the foot of State St., is a solid and handsome building. Near the Exchange, on State St., is the hall of the *Young Men's Association*, with a library of 12,000 volumes and a reading-room. The *State Geological and Agricultural Hall*, on State St., has valuable collections in Natural History, Geology, and Agriculture, and many curious relics. The *Medical College*, cor. Eagle and Jay Sts., is a prosperous institution with an extensive museum ; and near by is the Law School of the Albany University, one of the best in the country. Of the 54 churches in the city the *Cathedral of the Immaculate Conception* (in Eagle St.) and the *Church of St. Joseph* (cor. Ten Broeck and 2d Sts.) are the most noteworthy. The Cathedral seats 4,000 persons, and its stained-glass windows are among the richest in America. *St. Peter's* (Episcopal), cor. Lodge and State Sts., is a handsome Gothic structure, and owns a service of communion plate presented by Queen Anne to the Onondaga Indians. **Dudley Observatory,** founded and liberally endowed by Mrs. Blandina Dudley, stands on Observatory Hill, near the N. limits of the city. It has a valuable special library, and some fine instruments. The *Penitentiary*, 1 mile W. of the city, is a model prison conducted on the contract system.

Interesting relics of the early days of the city are the *Van Rensselaer Manor House*, in the N. part of the city near Broadway, portions of which were built in 1765 ; and the old *Schuyler House*, in Schuyler St. near S. Pearl, which was burned down in 1759, and immediately rebuilt, portions of the original walls remaining. The former is a fine mansion, and the latter was the residence of Col. Peter Schuyler, the first Mayor of Albany. *Washington Park*, in the W. part of the city, has been set apart as a pleasure-ground, but little work has been done on it. *Greenbush* (reached by ferry) is a populous suburb on the opposite side of the river.

* **Troy** (reached from Albany by railroad, steamboats, and horse-cars) lies on the W. bank of the Hudson, 6 miles above Albany, and at the head of river navigation. Its population in 1875 was 48,821, and it has a large commerce, with extensive manufactures of iron, steel, cars, cotton and woolen goods, hosiery, and shoes. *River St.*, running parallel with the river, is the chief thoroughfare ; and near 1st, 2d, and 3d Sts. are the finest churches and private residences. The *Savings Bank*, on State St., is an elegant edifice costing $450,000 ; the new *City Hall* is a fine building ; and there are many handsome business structures. The *Athenæum* is a beautiful freestone edifice, in which are the Post-Office and a library. The buildings of * *St. Joseph's Theological Seminary* (on Mt. Ida, E. of the city) are noble specimens of Byzantine architecture. In West Troy is the great *Watervliet Arsenal*, with 40 buildings in a park of 105 acres.

10. The Catskill Mountains.

Catskill Landing, on the Hudson River, is the point from which the mountains are usually entered. It may be reached from New York *via* steamboat on the river (see previous Route), or *via* Hudson River R. R. to Catskill Station, whence a ferry-boat crosses to Catskill. Passengers from the north can take the morning boat at Albany, and reach Catskill at 11 A. M., or can come by rail to Catskill Station as above. Omnibuses run from the landing to the village, which lies half a mile inland; and a regular line of stages runs to the *Mountain House* (distance, 12 miles ; fare, $2.50). The hotels and some of the larger boarding-houses have stages or carriages, which run daily to and from them and the landing and village ; while from other houses carriages are sent to meet such as are coming to them as boarders at times previ 'sly agreed upon. The mountains are sometimes entered by way ' the *Ove ,,ok Mountain House*, which is reached *via* railway from Rondout (see p. 62) to West Hurley Station, and thence by stage.

THE CATSKILLS, or Kaatskills, are a part of the great Appalachian chain, which extends through the eastern portion of the United States, from Canada to the Gulf of Mexico. Their principal ranges follow the cour.. of the Hudson for 20 or 30 miles, lying W. of it, and separated from it by a valley 10 or 12 miles wide. Their chief interest lies in the beauty and variety of their scenery. In a field of very limited area, easy of access and soon explored, they present a multitude of pictu-resque objects which have long made them a favorite resort of artists and of all who find pleasure in the wild haunts of the mountains. In-dian traditions singled them out as the favorite dwelling-place of spirits, and they, with the exception of the Hudson Highlands, are the only faëry ground that American literature has ventured to appropriate.

The village of **Catskill** ($\frac{1}{2}$ mile from the landing) occupies an ele-vated and attractive site at the mouth of Catskill Creek, and has about 4,000 inhabitants. The scenery in the neighborhood, especially along the banks of the creek, is very pleasing. The *Prospect Park Hotel* ($3 a day), near the landing, is spacious and handsome, located on a high plateau and surrounded by extensive grounds. In the village are the *Irving House* and *Gunn's Hotel ;* and about a mile to the W. is the *Grant House*, situated on a commanding elevation, with a noble out-look to the mountains.

The stage-ride from the village to the Mountain House occupies about three hours, and during the latter part affords some admirable views. Shortly after leaving the village Catskill Creek is crossed, and 6 miles out the *Half-Way House* is passed. Two miles from the sum-mit the coach pauses in a secluded dell which local tradition affirms to be the site of Rip Van Winkle's famous nap. The * **Mountain House** ($3 to $4 a day) is a spacious edifice, perched upon one of the terraces of Pine Orchard Mountain, at an elevation of 2,500 ft. above the river. From the broad rock platform in front of the hotel, a view of surpassing beauty may be obtained. Directly in front, the moun-tain falls almost perpendicularly to the plain ; to the right, the broad Hudson winds through its noble valley ; in the dim distance Albany may be descried with a glass ; and on the horizon the Hudson High-lands, the Berkshire Hills, and the Green Mountains unite their chains, forming a continuous line of misty blue. The views from the Mountain

House are said to embrace an area of 10,000 square miles, including portions of Vermont, Massachusetts, and Connecticut. The sunrise and thunder-storms are among the special attractions of the place; and occasionally an apparition like the "Specter of the Brocken" enlivens a foggy morning. The *North Mountain* is easily ascended from the Mountain House; the best view is from Table Rock, ¾ of a mile N. of the hotel. On the N. side of this rock a fine echo may be heard with four distinct reverberations. Another favorite excursion is to the top of *South Mountain*, which commands a fine view of the Catskill Pass and some distant peaks of New Jersey. * **High Peak** (6 miles

Catterskill Falls.

W. of the Mountain House) is the loftiest of the Catskill summits, and should certainly be climbed in order to see the region fairly. The ascent is toilsome, but ladies often accomplish it, and the view from the summit (3,804 ft. high) well repays the labor of reaching it.

The *Two Lakes* (North and South) are back of the Mountain House, on the road to the famous * **Catterskill Falls,** which are 2 miles distant. At the head of the falls is the *Laurel House* ($12 to $20 per week), an excellent hotel, commanding fine views of the falls, and of Round Top and High Peak in the immediate neighborhood. The falls are formed by the outlet of the lakes plunging into a deep hollow where the mountain divides like the cleft foot of a deer. The descent of the first cascade is 180 ft., that of the second 80, and below these there is another fall (the Bastion) of 40 ft. Below the falls the sides of the gorge rise in a succession of walls of rock to the height of 300 feet or more. To see the falls to the best advantage, the visitor should descend the winding stairs leading from the terrace of the hotel (fee 25c.) and spend an

hour or two in exploring the gorge and glen below. As the supp.,
of water is limited, the stream has been dammed at the verge of the
cliff and is only turned on at intervals for the benefit of visitors.
Below the falls, the Catterskill has a devious and winding course of 8
miles to the Catskill, which it enters near the village. Some ruggedly
picturesque scenery may be enjoyed by descending the glen to the road
in the Clove, about a mile from the falls. *Sunset Rock*, commanding
noble views, is reached from the Laurel House by a walk of a mile and
a half through the forest.

A favorite excursion from either the Mountain House or the Laurel
House is to **Haines's Falls,** a spot much frequented by artists. At
the Haines House, near by, one pays the usual fee (25c.) for viewing
the scene. The fall has two leaps, the first of 150 and the second of
80 ft., with a third one below of 60 ft., and others still, so that in
less than a quarter of a mile the stream falls 475 ft. From Haines's
Falls a rugged and picturesque ravine, called the *Catterskill Clove*,
traversed by a tolerable road, leads down to the plain below. In this
ravine are the High Rocks, and 200 or 300 yards below are the beautiful **Fawn Leap Falls** (fee 25c.), where the stream makes a perpendicular leap of 30 ft. over an immense concave ledge into a prodigious
caldron. At the mouth of the Clove is the sequestered village of **Pa-
lenvil.** (*Winchelsea House*), where there are many large boarding-
houses, and where artists most do congregate. It is 10 miles from
Catskill village, with which it is connected by stages. Above Palenville, on a lofty spur of South Mountain, is the *Grand View Hotel*, the
view from which is very impressive. Six miles from Palenville is the
Plattekill Clove, a deep and rugged gorge extending from the plain ᷇ᴼ
the plat ᴜ above, and traversed by a difficult road. In this clove are
the *Blac. Chasm Falls*, 300 ft. high.

Another pleasant ride is along the ridge 5 or 6 miles to the entr ᷇ᴄᴇ
of the *Stony Clove*, and thence through the wilderness of this fine pass,
within whose depths ice remains throughout the year. At the head of
the Clove is *Roggen's Hotel*, a favorite resort for sportsmen. On the
road from the Mountain House is the pretty little hamlet of *Tanners-
ville* (Mountain Summit and Roggen's Hotel) ; and 4 miles W., beyond
the entrance to Stony Clove, is *Hunter* (Breeze Lawn House), nestling
in a narrow glen, with Hunter Mountain (4,082 ft. high) towering
above it.

Stages connect Catskill with the mountain villages of *Cairo* (10
miles), *South Durham* (16 miles), and *Windham* (26 miles), in all of
which are numerous summer boarding-houses. *Prattsville*, 36 miles W.
of Catskill, is a popular resort. Near it are the celebrated Pratts'
Rocks, on which are cut busts of the Pratts, who founded the town.
The *Overlook Mountain House* is situated on one of the most southerly
of the Catskill group, and commands extensive views over the Hudson
Highlands and Valley. It is somewhat isolated from the portion of the
mountains previously described, but may be reached by a road leading
S. from Palenville.

11. New York to Boston via New Haven, Hartford, and Springfield.

This is the most popular of the railway routes between New York and Boston, and is traversed by several express trains daily, running through in 8 to 9 hrs. Distance, 233 miles ; fare, $5.

LEAVING the Grand Central Depot, the train runs on the track of the New York & Harlem R. R. as far as Williams Bridge (14 miles), and then takes the New York & New Haven R. R., which runs through several pretty suburban towns. *New Rochelle* (17 miles), *Mamaroneck* (21 miles), and **Rye** (24 miles), are especially attractive, the latter drawing many summer visitors owing to its convenience to the city and its proximity to the favorite Rye Beach, on Long Island Sound, which affords excellent salt-water bathing, boating, etc. (Hotels: the " Rye Beach " and the " Cliff House "). *Greenwich* (28 miles), the first station in Connecticut, is a picturesque old town, pleasantly situated on hill-slopes commanding fine views of Long Island Sound. The Lenox House and the City Hotel are favorite houses, open only in summer. A short distance S. E. is *Indian Harbor*, where is the Morton House ($4 a day), a popular summer hotel. **Stamford** (34 miles) is a favorite resort of New York merchants, many of whom have embellished its heights with handsome mansions and villas. The town is embowered in trees, and there are several fine churches and public buildings. *Shippan Point*, 2 miles S. of Stamford, is resorted to in summer by many hundreds, who crowd the spacious Ocean House and numerous smaller places of entertainment. *S. Norwalk* (42 miles) is near the beautiful village of **Norwalk** (reached by horse-cars), which is also much resorted to in summer. Its harbor is a picturesque bay, which affords oysters in great abundance and of excellent quality. The hotels are the *Allin* and the *Lucas* in S. Norwalk, and the *Connecticut* in Norwalk. **Fairfield** (51 miles), still another popular summer resort, has the finest beach on the Sound, and supports a large hotel, the Marine Pavilion or Fairfield House ($8 to $12 per week). The adjacent scenery is very attractive. **＊Bridgeport** (56 miles) is a flourishing city of 25,000 inhabitants, situated on an arm of Long Island Sound, and noted for the extent and variety of its manufactures, chief among which are sewing-machines, carriages, arms, cutlery, and locks. The city is handsomely built, and Golden Hill is crowned with fine villas. The hotels are the *Sterling House* and the *Atlantic* ($3 a day each). Passing now the pretty villages of *Stratford* (59 miles) and *Milford* (64 miles), the train approaches New Haven (73 miles) across extensive salt-meadows.

New Haven.

Hotels, etc.—The *New Haven House* ($4 a day), cor. College and Chapel Sts., is the leading hotel. The *Tontine* ($3 a day), cor. Church and Court Sts., and the *Elliot* ($3 a day), cor. Chapel and Olive, are good. There are *Reading-rooms* at the Y. M. C. A., in the Palladium Building, and at the Young Men's Institute, in Chapel St. *Horse-cars* traverse all parts of the city, and run to the suburbs. *Carriages* are allowed to charge· 50c. for one passenger one course; two passengers, 35c. each. *Steamboats* run to New York twice daily (fare $1).

New Haven, the largest city of Connecticut, is situated at the head of New Haven Bay, 4 miles from Long Island Sound, on a broad plain surrounded by rolling hills. It was settled in 1638, was incorporated as a city in 1784, and from 1701 to 1875 was one of the capitals of the State. It is the center of 5 railroads, has a large coasting-trade, and considerable fc 'ign commerce, chiefly with the West Indies. Its manufactures are very extensive, including machinery, hardware, locks, clocks, .earms, carriages, pianos, jewelry, India-rubber goods, etc. In 1870 the population was 50,840.

Chapel St., the principal thoroughfare, extends in a W. N. W. direction from end to end of the city. *State* and *Church* are also important business streets, and * **Hillhouse Ave.** is lined with handsome private residences. The number of magnificent elms with which its principal streets are planted has caused New Haven to be called the " City of Elms." The * **Public Green,** in the center of the city, is a fine lawn shaded by noble elms, and contains the *State House* (where the State Legislature met on alternate years till 1874), the *Center Church*, the *North Church*, and *Trinity Church*. Back of Center Church is the grave and monument of the regicide John Dixwell. On the E. side of the Green is the * **City Hall,** a very handsome building, containing the municipal offices. The *Custom-House* (which also contains the *Post-Office*) is a spacious granite edifice in Church St. near Chapel St. The other principal public buildings are the *Court-House*, in Church St., the *State Hospital*, the *Medical College*, the *Orphan Asylum*, the *County Prison*, and the *Almshouse*. The last three are in the W. part of the city. The new **Union Depot** is a large brick building, erected on made land fronting the harbor. On Chapel St. is the splendid granite edifir~ of the *American Life and Trust Co.*

Across College St. from the Green are the grounds of * **Yale College,** one of the oldest and most important educational institutions in America. It was founded in 1700, established at New Haven in 1717, and in 1878-'79 had 90 instructors and 1,022 students. Besides its Academic Department, the College has a Law School, a Medical School, a Scientific School, a Theological School, and a School of the Fine Arts. The grounds include 9 acres, and contain many buildings. The most noteworthy are the Gothic *Library*, with 90,000 volumes; the elaborate *Art Building* (at the W. corner of the Square), containing a fine collection of paintings, statuary, and casts, and a number of studios; the *Alumni Hall* (on the N. corner), used for the annual examinations and graduates' meetings; and the new dormitories, *Durfee Hall* and *Farnam Hall*, with the elegant *Battell Chapel* on the corner between them at the N. E. end. In Elm St., close by, are the two handsome buildings of the *Divinity School*, with the dainty little *Marquand Chapel* between. At the head of College St. is *Sheffield Hall*, and in Prospect St. is *North Sheffield Hall*, containing the laboratories and collections of the Sheffield Scientific School. In the *Peabody

Museum, cor. Elm and High Sts., are the collections of the University in geology, mineralogy, and the natural sciences, including the famous collection of Prof. Marsh. The *Gymnasium*, said to be the most complete in the country, is in Library St.

The *Old Burying-Ground* (on Grove St., near High) contains many interesting and venerable monuments, and the *Evergreen Cemetery* (on the bank of West River) is tastefully adorned. *Sachems' Wood* (the Hillhouse residence), at the head of Hillhouse Ave., is a pleasant spot. The most popular drive is down the E. side of the harbor to *Fort Wooster*, an old ruin dating from 1814, whence there is a fine view. Rising above the plain near the city are the lofty promontories known as East

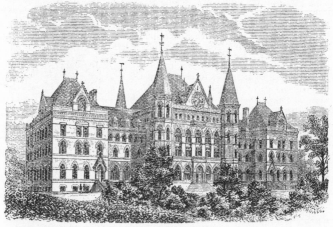

Peabody Museum.

and West Rocks. **East Rock** (reached by horse-cars from the Green) is 300 ft. high, and commands a wide and beautiful view. ***West Rock** (reached by cars from Chapel St.) is 400 ft. high, and also commands a fine view. On the top there is a group of bowlders called the "Judges' Cave," because Goffe and Whalley, two of the judges of King Charles I. of England, were secreted here for a while in 1661. Near the base of the rock on the N. is Wintergreen Fall, a pretty cascade. Near by is *Maltby Park*, 800 acres in extent, containing the city water-works and some picturesque drives and rambles. *Savin Rock*, a bathing-place, with summer hotels, on Long Island Sound, 4 m. S. W. of the city, is a favorite resort (reached by horse-cars from the Green).

The first important station beyond New Haven is *Wallingford* (85 miles), a pretty town much resorted to in summer (*Beach House*).

Meriden (91 miles), *Berlin* (98 miles), and *Newington* (104 miles) are the other principal stations before reaching *Hartford* (109 miles).

Hartford.

Hotels, etc.—The *Allyn House* ($4 a day), near the depot, is the largest and best. The *City Hotel* ($3 a day) and the *United States* ($3 a day) are good. *Horse-cars* connect the different portions of the city. *Carriages* charge for one passenger per course, 50c.; for two passengers, 75c.; for three passengers, $1; by the hour, $2. *Steamboats* run to New York daily. The *Post-Office* is at 252 Main St.

Hartford, the capital of Connecticut, and one of the handsomest cities in New England, is situated at the head of sloop navigation on the Connecticut River, 50 miles from Long Island Sound. It had a population in 1876 of about 50,000, and, besides an immense manufacturing business, is one of the great centers of fire and life insurance. Its manufactures include iron and brass ware, steam-engines, machinery, tool sewing-machines, firearms, silver-plated ware, stone-ware, woolens, cigars, fertilizers, etc. The city is regularly laid out, and comprises an area of about 10 square miles, intersected by Park River, which is spanned by numerous bridges. *Main St.*, running N. and S., is the leading thoroughfare. *State, Commerce,* and *Asylum Sts.* are active business streets. In the outskirts are many tasteful villas, and the city as a whole is remarkably well built.

The *Union Depot*, where the train stops, is one of the finest in the country. S of the depot, in a bend of Park River, is the beautiful * **Bushnell Park** (46 acres), shaded by noble elms and containing a fountain and several fine statues. Just S. of the park is the new * **State House,** of marble, in the secular Gothic style, 300 ft. long by 200 ft. wide and 250 ft. high to the top of the dome, completed in 1878 at a cost of $1,500,000. Besides spacious chambers for the two Houses of the Legislature it contains rooms for the Supreme Court and the State Library. Near the park is the *High School*, a very handsome building in the Norman style. On Asylum St. near the depot, is the *Asylum for the Deaf and Dumb*, beautifully situated amid extensive grounds; it was founded in 1817, and was the first institution of the kind in America. The *Retreat for the Insane* stands on elevated ground in the S. W. part of the city, whence there are broad views. The *Hartford Hospital*, in Hudson St. near the Retreat, is a handsome stone edifice. State House Square, in the center of the city, is the site of the *Old State House*, erected in 1794. To the N., fronting on Kingsley St., is the *City Hall*, a handsome building in the Grecian style. The building of *Cheney Bros.* (cor. Main and Temple Sts.) is one of the largest and finest in the State; and those of the *Connecticut Mutual Life Ins. Co.* (opposite State House Square) and the *Charter-Oak Life* (in Main St.) are very striking. The *Opera-House* (395 Main St.) is fine.

Among the many fine churches the most noteworthy are the * **Church of the Good Shepherd** (Episcopal), erected by Mrs. Colt as a memorial of her husband and children; *Christ Church* (Episcopal), cor. Main and Church Sts.; the *Park Congregational* and the *Pearl St.*

Congregational ; the *South Baptist,* the *First Methodist,* and the new
Roman Catholic *Cathedral* in Farmington Ave. The * **Wadsworth
Athenæum** (in Main St.) is a fine granite edifice in the castellated
style, containing a fine-art gallery, in which are some good pictures
and statuary ; the library and collections of the State Historical Society ; the free Watkinson Library, with 27,000 volumes ; and the Young
Men's Institute, with a library of 23,000 volumes. The magnificent
buildings of * **Trinity College** are slowly rising on Rocky Hill,

New State House.

about a mile S. of the Union Depot. They form a quadrangle 1,050 ft.
long and 376 ft. wide, inclosing 3 courts containing an area of 4 acres.
The architecture is early English, the design of William Burges, of
London. The grounds (78 acres) are handsomely adorned. There are
10 instructors and 100 students.

Colt's Firearms Manufactory and the *Willow Works* form a village
of themselves in the S. E. portion of the city. The grounds extend
from the river to Main St., upon which stands the elegant Colt mansion

("Armsmear"), surrounded by immense greenhouses, graperies, etc.
The *Ancient Burying-Ground*, containing the ashes of the first settlers,
is in the rear of Center Church, in Main St. *Cedar Hill Cemetery*
should be visited to see the Colt monument, the Beach monument, and
the fine prospect over the surrounding country. The favorite drives in
the vicinity of Hartford are to *Tumble-down Brook*, 8 m. W., on the
Albany road; to *Talcott Mountain*, 9 m. W.; to *Trout-Brook Reservoir*,
on the Farmington road; to *Prospect Hill ;* and to *Wethersfield* (4 m.
S.), the most ancient town on the river. *East Hartford* (reached by
a long bridge) contains some quaint old houses.

Between Hartford and Boston the only places requiring mention
are *Springfield* (135 miles) and *Worcester* 189 miles), both in Massachusetts. **Springfield** (*Massasoit House* and *Hayne's Hotel*, both first
class, $3 to $4 a day) is one of the prettiest among the smaller American cities, and is noted for the great variety of its industries. It is
situated on the Connecticut River, 26 miles N. of Hartford, is well built,
and its wide streets are shaded with elms and maples. The principal
point of interest is the * *United States Arsenal*, located in spacious
grounds on Arsenal Hill (reached by State St.) and commanding fine
views. This establishment employs 700 hands, and 175,000 stand of
arms are kept constantly in stock. During the civil war the works
were run night and day, and over 800,000 guns were made, at a cost
of $12,000,000. The *City Hall* is a noble building in the Romanesque
style, containing a public hall seating 2,700 persons. The * *Court
House* is a massive granite structure costing $200,000 ; and the build-
ing of the *City Free Library* (containing 40,000 volumes and a museum
of natural history) is very handsome There are also several fine
churches, of which the most noteworthy are the * *Church of the Unity*
(in State St.), the *Memorial Church*, and the *Cathedral of St. Patrick*
(Roman Catholic). The *Cemetery* (located near the Armory) is small
but beautiful. *Hampden Park* has fine race-tracks and is used for
cattle-shows, etc.

Worcester (*Bay-State House*, $3 a day, and *Lincoln House*, $2.50
a day) is a vast manufacturing center, the second city in Massachusetts
in wealth and population, but not particularly interesting to the sight-
seeing tourist. Its population was 49,265 in 1875, and its principal
manufactures are of boots and shoes, machinery and tools, stone ware,
jewelry, carpets, etc., etc. The city is regularly laid out with wide
and pleasant streets, *Main St.* being the leading thoroughfare. Near
the center of the city is the Common, on which are a beautiful **Soldiers'*
Monument designed by Randolph Rogers, and a monument to Timothy
Bigelow, a Revolutionary officer. Among the public buildings are two
county *Court-Houses*, adjacent to each other on Lincoln Square, the
City Hall, the *High School*, *Mechanics' Hall* (seating 3,000), and the
spacious *Union Depot*. Near the Court-Houses is the fire-proof building of the * *American Antiquarian Society*, containing a library of
50,000 volumes and a valuable cabinet of antiquities. The *Free Public
Library* (in Elm St.) has 37,500 volumes and a reading-room (open
from 9 A. M. to 9 P. M.). The *Lyceum and Natural History Society* (on

4

Foster St.) has interesting collections. Worcester is justly proud of
its educational institutions, among which are the *Worcester Academy*,
the *Oread Institute* for young ladies, the *Highland Military Academy*,
the *State Normal School*, the *College of the Holy Cross* (Roman Catholic), and the *Free Institute of Industrial Science* (handsomely endowed).
All these have fine buildings in or near the city. The new * *State
Lunatic Asylum* is a vast stone pile on a hill E. of the city, erected at
a cost of $1,350,000.

Beyond Worcester the train passes for 25 miles through a thickly
settled region, with numerous small towns, and stops at *S. Framingham*, a thriving manufacturing village, and center of an important system of railways. Four miles beyond, near the foot of Cochituate Lake,
whence Boston draws its water-supply, is the large village of *Natick*,
celebrated for its shoe-manufactures. Next come the wealthy suburban
towns of *Wellesley*, *Newton*, *Brighton*, and *Brookline*, and the train enters Boston over the Back Bay lands.

12. New York to Boston via Providence.

This is called the "Shore Line Route," and comprises the New York & New
Haven R. R., the Shore Line R. R., and the Boston & Providence R. R. The total
distance is 228 miles ; time, 8 to 9 hrs.; fare, $5.

As far as *New Haven* (73 miles) this route is identical with Route
11. Beyond New Haven the road runs close along the shore of the
Sound, passing several popular summer resorts. *Branford* (81 miles)
has within its limits Branford Point, a favorite watering-place, on and
near which are several large summer hotels. *Guilford* (89 miles) is a
pretty town, built round a finely shaded public square, and noted as
the birthplace of Fitz-Greene Halleck, the poet, who died there Nov.
17, 1867. *Guilford Point*, S. of the village, has a number of hotels
and is a popular summer resort. *Saybrook* (105 miles) is an old and
quaintly rural village, whence the Connecticut Valley R. R. runs S. to
the venerable town of *Old Saybrook*, and to the shore. Shortly beyond Saybrook the train crosses the Connecticut River, and, passing
several small villages, of which *East Lyme* is a place of some resort,
soon reaches **New London** (123 miles), a city of 12,000 inhabitants,
pleasantly situated on the W. bank of the river Thames, and possessing one of the finest harbors in the United States. A *City Hall* of
polished freestone, a granite *Custom-House*, several fine churches, and
a great number of costly residences, are among the architectural features of the city. *Cedar Grove Cemetery* is pleasantly situated, and
the ancient burial-ground of the town is of special interest to the antiquarian. The *Crocker House*, in the city, is first class ; and 2 miles
S. at the mouth of the Thames is the famous * *Pequot House* (500
guests, $5 a day), the most fashionable summer resort along the Sound
shore. Across the river from New London is *Groton*, where is a tall
granite monument commemorating the cruel Fort Griswold massacre
(Sept. 6, 1781). **Stonington** (135 miles) is the last station in Connecticut, and is much frequented in summer. It is a quiet, sleepy

town, with quaint houses surrounded by beautiful grounds, and with
notably good facilities for fishing, bathing, and boating. The *Wada-
wannuck House* ($4 a day) is a fine hotel, and there are several smaller
ones. The well-known "Stonington Line" of steamers plies daily to
and from New York. Steamers also run to *Block Island*, on which are
summer hotels; and several times daily to *Watch Hill Point,*
which, after Newport and Narragansett Pier, is the most popular summer resort in Rhode Island. The Point is also reached by steamer
from New London and from Westerly on the Stonington & Providence
R. R. It is the extreme S. W. tip of Rhode Island, has a superb
beach, and is surrounded by attractive scenery. The leading hotels
are the *Ocean House*, the *Watch Hill House*, the *Atlantic*, the *Larkin*,
the *Plimpton*, and the *Bay View*.

From Stonington to Providence the distance is 50 miles, and there
are a number of prosperous little towns *en route*, none of which require
special mention. At *Kingston* (158 miles from New York) a branch
line diverges to *Narragansett Pier,* next to Newport the chief
summer resort in Rhode Island, situated at the mouth of Narragansett
Bay, and possessing one of the finest beaches on the Atlantic coast.
Fishing and boating are excellent, and there are fine drives and views.
The leading hotel is the *Tower Hill House* ($4 a day), 3 miles from the
Pier on Narragansett Heights, 400 ft. above the bay, and commanding
a magnificent view. Other good hotels are the *Atwood, Continental,
Delavan, Atlantic, Metatoxet*, etc., etc. The Heights are reached from
the beach by horse-cars. On the plateau near the Tower Hill House is
Silver Lake, a sequestered and picturesque spot.

Providence.

Hotels, etc.—The *Narragansett* and the *City*, in Broad St., are the best.
The *Aldrich*, the *Perrin*, and the *Providence* are good. The *Central* is on the
European plan. *Horse-cars* run to all parts of the city and to the adjoining towns.
Steamboats daily to New York, and 4 times daily to Newport.

Providence, the second city of New England in wealth and population, and the chief city and one of the capitals of Rhode Island, is
picturesquely situated on the northern arm of Narragansett Bay, known
as Providence River. The river extends to the center of the city, where
it expands into a beautiful cove nearly a mile in circumference, which
is surrounded by an elm-shaded park. Providence was founded in
1636 by Roger Williams, who had been banished from Massachusetts
on account of his religious opinions. It was incorporated in 1832, and
in 1875 had a population of 100,675. Its manufactures are very
extensive, including "prints," cotton and woolen goods, iron, jewelry, etc.

The surface of the city is very irregular, and the sides and summits
of the hills are covered with dwelling-houses, surrounded by ornamental gardens. *Westminster St.* is the main business thoroughfare, and
extending from it to Weybosset St. is the *Arcade*, the largest of the
kind in the United States, 225 ft. long, 80 ft. wide, and 3 stories high.
Near by is the massive granite building of the *Custom-House* and *Post-*

Office. The *State House* is a plain brick building at the corner of N. Main and S. Court Sts. The *Union Depot* is a large and handsome brick building in the heart of the city, fronting on Exchange Place. At the head of Exchange Place stands the * **City Hall,** one of the finest municipal buildings in New England, erected at a cost of over $1,000,-000. Directly in front of it is the * **Soldiers' and Sailors' Monument,** erected by the State in memory of its citizens (1,741 in number) who fell in the civil war. It was designed by Randolph Rogers, cost $60,000, and consists of a base of blue granite with 5 bronze statues. The **County Court-House** is an imposing edifice cor. College and Benefit Sts. The new *Opera-House* and the *Butler Exchange* (in Westminster St.) are fine structures. Of the numerous churches the most noteworthy are * *St. Stephen's* (Episcopal), with rich stained-glass windows; *Grace* (Episcopal), a handsome stone edifice with exceedingly graceful spire; the quaint old *First Baptist* (belonging to the oldest Baptist Society in America, founded in 1639); the *Roger Williams Baptist,* the *Union Congregational,* the *First Universalist,* and the Roman Catholic churches of *St. Joseph* and *St. Mary.* A costly stone cathedral is in process of construction on High St.

On the heights (Prospect St.) in the E. section of the city are the spacious grounds and substantial buildings of * **Brown University,** an old and important institution of learning, founded in 1764. Its library numbers over 50,000 volumes and is housed in a handsome fireproof building, which has room for 100,000 volumes more. The Museum of Natural History is rich in specimens, and the Art Collection includes some good portraits. The grounds comprise 16 acres, and are shaded with grand old elms. The *Rhode Island Historical Society* has a fine brick and granite building opposite the University grounds, in which are a valuable library and some interesting historical relics. The * **Athenæum** (cor. College and Benefit Sts., just below the University) is a substantial granite building, containing a reading-room, a library of 38,000 volumes, and some valuable paintings, among which are portraits by Allston and Sir Joshua Reynolds, and Malbone's masterpiece (" The Hours "). The *Butler Hospital for the Insane* occupies large and imposing buildings on the W. bank of Seekonk River, surrounded by extensive grounds and commanding broad views. The *Dexter Asylum for the Poor* is a fine edifice of brick, situated on elevated land in the N. E. part of the city. The *Rhode Island Hospital* has stately buildings surrounded by pleasant grounds in the S. part of the city, fronting on the harbor. The *Reform School* is in the S. E. section of the city, and near by is the *Home for Aged Women.* The *State Farm,* in Cranston, comprises 500 acres, and contains the State Prison, Workhouse, House of Correction, Almshouse, and State Hospital for the Insane.

There are several public squares and small parks. *Roger Williams Park,* containing about 100 acres, is near the W. shore of Narragansett Bay, in the S. part of the city; it was devised to the city in 1871 by Betsey Williams, a descendant of Roger Williams. *Prospect Terrace,* on Congdon St., commands an unrivaled view of the city.

*Swan Point Cemetery, tastefully laid out and ornamented, is on the E. bank of Seekonk River, near the Butler Hospital for the Insane.

At Cranston, 4 m. W. of Providence, is the famous *Narragansett Trotting Park.* A favorite drive is to *Hunt's Mill* (3½ m.), where there is a beautiful brook with a picturesque little cascade. *Pawtuxet,* 5 m. from the city on the W. shore of the Bay, has a fine beach and excellent bathing. In summer time, steamers leave Providence every fifteen minutes for the various resorts on the Bay, and 4 times daily for Newport. ***Rocky Point,** midway between Providence and Newport, has a fine hotel, and a far-viewing observatory on the summit of a hill near by. It is famous for its clam-bakes, sharing the honor with *Silver Spring,* higher up, on the E. shore of the Bay. *Squantum,* near Silver Spring, is owned by the Squantum Club, has been fitted up at an expense of $60,000, and is a noted resort for the private clam-bakes of the Club and its guests.

Between Providence and Boston the distance is 44 miles, and *en route* are half a dozen busy but uninteresting manufacturing towns, chief among which is *Pawtucket,* 5 miles from Providence. Here are made immense quantities of calico, thread, tacks, rope, braid, etc., and there is a fine water-power. As the train nears Boston the beautiful suburban villages of *Hyde Park* and *Roxbury* are passed, and the train stops at the fine depot on Columbus Ave. near the Common.

13. New York to Boston via "Air Line R. R."

This route is composed of the New York & New Haven R. R. to New Haven; the Air Line R. R. from New Haven to Willimantic; and the New York & New England R. R. from Willimantic to Boston. Total distance, 213 miles; time, 8½ hrs.; fare, $6. This is part of the "through line" from Boston to Philadelphia, passengers (with cars) being transferred by steamer from Harlem River to Jersey City, where connection is made with the Pennsylvania R. R.

As far as New Haven this route is identical with Route 11. *Wallingford* (12 miles) is described on p. 70. **Middletown** (23 miles from New Haven, 96 from New York) is one of the most beautiful cities in Connecticut. It occupies some gentle slopes on the W. bank of the Connecticut River, and is remarkably well built. *Main St.* is the leading business thoroughfare, and *High St.* is lined with fine residences. Upon an eminence overlooking the city (reached by High St.) stand the buildings of the *Wesleyan University* (Methodist), the most striking of which are the Memorial Chapel, Rich Hall, and Judd Hall. In Rich Hall is the library (25,000 volumes), and in Judd Hall some rich natural-history cabinets. The *view from the tower of the old chapel is extremely fine, and another scarcely inferior may be obtained from *Indian Hill Cemetery,* which contains some handsome monuments. The *Berkeley Divinity School* (Episcopal) is located in Main St.; its chapel is an exquisite specimen of Gothic architecture. The vast and stately buildings of the *State Hospital for the Insane* stand on a high hill S. E. of the city, and command a wide-extended view. (Hotel: *McDonough House.*)—*Willimantic* (127 miles) is a prosperous manufacturing village and railroad center, where are produced large quantities of thread, silk, cotton goods, etc. *Putnam* (151 miles) is another thriving manufacturing town, at the crossing of the New London Northern R. R. Daily stages run from Putnam to **Woodstock** (*Elmwood Hall*), one of the most beautiful villages in New England, delightfully situated amid wonderfully picturesque scenery. "Its like," says Mr. Beecher, "I do not know anywhere. It is a miniature Mt. Holyoke, and its prospect the Connecticut Valley in miniature." About a mile from the village is Woodstock Lake, skirted by primeval woods and abounding in fish. At *E. Thompson* (160 miles) a branch line diverges to the busy town of *Southbridge ;* and then follow in rapid succession the stations of *Blackstone* (177 miles), *Wadsworth, Franklin* (186 miles), and *Walpole* (194 miles). Passing then through the suburban towns of *Dedham, Hyde Park,* and *Dorchester,* the train stops at the Boston depot (foot of Summer St.).

14. Steamboat Routes to Boston.

a. Via Newport and Fall River.

THIS route is by steamer to Fall River, Mass., and thence by the Old Colony R. R. (time 10 to 12 hrs.). The steamers Bristol and Providence, of the Fall River line, are among the largest and finest in American waters, and there are few trips more enjoyable than that part of the present journey which is made on them. Their route in leaving New York (from Pier 28 North River at 4.30 P. M.) is such as to afford an excellent view of the harbor and city, of Brooklyn and the Long Island shore, of the islands in the East River (see p. 18), of the famous Hell Gate, and of the tranquil waters of Long Island Sound. The greater part of the voyage is on the Sound, and when *Point Judith* is passed and the turbulent Atlantic entered upon, the steamer's destination is close at hand. One stoppage only is made between New York and Fall River—namely, at *Newport,* which is reached at an early hour of the morning.

Newport.

Another route from New York to Newport is *via* Route 12 to *Wickford* and thence by ferry (fare, $5). From Boston, Newport is reached *via* Old Colony R. R. (distance, 68 miles ; fare, $2). From Providence by steamer 4 times daily.

Hotels.—The *Ocean House* ($4.50 a day), on Bellevue Ave., is the largest and most fashionable. It can accommodate 600 guests, and is generally open from June 15th to September 10th. The *Aquidneck House* ($3.50 to $4 a day), at the cor. of Pelham and Corne Sts., is cozy and quiet. The *Perry House* ($3 a day) is frequented by business men, and *Perrier's* by the diplomatic corps and foreign visitors. The *United States* ($2.50 to $3 a day), cor. Thames and Pelham Sts. is in the business quarter. The *Cliff House* and *Cottage* are near First Beach. The private-cottage system largely prevails at Newport, and hotel-life is quite subordinate to it. Furnished cottages cost $500 to $5,000 for the season. Board in private houses is $10 to $20 a week.

Newport, one of the most fashionable and frequented of all the American summer resorts, is situated on the W. shore of Rhode Island

and on Narragansett Bay, 5 miles from the ocean. It is a port of entry, and has a fine harbor, the approach to which from the sea is charming. Newport was settled in 1637, incorporated in 1700, and as late as 1769 exceeded New York in the extent of its commerce; but it suffered greatly during the Revolution, and never recovered its commercial importance. The old town lies near the water; but, since Newport has become popular as a summer resort, a new city of charming villas and sumptuous mansions has sprung up, extending along the terraces which overlook the sea.

Of the places of interest within the city proper, the first is * **Touro Park,** between Pelham and Mill Sts. Here is the * *Old Stone Mill* (sometimes called the "Round Tower"), whose origin and purpose were once the theme of much learned discussion, and which is still asserted by some antiquaries to have been built by the Norsemen 500 years before the arrival of Columbus. The weight of evidence appears to favor the theory that it was erected by Governor Benedict Arnold, who died in 1678. Near the Old Mill is J. Q. A. Ward's fine bronze statue of Commodore Perry, who was a native of Newport.

Old Stone Mill.

The **State House** (for Newport is one of the capitals of Rhode Island) is a venerable old building (dating from 1742), fronting on Washington Square in the center of the town. In its Senate-chamber is one of Stuart's celebrated portraits of Washington. The *Perry Mansion,* occupied by Commodore Perry after his victory on Lake Erie, fronts on this square; also the *City Hall* and the *Perry House.* Other objects of historical or antiquarian interest are the *Jewish Cemetery,* in Touro St., and the

Synagogue erected in 1762, when there were many wealthy Jews in Newport, and still kept in order by a bequest of $20,000 left for that purpose by Abraham Touro. * **Trinity Church** (Episcopal), in Church St., is a venerable edifice, dating from the beginning of the last century, and possessing a special interest from the fact that Bishop (then Dean) Berkeley often preached in it during his residence in New-port (1729 to 1731). The *First Baptist Church*, in Spring St., dates from 1638, and is said to be the oldest church in Rhode Island. The *Central Baptist Church*, built in 1733, stands on Clarke St., and adjoining it is the *Armory* of the Newport Artillery Company, organized in 1741. The *Vernon House*, cor. Clarke and Mary Sts., was the head-quarters of Rochambeau in 1780. The * **Redwood Library** (in Touro St.) is a substantial building in the Doric style; it contains 20,000 volumes, and some choice paintings and statuary. The *People's Library* (free) is in Thames St., and contains 15,000 volumes. The *Opera-House*, on Washington Square, is a handsome edifice.

The surf-bathing at Newport is unsurpassed. There are three fine beaches, of which * **First Beach** is the one principally used. It is ½ mile from the Ocean House, and stages ply regularly to and fro. When the red flag is displayed, gentlemen are allowed to bathe without costume; when the white flag is displayed, bathers must wear costume. **Sachuest Beach** (Second) is about a mile E. of the First, and is used only by the more adventurous, the breakers being very heavy. At the W. end of this beach is * **Purgatory,** a dark chasm 160 ft. long, 50 ft. deep, and from 8 to 14 ft. across. *Third Beach* is a long, secluded strip of sand, and beyond it are the picturesque * **Hanging Rocks,** within whose shadow Bishop Berkeley is said to have written his " Minute Philosopher." The view from this point is very attractive. The *Forty Steps*, leading from the summit of the bluff to the beach, are at the foot of Narragansett Ave.

The grand drive of Newport is * **Bellevue Avenue,** 2 miles long and lined with villas, and during the fashionable hours it is thronged with costly equipages. *Ocean Avenue* begins at Bellevue Ave., and runs 10 miles along the S. shore of the island, affording an uninterrupted view of the ocean for nearly the entire distance. The * **Spouting Cave** (reached by Bellevue Ave.) is a popular resort of excursion-parties. It is a deep cavern, running back from the sea into the rocky cliffs, and is quiet enough in ordinary weather; but after a S. E. storm the waves rush madly in and dash through an opening in the roof, sometimes to the height of 50 ft. The view from the cliffs above is considered one of the finest that Newport affords. Another favorite excursion is to the **Glen,** a quiet and sequestered retreat, where an old mill stands near a pond. It is 7 miles out, on the Stone Bridge road. The *Pirate's Cave*, 4¼ miles from the city, and *Miantonomi Hill*, 1½ mile, are often visited. The latter affords a superb view. *Lily Pond*, the largest sheet of spring-water on the island, is easily reached from Spouting Cave. **Fort Adams,** on Brenton's Point, 3½ miles from the city, is one of the largest and strongest fortresses in the United States, mounting 460 guns. Twice a week occur what are called the "fort days," when the band discourses its best music, attracting crowds of visitors. On *Conanicut Island*, opposite Fort Adams, are some summer cottages and a hotel. *Brenton's Cove* is approached by a causeway leading to Fort Adams, and affords a charming view of the city. *Goat Island*, opposite the city wharves, is the headquarters of the torpedo division of the U. S. Naval Service. *Lime Rock*, famous as the home of Ida Lewis, lies in the harbor beyond Goat Island. A popular excursion is by Providence steamer to *Rocky Point* (see p. 77).

Beyond Newport the steamer plows the lovely waters of Narragansett Bay, and soon stops at **Fall River** (*Mt. Hope House, Wilbur House*), one of the great manufacturing cities of Massachusetts, with a population of about 45,000. Cotton cloth is the great article of manufacture, and more spindles are said to be in operation than in any other American city. Fall River is well built, many of the edifices being of granite, and the vast factories are worth inspecting. North and South Main St. is the principal thoroughfare. Here passengers take the cars of the Old Colony R. R. and are conveyed to Boston (49 miles) in about 2 hours. The route is through a well-cultivated and populous farming country. Many towns and villages cluster along the line, of which the principal are **Taunton** (*City Hotel*), another prosperous manufacturing city, with 20,000 inhabitants; and **Quincy,** a beautiful old town, noteworthy as the home of the Adams and Quincy families. Leaving Quincy, the train crosses the Neponset River, runs through Dorchester and S. Boston, and stops at the depot cor. Kneeland and South Sts. (There is another route from Fall River to Boston *via* Bridgewater. It is the same as the one here described, except that Taunton is not passed.)

b. Via "Stonington Line."

Next to the Fall River Line this is the most popular of the steamboat routes to Boston, and runs fine and commodious steamers daily (except Sundays) from Pier 33 North River at 4.30 P. M. The route is nearly the same as that of the Fall River boats; but the distance traveled by steamer is shorter, and the occasionally stormy ocean passage around Point Judith is avoided. At **Stonington** (see p. 75) passengers are transferred to the cars of the Stonington & Providence R. R., and the remainder of the route is identical with Route 12.

c. Via "Norwich Line."

The boats of this line run from Pier 40 North River daily (Sundays excepted) at 4.30 P. M. by Long Island Sound to New London, Conn., which is reached in the early morning. **New London** has already been described on p. 74. Here the cars of the New London Northern R. R. are taken, and in 13 miles we reach **Norwich** (*Wauregan House, American House, Uncas House*), a beautiful city, built upon a series of terraces, lying between the Yantic and Shetucket Rivers, which there unite and form the Thames. The city is laid out in broad avenues, bordered with fine trees, and the churches, public buildings, and private houses are very attractive. Washington St. and Broadway are

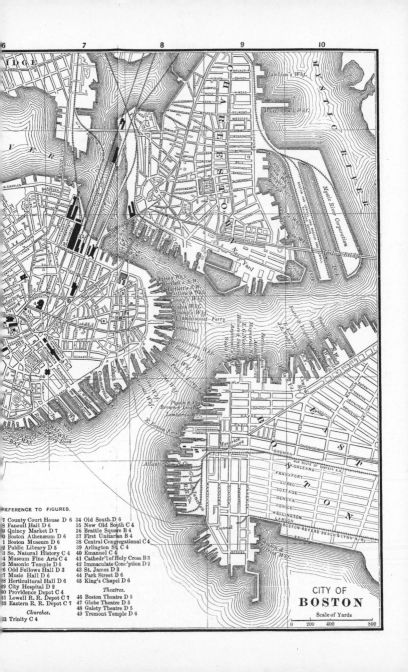

CITY OF
BOSTON

Scale of Yards

0   200   400   800

lined with handsome dwellings, surrounded by shade-trees and ornamental gardens. Main St. is the leading business thoroughfare. The
Free Academy is an imposing building near the Parade, or Williams
Park (reached by Washington St.). Near by is the *Park Congregational
Church*, and in Washington St. is the ivy-clad *Christ Church* (Episcopal). The *Yantic Cemetery* and the old burying-ground contain some
interesting monuments; and in the ancient Indian burying-ground in
Sachem St. a granite obelisk marks the grave of Uncas. Near Greenville is the battle-field, where a granite block marks the site of Mian-
tonomoh's capture; and a drive of 5 miles toward New London leads
to *Mohegan*, where a remnant of the aborigines still live. The once
famous *Falls in the Yantic* have been sacrificed to the need of water-
power for factories.—Beyond Norwich the train stops at the busy
manufacturing villages of *Wauregan*, *Danielsonville*, and *Daysville*. At
Putnam (34 miles from Norwich) the main line of the New York &
New England R. R. is reached, and the route thence is identical with
Route 13.

d. Via " Providence Line."

The steamers of this line leave Pier 29 North River daily (Sundays
excepted) at 4 P. M. and run to Providence direct, where the morning
trains to Boston may be taken. From Providence to Boston the route
is the same as Route 12. This is primarily a freight line, and the accommodations for passengers are not equal to those on either of the
preceding lines.

15. Boston.

Hotels.—The *Hotel Brunswick* (cor. Boylston and Clarendon Sts.) is one of
the finest in the country. Other first-class houses on the American plan are the
Revere (on Bowdoin Square); the *Tremont* (cor. Tremont and Beacon Sts.); the
Evans House ($4 a day), at 175 Tremont St., fronting on Boston Common; the
American House ($3.50 to $4 a day), in Hanover St., centrally located; the *St.
James* ($4 a day), on Franklin Square, at the S. End; the *Commonwealth* ($4 a
day), Washington St., cor. Worcester, also at the S. End; the *Clarendon* ($3.50 a
day), 521 and 523 Tremont St.; and the *United States*, opposite the New York and
Albany depot. Among the less expensive houses are the *Adams House* ($2.50 a
day), 371 Washington St.; the *Quincy House* ($2.50 a day), Brattle Square; the
Metropolitan ($2.50 a day), Washington St., near Dover; the *Creighton House*
($2.50), 245 Tremont St.; the *New England*, cor. Blackstone and Clinton Sts.; and
the *National*, in Haymarket Square. Of the hotels on the European plan, the
Parker House, in School St., opposite the City Hall, is the most famous in New
England. Other first-class ones are *Young's Hotel*, in Court Ave.; the *Hotel Boyls-
ton*, cor. Tremont and Boylston Sts.; the *Crawford House*, cor. Court and Brattle
Sts.; and the *Belmont*, in Washington St., near Boylston. Rooms at these hotels
are from $1 to $3 a day; meals *à la carte* in restaurants attached or elsewhere.
Restaurants.—The restaurant of the *Parker House* has long been famous.
Young's, in Cornhill Road, leading from Washington St., is noted for good dinners.
Charles Copeland's (No. 4 Tremont Row and 128 Tremont St.) and *Weber's* (in
Temple Place) are much frequented by ladies. The *Hotel Boylston Café* (in
Tremont St. near Boylston) is one of the best in the city; and at *Ober's Restaurant Parisien* (4 Winter Place) will be found the French *cuisine*. In the busi-
ness quarter are numerous lunch-rooms. Good restaurants are attached to all the
railway stations.
Modes of Conveyance.—The *horse-car* system of Boston is very complete,
and affords easy access to all parts of the city and to most of the suburbs. Fare
usually 6c. *Carriages* are in waiting at the depots and at stands in various parts

of the city, and Boston hackmen have an excellent reputation. The fares are regulated by law, and are as follows : For 1 passenger per course in city proper, 50c. ; from points S. of Dover St. or W. of Berkeley St. to points N. of State, Court, and Cambridge Sts., $1 ; each additional passenger, 50c. From midnight until 6 A. M. double the above rates. Complaints of overcharges should be made to the Supt. of Hacks, City Hall. *Omnibuses* run on the principal streets. There are 2 *ferries* to East Boston—North Ferry, from Battery St. to Border St. ; and South Ferry, from Eastern Ave. to Lewis St. (fare, 2c.). The Winnisimmet Ferry connects the city with Chelsea (fare, 5c.).

Railroad Depots.—The *Lowell Railroad Depot* (Causeway St. near Lowell St.) is one of the largest and finest in the country. It is of brick trimmed with Nova Scotia freestone, 700 ft. long and 205 ft. wide. Just beside it, in Causeway St., stands the depot of the *Eastern Railroad ;* and a few paces from the latter is the depot of the *Fitchburg Railroad.* The *Boston & Albany* depot is in Beach St., between Albany and Lincoln Sts. ; the depot of the *Maine Central* is on Haymarket Square, at the end of Union St. ; that of the *Providence R. R.* is on Columbus Ave. near the Common, and is a splendid edifice; that of the *Old Colony R. R.* is at the cor. of Kneeland and South Sts. ; and that of the *New York & New England R. R.* at the foot of Summer St.

Theatres and Amusements.—The *Boston Theatre* (in Washington St. near West St.) is the largest in New England. The *Globe Theatre* (in Washington St. near Boylston) is the place where operatic and star performances are given. The *Museum Theatre*, in the Boston Museum (Tremont St. near School St.) is select. In the Museum are pictures, casts, wax figures, and curiosities of all sorts (admission, 30c.). The *Howard Athenæum* (Howard St. near Court St.) is devoted to varieties and negro minstrelsy. The *Gaiety*, devoted mainly to vaudeville and comic opera, is a few doors from the Boston Theatre. *Music Hall* (15 Winter St.) is one of the finest in the country, and contains the second largest organ in the world, built in Germany at a cost of $60,000. Classic music is performed here. Lectures, concerts, and readings are given at Music Hall; at *Tremont Temple* (in Tremont St. opposite the Tremont House); at *Beethoven Hall* (in Washington St. near Boylston); at *Horticultural Hall* (No. 100 Tremont St.); and at the *Hawthorne Rooms*, in Park St. *Horse-races* occur at Beacon Park and Mystic Park, in the suburbs of the city.

Reading-Rooms.—In the leading hotels are reading-rooms (supplied with newspapers) for the use of guests. The *Public Library* (in Boylston St. opposite the Common) is free to all. The *Athenæum* (in Beacon St. near Bowdoin) has excellent reading-rooms, but introduction by a member is necessary. Free reading-rooms may be found at the *Young Men's Christian Union* (20 Boylston St.) and the *Young Men's Christian Ass.* (cor. Tremont and Eliot Sts.).

Art Collections.—The *Museum of Arts*, on Art Square (St. James Ave. and Dartmouth St.), is a splendid building, and contains an extensive collection of pictures, statuary, casts, and antiquities (admission, 25c.). Art Exhibitions are held at the *Boston Art Club* (64 Boylston St.) and at the *Studio Building* (in Tremont St. next to Horticultural Hall). Good pictures, engravings, etc., may be seen (free) at the sales galleries of *Williams & Everett*, 508 Washington St.

Clubs.—The *Somerset Club* has a fine granite-front house in Beacon St., elegantly furnished. The *Union Club* owns a handsome house in Park St., containing a valuable library and paintings. The *Central Club* is housed in a handsome brown-stone mansion at the cor. of Washington St. and Worcester Square. All these clubs are for social purposes, and admission is obtained by a member's introduction.

Post-Office.—The Post-Office is in Milk St. cor. Devonshire and Water Sts. It is open for the delivery of letters from 7.30 A. M. to 7.30 P. M., and to boxholders throughout the 24 hours. Letters may also be mailed in the lamp-post boxes, whence they are collected at frequent intervals.

BOSTON, the capital of Massachusetts, and chief city of New England, is situated at the W. extremity of Massachusetts Bay, in latitude 42° N. and longitude 71° W. The city embraces Boston proper, East Boston, South Boston, Roxbury, Dorchester, Charlestown, Brighton, and West Roxbury, containing in all about 22,000 acres. Boston proper, or old Boston, occupies a peninsula of some 700 acres, very uneven in surface, and originally presenting three hills, Beacon, Copp's, and Fort, the former of which is about 130 ft. above the sea. The Indian name of this peninsula was Shawmut, meaning "Sweet Waters." It was called by the earlier settlers Trimountain or Tremont. *East Boston* occupies the W. portion of Noddle's or Maverick's Island. Here is the deepest water of the harbor, and here the ocean steamers chiefly lie. *South Boston* extends about 2 m. along the S. side of the harbor, an arm of which separates it from Boston proper. Near the center are Dorchester Heights, which attain an elevation of about 130

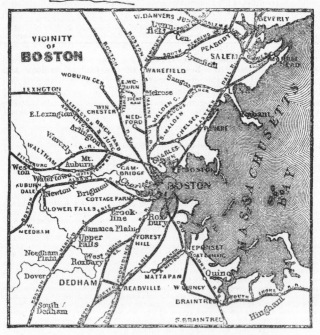

ft. above the ocean, and afford a fine view of the city, bay, and sur- rounding country. The city is connected with Charlestown by the Charles River bridge, 1,503 ft. long, and the Warren bridge, 1,300 ft. long; and with Cambridge by the West Boston bridge, which crosses Charles River from Cambridge St., Boston, and is 2,756 ft. long, with a causeway 3,432 ft. long. Craigie's bridge, 2,796 ft. long, extends from Leverett St. to E. Cambridge; from this bridge another, 1,820 ft. long, extends to Prison Point, Charlestown. South Boston is reached by the Federal St. bridge, about 500 ft. long, and the South Boston bridge, 1,550 ft. long. All these bridges are free. A causeway, built across Back Bay on a substantial dam 1½ m. long, extends from the foot of Beacon St. to Sewall's Point in Brookline. The harbor is a spacious indentation of Massachusetts Bay, embracing about 75 square miles, including several arms. A wide sheet of water at the mouth of Charles River is commonly known as Back Bay. There are more than 50 islands or islets in the harbor, and it offers many picturesque views.

In the older portions of the city the streets are irregular, and generally narrow, though somewhat has been done toward widening and straightening them since the fire. Those in the new section built on the made land of Back Bay are wide, well paved, regularly laid out, and present a handsome appearance. *Washington St.* is the principal thoroughfare for general retail stores. *Tremont* and *Winter Sts.* also contain many, and are much frequented. *State St.* is the financial center, and contains the headquarters of the leading bankers and brokers. *Pearl St.* is the largest boot and shoe market in the world ; and in Franklin, Chauncey, Sumner, and the neighboring streets are the great wholesale dry-goods establishments. **Commonwealth Ave.,** running through the newer portion of the city, is one of its finest streets. It is 240 ft. wide, and through the center runs a long park with rows of trees. The most "fashionable quarter" of the town lies on the made land of the Back Bay, W. of the Common. Nearly all the streets in this section contain costly and handsome private residences. The beauty of its surroundings is such that there are pleasant drives out of Boston in almost any direction. The most popular drive is to and around Chestnut Hill Reservoir (5 miles).

The first white inhabitant of Boston was the Rev. John Blackstone, supposed to have been an Episcopal clergyman, and to have arrived in 1628. Here he lived alone until 1630, when John Winthrop (afterward the first Governor of Massachusetts) came across the river from Charlestown, where he had dwelt with some fellow immigrants for a short time. About 1635 Mr. Blackstone sold his claim to the now populous peninsula for £30, and removed to Rhode Island. The first church was built in 1632; the first wharf in 1673. Four years later a postmaster was appointed, and in 1704 (April 24th) the first newspaper, called the "Boston News Letter," was published. The "Boston Massacre" occurred March 5, 1770, when 3 persons were killed and 8 wounded by the fire of the soldiery. On Dec. 16, 1773, the tea was destroyed in the harbor, and Boston bore a conspicuous part in the opening scenes of the Revolution. The city was incorporated in 1822, with a population of 45,000, which had increased to 136,881 in 1850, to 177,840 in 1860, and 250,526 in 1870. By the recent annexation of the suburbs of Brighton, Charlestown, and W. Roxbury, the population has been increased to 357,254. On the 9th of November, 1872, one of the most terrible conflagrations ever known in the United States swept away the principal business portion of Boston. The district burned over extended from Sumner and Bedford Sts. on the S. to near State St. on the N., and from Washington St. east to the harbor. About 775 of the finest buildings in the city were destroyed, causing a loss of $70,000,000.

Perhaps the most interesting and attractive spot in Boston is the *****Common,** a park of 48 acres in the heart of the city, surrounded by an iron fence, laid out in sloping lawns and winding walks, and shaded by magnificent trees. The Common is considered to date from 1634, and by the city charter it is made public property for ever. A pond and fountain, on the site of the ancient and historic *Frog Pond,*

occupy a central point in the grounds. On Flagstaff Hill, overlooking
the Pond, is the costly *Soldiers' Monument*, 90 ft. high, with 4 statues
of heroic size at the base, and surmounted by a colossal figure of
America, standing on a hemisphere and guarded by 4 eagles with outspread wings. Near the monument stood the famous *Old Elm*, which
antedated the birth of the city, and was finally blown down in the gale
of Feb. 15, 1876. Near Park St. is the beautiful *Brewer Fountain*,
of bronze, cast in Paris, and adorned with statues.—The **Public
Gardens**, once a part of the Common, are now separated from it by
Charles St. They comprise 22 acres, beautifully laid out, and contain
a conservatory, Ball's noble equestrian statue of Washington, Story's
bronze statue of Edward Everett, one representing "Venus rising from

the Sea," and the
beautiful monu-
ment in honor of
the discovery of
ether as an anæs-
thetic. In the cen-
ter is a serpentine
pond covering 4
acres and crossed
by a handsome
bridge.

N. of the Com-
mon is Beacon Hill,
on the summit of
which stands the
State House,
an imposing edi-
fice 173 ft. long
and 61 ft. deep,
with a stately col-
onnade in front,
and surmounted by
a gilded dome. On
the terrace in front
are statues of Dan-

State House.

iel Webster and Horace Mann. On the entrance floor (Doric Hall) are
Ball's statue of Governor Andrew, busts of Samuel Adams, Lincoln, and
Sumner, and a collection of battle-flags. In the Rotunda, opening off
Doric Hall, are Chantrey's statue of Washington, copies of the tomb-
stones of the Washington family in Brighton Parish, England, and many
historical relics. The *view from the dome (open when the General
Court is not in session) is very fine, including the city, the harbor and
ocean beyond, and a vast extent of country. On Beacon St., near the
State House, is the **Boston Athenæum,** an imposing freestone edifice in the Palladian style, containing a library of 110,000 volumes, a reading-room, and some choice pieces of sculpture. The Athenæum was incorporated in 1807, and is one of the best endowed institutions of the

kind in the world. Access to the library is obtained only on introduction by a member. The *American Academy of Arts and Sciences*
has its rooms and library (15,000 volumes) in the Athenæum building.
Near the Athenæum is *Pemberton Square*, the site of an old Indian
burying-ground; and on the farther slope of Beacon Hill is *Louisburg
Square*, containing statues of Columbus and Aristides. Near the State
House is the *Beacon Hill Reservoir*, a solid granite structure with a
capacity of 2,700,000 gallons. At No. 20 Beacon St. are the offices of
Boston University, founded in 1869 by Isaac Rich, who bequeathed it
$2,000,000.

In Boylston St., opposite the Common, is the * **Boston Public
Library,** next to the Library of Congress the largest in America. It
contains 300,000 volumes, besides 150,000 pamphlets, and the valuable
Tosti collection of engravings. The library and reading-room are free
to all, but only residents of the city can take books away. Next door
to the library is the lofty *Hotel Pelham*, opposite which is the spacious
and ornate *Hotel Boylston*, opposite which again (at the cor. of Tremont
St.) is the **Masonic Temple,** a lofty structure of light-colored granite,
highly ornamental and unique in style, with noble halls in the interior.
Opposite the Temple (No. 20 Boylston St.) is the handsome Gothic
building of the *Young Men's Christian Union*, containing a library
(5,000 volumes), reading-rooms, refreshment-rooms, gymnasium, etc.
From this point Boylston St. leads W. past the Public Gardens to the
aristocratic West End. Beyond the Garden, at the cor. of Berkeley
St., is the fine building of the * **Society of Natural History,** with
a library of 12,000 volumes, and valuable cabinets (open to the public
from 9 A. M. to 5 P. M. on Wednesdays and Saturdays). Near by is
the *Institute of Technology*, and at the cor. of Clarendon St. is the
magnificent **Hotel Brunswick*. Close by is the *Second Church* (Unitarian), with a rich interior; nearly opposite which (cor. Clarendon
St. and Huntington Ave.) is * **Trinity Church** (Episcopal—Phillips
Brooks, pastor), one of the largest, finest, and most splendidly decorated churches in America, finished in 1877 at a cost of $750,000. One
block beyond (cor. Boylston and Dartmouth Sts.) is the new * **Old
South Church,** an imposing group of stone buildings—church, chapel,
and parsonage. The interior is extremely ornate, and the tower is
248 ft. high. A block S. on Art Square (cor. Dartmouth St. and Huntington Ave.) is the * **Museum of Fine Arts,** a substantial red-brick
building, elaborately adorned with terra-cotta bas-reliefs, copings,
and moldings. In the lower halls are statuary, casts, and Egyptian
antiquities; and in the upper galleries a library and one of the richest
collections of paintings and engravings in the country. (Admission
free 2 days in the week; other days, 25c.)—In this opulent quarter
are other noteworthy churches. The * **Brattle-Square Church**
(Unitarian), cor. Clarendon St. and Commonwealth Ave., is a massive
stone edifice in the form of a Greek cross, with a campanile 176 ft.
high, surrounded near the top with a frieze containing colossal statues in high relief, after designs by Bartholdi. The *First Church*
(Unitarian), cor. Berkeley and Marlborough Sts., is one of the most

beautiful in the city, with stained-glass windows and a richly decorated interior. Close by, at the cor. of Berkeley and Newbury Sts., is the elegant little *Central Congregational Church*, cruciform in shape, with rich stained windows and a stone spire 240 ft. high; near which, in Newbury St., is the ornate *Emanuel Church* (Episcopal). The *Arlington St. Church* (Unitarian), in Arlington St., fronting the Public Garden, is a handsome freestone structure with a fine chime of bells in the tower. The *Providence Depot*, on Columbus Ave., near the Common, is worthy of attention as one of the finest in New England.

On Dock Square, in the heart of the business quarter, stands *** Faneuil Hall,** the most interesting building in the United States, next to Independence Hall, Philadelphia. This famous edifice, the

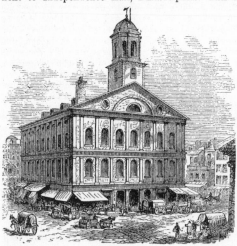

"cradle of liberty," was erected in 1742 and presented to the town by Peter Faneuil, a Huguenot merchant. Destroyed by fire in 1761, it was rebuilt in 1768, and enlarged to its present dimensions in 1805. The basement is a market with shops. The public hall is on the second floor, and adorned with a full-length portrait of the founder, and with portraits of Washington, Samuel Adams, J. Q. Adams, Webster, Everett,

Faneuil Hall.

Lincoln, Governor Andrew, Henry Wilson, and Charles Sumner. Just E. of Faneuil Hall is **Quincy Market,** a vast granite building, 530 by 50 ft., and 2 stories high; and near by (in State St.) is the massive and stately *** U. S. Custom-House,** of granite, in the form of a Greek cross, with handsome porticoes on either front, erected from 1837 to 1849 at a cost of $1,076,000. The old *Merchants' Exchange* (No. 55 State St.) was noted for its large size and massive architecture, but it suffered greatly in the fire of 1872, and has since lost much in remodeling. At the head of State St., in Washington St., is the *Old State House*, built in 1748, and often mentioned in Revolutionary annals; but now remodeled inside and outside, and given over to business uses. Just above, in Court Square, is the *County Court-House*, a fine building of Quincy granite. In rear of the Court-

House, fronting on School St., is the * **City Hall,** one of the most imposing edifices in the city, completed in 1865 at a cost of $505,691. It is of white Concord granite, in the Italian Renaissance stlye, and surmounted by a Louvre dome, 109 ft. high. The interior is striking, and on the lawn in front is Greenough's bronze statue of Franklin.

Opposite the City Hall is the *Parker House*, and just above (at the cor. of School and Tremont Sts.) is the venerable *King's Chapel*, built in 1754 by the Episcopalians on the site of the first church of that sect in Boston. Adjoining it is the first burying-ground established in Boston, containing the graves of Isaac Johnson, "the father of Boston," Governor Winthrop, John Cotton, and other distinguished men. On Tremont St. to the right of School St. is a granite building in which are the rooms of the *Massachusetts Historical Society*, with a library of 25,000 volumes and many valuable MSS., coins, maps, charts, portraits, and historical relics. Close by is the *Boston Museum* (admission 30c.), containing pictures, casts, wax figures, and curiosities from all parts of the world. Turning down Tremont St. to the left from School St., we pass *Tremont Temple* (used for lectures, readings, etc.), and soon reach * **Horticultural Hall,** an ornate white granite structure, in which annual floral shows are held; also fairs, concerts, and lectures. Just beyond is **Music Hall,** one of the finest in the country, with the second largest organ in the world (entrances on Tremont St., Winter St., and Central Place). Opposite is the famous old *Park Street Church* (Congregational), founded in 1809; adjoining which is the *Old Granary Burying-Ground*, in which are buried Peter Faneuil, Samuel Adams, John Hancock, and other distinguished men. Near Temple Place is the church of *St. Paul's* (Episcopal), of gray granite in the Ionic style, with a classic portico of 6 columns; and next to it (cor. Temple Place) is the granite *U. S. Court-House*, formely Masonic Hall. Still beyond are the Public Library and Masonic Temple, already described (see page 87); and farther still (cor. Berkeley St.) is **Odd Fellows' Hall,** a white granite building of chaste and pleasing design. Near Concord St. is the *Methodist Church*, a quaint structure, with two spires. In Harrison Ave. near Concord St. is the **City Hospital,** a spacious granite edifice standing in 7 acres of grounds; and near it is the Roman Catholic *Home for Orphans*, the *Church of the Immaculate Conception* (famed for its music and its fine interior), and *Boston College*, a Jesuit institution with many pupils. Also in Harrison Ave. is the *Church of St. James* (Roman Catholic), in the purest form of the classical basilica, with richly adorned interior. At the cor. of Washington and Malden Sts. is the new * **Cathedral of the Holy Cross** (Roman Catholic), the largest and finest church edifice in New England. It is in the mediæval Gothic style, 364 ft. long and 170 ft. broad, with two spires 300 and 200 ft. high, and a splendid interior.

Returning now to the business quarter, we find at the cor. of Washington and Milk Sts. the * **Old South Church,** an historic relic of much interest. It was built in 1729, and was used as a place of meeting by the heroes of '76, and subsequently by the British as a place for cavalry-drill. It barely escaped the flames in the great fire of 1872, and immediately afterward was leased to the Government for a post-office. A public subscription is being raised to preserve it as public property. In Milk St., between Devonshire and Water Sts., is the new * **Post-Office,** completed in 1875 at a cost of over $3,000,000. It is of granite, highly ornate in style, and is said to be the finest building in New England. The upper stories are used by the *U. S. Sub-Treasury ;* the Cash-Room is very richly adorned.

The new buildings and "blocks" that have been erected in the burnt district since 1872 comprise some of the finest and costliest commercial structures in America. Most noteworthy among them are the *Sears Building,* cor. Washington and Court Sts. ; the *Brewer Building,* covering an entire block on Devonshire, Franklin, and Federal Sts. ; the *Franklin Building,* cor. Franklin and Federal Sts. ; the *Rialto Building,* cor. Devonshire and Milk Sts. ; the *Simmons Building,* cor. Congress and Water Sts. ; the *Cathedral Building,* in Winthrop Square ; and especially those of the *N. Y. Mutual Life Ins. Co.* (cor. Milk and Pearl Sts.), the *Equitable Life Ins. Co.* (cor. Milk and Federal Sts., opposite the Post-Office), and the *New England Mutual Life Ins. Co.* (cor. Milk and Congress Sts.).

On **Copp's Hill,** in the N. E. part of the city, is the old *North Burying-Ground,* the second established in Boston, and still sacredly preserved. Here lie three fathers of the Puritan Church, Drs. Increase, Cotton, and Samuel Mather. *Christ Church,* in Salem St. near Copp's Hill, is the oldest in the city, having been erected in 1722. In the tower is a fine chime of bells.

Of the charitable institutions of Boston, the *Perkins Institution for the Blind* is famous all over the world. It was founded in 1831 by Dr. Samuel G. Howe, under whose charge it remained until his death, and occupies spacious buildings on Mt. Washington, in S. Boston. Near by on the hill is *Carney Hospital,* managed by the Sisters of Charity. The *Massachusetts General Hospital* is a vast granite structure on Charles River, between Allen and Bridge Sts. The *City Hospital* has already been described (see page 89). The *Marine Hospital* (for invalid seamen) occupies a commanding site in Chelsea, and is a spacious and stately building. The *U. S. Naval Hospital* is near by. The *House of Industry* and the *Almshouse* are on Deer Island in the harbor ; and the *House of Correction* and *Lunatic Asylum* in S. Boston.

The environs of Boston are remarkably attractive. On almost all sides lie picturesque and venerable towns, and the country between, even when not strictly beautiful, is never flat and tame. Charlestown, Brighton, Jamaica Plain, and W. Roxbury were annexed in 1875, and now form part of the city. Roxbury and Dorchester had been previously annexed. In all of them are the fine villa residences of Boston merchants, and other features of interest which make them worth a visit. At *Charlestown,* on the N. (reached by horse-cars from Scollay Square), is the famous * **Bunker Hill Monument,** occupying the site of the old redoubt at Breed's Hill, and commemorative of the eventful battle fought on the spot, June 17, 1775. It is a plain but massive obelisk of Quincy granite, 30 ft. square at the base, and 221 ft. high. From the observatory at the top, reached by a spiral flight of 295 steps, is obtained a magnificent view, including the entire vicinity of Boston. The monument was dedicated June 17, 1843, in the presence of President Tyler and his cabinet, on which occasion Daniel Webster delivered an oration which is considered his finest oratorical effort. In the house near the monument is a fine statue of General Warren, who was killed on the Hill; and a stone marks the spot where he fell. The *U. S. Navy Yard* is also located in Charlestown. It comprises about 100 acres, and contains, among other objects of interest, the longest rope-walk in the country, and an immense dry dock. In *Chelsea* (connected with Boston by ferry, and with Charlestown by a bridge over the Mystic River) are Woodlawn Cemetery, Marine Hospital, and Naval Hospital, which have already been described. *Chelsea Beach,* 5 miles from Boston (reached by horse-cars or by Eastern R. R., and Revere & Lynn R. R.), is a smooth, hard, sandy beach, well adapted for driving or walking. It is much visited by citizens on Sundays and holidays. *Brighton*, a station on the Albany R. R., 5 miles W. of the city proper, is famous for its cattle-market. *Point Shirley*, 5 miles from Boston, affords a pleasant drive. The most direct route is *via* the E. Boston ferry. Ex-

Bunker Hill Monument.

cellent fish and game dinners and suppers may be obtained here, at Taft's Hotel. *** Brookline** is a beautiful town on the Boston & Albany R. R. (reached also by the Mill-Dam from Boston). In it is the Brookline Reservoir, with a capacity of 120,000,000 gallons. About 1 m. distant, on the boundaries of Brookline, Brighton, and Newton, is the great *Chestnut Hill Reservoir*, with a capacity of 800,000,000 gallons. From Boston to and around this point is a favorite drive. *Lexington* and *Concord* are reached by the Lexington Branch R. R. from the Lowell depot; Concord may also be reached by the Fitchburg line.

*** Cambridge,** most renowned of American academic cities, lies 3 miles W. of Boston (horse-cars from Bowdoin Square), and has a population of about 50,000. It covers an extensive area, generally level, and is laid out in broad streets and avenues, lined with elms and

other shade trees. Its greatest attraction is **Harvard University,**
the oldest and most richly endowed institution of learning in America. It was founded in 1638 by the Rev. John Harvard, and embraces,
besides its collegiate department, law, medical, dental, scientific, art,
and theological schools. In 1877–'78 there were 125 instructors and
1,344 students. The university lands in various parts of Cambridge
comprise 60 acres. The college yard contains about 15 acres, tastefully laid out and adorned by stately elms. Here, forming a large
quadrangle, are clustered 15 buildings, of brick or stone, from 2 to 5
stories high. The most notable of these are *Matthews's Hall,* a large
and ornate structure used as a dormitory; *Massachusetts Hall,* an
ancient building dating from 1720; *Holden Chapel ; Harvard, Univer-*

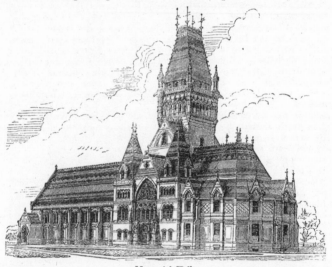

Memorial Hall.

sity, Gray, and *Boylston Halls ; Appleton Chapel ; Thayer Hall* and
Dane Hall, for the law school. * *Gore Hall,* beyond the quadrangle,
contains the university library (160,000 volumes). N. of the quadrangle is * *Memorial Hall,* erected by the alumni and friends of the university in commemoration of the students and graduates who lost
their lives during the civil war. It is a handsome edifice of brick and
Nova Scotia stone, 310 ft. long by 115 wide, with a tower 200 ft. high.
It is one of the finest college buildings in the world, and cost $575,-
000. It contains, besides Memorial Hall proper, a theatre, and a spacious dining-hall. Near the college yard are the *Gymnasium* and the
* *Zoölogical Museum ;* and about ¾ mile N. W. are the *Botanical Garden,* containing a valuable herbarium, and the *Observatory.*

W. of the college yard is *The Common*, on which stands a granite monument erected by the city in honor of her soldiers who fell in the civil war.   Near the Common are *Christ Church* (Episcopal), a venerable edifice; the *First Unitarian* Church; and the * *Shepard Memorial Church* (Congregational), erected in honor of Thomas Shepard, who was pastor at Cambridge from 1635 to 1649.   In front of the latter is the famous * *Washington Elm*, beneath which Washington assumed the command of the American army in 1775, and which is thought to be 300 years old.   Many structures erected before the Revolution are still standing, among them the house used by Washington for his headquarters and now inhabited by the poet Longfellow, and *Elmwood*, the home of James Russell Lowell.

The cemetery of * **Mount Auburn** is in Cambridge (1 mile from Harvard Square, 4 miles from Boston), and is one of the oldest and most beautiful in America.   It contains 125 acres, and is embellished by landscape and horticultural art and many elegant and costly monuments.   The gateway is of Quincy granite in the Egyptian style; and near it is the *Chapel*, an ornamented Gothic edifice, containing statues of Winthrop, Otis, John Adams, and Judge Story.   Central, Maple, Chapel, Spruce, and other leading avenues afford a circuit of the entire grounds, with a view of the principal monuments.   The *Tower*, 60 ft. high, in the rear of the grounds, is 187 ft. above Charles River, and commands a fine view.   It is reached by Central, Walnut, and Mountain Avenues.   Numerous lakes, ponds, and fountains in various parts of the cemetery add to its beauty.

16. Boston to Portland via "Eastern Shore."

By the phrase "Eastern Shore" is meant that part of the New England coast lying between Boston and Portland.   The *Eastern R. R.* traverses the entire distance, affording many pleasant glimpses of the ocean, and rendering easily accessible the various watering-places and maritime towns along shore.   Distance from Boston to Portland, 108 miles; fare, $3.   There is also a line of steamers from Boston to Portland daily from India Wharf (fare, $1.50).

LEAVING Boston by the Eastern R. R., *Chelsea* (4 miles out) is speedily reached, and affords a convenient point from which to visit the Chelsea or **Revere Beach,** a favorite summer resort of the less well-to-do classes of Boston, who throng it on Sundays and holidays.   It is reached from the city by horse-cars and also by the Boston, Revere Beach & Lynn R. R., and affords a delightful promenade and drive as well as excellent sea-bathing.   **Lynn** (11 miles from Boston) is a flourishing city of 28,231 inhabitants, situated on the shore of Massachusetts Bay, and surrounded by pleasing scenery.   It contains some handsome churches and schoolhouses, numerous fine villas of Boston merchants, a costly Soldiers' Monument, and a very fine City Hall. *High Rock* is a commanding eminence in the center of the city, which affords a wide-extended view.   *Pine Grove Cemetery* is a beautiful rural burying-ground.   Four miles from Lynn (reached by stage) is **Nahant,** a bold promontory connected with the mainland by narrow ridges of sand and stone thrown up by the ocean, above which the highest point

rises 150 ft. A large and splendid hotel was built here in 1824, and
numerous summer residents filled the place with their cottages, making
it the most fashionable watering-place in New England; but the hotel
was burned down in 1861, and since then the tide of pleasur-eseekers
has gone in other directions, especially toward Swampscott. Several
small hotels still remain, however, and the villas give it a gay aspect in
summer. The beach of Nahant (1½ mile long) is hard and smooth,
shelving gently, and with a splendid surf. There are many natural
wonders and curiosities in the vicinity; and on the N. side the *Garden
of Maolis* (entrance, 25c.) offers a picturesque retreat where good fish
or clam dinners may be enjoyed. Nahant is reached from Boston by
steamer as well as by railway.[1]

A mile beyond Lynn the train reaches **Swampscott,** which is to
Boston what Long Branch is to New York, the favorite summer resort of its wealthiest citizens. The leading hotels are the *Great Anawan House,* the *Little Anawan House,* the *Lincoln House,* and the *Ocean
House.* The shore is lined with tasteful villas, and wealth has fairly
turned poverty out of the place. There are 3 beaches of varying length,
and picturesque headlands jut out into the sea. The bathing is excellent, with no undertow, and the water is thought to be warmer than at
Nahant or Rye Beach. The permanent residents are chiefly engaged in
the cod and haddock fishing, and supply the market with fresh fish. The
Swampscott Branch of the Eastern R. R. diverges here to Marblehead,
passing *Phillips Beach, Beach Bluff,* and *Clifton,* all popular resorts.

Salem (16 miles from Boston) is a venerable town, the site of the
first permanent settlement in the old Massachusetts colony. Many interesting historical associations cluster around Salem, and every period
in her annals has been illustrated by some important event or illustrious
name. The year 1692 is remarkable as the date of the witchcraft delu-
sion at Salem village, now Danvers, for which several persons were
tried and executed. In the Court-House are deposited the documents
that relate to these curious trials. The house is still standing (at the
corner of Essex and North Sts.) in which some of the preliminary examinations were made. The place of execution is in the western part
of the city, an eminence overlooking the city, harbor, and surrounding
shores, and known as *Gallows Hill.* A pleasant drive of 5 or 6 miles
will enable the visitor to examine the several places of interest mentioned in Mr. Upham's work on the subject. *Plummer Hall* is a handsome building in Essex St. containing the library of the Salem Athenæum (14,000 volumes), and that of the Essex Institute (25,000
volumes, and a large collection of newspapers, pamphlets, manuscripts,
and various historical relics). In rear of Plummer Hall is the oldest
church edifice in New England, dating from 1634. * *East India Marine Hall* contains the museum of the East India Marine Society, and
the extensive and valuable scientific collections of the Essex Institute,
the whole being open to the public daily, except Sunday and Monday,

---

[1] Fuller particulars of these beaches as well as of other popular resorts mentioned in this Guide may be found in *Appletons' Illustrated Handbook of American
Summer Resorts.*

from 9 A. M. to 5 P. M.   The visitor to Salem should not fail to take the horse-cars to *Peabody* (2 miles distant) to visit the * *Peabody Institute*, in which are deposited many interesting works of art, and the various memorials of the founder, George Peabody, of which may be mentioned the portrait of Queen Victoria, the Congress Medal, etc.   A short distance in one direction from the Institute building is the house in which Mr. Peabody was born, and about the same distance in an opposite direction, in *Harmony Grove Cemetery*, is his grave.   The principal hotel of Salem is the *Essex House* ($3 a day).

Four miles from Salem (reached by Marblehead Branch R. R.) is the quaint and interesting old town of **Marblehead,** built on a rugged, rocky promontory, which juts far out into the sea and forms an excellent harbor.   This spot was one of the first settled in New England, the town of Marblehead having been incorporated by the Puritan colony just 15 years after the landing of the Pilgrims at Plymouth.   So bleak and bare are the Marblehead rocks, that Whitefield asked in wonder, "Where do they bury their dead?"   There are many queer houses still standing which were built and occupied before the Revolution; the most noteworthy being the old *Bank Building*, which is supposed to have been built in 1768 for a Colonel Lee, and which is a fine specimen of the palatial mansions of the nabobs of the last century.   A hundred years ago Marblehead was, next to Boston, the most populous town in Massachusetts, and had a large maritime commerce.   Now its character has almost wholly changed from the olden time, for it has become a center of the shoe-manufacture.   The *Old Fort* is a plain, hoary-looking edifice, standing on the rugged slope of the promontory looking toward the sea.   *Marblehead Neck*, easily reached by boats across the harbor, or by a ride of 2 miles along shore, is a favorite resort; many campers-out flock hither to pitch their canvas tents and spend a few weeks of the heated term.   Two hotels (open only in summer) have recently been erected here, and the place is growing in popularity.   *Lowell Island*, 2 miles distant, is reached by steamer from Marblehead several times daily.   It is noted for the purity of its air and the beauty of its views, and has a large summer hotel on it.

Two miles beyond Salem on the main line is *Beverly*, an ancient town now busy with shoe-factories.   The Beverly beaches are very pleasant, and from here to *Manchester* the strip of coast is lined with beautiful residences standing amid ornamental gardens.   At Manchester and Magnolia are new hotels, and tourists will find many attractive places along the Gloucester Branch of the E. R. R., running as it does to the extreme point of Cape Ann.   Next comes *Ipswich* (27 miles), and 9 miles beyond is **Newburyport** (*Merrimac House*, $2.50 a day, and *Ocean House*), an old, historic town, built on an abrupt declivity of the Merrimac River, 3 miles from the ocean.   Like Salem and Marblehead, it is one of those antique coast towns which have to a large extent lost their maritime importance, while preserving the relics and mementos of a former commercial prosperity.   The *Marine Museum* (on State St.) contains a number of these mementos. The *Public Library* was endowed by George Peabody and contains

15,000 volumes. There are several fine churches, and many quaint houses of the olden time. Stages run twice daily in summer from Newburyport to **Salisbury Beach,** which is one of the best on the coast. It extends about 6 miles, from the Merrimac to the Hampton River, and is so firm and hard that horses' hoofs make scarcely any impression. Twenty years ago there was nothing there but the lonely breaker and the windy beach-grass, and it was the same when Whittier's "Tent on the Beach" was pitched there; but now a comfortable hotel (the *Atlantic House*) and some 50 summer cottages have peopled it, and during the summer months the season is a lively one. The shore descends very gradually, and on its long slope the people of the surrounding country have had an annual reunion every September for more than 100 years. From *Hampton* (10 miles beyond Newburyport) stages run 3 miles to **Hampton Beach,** a much-frequented resort, with numerous summer cottages and hotels that are generally thronged in summer. The bathing and fishing at Hampton Beach are capital, the scenery charming, and the drives in the vicinity pleasant. **Rye Beach,** the most fashionable of the New Hampshire beaches, is reached by stage in 3 miles from N. Hampton, or by a delightful drive of 7 miles from Portsmouth. The bathing is excellent, the surf being particularly fine and without any undertow. The hotels are the *Farragut House,* the *Washington House,* and the *Sea-View House ;* there are also a number of boarding-houses and a colony of cottages.

Portsmouth (56 miles from Boston) the only seaport of New Hampshire, stands upon a peninsula on the S. side of Piscataqua River, and, excepting the narrow strip connecting it with the mainland, is entirely surrounded by water. The harbor is deep and safe, and in it are many islets, some accessible by bridges. Portsmouth is a singularly venerable and tranquil-looking old place, with beautifully shaded streets, ancient buildings, large gardens, and home-like residences. Among the objects of special interest are the old church of St. John, the Athenæum, Governor Wentworth's mansion (at Little Harbor), and the tomb of Sir William Pepperell, which is near the Navy Yard. The *United States Navy Yard* is admirably located upon Continental Island (reached by ferry from foot of Daniel St.), and contains, besides the usual ship-houses, shops, etc., a very fine balance dry-dock, which is an ingenious affair and with its appendages cost $800,000. The hotels of Portsmouth are the *Rockingham House,* the *American House,* and the *National House.* The population is about 13,000.

The Isles of Shoals.

These are a group of eight bare and rugged islands, lying about 9 miles off the coast and reached from Portsmouth by steamer daily in summer. The isles are small in extent, the largest (Appledore) containing only 350 acres. From the mainland they appear shadowy, almost fairy-like in their dim outline. As the steamboat approaches, they separate into distinct elevations of rock, all having a bleak and barren aspect, with little vegetation, and with jagged reefs running far out in all directions among the waves. *Appledore*, the principal island of the group, rises in the shape of a hog's back, and is the least irregular in appearance. Its ledges rise some 75 ft. above the sea, and it is divided by a narrow, picturesque little valley, wherein is situated the *Appledore House* (500 guests, $3 a day) and its cottages, the only buildings on the island. Just by Appledore is *Smutty Nose* or *Haley's Island*, low, flat, and insidious, on whose sullen reefs many a stalwart vessel has been dashed to destruction. About ¼ mile beyond is *Star Island*, once the site of the little village of Gosport, now occupied by the Oceanic Hotel, with its cottages. On the W., toward the mainland, is *Londoner's Island*, jagged and shapeless, with a diminutive beach; while 2 miles away is the most forbidding and dangerous of all these islands, *Duck Island*, many of whose ledges are hidden beneath the water at high tide, and at low tide are often seen covered with the big white sea-gulls, which shun the inhabited isles. *White Island*, the most picturesque of the group, is about a mile S. W. from Star Island, and has a powerful revolving light on it which is visible for 15 miles around.

Nine miles N. E. of Portsmouth (reached by steamer or stage) is the quiet little hamlet of *York*, near which is **York Beach** (*Marshall House, Sea-Foam Cottage*), a popular place of resort in summer. *Cape Nedáick* runs out into the sea at the N. end of the beach, and a short distance inland is *Mt. Agamenticus*, from the summit of which there are fine views of the White Mountains, of the ocean, and of the harbors of Portsmouth and Portland. *Bald Head Cliff* is a remarkable rocky promontory, 5 miles N. of York Beach, of peculiar conformation and commanding noble views. Beyond, stretching away to Wells, is the long *Ogunquit Beach*.

Beyond Portsmouth the train crosses the Piscataqua River into Maine and soon reaches Wells, whence stages run 6 miles to **Wells Beach** (*Island Ledge House*, and *Atlantic House*). The beach is 6 miles long, is covered with snipe and curlew, and is a great rendezvous for sportsmen. In the woods are partridges and woodcock, and a large trout-stream crosses the beach. **Biddeford** (37 miles from Portsmouth) is a thriving city of 10,000 inhabitants, opposite **Saco,** near the mouth of the Saco-River, which here falls 55 ft. and furnishes a fine water-power to both places. The **Saco Pool**, which is in Biddeford, though usually spoken of in connection with Saco, is a deep basin scooped out of the solid rock, about ¼ mile from the sea, with which it is connected by a narrow passage. It is emptied and filled with each changing tide, and is reached from Biddeford by a steamer which runs twice daily in summer. Four miles E. of Saco (reached by stage or by trains on the Boston & Maine R. R.) is **Old Orchard Beach,** the finest in New England, and, after Swampscott and Rye, the most frequented and fashionable. It is nearly 10 miles long, is hard and smooth as a floor, shelves gently to the water, and affords unsurpassed surf-bathing. The hotels are the *Old Orchard House*, the *Ocean, Sea Shore, Central, Fiske, St. Cloud, Lawrence, Belmont*, and *Blanchard*. The fishing in the vicinity is excellent, and sufficient game is always to be

5

found to tempt the sportsman. Eight miles beyond Saco is Scarborough station, whence stages run 3 miles E. to **Scarborough
Beach** (*Kirkwood House, Atlantic House,* and large ·boarding-houses).
There is good bathing on the beach, and fishing and hunting near by;
and the place has a large summer patronage. **Cápe Elizabeth,** on
the S. side of Portland Harbor, may be considered a part of Portland,
from which it is reached by a pleasant drive. It is a delightful summer resort, with excellent bathing and fishing. The hotels are the
Cape Cottage, a large stone building, and the *Ocean House.*

Portland.

Hotels, etc.—The *Falmouth House* ($2.50 to $3 a day), in Middle St., is the best·
The *Preble, United States,* and *City* are good. The *St. Julian* is on the European
plan. *Horse-cars* run through the main streets and to the suburbs. *Reading-
rooms* at the Portland Institute (in the City Hall), and at the Y. M. C. A., on Congress St.

Portland, the commercial metropolis of Maine, is picturesquely
situated on a high peninsula at the S. W. extremity of Casco Bay, and
is one of the most beautiful cities in the country. It was settled in
1632, and has had a steady growth; but on the night of July 4,
1866, a great fire swept away half the business portion, destroying
$10,000,000 worth of property. The entire district destroyed by the
fire has since been rebuilt. The streets are embellished with trees, and
so profusely, that before the fire they were said to number 3,000. The
population in 1860 was 26,341, and in 1875, 34,420. For a city of its
size, Portland has exceptionally fine public buildings. The * **City
Hall** is one of the largest and finest municipal structures in the country. Its front, of olive-colored freestone, elaborately dressed, is 150 ft.
long, its depth is 221 ft., and it is surmounted with a graceful dome
160 ft. high. The **Post-Office** is a beautiful building of white Vermont marble, in the mediæval Italian style, with a portico supported
by Corinthian columns. The **Custom-House,** erected at a cost of
$485,000, is a handsome granite structure, with elaborate ornamenta-
tion within. Some of the churches are worthy of attention. The *Society of Natural History* has a fine collection of ·birds, fishes, reptiles,
shells, and minerals. The *Library,* incorporated in 1867, contains
15,000 volumes. The *Marine Hospital,* erected in 1855 at a cost of
$80,000, is an imposing edifice.

There are many pleasant drives in the vicinity of Portland (to Cape
Elizabeth, around Deering's Woods, and along Falmouth Foreside); and
the scenery has been declared by travelers to be among the most enchanting in the world. The harbor is spacious and deep, dotted over
with lovely islands, and defended by three powerful forts. *Diamond
Island* is a favorite spot for picnics, and is noted for its groves of
noble trees; and *Peak's Island* is embowered in foliage, and contains
several small summer hotels. *Cushing's Island* is reached by ferry
from the city, and contains a large hotel, from the cupola of which
there is an exquisite view. No visitor to Portland should fail to ascend
the * **Observatory** on Munjoy's Hill, in order to enjoy the famous

view from the top. Near the Observatory is the *Eastern Promenade*, whence there is a pleasing outlook over the city and harbor. Congress St. leads thence to the *Western Promenade* on Bramhall's Hill. Each of these promenades is 150 ft. wide, and planted with rows of trees. *Lincoln Park*, in the center of the city, contains about 2½ acres. *Evergreen Cemetery*, containing 55 acres, is about 2½ miles distant (reached by stage or railway).

17. Boston to Portland via Boston & Maine R. R.

THE distance by this route is 115 miles, and the fare $3. Twelve miles from Boston is *Reading*, a thriving manufacturing village. **Andover** (*Elm House, Mansion House*) is a famous academic town, settled in 1643, and has several noted educational establishments. The *Theological Seminary* (Congregational) is the leading institution of that sect in America, and the Phillips Academy is of wide reputation and still older date (founded in 1778). The Albert Female Seminary and the Punchard High School rank high among schools of the kind. The scenery about Andover is very pleasing, and the society of the place is refined and cultivated. **Lawrence** (*Franklin House, Essex Hotel*) is 26 miles from Boston, and is one of the largest manufacturing cities of Massachusetts, with a population of 35,000. Its prosperity dates from 1845, when a dam was thrown across the Merrimac River (on both sides of which the city is built), giving a fall of water of 28 ft., and furnishing power for the numerous mills and factories located here. The leading manufactures are cotton cloth, woolens, shawls, paper, flour, and files. The vast mills are separated from the city by the canal which distributes the water-power. This canal runs parallel with the river for a mile, at a distance of about 400 ft. from it, and another canal has been cut on the S. side. The *Common* is a tasteful little park of 17½ acres, surrounded by handsome buildings, including several churches and the city and county buildings. The finest church in the city is *St. Mary's* (Roman Catholic), a beautiful stone structure in the Gothic style. There are a number of good public libraries, several of which pertain to the mills. On Prospect Hill is a neat park, with attractive views. *South Lawrence* is a busy manufacturing suburb across the river.

Beyond Lawrence the train skirts the bank of the Merrimac for 7 miles to **Haverhill** (*Eagle House, American House*), another lively manufacturing city, beautifully situated on hills which slope gently down to the river. Shoemaking is the leading industry, and in this Haverhill ranks next to Lynn. The city is well built and contains about 15,000 inhabitants. The Public Library is a very handsome building, with 20,000 volumes. The City Hall (on Main St.) is also handsome, and N. of it is a fine white marble Soldiers' Monument, erected in 1869. A mile N. E. of the city is *Lake Kenoza*, a pretty sheet, named and celebrated by the poet Whittier, who was born at Haverhill in 1807. Beyond Haverhill the train enters New Hampshire and soon reaches *Exeter* (51 miles), a pretty, elm-shaded village, seat of another Phillips Academy and of the Robinson Female Seminary. There are some important factories and machine-shops here, neat county buildings, and many tasteful residences. Seventeen miles beyond (with several intervening villages) is the busy little city of **Dover** (*American House*), the oldest place in New Hampshire, settled in 1623. It now has 10,000 inhabitants, 11 churches, and extensive manufactories, chiefly of cotton cloth. The Cocheco Mills and Print Works are among the largest of the kind in the country. From Dover the Dover & Winnepesaukee R. R. runs in 28 miles to Alton Bay on Lake Winnepesaukee (see p. 117).

The stations next after Dover (Rollinsford, Salmon Falls, North Berwick, and Wells) are small. About a mile from Wells is *Wells Beach*, already described (see p. 97). From *Kennebunk* (90 miles) stages run to **Cape Arundel** (*Ocean Bluff Hotel*), a bold promontory which is much resorted to in summer on account of its excellent bathing, boating, and fishing. Nine miles beyond Kennebunk the train crosses the Saco River between the twin manufacturing cities of **Saco** and **Biddeford** (see p. 97), and passes on direct to the famous *Old Orchard Beach*, already described (see p. 97). In five miles more the train reaches *Scarborough* (109 miles), whence stages run in 3 miles to *Scarborough Beach* (see p. 98), and then passing through Cape Elizabeth, with its spacious hotels, enters the city of Portland, which is described on page 98.

18. Portland to the White Mountains.

a. Via Portland & Ogdensburg R. R.

THE Portland & Ogdensburg R. R. runs through the heart of the White Mountain region, and offers some of the finest scenery to be found in America. Observation-cars, open on all sides, are run on the mountain section of the road. In the close cars, seats on the right are most desirable. Between Portland and the mountains the only point of interest is **Sebago Lake** (17 miles from Portland), a beautiful sheet, 12 miles long by 9 miles wide, with very deep, cool, and clear waters. A number of islands dot its surface, and its shores are diversified and pleasing, with half a dozen towns nestling here and there. At its N. W. end it connects by the Songo River with *Long Lake*, a river-like body of water nearly 14 miles long and only 2 miles wide. The distance between the two lakes is but 2½ miles "as the crow flies," but the Songo River makes 27 turns and thus secures for itself the length of 6 miles. Two steamers daily, during the summer season, make the round trip between *Sebago Lake Station* and *Harrison*, at the northern end of Long Lake (34 miles). A lock near the outlet of the latter raises the steamers and other craft plying upon these waters from the level of the lower to the upper lake. The trip to Harrison and return, including landings at *Naples* (Elm House), *Bridgton*, and *North Bridgton* (Lake House), is made in about 8 hours, and affords a very agreeable excursion. From Bridgton, stages run 1 mile west to **Bridgton Center** (*Bridgton House* and *Cumberland House*), a prettily situated village, which is becoming popular as a summer resort. In the vicinity are numerous small ponds, and the summit of Pleasant Mt. (8 miles distant) affords a beautiful view. From Harrison daily stages run to *South Paris*, on the Grand Trunk R. R. (14 miles; fare, $1).

Beyond Lake Sebago the train follows the valley of the Saco River, amid pleasing scenery. *Baldwin* (32 miles) is at the confluence of the Saco and Ossipee Rivers, and 3 miles beyond a fine view is obtained of the Great Falls of the Saco, where the river descends 72 ft. in successive pitches. **Fryeburg** (49 miles, *Oxford House*) is a pretty village on the river, surrounded by attractive scenery, and much resorted to in summer. Near the village are several eminences from which fine panoramic views of the distant White Mountains may be had. Beyond Fryeburg the State of New Hampshire is entered, and the mountain-views become increasingly impressive. At *North Conway* (60 miles) beautiful views are had from the cars, and at *Intervale Station*, 2½ miles beyond, the R. R. enters and follows for some distance the charming Conway Intervale. From *Glen Station* (66 miles), stages run in 2 miles to Jackson and in 14 miles to the *Glen House* (see p. 106). At this point, on clear days, look to the right for a fine view of the summit of Mt. Washington, with its gleaming white buildings. *Upper Bartlett* (72 miles) is a thriving lumbering village, situated amid picturesque scenery in a smiling intervale walled in by lofty hills. At *Bemis* (78 miles) the famous ride through the Notch may be said to commence. Near here the steeper grade of the R. R. begins, and the remainder of the journey to the summit at the Crawford House is only accomplished by a continuous ascending grade of over 100 ft. to the mile. The road rises above the valley at some points to an elevation of over 300 ft., affording much finer views than any to be obtained from the highway. Three miles from Bemis is the * *Frankenstein Trestle*, a graceful iron structure spanning a gorge 500 ft. wide and commanding a lovely valley-view to the S., and to the N. a noble view of Mt. Washington and the summits of the Presidential Peaks. Crossing the Trestle, the road soon curves to the left toward Mt. Willey, revealing the summit of that mountain in the W., and the shoulder of Mt. Webster in the E., these two eminences forming the walls of the Notch proper. Another and deeper gorge between Mts. Willey and Willard is crossed on an iron trestle, just beyond which a most lovely *view is obtained of the secluded Willey Valley. The train now follows the contour of Mt. Willard, soon enters the narrowest part of the Notch, dashes through the Great Cut and then through the Gate of the Notch, emerging upon the plateau of the *Crawford House* (see p. 110). Four miles from Crawford's the train reaches the *Fabyan House* (91 miles), where connection is made with the Mt. W. R. R. for the summit of Mt. Washington.

b. Via Grand Trunk R. R.

This route runs near the bases of the principal White Mountain peaks, and, like the preceding route, affords a succession of grand and impressive views. The stations are: Falmouth, 5 miles; Yarmouth, 11; Pownal, 18; New Gloucester, 22; Danville Junction, 27; Me-

chanics' Falls, 36; Oxford, 41; S. Paris, 47; W. Paris, 55; Locke's
Mills, 65; Bethel, 70; Gilead, 80; Shelburne, 86; Gorham, 91. All
these are small villages or hamlets, most of which require no further
mention at our hands.   **Bethel** (*Chandler House*) is a lovely village
in the Androscoggin Valley, with mineral springs, numerous summer
boarding-houses, and fine views of the mountains.   From Bethel to
Gorham the views are wonderfully varied and striking, including Mts.
Moriah, Washington, Madison, Adams, and Jefferson, and other towering peaks.   From **Gorham** (described on p. 108) the whole White Mountain region is easily accessible.

19. Boston to the White Mountains.

a. Via Eastern R. R.

THIS is the shortest and quickest route from Boston to the White
Mountains, the distance to North Conway (137 miles) being made in
less than 6 hrs. (fare $4).   As far as **Portsmouth** (56 miles), it is
identical with Route 16.   At *Conway Junction* (11 miles beyond Portsmouth) the Mountain Division diverges from the main line and passes
in 12 miles to **Rochester** (*Dodge's Hotel, Mansion House*), a large
manufacturing village of 5,000 inhabitants, where four railroads meet.
Milton (87 miles) and *Union* (93 miles) are small hamlets, frequented
in summer.   From *Wolfboro Junction* (97 miles) a branch railroad
runs in 12 miles to **Wolfboro** on Lake Winnepesaukee (see p. 117).
Stations, *Wakefield*, 99 miles; *Ossipee*, 111; *Center Ossipee*, 115; and
West Ossipee, 121.   The scenery now becomes more pleasing, and
Chocorua looms up on the left.   **Conway** (*Conway House, Pequawket
House*, and *Grove House*) stands at the vestibule of the mountain-region,
and commands noble views.   It is more quiet than North Conway, and
as all the objects of interest near the latter can be as well visited from
Conway, many prefer it to its more frequented neighbor.   *Echo Lake*,
the *Cathedral*, and *Diana's Bath* (described in connection with N. Conway) are as near to Conway; and excursions may be made to other
points of interest—to *Chocorua Lake* (8 miles), to *Champney's Falls,
Conway Center*, and *Chatham*.   At **North Conway** (see p. 105) connection is made with trains of the Portland & Ogdensburg R. R. without
change of cars, for the Crawford and Fabyan Houses, passing through
the White Mountain Notch, and for Glen House.

b. Via Boston, Concord & Montreal R. R.

As far as **Concord** (75 miles) this route is described in Route 26.
Leaving Concord a number of small stations are passed in succession.
Just beyond *Tilton* (90 miles from Boston) a fine view of the Sandwich
Range is had on the left, and from this point the scenery is very attractive.   **Laconia** (*Willard House*) is a busy manufacturing town on Lake
Winnesquam, from which the summit of *Mt. Belknap* (see p. 117) may be
reached in 8½ miles.   **Weirs** (105 miles) is described in Route 21.   Here
connection is made with the Lake Winnepesaukee steamers; and N. Conway may be reached by crossing to Wolfboro and taking the preceding

route. Stations, *Meredith*, 109 miles; *Ashland*, 117; and *Bridgewater*, 120. **Plymouth** (*Pemigewasset House*) lies in the lovely Pemigewasset Valley, on the outskirts of the White Mountain region, and amid charming scenery. There are several natural curiosities within excursion distance, and 4 miles N. E. (ascended by carriage-road) is *** Mt. Prospect** (2,963 ft. high), affording what is said to be the finest view south of the mountains. Several small stations are now passed, and then (145 miles from Boston) comes **Warren** (*Moosilaukee House*), a much-visited highland village, 9 miles from *** Mt. Moosilaukee,** the highest peak in New Hampshire outside of the White and Franconia groups, and commanding magnificent views. From the *Prospect House* may be seen the valley of the Connecticut, the White and Franconia Mountains, Lake Winnepesaukee, nearly the whole of Vermont and New Hampshire, and several Canadian peaks. Stations, *E. Haverhill*, 151 miles; *Haverhill* and *Newbury*, 156; *Woodsville*, 166; and **Wells River** (169 miles), the junction of the Connecticut & Passumpsic R. R. and the Montpelier & Wells River R. R. with the present route. From *Littleton* (185 miles) stages run to the Profile House (see p. 114). At **Wing Road** (192 miles) the present route diverges to the *Twin Mountain House* (201 miles), the *White Mountain House* (205 miles), and the *Fabyan House* (206 miles). (All these are described in Route 20.) At the Fabyan House the train connects with the railway up Mt. Washington.

c. Via Boston & Maine R. R.

This route takes Lake Winnepesaukee *en route.* As far as **Dover** (68 miles) it is the same as Route 17. The line from Dover traverses the Cocheco Valley, passing *Rochester* (see p. 102), *Farmington* (86 miles), and *New Durham* (92 miles), and stops at **Alton Bay** (96 miles). From Alton Bay the traveler may go by steamer to *Weirs*, and thence by Route *b ;* or to *Wolfboro*, and thence by Route *a* to *North Conway ;* or to *Center Harbor*, and thence by stage through Sandwich to Conway. (See Route 21.)

20. The White Mountains.

The routes from Boston to the White Mountains are described in Route 19. From Portland, in Route 18. From New York the White Mountains may be reached *via* Boston, or direct by either of the following routes : (1.) *Via* Route 28 to Wells River, and thence to the Twin Mountain, White Mountain, and Fabyan Houses, as in Route 19, *b ;* distance to the Twin Mountain House, 338 miles. (2.) *Via* New Haven or New London to Norwich, Worcester, and Nashua, to Concord, and thence as in Route 19, *b*. (3.) *Via* steamer to New London, thence *via* Route 29 to Brattleboro and Wells River, and from the latter point as in Route 19, *b*. (4.) *Via* Albany, Rutland, and Bellows Falls, to Wells River (Routes 35 and 27), and thence as in preceding route. From Montreal or Quebec *via* Grand Trunk R. R. to Gorham. Also from Montreal *via* Southeastern R. R. to Wells River, and thence *via* B. C. & M. R. R.

THE WHITE MOUNTAINS (the "Switzerland of America") rise from a plateau in Grafton and Coös Counties, New Hampshire, about 45 miles long by 30 broad, and 1,600 ft. above the sea. Some 20 peaks of various elevations rise from the plateau, which is traversed by several deep, narrow valleys. The peaks cluster in two groups, of which the

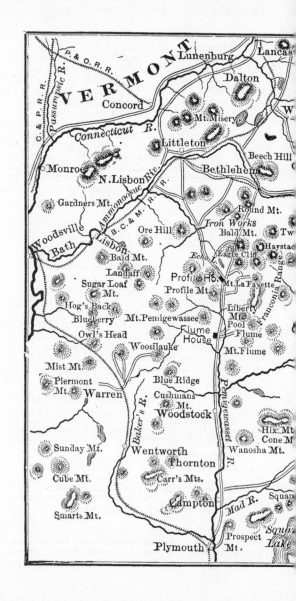

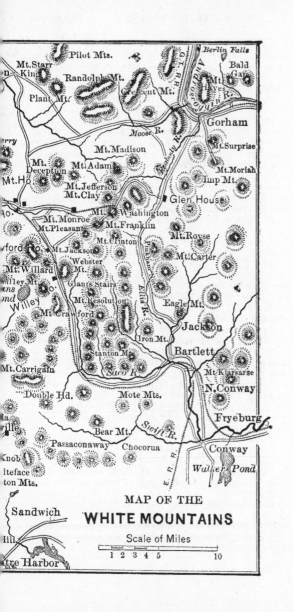

MAP OF THE

WHITE MOUNTAINS

Scale of Miles

1 2 3 4 5   10

eastern is known locally as the White Mountains, and the western as the Franconia Group. They are separated by a table-land varying from 10 to 20 miles in breadth. The principal summits of the eastern group are Mounts Washington (6,293 ft. high), Adams (5,759), Jefferson (5,657), Madison (5,361), Monroe (5,349), Franklin (4,850), Pleasant (4,712), Webster, Clinton, and Clay. The principal summits of the Franconia Group are Mounts Pleasant, Lafayette (5,280 ft.), Liberty, Cherry Mountain, and Moosilauke. Near the S. border of the plateau rise Whiteface Mountain, Chocorua Peak, Red Hill, and Mount Ossipee; and in the S. E., Mount Kearsarge. With the exception of the Black Mountains of North Carolina, several of these peaks are the highest elevations in the United States E. of the Rocky Mountains. Multitudes of little streams force their way down steep glens from springs far up the mountain-sides, and flow through narrow valleys among the hills. The courses of these rivulets furnish irregular but certain pathways for the rough roads that have been cut beside them, and by which the traveler gains access to these wild mountain-retreats.

The aboriginal name of the White Mountains was *Agiochook* or *Agiocochook*, signifying "Mountain of the Snowy Forehead and Home of the Great Spirit." The first white man to visit them, according to Belknap, the State historian, was Walter Neal, in 1632. The Notch was discovered in 1771, the first inn was erected in 1803, a bridle-path to the summit of Mount Washington was cut in 1819, and the first hotel was opened in 1852. Since this latter date the popularity of the mountains has steadily increased, until they are now, next to Saratoga and Long Branch, the most frequented of any American summer resort. As to the time to visit them, Starr King recommends the early summer. "From the middle of June to the middle of July, foliage is more fresh; the cloud-scenery is nobler; the meadow-grass has a more golden color; the streams are usually more full and musical; and there is a larger proportion of the 'long light' of the afternoon, which kindles the atmosphere into the richest loveliness. The mass of visitors to the White Mountains go during the dog-days, and leave when the finer September weather sets in, with its prelude touches of the October splendor. In August there are fewer clear skies; there is more fog; the meadows are appareled in more sober green; the highest rocky crests may be wrapped in mists for days in succession; and a traveler has fewer chances of making acquaintance with a bracing mountain-breeze. The latter half of June is the blossom-season of beauty in the mountain-districts; the first half of October is the time of its full-hued fruitage."

In describing the mountains we shall begin at North Conway, the S. E. portal, and proceed by the usual routes to different points, describing in connection with each the various features of interest in its neighborhood. Of course, the tourist can arrange his routes differently, and still find the description equally serviceable.

North Conway.

This is one of the prettiest towns in the entire mountain-region, and is a favorite rendezvous for artists and tourists who wish to be within easy excursion-distance of the mountains, while avoiding the excitement and expense of the larger hôtels. It is beautifully situated on a terrace overlooking the intervales of the Saco, and is surrounded on all sides by mountains. On the E. the rugged Rattlesnake Ridge walls it in, Kearsarge or Pequawket rising in lonely dignity a little to the N. ; on the W. are the Moat Mountains, with the peak of Chocorua in the distance ; and on the N. and N. W. almost the whole line of the White Mountains proper, crowned in the center with the dome of Mount Washington, closes in the view. The leading hotel of the village is the *Kearsarge House* ($3 a day), a large and well-kept house with accommodations for 300 guests. The *Intervale House* ($3 a day), 1½ mile from the village, is large and excellent, and commands a unique and beautiful view of the mountains up a long valley-vista. Other hotels (charging $2.50 to $3 a day) are the *Sunset Pavilion,* the *Mc-Millan House,* the *Washington House,* the *North Conway House,* and the *Randall House.* There are also many boarding-houses in the village ($7 to $12 a week).

There are several points of interest in the immediate neighborhood of North Conway. The *Artist's Falls* is a picturesque and much-visited spot in the forest 1½ mile distant. On the opposite side of the river, and 3 miles distant, are *The Ledges,* a series of cliffs from 100 to 900 ft. high, which extend along the mountain-side for 4 or 5 miles. A figure of a horse (called the " White Horse ") is pictured on the perpendicular side of these cliffs, and is visible from the village. *Echo Lake** is a beautiful sheet of water lying at the very base of the cliffs (Moat Mountain), and is celebrated for the distinctness of the echo which it throws back. Above Echo Lake (reached by climbing the cliff) is the *Cathedral,** a natural cavity formed in the solid granite. The wall gradually inclines outward, forming a magnificent Gothic arch 40 ft. long, 20 wide, and 60 high, with noble forest-trees constituting the outer wall. A little north of the Cathedral, approached by a pleasant woodland path, is *Diana's Bath,* a crystal pool, 10 ft. in diameter and more than 10 ft. deep, overhung with trees, and having a beautiful cascade just below. Favorite drives are *Around the Square* (5 miles) and the *Thorn Hill Drive,* which ascends one of the spurs of Thorn Mountain and affords a fine view. *Mt. Kearsarge** (or Pequawket), 3 miles from the village, is 3,367 ft. high, and is easily ascended. Parties of 2 or 3 persons are carried from North Conway to the foot of the mountain for 50c. each. A fair carriage-road leads to the summit. As this is the highest peak S. of the mountains in this direction, the view from its summit is extremely fine, embracing the whole White Mountain range, and an especially good view of Mt. Washington. The sharp peaks of Chocorua, with the Moat Mountain in the foreground, can also be seen with great distinctness ; the course of the Saco River can be traced almost from its source, as it winds

among the intervales, and finally bends away into Maine; and in the
broad level expanse toward the S. E. the eye is caught by Sebago Lake,
Lovewell's Pond, and numerous smaller bodies of water. There is a
small hotel on the summit, at which those wishing to see the gorgeous
sunset and sunrise views can remain overnight ($4 a day).

North Conway to the Glen House.

Stages leave Glen Station (Portland & Ogdensburg R. R.), on the arrival of the
trains, for the Glen House, and this is the quickest way of reaching it; but if the
tourist have time he should not adhere too closely to the railway-routes, but should
traverse some of the picturesque stage-roads which used to form the only mode of
transit from point to point. By hiring a private conveyance at N. Conway, and
taking the old stage-route to the Glen House, he can secure a very enjoyable ride
of 20 miles. This route we shall now describe.

For a few miles after leaving North Conway the road passes up
the valley of the Saco, amid delightful scenery, with Mt. Kearsarge
looming up grandly on the right and presenting an endless variety of
forms. At *Bartlett* the old stage-road to the Notch diverges to the
W., while the one we are pursuing runs nearly due N. At the crossing of the Ellis River, the former site of the *Goodrich Falls* is seen.
These falls were among the heaviest and finest in the White Mountains, but were spoiled in 1875 by the erection of a mill. In seasons
of high water they are still imposing. For the next mile the road is
bordered by heavily wooded hills, between which occasional glimpses
are had of the summits of the Washington range, and the little hamlet
of **Jackson** is reached. There is a church here (Baptist), two hotels
(the *Jackson Falls House* and the *Thorn Mountain House*), and some
half a dozen houses. From the portico of the first-mentioned hotel
there is a noble view of the surrounding mountains, with *Iron Mountain* (2,900 feet high) on the right, and the bold peak of *Tin Mountain*
on the left. Within three minutes' walk of the hotel are *Jackson
Falls*, a romantic cascade on the Wild-Cat Brook. In this vicinity is
some of the best trout-fishing to be found among the mountains, and
the place is much frequented by sportsmen and artists. On leaving
Jackson, there is an impressive view of the dark gorges, which open
miles away toward Mt. Washington, and then the road ascends
through the desolate *Pinkham Notch*, filled with an almost unbroken
forest. About 7 miles beyond Jackson, a path to the right leads to
the Glen Ellis Falls, which are quite near the road, and a little farther
on is the entrance to the Crystal Cascade (see p. 107). Here the Peabody River is crossed twice in quick succession, and a further ride of
3 miles brings us to our destination.

The **Glen House** is one of the largest and best hotels in the
mountain-region (600 guests; $4.50 a day). It fronts the Peabody
River and the Washington range, to which it is nearer than any other
hotel in the mountains, five of the highest peaks being in full view
from the portico. Directly in front are the outworks and huge shoulder of Mt. Washington itself. Next comes Mt. Clay (5,400 ft.), rising
over the huge "Gulf of Mexico"; then the massive Jefferson (5,700

ft.) ; then the Adams (5,800 ft.), with its sharp and symmetrical peak; and, finally, Madison (5,361 ft.). From the balcony of the hotel, parties ascending and descending Mt. Washington may readily be seen with the aid of a glass ; and a still better view is obtained by climbing a few hundred feet up the mountain behind the hotel. Stages run from the Glen House to Gorham on the Grand Trunk R. R., and to Glen Station on the P. & O. R. R.

In the vicinity of the hotel are many points of interest. The *Garnet Pools*, about ½ mile distant, near the Gorham road, are a series of basins in the Peabody River, some of them 15 and 20 ft. deep, worn in the granite rock by the action of the water. *** Thompson's Falls** are a series of picturesque cascades in an affluent of the Peabody River, 2 miles from the hotel, on the road to North Conway. The view of Mt. Washington and Tuckerman's Ravine, from the upper fall, is the finest that is obtained from any point. *Emerald Pool*, noted for its quiet sylvan beauty, is a short distance from the road just before reaching Thompson's Falls. On the North Conway road, 3 miles from the hotel, a path through the woods leads to the **Crystal Cascade,** " an inverted liquid plume," 80 ft. high, situated near the mouth of Tuckerman's Ravine. The best view of the cascade is not from the foot, but from a high, moss-covered bank opposite. A mile beyond (4 miles from the hotel), a plank-walk to the left leads to the *** Glen-Ellis Fall,** where the Ellis River slides 20 ft. over the cliff at a sharp angle and then plunges 60 ft. into a dark-green pool below. This is one of the loveliest cascades in the entire region. *** Tuckerman's Ravine** is a tremendous chasm in the S. side of Mt. Washington, whose frowning walls, 1,000 ft. high, are plainly visible from the hotel. It is filled, hundreds of feet deep, by the winter snows, through which a brook steals as summer draws near, gradually widening its channel until it flows through a grand snow-cave, which was found, by actual measurement one season, to be 84 ft. wide on the inside, 40 ft. high, and 180 ft. long. The snow forming the arch was 20 ft. thick. The engineers of the carriage-road up Mt. Washington dined in that snow-arch July 16, 1854. After rain the cliffs back of the ravine present an appearance which has gained for them the name of the " Fall of a Thousand Streams." The ravine is reached from the Glen House by Thompson's Path, which diverges from the carriage-road about 2 miles up the mountain (distance, 4½ miles), or by a rugged and difficult path by the brook-side from Crystal Cascade. The more common way of visiting it, however, is to descend into it from the summit of Mt. Washington. The distance from the summit to the bottom of the ravine is about a mile.

The **Carriage-road up Mt. Washington** from the Glen was, until the completion of the steam-railway, the easiest and most popular way of reaching the summit, and is still preferred by many. The road was begun in 1855 and completed in 1861, and is a noble piece of engineering. The average grade is 12 ft. in 100, and the steepest, which is 2½ miles from the base, is 16 in 100 for a short distance only. The tolls are, for each person on foot, 32c. ; on horseback or in car-

riages, 80c. The fare for a seat in one of the regular mountain-car-
riages, which leave the Glen House morning and afternoon, is $5 for
the round trip, $3 either way. The time required for the ascent is
about 3 hours, and for the descent 1½ hour.

The Glen House to Gorham.

Stages run twice a day from the Glen House to Gorham, which is 8
miles N. E. (fare, $1.50). The ride is a pleasant one down the valley
of the Peabody, with fine mountain-views nearly all the way. About
2½ miles from the Glen is a bridge over the Peabody River, by crossing
which and proceeding to a point near a farmhouse, ½ mile from the road,
the traveler may see **The Imp,** a peak of Mt. Moriah, so named from
the marked resemblance which the summit bears to a grotesque human countenance.

Gorham (*Alpine House, Gorham House, Eagle House*), the N. E.
gateway to the mountain-region, is a thriving village, situated in a
broad and beautiful valley at the confluence of the Androscoggin and
Peabody Rivers, 800 ft. above the sea. It is a station on the Grand
Trunk R. R., whose repair-shops are located here. The scenery in the
vicinity of the village is remarkably striking, both in the views of the
mountain-ranges and isolated mountains, and of rivers and waterfalls.
The range of Mts. Moriah, Carter, and The Imp, in particular, is
seen to great advantage. Mt. Carter is one of the highest and Mt.
Moriah the most graceful of the larger New Hampshire hills; the best
view of them is from the Alpine House. The noble chain of hills to
the N. W. of Gorham is known as the Pilot Range; while on the E.
and S. E. the valley is walled in by the stalwart and brawny Androscoggin Hills. ***Mt. Hayes,** the highest of these latter (2,500 ft.), is
directly N. E. of the village, and may be ascended by a path leading
directly to the summit in two hours. "The picture from the summit
can not be sufficiently praised. The view of Adams and Jefferson,
sweeping from the uplands of Randolph, will never be forgotten. And
Mt. Washington shows no such height, or grandeur, when seen from
any other point." ***Mt. Surprise,** a spur of Mt. Moriah, fronts Mt.
Hayes on the opposite side of the valley, and a bridle-path leads from
the village to its summit (2¼ miles). This bridle-path was formerly
feasible for horses, but it has been allowed to get so much out of repair as to be no longer safe even for pedestrians without the aid of a
guide. Mt. Surprise is 1,200 ft. high, and its summit affords a grand
view of the "Presidential group" (Adams, Washington, Jefferson, and
Madison). "There is no other eminence where one can get so near to
these monarchs, and receive such an impression of their sublimity, the
vigor of their outlines, their awful solitude, and the extent of the wilderness which they bear upon their slopes." The highest summits of
the range rise directly against the eye, with no intervening ridge or
obstacle. **Mt. Moriah,** 4,700 ft. high, can now only be ascended on
foot, though there was once a good bridle-path. The ascent is tedious
but not otherwise difficult, and the view from the summit is very
striking.

Randolph Hill, 600 ft. higher than the valley, is reached by a pleasant carriage-drive of 5 miles from Gorham, and from its summit a superb view is obtained of the whole northerly wall of the Mt. Washington range. From the foot of Randolph Hill a path has been " blazed " through the forest to the summit of *Mt. Madison,* which may be ascended with guides. The summit is 5,361 ft. high, and the outlook which it affords is only inferior to that from the peak of Mt. Washington. It is possible for a strong pedestrian (with guides) to start from Gorham early in the morning, and, ascending Mt. Madison, pass over its summit, around or over the sharp pyramid of Adams, over Jefferson, between the humps of Mt. Clay, and reach the hotels on the summit of Mt. Washington before sunset. This route would lie among and over the largest mountains of the White Mountain range, and would afford a continuous succession of unrivaled views. From the *Lead-Mine Bridge,* 4 miles E. of the village, a pleasing view is obtained of the Androscoggin, dotted with islands in the foreground, with the mountains in the distance. It should be visited between 5 and 7 o'clock P. M., in order to see the sun set behind the mountains. An extremely attractive drive of 6 miles along the W. bank of the river leads to the * **Berlin Falls,** where the whole volume of the Androscoggin pours over a granite ledge, descending nearly 200 ft. in the course of a mile. The best views of the cataract are obtained from a jutting rock near the lower end, and from the bridge above which spans the narrowest part of the stream. There is an hotel at Berlin called the *Mount Forist House* ($8 to $15 a week).

Stages leave Gorham, on the arrival of the trains, for the Glen House (8 miles; fare, $1.50). The ascent of Mt. Washington may be made from Gorham in a day *via* the Glen House.

Gorham to the Notch.

Since the completion of the carriage-road on the E. side, and of the railroad on the W. side, nearly all the travel through the mountains passes over Mt. Washington, and comparatively few tourists go by the old stage-routes. These, however, have not lost their charm, and whoever can spare the time should certainly make the trip from Gorham to the Notch, *via* the " Cherry Mountain Road," now to be described. The scenery along its entire length is grander than is afforded by any other route among the mountains. The distance is 32 miles. There is no regular stage, but mountain-wagons can be hired at Gorham on reasonable terms. The beauties of the road begin almost before the village is left behind. It takes in the glorious outlook from Randolph Hill, of which we have already spoken; it commands every slope and summit of the Mt. Washington range from the N.; and for 12 miles of the way they are all in view at once, with no intervening hills to break the impression of their majesty. The mountain-forms are much grander on the northerly than on the southern side, and the road we are traversing commands the finest views obtainable in this direction. " From the village of *Jefferson* (Starr King House), through which this Cherry Mountain road runs, not only is every one of the great White Mountain group visible, but also the Franconia Mountains, the side of the Willey Mountain, in the Notch, the line of the nearer Green Mountains beyond the Connecticut—in fact, a panorama of hills to the northwest and north almost as fine as the prospect in that direction from the summit of Mt. Washington." The finest point of view is *Jefferson Hill (17 miles from Gorham), which is becoming one of the most frequented resorts in the White Mountain region. Here are the *Waumbek House*, the *Plaisted House*, the *Jefferson Hill House*, the *Starr King*, the *Sunnyside*, and numerous boarding-houses. The rates at the hotels are $9 to $18 per week; at the boarding-houses, $7 to $12. The view of the mountains, above described, is incomparably fine from the Waumbek House; and from the piazza, with a glass, people on the summit of Mt. Washington can be distinctly seen, and the trains moving up and down the steep side. The remainder of the road to the Crawford House (16 miles) is scarcely inferior in scenic grandeur to that already described, and the entrance of the Notch is extremely fine. The White Mountain House and the Fabyan House are passed *en route*. There is a shorter route from Gorham to the Notch than the preceding, but it is much less attractive, and in engaging the carriage care should be taken to stipulate for Jefferson Hill.

The Crawford House and Vicinity.

The Crawford House (350 guests; $4.50 a day) is a large and popular summer hotel, situated on a little plateau 2,000 ft. above the sea, and facing the Notch. It bears the name of one of the earliest hosts of these mountain-gorges, and is near the site of the old Notch House, one of the first taverns opened in the White Mountain region. The Crawford House and adjacent hotels are now connected with the outside world by two lines of railway, and passengers can run through from Boston to the very doors (see Routes 18 and 19). The station of the P. & O. R. R. stands a few rods from the front of the hotel. Stages also connect the Crawford House with the other mountain hotels. Within a stone's-throw of the hotel and of each other there are two springs, one of which discharges its waters into the Saco, while the other empties into a tributary of the Ammonoosuc, and reaches the sea through the Connecticut. In front of the house, near the gate of the Notch, is a tiny lakelet, which forms the head-waters of the Saco.

A favorite excursion from the hotel is the ascent of * Mt. Willard, which is easily made by a road 2 miles long, either in carriages or on foot. The summit is 2,000 ft. high, and commands a wonderful view of the tremendous gulf of the Notch, and of the mountain-peaks far and near. Speaking of the view of the Notch from this point, Bayard Taylor says : " As a simple picture of a mountain-pass, seen from above, it can not be surpassed in Switzerland." Near the summit of the mountain, on the S. side, is the *Devil's Den*, a dark, cold cave, about 20 ft. deep, 15 high, and 20 wide, only accessible by means of ropes. *Gibbs's Falls* are a series of romantic cascades, reached by a walk of half an hour from the hotel, along the aqueduct by which it is supplied with water, and then along the brook-side. The falls are about ¼ of a mile from where the aqueduct issues from the brook. *Beecher's Falls* (named after Rev. Henry Ward Beecher, who is said to have taken an involuntary bath in one of the basins) are situated on the slope of Mt. Lincoln, and may be reached by an easy path through the woods to the right of the hotel. They consist of a series of beautiful cascades extending for ⅛ mile along a mountain-brook. From some shelving rocks at the head of the uppermost fall, called the "Flume Cascade," there is a fine view of the summit of Mt. Washington.

The favorite excursion from the Crawford House is through the famous *** Notch,** which is seen to the best advantage as approached from this direction, the giant masses of Webster, Willard, and Willey being directly in front. The Notch is a tremendous gorge or rift in the mountains which rise on either side to the height of 2,000 ft., and which, in one spot, called the "Gateway," are only 22 ft. apart. The Saco River runs through it, and also the P. & O. R. R., which along the slopes of Mt. Willey is 300 ft. above the stage-road. The *Elephant's Head* is a rocky bluff on the E. side of the Notch, about ¼ mile from the hotel, the supposed resemblance of which to an elephant's head, as seen from the hotel-piazza, gives it its name. Just within the Gate, a view is obtained of the *Old Maid of the Mountain*, a great stone face on a spur of Mt. Webster. An overhanging rock on the same side of the road is called the *Devil's Pulpit*, and on the face of this the profile of *The Infant* is visible to imaginative minds. Directly opposite the Devil's Pulpit is another profile called the *Young Man of the Mountain ;* and far up the slopes of Mt. Willard is the black mouth of the Devil's Den, already mentioned. *The Flume* is a portion of a little mountain-stream, to the left of the road about ¾ mile from the hotel. A little farther down the Notch is the *** Silver Cascade,** the finest waterfall on the W. side of the mountains. The stream, the upper part of which is visible from the piazza of the hotel, descends 800 ft. in the course of a mile, 400 of which are nearly perpendicular. The best view is from the bridge, near which the current rushes through a narrow flume, like that already described. Passing down the Notch between Mts. Willey and Webster, we come to the *Willey House* (3 miles from the hotel), where the whole Willey family, 9 in number, were crushed by an avalanche from which they were trying to escape, August 28, 1826. A rock 30 ft. high split the avalanche and saved the house from which they fled to their death. The house is occupied and a small entrance-fee is charged, but there is nothing inside to interest. Three miles beyond the Willey House, on Avalanche Brook, a small mountain-stream emptying into the Saco, is the *** Sylvan Glade Cataract,** regarded by many as the finest waterfall in the mountains. It is 2 miles from the road, in a steep ravine, whose cliffs, crowned with a dense forest of spruce, are singularly grand. The cascade leaps first over 4 rocky ledges, each about 6 ft. high, and then glides at an angle of 45° down a solid bed of granite 150 ft. into the pool below. It is about 75 ft. wide at the base, and 50 at the summit. A mile above the cataract, there are several other falls, the finest of which is called the *Sparkling Cascade*. This is the limit of the ordinary excursions, but it is quite worth while to engage a vehicle and drive farther along the old stage-route to North Conway. As we proceed down the Saco we pass through a dense forest and come in succession to the *Giant's Stairs*, 5,500 ft. high ; *Mt. Resolution*, 3,400 ; and *Mt. Crawford*, 3,200. Next, the *Mt. Crawford House*, once the most popular of the mountain inns, is passed ; and ½ mile beyond we cross *Nancy's Brook and Bridge*, so named after a young woman who perished here from exposure when in pursuit of a faithless lover. Near by is the grave of Abel Crawford, the "patriarch of the mountains."

The * **Bridle-Path up Mt. Washington** from the Crawford House commands finer views than any other route, leading over the summits of Mts. Clinton, Pleasant, Franklin, and Monroe. It can only be traversed on foot, but the path is plain and safe, *except in case of a fog*, when great caution should be exercised, as several fatal accidents have occurred.

The Fabyan and Twin Mountain Houses.

The **Fabyan House** (500 guests ; $4.50 a day) is the largest and finest hotel in the mountains, with all the appointments and conveniences of a first-class city hotel. It stands on the Giant's Grave, a lofty, grave-shaped mound, and commands a noble view of the whole White Mountain range. It is at the junction of the Portland & Ogdensburg and Boston, Concord & Montreal Railways, and is also the nearest of the large hotels to the lower terminus of the Mt. Washington Railway. It is likewise a convenient point for excursions to Mt. Willard, the Notch, and the Willey House, the intervening 5 miles being over a good road with fine views. Between the railroads (about ½ mile from the Fabyan House) is the *Mount Pleasant House*, new and attractively situated, and charging only $2 a day. About a mile beyond Fabyan's is the *White Mountain House* ($2.50 a day), an old and favorite hostelry, pleasantly situated in the midst of an open tract of country. In the rear is a fine view of the Presidential peaks, and in front, beyond the Ammonoosuc, rises the lofty range which connects the Great Notch with Franconia. There are pleasant rambles in the neighborhood, and varied views from the adjacent hills. The once famous *Lower Ammonoosuc Falls* have been spoiled by the erection of a saw-mill above. The * *Upper Ammonoosuc Falls* (3½ miles from the Fabyan House on the road to Mt. Washington) are very fine. The **Twin Mountain House** (300 guests, $4.50 a day) is a large and highly popular hotel, 5 miles W. of Fabyan's, pleasantly situated on heights above the Ammonoosuc River. The Boston, Concord & Montreal R. R. has a station here, and it is a convenient point from which to visit the various places of interest.

Bethlehem (*Sinclair House, Maplewood House, Strawberry Hill House, Prospect House*, the *Bellevue*, and numerous boarding-houses) is a highly popular summer resort on the Boston, Concord, Montreal & White Mts. R. R., 5 miles from the Twin Mountain House. It claims to be the highest village E. of the Rocky Mountains, and is the meeting-place of the American Hay-Fever Association. Starr King said of it that "no village commands so grand a panoramic view." Several interesting excursions may be made from Bethlehem, the best being to the summit of *Mt. Agassiz* (1¾ mile distant). Daily stages run to the Profile House (10 miles) and to Littleton (5 miles). A railroad from Bethlehem to the Profile House is approaching completion.

Mount Washington.

The ascent of Mt. Washington by the Carriage-Road from the Glen House is described on p. 107. The ascent by the Crawford House Bridle-Path on p. 112.

The *Mt. Washington Railway* connects with the Mt. Washington Branch of the B. C. & M. R. R. near *Marshfield* (Ammonoosuc Station). The distance from Marshfield to the summit is about 3 miles. The fare for the ascent or descent is $3 ; round trip, $4 ; trunks are charged extra. The Mt. Washington Railway was begun in 1866, and opened in 1869, and is similar to that up the Righi. The grade is enormous, being 3,596 ft. in 3 miles, and in places 1 foot in 3. The track is of three rails bolted to a trestle-work of heavy timber. The third or center rail is like a wrought-iron ladder with rounds 4 inches apart. Into this fits a cog-wheel which fairly pulls the train up the mountain. The seats for the passengers are so swung as to be horizontal, whatever may be the inclination of the track. The safety of the train is secured by independent, self-acting brakes. The time occupied by the ascent is 1½ hour, but the slow progress is forgotten in the splendid panorama of the gradually widening views.

The summit (6,293 ft. high) is an acre of comparatively level ground, on which stand the *Mount Washington Summit Hotel* ($1.50 for each meal, and the same for a night's lodging), the old Tip-Top and Summit Houses (which are no longer in use), the engine-house of the railway, and the U. S. Signal-Service observatory. At this station, which is occupied in winter, observers have recorded a temperature of 59° below zero, while the wind blew with a velocity of 190 miles an hour. Visitors to Mount Washington should always go well clad. The range of the thermometer, even in midsummer, is from 30° to 45°. It frequently falls as low as 25°, and sometimes to 20°, or 12° below freezing. The tourist should spend one night on the summit, in order to see the wonderful sunrise and sunset views. The enjoyableness of the trip is greatly increased by going up the mountain one way and down the other (up by railway and down by stage, or *vice versa*).

The * view from Mt. Washington is incomparably grand. In the W., through the blue haze, are seen in the distance the ranges of the Green Mountains; the remarkable outlines of the summits of Camel's Hump and Mount Mansfield being easily distinguished when the atmosphere is clear. To the N. W., under your feet, are the clearings and settlement of Jefferson, and the waters of Cherry Pond; and, farther distant, the village of Lancaster, with the waters of Israel's River. The Connecticut is barely visible; and often its appearance for miles is counterfeited by the fog arising from its surface. To the N. and

N. E., only a few miles distant, rise boldly the great northeastern peaks of the White Mountain range—Jefferson, Adams, and Madison—with their ragged tops of loose, dark rocks. A little farther to the E. are seen the numerous and distant summits of the mountains of Maine. On the S. E., close at hand, are the dark and crowded ridges of the mountains of Jackson; and beyond, the conical summit of Kearsarge, standing by itself on the outskirts of the mountains; and, farther over, the low country of Maine and Sebago Lake, near Portland. Still farther, it is said, the ocean itself has sometimes been distinctly visible. Farther to the S. are the intervales of the Saco, and the settlements of Bartlett and Conway, the sister ponds of Lovewell, in Fryeburg; and, still farther, the remarkable four-toothed summit of Chocorua, the peak to the right being much the largest, and sharply pyramidal. Almost exactly S. are the shining waters of the beautiful Winnepesaukee, seen with the greatest distinctness on a favorable day. To the S. W., near at hand, are the peaks of the southwestern range of the White Mountains: Monroe, with its two little Alpine ponds sleeping under its rocky and pointed summits; the flat surface of Franklin, and the rounded top of Pleasant, with their ridges and spurs. Beyond these, the Willey Mountain, with its high, ridged summit; and, beyond that, several parallel ranges of high, wooded mountains. Farther W., and over all, is seen the lofty, bare summit of Mt. Lafayette, in Franconia. There is no observatory on the summit, nor any one spot whence the whole horizon may be surveyed; the observer, therefore, must move from point to point in order to obtain the full view.

The Franconia Mountains.

These mountains, though in popular estimation inferior in interest to the eastern cluster, are really not so, except it be in the wonders of the mountain ascents; and even in this the panorama from the summit of *Lafayette* is scarcely less extensive or less imposing than the scene from the crown of Mount Washington, while the exquisite little lakes, and the singular natural eccentricities in the Franconia group, have no counterpart in the other. They lie W. S. W. of the White Mountains, from which they are separated by the Field Willey and Twin Mountain ranges, and consist of sharp and lofty peaks, covered almost to their summits with dense forests. The name is usually applied to all the mountains around the Notch, but belongs more properly to the majestic range on the E. side. The **Franconia Notch** is a fine pass between the Franconia and Pemigewasset ranges, 5 miles long and ½ mile wide, walled in by precipitous cliffs, filled with forests, and traversed by the crystal waters of the upper Pemigewasset River.

The **Profile House** (500 guests, $4.50 a day) is the headquarters of the Franconia range, and is one of the largest and best hotels in the White Mountain region. It is situated in a narrow glen near the N. end of the Franconia Notch, 1,974 ft. above the sea.

Through tickets to the Profile House may be had *via* any of the routes mentioned in Routes 18 and 19, or at the beginning of the present route. Stages run to it twice a day from Littleton on the B. C. & M. R. R. (distance, 11 miles; fare, $2); and daily from Bethlehem, on the Mt. Washington Branch of the B. C. & M. R. R. (distance, 10 miles; fare, $2). A railroad from Bethlehem will be completed during the coming season. Daily stages also from Plymouth (see p. 103); distance, 29 miles ; fare, $4.

Of the many objects of interest in the neighborhood of the Profile House, one of the most charming is * **Echo Lake,** a diminutive but very deep and beautiful sheet of water about ¾ mile N. of the hotel, entirely inclosed by high mountains. From the center of this fairy-water, a voice, in ordinary tone, will be echoed distinctly several times, and the report of a gun breaks upon the rocks like the roar of artillery. The Indian superstition was, that these echoes were the voice of the Great Spirit, speaking in gentleness or in anger. The best time to visit the lake is toward evening, when the flush of sunset is on the mountains. *Eagle Cliff* is a magnificently bold and rocky promontory, almost overhanging the hotel on the N. Directly opposite Eagle Cliff, and forming the southern side of the Notch, is **Profile Mountain** (or Mt. Cannon), 2,000 ft. above the road, and 4,000 ft. above the sea. Away up on its crown is a group of mighty rocks which, as seen from the hotel, bears an exact resemblance to a mounted cannon. The mountain is ascended by a difficult footpath in about 2 hours, and the view from the summit is surpassingly fine, including the surrounding peaks, the towering heights of Washington and his peers, the softly swelling hills sloping away to the S., and the lovely valley of the Pemigewasset. It is upon this mountain, also, that we find the * **Profile,** or "Old Man of the Mountain." This strange freak of Nature, so admirably counterfeiting the human face, is 40 ft. long from the chin to the top of the forehead, and is 1,200 ft. above the road, though far below the summit of the mountain. It is formed of three distinct masses of rock, one forming the forehead, another the nose and upper lip, and a third the chin. The rocks are brought into the proper relation to form the profile at one point only, namely, upon the road through the Notch, ¼ mile S. of the hotel (indicated by a sign-board). The face is boldly and clearly relieved against the sky, and, except in a suspicion of weakness about the mouth, has the air of a stern, strong character, well able to bear, as he has done unflinchingly for centuries; the scorching suns of summer and the tempest-blasts of winter. Passing down the road a little way, the Old Man is transformed into "a toothless old woman in a mob-cap," and soon after melts into thin air, and is seen no more. Hawthorne has found in this scene the theme of one of the pleasantest of his "Twice-Told Tales," that of "The Great Stone Face." At the base of the mountain, immediately under the ever-watchful eye of the Old Man, is the exquisite little **Profile Lake,** sometimes called the "Old Man's Washbowl." It is full of the finest trout, and near by is the *Trout House,* where several hundred of this beautiful fish are kept for breeding purposes. From the shore of this lake the best view of Eagle Cliff is had. There is a foot-path from the Profile House to the summit of *Bald Mountain,* 1¾ mile distant, whence a noble view is obtained without undergoing the fatigue consequent upon the ascent

of the more lofty peaks.   * **Mt. Lafayette** is the monarch of the
Franconia kingdom, towering skyward to the height of 5,280 ft. Its
lofty pyramidal peaks are the chief objects in all views for many miles
around.   The summit is reached from the Profile House in 3¾ miles by
a good bridle-path (toll for pedestrians, 50c. each; charge for horse
with guide, $3.50).   On the summit stand the walls of an old house,
erected as a shelter for visitors.   From this point is obtained "a view
more beautiful, in some respects, though it may be less grand and majestic, than that from Mt. Washington."   The Green Mountains are
plainly seen, as well as the entire White Mountain range; the peak of
Katahdin cleaves the air to the N. E., and to the S. the Pemigewasset
Valley shows its contour for a distance of 40 miles.

   Walker's Falls, reached by following for ½ mile a rivulet which
crosses the road 2½ miles S. of the hotel, is one of the most picturesque
of the mountain cascades, though the volume of water is not very great,
nor the height of the fall at all remarkable. Half a mile farther up the
stream is a larger fall. A mile farther S. is **The Basin,** a granite
bowl, 60 ft. in circumference and 15 ft. deep, filled with cold, pellucid
water. It lies near the roadside, where the Pemigewasset has worn
deep and curious cavities in the solid rock. The water, as it flows from
the Basin, falls into most charming cascades; and at the outlet, the lower
edge of the rocks has been worn into a remarkable likeness of the human leg and foot, called the "Old Man's Leg." Across the brook, below the basin, is thrown a bridge of logs, which enables the visitor to
reach a path leading ½ mile to a succession of the most exquisitely
lovely *Cascades* in this whole region. These cascades should be followed to the point where they end in a waterfall (*Tunnel Falls*), 30 ft.
high.   About 1½ mile beyond the Basin (5 miles from the Profile House)
is the **Flume House** ($3 a day), a small but excellent hotel, beauti-
fully situated at the head of the valley, with Mt. Liberty in front and
Mt. Pemigewasset behind. The views northward toward the Notch,
and southward toward the Pemigewasset Valley, are surpassingly fine.
Opposite the hotel a path through the forest leads ¾ of a mile to * **The
Pool,** a wonderful excavation in the solid rock, smooth as though
hewn by human hands. It is about 150 ft. wide and 40 ft. deep, the
water entering by a cascade, and escaping through the rocks at its
lower extremity; from the top of the rocks above to the surface of the
pool the distance is nearly 150 ft.

   * **The Flume,** one of the most famous of all the Franconia wonders, is ¾ of a mile from the hotel, and is reached by a carriage-road
leading to the part of the *Cascade* below the Flume. The cascade is a
continuous succession of gentle rapids, 600 ft. long, and at its upper
end is the entrance to the Flume itself, which is a rugged ravine 700
ft. long, with precipitous, rocky walls 60 ft. high, and not more than
20 ft. apart.   Through this grand fissure comes the little brook which
we have just seen; and a plank-walk leads along its bed to the upper
end of the ravine, where the walls approach within 10 ft. of each
other. At this point, about half-way up, a huge granite bowlder, several tons in weight, hangs suspended between the cliffs, where it has

been caught in its descent from the mountain above. So nicely is it adjusted, and so slight appears its hold, that it seems as if the gentlest touch would be sufficient to dislodge it from its resting-place, and precipitate it into the gorge below. The **Georgianna Falls** (or *Harvard Falls*, as they are sometimes called) are of greater magnitude than any yet discovered in these mountains. They plunge over the precipice in two leaps of 80 ft. each, and are reached by a path from a small farmhouse about a mile S. of the Flume House, on the Plymouth road (guide at the farmhouse).

21. Lake Winnepesaukee.

Lake Winnepesaukee is reached from Boston, Portland, or New York, by any of the routes described in Routes 18 and 19 and at the beginning of Route 20. The best approach for those who wish to make the tour of the lake on the way to the White Mts. is *via* Boston & Maine and Dover & Winnepesaukee R. R. to Alton Bay, whence steamers run to Wolfboro and Center Harbor, connecting at Wolfboro for Weirs.

LAKE WINNEPESAUKEE, the largest and most beautiful sheet of water in New Hampshire, lies in the two counties of Belknap and Carroll, and is a sort of portal to the White Mountain region from the S. It is very irregular in form, its extreme length from N. E. to S. W. being about 25 miles, and its width varying from 1 to 10 miles. Its waters are wonderfully pure and translucent, numerous islands are dotted over its surface, and lofty hills and mountains close it in on all sides. Its name is of Indian origin, and means "The smile of the Great Spirit," or, as some maintain, "The beautiful water in a high place."

Alton Bay (*Winnepesaukee House*) is the most southern point of the lake, and is situated at the head of a narrow estuary, which appears more like a river than a lake. There are several points of interest in the vicinity. From *Sheep Mountain*, 2 miles N., there is a fine view of the lake; also from *Prospect Hill* and *Mt. Major*. *Lougee Pond*, 7 miles S. W., is noted for its tame fish; and *Merry-Meeting Lake*, 7 miles E., is a beautiful sheet of water. The pleasantest excursion, however, is to the summit of * **Mt. Belknap**, 10 miles distant. The fare for a party in a regular mountain-wagon is $1.50 each, and the excursion occupies an entire day. The view from the summit is very fine. The distance from Alton Bay to Wolfboro is 11 miles, and to Center Harbor 30 miles; so that the sail includes nearly the entire length of the lake. **Wolfboro** (the *Pavilion*, *Glendon House*, *Bellevue House*, and *Lake House*) is picturesquely situated on two beautiful slopes of land rising gradually from the lake. It is the most important point on the lake, and has 2,000 inhabitants. A branch of the Eastern R. R. connects Wolfboro with North Conway; stages run daily to *Melvin Village*, on the shore of Moultonboro Bay; and steamers run to Weirs, Center Harbor, and Alton Bay. A highly popular excursion from Wolfboro is to **Copple Crown Mountain,** 2,100 ft. high, and 6¼ miles distant. Carriages from the hotel run to within a mile of the summit, from which point horses may be obtained, or the ascent may be easily made on foot. The carriage fare is $1.50

for each person of a party. The view from the summit is very fine.
The lake can be seen for nearly its entire length. To the S. is a vast
level expanse, dotted with lakes and villages and patches of woodland ;
Belknap and Gunstock, with the mountains of the Merrimac Valley,
stretch away toward the W., with the Ossipee and Sandwich ranges
closing in the head of the lake; and almost due N. Chocorua looms
up in massive grandeur, with the distant peak of Mt. Washington above
its shoulder. The ocean is visible to the S. E. on a clear day. A mile
N. of Copple Crown (6 miles from Wolfboro) is a smaller mountain
called *Tumble-Down Dick*, which is more easily ascended, and affords
a scarcely inferior view. In the middle of the lake, about equidistant
from Wolfboro, Weirs, and Alton Bay, is *Diamond Island*, on which
is the *Island House*, a favorite resort for picnic and excursion parties. A short distance above, on Long Island, there is another small
hotel.

The sail from Wolfboro to Center Harbor affords a constant succession of striking views. First Ossipee and Chocorua attract the attention as they loom up against the northern horizon ; and then, about
midway of the lake, the dim but majestic peak of Mt. Washington is
seen 40 miles away. **Center Harbor** (20 miles from Wolfboro and
10 from Weirs) is a very small village, but, being a highly popular
summer resort, has a commodious hotel so located as to command
charming views of the lake and vicinity. This is the *Senter House*
($3 a day); another and smaller hotel, the *Moulton House* ($7 to $12
a week), is well kept. Stages leave Center Harbor daily for Moulton-
boro, S. Tamworth, and West Ossipee. Steamers run to Weirs, Wolfboro, and Alton Bay. The drives in the vicinity of the village are very
attractive, but the chief objects of interest are Red Hill and Squam
Lake. *** Red Hill** is a remarkably beautiful eminence, 2,000 ft. high,
about 6 miles N. W. of the lake. Carriages run to the foot of the
hill, where horses are always in readiness to convey passengers to the
summit by a bridle-path 1½ mile long. In order to obtain the best
views, the ascent should be made in the forenoon, or in the afternoon
between 3 and 5 o'clock. At the latter hour the view of the lake and
its islands is charming. The view as a whole is one of the finest in
New England, and has been compared to that from the summit of Mt.
Holyoke. *** Squam Lake,** lying W. from Red Hill and 2 miles
N. W. of Center Harbor, is another lovely sheet of water. It is about
6 miles long and 3 miles wide at its widest part, and, like Winnepesaukee, is studded with a succession of romantic islands. This lake
abounds in fish, and is noted for the limpid purity of its water. The
drive around Squam Lake from Center Harbor (21 miles) affords a delightful day's excursion.

From Center Harbor a steamer runs several times daily to **Weirs**
(10 miles), the principal point on the W. side of the lake. This short
sail is delightful, and from a point about 3 miles below Center Harbor
is obtained the finest view on the lake. Weirs is simply a station on
the B. C. & M. R. R., where the trains connect with the steamboats.
Near Weirs is *Endicott Rock*, supposed to have been set up as a monu-

ment or boundary by the surveyors sent out in 1652 by Governor Endicott of Massachusetts.

22. Portland to Mount Desert.

A popular way of reaching Mt. Desert is by steamer from Portland twice a
week (Tuesdays and Fridays), landing at Bar Harbor. The steamer leaves Portland at 11 P. M., on the arrival of the train which leaves Boston *via* B. & M. R. R.
at 6 P. M., and Eastern R. R. at 7 P. M., and reaches Bar Harbor about noon the
next day (fare $5.50). As far as Rockland, this journey is made by night. The route
from Rockland is described below. Another line of steamers, connecting with the
trains of the Maine Central R. R., runs from Rockland on Tuesdays, Thursdays,
and Saturdays, returning alternate days. By this line the entire trip is made by
daylight, and the running time is so arranged that the journey to or from New York
can be made in a day and night. This line also has the advantage, for those who
object to a sea-voyage, of requiring but a few hours of travel on the boat.

THE distance from Portland to Rockland by the Maine Central and
Knox & Lincoln Railways is 89 miles. On the line, 29 miles from
Portland, is **Brunswick** (*Bowdoin House, Tontine Hotel*), a thriving
town at the head of tide-water on the Androscoggin River, noted as
the seat of *Bowdoin College* (incorporated in 1794). The college buildings, situated amid a beautiful grove of pine-trees near the station, are
worthy of a visit, and the gallery of paintings is famous. A few miles
beyond Brunswick is **Bath** (*Sagadahoc House, Shannon's Hotel*), a busy
little city of 12,000 inhabitants, situated on the Kennebec River, 12
miles from the sea. Ship-building is the leading industry, and there
are several fine churches and other buildings. At Bath the cars are
carried by ferry across the Kennebec River, and passing on to the
rails of the Knox & Lincoln R. R. reach Rockland in 49 miles, passing
en route the small towns of *Wiscasset* (on the Sheepscot River), *Newcastle,
Damariscotta, Warren,* and *Thomaston.* The latter contains the Maine
State Prison. **Rockland** (*Thorndike Hotel, Lynde*) is a city of
nearly 10,000 inhabitants, situated on Owl's-Head Bay, an inlet of
Penobscot Bay. The town is well built, and the adjacent scenery
is remarkably picturesque. At Rockland, passengers for Mt. Desert
take the steamer, which pursues a devious course across Penobscot
Bay and through intricate channels to the island, stopping by the way
at **Castine,** a pretty and wealthy village, situated on a narrow peninsula projecting into the bay, and much resorted to in summer for its
coolness, seclusion, and boating and fishing facilities. (This is the
route followed by the Portland steamers, while those running from
Rockland direct pursue a nearly straight course through Fisherman's
Reach.)

Mount Desert.

Mount Desert lies in Frenchman's Bay, just off the coast of Maine,
about 110 miles E. of Portland, and 40 miles S. E. of Bangor. The
island is 14 miles long and 8 miles wide, at the widest part, and has
an area of 100 square miles. At its northern end it approaches so
nearly to the mainland that a bridge affords permanent connection between the two; and nearly midway it is pierced by an inlet known as
Somes's Sound, which is 7 miles long. "The island," says Mr. Carter,

in his "Summer Cruise," "is a mass of mountains crowded together, and seemingly rising from the water. As you draw near, they resolve themselves into 13 distinct peaks, the highest of which is about 2,000 ft. above the ocean. Certainly only in the tropics can the scene be excelled—only in the gorgeous islands of the Indian and Pacific Oceans. On the coast of America it has no rival, except, perhaps, at the Bay of Rio Janeiro." The mountains are mainly upon the southern half of the island, and lie in 7 ridges, running nearly N. and S. The highest peak is *Green Mountain ;* and the next, which is separated from Green Mountain by a deep, narrow gorge, is called *Newport.* The western sides of the range slope gradually upward to the summits, but on the east they confront the ocean with a series of stupendous cliffs. High up among the mountains are many beautiful lakes, the largest of which is several miles in length. These lakes, and the streams that flow into them, abound in trout. There are several harbors on the island, the best known of which are Southwest, Northeast, and Bar Harbor.

Bar Harbor (*Grand Central Hotel, Rodick, Rockaway, Atlantic, Bay View, Ocean, Deering, Hamon, Newport, Harbor, Eden, St. Sauveur, Hayward*) is on the E. shore of the island, opposite the Porcupine Islands, and derives its name from a sandy bar, visible only at low water, which connects Mt. Desert with the largest of the Porcupine group. The village is known locally as "East Eden," and is the favorite stopping-place for travelers. The scenery in the neighborhood is pleasing, and many excursion-points are near. The first excursion should be to the summit of * **Green Mountain,** in order to get a general idea of the position and conformation of the island. There is a small hotel on the mountain-top, and a rough road leads from the village (in 4 miles) to the hotel, and enables vehicles to ascend the entire distance. Pleasure-parties commonly prefer to ascend on foot, and it is customary to remain overnight at the hotel in order to view the sunrise from this altitude (1,762 ft.). The view from the summit is very fine, embracing the whole of Mt. Desert, Frenchman's Bay with its many islands, the boundless ocean on the one hand, and a vast stretch of the Maine coast on the other. **Eagle Lake,** so named by Church, the artist, is visible at intervals during the entire ascent of the mountain ; and, half-way up, a short *détour* from the road will bring the tourist to its pebbly shore. *Mt. Newport* is ascended from the Schooner Head road, and *Kebo,* which may be reached in half an hour from the hotels at Bar Harbor, affords a pleasing prospect. The several points along the coast to which the visitor's attention is directed are The Ovens, which lie 6 or 7 miles up the bay, and Schooner Head, Great Head, and Otter Creek Cliffs, lying on the seaward shore of the island. *The Ovens* may be reached by boat or by a pleasant drive of 7 miles through the woods. They are a series of cavities worn in the cliffs by the action of the tides, some of which are large enough to contain 30 or 40 people at a time. They can only be visited at low tide, and are then a favorite picnic-ground for summer residents in Bar Harbor. The *Via Mala* is a curious archway in one of the projecting cliffs. * **Schooner Head,** so named from the fancy that a mass of white rock on its sea-face has the appearance of a small schooner, is on the seaward side of the island, 4 miles S. of Bar Harbor. The *Spouting Horn* is a wide chasm in the cliff, which extends down to the water and opens to the sea through a small arch-way below high-water mark. At high tide, and especially in stormy weather, the waves rush through this archway and send a spout of water far above the summit of the cliff. *** Great Head,** 2 miles S. of Schooner Head, is the highest headland between Cape Cod and New Brunswick. It is a bold, projecting mass, whose base has been deeply gashed by the waves. Still farther S. are the **Otter Creek Cliffs,** situated near a small stream known as Otter Creek. The most inter-esting feature of these cliffs is *Thunder Cave* (reached from the road by a superb forest-walk). The cave is a long, low gallery in the cliff-side, into which the waves rush with impetuous force, and, dashing themselves against the hollow cavity within, produce a sound closely resembling thunder. In fair weather the sound is apparent only when near, but in great storms it may be heard distinctly at the distance of 7 miles. About 9 miles S. W. of Bar Harbor is *** Jordan's Pond,** a beautiful lake 2 miles long and ½ mile wide, surrounded by pictu-resque mountain scenery and abounding in fish. *Cromwell's Cove* is 1½ mile S. of the village. The Pulpit, the Indian's Foot, and the Assyrian (a rock figure in one of the cliff-sides) are in this vicinity.

Somes's Sound, which divides the lower portion of the island into two distinct portions, possesses many attractions for those who admire bold headlands. It is usual to ascend the Sound in boats from Southwest Harbor; but explorers sometimes drive to **Somesville,** a neat little village at the head of the Sound (8 miles from Bar Harbor, and 6 miles from Southwest Harbor), and there take boats for a sail down stream. The Sound cuts through the center of the mountain-range at right angles between Dog Mountain and Mt. Mansfield, and has striking views on either hand. *Eagle Cliff* is one of the cliffs of Dog Mountain, and rises perpendicularly to a height of nearly 1,000 ft. *Fernald's Point,* on the W. shore of the Sound, is the site of the an-cient Jesuit settlement of St. Sauveur, and near by is Father Biard's Spring. The Sound affords excellent fishing and boating, though it is necessary to guard against the sudden gusts which rush down from the mountains.

Southwest Harbor (*Island House, Freeman House,* and *Ocean Hotel*) is less picturesque in its surroundings than the eastern and northern shores of the island, but there are several points of interest in the vicinity. Chief of these is the **Sea Wall** (3 miles S. W.), a *cheval-de-frise* of shattered rock skirting the shore for the distance of a mile, and against which the sea beats with tireless impetuosity. Beech Mountain (affording a noble view), Dog Mountain, Flying Moun-tain, Mt. Mansell, and Sargent's Mountain may all be ascended from Southwest Harbor. *Long Lake* is 2½ miles N. W.; *Denning's Lake* about 3 miles N.; and *Seal Cove,* 5 miles W. These are all in the neighborhood of fine scenery, and the lakes abound in fish.

6

23. Portland to Moosehead Lake.

The regular route *via* Bangor and Blanchard is described below. Another route is *via* Maine Central R. R. to *Newport* (114 miles from Portland), thence *via* Dexter & Newport R. R. to *Dexter* (15 miles), whence stages run to Greenville, passing through Blanchard. Still another route is *via* Maine Central R. R. to *Skowhegan* (100 miles from Portland), and thence by stage (distance, 50 miles; fare, $3.50). The two latter routes are not much traveled, round-trip tickets from Boston ($15) being sold only *via* Bangor and Blanchard.

The distance from Portland to Bangor *via* Maine Central R. R. is 136 miles; to Augusta, 62 miles. The first important station after leaving Portland is *Brunswick* (described on p. 119). Beyond Brunswick the train crosses the Androscoggin and passes in 27 miles to *Gardiner* (Johnson House, Evans House), a leading center of the lumber industry, with a population of about 4,000. Four miles beyond Gardiner, on the banks of the Kennebec, is *Hallowell* (Hallowell House), a town of 3,000 inhabitants, with extensive granite quarries in the neighborhood. Two miles above, at the head of navigation on the Kennebec, is **Augusta** (*Augusta House, Cony House*), the capital of the State of Maine. It is a beautifully situated and well-built city of 8,000 inhabitants, owing much of its loveliness to a great abundance of shade-trees and shrubbery. Among the noteworthy buildings are the **State House*, built of white granite, and one of the finest public edifices in New England ; the *Court-House* of Kennebec County ; the *State Insane Asylum*, a handsome granite structure on the heights E. of the river ; and the *Kennebec Arsenal*, with well-arranged grounds and neat buildings. The great dam across the Kennebec, $\frac{1}{4}$ mile above the city, is 584 ft. long, and furnishes immense water-power.—Beyond Augusta several small stations are passed, and then come *Waterville* (81 miles from Portland), a beautiful town of 5,000 inhabitants near the Ticonic Falls of the Kennebec, seat of Colby University (Baptist) ; *Burnham*, whence the Belfast Division runs to **Belfast,** a prosperous maritime city of 6,000 inhabitants, on Penobscot Bay ; and *Newport* (108 miles), whence the Dexter Division runs N. to Dexter. **Bangor** (*Bangor House, Penobscot Exchange, Franklin House*), the second city of Maine, and one of the greatest lumber-marts in the world, is situated at the head of navigation on the Penobscot River, 60 miles from the ocean, and contains about 20,000 inhabitants. It is solidly and handsomely built, and very wealthy for its size. Besides the lumber industry, for which all the vast forest country above, drained by the Penobscot and its affluents, is laid under contribution, ship-building is extensively carried on. The granite *Custom-House* and *Post-Office* (on the Kenduskeag Bridge) is a handsome structure. The *Bangor Theological Seminary*, situated in the higher part of the city, and several of the churches are noteworthy edifices. *Norembega Hall*, with seats for 2,000 persons, is on the Kenduskeag Bridge ; the lower story is used as a market. Steamers run tri-weekly between Bangor and Portland and Boston.

At Bangor the Bangor & Piscataquis R. R. is taken to **Blanchard** (75 miles), the only station *en route* requiring mention being *South*

Sebec, whence stages run in 6 miles to **Sebec Lake,** a beautiful sheet of water 12 miles long and abounding in fish. The stage-route of 12 miles from Blanchard to Greenville, on Moosehead Lake, leads through a thinly settled and picturesque region, and affords several fine mountain-views.

Moosehead Lake.

Moosehead Lake, the largest in Maine, lies among the northern hills on the verge of the great Maine forest. It is 40 miles long, and at one point is 18 miles wide, though near the center there is a pass which is not more than a mile across. It is 1,023 ft. above the sea, into which it empties by way of the Kennebec River. Its waters are deep, and furnish ample occupation to the angler in their stores of trout and other fish. The best time for visiting Moosehead Lake, or any portion of the Maine woods, is from the 15th of May to the 15th of June (*before* "fly-time"), and from August 10th to October 10th (*after* "fly-time").

Greenville (*Lake House, Eveleth House*) is a small hamlet on the S. shore, and the only permanent settlement on the lake. Small steamers leave Greenville daily for Mt. Kineo and the other end of the lake, the passage to which affords a panoramic succession of fine scenery. On the W. side **Mt. Kineo** overhangs the water with a precipitous front over 800 ft. high. On a long peninsula jutting out from its base into the lake the popular *Kineo House* is situated, and close by are the best fishing-grounds on the lake. The mountain is easily ascended (with a guide) from the hotel, and its summit reveals a picture of forest beauty well worth the climbing to see. The lake is visible from end to end, and to the northeast Katahdin stands out in massive grandeur against the horizon. About 18 miles N. of Mt. Kineo the landing-place at the end of the lake is reached, whence a portage 2 miles long leads across to the Penobscot River. This river may be descended in canoes in 7 to 10 days to Oldtown, and for those who enjoy roughing it the journey will prove a genuine "experience." "Birches," as the boats are called, and guides may be procured either at Greenville or at the Kineo House. By this approach *Mt. Katahdin* (5,385 ft. high) is seen in much finer outline than from the E., and may be ascended from the river with the canoe-guides.

24. Portland to the Rangeley Lakes.

THE route is *via* the Androscoggin Division of the Maine Central R. R. to Farmington, and thence by daily stage to Greenvale (37 miles) and Rangeley City (40 miles). As far as Brunswick the route is the same as Route 23. Beyond Brunswick, a number of small villages and hamlets are passed, lying amid a rich farming and grazing region. At *Livermore Falls* the Androscoggin River is reached. From *Wilton* stages run daily to *Weld,* a small village on the shore of a mountain-surrounded lake. **Farmington** (*Stoddard House, Forest House, Elm House*) is a frontier town of about 3,500 inhabitants, the terminus of the railroad in this direction. (Another route from Portland to Farmington is *via* Lewiston, and is 10 miles shorter than the preceding.)

The stage for Rangeley leaves on the arrival of the train, and traverses between Farmington and Phillips one of the most beautiful sections of the State, passing as it does the entire distance along the banks of the Sandy River through what is called the " Garden of Maine," on account of its splendid farms. **Phillips** (*Barden House, Elmwood*) is about half-way, and is an attractive resort, being near some excellent trout-streams, and within easy excursion distance of *Mt. Blue* and *Saddleback Mountain*, both of which command fine views. The latter is 4,000 ft. high, and from its summit may be seen the whole Rangeley region, the White Mountains, the Valley of the Upper Kennebec, and portions of Canada. Travelers usually stop overnight at Phillips, and, taking stage in the morning, pass through the hamlet of *Madrid*, beyond which a rugged wilderness stretches to the lakes.

The Rangeley Lakes.

This remote and romantic series of lakes lies in the N. W. corner of Maine, within the borders of its great forest-region, and in what is perhaps the most picturesque portion of the State. It consists of several distinct lakes, connected by narrows and streams, extending from the Oquossoc or Rangeley Lake (1,511 ft. above the sea) to Lake Umbagog (1,256 ft. above the sea), forming one continuous water-way for a distance of nearly 50 miles ; embracing 80 square miles of water-surface, and abounding in blue-back trout and other game-fish. Each lake has its individual name, but the chain is known collectively as " The Rangeley Lakes " ; and there is probably no equally accessible portion of the country which offers such attractions to sportsmen, and especially to trout-fishers. It is claimed that there are two distinct species of trout in these waters, one of which is found nowhere else, and produces specimens weighing as much as 10 pounds, while the smaller kind is caught with an ease and in quantities which can be equaled in no other known locality.

At the head of Rangeley Lake, 37 miles from Farmington, is **Greenvale** (*Greenvale House*), a much-frequented resort; and 3 miles distant, also on the lake, is **Rangeley City** (several excellent hotels), which draws many summer visitors. From both these points connection is made daily, by the little steamer "Molly Chunkamunk," with the *Mountain-View House*, at the foot of the lake, and with the *Outlet*, whence a short and easy " carry " leads to Indian Rock and Camp Kennebago, the headquarters of the Oquossoc Angling Association. *Indian Rock* is a famous old Indian camping-ground, and is the favorite resort of sportsmen, being the most central point of the region, and within half a mile of the lakes Mooselucmaguntic and Capsuptic. Lake Oquossoc, or Rangeley, is 7 miles long and 2 miles wide at the widest part, and is surrounded by forest-clad hills. Lake Mooselucmaguntic is the largest of the series, and is 10 miles long and 2 to 4 miles wide. Four small steamers ply on the lakes, forming an almost continuous and connecting line from the head of Rangeley to the foot of Umbagog. Traveling in this remote wilderness is difficult, and guides should be procured by those who leave the more frequented localities. **Upton** (*Lake House*) is a small town of 200 inhabitants at the foot of Lake Umbagog. A small steamer runs thence in 13 miles to *Errol Dam*, a rude lumbermen's village in New Hampshire, at the head-waters of the Androscoggin.

Another route from Portland to the Rangeley Lakes is *via* Grand Trunk R. R. to either *Bryant's Pond* or *Bethel*, and thence by stage to *Upton*, at the foot of Lake Umbagog (distance, 26 miles; fare, $2.50); or to *Andover*, and thence to the S. arm of Richardson Lake, connecting there with steamer running in connection with others for the Upper Lakes. The railroad journey is described in Route 18. The stage-route traverses a wild but picturesque region.

25. Portland to Montreal and Quebec.

Via Grand Trunk R. R.   Distance to Montreal, 297 miles.   To Quebec, 317 miles.

THE Grand Trunk R. R. is an important thoroughfare, used chiefly for freight, connecting the maritime city of Portland with the St. Lawrence and the Great Lakes of the interior. Its route traverses a fertile and productive country, for the most part under fine cultivation, the streams in its vicinity affording to the manufacturer water-power of the greatest value, and to the tourist a variety of picturesque and romantic scenery. As far as **Gorham** (91 miles), the entrance from this direction of the White Mountain region, it has already been described in Route 18. Beyond Gorham it follows the line of the Androscoggin and the Upper Ammonoosuc to *Northumberland* (122 miles), and thence passes into the valley of the Connecticut, reaching the banks of that river at *North Stratford* (134 miles), the last station in New Hampshire. From N. Stratford daily stages run in 13 miles to *Colebrook* (Parsons House), near which is *Mt. Monadnock*, and from which it is easy to reach the * **Dixville Notch,** 10 miles S. E. This remarkable pass is much narrower than either of the great Notches in the White Mountains, and no portion of the White Mts. surpasses it in sublimity or in a certain desolate and wild grandeur. It is $1\frac{1}{2}$ mile long, and about half-way through is a lofty projecting pinnacle called *Table Rock*, 600 ft. high, from which one can look into Maine, Vermont, and Canada. The *Dix House* is a summer hotel at the mouth of the Notch.

Beyond N. Stratford the route enters Vermont and passes in 15 miles to **Island Pond** (*Island Pond Hotel*), where the railway company has erected handsome buildings, and where the border custom-house is located. Eleven miles beyond, the train passes *Norton Mills* (160 miles), and enters the Dominion of Canada. At *Lennoxville* (193 miles) connection is made with the Massawippi Valley R. R., and 3 miles beyond is **Sherbrooke** (*Sherbrooke House, Magog House*), the most important station between Portland and Montreal, only 16 miles from Lake Memphremagog (see p. 137). At *Richmond* (221 miles) the Quebec Branch diverges, while the main line runs almost due west in 76 miles to Montreal (297 miles). *St. Hyacinthe* (262 miles) is a quaint old French-Canadian city on the Yamaska River, with a fine cathedral and famous Jesuit college. At *St. Lambert*, the train crosses the St.

Lawrence on the magnificent Victoria Bridge and enters **Montreal** (see Route 57).

The *Quebec Branch* runs N. E. from Richmond to Quebec in 96 miles, traversing a thinly populated but picturesque region, and stopping at a number of small stations, of which the principal are *Danville* (12 miles from Richmond) and *Arthabaska* (32 miles). From the latter a branch road runs in 35 miles to *Three Rivers*, on the St. Lawrence. The train stops at *Point Levi*, opposite Quebec, and passengers cross the St. Lawrence in ferry-boats. **Quebec** (see Route 57).

26. Boston to Montreal via Lowell and Concord.

Via the Boston & Lowell, Nashua & Lowell, Northern, and Central Vermont Railroads. Distances : to Lowell, 26 miles ; to Concord, 75 ; to Montreal, 334.

THIS route traverses the most populous portion of three States, passing very many cities, towns, and villages, of which only the most important can be even mentioned. **Lowell** (*Merrimac House, American, Washington*) is 26 miles from Boston, and is the second city of Mass. in point of population (52,000), and one of the most noted manufacturing cities in the Union. It is situated on the Merrimac, at the mouth of the Concord, and the source of its prosperity are the Pawtucket Falls in the Merrimac, which have a descent of 30 ft. and furnish water-power to the extent of about 10,000 horse-power. The city is regularly laid out and well built, Belvidere, the E. part, being the handsomest portion. The principal public buildings are the *Court-House*, the *City Hall*, and several fine churches and school-houses. The vast mills are among the most noteworthy structures. There are several tastefully ornamented public squares ; and in one of them (on Merrimac St.) is a monument erected to the memory of Ladd and Whitney, who fell in the attack upon the 6th Massachusetts in Baltimore, April 19, 1861. Near this monument is * Rauch's fine bronze statue of Victory, erected as a memorial of the Lowell men who fell in the civil war. Beyond Lowell the line follows the Merrimac to Concord, entering New Hampshire just beyond *Tyngsboro* (38 miles), and soon after reaching **Nashua** (*Indian Head Hotel, Tremont, Merrimac*), a pretty manufacturing city of 12,000 inhabitants, at the confluence of the Merrimac and Nashua Rivers. Here the cars pass on to the tracks of the Concord R. R., and in 17 miles reach **Manchester** (*Haseltine House, National, Manchester*), the largest city of New Hampshire, with a population of about 30,000, and extensive manufactures, chiefly of prints. The water-power is furnished by a canal around the Amoskeag Falls of the Merrimac, and on the canal are located the immense factories. In the city are a number of neat public squares, several fine churches, and a public library with 20,000 volumes.

Nine miles beyond Manchester is *Hooksett*, the site of several cotton factories and extensive brick-yards. Here the Merrimac is crossed on a bridge 550 ft. long. W. of the town is *Pinnacle Mountain*, the summit of which commands broad views. Nine miles from Hooksett is **Concord** (*Eagle Hotel, Phenix Hotel*), the capital of New Hampshire, handsomely built on the sloping W. bank of the Merrimac River, with streets regularly laid out and shaded with an abundance of trees. The city is celebrated for its carriage manufactories and for the superior quality of the granite quarried in the vicinity, some of the finest structures in the country being built of it. Main St. and State St. are the leading streets. The * *State Capitol* is a fine building of Concord granite, situated in a square bounded by Main, State, Park, and Capitol Sts. The *City Hall and Court-House* is a brick structure on Main St., N. of the Capitol. The *State Prison* is a granite building on Main St., and the *Asylum for the Insane* has handsome buildings in the W. part of the city. The population of Concord is about 15,000.

At Concord the train takes the Northern R. R. of New Hampshire, and passes in 69 miles to White River Junction, with numerous small stations *en route.* Near *Franklin* (19 miles) Daniel Webster was born in 1782. From *Potter Place* (31 miles) stages run in 4 miles to **Mt. Kearsarge,** from the summit of which (2,461 ft. above the sea) there is a noble view. (This must not be confounded with the White Mountain peak of the same name, described elsewhere.) About half way

State House, Concord.

from base to summit is the Winslow House, a commodious summer hotel. At *W. Lebanon* (67 miles) the train crosses the Connecticut, on a bridge which commands fine views of the river, and enters **White River Junction** (*Junction House*), the converging point of 4 important railroads. There is a good restaurant in the depot, and trains usually stop long enough for a meal to be eaten.

At White River Junction the Central Vermont R. R. is taken, and the train passes it into Vermont, following the White River for 25 miles, and crossing it several times. Sharon Station (13 miles from the Junction) is opposite the village of *Sharon,* where Joseph Smith, the founder of Mormonism, was born in 1805. The scenery now becomes more bold and rugged, the hills increase in height, and beyond *W. Randolph* (32 miles) the highest peaks of the **Green Mountains** come into view, on the left. At *Roxbury* (46 miles) the road leaves the White River, and, crossing the summit of the pass (1,000 ft. above the sea), reaches the source of Dog River and descends to *Northfield* (53 miles), where is located the Norwich University, a military college. Ten miles beyond Northfield is *Montpelier Junction,* whence a short branch road runs to **Montpelier** (*Pavilion Hotel, American*), the capital of Vermont, beautifully situated on the Winooski River, in a narrow valley surrounded by hills. The village is compactly built, and has a population of about 4,000. The *State Capitol* is a fine edifice of light-colored granite, in the form of a cross, the main building being 72 ft. long, and each of the wings 52 ft. The main building is 113 ft. deep and 124 ft. high to the top of the dome, which is surmounted by a graceful statue of Ceres. The entrance is approached from a Common by granite steps in terraces. In the portico is a marble statue of Ethan Allen, by the Vermont sculptor, Larkin G. Mead; and in the building are historical and geological cabinets, a State library with 15,000 volumes, and the flags carried by the Vermont volunteers during the civil war. *Mt. Hunga* is 7 miles from Montpelier, and from it may be had a very fine view. A carriage-road has been constructed to within ½ mile of the summit. The picturesque *Benjamin's Falls* are within a mile of Montpelier.

From *Waterbury* (7 miles beyond Montpelier) stages run in 10 miles to **Stowe** (*Mt. Mansfield House,* 400 guests, $3 a day), a much-frequented summer resort, delightfully situated on a plain surrounded by noble mountain scenery. Favorite excursions from Stowe are to *Moss-Glen Falls* (3 miles), *Gold Brook* (3 miles), *Bingham's Falls* (5 miles), *Morrisville Falls* (8 miles), and *Smuggler's Notch* (8 miles). The latter is a wild and picturesque pass between Mts. Mansfield and Stirling. But the great excursion is to the top of * **Mt. Mansfield,** the loftiest peak of the Green Mountains (4,348 ft. high). Its summit, as seen from Stowe, is likened to the upturned face of a giant, showing the Forehead, Nose, and Chin in three separate peaks. The *Nose* has a projection of 400 ft., and the *Chin* all the decision of character indicated by a forward thrust of 800 ft. A good carriage-road leads from Stowe to the *Summit House* ($3.50 a day) at the base of the Nose, whence a steep and rugged path leads to the top, the view from which is little if at all inferior to that from Mt. Washington. The Chin is 400 ft. higher than the Nose, and may be ascended from the Summit House by a path 2 miles long. The view is in all respects similar to that from the Nose. One night, at least, should be spent at the Summit House in order to enjoy the glorious sunrise and sunset views.

From *Ridley's Station* (5 miles beyond Waterbury) carriages run in 6 miles to **Camel's Hump,** the second highest of the Green Mountain peaks (4,188 ft. high). A carriage-road extends about half way to the summit, and the remainder of the ascent may be made either on horseback or on foot. The view closely resembles that from Mt. Mansfield, but this noble peak itself now forms one of the most striking features of the landscape. The beautiful *Bolton Falls* are near Ridley's Station.

Beyond this point, the route traverses the picturesque valley of the Winooski, and at *Williston* (91 miles) emerges into a more open country. On the right of the cars are now visible the summits of the Green Mountains; on the left, beyond Lake Champlain, those of the Adirondacks. At *Essex Junction* (94 miles) a branch road runs in 8 miles to *Burlington* (see p. 132). The main line continues N., with the Green Mts. constantly in view on the right, and Lake Champlain frequently in sight on the left. **St. Albans** (*Welden House, American, St. Albans*) is 121 miles from White River Junction, and 265 miles from Boston. It is built upon an elevated plateau 3 miles from Lake Champlain, and is one of the prettiest villages in the country. "St. Albans," says Mr. Beecher, "is a place in the midst of greater variety of scenic beauty than any other I remember in America." The public square of 4 acres in the center of the village is an ornamental ground, surrounded by the principal buildings. The extensive shops of the Central Vermont R. R. are located at St. Albans, and the village is noted as the market-place of the great butter and cheese business of Franklin Co. Magnificent views are obtained from *Aldis Hill* ($\frac{1}{2}$ mile N. E. of the village) and from *Bellevue Hill* (2 miles S. W.). Ten miles N. E. of St. Albans (on the Missisquoi R. R.) are the **Missisquoi Springs** and **Sheldon Springs,** both noted for the cure of cancer. There are nearly 20 medicinal springs in Sheldon. The hotels are *Congress Hall* and the *Portland House.*

Beyond St. Albans the route reaches *Swanton Junction,* whence a branch line diverges to *Rouse's Point* and Ogdensburg, passing the *Alburgh Springs,* whose waters are a specific for cutaneous diseases. On the main line to Montreal, 12 miles N. of St. Albans, are *Highgate Springs* (Franklin House), another valued mineral water; and 3 miles beyond, the train crosses the boundary and enters the Dominion of Canada, passing 6 or 8 small stations. At *St. Johns* (42 miles from St. Albans) the Montreal & Champlain Div. of the Grand Trunk R. R. is taken, and the train passes in 27 miles to **Montreal** (see Route 56).

27. Boston to Montreal via Rutland and Burlington.

Via Fitchburg R. R., Cheshire R. R., and Central Vermont R. R. Distance to Fitchburg, 50 miles; to Bellows Falls, 114 miles; to Rutland, 166 miles; to Burlington, 234 miles; to Montreal, 329 miles.

LEAVING Boston by the Fitchburg R. R. (depot on Causeway St., near the Warren Bridge), the train passes Charlestown, Somerville, and Cambridge (described in connection with Boston), and in 10 miles reaches **Waltham** (*Central House, Prospect House*), a flourishing

manufacturing village of 10,000 inhabitants on the Charles River, noted
as the site of the Waltham Watch Company's Works, which are the
most extensive in the world. The first cotton-mill in the United States
was erected at Waltham in 1814. Near the village is Prospect Hill
(480 ft. high), affording broad views. Ten miles farther (20 miles
from Boston) is **Concord** (*Middlesex Hotel*), a handsome manufacturing village of 2,500 inhabitants, on both sides of the Concord River.
Here, on April 19, 1775, the same day as the Battle of Lexington,
blood was shed, and the great drama of the Revolution begun.   A
granite obelisk, 25 ft. in height, marks the spot.   **Lexington** (*Massachusetts House*) is 11 miles from Concord by a branch road.   On the village green stands a monument, erected by the State, to the memory of
the 8 men who were killed in the battle.   *Ayer Junction* (35 miles)
was formerly called Groton Junction, and is a thriving village and railroad center. **Fitchburg** (*American House, Fitchburg*) is a busy manufacturing city of about 15,000 inhabitants, built along the Nashua
River, which affords a fine water-power.   Its principal manufactures
are machinery and agricultural implements, paper, chairs, and cotton
goods.   A bronze monument, in memory of her soldiers who fell in
the civil war, has been erected by the city, from designs by Millmore.
Rollstone Hill and Pearl Hill, near the city, afford fine views.

At Fitchburg the Cheshire R. R. is taken, and several small stations are passed in quick succession, of which the principal is *Winchendon* (18 miles).   Just beyond Winchendon the State line is crossed,
and the train enters New Hampshire, stopping at *Fitzwilliam* (Fitzwilliam Hotel, Cheshire House), a hilly town, watered by several streams
and ponds well stocked with fish.   Five miles beyond is *Troy*, whence
stages run in 5 miles to *****Monadnock Mountain,** in the town of
Jaffrey.   It is 3,186 ft. high, and from its summit 40 lakes and a large
number of villages are in view, while the scenery immediately around
is grand and beautiful.   A large summer hotel has been erected half
way up the mountain.   **Keene** (42 miles; *Cheshire House, Eagle
House*) has thriving manufactures of leather, boots and shoes, furniture, organs, etc., and is said to be one of the handsomest villages in
New England.   It is built on a flat E. of the Ashuelot River, and has
broad and pleasantly shaded streets.   *Walpole* (60 miles) is a pretty
village near the base of Mt. Kilburn, much resorted to in summer on
account of its scenic attractions.   From the summit of Derry Hill an
extensive and pleasing view may be had.   Four miles beyond Walpole
the train crosses the river into Vermont, and stops at **Bellows Falls**
(*Island House, Towns House*), a famous railroad center and popular
summer resort.   The Falls are a series of rapids in the Connecticut,
extending about a mile along the base of a high and precipitous hill,
known as *Mt. Kilburn*, which skirts the river on the New Hampshire
side.   At the bridge which crosses the river at this place the visitor
can stand directly over the boiling flood; viewed from whence, the
whole scene is very effective.   In the immediate neighborhood are the
Abenâquis Springs, highly tonic and possessing medicinal properties.
Fall Mountain Hotel is located near the springs at the base of Mt. Kil-

burn, and is a pleasant resort for invalids. There is a good path from the hotel to *Table Rock* on the top of the mountain, from which an extended view of the valley of the Connecticut is had.

From Bellows Falls the route is *via* the Rutland Div. of the Central Vermont R. R., which passes through the marble district, through the Green Mountains, and near the shore of Lake Champlain, affording fine views along nearly the whole line. At *Bartonsville* (10 miles from Bellows Falls) the ascent of the mountains begins, and between this and *Chester* (14 miles) is a deep ravine spanned by a bridge. At *Healdville* (33 miles) the grades become heavy, and in a mile the train reaches *Summit*, the highest point on the line. In the 18 miles between Summit and Rutland there is a descent of 1,000 ft. **Rutland** (*Bardwell House, Bates House*) is a prosperous town of 10,000 inhabitants, at the junction of the present route with the Rensselaer & Saratoga and Harlem Extension Railways, 166 miles from Boston, 230 from New York (*via* New York & Harlem and Harlem Extension R. R.), and 68 from Burlington. The town is picturesquely situated, contains some fine public and commercial buildings, including the State Workhouse and the extensive Howe Scale Works, has extensive quarries and marble-works in its vicinity, and is a center from which several pleasant excursions may be made. The road to *Killington Peak* (7 miles E.) is unattractive, and the ascent arduous, but the view from its summit, which is 3,924 ft. high, is extremely fine. *Mt. Ida*, too, is near by, and beyond Killington Peak, as seen from Rutland, are *Mt. Pico* and *Castleton Ridge*, shutting out the view of Lake Champlain. Another pleasant excursion from Rutland is to the **Clarendon Springs,** 6 miles distant. These mineral springs are a highly popular resort, and the hotel can accommodate 250 guests ($10 to $12 a week).

Sutherland Falls (6 miles N. of Rutland) is the site of large marble-works, and 3 miles beyond is *Pittsford*, noted for its beds of iron-ore and extensive marble-quarries. Seventeen miles from Rutland is **Brandon** (*Brandon House, Douglass*), a manufacturing village of 3,500 inhabitants, with marble-quarries, vast deposits of excellent bog-iron ore, and several factories where mineral paint is made from kaolin mines in the vicinity. It is pleasantly situated, near fine scenery, and draws many summer visitors. From *Salisbury* (10 miles beyond Brandon) stages run in 5 miles to **Lake Dunmore,** a lovely mountain-lake, nestling at the foot of the loftiest range of the Green Mountains, and almost surrounded by bold hills, seen here in verdant slopes and there in rocky bluff and precipitous cliff. It is about 4 miles long and 1½ mile wide at the widest part, and its clear and limpid waters afford excellent bathing, boating, and fishing. On the W. shore is a summer hotel with cottages. The drives in the vicinity are exceptionally pleasant. Six miles beyond Salisbury is the picturesque and handsomely built village of **Middlebury** (*Addison House*), situated on Otter Creek at some fine falls in that stream, and surrounded on all sides by most attractive mountain scenery. It has a population of about 2,000, and is distinguished as the seat of *Middlebury College*, founded in 1800. The college has 3 large stone buildings in the midst of extensive grounds, with a library of 14,000 volumes and a small natural-history collection. The favorite excursions from Middlebury are to *Belden's Falls* (2½ miles), to *Lake Dunmore* (8 miles), to *Bristol* (11 miles), and to *Snake Mountain* (10 miles), from the summit of which there is a remarkably fine view of the Green Mountain range from Mt. Mansfield to Rutland, of the clustering Adirondack peaks, of the northern part of Lake George, and of Lake Champlain, from Ticonderoga to the great bay above Burlington.   On the summit are a small hotel and a wooden tower 80 ft. high (fee, 25c.). The famous *Bread-Loaf Inn* at Ripton is reached by stage from Middlebury in 8½ miles.

Fourteen miles beyond Middlebury (47 from Rutland) is **Vergen-nes** (*Stevens House, Franklin*), the oldest city in Vermont (incorporated in 1783), and the smallest in the Union, with a population of little more than 1,500. It is at the head of navigation on Otter Creek, 8 miles from Lake Champlain, and near the *Falls*, which have a descent of 37 ft.   Commodore McDonough's fleet, which won the naval battle of Lake Champlain (Sept. 11, 1814), was fitted out at Vergennes.

Burlington (*American House, Van Ness House*), the largest city of Vermont, is finely situated upon the E. shore of Lake Champlain, on ground which gradually rises from the water to a height of 367 ft.   The first permanent settlement at Burlington was made in 1783, and it has since become one of the great lumber-marts of the country.   In 1865 the township was divided into the city of Burlington and the town of South Burlington.   The city has grown rapidly, for an Eastern city, and has now about 17,000 inhabitants.   It has several of the largest mills in the country for planing and dressing lumber, and extensive manufactories of articles of wood, as of doors, packing-boxes, furniture, spools, etc.   The city is regularly laid out and handsomely built, and many of the residences and churches are noticeable for their beauty. The *Cathedral of St. Mary* (Roman Catholic) is a large and striking structure; and *St. Paul's Church* (Episcopal) is a fine old stone build-ing, in the Gothic style, with windows of stained glass.   The *Court-House* and the *Custom-House and Post-Office* are handsome buildings, on the public square in the center of the city.   The *City Hall* and the *Fletcher Library* (containing 10,000 volumes) are also on the square. On Church St. is a spacious and handsome *Opera-House*, completed in 1879.   The depot of the Vermont Central and the Vermont & Canada Railways, near the wharf, is an extensive building.   The *University of Vermont*, whose buildings crown the summit of the hill back of the city, was incorporated in 1791 and organized in 1800.   The corner-stone was laid by Lafayette in 1825.   In 1865 the State Agricultural College was united with it.   It has a library of 17,000 volumes, and a museum containing upward of 50,000 specimens in natural history. The view from the dome of the university building is superb, and is only surpassed by the *view from the top of the costly *Mary Fletcher Hospital*, a little to the N. E., which has been pronounced the finest lake-view in America.   The 10 miles width of the lake makes an admirable foreground for the towering Adirondack peaks on the W., while to the E. the chain of the Green Mountains lifts against the sky, and N. and S. lies a great expanse of lake. Near the university is the *Green-Mount Cemetery*, where Ethan Allen lies, under a granite shaft 42 ft. high, surmounted by a marble statue of the old hero. *Lake View Cemetery*, in the N. W. part of the city, directly on the shore of the lake, is one of the finest in the State.

From Burlington to *Essex Junction*, the distance is 8 miles, and the train passes *en route* the picturesque falls of the Winooski River. From Essex Junction the route is the same as in Route 26. The distance from Burlington to Montreal is 95 miles.

28. New York to Montreal and Quebec by the Connecticut Valley.

Via New York, New Haven & Hartford R. R., Connecticut River R. R., New London Northern R. R., Central Vermont R. R., and Passumpsic R. R.   Distances: New York to Springfield, 135 miles; to Bellows Falls, 219 miles; to White River Junction, 259 miles; to Quebec, 525 miles; to Montreal, 505 miles (*via* Sherbrooke), 444 miles (*via* Montpelier and St. Albans).

As far as **Springfield, Mass.,** this route has already been described in Route 11. Leaving Springfield, the train passes over level meadow-lands along the Connecticut River, and in 4 miles reaches *Chicopee* (*Cabot House*), a handsome village of 6,000 inhabitants, noteworthy as the site of the Ames Manufacturing Co., which produces so many fine arms and bronzes. Here were cast the bronze doors of the Senate wing of the Capitol at Washington (see p. 51), and Ball's equestrian statue of Washington, in the Public Garden at Boston. Four miles beyond is **Holyoke** (*Holyoke House*), which possesses the greatest water-power in New England, being the site of the great dam of the Holyoke Water-Power Co. The river has a fall here of 60 ft. in ¾ mile, and is dammed by an immense structure 1,000 ft. in length and 30 ft. in height, built of wood spiked to the rock of the river-bed and covered with plates of boiler-iron. This dam throws the water into a canal which distributes it to the various factories. Holyoke has about 18,000 inhabitants, is well built, and boasts of one of the finest City Halls in Massachusetts, and of a handsome soldiers' monument. Beyond Holyoke the scenery grows more picturesque, the hills on either side beginning to assume the name and aspect of mountains; and soon the train passes between Mount Tom (on the left) and Mount Holyoke (on the right), and stops at **Northampton** (*Mansion House* and *Hampshire House*), which is said to be the most beautiful village in America. The village is built on alluvial meadows about a mile W. of the river. Its streets are laid out with picturesque irregularity, and abound in shade-trees of venerable age and noble size; even the business quarter has a cozy, rural air, and all around are charming villas, nestled amid green lawns and shrubbery. Near the center of the village is the *Smith Female College*, founded by Miss Sophia Smith, of Hatfield, and endowed with a fund of about $500,000. The free *Public Library* (with 12,000 volumes) is lodged in a fine building, with which is connected *Memorial Hall*, erected in memory of the men of Northampton who fell during the civil war. On a fine eminence W. of the village is the *Round Hill Hotel*, formerly a water-cure, now a first-class hotel. On the same hill is the *Clarke Institution for Deaf Mutes* (endowed with $300,000), and near by are the spacious and handsome buildings of the *State Lunatic Asylum.* The vicinity of Northampton is the most beautiful portion of the Connecticut Valley, and attractive drives lead in all directions.

On the opposite side of the river from Northampton, 3 miles distant, is * **Mt. Holyoke,** " the gem of Massachusetts mountains." It can be reached by private conveyance, crossing the river at Hockanum Ferry, either by ascending the carriage-road to the top or to the foot of the inclined railway (600 ft. long) by which passengers are carried up the steepest part of the mountain. An easier way is *via* Connecticut River R. R. to Mt. Tom Station, thence by steamer to the foot of the mountain, whence there is a conveyance to the inclined railway. On the summit, 1,120 ft. above the sea, stand the *Prospect House* and an observatory. The view from the Prospect House has been often pronounced by tourists the finest in America.

The view embraces no less than 10 mountains in 4 States, and about 40 villages. " On the W., and a little elevated above the general level, the eye turns with delight to the populous village of Northampton, exhibiting in its public edifices and private dwellings an unusual degree of neatness and elegance. A little more to the right the quiet and substantial villages of Hadley and Hatfield ; and still farther E., and more distant, Amherst, with its colleges, observatory, cabinet, and academy, on a commanding eminence, form pleasant resting-places for the eye. Facing the S. W., the observer has before him, on the opposite side of the river, the ridge called Mt. Tom, rising 200 ft. higher than Holyoke, and dividing the valley of the Connecticut longitudinally. The western branch of this valley is bounded on the W. by the Hoosic range of mountains, which, as seen from Holyoke, rises ridge above ridge for more than 20 miles, checkered with cultivated fields and forests, and not unfrequently enlivened by villages and church-spires. In the N. W., Graylock may be seen peering above the Hoosic ; and, still farther N., several of the Green Mountains, in Vermont, shoot up beyond the region of the clouds in imposing grandeur. A little to the S. of W., the beautiful outline of Mt. Everett is often visible. Nearer at hand, and in the valley of the Connecticut, the insulated Sugar-Loaf and Mt. Toby present their fantastic outlines, while far in the N. E. ascends in dim and misty grandeur the cloud-capped Monadnock."

Mt. Tom is about 5 miles S. of Northampton, on the same side of the river. It is 200 ft. higher than Mt. Holyoke, but is comparatively seldom visited on account of the difficulty of the ascent. *Mt. Nonotuck,* the northern peak of the Mt. Tom range, is easily reached from the Mt. Tom station. On its summit is a well-kept hotel, and the view is nearly if not quite equal to that from Mt. Holyoke.

About a mile beyond Northampton the train passes in sight of **Hadley,** a venerable and interesting old village, lying in the Great Bend of the Connecticut, which here makes a détour of 7 miles in order to accomplish a mile of direct distance. Hadley is connected with Northampton by a bridge across the river. Here we take our last view of the river until South Vernon is reached, 33 miles distant. From *S. Deerfield* (11 miles from Northampton) a carriage-road leads to the Mountain House on the summit of *Sugar-Loaf Mountain,* a conical peak of red sandstone rising almost perpendicularly 500 ft. above the plain, and commanding broad and pleasing views. This peak is said to have been the headquarters of King Philip during the Indian wars, and the valley which it overlooks was the scene of some of the bloodiest incidents of those cruel wars. On the battle-field of Bloody Brook, where Captain Lathrop with 80 youths, "the flower of Essex County," were drawn into an ambuscade and slain, a monument has been erected. The train passes in sight of the monument, and in 5 miles reaches *Deerfield* (Pocomtuck House), a pretty village near the foot of *Deerfield Mountain*, which is 700 ft. high, and commands a much-admired view. Stages run S. E. in 2 miles to *Sunderland*, whence a carriage-road leads to the summit of *Mt. Toby*, from which another beautiful view may be had. A tower 63 ft. high, containing rooms for a night's lodging, stands on the crest.

Nineteen miles above Northampton is the beautiful village of **Greenfield** (*Mansion House, American House*), with elm-shaded streets and garden-surrounded villas. The hill-ranges in the neighborhood open fine pictures of the valleys and windings of the great river; and the vicinity abounds in delightful drives. This is one of the most popular summer resorts in the valley. Directly E., on the Connecticut, is Turner's Falls, the site of an immense water-power, second only to that of Holyoke; and frequent excursions are made to the Coleraine, Shelburne, and Leyden Gorges. Just beyond *Bernardston* (7 miles from Greenfield) the river again comes in sight, and soon after the train crosses the boundary-line and enters the State of Vermont. From *South Vernon* (14 miles from Greenfield) the summit of Mt. Monadnock (see p. 130) may be seen 30 miles E. through the valley of the Ashuelot. Here the Connecticut River R. R. ends, and the New London Northern R. R. is taken to **Brattleboro** (*Brooks House, Brattleboro House*), a large and handsomely built village on the W. side of the Connecticut at the mouth of Whetstone Creek. The situation is very fine, and the scenery and drives in the vicinity romantic and pleasing. The Vermont Asylum for the Insane is located here, and numerous factories, including the Estey Cottage-Organ Works, the largest in the world. In the cemetery is a costly monument to James Fisk, Jr., and from Cemetery Hill there is a fine view of the Connecticut Valley and of Wantastiquet and Mine Mts. on the opposite side of the river. Across the river (reached by bridge) is the pretty town of *Hinsdale*, New Hampshire.

Twenty-four miles above Brattleboro (several small stations *en route*) is **Bellows Falls,** which has been described elsewhere (see p. 130). Here the Central Vermont R. R. is taken, and the train passes N. by *Charlestown, Claremont,* and *Windsor.* The latter is a pretty highland village, with considerable manufactures and trade, and surrounded by attractive scenery. At the Windsor House guides and horses may be procured for the ascent of **Ascutney Mountain,** in 5 miles by a good road. Ascutney (or "Three Brothers") is an isolated peak, 3,320 ft. high, and the view from its summit is the finest and most extensive of any in Eastern Vermont. At *White River Junction* (40 miles from Bellows Falls, 154 from Boston, and 259 from New York) the regular Montreal through route diverges from the present

route and proceeds *via* Montpelier and St. Albans (see Route 26). Such
Montreal passengers as prefer it can continue on present route to either
Newport or Sherbrooke, *via* Passumpsic River R. R.

Just beyond the Junction the train crosses White River and passes
in 4 miles to *Norwich*, whence stages run in ¾ mile to *Hanover, N. H.*,
the seat of **Dartmouth College**, one of the most famous institutions

Dartmouth College.

of learning in America. It was founded in 1769; and Daniel Webster,
Rufus Choate, and Chief-Justice Chase were among its alumni. The
college buildings are grouped around a square of 12 acres in the center of
the plain on which the village stands. The most notable are Dartmouth
Hall, Reed Hall (containing the library of 40,000 volumes), Culver Hall,
and the new Gymnasium. Still running N. along the boundary between
Vermont and New Hampshire the train passes several small stations
and in 30 miles reaches **Newbury** (*Spring Hotel*), one of the prettiest
towns in the upper Connecticut Valley. It is built on a terrace 100 ft.
above the river, and is much visited on account of its celebrated Sulphur Spring and its beautiful scenery. The great *Ox-Bow* of the Connecticut and *Mt. Pulaski* are both in this township. The latter is easily ascended from the village, and affords a noble view. **Wells River**
(4 miles above Newbury) is at the junction of the B. C. & M. R. R. to
the White Mts. (see Route 19).

The scenery now becomes more rugged and impressive, and fine
views are had from the car-windows on either side. Numerous small
villages are passed, and then, at the head of the Connecticut Valley,
comes **St. Johnsbury** (*St. Johnsbury House, Avenue House*), the most
important and attractive town in this portion of Vermont. Many of
the dwellings are elegant, there are several fine churches, and the
Court-House is a handsome structure. In front of the latter is a Sol-

diers' Monument designed by Larkin G. Mead. The Athenæum contains 10,000 volumes and an art-gallery. Here the Connecticut Valley
ends, and the train passes on through a picturesque hill country toward
Lake Memphremagog. From *W. Burke* (16 miles from St. Johnsbury)
carriages run in 6 miles to **Willoughby Lake,** a lovely sheet of water 7 miles long and from ½ to 2 miles wide, lying between Mt. Annanance (2,638 ft. high) and Mt. Hor (1,500 ft. high), and teeming with
muscalonge and trout. A good hotel stands on the lake-shore, whence
a bridle-path leads to the summit of Mt. Annanance, the view from
which is extremely fine. Other small stations are passed, and the train
speedily reaches **Newport** (*Memphremagog House, Bellevue House*)
at the head of Lake Memphremagog. The village is built on Pickerel
Point, and contains 1,000 inhabitants. *Prospect Hill*, just S., affords a
fine view of the lake and surrounding elevations; and *Jay Peak* (12
miles W., 4,018 ft. high) commands a view which includes the Green
and White Mts., Lake Champlain, and the Adirondacks. Pleasant excursions are to *Clyde River Falls* (2 miles), *Bear Mountain* (7 miles),
and *Bolton Springs* (15 miles). The latter are in Canada.

Lake Memphremagog.

Lake Memphremagog is a beautiful sheet of water, 30 miles long
and 2 to 4 miles wide, lying partly in Vermont and partly in Canada.
Its shores are rock-bound and indented with beautiful bays, between
which jut out bold, wooded headlands, backed by mountain-ranges.
Its waters are deliciously cool and transparent, and numerous picturesque islands dot its surface. Muscalonge, a fish peculiar to these
waters, and trout are taken here in perfection, and other varieties of
fish are abundant. A steamer leaves the pier in front of the Memphremagog House in Newport every morning, for Magog, at the other end
of the lake, returning in the afternoon (fare to Magog, $1.50; to Owl's
Head, 75c.). In ascending the Lake, *Indian Point*, the *Twin Sisters*,
and *Province Island* are passed within a few miles of Newport. E. of
Province Island, and near the shore, is *Tea-Table Island*, a charming
rural picnic resort; and on the W. shore the boundary-line between
Vermont and Canada strikes the lake. About half way down the lake,
on the W. side, is the *Mountain House*, nestling in a lovely nook at
the foot of * **Owl's Head** (2,743 ft. high). A footpath leads from
the hotel to the summit, which can be reached in 1 to 2 hours. The
view in clear weather is very extensive, including the entire length of
Memphremagog, the White Mountains, Lake Champlain, Willoughby
Lake and Mountain, the St. Lawrence River, and the white pinnacles
of Montreal. At and near the Mountain House are the best fishing-
grounds on the Lake; and *Fitch's Bay* and *Whetstone Island, Magoon
Point, Round* and *Minnow Islands*, are in the vicinity, affording pleasant
picnic and excursion points for visitors sojourning there. *Skinner's
Island* and *Cave*, said to have been the haunt of Uriah Skinner, "the
bold smuggler of Magog," during the war of 1812, are also near by.
Balance Rock, on the S. shore of Long Island, is frequently visited.
The E. shore of the Lake, in this vicinity, is much improved and

adorned with some handsome summer villas. About a mile N. of the
hotel, on the W. side, is a series of precipitous cliffs 700 ft. high,
and the water beneath is of unfathomed depth. *Mt. Elephantis* (or
Sugar Loaf) is seen to advantage from Allen's Landing; its outline is
supposed to resemble that of an elephant's head and back. *Concert
Pond*, W. of Mt. Elephantis, abounds in brook-trout, and attracts numerous visitors. *Georgetown*, 20 miles from Newport and 12 from Magog, has an hotel (the *Camperdown House*) and several stores, and is a
favorite summer resort with the Canadians. **Magog** (*Parks House*) is
a small hamlet at the N. end of the lake, where the Memphremagog
discharges its waters through the Magog River into the St. Francis.
There is excellent trout-fishing in the vicinity of Magog; and from the
summit of *Mt. Orford*, 5 miles W., and reached by carriage-road, an
exceedingly striking outlook is obtained over the somber and far-
stretching Canadian forests.

From Newport the Southeastern R. R. runs N. W. to Montreal in 65 miles, passing *Richford, W. Farnham*, and *St. Johns*. This road forms a part of the **Boston
& Montreal Air Line**, which follows Route 26 to White River Junction, the
present route thence to Newport, where the Southeastern R. R. is taken. The
total distance from Boston to Montreal by this route is 314 miles.

Soon after leaving Newport an arm of the lake is crossed, and the
train speedily passes the frontier and enters Canada, traversing for
many miles the Eastern Townships, "as beautiful a tract of country
perhaps as any on the continent, both with regard to mountain and
lake scenery, beautiful rivers, and fertile valleys." *Massawippi* (20
miles from Newport) is near the lovely and fish-teeming *Lake Massawippi*, and beyond this the train follows the Massawippi River for 16
miles, reaching **Sherbrooke** (40 miles from Newport), an important
station on the Grand Trunk R. R. The route from Sherbrooke to
Quebec and Montreal is described in Route 25.

29. New London to Brattleboro.

Via New London Northern R. R. Distance, 121 miles

THIS route crosses the two States of Connecticut and Massachusetts, and forms part of a popular through route from New York to
the north. **New London** is described in Route 12. It is connected with New York by the Shore Line R. R. and by the Norwich
Line of steamers. The present route runs N., following the Thames
River for 13 miles to **Norwich,** which has already been described
(see p. 81). A seat on the right-hand side of the car on this portion
of the route will afford some pleasing views. *Willimantic* (30 miles
from New London) is a busy manufacturing town at the crossing of
the New York & Boston Air Line R. R. (see Route 13). Beyond
Willimantic the train follows the Willimantic River, and passing several small stations reaches **Stafford,** celebrated for its mineral springs,
one of which is regarded as one of the best chalybeate springs in the
United States. The Indians estimated the curative properties of these
springs very highly, and the whites have used them for more than a

hundred years. The springs and a large hotel (the *Stafford Springs House*) are close by the depot on the W. side of the track. The village is 2 miles distant.

Ten miles beyond Stafford the train crosses the State Line and enters Massachusetts. *Monson* (61 miles from New London) is the first station in Massachusetts, and is near some excellent granite-quarries. *Palmer* (65 miles) is at the junction of the Boston & Albany with the New London Northern R. R., and has fine water-power which is extensively used for manufactories. Stations, *Barrett's Junction*, at the crossing of the Springfield, Athol & Northeastern R. R., *Belchertown* (76 miles), and *Amherst* (85 miles). Just beyond Belchertown a fine view of the Connecticut Valley and Mt. Holyoke appears on the W. of the road. **Amherst** (*Amherst House*) is charmingly situated, and is noted for its college, its picturesque surroundings, and its refined and cultivated society. It is irregularly built upon a hill, commanding extensive views, and has a population of about 4,000. *Grace Church* (Episcopal) and the *First Congregational* are fine edifices. **Amherst College** was founded in 1821, and is one of the leading educational institutions of New England. Its buildings occupy an eminence on the S. side of the village, and command a prospect of exceeding beauty. The college collections in zoölogy, botany, geology, mineralogy, etc., are among the richest in the country, and are accessible to visitors. The Shepard cabinet of minerals is of immense value, and is said to be surpassed only by those of the British Museum and the Imperial Cabinet at Vienna; and the collection of 20,000 specimens of ancient tracks of birds, beasts, and reptiles in stone is without a rival. The Memorial Chapel is a fine building, and so are Walker and Williston Halls. The *Massachusetts Agricultural College* has extensive and handsome buildings about a mile N. of the village green, and possesses, besides other objects of interest, the Durfee Plant-House, containing many rare and beautiful plants. Founded in 1866, this institution has become the most successful agricultural school in the country. Amherst is within excursion distance (7 miles) of Northampton and Mt. Holyoke (see p. 133).

Beyond Amherst the scenery is very pleasing, and may be enjoyed from the left-hand side of the cars. From *Leverett* (90 miles) there is an impressive view of Mt. Toby (see p. 134). *Miller's Falls* (100 miles) is at the crossing of the Vermont & Massachusetts R. R. (Route 33). *Northfield* (109 miles) is an attractive village, and the last station in Massachusetts. Just beyond it, the train crosses the Connecticut River, affording fine views from the bridge, and passes to *South Vernon* (111 miles). From this point the route is the same as that described in Route 28, and passes on to the White Mts., the Green Mts., and Canada.

30. Boston to Plymouth.

Via Old Colony R. R.   Distance, 38 miles.

From Boston to *S. Braintree* (11 miles), this is the same as Route 14 (*a*), taken in reverse.   *S. Abington* (20 miles) is noted for its shoe-factories.   A short branch line runs thence in 7 miles to the ancient town of *Bridgewater*.   Beyond S. Abington the road traverses the great forest and lake region of the Old Colony, skirts the W. shore of Plymouth Harbor, and stops at Plymouth.

Plymouth (*Samoset House*) is a flourishing manufacturing village of 7,000 inhabitants on Cape Cod Bay.   Its interest is chiefly historical, and it will be for ever famous as the landing-place of the Pilgrim Fathers (Dec. 22, 1620), and as the site of the first settlement made in New England.   * **Plymouth Rock,** on which the Pilgrims first landed, is in Water St., and is covered by a handsome granite canopy, in the attic of which are inclosed the bones of several men who died during the first year of the settlement.   A portion of the rock has been placed in front of Pilgrim Hall, and surrounded by an iron fence. * **Pilgrim Hall** is in Court St., and contains a large hall, the public library, portraits and busts, and many interesting relics of the Mayflower pilgrims and other early settlers of Massachusetts.   Near the Hall are the County Court House and House of Correction, both fine buildings.   The Town Green is at the end of Main St.   *Leyden St.*, the oldest street in New England, runs E. from Town Square to the water. The * **Burying Hill,** where some of the Pilgrims were interred, is a place of much interest.   It contains some ancient and venerable tombs, and commands a wide view.   *Cole's Hill*, W. of the canopied rock, is noted as the spot where nearly half the Mayflower pilgrims were buried the first winter; but no trace of their graves remains.   The *National Monument to the Pilgrims*, the corner-stone of which was laid Aug. 1, 1859, stands on a high hill near the Samoset House.   It consists of a granite pedestal 40 ft. high, surrounded by statues 20 ft. high; and surmounted by a colossal granite statue of "Faith," 40 ft. high.   (Not yet finished.)

The environs of Plymouth are very attractive, and in the township are about 200 ponds, one of the largest, *Billington Sea*, being stocked with fish.   It is about 2 miles from the village.

31. Boston to Cape Cod.

Via Cape Cod Division of the Old Colony R. R.   Distance, Boston to Province town, 120 miles.   Fare, $3.

As far as *S. Braintree*, this is the same as Route 30.   The first station beyond S. Braintree is *Holbrook* (15 miles), a small manufacturing village, and 5 miles farther is **Brockton** (*Brockton House*), a prosperous town of 12,000 inhabitants, with extensive factories of shoes, furniture, carriages, etc.   **Bridgewater** (*Highland House*) is 27 miles from Boston, and is the site of extensive iron-foundries, rolling-mills, machine-shops, and brickyards. The Bridgewater Iron-Works are among the largest on the continent. At *Middleboro* (34 miles) the Cape Cod Div. of the Old Colony R. R. begins. Stations, *S. Middleboro* (42 miles), *Tremont* (45 miles), *Wareham* (49 miles), and *Cohasset Narrows* (54 miles). From the latter, a branch road diverges to Wood's Holl, whence steamers run to Martha's Vineyard (see Route 32). The present route continues on past the small stations of *N. Sandwich* (58 miles), *W. Sandwich* (59 miles), and *Sandwich* (62 miles). At Sandwich the Cape begins, and extends E. about 35 miles, with a width rarely exceeding 8 miles, and then bends N., and gradually N. W., extending about 30 miles farther. The curve still continues around to the W., S., and E., inclosing the fine land-locked harbor of Provincetown. This latter portion does not average half the width of the former, and is greatly indented by bays both on the outer and inner sides.

"The ride throughout the Cape," says Mr. Samuel Adams Drake, "affords the most impressive example of the tenacity with which a population clings to locality that has ever come under my observation. To one accustomed to the fertile shores of Narragansett Bay or the valley of the Connecticut, the region between Sandwich, where you enter upon the Cape, and Orleans, where you reach the bend of the forearm, is bad enough, though no desert. Beyond this is simply a wilderness of sand. The surface of the country about Brewster and Orleans is rolling prairie, barren, yet thinly covered with an appearance of soil. Stone-walls divide the fields, but from here down the Cape you will seldom see a stone of any size in going 30 miles. . . . Eastham, Wellfleet, and Truro grow more and more forbidding, as you approach the *Ultima Thule*, or land's end. . . . It was something to conceive, and more to execute, such a tramp as Thoreau's (from Orleans to Provincetown on the ocean side of the Cape), for no one ought to attempt it who can not rise superior to his surroundings, and shake off the gloom the weird and widespread desolateness of the landscape inspires. I would as lief have marched with Napoleon from Acre, by Mt. Carmel, through the moving sands of Tentoura."

Seven miles beyond Sandwich is *W. Barnstable*, whence stages run in 6 miles to *Cotuit Port*, on the S. shore, a favorite resort of sportsmen. *Yarmouth* (75 miles) is near a camp-meeting ground, and is the junction of a branch road which runs in 4 miles to **Hyannis** (*Iyanough House, Hallet*), on the S. shore, which is becoming a popular summer resort. Beyond Yarmouth are the small stations of *S. Yarmouth* (80 miles), *Harwich* (84 miles), *Brewster* (89 miles), *Eastham* (97 miles), and *Wellfleet* (109 miles). Near *Truro* (114 miles) is one of the most fatal beaches on the New England coast; and on Clay Pounds, on the outer shore of Truro, is the famous *Highland Light,* 200 ft. above high-water mark, and provided with Fresnel burners. Six miles beyond Truro is **Provincetown** (*Gifford House, Central, Pilgrim*), a thriving fishing village, with a magnificent land-locked harbor, which is frequently crowded with shipping seeking a haven of refuge. Near here are the principal cod and mackerel fisheries on the coast, and nearly all the inhabitants are in one way or another connected with the sea-going business. From the summit of Town Hill there is an impressive view, with the Atlantic Ocean on one side and Massachusetts Bay on the other. *Race Point* is the outermost land of the Cape and has a revolving light 150 ft. above high water. It is

reached from Provincetown by a walk of 3 miles across the sand-dunes.
"Standing here," says Mr. Drake, "I felt as if I had not lived in vain.
I was as near Europe as my legs would carry me, at the extreme of
this withered arm with a town in the hollow of its hand. For centuries the storms have beaten upon this narrow strip of sand, behind
which the commerce of a State lies intrenched. The assault is unflag-
ging, the defense obstinate. Fresh columns are always forming outside for the attack, and the roll of ocean is for ever beating the charge.
Yet the Cape stands fast, and will not budge."

32. Boston to Martha's Vineyard and Nantucket.

Via Old Colony R. R. to Wood's Holl (78 miles), and thence by steamer.

FROM Boston to *Cohasset Narrows* (54 miles) this route is the same
as Route 31. Beyond Cohasset Narrows, the train runs along the shore
of Buzzard's Bay, passing the small stations of *Monument Beach*, *Po-
casset*, and *Falmouth*. A mile S. E. of the latter is the popular summer
resort of **Falmouth Heights** (*Tower's Hotel*), a line of high and picturesque bluffs fronting on Vineyard Sound, with a good beach and other
attractions. At *Wood's Holl* (71 miles from Boston), connection is made
with the steamer for Martha's Vineyard, 7 miles distant.

Martha's Vineyard.

From New York Martha's Vineyard is reached *via* Fall River steamers to Fall
River (Route 14), thence *via* Old Colony R. R. to *Myrick's*, thence *via* New Bedford
R. R. to *New Bedford*, and thence by a charming steamboat ride of 30 miles to
Martha's Vineyard. Total distance, 225 miles; fare $5. Another route is by steamer
to Fall River, as before, thence by rail to Wood's Holl, and thence by steamer.

Hotels.—The *Sea-View House* ($4 a day), is a large, handsomely furnished,
and well-kept hotel with accommodations for about 300 guests. The *Highland
House* is also first-class. Smaller hotels, in the village of Oak Bluffs, are the *Island*,
the *Baxter*, the *Pawnee*, the *Central*, the *Grover*, and the *Wesley*. The last five
are on the European plan, with restaurants attached.

Martha's Vineyard is an island 20 miles long and 6 miles in average
width, lying off the S. coast of Massachusetts, and separated from the
mainland by Vineyard Sound. Its surface is generally level, though
there are elevations rising to the height of 150 ft. above the sea. The
soil is generally light, and a great part of the surface is covered with
low forests. The inhabitants, of whom there were 3,688 in 1870, are
chiefly engaged in navigation and fishing. Martha's Vineyard was discovered by Bartholomew Gosnold in 1602, was settled by Thomas
Mayhew in 1642, and suffered much from the British during the Revolutionary War. Of late years it has become noted for its annual camp-
meetings and as a summer resort.

Near the Sea-View Hotel is the great Methodist *Camp-Meeting
Ground, where 20,000 to 30,000 people are gathered every August.
The grounds are regularly and tastefully laid out, and comprise a tabernacle capable of seating 5,000 persons. E. of the camp-ground, on
bluffs 30 ft. high, overlooking the sea, the village of **Oak Bluffs** was
laid out in 1868, and has become a popular summer resort; besides the

hotels named above, it contains numerous cottages of summer residents. A narrow-gauge railway connects Oak Bluffs with Edgartown and Katama, and the *Sea-View Boulevard*, an admirable drive along the coast, runs to the same places. **Edgartown** (*Atlantic House, Sea-Side House*, and *Vineyard House*) is a neat village, 6 miles E. of Oak Bluffs, containing several churches, a town-hall, the county buildings, and the Martha's Vineyard National Bank. Its harbor is well sheltered, and at the entrance is a lighthouse showing a fixed light 50 ft. above the sea, erected on a pier 1,000 ft. long. Beyond Edgartown the railway and the boulevard extend to **Katama Bay,** noted for its clam-bakes and for its attractive scenery. The *Mattakeset Lodge* here is one of the best hotels on the island. A short distance W. of Oak Bluffs is the East Chop Light, whence a fine view is obtained of **Vineyard Haven,** one of the most celebrated harbors on the coast.
*** Gayhead,** the westerly end of Martha's Vineyard (20 miles from Oak Bluffs), is a spot well worth the attention of the visitor. It is of volcanic origin, and was pronounced by Prof. Hitchcock one of the most remarkable geological formations in America. "Never," said General Twiggs, as he looked from the top of this bold promontory, "since I stood on Table Rock, have I seen a sight so grand and beautiful as this!"

Nantucket.

Nantucket is about 30 miles from Martha's Vineyard, from which it is reached by a daily steamer. The island is of an irregular triangular form, about 16 miles long from E. to W., and for the most part from 3 to 4 miles wide. It has a level surface in the S., and in the N. is slightly hilly. The soil is light, and, with the exception of some low pines and the shade-trees in the town, the island is treeless. Farming and fishing are the chief occupations of the inhabitants (of whom there were 3,200 in 1875), the surrounding waters abounding in fish of various kinds. The climate in summer is remarkably cool, and the island is fast becoming a favorite summer resort.

The town of **Nantucket** (*Ocean, Bay View, Sherburne*, and *Springfield Houses*, $2 to $3 a day) was at one time the chief whaling-port of the world, and increased rapidly in size and prosperity until 1846, when it was visited by a severe conflagration that destroyed nearly a million dollars' worth of property. After this the whale-fishery, and with it the prosperity of the town, rapidly declined; and until the stream of summer visitors began to flow in, it had a distinct air of decrepitude and decay. It is picturesquely situated, and presents an appearance from the water which is hardly confirmed on closer scrutiny. The streets are cleanly, and, having trees and flower-gardens, are often pretty and cheerful. The roofs of many houses are surmounted by a railed platform, a reminder of old whaling-times. The town contains 9 churches, a town-hall, a national bank, a savings-bank, 5 public halls, a custom-house, and several good public schools. In the *Athenæum* is a public library of 5,000 volumes, and some interesting relics of whales and whaling. Three excursions must be made from the town

before one can say that he has "seen Nantucket." One is to a cliff
at the North Shore whence a wide view is had; and another to the
beaches of the South Shore, where the waves roll in grandly after a
storm. But "**Siasconset** (pronounced Sconset) is the paradise of
the islander: not to see it would be in his eyes unpardonable." It is
a quaint little fishing hamlet on the S. E. shore of the island, 7 miles
from Nantucket. It is noted for the purity and salubrity of its air,
and is much resorted to in summer by the denizens of Nantucket. On
Sankoty Head, 1 mile N. of Siasconset, there is a lighthouse, and from
the eminence on which it stands the broad Atlantic Ocean is visible on
all sides of the island.

33. Boston to Hoosac Tunnel and Troy.

Via Fitchburg R. R.   Distance, to Hoosac Tunnel, 136 miles; to North Adams,
143 miles.

As far as and including **Fitchburg** (50 miles), this route has been
described in Route 27. (There is another division of the Fitchburg
R. R., passing through Framingham, S. Marlboro, and Clinton, by which
the distance from Boston to Fitchburg is only 37 miles). Soon after
leaving Fitchburg the train reaches *Wachusett*, whence stages run in
6 miles to **Mt. Wachusett,** from the summit of which (2,480 ft. high)
there is one of the grandest views to be obtained in all New England.
It is said that 300 villages and portions of 6 States are included in it.
Stations, *Ashburnham* (60 miles), *Gardner* (65 miles), *Baldwinville* (71
miles), and *Athol* (83 miles). *Miller's Falls* (98 miles), where the Connecticut and Deerfield Rivers are crossed, and the beautiful village of
Greenfield (106 miles) have been described in Route 28. Beyond
Greenfield the route follows the Deerfield River, passing amid extremely
picturesque scenery, the most striking feature of which is the narrow
and romantic * Deerfield Gorge, traversed just before reaching the village of *Shelburne Falls* (119 miles). At Shelburne Falls the Deerfield
River makes a descent of 150 ft. in a few hundred yards, roaring through
a narrow channel. The scenery beyond is very charming, and at
Charlemont (128 miles) the Hoosac Mountains are in full view. Passing now for 8 miles through a savage, rugged, and desolate region, the
train stops for a moment at Hoosac Tunnel Station, and then plunges
into the profound darkness of the tunnel. The * **Hoosac Tunnel** is,
next to that under Mt. Cenis, the longest in the world, and is one of the
most wonderful achievements of modern engineering. It pierces the
solid micaceous slate of the Hoosac Mountain, is 4¾ miles long, was
nearly 20 years in constructing (1855 to 1874), and cost the State of
Mass. about $16,000,000. The cut-stone façade of the entrance is
worthy of notice.

Just beyond the W. end of the tunnel is the town of *N. Adams* (see p. 151).
Here connection is made with the Troy & Boston R. R , which runs past Williamstown (see p. 151), Pownal, Petersburg, Hoosic Falls, Johnsonville, and Lansingburg
to **Troy** (in 48 miles). This forms the new through route between Boston and the
West, to obtain which the vast expenditures for the Hoosac Tunnel were incurred.

34. Boston to Albany and the West.

Via Boston & Albany R. R.   Distance to Albany, 200 miles.

THIS is the most popular passenger route from Boston to the West, and traverses some of the most attractive portions of New England. The Boston & Albany R. R. was among the first constructed in America, being completed to Worcester in 1835, to Springfield in 1839, and to Albany in 1842. Its completion was the occasion of festivities in both Boston and Albany, the memory of which has not yet died out. As far as **Springfield** (98 miles) the route is the same as Route 11 taken in reverse. Immediately after leaving Springfield the train crosses the Connecticut River on a long bridge, and follows the Agawam River to **Westfield** (*Willmarth House, Central*), a beautiful village on the bank of the river, surrounded by hills. In the center of the village is a neat public square, surrounded by churches and other buildings, and adorned with a handsome soldiers' monument. The State Normal School here has a wide reputation. The New Haven & Northampton R. R. crosses here. Beyond Westfield the route leads up Westfield River, amid picturesque scenery, which rapidly becomes mountainous. At *Chester* (28 miles from Springfield) the grades become very heavy, and the train enters the Berkshire hills, which are described in Route 36. The scenery along all this portion of the route is extremely fine, and at Summit the track is 1,211 ft. above the sea. *Beeket, Washington,* and *Hinsdale* are high-perched mountain towns; and *Dalton* (146 miles from Boston) is a manufacturing village on the W. side of the range of hills that has just been crossed. Five miles beyond Dalton, in the heart of the Berkshire hills, is **Pittsfield** (described in Route 36). Three miles beyond Pittsfield is *Shaker Village*, one of the settlements of the curious sect of Shakers; and a short distance N. of the village is the mountain where, according to tradition, the Shakers hunted Satan through a long summer night, and finally killed and buried him. Eleven miles beyond Pittsfield the road crosses the State line and enters New York State, running by *Chatham*, where connection is made with the Harlem R. R. and the Hudson & Boston R. R., *Kinderhook*, and *Schodack* to *Greenbush*, whence the train crosses a fine bridge and enters **Albany** (see p. 63).

35. Albany to Rutland.

a. Via Rensselaer & Saratoga Railroad.   Distance, 100 miles.

FROM Albany to *Whitehall* (76 miles) this route is described in Route 40. Beyond Whitehall the line runs N. E. to *Fairhaven* (85 miles), where there are extensive slate-quarries, and *Hydeville* (86 miles), a pretty village at the foot of *Lake Bomoseen*, a beautiful sheet of water, 8 miles long and 1 to 1½ wide, famed for its boating and fishing. Four miles farther is **Castleton** (*Lake Bomoseen House*), a neatly built village, situated on a plain near the Castleton River, and surrounded by pleasing scenery. The township in which it is located is noted for its

7

slate-stone, which is extensively quarried, and from which is made an imitation of marble "so perfect that it challenges the closest scrutiny." There are 5 churches in the village and a State Normal School. *W. Rutland* (96 miles) is noted for its vast marble-works, and stages run thence in 4 miles to *Clarendon Springs* (see p. 131). **Rutland** (100 miles) has already been described (see p. 131.)

b. Via Rutland & Washing:on Div. of the Hudson Canal Co.'s R. R. Distance, 98 miles.

As far as *Eagle Bridge* (23 miles) this route follows the Troy & Boston R. R., passing *Lansingburg*, a thriving manufacturing village on the Hudson River, and *Schaghticoke* (13 miles), a manufacturing village on the Hoosic River, which furnishes a fine water-power. *Salem* (41 miles) is a pretty village on White Creek. From this station the road makes a détour into Vermont, and runs near the boundary for some miles until at *Granville* (60 miles) it again enters New York, finally leaving the State near Poultney (68 miles). **Poultney** (*Poultney House, Beaman's*) is a beautiful village, noted for its coolness in summer, and then much resorted to. It lies amid varied and picturesque scenery, and the walks and drives in the vicinity are very attractive. Among its many pleasant excursions are those to the *Gorge*, the *Bowl, Carter's Falls, Lake Bomoseen* (see p. 145), and *Lake St. Catherine* (or Austin). The latter is 3 miles from Poultney, is about 6 miles long, and has a summer hotel at its lower end. Daily stages run in eight miles to **Middletown Springs** (*Montvert Hotel*), one of the most famous mineral springs in Vermont. The waters are impregnated with iron, and are an excellent tonic. Two miles beyond Poultney the present route connects with the preceding one at Castleton, and proceeds to Rutland in 12 miles.

36. The Housatonic Valley and the Berkshire Hills.

The point of departure for the trip up the Housatonic is **Bridgeport**, Conn., which is reached from New York *via* Route 11 (fare, $1.70) or by steamboat daily from Pier 35 East River (fare, $1). From Bridgeport to Pittsfield the distance is 110 miles, and the fare $3.30. But the through fare from New York to Pittsfield is only $3.50.

THE Housatonic River rises in Berkshire Co., Massachusetts, and flowing S. enters the State of Connecticut, where, after winding through Litchfield Co., and forming the boundary between New Haven and Fairfield Counties, it meets the tide-water at Derby, about 14 miles from Long Island Sound. The sources of the stream are more than 1,200 ft. above the level of the sea, and in its course of 150 miles it offers some exquisitely beautiful scenery. The Housatonic Railway runs along its bank for about 75 miles. "Of all the railroads near New York," says Mr. Beecher in his "Star Papers," "none can compare, for beauty of scenery, with the Housatonic, from Newtown up to Pittsfield, but especially from New Milford to Lenox."

Bridgeport, our point of departure, has already been described (see p. 68). For some miles after leaving Bridgeport the route traverses a level and thinly settled country, destitute of picturesque features; but at *Newtown* (19 miles) the hills begin to show mountainous symptoms, and the traveler obtains glimpses of forest-clad hills and lovely intervales. **New Milford** (35 miles) is a large and beautiful village, with broad, well-shaded streets, and surrounded by delightful scenery. It has some popularity as a summer resort, and is also the site of several manufactories. From New Milford to the terminus of the road, the scenery is ever changing and of rare beauty. **Kent** (48 miles, *Elmore House*) is a quiet little village, with the river running through it, situated in the midst of the charming Kent Plains. Hatch and Swift Lakes or Ponds are visible from the cars; and on a lofty plateau W. of Kent are the *Spectacle Ponds*, a pair of twin lakelets, of oval shape, fringed by dense woods and connected by a narrow strait. From the lofty hill just above them the view is grand. *Cornwall Bridge* (57 miles) is a small manufacturing village surrounded by exquisite scenery. Daily stages run thence to *Litchfield*, said to be the most beautiful village in Connecticut, and to *Sharon*. From *W. Cornwall* (61 miles) stages run to *Goshen*, a pretty highland town, celebrated for its butter and cheese. **Falls Village** (67 miles, *Dudley House*) is at the Great Falls of the Housatonic, which are the largest and finest in the State, descending 60 ft. over a ledge of limestone. About 2 miles N. W. of the village is *Mt. Prospect* (reached by carriage-road), from the summit of which there is a fine view over the valley and the out-lying villages. At the foot of this hill is a deep, dark, and ugly fissure in the rocks, known as the *Wolf's Den*. Stages run from Falls Village to **Salisbury** (*Maple Shade Hotel, Barnard House*), situated in the township of the same name, and noted for its varied and beautiful scenery.

In his "Star Papers," Mr. Beecher writes lovingly of all this region, and we quote a paragraph which may prove useful to the tourist: "If one has not the leisure for detailed exploration, and can spend but a week, let him begin, say, at *Sharon* (reached by stage from Cornwall Bridge on the Housatonic R. R.) or at *Salisbury*. On either side to the E. and to the W. ever-varying mountain-forms frame the horizon. There is a constant succession of hills swelling into mountains, and of mountains flowing down into hills. The hues of green in the trees, in grasses, and in various harvests, are endlessly contrasted. There are no forests so beautiful as those made up of both evergreen and deciduous trees. At Salisbury, you come under the shadow of the Taconic range. Here you may well spend a week, for the sake of the rides and the objects of curiosity. Four miles to the E. are the Falls of the Housatonic, very beautiful and worthy of much longer study than they usually get. . . . On the W. of Salisbury you ascend *Mt. Riga* to *Bald Peak*, thence to *Brace Mountain*, thence to the *Dome*, thence to that grand ravine and its wild water, *Bash-Bish*, a ride in all of about 18 miles, and wholly along the mountain-bowl. On the E. side of this range, and about 4 miles from Salisbury, is *Sage's Ravine*, which is the antithesis of *Bash-Bish*. Sage's Ravine, not without grandeur, has its principal attractions in its beauty; Bash-Bish, far from destitute of

beauty, is yet most remarkable for grandeur. I would willingly make
the journey once a month to see either of them. Just beyond Sage's
Ravine, very beautiful falls may be seen just after heavy rains, which
have been named *Norton's Falls.* Besides these and other mountain
scenery, there are the *Twin Lakes* on the N. of Salisbury, and the two
lakes on the S., around which the rides are extremely beautiful."

Just beyond *Canaan* (73 miles), a pretty village at the intersection
of the Housatonic and Connecticut Western Railways, the train crosses
the boundary-line of Massachusetts and enters the renowned

Berkshire Hills,

" a region not surpassed in picturesque loveliness, throughout its whole
longitude of 50 miles and its average latitude of 20 miles, by any equal
area in New England, and perhaps not in all this Western world."
From *Sheffield* (138 miles), a quiet town at the base of the Taconic
Mountains, the ascent of *Mt. Washington* is easily made and affords a
far-viewing prospect. This mountain was once a part of the great
Livingston Manor, and its summit overlooks the rich and lordly domain
once included in that now forgotten name. Six miles above Sheffield is
Great Barrington (*Berkshire House, Collins House, Miller's Hotel*), of
which Mr. Beecher says that it "is one of those places which one never
enters without wishing never to leave it. It rests beneath the branches
of great numbers of the stateliest elms. It is a place to be desired
as a summer residence." The Congregational and Episcopal Churches,
and the High-School, are handsome buildings, and there are several fine
villas in the outskirts. *South Egremont,* 4 miles S. E. of Great Barrington, is reached by daily stage from Great Barrington and also by 6
miles' staging from Hillsdale on the Harlem R. R. The *Mt. Everett
House* here is an excellent summer hotel, situated just under the lofty
crest of Mt. Everett, whose summit may be scaled by way of " its vast,
uncultivated slope, to a height of 2,000 ft." On the summit is a village of about 250 inhabitants, and the view is exceedingly fine, taking
in half the whole stretch of the Housatonic Valley, the Catskills, and
the Hudson. The trout-fishing in the vicinity of S. Egremont is exceptionally good. The *Berkshire Soda Springs* are about 3 miles S. E.
of Great Barrington, amid wild and romantic scenery. "Next to the
north of Great Barrington," says Mr. Beecher, "is **Stockbridge,**
famed for its meadow-elms, for the picturesque beauty adjacent, for
the quiet beauty of a village which sleeps along a level plain just under
the rim of hills. If you wish to be filled and satisfied with the serenest
delight, ride to the summit of this encircling hill-ridge, in a summer's
afternoon, while the sun is but an hour high. The Housatonic winds
in great circuits, all through the valley, carrying willows and alders
with it wherever it goes. The horizon on every side is piled and terraced with mountains. Abrupt and isolated mountains bolt up here
and there over the whole stretch of plain, covered with evergreens."
The distance by railway from Great Barrington to Stockbridge is 8
miles, but it is only 6½ miles by the highway, and this latter should be

chosen, if the tourist have time. The entire ride is through the most delightful scenery, and about half way is *Monument Mountain*, one of the special attractions of the vicinity. The view from the summit is very fine, resembling that from Mt. Everett. Stockbridge contains many handsome villa residences. The *Stockbridge House* is an excellent hotel, open only in summer. It is situated on the main street of the village, and near by are an elegant Italian fountain, a fine soldiers' monument, a memorial monument to Jonathan Edwards, and the house in which that famous divine wrote his celebrated treatise on "The Freedom of the Will." Among the most interesting features of Stockbridge are the old burying-ground of the Mohegan Indians, and the fine antique mansion built by Judge Theodore Sedgwick and afterward occupied by his famous daughter Catharine. There is a handsome stone library building containing 5,000 volumes, and the Hon. David Dudley Field has presented the town with a bell-tower of stone, containing a silvery chime of bells and a clock. The Episcopal and Congregational Churches are noteworthy structures, and on the heights above the village is an old Mission-House, erected early in the last century. The view from these heights is one of the loveliest imaginable. The drives in the vicinity of Stockbridge are extremely picturesque, and there are several points of interest besides Monument Mountain, already mentioned. About 3 miles N. is *Lake Mahkeenac* (formerly called "Stockbridge Bowl"), a capacious basin of crystal-clear water, on whose margin Hawthorne once lived for a year and a half. About 1½ mile from the village is the wonderful *Ice-Glen*, piercing the northern spur of Bear Mountain. "In its long and awesome corridors and crypts, formed by massive and gloomy rocks, and huge but prostrate trees, the explorer may sometimes find masses of ice in the heart and heat of midsummer."

Six miles N. of Stockbridge is the flourishing town of **Lee** (*Morgan House, Norton*), which owes its prosperity to its extensive paper-mills and woolen fabrics. It is also celebrated for its marble, which is among the best in the world. Large quantities of it were used in constructing the new portions of the Capitol at Washington. The village contains several fine churches and private residences, and there are many attractive drives in the vicinity. That down the valley of the Hopbrook and up the mountain to *Monterey* is said not to be excelled in beauty in any part of Europe. Three miles beyond Lee we come to **Lenox** (*Curtis's Hotel*), a favorite resort of Bostonians and New Yorkers. It is a place of little business, except in that part called the Furnace, which lies near the railway, and contains extensive factories of plate-glass and iron ; but it "is known for the singular purity and exhilarating effects of its air, and for the beauty of its mountain scenery." Beecher's "Star Papers," from which the above is a quotation, were written in a house which stood near the site now occupied by General Rathbone's mansion. Fanny Kemble Butler, who long resided here, said of the graveyard at Lenox : "I will not rise to trouble any one if they will let me sleep there. I will only ask to be permitted, once in a while, to raise my head and look out upon this glorious scene." Lenox having ceased to be the shire town of the county the former court-house has been transformed into a handsome building containing a library, public hall, club-rooms, etc. There are numerous pleasant excursions from Lenox, a popular one being to the summit of *Bald Head* (carriages all the way), which commands a very fine view of the village, and of the valley to the south, including Monument Mountain. Other excursions are to the *Ledge, Richmond Hill,* and *Perry's Peak.* This isolated summit is 6 miles from the town, over 2,000 ft. high, and overlooks a vast range of country from the Catskills to the Green Mountains.

Six miles above Lenox (110 from Bridgeport, and 151 from Boston *via* Route 34) is **Pittsfield** (*American House, Burbank's*), a flourishing city of 13,000 inhabitants, the capital of the Berkshire region. It is beautifully situated on a lofty plateau, with the Taconics on the W. and the Hoosacs on the E. ; and contains many handsome public and commercial buildings and private dwellings. The new *Court-House* is a costly white-marble edifice, and the *Roman Catholic Church* is the finest in Western Massachusetts. There are several other handsome churches, including the spacious and costly *Methodist Church,* and the *Maplewood Female Seminary* comprises several admirable buildings situated in the midst of charming grounds. In the park, near the center of the town, is a *Soldiers' Monument,* which was dedicated with imposing ceremonies on September 24, 1872. The * *Berkshire Athenœum* is a unique building of bluestone, freestone, and red granite, and contains a valuable library, museum, cabinets, and reading-rooms, all free and open constantly. The drives in the vicinity of Pittsfield are very fine, especially those to Williamstown (20 miles), described below, and to Lebanon Springs (9 miles). On the charming mountain-road thither is *Lake Onota,* a lovely and romantic sheet of water, about 2 miles W. of Pittsfield, and a favorite excursion. Other drives which the stranger should not miss are those to *Wahconah Falls,* in Windsor (10 miles), and to *Potter's Mountain* (6 miles). *Ashley Pond,* from which the water-supply of the town is drawn, lies E. on the crest of the Washington Hills; and near by is *Roaring Brook,* a wild mountain-torrent that dashes down the side of the mountain in a rugged cleft known as *Tories' Gorge.* N. of Onota, on the slopes of the Taconics, are the romantic *Lulu Cascade ; Balance Rock,* a huge and nicely poised bowlder ; and, on the plateau of a giant crest above, a lovely mountain lakelet called *Berry Pond.* About 3 miles N. of Pittsfield is *Pontoosuc Lake,* once known as Lanesboro Pond, and about 2½ miles S. is the *South Mountain,* from the summit of which there is a fine view. **Lebanon Springs** (mentioned above) are among the most famous and frequented in the country, and the waters are regarded as remedial for rheumatism, liver-complaint, and cutaneous affections. Two miles from the Springs is **Shaker Village,** founded over a century ago by the disciples of Ann Lee, and now the headquarters of the "Millennial Church." On Sundays their singular form of worship may be witnessed.

At Pittsfield the Housatonic R. R. comes to an end, and the region N. of it (known as "Northern Berkshire") is penetrated by the Pittsfield & North Adams Branch R. R., which we shall now follow as far

as Williamstown. If the tourist have time he can make his trip much
more enjoyable by hiring a suitable conveyance and taking the highways instead of the railway. The road from Pittsfield to Williamstown
(20 miles) presents a continuous panorama of beautiful scenery, and
other drives are scarcely less attractive. On the railroad, the first
noteworthy station above Pittsfield is *Cheshire* (9 miles), famous for
butter, cheese, and lumber. For 50 years the inhabitants were almost
unanimously democratic in politics ; and, to show their appreciation of
President Jefferson, they made him a present, on January 1, 1802, of
an enormous cheese weighing 1,450 pounds. From this point to N.
Adams the road follows the valley of the Hoosac River, with the lofty
Saddleback Range on the W. for the greater part of the way. *South
Adams* (7 miles from Cheshire) is the best point from which to visit
✳ Greylock Mountain, which rises majestically over the valley to the
height of 3,500 ft., and is the highest elevation in Massachusetts. The
ascent is tedious and difficult, but the view from the summit is surpassingly grand, taking in all the Berkshire Hills, the valleys of the
Hoosac and Housatonic, the Green Mountains on the N., and the Catskills on the S., and Mounts Monadnock, Tom, and Holyoke. There is
a still longer and more difficult but very romantic route to the top of
Greylock from North Adams. Four miles above South Adams is
North Adams (*Wilson House, Richmond House, Commercial*), a busy
manufacturing village, where "Chinese cheap labor" has been a specialty and a success for years in the shoe-shops. It is the metropolis
of Northern Berkshire, and is even more thickly studded about with
wild and romantic spots than its southern sister. About a mile E. of
the village is the *Natural Bridge,* a vast roof of marble through and
under which Hudson's Brook has excavated a tunnel 15 ft. wide and
150 long. In the ravine of this brook there are several picturesque
points ; but next in interest to the bridge itself is a strange, columnar
group of rocks, which at its overhanging crest assumes the aspect of
gigantic features, and is called *Profile Rock.* The *Cascade* is in a romantic glen 1½ mile from the hotel, and is 30 ft. high. About 2 miles
S. is the W. entrance to the famous **Hoosac Tunnel** (see p. 144).
The old stage-road across the Hoosacs from N. Adams to the E. end of
the tunnel (8 miles) affords an interesting mountain-drive. Hawthorne
says of it : "I have never driven through such romantic scenery,
where there were such variety and boldness of mountain-shapes as
this ; and, though it was a sunny day, the mountains diversified the
view with sunshine and shadow, glory and gloom."

Five miles W. of North Adams is the academic **Williamstown**
(*Mansion House*), beautifully situated in a mountain-inclosed valley, and
noted as the site of *Williams College,* founded in 1793, and a highly
prosperous institution. The college buildings are the only architectural
features of the town, and embrace 10 or 12 structures, of which the finest
is Goodrich Hall. The library of 20,000 volumes is in Lawrence Hall ;
and the residence of President Chadbourne is opposite West College, on
the main street. Near by is *Mills's Park*, an inclosure of 10 acres, in
which a marble shaft, surmounted by a globe, marks the spot where

Samuel J. Mills and his associate students met by a haystack in 1807
to consecrate themselves to the work of foreign missions.   There is a
bronze soldiers' monument on a granite pedestal in the main street.
Among the many attractive resorts in the vicinity of Williamstown are
Flora's Glen, where Bryant, then a student at Williams College, wrote
"Thanatopsis"; the *Cascades*, and *Snow Glen*, a gorge in the mountain where the snow never entirely melts.   At *Sand Springs*, 1½ mile
N. of the village, is an excellent summer hotel called *Greylock Hall*.
The waters of the spring are thought to be efficacious in cutaneous diseases, and bathing-houses are provided for their use.   *Mount Hopkins*
(2,800 ft. high) is a short distance S. of Williamstown, and is often
ascended for its broad and striking view.   The ascent of Greylock is
often made from this side.   *The Hopper* is a stupendous gorge between
Greylock, Prospect, and Bald Mountains, through which flows the picturesque Money Brook.   In the remote recesses of this wild gorge is a
series of cascades said to be the finest in Berkshire.

37. New York to Vermont via Harlem R. R.

THE Harlem R. R. is no longer available as a through route between
New York and Albany, but in connection with the Harlem Extension
R. R. forms a short and popular route to Vermont and the North.   It
skirts the eastern portions of all those counties lying upon the Hudson
River and traversed by the Hudson River R. R. (see Route 9).   The
stations and towns along the line are, for the most part, inconsiderable
places, many of them having grown up with the road.   The country
traversed is varied and picturesque in surface, much of it being rich
agricultural land; but it does not compare with the river route in
scenic attractions.

Leaving the Grand Central Depot, the train passes through long
tunnels under the city, and at Harlem (4 miles) crosses the Harlem
River.   *Fordham* (9 miles) is the seat of St. John's College, a noted
Jesuit institution; and 1½ mile W. is **Jerome Park,** the finest race-
course in America.   *Williams Bridge* (10½ miles) is at the junction
with the New York & New Haven R. R. (see Route 11).   One mile
beyond is *Woodlawn Cemetery*, one of the most beautiful near New
York.   *White Plains* (22 miles) was the scene of the eventful Revolutionary battle of Oct. 28, 1776.   Stations, *Chappaqua* (32 miles), *Bedford* (39 miles), and *Katonah* (41 miles).   From *Golden's Bridge* (44
miles), a branch road runs in 7 miles to **Lake Mahopac,** a highly
popular summer resort.   The lake is 1,000 ft. above the sea, is 9 miles
in circumference, with very irregular shores, and is the center of a
group of 22 lakes, lying within a circle of 12 miles' radius, and amid
pleasing scenery.   The boating on the lakes is excellent, and the fishing good.   The drives are fine, and there are many pleasant excursions.
The leading hotel, the *Gregory House*, was burned down in 1878.
Thompson's Hotel is first class, and there are many boarding-houses.

Beyond Golden's Bridge, the train passes the small stations of
Brewster's (52 miles), *Paterson* (60 miles), *Pawling* (64), and *Dover*

Plains (77). Beyond the latter, the scenery becomes mountainous and fine. From *Amenia* (85 miles), stages run in 3 miles to *Sharon* (see p. 147) ; and at *Boston Corners* (99 miles) the Berkshire Hills come in sight on the right. *Copake* (105 miles) is only 2 miles from the Bash-Bish Fall (see p. 147). At *Chatham Four Corners* (127 miles) connection is made with the Boston & Albany R. R. (see Route 34), by which the distance to Albany is 24 miles. Connection is also made here with the *Harlem Extension R. R.*, which runs N. in 58 miles to Bennington, Vt., where connection is made with the Bennington & Rutland R. R., which runs in 55 miles to Rutland. Nineteen miles beyond Chatham Four Corners the train reaches **Lebanon Springs** (see p. 150). At *Petersburg* (166 miles) the Troy & Boston R. R. is intersected, and shortly beyond the train enters the State of Vermont, and soon reaches **Bennington** (*Putnam House, Gates House*), one of the prettiest towns in the State. It is situated in a picturesque mountain-inclosed valley, 800 ft. above the sea, is solidly and handsomely built, and contains about 7,000 inhabitants. Manufacturing is extensively carried on, the chief products being cotton goods and knit underclothing. *Bennington Center*, one mile distant, is the Revolutionary village, and was the site of the old Catamount Tavern which was burned in 1871. *Hoosac*, New York, the adjoining township, was the scene of the battle of Bennington (Aug. 16, 1777), in which a detachment of the British forces under Col. Baum was utterly defeated by the Green Mountain Boys, led by the intrepid Col. Stark. About 2 miles from Bennington, by footpath (4½ by carriage-road), is * *Mt. Anthony*, on whose summit is a tower from which a broad and beautiful view may be obtained. Among numerous and pleasant drives in the vicinity are those to *Petersburg*, to *Prospect Mt.*, and to *Big Pond*.

Between Bennington and Rutland a mountainous region, affording much pleasing scenery, is traversed. There are several pretty towns *en route*, of which the only one requiring mention is **Manchester** (*Equinox House, Elm House, Taconic Hotel*), a beautiful village nestling in a valley between the Green and Equinox ranges. Many visitors are attracted thither in summer by its pure and invigorating air, fine scenery, trout-fishing, and driving. A noticeable feature of the village is its white-marble pavements, there being numerous marble quarries in the vicinity. *Mt. Æolus* is 5 miles from the village, and to the S. E. is *Stratton Mountain*. Near the latter is *Stratton Gap*, a beautiful glen, which furnished the subject of one of A. B. Durand's best paintings. * **Mt. Equinox** (3,706 ft. above the sea) is ascended by a road from the village, and is noted for its glorious views, the following points being visible in clear weather : Lakes George and Champlain, Kearsarge and the Franconia Mountains in New Hampshire, Greylock in Massachusetts, Killington Peak in Vermont, and the Catskill Mountains and Saratoga village in New York. *Skinner Hollow* is a deep gulf on the S. side of the mountain, containing a cave in which the snow never entirely melts, a stream which finds an outlet through a cavern, and a marble-quarry. **Rutland** (240 miles) is described on page 131.

38. New York to Buffalo and Niagara Falls.

Via New York Central and Hudson River R. R.   Distance to Buffalo, 440 miles;
fare, $9.25.   To Niagara Falls, 449 miles; fare, $9.25.

FROM New York City to Albany (143 miles) this route has already
been described in Route 9.   The railway runs close along the E. bank
of the Hudson River, affording good views of the river itself and of the
opposite bank, but losing many of the most attractive views described
in connection with the steamboat journey.   Seats on the left-hand side
of the cars should be obtained going N. ; on the right-hand side going
S.   At Albany the Hudson River R. R. ends.   The New York Central
R. R. traverses from E. to W. the entire length of New York State,
passing through the rich midland counties.   It has two termini at the
E. end, one at Albany and the other at Troy, the branches meeting
after 17 miles at Schenectady.   It then continues in one line to Syracuse (148 miles from Albany) where it again divides and is a double
route to Rochester, whence the Niagara Falls branch diverges to the
Falls and the main line passes on to Buffalo.   The great Erie Canal
traverses the State from Albany to Buffalo nearly on the same line
with the railroad, and often in sight from the cars.   The quadruple
tracks of the road are laid with steel rails, and Wagner drawing-
room and sleeping-cars are attached to the through trains.

Leaving Albany (which is described on p. 63) the train passes *W.
Albany*, with its extensive machine-shops and cattle-yards, and in 17
miles reaches **Schenectady** (*Carley House, Given's Hotel*), a city of
13,000 inhabitants, situated on the right bank of the Mohawk River, on
a spot which once formed the council grounds of the Mohawks.   It is
one of the oldest towns in the State, a trading port having been established here by the Dutch in 1620, and is distinguished as the seat of
Union College, founded in 1795, and now an important institution.
Here the Rensselaer & Saratoga R. R. diverges and leads to Saratoga
Springs and Lakes George and Champlain (see Route 40).   Leaving
Schenectady, the train crosses the Mohawk River and the Erie Canal
on a bridge nearly 1,000 ft. long, and traverses a rich farming country
to *Amsterdam* (33 miles) and *Fonda* (44 miles).   From Fonda a railway runs in 26 miles to *Northville*, where connection is made with
daily stages which run in 29 miles to *Lake Pleasant* in the Adirondack
region (see p. 195).   From *Palatine Bridge* (55 miles) stages run in 10
miles to *Sharon Springs* (see p. 219).   *Fort Plain* (58 miles) is a flourishing village 2 miles from old Fort Plain of Revolutionary memory ; and
St. Johnsville (64 miles) is a prosperous manufacturing town on the
banks of the Mohawk, with fine scenery in the vicinity.   Ten miles
beyond is **Little Falls** (*Benton House*), which is remarkable for a
bold passage of the river and canal through a wild and most picturesque
defile.   The river falls 45 ft. in half a mile, and affords a water-power
which is extensively used in manufactures.   Twelve miles S. W. of
Little Falls is *Richfield Springs* (see p. 226).   Stations, *Herkimer* (81
miles) and *Ilion* (83 miles), and then (95 miles from Albany) comes the
large and handsome city of **Utica** (*Butterfield House, Bagg's, Ameri-*

can), situated on the S. bank of the Mohawk, on the site of old Fort Schuyler (built in 1756). The city has about 35,000 inhabitants, extensive and varied manufactures, and is the center of an important railway and canal system. Genesee St. is the leading thoroughfare; on it are the handsome *City Hall* and many fine commercial buildings, churches, and private residences. The *State Lunatic Asylum*, which holds a high rank among institutions of the kind, is a spacious building on a farm W. of the city (reached by horse-cars).

An easy and popular excursion from Utica is *via* Utica and Black River R. R. to Trenton Falls (distance 17 miles, fare 75c.). **** Trenton Falls** (*Moore's Trenton Falls Hotel, Perkins House*) are situated on the W. Canada (or Kanata) Creek, a tributary of the Mohawk. The descent of the stream, 312 ft. in a distance of 2 miles, is by a series of half a dozen cataracts, which have worn for themselves out of the limestone hills a bed which at some points is 200 ft. below the level of the surrounding country. The ravine is very narrow, with precipitous walls, and the path along the bottom, which was hewn out at considerable cost and is kept in admirable order by Mr. Moore, is passable only at low water. During high water the path along the cliff must be followed, and affords some striking views of the profound chasm below and of the torrent which in time of flood rages along with the force and tumult of a Niagara. It is difficult to say whether the falls are most impressive in times of high or of low water, but those who can should see them under both conditions. The usual way of visiting them is by a stairway which descends the precipice a few rods from Moore's Hotel (fee, 25c.). From the platform at the foot a pathway, difficult in places but entirely safe, leads up the ravine past **Sherman's Fall* (33 ft. high), **High Falls* (40 ft. high and extremely beautiful), *Mill Dam Fall* (14 ft. high), and the **Alhambra*, a great natural hall or amphitheatre which "has been the despair of artists and descriptive writers." At *Rocky Heart* most visitors turn back, but the adventurous may pass on to *Prospect Fall* (20 ft. high), at the head of the chasm. An easier way of reaching Prospect Fall is by a walk or drive of 3 miles along the cliff from the hotel.

Beyond Trenton Falls the Utica & Black River R. R. runs N. to *Sackett's Harbor* (104 miles from Utica) on Lake Ontario, and to *Clayton* (108 miles) and *Ogdensburg* (134 miles) on the St. Lawrence River. From Clayton steamers run in connection with the trains to **Alexandria Bay** (see Route 56). *Boonville* (35 miles from Utica) is the most convenient entrance to the **John Brown Tract**, which forms the S. portion of the great Adirondack wilderness, and being still unsettled and comparatively little visited, affords admirable sport both in hunting and fishing. Guides and outfit may be obtained at Boonville. The *Fulton Lakes* (see p. 190) are 26 miles N. E. of Boonville, and there are many other lakes in the vicinity abounding in fish.

Beyond Utica the train passes in 14 miles to **Rome** (*Stanwix Hall, Commercial Hotel*), a thriving city of 11,000 inhabitants at the junction of the present route with the Rome, Watertown & Ogdensburg R. R. and of the Erie and Black River canals. Large railroad shops and rolling-mills are located here, there is excellent water-power, and Rome

is one of the best lumber-markets in the State. There are a few fine
buildings, of which the *Seminary* is the handsomest.

The *Rome, Watertown & Ogdensburg R. R.* runs N. W. from Rome to *Watertown* (72 miles), *Cape Vincent* (96 miles), and *Ogdensburg* (see Route 56), 142 miles.
From Cape Vincent a steamer runs twice daily in summer to *Alexandria Bay* (see
Route 56), and there is a steam-ferry to *Kingston* Can. This is the favorite route
from New York to Kingston, Alexandria Bay, and the Thousand Islands. Fare
from New York to Cape Vincent, $8.20.

Leaving Rome the train passes *Verona* (118 miles), with a mineral
spring, and *Oneida* (122 miles), which is about 6 miles from **Oneida
Lake,** a beautiful sheet of water 19 miles long and 6 miles wide,
abounding in fish, and surrounded by a highly-cultivated country.
Chittenango (133 miles, *White Sulphur Springs Hotel*) lies at the
entrance of the deep and narrow valley through which the waters of
Cazenovia Lake are discharged into Oneida Lake, and is noted for its
iron and sulphur springs, which are much frequented by invalids. The
hotel and cottages will accommodate about 100 guests. Fifteen miles
beyond Chittenango is **Syracuse** (*Vanderbilt House, Globe Hotel, Congress Hall*), one of the largest of the interior cities, with a population
of about 50,000, and important manufactures and trade. It is pleasantly situated at the S. end of *Onondaga Lake* (which is 6 miles long
and about 1½ wide) and is regularly laid out and handsomely built.
The City Hall, County Court-House, High School, St. Vincent's Asylum,
and State Asylum for Idiots are all fine buildings. The Penitentiary is
a vast structure on a hill a mile N. E. of the city. The *Syracuse University* (Methodist) has a very fine building on a hill to the E., which commands a beautiful view. The famous *Salt Springs*, the most extensive
in America, are on the shore of the lake N. W. of the city (reached by
horse-cars). Between Syracuse and Rochester the N. Y. Central R. R.
has two lines: the "Old Route" *via* Canandaigua, 104 miles long, and
the "New Route," 81 miles long. The through trains follow the latter, but we shall describe both.

Syracuse to Rochester via "New Route."

This is the route followed by the through trains, but it is less interesting than the other. It runs parallel with the Erie Canal nearly all
the way through a level country, with numerous small towns along
the line, but none that require mention. *Lyons* (193 miles) is the
largest, and is a pretty village of 3,500 inhabitants, capital of Wayne
Co., which produces more dried fruit than any other in the country.
In a hillside near *Palmyra* (207 miles) Joe Smith claimed to have
found the golden plates of the Mormon Bible. *Rochester* (229 miles)
is described below.

Syracuse to Rochester via "Old Route."

The distance by this route (Auburn Division) is 104 miles, and is
traversed only by local trains. Leaving Syracuse the train passes several minor stations, and in 17 miles reaches *Skaneateles*, a thriving village at the foot of *** Skaneateles Lake,** a charming water 16 miles

long and 1 to 1½ wide, 860 ft. above the sea, and surrounded by hills
rising 1,200 ft. above the surface. Boating and fishing are excellent,
and the lake is much visited in summer, when a small steamer plies
between Skaneateles and the village of *Glen Haven* at the S. end.
About 10 miles S. E. of Skaneateles is the picturesque and romantic
Otisco Lake, 4 miles long and embosomed amid lofty hills. Eight miles
beyond Skaneateles is **Auburn** (*Osborne House, Gaylord House*), a
handsomely built city of 18,000 inhabitants situated near Owasco Lake,
which finds its outlet through the town. Genesee St. is the principal
thoroughfare, and nearly all the streets are pleasantly shaded. On
Genesee St. is the handsome *County Court-House;* and the churches of
St. Peter (Episcopal), *St. Mary's* (Roman Catholic), and the *First Presbyterian* are very fine edifices. The *Theological Seminary* (Presbyterian) has substantial stone buildings in the N. E. part of the city.
Near the depot is the vast and massive *Auburn State Prison*, covering
18 acres of ground, which are enclosed by a stone wall 30 ft. high.
Auburn was long the home of the late Wm. H. Seward, and his grave
is in the pleasant cemetery on Fort Hill (reached by Fort St.). **Owasco Lake** is 3 miles S. of Auburn, and is a favorite summer resort
with the citizens. It is 11 miles long and about a mile wide, and is
surrounded in part by bold hills. A little steamer plies in summer
between *Owasco Village* (Bennington House) and *Moravia* (Skidmore
House).

At *Cayuga* (11 miles beyond Auburn) the train crosses Cayuga
Lake by a bridge nearly a mile long, affording a fine view from the
cars to the left. From this point the Cayuga Lake R. R. runs S. in
38 miles to Ithaca, and steamboats also ply upon the lake. **Cayuga
Lake** is 38 miles long and from 1 to 3¼ wide, and affords every variety
of sport in the way of fishing, boating, sailing, and bathing. At the N.
end lies **Ithaca** (*Ithaca Hotel, Clinton House*), one of the most beautiful cities in the State, noted as the seat of Cornell University, and surrounded by most charming and picturesque scenery. The buildings of
* *Cornell University*, on the hills E. of the village, 400 ft. above the
lake, are worth a visit. This institution was founded in 1865 and has
already become one of the leading educational establishments of the
country. In the immediate vicinity of the village there are said to be
no less than 15 cascades and waterfalls, varying from 30 to 160 ft. in
height, 5 of them being over 100 ft. The beautiful **Ithaca Fall,** 150
ft. broad and 160 ft. high, is about a mile distant in *Ithaca Gorge*,
which is said to contain more waterfalls within the space of a mile
than any other place in America. The celebrated * **Taghkanic
Falls** are 10 miles from Ithaca, and may be reached by a pleasant
drive along the shore of the lake, by the lake-steamers, or by the
Ithaca and Geneva R. R. Near the Falls is the Taghkanic House.
Taghkanic Creek flows through a comparatively level country until
about 1½ mile from the lake it encounters a rocky ledge lying directly
across its course. But the stream has succeeded in excavating for
itself a channel from 100 to 400 ft. in depth and 400 across at its lower
extremity. Through this chasm the waters hurry on to the precipice,

where they fall perpendicularly 215 ft. into a rocky basin, forming a cataract more than 50 ft. higher than Niagara. At the bottom of the Fall the walls of the ravine are nearly perpendicular and 400 ft. high. Paths and stairways assist the passage through the gorge. (Ithaca is also reached by the Cayuga division of the Erie R. R.)

Five miles beyond Cayuga is the manufacturing village of *Seneca Falls*, pleasantly situated at the falls of the Seneca River; and 10 miles farther is the academic city of **Geneva** (*Franklin House, American*), beautifully situated at the foot of Seneca Lake, and noted for its educational institutions, of which *Hobart College* (Episcopal) is the most important. **＊ Seneca Lake,** one of the largest and most beautiful in New York State, is 35 miles long and 1 to 4 miles wide, is very deep, and never freezes over. Steamboats run 3 times daily in summer from Geneva to *Watkins* at the S. end of the lake, stopping *en route* at *Ovid* and *Dresden*. Near Watkins is the famous *Watkins Glen* (see Route 55).

Twelve miles beyond Geneva are the **Clifton Springs** (*Clifton Springs Sanitarium, Foster House*), the most frequented resort on the line of the Central R. R. The waters are sulphurous in character and are considered efficacious in bilious and cutaneous disorders. Eleven miles further is *Canandaigua* (Canandaigua Hotel), a pretty village of 5,000 inhabitants at the N. end of Canandaigua Lake, 28 miles from Rochester. **Canandaigua Lake** is 16 miles long, narrow and deep, is bordered by numerous vineyards, abounds in fish, and is much visited in summer. Small steamers run down the lake to *Seneca Point* (Lake House) and *Woodville*. Canandaigua is the N. terminus of the Northern Central R. R. (see Route 55). Between Canandaigua and Rochester there are no important stations.

Rochester.

Hotels, etc.—*Osburn House* ($3 to $4 a day), in Main St. ; *Whitcomb House*, cor. Main and Clinton Sts. ; *Brackett's*, *Congress Hall*, and *Reed's*, near the Central depot; and *Clinton House*, in Exchange St. *Horse-cars* on the principal streets and to the suburbs; *stages* to adjacent towns. *Reading-room* at the Athenæum on W. Main St. *Post-Office* in the Arcade, W. Main St.

Rochester is situated on both sides of the Genesee River, 7 miles from its mouth in Lake Ontario. Soon after it enters the city the river makes a rapid descent, there being a perpendicular fall of 96 ft. near the center, and two others of 25 ft. near the northern limit. It is to the prodigious water-power thus afforded that much of the prosperity of the city is attributable, and it contains several of the largest flour-mills in the country. Other important industries are the production of clothing, boots and shoes, engines and boilers, agricultural implements, trees, and garden and flower seeds. The immense ＊ nurseries in which these latter are produced are well worth a visit (reached by Mt. Hope Ave.). Rochester was first settled in 1810, was incorporated as a city in 1834, and in 1875 had a population of 81,813. The streets are nearly all laid out at right angles, many of them are well paved with stone, and most of them are bordered with shade-trees. *Main*

St. is the principal thoroughfare, and contains many fine buildings. At the corner of W. Main and State Sts. are the *** Powers Buildings,** a tubular block of stores, built of stone, glass, and iron, 7 stories high. In the upper halls is a fine collection of paintings, and on the top is a tower (open to visitors) from which may be obtained a fine view of the city and i^ts surroundings. Near the Powers Buildings is the *Arcade*, roofed over with glass, and containing numerous shops. Nearly opposite is the *County Court-House*, of brick with limestone trimmings, in which is the *Athenæum* with a library of 20,000 volumes. Back of the Court-House is the **City Hall,** a handsome building of gray limestone, 138 by 80 ft., with a tower 175 ft. high. In the same vicinity is the *High School*, a large brick building with sandstone trimmings. The most ornate business block in the city is the *Rochester Savings-Bank*, cor. W. Main and Fitzhugh Sts. The finest church edifices are the *First Baptist*, in Fitzhugh St., the *First Presbyterian*, in Spring St., and *St. Patrick's Cathedral* (Roman Catholic), in Frank St. The *** University of Rochester** was founded by the Baptists in 1850, and in 1875 had 9 professors and 160 students. It is situated in the E. part of the city (on University Ave.), where it has 23½ acres beautifully laid out, and occupies a massive building of red sandstone. The library contains 12,000 volumes, and the geological cabinets, collected by Professor Henry A. Ward, are said to be the finest in the country. The library and cabinets are in a handsome fire-proof building. There is also a Baptist *Theological Seminary*, founded in 1850. Its library numbers more than 15,000 volumes, including 4,600 which constituted the library of Neander, the German church historian. The *City Hospital* (West Ave.) has a fine building with accommodations for 150 patients. *St. Mary's Hospital* (in West Ave.) is an imposing edifice of cut-stone with accommodations for 500 patients. The *Western House o Refuge*, a State institution, is an extensive brick buildˈg surrounded by grounds 42 acres in extent, about one mile N. from the center of the city. Near this, on the S., is the *Reformatory for Girls*, a fine edifice. Other points of interest are *** Mount Hope Cemetery,** picturesquely situated in the S. part of the city (reached by horse-cars); and the cut-stone *Aqueduct*, 848 ft. long with a channel 45 ft. wide, by which the Erie Canal is carried across the Genesee River.

The *** Genesee Falls** are seen to the best advantage from the E. side of the stream. The railroad cars pass about 100 yards S. of the most southerly fall, so that passengers in crossing lose the view. To view the scene properly, the visitor should cross the bridge over the Genesee above the mill, and place himself immediately in front of the fall. By descending a stairway to the bottom of the ravine the impressiveness of the view is greatly increased. The first fall is 80 rods below the Aqueduct, and is 96 ft. high. From Table Rock, in the center of it, Sam Patch made his last and fatal leap. The river below the first cataract is broad and deep, with occasional rapids to the second fall, where it again descends perpendicularly 25 ft. A short distance below is the third fall, which is 84 ft. high.

Charlotte, the port of Rochester, is 7 miles distant on Lake Ontario (reached by branch R. R.). The adjacent beaches are much visited in summer, and daily steamers cross the lake to Toronto (70 miles).

The distance from Rochester to Buffalo is 69 miles. Of the five small towns *en route* the only one requiring mention is **Batavia** (*St. James's Hotel*), a pretty village of 4,000 inhabitants, noted as the site of the *State Institution for the Blind*, one of the finest structures of its kind in the country. The village is laid out in broad streets which are beautifully shaded, and the County Court-House is a handsome building.

Buffalo.

Hotels, etc.—The best are *Pierce's Hotel*, the *Mansion House*, and *Tifft House*, in Main St. Good houses on a smaller scale are *Bonney's*, cor. Washington and Carrol Sts., and the *Continental* at the depot. *Horse-cars* run through the principal streets and to the suburbs. *Stages* to the adjacent towns. *Steamboats* run to the principal ports on the Great Lakes (see Route 96). *Reading-rooms* at the Young Men's Association, cor. Main and Eagle Sts., and at the Y. M. C. A., 319 Main St. *Post-Office* at the cor. of Washington and Seneca Sts.

Buffalo, the third city in size in the State of New York, is situated at the mouth of Buffalo Creek and head of Niagara River, at the E. end of Lake Erie, and possesses the largest and finest harbor on the Lake. It is the terminus of the Erie Canal, the New York Central R. R., the Erie R. R., and eight other railroads, connecting it with all parts of the country. The city has a water-front of about 5 miles, half of which is upon the Lake and half upon Niagara River. Its commerce is very large, as its position at the foot of the great chain of lakes makes it the *entrepôt* for a large part of the traffic between the East and the great Northwest. During the year 1872 the number of vessels entered and cleared was 10,303, with an aggregate tonnage of 4,678,058 tons. The manufactures are also large, the most important being of iron, tin, brass, and copper ware. Malting and brewing, for which the climate is highly favorable, are extensively carried on. Buffalo was first settled in 1801; it became a military post during the war of 1812, and was burned by a force of Indians and British in 1814; and it was incorporated as a city in 1832. Since the completion of the Erie Canal in 1825 its growth has been very rapid, and in 1875 it had a population of 134,573.

Buffalo, in the main, is handsomely built. Its streets are broad and straight, and for the most part laid out at right angles. *Main*, *Niagara*, and *Delaware Sts.* are the principal thoroughfares. The streets in the more elevated portions of the city are bordered with a profusion of shade-trees, and the more important avenues have many fine residences. Shade-trees adorn the public squares, 5 in all, named respectively Niagara, Lafayette Place, Franklin, Washington, Johnson's, and the Terrace. The latter is a broad open square in the busiest section of the city. A portion of the river front is a bold bluff, 60 ft. above the level of the river, and the more elevated portions afford fine views of the city, river, lake, Canada shore, and the hilly country to the S. E. The prominent public buildings are: the *Custom-House* and *Post-Office*, a large but plain freestone edifice, at the cor. of Washington and Seneca Sts.; the *** State Arsenal,** a handsome turreted structure of stone in

Batavia St.; the *State Armory* in Virginia St., a large plain edifice of brick; the *Erie County Penitentiary*, a capacious building of brick and stone; and the *General Hospital*, in High St., of which only one wing has been erected. A fine granite court-house and city hall, fronting on Franklin St., is in process of construction, and is estimated to cost nearly $1,500,000. Several of the bank buildings in the city are costly and imposing edifices, especially those of the Erie County, the Buffalo, and the Western savings-banks. The most notable church edifices are **St. Paul's Cathedral** (Episcopal), in Pearl St., built of red sandstone in the early English style and containing a fine chime of bells; * **St. Joseph's Cathedral** (Roman Catholic), in Franklin St., of blue-stone trimmed with white-stone, in the florid Gothic style, with a stained-glass chancel-window and a chime of 42 bells; the *Church of the Messiah* (Universalist), in Main St.; the *North Presbyterian*, in Main St., and the *Calvary Presbyterian*, in Delaware St., which h · a lofty spire. The leading educational institutions are the *Medical College*, of the University of Buffalo, in Main St.; *Canisius College*, a Jesuit institution, occupying a handsome building of stone and brick in Washington St. near Tupper; *St. Joseph's College*, on the terrace in the rear of St. Joseph's Cathedral, a flourishing institution, conducted by the Christian Brothers; *St. Mary's Academy*, on the same square, in Franklin and Church Sts.; the *Buffalo Female Academy*, in Delaware St.; the *Heathcote School*, in Pearl St., a classical academy established under the patronage of the Episcopal Church; and the *State Normal School*, in North St., a large and imposing building. The *Young Men's Association* (cor. Main and Eagle Sts.) has a circulating library of 30,000 volumes and a well-supplied reading-room. In the same building are the Buffalo Historical Society, with : .arge library and cabinets; the Society of Natural Sciences, which has a very complete and valuable collection of minerals, a good botanical and c· .1-chological cabinet, and a complete set of Prof. Ward's fossil casts; the Academy of Fine Arts, which is founding a fine gallery of painting and sculpture; and the Mechanics' Institute. Adjoining the library building is *St. James's Hall*, where lectures, concerts, etc., are given. The *Grosvenor Library* is a public library for reference, founded by a bequest of Seth Grosvenor, of Buffalo. It is liberally endowed, and contains about 12,000 volumes, chiefly important books not easy of access elsewhere. The *Church Charity Foundation* (Episcopal), in Rhode Island St., near Niagara, is a fine building, embracing a home for aged and destitute women, and an orphan ward. The *Ingleside Home*, with an excellent building in Seneca St., is designed for the reclamation of fallen women, and has been very successful since its organization in 1849. The *Buffalo Orphan Asylum* (Protestant) has a commodious building in Virginia St.; and the *St. Vincent Female Orphan Asylum*, cor. Batavia and Ellicott Sts., and the *St. Joseph's Boys' Orphan Asylum*, at Limestone Hill, are large and successful Roman Catholic institutions. The * **State Insane Asylum**, in process of construction, will be the largest institution of the kind in the United States if not in the world; it will have a front of about 2,700 ft. The grounds attached to it embrace 203 acres, and are laid out in harmony with the plan of the Buffalo Park, which they adjoin.

A superb public **Park,* or system of parks, has been designed and laid out by Frederick Law Olmsted, the architect of Central Park in New York City. The land embraces about 530 acres ; and is divided into three plots, situated in the western, northern, and eastern parts of the city, with broad boulevards connecting them, forming a continuous drive of nearly 10 miles. The *Forest Lawn Cemetery,* bounded on two sides by the Park, is tastefully laid out and contains some fine monuments. From Black Rock, a suburb of Buffalo (reached by Niagara St.), the magnificent **International Bridge,* completed in 1873 at a cost of $1,500,000, crosses the Niagara River to the Canadian village of Fort Erie. *Niagara Falls* (see p. 163) are 22 miles from Buffalo *via* N. Y. Central R. R., 23 miles *via* Erie R. R., and 26 miles *via* Canada Southern R. R.

No visitor should leave Buffalo without having seen the great canal-basins, the piers, the grain-elevators, and some of the iron-works. The spacious passenger depots of the Central and Erie R. R. and the immense freight depots of the same roads are also worth a visit.

Rochester to Niagara Falls.

At Rochester the Niagara Falls branch of the Central R. R. diverges from the main line and runs to the Falls in 77 miles. Though it is called a branch this is in reality the continuation of the main trunk line, as by far the greater portion of the freight and passengers never go to Buffalo at all, but pass east and west by way of Suspension Bridge. Rochester is described on p. 158. Leaving Rochester the train runs through a rich agricultural region, passing two or three small stations to *Brockport* (17 miles from Rochester), a pretty village of 3,000 inhabitants on the Erie Canal, containing the fine building of the State Normal School. *Albion* (30 miles) is another attractive village, capital of Orleans County, with a handsome Court-House and substantial jail, and a costly Soldiers' Monument. *Medina* (39 miles) is noted for its quarries of dark-red sandstone, known as "Medina sandstone"; and 16 miles beyond is **Lockport** (*Judson House*), a prosperous city of 15,000 inhabitants, famous for its limestone-quarries and its manufacture of flour. It is situated at the point where the Erie Canal descends by ten double locks from the level of Lake Erie to the Genesee level. These locks may be seen from the cars. By means of them an immense water-power is obtained, which is utilized by the factories and flour-mills. Nineteen miles beyond Lockport is *Suspension Bridge* (448 miles from New York), over which the through trains cross the Niagara River in full view of the Falls and of the rapids rushing to the whirlpool below. The ** Bridge itself is worth attention as one of the triumphs of modern engineering. It is 821 ft. long from tower to tower, is 245 ft. above the water, and was finished in 1855 at a cost of $500,000. A carriage and foot way is suspended 28 ft. below the railway-tracks. The Falls and village are 2 miles distant, and are reached without changing cars.

Niagara Falls.

Hotels, etc.—On the American side are the *International Hotel* ($3.50 to $4.50 a day) and the *Cataract House* ($3.50 to $4.50 a day), both close to the Falls and alongside the rapids; the *Spencer House* ($3.50 a day) near the R. R. station; and the *Park Place Hotel* ($3 a day). In the village are several small hotels and large boarding-houses at which the charges are $7 to $12 a week. On the Canadian side are the *Clifton House* ($3.50 a day), commanding an excellent view of the Falls; and the *Victoria Hall Hotel* ($2 to $3 a day).

The extortions practiced at Niagara Falls have become proverbial, but are much exaggerated. The hackmen are the most troublesome feature, but it is easy to thwart their impositions by making an explicit agreement before starting, designating the places to be visited and the total charge to be paid. The legal tariff is $2 per hour, but special terms can be secured at a lower rate. Besides the price agreed upon for the carriage the tourist will have to pay all tolls and fees. A still better way of avoiding the annoyance and impositions of the hackmen is to walk, and this is becoming quite customary. There are scarcely any points of interest connected with the Falls which are not within the compass of an easy walk; especially if a day or two can be devoted to the American side and the same length of time to the Canadian side. Moreover, in the number and variety of the attractions seen, the pedestrian will be apt to enjoy a marked advantage over the carriage-traveler. As far as the fees and tolls are concerned, it should be remembered that they secure for the visitor the enjoyment of conveniences and facilities which have cost immense amounts of money and which are profitable for only a brief portion of the year. Season-tickets at a price much lower than the regular rates can be availed of by those purposing to spend several days at the Falls.

The Falls of Niagara are situated on the Niagara River, about 22 miles from Lake Erie and 14 miles from Lake Ontario. This river is the channel by which all the waters of the four great upper lakes flow toward the Gulf of St. Lawrence, and has a total descent of 333 ft., leaving Lake Ontario still 231 ft. above the sea. From the N. E. extremity of Lake Erie the Niagara flows in a N. direction with a swift current for the first 2 miles, and then more gently with a widening current, which divides as a portion passes on each side of Grand Island. As these unite below the island, the stream spreads out to 2 or 3 miles in width, and appears like a quiet lake studded with small low islands. About 16 miles from Lake Erie

NIAGARA RIVER

the current becomes narrow and begins to descend with great velocity. This is the commencement of the Rapids, which continue for about a mile, the waters accomplishing in this distance a fall of 52 ft. The Rapids terminate below in a great cataract, the descent of which is 164 ft.

on the American side and 158 ft. on the Canadian. At this point the
river, making a curve from W. to N., spreads out to an extreme width
of 4,750 ft. Goat Island, which extends down to the brink of the
cataract, occupies about one fourth of this space, leaving the river on
the American side about 1,100 ft. wide, and on the Canadian side
about double this width. The line along the verge of the Canadian Fall
is much longer than the breadth of this portion of the river, by reason
of its horseshoe form, the curve extending up the central part of the
current. The waters sweeping down the Rapids form a grand curve
as they fall clear of the rocky wall into the deep pool at the base. In
the profound chasm below the fall, the current, contracted in width to
less than 1,000 ft., is tossed tumultuously about, and forms great whirlpools and eddies as it is borne along its rapidly descending bed. Dangerous as it appears, the river is here crossed by small row-boats.
For 7 miles below the Falls the narrow gorge continues, varying in
width from 200 to 400 yards. The river then emerges at Lewiston
into a lower district, having descended 104 ft. from the foot of the
cataract.

The gorge through which the Niagara River flows below the Falls bears evidence
of having been excavated by the river itself. Within comparatively recent years
changes have taken place by the falling down of masses of rock, the effect of which
has been to cause a slight recession of the cataract, and extend the gorge to the same
amount upward toward Lake Erie. Thus in 1818 great fragments descended at the
Horseshoe Fall, and since 1855 several others, which have materially changed the
aspect of the Falls. Table Rock, once a striking feature, has wholly disappeared.
Lyell estimates the rate of recession to be about a foot a year, but the rate is not
uniform. For several successive years there will be no apparent change; and then,
the soft underlying strata having been gradually worn away, great masses of the
upper harder ones fall down, causing a very noticeable change in a very brief time.
At the present site of the Falls a layer of hard limestone rock, of the formation
known as the Niagara limestone, covers the surface of the country, and forms the
edge of the cataract to the depth of between 80 and 90 ft. Professor Hall, of the State
geological survey, points out that, after a further recession of about 2 miles, this
limestone layer, with the soft layers under it, will have been swept away, and the
Fall will become almost stationary on the lower sandstone formation, with a height
of only 80 ft. As, however, it will take rather more than 10,000 years to excavate
this 2 miles, the tourists of our day need feel no alarm lest the stupendous torrent
dwindle beneath their gaze! In regard to the volume of water which passes over
the Falls, Lyell estimates it at 90,000,000,000 cubic ft. per hour, and Dwight at 100,-
000,000 tons per hour.

* **Goat Island** is the point usually visited first. It is reached by
a bridge 360 ft. long, the approach to which is just in rear of the
Cataract House. The charge for crossing to the island is 50 cents for
each person, or $1 for a season-ticket. The bridge itself is an object
of interest, from its apparently dangerous position. It is, however, perfectly safe, and is crossed constantly by heavily laden carriages. The
view of the * **Rapids** from the bridge is one of the most impressive
features of the Niagara scenery. The river descends 52 feet in a distance of three quarters of a mile by this inextricable turmoil of waters.
Below the bridge, a short distance from the verge of the American Fall,
is *Chapin's Island*, so named in memory of a workman who fell into the
stream while at work on the bridge. He lodged on this islet, and was
rescued by a Mr. Robinson, who gallantly went to his relief in a skiff.

About midway of the stream the road crosses *Bath Island*, on which is an extensive paper-mill, run by water-power. From the island end of the bridge 3 paths diverge, that to the right being the one usually followed. A short walk brings us to the foot-bridge leading to **Luna Island,** a huge rock-mass of some three quarters of an acre, lying between the Center Fall and the American Fall. The exquisite lunar rainbows seen at this point, when the moon is full, have given it the name it bears. A little girl, 8 years old, fell into the torrent here in 1848, and was swept over the Falls, together with a gentleman who jumped in to rescue her. The width of the **American Fall** from Luna Island is over 1,100 ft., and the precipice over which it plunges is 164 ft. high. Just beyond Luna Island a spiral stairway (called "Biddle's Stairs," after Nicholas Biddle, of United States Bank fame, by whose order they were built) leads to the foot of the cliff. From the foot of the stairs, which are secured to the rocks by strong iron fastenings, there are two diverging paths. That to the right leads to the * **Cave of the Winds,** a spacious recess back of the Center Fall. Guides and water-proof suits for visiting the Cave may be obtained at the stairs (fee, $1.50); and the excursion is well worth making. You can pass safely into the recess behind the water to a platform beyond. Magical rainbow pictures are found at this spot; sometimes bows of entire circles, and two or three at once, are seen. A plank-walk has been carried out to a cluster of rocks near the foot of the fall, and from it one of the best * views of the American Fall may be obtained. The up-river way, along the base of the cliff toward the Horseshoe Fall, is difficult, and much obstructed by fallen rocks. It was from a point near Biddle's Stairs that the renowned jumper, Sam Patch, made two successful leaps into the waters below (in 1829), saying to the throng of spectators, as he went off, that "one thing might be done as well as another." Reascending the stairs, a few minutes' walk along the summit of the cliff brings us to a bridge leading to the islet on which stood the famous Terrapin Tower, which, having become dangerous, was blown up with gunpowder in 1873. The view of the * **Horseshoe Fall** from this point is surpassingly grand. The mighty cataract is here 2,200 ft. across, with a perpendicular plunge of 158 ft., and it was estimated by Lyell that 1,500,-000,000 cubic feet of water pass over the ledges every hour. One of the condemned lake-ships (the Detroit) was sent over this Fall in 1829; and though she drew 18 ft. of water, she did not touch the rocks in passing over the brink of the precipice, showing that the water is at least 20 ft. deep *above* the ledge.

At the other end of Goat Island (reached by a road from the Horseshoe Fall), a series of graceful bridges leads to the * **Three Sisters,** as three small islets lying in the Rapids are called. The islands are rugged masses of rock, covered with a profuse and tangled vegetation, and afford fine views of the Rapids at their widest and wildest part. On Goat Island, near the Three Sisters, is the *Hermit's Bathing-Place*, so called after Francis Abbott, "the Hermit of Niagara," who used to bathe here, and who was finally drowned while doing so. At the foot of Grand Island, near the Canada shore, is *Navy Island*, which was the

scene of some interesting incidents in the Canadian Rebellion of 1837–
'38, known as the Mackenzie War. *Chippewa*, which held at that period some 5,000 British troops, is upon the Canadian shore, nearly opposite. It was near *Schlosser Landing*, about 2 miles above the Falls,
on the American side, that during the war the American steamer Car-
oline, which had been perverted to the use of the insurgents, was set
on fire and sent over the Falls, by the order of Sir Allan McNab, a
Canadian officer. Above Navy Island is *Grand Island* (17,000 acres),
somewhat noted as the spot on which, in 1820, Major Mordecai M.
Noah founded "Ararat, a city of refuge for the Jews," in the vain
hope of assembling there all the Hebrew population of the world.

Returning to the mainland, the next point of interest is *** Prospect
Park** (entrance fee, 20c.; season ticket, 50c.), which lies beside the
American Fall, of which it affords a noble and impressive view. A
" vertical railway," running on a steep incline, leads from the Park to
the base of the cliff; and from its foot the river may be crossed in a
large row-boat (railway, and ferriage over and back, 25c. each). The
passage across the river is perfectly safe, and is worth making for the
very fine * view of the Falls obtained in mid-stream. A winding road
along the cliff side leads from the landing on the Canadian side to the
top of the bluff, near the Clifton House. By climbing over the rocks
at the base of the cliff on the American side (turn to the left after descending the railway), the tourist may penetrate to a point within the
spray of the American Fall, and get what is perhaps, on the whole, the
finest view of it to be had.

The usual way of crossing to the Canadian side is over the *** New
Suspension Bridge,** which arches the river about $\frac{1}{3}$ of a mile below
the Falls, and is one of the curiosities of the locality (fee for pedestrians 25c.). It was finished in 1869, at a cost of $175,000; is 1,190
ft. from cliff to cliff, and 1,268 ft. from tower to tower; and is 190 ft.
above the river. The view of the Falls and of the gorge below from
the bridge is much admired; and a still finer one may be obtained
by ascending one of the towers. The tower on the American side is
100 ft. high (fee for ascent 10c.), and that on the Canadian side
105 ft. high (ascent by elevator, 25c.). A road to the left from the
bridge terminus leads along the cliff, affording good views of the American and Center Falls. On the terrace, near the Falls, is the **Museum**
(admission 50c.), containing more than 10,000 specimens of minerals,
birds, fishes, and animals; a collection of coins; some Egyptian and
Assyrian curiosities; and a few wax figures. The view from the upper
balconies is comprehensive, overlooking both Falls. A short distance
above the Museum is the spot still called **** Table Rock,** though the
immense overhanging platform originally known by that name has long
since fallen over the precipice. From this point the best front view of
the Falls is obtained, and that of the Horseshoe Fall is incomparably
grand. The concussion of the falling waters with those in the depths
below produces a spray that veils the cataract two thirds up its height.
Above this impenetrable foam, to the height of 50 ft. above the Fall, a
cloud of lighter spray rises, which, when the sun shines upon it in the

proper direction, displays magnificent solar rainbows. The appropri-
ateness of the name Niagara ("Thunder of Waters") is very evident
here.

Guides and water-proof suits for the passage under the Horseshoe Falls may be
procured at the Museum (fee, $1). This passage (which no nervous person should
attempt) is described as follows by a writer in "Picturesque America": "The
wooden stairways are narrow and steep, but perfectly safe; and a couple of minutes brings us to the bottom. Here we are in spray-land indeed; for we have
hardly begun to traverse the pathway of broken bits of shale when, with a mis-
chievous sweep, the wind sends a baby cataract in our direction, and fairly inundates us. The mysterious gloom, with the thundering noises of the falling waters,
impresses every one; but, as the pathway is broad, and the walking easy, new-
comers are apt to think that there is nothing in it. The tall, stalwart negro, who
acts as guide, listens with amusement to such comments, and confidently awaits a
change in the tone of the scoffers. More and more arched do the rocks become as
we proceed. The top part is of hard limestone, and the lower of shale, which has
been so battered away by the fury of the waters that there is an arched passage behind the entire Horseshoe Fall, which could easily be traversed if the currents of
air would let us pass. But, as we proceed, we begin to notice that it blows a trifle,
and from every one of the 32 points of the compass. At first, however, we get
them separately. A gust at a time inundates us with spray; but the farther we
march the more unruly is the Prince of Air. First, like single spies, come his
winds; but soon they advance like skirmishers; and, at last, where a thin column
of water falls across the path, they oppose a solid phalanx to our efforts. It is a
point of honor to see who can go farthest through these corridors of Æolus. It is
on record that a man, with an herculean effort, once burst through the column of
water, but was immediately thrown to the ground, and only rejoined his comrades
by crawling face downward, and digging his hands into the loose shale of the pathway. Professor Tyndall has gone as far as mortal man, and he describes the buffet-
ing of the air as indescribable, the effect being like actual blows with the fist."

Termination Rock is a short distance beyond Table Rock at the
verge of the Fall. The spray here is blinding and the roar of waters
deafening. On an island in the Rapids above the Fall is a tower (*Prince
of Wales's Tower*), from whose summit there is an imposing view of
the Falls, Rapids, and adjacent islands and shores (fee, 50c.). The
island is reached by a pretty bridge. Two miles above the Falls
(reached by the river road) is the famous * **Burning Spring,** whose
waters emit into the air sulphuretted-hydrogen gas, which burns with
a brilliant flame when ignited. The spring is so arranged as to show
off the phenomenon to the best advantage (admission, 40c.).

Below the Falls are several points of interest, which are best visited on the American side. The first of these is the old *Suspension
Bridge,* which spans the gorge 2 miles below the Falls, and supports
railway-tracks, a roadway, and footways. The bridge is 245 ft. above
the water, and supported by towers on each bank, the centers of which
are 821 ft. apart. It was built in 1855 by the late John A. Roebling,
and cost $500,000. The fee for crossing the bridge is 25c. for pedes-
trians, which confers the right to return free on the same day. From
one side of this bridge a fine distant view of the Falls is had, and
from the other a bird's-eye view of the seething and tumultuous * *Whirlpool Rapids*. By descending the elevator (50c.) which leads from the
top to the base of the cliff near the site of the old Monteagle House,
a nearer view is obtained of these wonderful Rapids, in which the
waters rush along with such velocity that the middle of the current is

30 ft. higher than the sides.   Three miles below the Falls is the
* Whirlpool, occasioned by a sharp bend in the river which is here
contracted to a width of 220 ft.   The water rushes against the bank
with prodigious fury, and being turned back almost at a right angle
is converted into an angry and swirling eddy.

In the vicinity of Niagara is *Lewiston* (7 miles N.), at the head of
navigation on Lake Ontario; and directly opposite (on the Canadian
side) is Queenston.   *Queenston* is well worth a visit, and affords a
pleasant drive from the Falls.   It is historically as well as pictorially
interesting.   Here General Brock and his aide-de-camp McDonnell fell,
October 11, 1812.   *** Brock's Monument,** which crowns the
heights above the village, is 185 ft. high, surmounted by a dome of 9
ft., which is reached by a spiral flight of 250 steps inside.   The remains
of Brock and his comrade lie in stone sarcophagi beneath, having been
removed thither from Fort George.   This is the second monument
erected on the spot, the first having been destroyed by the scoundrel
Lett, in 1840.   At *Drummondville,* 1½ mile W. of the Falls, is a tower
which overlooks the battle-field of Lundy's Lane.

39. New York to Buffalo and Niagara Falls via Erie Railway.

Distances : To Middletown, 67 miles; to Port Jervis, 88 ; to Susquehanna, 193 ;
to Binghamton, 215; to Elmira, 274 ; to Hornellsville, 332 ; to Buffalo, 423 ; to
Niagara Falls, 442.   The time to Buffalo or Niagara Falls is about 16 hours, and the
fare $9.25.

THE Erie Railway is one of the greatest triumphs of engineering
skill in this or any other country, and affords some of the grandest
and most varied scenery to be found E. of the Rocky Mountains.
Prior to its construction, portions of the line were considered impassable to any other than a winged creature, yet mountains were scaled or
pierced and river-cañons passed by blasting a path from the face of
stupendous precipices; gorges of fearful depth were spanned by
bridges swung into the air; and broad, deep valleys crossed by massive viaducts.   The road was begun in 1836 and completed in 1851,
and has cost to date upward of $60,000,000.   Pullman palace draw-
ing-room and sleeping cars are attached to all the through trains.

The terminal station in Hoboken is reached by ferry from foot of
Chambers St. and W. 23d St.   Leaving Hoboken the train traverses a
series of dreary marshes, and in 17 miles reaches **Paterson** (*Hamilton
House, Franklin*), a busy manufacturing city of about 35,000 inhabitants, situated on the right bank of the Passaic River immediately
below the falls.   It was founded in 1791 by Alexander Hamilton, in
the cotton interest, and its cotton factories are now very extensive.
It is also the site of the largest silk-mill in America, employing 800
hands, and of the mills of the Am. Velvet Co.   Next to Newark it
is the largest manufacturing city of New Jersey.   The ** Passaic Falls*
have a perpendicular descent of 50 ft., and the scenery in the vicinity
is very picturesque.   A small and rugged park surrounds them ; and

on a hill in the vicinity are a costly Soldiers' Monument and a belvidere tower whence there is a fine view. Beyond Paterson the route traverses a fertile but uninteresting country, and just this side of *Suffern* (32 miles) crosses the boundary line and enters New York State. From Suffern a branch line runs in 18 miles to Piermont on the Hudson River (see p. 59). Here the beautiful Ramapo Valley begins and the scenery becomes increasingly picturesque and impressive. *Ramapo* (34 miles) is near Tom Mountain, from the summit of which there is a wide-extended view. During the campaign of 1777 Washington often ascended this mountain to watch the movements of the British army and fleet around New York. Beyond *Sloatsburg* (36 miles), on the right, are seen the ruins of the Augusta Iron Works, where was forged the chain that was stretched across the Hudson to check the advance of the British ships. At *Turner's* (48 miles) a branch road diverges to Newburg on the Hudson (see p. 62). From *Monroe* (50 miles) and also from *Greycourt* (54 miles) stages run in 8–10 miles to * **Greenwood Lake** (*Windermere House, Brandon, Traphagen*), a highly popular summer resort, which is also reached from New York *via* Montclair & Greenwood Lake R. R. (50 miles). This "miniature Lake George" is a beautiful, river-like body of water, 10 miles long and 1 mile wide, nearly inclosed by mountains, and offering some extremely picturesque scenery. Its waters are clear and deep, and abound in fish. A small steamer plies on the lake, making two trips daily. In the vicinity are the smaller but scarcely less charming Lakes Macopin, Sterling, and Wawayandah. **Turner's** is the most attractive station on this portion of the line, and is near some lovely little lakelets. The view from the hill N. of the station is superb, the Hudson River, with Fishkill and Newburg, being in sight.

From Greycourt another branch line runs to Newburg in 18 miles, and the Warwick branch diverges to Warwick. On the main line, 6 miles beyond Greycourt, is the pretty little village of *Goshen*, one of the capitals of Orange County, and celebrated for its milk, butter, and cheese. Here the Walkill Valley Branch diverges and runs in 43 miles to Kingston and Rondout on the Hudson (see p. 62), passing *New Paltz*, whence stages run in 6 miles to *Lake Mohonk* (see p. 62). Seven miles beyond Goshen, at the crossing of the New York & Oswego Midland R. R., is the busy manufacturing village of **Middletown** (*Grand Central Hotel*) with 6,000 inhabitants. Four miles beyond, at *Howell's* (71 miles), the most picturesque section of the line begins, and fine views are had all the way to Port Jervis. On approaching *Otisville* (76 miles), the eye is attracted by the bold flanks of the Shawangunk Mountain, the passage of which great barrier (once deemed insurmountable) is a miracle of engineering skill. A mile beyond Otisville, after traversing an ascending grade of 40 ft. to the mile, the road runs through a rock cutting 50 ft. deep and 2,500 ft. long. This passed, the summit of the ascent is reached, and thence we go down the mountain's side many sloping miles to the valley beneath, through the midst of grand and picturesque scenery. Onward the way increases in interest, until it opens in a glimpse, away

8

over the valley, of the mountain-spur known as the *Cuddeback ;* and
at its base the glittering water is seen, now for the first time, of the
Delaware & Hudson Canal. Eight miles beyond Otisville we are imprisoned in a deep cut for nearly a mile, and, on emerging from it,
there lie spread before us (on the right) the rich and lovely valley
and waters of the *Neversink.* Beyond sweeps a chain of blue hills,
and at their feet, terraced high, gleam the roofs and spires of the
town of *Port Jervis* (88 miles) ; while to the S. the eye rests upon the
waters of the Delaware, along the banks of which the line runs for the
next 90 miles.

Port Jervis (*Delaware House, Fowler House*) is situated at the
confluence of the Delaware and Neversink Rivers, and contains about
9,000 inhabitants. Extensive railroad shops are located here, and it
is the terminus of the E. division of the Erie road. The scenery in
the vicinity is delightful, and the village itself is a very pretty one.
Riding, driving, hunting, and fishing may be enjoyed to any extent,
and many summer visitors are attracted to it. *Point Peter* is ascended
from the village, and affords a pleasing outlook over the Delaware
and Neversink Valleys. Six miles distant are the *Falls of the Sawkill,*
where a mountain-brook is precipitated 80 ft. over two perpendicular
ledges of slate-rock into a wild and romantic gorge. **Milford** (*Dim-
mick House*) is a lovely mountain-surrounded town about an hour's
stage-ride S. W. of Port Jervis. Shortly beyond are the beautiful
falls of the *Raymondskill,* and there are fine trout-streams in the neighborhood.

Three miles beyond Port Jervis the train crosses the Delaware
into the State of Pennsylvania, which it traverses for 26 miles to *Tusten,* where it again enters New York. Near *Shohola* (107 miles) some
of the greatest obstacles of the entire route were encountered, and for
several miles the roadway was hewed out of the solid cliff-side at a
cost of $100,000 a mile. *Lackawaxen* (111 miles) is a pretty village at
the confluence of the Lackawaxen Creek and Delaware River. Here
the Delaware is spanned by an iron suspension bridge supporting the
aqueduct by which the D. & H. Canal crosses the river. The country
around *Narrowsburg* (123 miles) was the theatre of the stirring incidents of Cooper's novel, "The Last of the Mohicans." Beyond Narrowsburg for some miles the scenery is uninteresting and the stations
unimportant. Near *Callicoon* (136 miles) is the romantic and trout-
teeming Callicoon Brook ; and *Hancock* (164 miles) is attractively situated. At *Deposit* (177 miles) the train leaves the valley of the Delaware and begins the ascent of the high mountain-ridge which separates it from the lovely valley of the Susquehanna. As the train
descends into the latter valley there opens suddenly on the right a
* picture of rare and bewitching beauty. This first glimpse of the
Susquehanna is esteemed one of the finest points of the varied scenery
of the Erie route. A short distance below, the train crosses the great
* *Starucca Viaduct,* 1,200 ft. long and 110 ft. high, constructed at a
cost of $320,000, and spanning the Starucca Valley with 18 arches.
From *Susquehanna* (193 miles) the viaduct itself is a most effective

feature of the valley views. **Susquehanna** (*Starucca Hotel*, at the station) contains the vast repair-shops of the Company, and is one of the stopping-places for meals.

For a few miles beyond Susquehanna the route still lies amid mountain-ridges, but these are soon left behind, and the train enters upon a beautiful hilly and rolling country, thickly dotted with villages and towns. At *Great Bend* (201 miles) the Delaware, Lackawanna & Western R. R. comes in from the Pennsylvania coal-fields. *Kirkwood* (207 miles) has some title to fame as the birthplace of Joe Smith, the Mormon prophet. Eight miles beyond Kirkwood is **Binghamton** (*Spaulding House, Exchange Hotel*), an important railroad and manufacturing center, pleasantly situated on a wide plain in an angle formed by the confluence of the Susquehanna and Chenango Rivers. It contains about 16,000 inhabitants, and is a leading seat of the coal and iron industry. Four railways converge here, and the Chenango Canal, 95 miles long, connects it with the Erie Canal at Utica (see p. 154.) The *Court-House* (on Court St.) is a handsome building, the *Bank Building* (cor. Court and Chenango Sts.) is another, and there are several fine churches. The *State Inebriate Asylum* is a vast stone structure on a commanding eminence a mile from the city (reached by horse-cars). On the far-viewing *Mt. Prospect* is a popular water-cure hotel.

Twenty-two miles beyond Binghamton is **Owego** (*Ahwaga House, Central House*), a prosperous town of about 10,000 inhabitants, situated on the Susquehanna at the mouth of Owego Creek, and surrounded by pleasing scenery. The Southern Central R. R. connects here, and the Cayuga Division of the Del., Lack., & Western R. R. runs N. E. 35 miles to Ithaca (see p. 157). *Evergreen Cemetery* is on the N. side of the Susquehanna River on a hill 200 ft. high, which commands fine views. On Owego Creek, a short distance from the village, is *Glennary*, once the home of N. P. Willis and the place where he wrote his charming "Letters from under a Bridge." Beyond Owego, passing several small stations of which *Waverly* (256 miles) is the principal, the train runs in 37 miles to **Elmira** (*Rathbun House, American, C. T. A. Hotel*), the largest city of the Southern Tier, with 20,000 inhabitants, and extensive manufactures, among which are the vast car-shops of the Erie R. R. *Water St.* is the business thoroughfare. The *Court-House* is a handsome edifice, and the *Elmira Female College* has a spacious brick building in the N. portion of the city. On a hill E. of the city is the *Elmira Water Cure*, which is well patronized. The *State Reformatory* and the *Southern Tier Orphans' Home* are also located here. * *Eldridge Park* contains 100 acres tastefully laid out and adorned with numerous statues. The Northern Central R. R. (Route 55) intersects the present route at Elmira. The Lehigh Valley R. R. also comes in from the coal regions of Pennsylvania; and the Utica, Ithaca & Elmira R. R. runs in 50 miles to Ithaca (see p. 157). **Corning** (291 miles) is a busy manufacturing village of about 7,000 inhabitants on the Chemung River. The Corning & Blossburg R. R. connects here, and the Rochester Division of the Erie R. R. diverges from the main line.

The Rochester Division of the Erie. R. R. runs N. W. to Rochester in 95 miles and to Attica (111 miles), where a junction is made with the Buffalo Div. described below. The distance from New York to Buffalo by this route is 433 miles, being 10 miles longer than the route *via* Hornellsville. There are many small towns between Corning and Rochester, of which the most important is *Bath,* a thriving manufacturing village, surrounded by a rich and populous agricul·ural country. *Avon* (76 miles from Corning and 19 from Rochester) is noted as the site of the much-frequented **Avon Springs** (*Knickerbocker Hall, Congress Hall, Avon Springs Hotel*). The springs, 3 in number, are about a mile S. W. of the station, and the Lower Spring discharges 54 gallons a minute. The waters are saline-sulphurous, are taken both internally and in the form of baths, and are considered remedial in rheumatism, indigestion, and cutaneous diseases. **Rochester** (386 miles from New York) is described on page 158.

Beyond Corning the main line runs for 2 miles parallel with the Rochester Division, then passes six small stations, and in 41 miles reaches **Hornellsville** (*Sherman House*), a village of about 5,000 inhabitants, with extensive repair-shops, engine-houses, etc. Here the Buffalo and Western Divisions diverge; the former running N. W. to Buffalo and Niagara Falls (described below), and the latter running almost due W. to Dunkirk on Lake Erie. The section between Hornellsville and Dunkirk is the least attractive of the Erie line, the country being comparatively unsettled, and no important towns having grown up within it. Soon after leaving Hornellsville the train enters the valley of the Canisteo River, on the banks of which are the hamlets of Almona and Alfred. At *Tip Top Summit* the road reaches its highest point (1,760 ft. above tide-water), and the descent is begun into the valley of the Genesee. The country *en route* is peculiarly wild and lonely, desolate and somber forest tracts alternating with the stations and little villages along the line. At *Cuba Summit* the train crosses the Alleghany water-shed, 1,680 ft. above the sea, and just beyond are many brooks and glens of rugged beauty. Passing *Olean* (395 miles) and *Carrollton* (408 miles) the route enters the Reservation of the Seneca Indians (embracing 42 square miles) and follows the wild banks of the Alleghany River, flowing amid hills as wild and desolate as itself. At *Salamanca* (414 miles) the Atlantic & Great Western R. R. connects with the Erie and forms the route taken by the "through trains" to the West (see Route 63). Beyond Salamanca the Erie traverses for nearly 50 miles a dreary and monotonous forest region, and reaches its terminus at **Dunkirk** (*Erie Hotel*), a village of 5,000 inhabitants on Lake Erie, 460 miles from New York. Dunkirk has a safe and commodious harbor, protected by a breakwater, considerable trade, and some manufactures. Connection is made here with the Lake Shore & Michigan Southern R. R., which begins at Buffalo and runs W. to Cleveland and Chicago (see Route 62).

The Buffalo Division.

Leaving Hornellsville the train passes a number of small stations, and in 30 miles (362 miles from New York) reaches **Portage** (*Cascade House, Ingham House*), the most attractive point on the entire Erie line. Here are the ***Portage Falls,** 3 in number, and each of sufficient beauty to repay the tourist for the journey from New York.

They are formed by the descent of the Genesee River from the plateau on which it has flowed tranquilly for many miles to the lake-level. The Upper or *Horseshoe Falls* are just below the R. R. bridge and have a vertical descent of 70 ft. Half a mile below is the * *Middle Fall*, where the river plunges 110 ft. into a chasm formed by perpendicular ledges of rock. The action of the water has worn a cave or hollow in the W. bank, which is called the *Devil's Oven*. In time of high water this cavern is submerged; but when the river is low it will hold 100 people. For 2 miles below the Middle Fall the river rushes through a deep and narrow gorge, and at the * *Lower Falls* roars down a wonderful series of cascades and rapids, descending 150 ft. in ½ mile. The railroad crosses the river on an iron * bridge, 818 ft. long and 234 ft. high. The Upper Falls are visible from the bridge, but no idea of their grandeur can be formed until they are seen from below. Also visible from the bridge is the long *Aqueduct* by which the Genesee Canal crosses the river.

Six miles beyond Portage is *Gainesville* (368 miles), whence a railway runs in 7 miles to the lovely **Silver Lake**, where the sea-serpent was said to have been seen in 1855. *Warsaw* (375 miles) is a pleasant village, at the entrance of the romantic O-at-ka Valley, and surrounded by rich pastoral scenery. It is much visited in summer. At *Attica* (392 miles) the Rochester Div. (see p. 172) joins the main line, which then passes on to **Buffalo** (423 miles) and **Niagara Falls** (442 miles). Both these places are described in Route 38.

40. New York to Montreal via Saratoga Springs and Lake Champlain.

Via steamboat or Hudson River R. R. (Route 9) to Albany or Troy, and thence *via* Delaware & Hudson Canal Company's R. R. Distances: To Albany, 143 miles; to Saratoga Springs, 181; to Whitehall, 219; to Rouse's Point, 341; to Montreal, 391. This is the shortest and most direct route between New York and Montreal, and the through trains make the journey in 15 hours. Wagner drawing-room and sleeping cars are attached to the through trains.

As far as Albany or Troy this route has already been described in Route 9. At Albany (143 miles) the cars take the track of the Rensselaer & Saratoga R. R. and run N. past the Rural Cemetery to *W. Troy* (149 miles); *Cohoes* (152 miles), a busy manufacturing city at the crossing of the Mohawk River; *Waterford* (154 miles), a large manufacturing village on the Hudson; and *Albany Junction* (155 miles), where the Albany Div. joins the main line from Troy, 6 miles distant. *Round Lake* (168 miles) is a celebrated Methodist camp-meeting ground; and 6 miles beyond is **Ballston Spa** (*Sans-Souci Hotel, Ballston House*), a once fashionable and still frequented resort, noted for its mineral springs, whose fame, however, has been overshadowed by the more popular Saratoga waters. The village of 5,000 inhabitants is situated upon the Kayaderosseras Creek, and contains several factories. Seven miles beyond (181 from New York) the train stops at

Saratoga Springs.

Hotels, etc.—The hotels of Saratoga are among the largest in the world. *Congress Hall* ($3 to $5 a day) is an immense brick structure on Broadway, adjoining Congress Park, with an imposing front of 5 stories on 3 streets, and contains 800 rooms accommodating 1,200 guests. There are broad piazzas, roof promenades, observatories, an immense dining-room, a handsome ballroom, and spacious parlors. The *Grand Union Hotel* ($3 to $5 a day), opposite Congress Hall, is another vast building. It has a frontage of 1,364 ft. on Broadway, contains 1,000 rooms, and can accommodate 1,800 guests. It is handsomely furnished, and the parlors, office, and dining-room are richly decorated. Its grounds are beautifully shaded by elms, under which the band plays every afternoon. The *United States Hotel* ($4 to $5 a day) is a spacious brick edifice, containing 1,100 rooms with a capacity for nearly 2,000 guests. It is surrounded by spacious piazzas and delightful promenades, and is richly furnished. The *Clarendon* ($5 a day) fronts Congress Park, and accommodates 500 guests. It is very aristocratic, and is patronized by the wealthy visitors who prefer to keep a little outside of the whirl of gayety and dissipation which characterizes the larger hotels. The *Windsor Hotel*, opposite the Clarendon, is new, and can accommodate 500 guests. The *Marvin House*, corner of Broadway and Division St., accommodates 250 guests; the *American*, 450; the *Everett*, 200; the *Columbian*, 200; the *Continental*, 200; and the *Adelphi*, 350. *Dr. Strong's Remedial Institute*, on Circular Street, has fine grounds and cultured society. It is near the principal springs, hotels, and Congress Park, and accommodates about 200 guests. Besides those enumerated, there are upward of 40 hotels of various kinds; and there are numerous boarding-houses in Franklin St. and the upper part of the town, where good board can be obtained at from $8 to $20 a week. From the R. R. station to most of the hotels is only a short walk. Hotel omnibuses convey passengers from the station to the hotels free of charge.

Saratoga Springs is one of the most famous places of summer resort in the United States, and is frequented by Americans from all sections, and by foreign tourists from all parts of Europe. Its resident population is about 11,000, but during the season, which lasts from June 15th to September 15th, there are often not less than 30,000 people in the village. The Mineral Springs, which have given the place its celebrity, and the magnificent elms which shade many of its streets, are almost the only natural attractions. The site is a level and somewhat barren plateau, and the spot would be uninteresting enough but for the virtues of its waters and the dissipations of its society; yet as a mere spectacle America has nothing more brilliant to show than Saratoga at the height of the season (August).

The medicinal properties of the High Rock Spring were known to the Iroquois Indians at the period of Jacques Cartier's visit to the St. Lawrence in 1535. In 1767 Sir William Johnson was carried thither on a litter by the Mohawks, and he is believed to have been the first white man to visit the spring. The first log cabin was erected in 1773, and the first framed house in 1784 by General Schuyler, who in the same year cut a road through the forest to the High Rock from Schuylerville. Hotels began to be erected about 1815, and since then the fame of the Springs has spread so widely that, in addition to the hosts of visitors, immense quantities of the waters are bottled and sent to all parts of the United States and Europe. The name Saratoga (Indian, *Saraghoga*) signifies "the place of the herrings," which formerly passed up the Hudson into Saratoga Lake.

The principal street of the village is *Broadway*, on which are situated the large hotels, the Park, several of the leading springs, and at its upper and lower ends fine private residences. There are also handsome residences on *Circular St.*, on *Lake Avenue*, and on *Franklin St.* The *Boulevard*, 100 feet wide and lined with three rows of trees, leads

from Broadway to Saratoga Lake (4 miles), and is the grand drive.
* **Congress Park** is a low ridge in the shape of a horseshoe, encircling the lower ground on which the Congress and Columbia Springs
are situated. It is opposite the principal hotels, is shaded by noble
trees and laid out in smooth walks, and is the favorite ramble. A
small entrance-fee is charged. The *Indian Camp* lies a short distance
N. of the Park, and here during the summer a band of Indians and
Canadian half-breeds ply a lucrative traffic in moccasins, bead-work,
baskets, etc. Near by is the *Circular Railway*, a favorite resort for
" exercise."

There are in all at Saratoga 28 springs (including 6 spouting) ; some
chalybeate, others impregnated with iodine, sulphur, and magnesia,
and all powerfully charged with carbonic-acid gas. The most popular
is the *Congress Spring*, which is in Congress Park, protected by a neat
canopy. Each pint of its waters contains 75 grains of mineral constituents, and 49 cubic inches of carbonic-acid gas. The water is
cathartic and alterative, and should be drunk in the morning before
breakfast. The *Columbian Spring* is but a few rods S. W. of the Congress, in Congress Park. It contains much more iron than the Congress Spring, and acts as a tonic and diuretic. It should be drunk
after dinner ; if taken on an empty stomach it is apt to cause headache. The *Washington Spring* is situated in the grounds of the Clarendon Hotel, 600 ft. S. W. of Congress Spring. It is less ferruginous
than the Columbian, but is an excellent tonic and is pleasant to take.
The *Hathorn Spring*, one of the most popular, is in Spring St., opposite Congress Hall. The water contains nearly 94 grains of mineral
constituents and 47 cubic inches of carbonic-acid gas in each pint, is
a powerful cathartic, and acts also as a tonic and diuretic. The *Hamilton Spring* is at the cor. of Spring and Putnam Sts. (back of Congress Hall); its water is mildly cathartic and alterative. About 20
rods N. of the Hamilton (approached through an alley-way from Broadway) is the *Putnam Spring*, which is chalybeate, and has a bathing
establishment attached. Still to the N., in a trim little park on Lake
Ave., near Broadway, is the *Pavilion Spring*, which is one of the best
of the cathartic waters. Close by is the *United States Spring ;* its
water is tonic and alterative, and very agreeable to drink. Next to
the N. is the *Seltzer Spring*, which rises through a glass tube 3 ft. in
height, over the rim of which it flows. Its water closely resembles the
celebrated Seltzer of Germany, and is a sparkling and invigorating
drink. Less than 100 ft. N. of the Seltzer is the *High Rock Spring*,
the earliest known of the Saratoga springs. It bubbles up through
an aperture in a conical rock 4 ft. high, which has been formed by
deposits of the mineral substance of the water. A tasteful pagoda has
been erected over it, and a bottling-house stands by its side. The
water contains 69.5 grains of mineral constituents and 51 cubic inches
of carbonic-acid gas to each pint, and is strongly cathartic and tonic.
The *Star Spring* (formerly called " the President " and " the Iodine ")
is a few rods N. of the High Rock ; and next comes the celebrated
Empire Spring, whose water closely resembles that of the Congress

Spring. Near by is the *Red Spring*, containing an unusual proportion of iron ; and the *Saratoga Spring*, whose waters are mildly cathartic. The *Excelsior Spring* is situated in Excelsior Park, nearly 2 miles N. E. of the hotels, and is reached by a beautiful walk through woods and by a pleasant drive. It is one of 10 springs, none of which are used except this, and its waters are mildly cathartic. The *Eureka Spring* is a short distance beyond, and is surrounded by charming scenery (reached by stages : fare, 20c.). Its waters also are cathartic. Near by is the *Eureka White Sulphur Spring*, strongly impregnated with sulphuretted hydrogen, and used chiefly for bathing. There are bath-houses in the vicinity, where a bath may be had for 50 cents. The *Geyser Spring* is situated on Ballston Road, 1½ mile from Saratoga (reached by stages : fare, 20c.). Its water rises through a tin pipe and " spouts " 25 ft. into the air. The water is so highly charged with carbonic-acid gas that it foams like soda-water when drawn from a faucet, and exhilarates like champagne, and it is deliciously cold. The *Glacier Spring* is near the Geyser, and was formed by sinking an artesian well to the depth of 300 ft. The water spouts high above the pipe, and is powerfully cathartic. There are numerous other springs, but none calling for special mention. (R. L. Allen's " Analysis of the Principal Mineral Fountains at Saratoga " is a good guide to the use of the waters.)

The favorite resort in the vicinity of the Springs is *** Saratoga Lake,** a beautiful body of water, 8 miles long by 2½ wide, lying about 4 miles from the village (reached by omnibus : fare for the round trip, 75c.). On the shore of the lake is *Moon's Lake House*, where excellent fish and game dinners may be obtained at high prices. The fried potatoes of this house are famous, and are sold done up in papers like confectionery. On either side of the lake the drive is pleasant, and the view from *Snake Hill*, an eminence on the E. side, is the most attractive in the neighborhood. *Lake Lovely*, a pretty lakelet with wooded shores, lying near the Boulevard, and between Saratoga Lake and the village, is a favorite resort for picnics and rambles. The *Race-Course* is also on the Boulevard, ½ mile from the hotels. It is the finest mile-track in the country, has commodious stands, and is kept in excellent order. The *Saratoga Battle-Ground* is at Stillwater, 15 miles S. E. of the Springs (reached by a good carriage-road). A drive of 16 miles on the road to Mt. Pleasant leads to *Waring Hill*, which commands a fine view. *Lake Luzerne*, one of the loveliest lakes in the Adirondack region, may be visited from Saratoga, either by a carriage-drive or by the Adirondack Railway. (See p. 194.) The Greenfield Hills and the falls at Corinth are also within excursion distance. The Delaware & Hudson R. R. Co. have arranged a series of excursions to Lake George and Lake Champlain, particulars of which may be obtained at their ticket-offices.

Leaving the spacious depot at Saratoga, the train runs N. E. through an uninteresting country, and in 16 miles reaches **Fort Edward** (*Eldridge's Hotel, St. James*), whence a branch line diverges to Glens Falls

on the way to Lake George (see Route 41). Beyond Fort Edward there
is no important station until Whitehall (219 miles from New York) is
reached. **Whitehall** (*Hall's Hotel*) is a lumbering village of 4,500
inhabitants, situated at the head or S. end of Lake Champlain. It lies
in a rude, rocky ravine at the foot of Skene's Mt., and was a point of
much importance during the French and Indian Wars and the Revolution, but contains nothing now to detain the traveler. From Whitehall one route to Montreal passes N. E. *via* Castleton and Rutland, Vt.
(see Routes 27 and 35). The present route runs almost due N. along
the W. shore of Lake Champlain. The lake and the principal points
of interest on its shores are described in Route 41. Here we shall
only mention the special features which make the railway journey n-
joyable.

　Soon after leaving Whitehall the fine scenery begins (seats should
be obtained on the right-hand side of the cars). The R. R. track runs
close along the margin of the lake at the foot of steep bluffs, with fine
views across the water of the Vermont shore. At *Fort Ticonderoga*
(see p. 182) a branch line diverges and runs in three miles to Baldwin
on Lake George (see p. 181). At *Addison Junction*, 2 miles from Ticonderoga, connection is made with a railroad which connects with the
Central Vermont R. R. at Leicester Junction, and affords a direct
through route between Lake George and the White Mountains, the
trip being made in a day. From Ticonderoga to *Port Kent* (see p. 183),
a distance of about 55 miles, the scenery is remarkably varied and
beautiful, the train running now on high terraces along the mountain-
sides, now through black tunnels and deep rock-cuttings, now at the
base of towering cliffs, and affording at frequent intervals the most
exquisite lake-views. Port Kent is one of the entrances to the Adirondack region (see Route 42). Between Port Kent and *Plattsburg*
(309 miles from New York) the scenery is less impressive, but fine
views are had of the distant mountains. Plattsburg is described on p.
183. Beyond Plattsburg the route leaves the lake and traverses a
comparatively flat and uninteresting country. At *Rouse's Point* (334
miles), the train takes the track of the Champlain Div. of the Grand
Trunk R. R. and passes in 50 miles to Montreal (see Route 26). For
description of **Montreal,** see Route 56.

41. Lake George and Lake Champlain.

　THE usual approach to Lake George is by Route 40 to Fort Edward,
whence a branch road runs in 6 miles to **Glens Falls** (*Rockwell House,
American*), a village of 9,000 inhabitants, situated on the Hudson
River, at a cataract 50 ft. high. The falls are very fine, and the spot
is of peculiar interest as the scene of some of the most thrilling incidents of Cooper's romance, "The Last of the Mohicans." Stages connect with the trains at Glens Falls and run in 9 miles to *Caldwell*, at the
head of Lake George (fare from New York, $6.20). The stage-ride is
a pleasant one, and affords some striking views. About 2 miles from
the lake, in a dark glen, the road passes in sight of the *Williams Mon-*

ument, a plain marble shaft erected on the spot where Col. Williams, of Mass., founder of Williams College, fell in a battle with the French and English, Sept. 8, 1755. Near by is the storied *Bloody Pond,* into which the bodies of the slain were cast after the battle, tingeing its waters for many years (according to the legend) with a sanguine hue. The approach to the lake is very impressive, fine but fleeting glimpses being caught of its gleaming waters and blue hills. Finally, as the coach emerges into **Caldwell** (*Fort William Henry Hotel, Lake House, Fort George Hotel, Nelson's, Carpenter's*), the whole glorious scene bursts upon the view. Caldwell is a small village at the S. end of Lake George, much visited in summer, and chiefly noted for its hotels. The *Fort William Henry Hotel* ($3 to $5 a day) is one of the largest and finest summer hotels in the country. It stands on the site of the old Fort William Henry, remnants of which are still visible, and from its spacious piazzas an unrivaled view of the lake is obtained. About ½ mile to the S. E. are the picturesque ruins of Fort George, and the outlook embraces French and Prospect Mountains, and Rattlesnake Hill, all of which may be ascended from the village. Other fine hotels are the *Lake House* ($3 a day), and *Fort George Hotel* ($3 a day) near the ruins of Old Fort George. Many persons spend the season at Caldwell, making excursions to the various points of interest on the lake. The fishing is excellent, and pleasure-boats may be obtained in any numbers.

Lake George is a picturesque sheet of water in Warren and Washington Counties, N. Y., 33 miles long from N. E. to S. W., and from ¾ of a mile to 4 miles wide. It is the most famous and most frequented of American lakes, and is remarkable alike for the pellucid clearness of its water, its multitude of little islands, popularly supposed to correspond in number with the days of the year, and the beautiful scenery of its banks. The lake is bordered on either side by high hills, which here recede from the undulating shore, there lift their wooded crests in the distance, and again hang rugged cliffs over the water, or project bold promontories into its placid depths. It empties to the N. into Lake Champlain, from which it is separated by a narrow ridge only 4 miles wide; and, except in its widest part, seems more like a river than a lake. The Indian name of Lake George was "Horicon," meaning "silvery waters," and it is a great pity that this picturesque and expressive designation should have been superseded by its present commonplace title. When the French discovered it, early in the seventeenth century, they named it "Le Lac du St. Sacrement" (Lake of the Holy Sacrament), but its English conquerors called it after King George II., then on the throne.

Lake George fills a conspicuous and romantic place in American his'ory. For more than a century it was a channel of communication between Canada and the settlements on the Hudson. In the French and Indian War it was repeatedly occupied by large armies, and was the scene of several battles. In an engagement near the S. end of the lake, September 8, 1755, between the French and the English, Colonel Williams, of Massachusetts, the founder of Williams College, was killed, Baron Dieskau, the French commander, severely wounded, and the French totally defeated (see above). In 1757, Fort William Henry, at the same end of the lake, was besieged by the French General Montcalm, at the head of 8,000 men. The garrison capitulated after a gallant defense, and were barbarously massacred by the Indian allies of the French. In July, 1758, the army of General Abercrombie, about 15,000 strong, passed up the lake in 1,000 boats, and made an unsuccessful attack on Ticonderoga. A year later (July, 1759) General Amherst, with an almost equal force, also traversed the lake, and took Ticonderoga and Crown Point. The head of Lake George was the depot for the stores of the army of General Burgoyne before he began his march to Saratoga.

Two steamers daily (one in the morning and one in the afternoon) run between Caldwell and Baldwin at the N. end of the lake (fare ei'her way $2, which entitles the passenger to return free the same day). Leaving the pier in front of Fort William Henry Hotel, the steamer touches at the docks of the Lake House and Fort George Hotel, and then crosses to *Crosbyside*, opposite Caldwell, and the site of the spacious *Crosbyside Hotel* (250 guests, $10 to $17.50 per week). About a mile N. of Crosbyside is *St. Mary's on the Lake*, the summer retreat of the Paulist Fathers. The nearest island to Caldwell, about 1 mile distant, is *Tea Island*, so called from a " tea-house " once erected there for the entertainment of visitors, but of which only the stone walls now remain. This island is covered with noble trees, and bordered with picturesque rocks, and is a favorite resort for picnic and boating parties. A mile and a half beyond is **Diamond Island,** so named on account of the beautiful quartz-crystals found on it in abundance. Here, in 1777, was a military depot of Burgoyne's army, and here a severe skirmish occurred in that year between the garrison and a detachment of New England militia, in which the latter were signally worsted. Next beyond are the two diminutive islets known as the *Two Sisters*, and along the E. shore is *Long Island*, which appears from the boat to be part of the main shore. Just above is *Ferris's Bay*, where Montcalm moored his boats and landed his troops in 1757. **Dome Island,** a richly wooded island, is about 10 miles from Caldwell, near the center of the widest part of the lake. Putnam's troops took shelter here, while he went to apprise General Webb of the movements of the enemy at the mouth of *Northwest Bay*, which here runs in to the W. A little W. of Dome Island is the " Hermitage," or *Recluse Island*, where a gentleman from New York has erected a neat villa among the trees, and thrown a graceful bridge to a little dot of an island close at hand, named *Sloop Island*, from its fancied resemblance to a sloop, when seen from a certain point of view. *Pilot Mountain* is a precipitous peak on the E. shore, at the foot of which are the *Trout Pavilion* ($8 to $12 per week) and the *Kaatskill House* ($10 to $12 per week). Near these hotels are the best fishing-places on the lake, and the wooded mountains in the rear afford good hunting. From this point, the steamer runs nearly due N. to Bolton, passing between Dome and Recluse Islands, already mentioned. **Bolton** is a snug little village on the W. shore, the largest on the lake after Caldwell, and has fine hotels (the *Mohican House, Bolton, Lake View*, and *Wells*). Back of the village is *Prospect Mountain*, whence there is a fine view, and on the high plateau to the W. are several charming little lakelets. *Ganouskie Bay* extends for 5 miles above Bolton, and is

closed in on the E. by *Tongue Mountain*, which comes in literally like
a tongue of the lake, into the center of which it seems to protrude,
with the bay on one side, and the main passage of the waters on the
other. On the right or E. shore, nearly opposite the Tongue, is the
bold semicircular palisade called *Shelving Rock*. Passing this picturesque feature of the landscape, and afterward the point of Tongue
Mountain, we come to *Fourteen-Mile Island*, at the entrance of the
"Narrows," where there is a large hotel ($10 to $12 a week). On the
mainland, about 1 mile S. of Fourteen-Mile Island, is *Shelving-Rock
Fall*, situated on a small stream, which empties into Shelving-Rock
Bay. It is a very picturesque cascade, and is much resorted to by
picnic-parties. At * **The Narrows** the shores of the lake approach
each other, the space between being crowded with islands. This is the
most picturesque and striking portion of the lake scenery, and enthu-
siastic visitors have declared it to be unsurpassed for beauty by any
of the famous lakes of Switzerland or Scotland. On the E. is *Black
Mountain*, the highest of the peaks that line the lake-shore. It is
well wooded at its base, though frequent fires have swept over its surface, while the summit of the mountain stands out rocky and bare.
Its height is 2,878 ft., and the view from the summit is very extensive.
The ascent is easy from either Black Mountain Point or Hulett's Landing. Beyond Black Mountain the steamer passes *Sugar-Loaf Mountain*, on the E.; *Bosom Bay*, with the little village of Hulett's Landing;
and *Deer's-Leap Mountain*, on the W., said to be so named from the
tragical fate of a buck, which, being hotly pursued by a hunter and his
dogs, leaped over the precipitous side of the mountain facing the lake,
and was impaled on a sharp-pointed tree below.

Emerging from the Narrows on the N., we approach a long, projecting slip of fertile land known as *Sabbath-Day Point*. This spot is
memorable as the scene of a fight in 1756 between the colonists and a
party of French and Indians. The former, sorely pressed, and unable
to escape across the lake, made a bold defense and defeated the enemy, killing very many of their men. In 1776 Sabbath-Day Point
was again the scene of a battle between some American militia and a
party of Indians and Tories, when the latter were repulsed, and some
40 of their number were killed and wounded. This part of Lake
George is even more charming in its views, both up and down the
lake, than it is in its numerous historical reminiscences. On a calm,
sunny day the romantic passage of the Narrows, as seen to the S., is
wonderfully fine; while in the other direction is the broad bay or
widening of the lake, entered as the boat passes Sabbath-Day Point.
On the W. side of this widening of the lake (which is here 4 miles
across) is the village of **Hague** (*Bay View House, Phœnix Hotel, Trout
House*, each $7 per week), near which are some good bass-fishing
grounds and two trout streams. Below Hague the lake narrows again
to a narrow pass between the precipitous *Anthony's Nose*, on the E.,
and *Rogers' Slide*, on the W. This pass is not unlike that of the
Highlands of the Hudson as approached from the S. Rogers' Slide is
a rugged and steep promontory, about 400 ft. high, down which the

Indians, to their great bewilderment, supposed the bold ranger, Major
Rogers, to have slid, when they pursued him to the brink of the cliff.
A short distance N. of it, on a bold promontory, is the *Rogers' Rock
Hotel*, one of the largest and best on the lake ($3 a day, $14 a week).
Stages run from the hotel to Addison Junction, where connection is
made with the White Mountain trains (see p. 177).   Beyond Rogers'
Slide the lake is narrow, the shores low and uninteresting, and soon
the voyage terminates at *Baldwin* (33 miles from Caldwell).   E. of the
landing is the low-lying *Prisoners' Island*, where, during the French
War, those taken captive by the English were confined; and to the
N. is *Lord Howe's Point*, where the English army under Lord Howe,
consisting of 16,000 men, landed previous to the attack on Ticonderoga.

From the steamboat-landing at Baldwin, a branch of the Delaware & Hudson
Canal Co.'s R. R. (see Route 40) runs to Fort Ticonderoga, on Lake Champlain, 5
miles distant.   At Ticonderoga village, about midway between the two lakes, the
stream which discharges Lake George into Lake Champlain tumbles down a rocky
descent in a highly picturesque fall.

Lake Champlain.

Lake Champlain lies between New York and Vermont, and extends
from Whitehall in the former State to St. John's in Canada.   It is 126
miles long, and varies in breadth from 40 rods to $12\frac{1}{8}$ miles.   Its outline is very irregular, the shores being indented by numerous bays, and
there are upward of 50 islands and islets.   Its depth varies from 54 to
399 ft., and vessels of 800 or 1,000 tons navigate its whole extent.
The principal rivers entering the lake are Wood Creek, at its head;
the outlet of Lake George, the Ausable, Saranac, and Chazy, from
New York; and Otter, Winooski, Lamoille, and Missisquoi, from Vermont.   The outlet of the lake is the Sorel or Richelieu River, sometimes called the St. John's, which empties into the St. Lawrence,
and, with the Chambly Canal, affords a passage for vessels to the
ocean.   On the south it communicates, by means of the Champlain
Canal, with the Hudson River at Troy.   Navigation is usually closed
by ice about the end of November, and opens early in April.   The
waters of the lake abound with bass, pickerel, muscalonge, and other
varieties of fish.   This lake, filling a valley inclosed by high mountains, is celebrated for its magnificent scenery, which embraces the
Green Mountains of Vermont on the E. and the Adirondack Mountains of New York on the W.   Several pleasant villages and watering-
places, with one or two important cities, are situated on its shores, and
it has always been one of the most attractive features of the Northern
Tour.

A writer in "Picturesque America" institutes the following comparison between the sister lakes: "On Lake George the mountains come down to the edge of
the waters, which lie embowered in an amphitheatre of cliffs and hills; but on
Lake Champlain there are mountain-ranges stretching in parallel lines far away to
the right and left, leaving, between them and the lake, wide areas of charming
champaign country, smiling with fields and orchards and nestling farmhouses.
There are on Lake Champlain noble panoramas; one is charmed with the shut-in

sylvan beauties of Lake George; but the wide expanses of Lake Champlain are, while different in character, as essentially beautiful. It is in every way a noble lake. Ontario is too large—a very sea; Lake George is perhaps too petty and confined; but Lake Champlain is not so large as to lose, for the voyager upon its waters, views of either shore, nor so small as to contract and limit the prospect." The name of the lake is derived from that of Samuel de Champlain, the French Governor of Canada, who discovered it on the 4th of July, 1609.

Whitehall, at the head or S. end of the lake, has already been described on p. 177. The Lake Champlain Steamers used to start from Whitehall, but since the completion of the railway along the W. shore (described in Route 40), they come no higher than Fort Ticonderoga (24 miles below). The narrowness of this upper portion of the lake gives it much more the appearance of a river than of a lake. For the first 20 miles the average width does not exceed ½ mile, and at one point it is not more than 40 rods across. Fort Ticonderoga is the point where the lake widens and becomes a lake in fact as well as in name.

Fort Ticonderoga (Fort Ticonderoga Hotel) is a station on the lake at the foot of Mt. Defiance, whence a branch railroad runs in 5 miles to Baldwin on Lake George (as described above), and whence the Lake Champlain steamers run daily in summer to Plattsburg. Ticonderoga village is 2 miles from the landing, and the ruins of the famous old * **Fort Ticonderoga** are on a high hill about a mile to the N. The view from the crumbling ramparts is extremely fine; and a still finer one may be obtained from the top of * *Mt. Defiance,* which is easily ascended from the village. *Mt. Independence* lies in Vermont opposite Ticonderoga, about a mile distant; remains of military works are still visible there. *Mt. Hope,* an elevation about a mile W. of Ticonderoga, was occupied by Burgoyne previous to the recapture of the fort, in 1777.

Fort Ticonderoga was first built by the French in 1756, and was called by them "Carillon." We have already mentioned Abercrombie's attempt to capture it in 1758, and Lord Amherst's more successful campaign in the following year. (See "Lake George.") The French, being unable to hold the fort, dismantled and abandoned it at the approach of the English forces; and soon afterward Crown Point was also abandoned. The English enlarged and greatly strengthened the two fortifications, expending thereon $10,000,000, which was at that time an immense sum for such a purpose. The fort and field-works of Ticonderoga embraced an area of several miles. After the cession of Canada to the English, in 1763, the fort was allowed to fall into partial decay; and at the outbreak of the Revolution it was one of the first strongholds captured by the Americans. Colonel Ethan Allen, of Vermont, at the head of the Green Mountain Boys, surprised the unsuspecting garrison, penetrated to the very bedside of the commandant, and, waking him, demanded the surrender of the fort. "In whose name and to whom?" exclaimed the surprised officer. "In the name of the great Jehovah and the Continental Congress!" thundered the intrepid Allen, and the fort was immediately surrendered. Afterward, however, in the campaign of 1777, Burgoyne easily reduced it by placing a battery of artillery on the summit of *Mount Defiance,* on the south side of the Lake George outlet and 750 feet above the lake, from which shot could be thrown into the midst of the American works. After the surrender of Burgoyne, the fort was dismantled, and from that time suffered to fall into ruin and decay.

Leaving the landing at Fort Ticonderoga (about 1 P. M.) the steamer runs N. to *Shoreham* on the Vermont shore, and thence crosses the lake to the village of *Crown Point* (Gunnison's Hotel), with fine mountain-views all the way. Six miles below on the W. side is the rugged promontory of *** Crown Point,** which was the site of Fort St. Frederic, erected by the French in 1731, and of a much stronger work subsequently erected by the English, the massive ruins of which are still plainly visible. The history of this fort is strikingly similar to that of Fort Ticonderoga, the fate of either fortress generally determining that of the other. In 1759 the English took possession of the whole region; in 1775 Crown Point was taken by Ethan Allen at the time he captured Ticonderoga; and in 1777 Burgoyne retook it and made it his chief depot of supplies in the advance to Saratoga. A light-house now stands on the peak of the promontory, but otherwise all is desolation. Fine views are obtained from the bastions of the old fort. Opposite Crown Point, on the Vermont shore, is *Chimney Point.* Be-tween them the lake is very narrow, but opens out above into the broad Bulwagga Bay, on the W. shore of which is the pretty village of *Port Henry* (20 miles from Fort Ticonderoga), with extensive iron-works and ore-beds. Just beyond Port Henry the scenery is exceed-ingly fine. To the E. the Green Mountains with their lofty peaks, Mt. Mansfield and Camel's Hump, rise against the distant horizon; and on the W. " the Adirondack Hills mingle their blue tops with the clouds." Eleven miles below Port Henry, on Northwest Bay, is **West-port** (*Weed House*), a favorite entrance to the Adirondack region by way of Elizabethtown (see Route 42). Ten miles below Westport, on the same side, is the small village of *Essex,* and between them the steamer passes *** Split Rock,** where a portion of the mountain ½ acre in extent and 30 ft. high is isolated by a remarkable fissure and converted into an island. Leaving Essex the steamer passes out into the broadest reach of the lake, bears over toward the Vermont shore, passes the islets called the Four Brothers and Rock Dunder, and soon reaches the beautiful city of **Burlington** (described on p. 132). The view of the city as approached from the lake is remarkably pleasing. Leaving Burlington, the steamer runs across the lake 10 miles to **Port Kent,** where tourists take the stage for Keeseville in visiting the famous **Ausable Chasm** (described on p. 192). From this point, whether on land or water, the views in every direction are striking and beautiful. The most interesting feature of the town is the old stone mansion of Elkanah Watson, on a hill near the lake. Port Kent is one of the entrances to the Adirondack region (see Route 42).

Three miles below Port Kent, the Ausable River comes in on the W., and 5 miles farther the steamer enters the narrow channel between the mainland and *Valcour Island,* which was the scene of the desperate naval battle between Arnold and Carleton, in 1776. Beyond, the steamer enters Cumberland Bay, and stops at **Plattsburg** (*Fouquet House,* $2.50 to $3 a day), a prosperous village of 8,000 inhabitants on the W. shore of the lake, at the mouth of the Saranac River. A branch railroad runs from Plattsburg to Ausable (20 miles), and this is the favorite entrance to the Adirondacks (see Route 42). The State R. R. runs 16 miles N. W. to *Dannemora,* the site of the Clinton State Prison, and 5 miles farther is the trout-teeming *Chazy Lake,* 4 miles

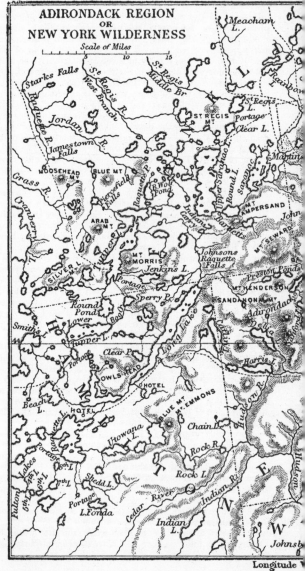

ADIRONDACK REGION
OR
NEW YORK WILDERNESS

Scale of Miles

5   10   15

long by 1½ wide. Six miles W. of Chazy Lake is the upper **Chateau-gay Lake,** 5 miles long and 2 miles wide, whence a navigable stream, 4 miles long, leads to the Lower Lake, 2½ miles long.

Cumberland Bay, on which Plattsburg is situated, was the scene of the victory of Macdonough and Macomb over the British naval and land forces, under Commodore Downie and Sir George Provost, familiarly known as the *Battle of Platts-burgh.* Here the American commodore awaited the arrival of the British fleet, which passed Cumberland Head about eight o'clock in the morning of September 11, 1814. The first gun from the fleet was the signal for commencing the attack on land. Sir George Provost, with about 14,000 men, furiously assaulted the defenses of the town, while the battle raged between the fleets, in full view of the armies. General Macomb, with about 3,000 men, mostly undisciplined, foiled the repeated assaults of the enemy, until the capture of the British fleet, after an action of about two hours, obliged the army to retire, with the loss of 2,500 men and a large portion of their baggage and ammunition.

The Lake Champlain steamers do not run beyond Plattsburg, so that the tourist loses the opportunity of seeing the interesting and diversified scenery of the N. portion of the lake. Those desiring to go farther can do so by Route 40. Daily steamers run across the lake in 25 miles to **St. Albans** (see p. 129), passing among beautiful islands.

42. The Adirondacks.

THIS remarkable tract, which, 30 years ago, was known even by name only to a few hunters, trappers, and lumbermen, lies in the northern part of New York State, between Lakes George and Champlain on the E., and the St. Lawrence on the N. W. It extends on the N. to Canada and on the S. nearly to the Mohawk River. The mountains rise from an elevated plateau, which extends over this portion of the country for 150 miles in latitude and 100 in longitude, and is itself nearly 2,000 ft. above the level of the sea. Five ranges of mountains, running nearly parallel, traverse this plateau from southwest to northeast, where they terminate on the shores of Lake Champlain. The most westerly, which bears the name of the Clinton Range, though it is also sometimes called the Adirondack Range, begins at Little Falls and terminates at Trembleau Point, on Lake Champlain. It contains the highest peaks of the entire region, the loftiest being Mt. Marcy (or Tahawus), 5,337 ft. high, while Mts. Seward, McIntyre, McMartin, Whiteface, Dix Peak, Colden, Santanoni, Snowy Mountain, and Pharaoh are none far from 5,000 ft. high. Though no one of these peaks attains to the height of the loftiest summits of the White Mountains of New Hampshire, or the Black Mountains of North Carolina, their general elevation surpasses that of any range east of the Rocky Mountains. The entire number of mountains in the Adirondack region is supposed to exceed 500, of which only a few have received separate names. They are all wild and savage, and covered with the "forest primeval," except the stony summits of the highest, which rise above all vegetation but that of mosses, grasses, and dwarf Alpine plants.

In the valleys between the mountains lie many beautiful lakes and ponds, more than 1,000 in number. The general level of these lakes is about 1,500 ft. above the sea, but Lake Perkins, the highest of them, has nearly three times that elevation. Some of them are 20 miles in length, while others cover only a few acres. The largest of these lakes are Long Lake, the Saranacs, Tupper, the Fulton Lakes, and Lakes Colden, Henderson, Sanford, Eckford, Raquette, Forked, Newcomb, and Pleasant. "Steep, densely wooded mountains," says a writer in "Picturesque America," describing these lakes, "rise from their margins; beautiful bays indent their borders, and leafy points jut out; spring brooks trickle in; while the shallows are fringed with water-grasses and flowering plants, and covered sometimes with acres of white and yellow water-lilies. The lakes are all lovely and romantic in everything except their names, and the scenery they offer, in combination with the towering mountains and the old and savage forest, is not surpassed on earth. In natural features it greatly resembles Switzerland and the Scottish Highlands, as they must have been before those regions were settled and cultivated." This labyrinth of lakes is connected by a very intricate system of rivers, rivulets, and brooks. The Saranac and the Ausable run in nearly parallel lines toward the N. E., discharging their waters into Lake Champlain. They define upon the map the position of the valleys, which have the same general arrangement throughout the whole chain, and to some extent the position of the ranges of mountains also. In the other direction, the Boreas, the Hudson, and the Cedar Rivers, which all unite below in the Hudson, define the extension of the valleys of the Ausable and its branches on the southern declivity of the great plateau; and farther W. the chain of lakes, including Long Lake, Raquette Lake, and the Fulton Lakes, lie in the same line with the valley of the Saranac, and mark its extension from the central elevation of the plateau toward the S. W. The largest and most beautiful river of the Adirondack region—its great highway and artery—is the Raquette, which rises in Raquette Lake, in the W. part of Hamilton County, and after a devious course of 120 miles flows into the St. Lawrence.

The mountains of the entire region are covered with forests, groves of birch, beech, maple, and ash, succeeding to the evergreens, among which the most common are the hemlock, spruce, fir, and cedar, with the valuable white pine intermixed with and overtopping the rest. In the lower lands along the streams a denser growth of the evergreens is more common, forming almost impenetrable swamps of cedar, tamarack or hackmatack, and hemlock. In these woods and mountain solitudes are found the panther, the great black bear, the wolf, the wild-cat, the lynx, and the wolverine. The moose is said to be extinct, but deer are abundant; and so, also, are the fisher, sable, otter, mink, muskrat, fox, badger, woodchuck, rabbit, and several varieties of the squirrel. There are scarcely any snakes, and none large or venomous. Among the birds are the grand black war-eagle, several kinds of hawk, owl, loon, and duck; the crane, heron, raven, crow, partridge, and numerous smaller birds. The salmon-trout and the speckled trout swarm in the lakes, and the latter also in the brooks and rivers. The lake-trout are caught sometimes of 20 pounds and more in weight; but the speckled trout are seldom large.

Outfit and Guides.—Nearly all traveling in the Adirondacks is done by means of boats of small size and slight build, rowed by a single guide, and made so light that the craft can be lifted from the water and carried on the guide's shoulders from lake to lake or from stream to stream. Competent guides, steady and intelligent men, can be hired at all the hotels for $2 to $3 a day, who will provide boats, tents, and everything requisite for a trip. Each traveler should have a guide and a boat to himself, and the cost of their maintenance in the woods is not more than $1 a week for each man of the party. The fare is chiefly trout and venison, of which an abundance is easily procured. A good-sized valise or carpet-bag will hold all the clothes that one person needs for a two months' trip in the woods, besides those he wears in. The following list comprises the essentials of an outfit for a man : A complete undersuit of woolen or flannel, with a "change"; stout pantaloons, vest, and coat; a felt hat; two pairs of stockings; a pair of common winter-boots and camp-shoes; a rubber blanket or coat; a pair of pliable buckskin gloves, with chamois-skin gauntlets tied or buttoned at the elbow; a hunting-knife, belt, and a pint tin cup; a pair of warm blankets, towel, soap, etc. A lady's outfit should comprise : A short walking-dress, with Turkish drawers fastened with a band tightly at the ankle; a flannel change throughout; thick balmoral boots, with rubbers; a pair of camp-shoes, warm and loose-fitting; a soft felt hat, rather broad in the brim; a water-proof or rubber coat and cap; a pair of buckskin gloves with armlets of chamois-skin or thick drilling, sewed on at the wrist of the glove and buttoned near the elbow so tightly as to prevent the entrance of flies; and a net of fine Swiss mull as a protection against mosquitoes, gnats, etc.

Game Laws.—By the laws of New York, the killing of *Quail* is prohibited between Jan. 1st and Nov. 1st; of *Partridge*, between Jan. 1st and Sept. 1st; of *Woodcock*, between Jan. 1st and Aug. 1st; of *wood-duck, wild duck, wild goose*, or *brant*, between May 1st and Sept. 1st. The killing of *Moose* and *Deer* is prohibited between Dec. 1st and Sept. 1st. It is unlawful to kill deer with any kind of trap or spring gun; to kill fawns in the spotted coat; or to chase deer with dogs. The taking of *speckled trout* is prohibited between Sept. 1st and April 1st; of *black bass*, between Jan. 1st and May 20th; of *salmon* or *lake trout*, between Oct. 1st and March 1st. "No person shall use any swivel or punt gun, or net, for killing or capturing any wild duck, goose, or brant; nor use any gun, except such as are habitually fired from the shoulder, under penalty of $100; nor shoot at wild fowl from a sail or steam vessel, or by the light of a lantern during the night, under penalty of $25. No blind, trap, net, or snare shall be used for taking any of the above-named birds, nor trout, black bass, or pickerel. Penalty $25 to $50."

Fares.—From New York to Plattsburg, $9.05; to Ausable Chasm, $9; to Elizabethtown, $8.50; to Port Kent, $8.50; to Westport, $7.50; to Lake Placid, $11; to Keeseville, $9; to Paul Smith's, $13.55; to Prospect House, $14.55; to Martin's, $13.55; to Bartlett's, $14.55; to Luzerne, $5.15; to North Creek, $6.40; to Blue Mt. Lake, $8.90; to Long Lake Village, $10.90; to Schroon Lake Village, $7.90; to Root's, $3.70. Local fares are given in the description of the routes.

There are several routes by which the Adirondack Wilderness may be entered, but very much the larger number of visitors choose that *via* **Plattsburg,** on Lake Champlain. From New York, Plattsburg is reached by Route 40 or Route 41. From Boston by Route 26 or Route 27 to Burlington, and thence by steamer across the lake. Plattsburg is described on page 183. In attempting to guide the tourist through the intricacies of the Adirondacks, we shall first take him on what we shall call the "Grand Through Route," embracing the principal points of interest, and extending through the region from N. E. to S. W.; next we shall indicate the several shorter excursions that may be advantageously made; and, finally, we shall enter the southern portion of the region by way of Schroon Lake.

I. Grand Through Route.

From Plattsburg (see p. 183) a railway runs S. W. to *Ausable*, on the Ausable River (20 miles, fare $1). At Ausable, stages connect with the trains and convey the traveler either to Martin's (fare, $3.50), to Paul Smith's (fare, $3.50), or to Keeseville (fare, $1.50). The ride to Martin's (37 miles) is over a good road, amid picturesque scenery, **Whiteface Mountain,** the great outpost of the Adirondacks, being in sight for a considerable portion of the way. At the village of *Ausable Forks*, 3 miles from the railway terminus, the traveler can (by hiring a special conveyance) turn off into a road which leads through the famous * **Wilmington Pass,** and can regain the main road about 2 miles before it reaches Saranac Lake. The distance by this route is not much longer than by the main road, and the scenery is incomparably finer. The view of Whiteface from Wilmington was pronounced by Prof. Agassiz to be one of the finest mountain-views he had ever seen. The mountain is easily ascended from *Wilmington*, where guides may always be had. A carriage-road leads nearly to the summit, and the remainder of the ascent is on horseback. There is a house near the summit, where a comfortable night's lodging may be obtained. The * view from Whiteface (4,918 ft. high) is indescribably grand, only surpassed by that from the top of Mount Marcy. The "Pass" is 6 miles beyond Wilmington. It is a profound chasm cloven boldly through the flank of Whiteface, scarcely wide enough for the road and the river, and 2 miles long. Through the Pass flows the Ausable River, with a succession of rapids and cataracts, and on either side rises a majestic mountain-wall, so high that the crowded row of pines along its broken and wavy crest is diminished to a fringe. At the foot of Whiteface, on the S. W. side (reached by a road which branches off to the right just beyond the Notch), lies * **Lake Placid,** one of the loveliest lakes of the Wilderness, 5 miles long and about 2 miles wide. There are several large hotels here (*Lake Placid House*, *Stevens*, *Grand View*, and *Nash's*, each $8 to $10 per week), and it is a favorite summer resort, the fishing being good, and the scenery delightful. One of the best views of Whiteface is obtained from Lake Placid, and near its southern shore is one of the curiosities of the region, *Paradox Pond*, whose outlet in high water flows back on the lake. Also near by is *Mirror Lake*, formerly called Bennett's Pond. Two miles S., on the road to Elizabethtown, is the hamlet of *North Elba* (Mountain View House), close to which (on the S.) is the house and farm of "John Brown, of Ossawattomie," who lies buried close by. The usual route to Lake Placid is by way of Westport (see p. 183) and Elizabethtown (sub-Route III.).

The regular stage route to Paul Smith's and Martin's leads from Ausable Station by Ausable Forks to *French's Hotel* (18 miles), where a stop is made for dinner. The Saranac River is then followed for 10 miles to **Bloomingdale** (*St. Armand House*), which is a convenient center from which to visit several resorts. Martin's is 8 miles distant, and Paul Smith's 10 miles. Seven miles N. (reached by private conveyance) is the fish-abounding *Rainbow Lake* (Wardner's Rainbow House, $8 per week), 3 miles long and about 1 mile wide. Near Wardner's are Jones Pond, Round and Mud Ponds, Loon Lake (all famous fishing-grounds); and 9 miles N. E. is Lewis Smith's *Hunter's Home*, on the N. Saranac. At Bloomingdale the road forks, one arm extending S. W. to Martin's (8 miles) and the other N. W. to Paul Smith's (10 miles). The route to Martin's passes up the valley of the Saranac.

*Martin's Saranac House (200 guests, $10 to $12 per week) is a large and comfortable hotel on the very edge of the beautiful *Lower Saranac Lake*, which is 7 miles long and 2 miles wide, studded with romantic islands, 52 in number. This is one of the best places in the Adirondacks to procure guides, boats, and camp-equipage, and is also an excellent point from which to make excursions. The Saranac River connects the lake with *Round Lake*, 3 miles W. Round Lake is about 2 miles in diameter, is a beautiful sheet of water, dotted with islets, and is famous for its storms. It is in turn connected with the *Upper Saranac Lake* by another stretch of the Saranac River, on which stands *Bartlett's Hotel*, one of the best and most frequented of the Adirondack taverns ($10 to $14 a week). A small steamer plies on the Lower Saranac, running from Martin's to the rapids below Round Lake, whence row-boats carry the passengers to Bartlett's. From a point near Bartlett's a fine view can be obtained of Round Lake and the surrounding mountains, and a guide will conduct the traveler to the summit of *Ampersand Mountain*, whence the view is superb. At the foot of the mountain, on the S., lies the sequestered *Ampersand Lake*, where Agassiz, Lowell, and Holmes used, a few years ago, to pitch their "Philosophers' Camp." A short "carry" of ½ mile conducts from Bartlett's to the *Upper Saranac Lake, the largest and one of the most beautiful of the Adirondack lakes. It is 8 miles long and from 1 to 3 miles wide, and its surface is studded with little islands. At its head is **Prospect House** ($10 to $17.50 a week), another favorite resort, commanding delightful views, and situated in the vicinity of excellent fishing-waters. A telegraph-line connects the hotel with the outer world, and good roads run out to Martin's (16 miles) and Paul Smith's (17 miles), and continue to the main stage-road already described. A small steamer plies on the lake, making the circuit from the Prospect House twice daily, and touching at the Sweeney Carry, Corey's, and Bartlett's (fare, $1). The "Route of the Nine Carries" conducts from the Upper Saranac to *St. Regis Lake*, on which is situated *Paul Smith's, the largest and by many considered the best hotel in the Wilderness (300 guests, $17.50 per week). It is equally popular with Martin's as a rendezvous and outfitting-point, for which it offers many advantages. It has a telegraph-office, and is connected by stage-road with Ausable, at the terminus of the Plattsburg R. R. (38 miles), with Martin's (14 miles), and with the Prospect House (17 miles). St. Regis Lake is one of the most picturesque of the group, and is surrounded by numerous small ponds. A short distance N. E. lies the *Rainbow Lake*, a favorite resort with fishermen (see above).

The "Round Trip" from Paul Smith's comprises a circuit of about 45 miles, including the St. Regis and Saranac Lakes, and the principal adjacent points of interest, and affording every variety of locomotion known to the Wilderness, without enough of any to become wearisome. The route is as follows : By boat across Lower St. Regis Lake, Spitfire Pond, and Upper St. Regis Lake, with connecting streams (4 miles); on horse or foot over the St. Germain Carry, 1¼ mile (horse $1.50); boat across Big Clear Pond (2 miles); carriage to the Prospect House at head of Upper Saranac Lake, 3 miles (boat $1.50, passengers 50c. each); on small steamer through Saranac Lake, 8 miles (fare $1); short carry to Bartlett's (50c.) and thence by river and Round Lake (3 miles); by steamer on Saranac River and Lower Saranac Lake to Martin's (9 miles); carriage from Martin's to Paul Smith's (14 miles). From Martin's the "Round Trip" may be made in reverse order.

At Bartlett's (see p. 188) three great Wilderness routes diverge: one N. to Paul Smith's, already described in the "Round Trip"; another W., to the Tupper Lake region ; and a third S., to Long and Raquette Lakes. The route to the Tupper Lakes is from Bartlett's or the Prospect House to the S. W. end of the Upper Saranac Lake, whence *Sweeney's Carry* leads across in 3 miles to the Raquette River (boats hauled across for $1.50). From the W. terminus of the Carry a small steamer runs down the river to Cronk's on * **Tupper Lake,** which is so named from the guide or hunter who first discovered it. It is a lovely sheet of water, 7 miles long by 1 to 3 miles wide, surrounded by primeval forests, and containing many picturesque rocky islands, covered with evergreens. At its head the wild and little-explored Bog River flows into the lake over a romantic cascade, which forms one of the great attractions of the Adirondacks, being a famous place for trout, and having near by one of the most popular hotels in the Wilderness (*Cronk's Lake Side House*). At the N. end of the lake is *Moody's Tupper Lake House,* and from this point the Raquette River may be descended to the pretty *Piercefield Falls* (9 miles), or to *Big Wolf Pond* (10 miles). The latter is reached by turning off from the river into Raquette Pond 2 miles below Lake Tupper, and then ascending Wolf Brook to *Little Wolf Pond,* whence a carry of ½ mile leads to Big Wolf Pond. From the S. end of Tupper Lake an easy route leads 9 miles S. through the lovely *Round Pond* to **Little Tupper Lake,** a lonely and sequestered sheet of water, 6 miles long, dotted with islands, and hedged in by rugged and precipitous shores. It is comparatively little visited on account of its remoteness, but affords excellent sport. On Sand Point, near the foot of the lake, is a small tavern and store. From Little Tupper a series of small ponds and carries leads E. to Long Lake.

From Cronk's a route leads over a 3-mile carry to *Horseshoe Pond,* and thence through a chain of ponds with an occasional short carry 12 miles farther to the dismal and deer-abounding **Mud Lake,** 4 miles in circumference. This lake is covered in their season with lily-pads and margined with rank wild grass, which attracts deer in greater numbers than any other spot in the Wilderness. It is also said to have been a favorite feeding-ground of the moose before they were exterminated. Seven miles N. of Mud Lake is **Cranberry Lake,** one of the largest of the Adirondack series, being 15 miles long and 1 to 5 miles wide. It discharges to the N. through the Oswegatchie River, and is usually visited from the W. via *Gouverneur,* a station on the Rome, Watertown & Ogdensburg R. R., 108 miles from Rome (see p. 155). The distance from Gouverneur to the lake is 36 miles. *Silver Lake, Pleasant Lake,* and numerous other ponds and lakelets lie scattered in every direction over this remote and desolate region.

The usual route from the Saranac region to Long Lake and Raquette Lake is via *Corey's*, a beautifully situated hotel at the S. end of the Upper Saranac Lake (2 miles from Sweeney's Carry), whence the *Indian Carry* leads across in 1 mile (75c. a load) to the *Stony Creek Ponds* (sometimes called Spectacle Ponds). *Farmer's Hotel* (40 guests) stands at the S. terminus of the carry close by the first of the Stony Creek Ponds, which are 3 in number and discharge by Stony Creek into the Raquette. The river is entered at a point 20 miles from Tupper Lake and about 13 miles from Long Lake. The route is up stream, and in 7 miles *Mother Johnson's* tavern, rendered famous by Murray, is reached. Mother Johnson died in 1875. A few rods above the house are the *Raquette Falls*, about 12 ft. high, around which the boats are hauled (1¼ mile, $1.50 a load). About 4 miles above Johnson's Carry, the mouth of Cold River, coming down from Mt. Seward, is passed; and a mile beyond the boat enters * **Long Lake,** with Buck Mt. on the right and the Blueberry Mts. on the left. Long Lake is the longest, though not the widest, of the Adirondack lakes, and for 20 miles resembles a great river. The scenery on the lake itself is varied and exquisite, and from it a noble view can be had of *Mt. Seward*, 4,348 ft. high. On the E. side of the lake (3½ miles from the head) is *Long Lake Village* (Long Lake Hotel, $8 a week), the center of supplies for all the adjacent region and the starting-point for routes radiating in all directions. Many noted guides live here, and the vicinity is much frequented by sportsmen. Stages run twice weekly in the sporting season *via* Newcomb and Minerva to *N. Creek* on the Adirondack R. R. and *Pottersville* at the foot of Schroon Lake (see p. 194), each about 40 miles distant (fare $4.50). The Carthage road runs S. W. past the N. end of Raquette Lake. *Little Tupper Lake* (see p. 189) is visited from Long Lake by a route of 15 miles leading through Slim and Clear Ponds. *Blue Mountain Lake* (see p. 191) is about 8 miles from the village *via* South Pond. *Grampus Lake* is reached from Long Lake by ascending the Big Brook ; and the Handsome and Mohegan Ponds may be visited from Grampus. Near the head of the lake on the W. is * *Owl's Head Mountain* (2,789 ft. high), which is easily ascended with guides, and which affords a fine view. At its base lie Clear Pond and Owl's Head Pond, famous for trout.

From the S. end of Long Lake an easy route of 10 miles with two carries leads through *Forked Lake*, a lovely sheet of water 5 miles long, to * **Raquette Lake,** the last of the great chain of lakes we have been following. Shortly after leaving Long Lake the picturesque *Buttermilk Falls* are passed, and the entire journey is through the midst of fine forest scenery with occasional mountain-views. Raquette Lake is 12 miles long and 5 miles wide at the widest part, and its surface is sprinkled with the most beautiful little islets. Dense forests close in on every side, and as it is comparatively unfrequented it makes rich returns to the sportsman. A short distance from its N. end is *Cary's Hotel*, which is connected by a rough stage-road with Long Lake Village (14 miles). *Hathorn's Forest Cottages* ($7 per week) are in a pleasant grove at South Beach, and *Blanchard's Camp* is at the head of Marryatt's Bay. Most visitors to the lake encamp on one of its projecting points. There is a multitude of lakelets and ponds in the vicinity of Raquette Lake, but only two or three require special mention. *Shallow Lake* (reached by an inlet from Marryatt Bay) and *Queer Lake* (2 miles S.) are noted for trout. *Beach's Lake,* a fine sheet of water, 3½ miles long, lies 4 miles N. W., and is reached by a long and tedious "carry." A series of ponds and carries leads from Beach's Lake to Little Tupper Lake (already described), but the route is long (15 miles) and difficult. *Salmon Lake* is N. of Beach's Lake, and may be reached by a carry of 2 miles. A pull of 4 miles up the Brown Tract Inlet, from the S. W. point of Raquette Lake, and a carry of 1½ mile lead to the upper or eighth of the chain of **Fulton Lakes,** which extend southwestward into the "John Brown Tract" (see p. 155). From the *Eighth Lake* a short portage leads to the *Seventh,* from which the *Sixth* can be reached by boat. There is a portage between *Sixth* and *Fifth,* and also one between *Fifth* and *Fourth.* *** Fourth Lake** is the largest of the chain; it is studded with islands and surrounded by rugged and precipitous shores. Hemlock grows down to the edge of the water; and in the undisturbed repose of the waters the fringes of foliage are clearly reflected. In the center of the lake is a beautiful rocky islet known as *Elba.* There is a passage for boats into *Third Lake,* close by which Bald Mountain frowns down; and the passage continues open to *Second Lake.* Second is hardly distinguishable from *First Lake,* there being a mere sand-bar between them. This section is seldom visited save by hunters and fishermen, to whom it yields rich returns. It is most easily reached from stations on the Utica and Black River R. R. (see Route 38). *Boonville* on this railway (see p. 155) is about 55 miles from Raquette Lake *via* the Fulton Lakes.

The Marion River (also called the E. Inlet) is the largest feeder of Raquette Lake, and by ascending it and passing through the Utowana and Eagle Lakes (total distance 12 miles, with but one carry of ¼ mile) we reach *** Blue Mountain Lake,** one of the loveliest of the Adirondack chain, 3 miles in diameter, irregular in shape, and 1,821 ft. above the sea. It is surrounded by dense forests, and in the lake and adjacent ponds are abundance of trout. The hotels are the *Blue Mt. Lake House* (100 guests, $10 per week), the *Ordway House* ($7 to $15 per week), and the *Blue Mt. House* ($7 per week). **Blue Mountain** (3,595 ft. high) overlooks the lake, and is ascended by a well-defined trail. The view from its summit is extremely fine.

Daily stages run in 30 miles to *N. Creek* on the Adirondack R. R. (fare $2.50), and the tourist may either pass out in this direction, or return toward Long Lake and visit the Indian Pass by a very rough journey through the wildest part of the Wilderness (see p. 195).

II. Port Kent to Ausable Chasm and the Saranac Lakes.

Port Kent is on the W. shore of Lake Champlain, 12 m. above Plattsburg and nearly opposite Burlington, with which it is connected by
steamer (see p. 183). Here stages connect with trains and steamers
and convey passengers to the *Lake View House* (3 miles) and to
Keeseville (5 miles). The Lake View House ($3 a day, and $12 to
$18 a week) stands on a far-viewing eminence just above the hamlet of
Birmingham, and is the most convenient point from which to visit the
Chasm. Near Keeseville, the Ausable River flows over the Alice Falls
and then descends a line of swirling rapids to the * **Birmingham
Falls,** where it plunges over a precipice 70 ft. high into a semicircular basin of great beauty. A few rods farther down are the Horseshoe
Falls, near which the gorge is entered from above by a stairway of 166
steps leading down a cleft in the rock (fee 50c.). Below this the stream
grows narrower and deeper, and rushes through * **Ausable Chasm,**
where at the narrowest point a wedged bowlder cramps the channel to
the width of 6 or 8 ft. Still lower down, the walls stand about 50 ft.
apart and are more than 100 ft. high, descending to the water's edge
in a sheer perpendicular line. The chasm is nearly 2 miles long, and
from the main stream branches run at right angles through fissures,
some of which offer very striking and beautiful effects. Stairways,
walks, and galleries enable the visitor to reach the principal points of
interest; and with the aid of boats constructed especially for the purpose the entire Chasm can be traversed. The entrance fee of 50c.
entitles the traveler to visit all points reached by the galleries and
walks, including the boat-ride from Table Rock to the Pool; for the
boat-ride from the Pool down the rapids to the basin at the end of the
gorge an additional fee of 50c. is charged.

Stages run from the Lake View House and Keeseville to Martin's or
Paul Smith's (fare, $4.50). From *Ausable Station* the route is the
same as that described in the preceding route. The only difference
between these two entrances to the Adirondack region is that Ausable
Station is reached by a railway-journey of 20 miles from Plattsburg
and by a stage-ride of 13 miles from Port Kent. The latter is usually
taken only by those who wish to include the Ausable Chasm *en route.*

III. Westport to Elizabethtown and Keene Valley.

Westport is on the shore of Lake Champlain, a few miles S. of
Port Kent, and is reached by railway (Route 40) or by steamer (Route
41). It is described on p. 183. From Westport stages run 8 miles W.
to **Elizabethtown,** a favorite summer resort, lying just within the
borders of the mountain region amid singularly picturesque and impressive scenery. The *Mansion House* ($10 to $15 per week) and the
Valley House ($6 to $10 per week) are good hotels, and there are several large boarding-houses. The village stands on a plateau, closed in
on all sides by lofty hills and mountain-peaks, most of which may be
ascended without difficulty. The *Hurricane Peak* lies 5 miles W., and

may be ascended with guides. The view from its summit is one of the most pleasing that the Adirondacks afford. The *Giant of the Valley* is also sometimes ascended from this place, though the route is long and difficult; and a singularly lovely view may be obtained from *Cobble Hill*, a dome-like elevation about a mile S. W. of the town. *Raven Hill* is a lofty peak to the E., from the summit of which Lake Champlain and the Green Mountains are combined in a noble view. A delightful drive from Elizabethtown is down Pleasant Valley to the romantic cascades of the Boquet River; or 8 miles S. W. to the *Split Rock Falls*, where a mountain-brook descends 100 ft. through a rugged and resounding gorge. There is good fishing in the vicinity of the village, in the Boquet River, in Black and Long Ponds, and in the trout-abounding New Pond.

Elizabethtown is the center from which several important stage-routes diverge. The State Road through the mountains here intersects the Great Northern Highway which runs S. to Schroon Lake (32 miles) and N. to Keeseville (21 miles). Stages connect with all trains at Westport, 8 miles distant (fare, $1). Daily stages run to the head of Keene Valley (17 miles, fare $1.50). Daily stages also run to Martin's on Saranac Lake, *via* Keene, N. Elba, and Lake Placid (distance, 35 miles; fare, $3). Stages run to Schroon Lake *via* Root's on Mondays, Wednesdays, and Fridays, returning alternate days (fare, $2.50).

About 10 miles W. of Elizabethtown is the beautiful ***Keene Valley,** nestling between two lofty mountain ranges, and watered by the S. branch of the Ausable River. From the village of *Keene* (Bell's Hotel) at the N. end to Beede's at the S. end the valley is nearly 8 miles long; and at different points in it are the *Tahawus House* ($7 to $10 per week), the *Maple Grove Mountain House* ($7 per week), *Crawford's* ($7 per week), *Hull's* ($7 per week), the *Astor House* ($6 to $8 per week), *Beede's* ($7 to $10 per week), and several others. Beede's, at the S. end, affords an excellent starting-point for several interesting excursions. Close by are **Roaring-Brook Falls*, where a brawling mountain brook dashes over a cliff 500 ft. high in a succession of cascades. Four miles away is the romantic *Hunter's Pass;* and nearer at hand is the lovely *Chapel Pond*, nestling at the base of Giant of the Valley, Camel's Hump, and Bald Peak, which almost close it in. About 5 miles from Beede's, reached by a rude forest-path, are the lonely and sequestered ***Ausable Ponds,** which are among the loveliest of the smaller Wilderness lakes. They are separated from each other by a rugged "carry" a mile long. Near the Lower Pond are the beautiful *Rainbow Falls;* and it is only 5 miles from the Upper Pond to the summit of ***Mount Marcy,** the monarch of the Adirondack group. Guides and an outfit may be obtained at the hotels in Keene Valley, and the ascent, which with the return requires 2 days, well repays the labor. The trail itself is wonderfully picturesque, and the view from the summit (5,337 ft. high) embraces the entire Adirondack region, together with Lake Champlain and the Green Mountains of Vermont.

Other routes to the summit of Mt. Marcy are from Adirondack (see p. 195) by a trail 12 miles long; from Root's Inn by a road, bridle-path, and trail in 20 miles (see p. 196); and from *Scott's* (see p. 194) by way of the Indian Pass in 14 miles.

The stages from Elizabethtown to Martin's cross Keene Valley at its N. end, traverse the picturesque pass between Pitch-Off and Long Pond Mountains, and stop for dinner at *Edmond Ponds* (4 miles from Keene). Seven miles farther (22 miles from Elizabethtown) is the *Mountain View House* ($8 per week), formerly known as *Scott's*, commanding fine views and a convenient center for excursions. About 2 miles beyond is John Brown's farm and grave, near which is the hamlet of *N. Elba*, and in 2 miles more *Lake Placid* is reached (fare from Elizabethtown, $2.50). Lake Placid and the route thence to Martin's (13 miles) are described on p. 187.

IV. Saratoga Springs to Schroon, Long, and Raquette Lakes.

By this route the tourist enters the Adirondack region from the S., taking it in the reverse direction to that followed in our "Grand Through Route." The Adirondack R. R. runs northward from Saratoga Springs to North Creek (58 miles ; fare, $2.50), and when completed will extend to Lake Ontario, near Cape Vincent, opening up the immense iron and lumber regions which lie in this portion of the State. It is a most picturesque route, running straight up the lovely Kayaderosseras Valley, from Saratoga, and passing at one place over a trestle-work 1,310 ft. long. It crosses the Sacandaga River by a bridge 450 ft. long and 96 ft. high, and passes near *Corinth Falls*, where the Hudson, with a width of only 50 ft., makes a leap of 60 ft. over the precipice. At *Hadley* (22 miles) passengers leave the train for **Lake Luzerne,** which, with the village of the same name, lies just across the Hudson. Lake Luzerne is a small but exceedingly picturesque body of water, and is a popular summer resort, and a favorite excursion from Saratoga Springs. There are several hotels in the village, of which the *Wayside Hotel* ($3 a day) and *Rockwell's* ($2.50 a day) are the best ; and the fishing, hunting, and boating are excellent. From *Potash Hill*, near the lake, an admirable view is obtained, and Lake George is only 10 miles distant (reached by a good road). From *Thurman* (36 miles from Saratoga), stages run in 9 miles to Caldwell, at the head of Lake George (see p. 178) ; and from *Riverside* (50 miles), stages run in 6 miles to **Pottersville,** which is only a mile from Schroon Lake (fare, $1).

* **Schroon Lake** is 10 miles long and about 2¼ wide, and is surrounded by lovely scenery. A boat plies on its waters, connecting the landing at Pottersville with *Schroon Lake Village*, the principal summer resort in this vicinity. The village lies on the W. shore of the lake, and, besides numerous boarding-houses, has several summer hotels (the *Leland House, Schroon Lake House,* and *Ondawa House*). The boating and fishing on the lake are unsurpassed, and excursions may be made (with guides) to the summit of *Mount Pharaoh*, to the top of *Mount Severn*, and to the beautiful **Paradox Lake,** which lies 4 miles above the N. end of Schroon Lake. At the foot of Mount Pharaoh is *Pharaoh Lake*, famous for the abundance of its trout.

Daily stages run from N. Creek *via* Indian Lake to *Blue Mt. Lake* (see p. 191). Stages also run twice a week from N. Creek (and also from Pottersville) to Minerva, Tahawus, Newcomb, and Long Lake Village (40 miles, fare $4.50). The Long Lake and Raquette Lake region is described on p. 190. *Tahawus* (Lower Iron Works) is a decayed hamlet in the very heart of the Adirondack mountain-system. At this point the road to Long Lake turns directly W. and soon reaches the village of **Newcomb** (*Newcomb House, Aunt Polly's Inn*), which is a good point at which to procure guides, boats, and camp equipage. Near Newcomb are *Lakes Harris, Delia,* and *Catlin,* and 12 miles W. is *Long Lake Village* on Long Lake (see p. 190).

From Tahawus, a rugged but picturesque road leads 11 miles N. to the hamlet of *Adirondack* (or Upper Iron Works), once a thriving mining town, but now deserted and desolate. It lies in the midst of singularly wild and impressive scenery, and there are several places of interest in the vicinity. A mile S. of the village is *Lake Sanford,* skirted by the road from Tahawus, and 5 miles long. On the N. are Henderson Mountain and Lake, and beyond these (2½ miles from the village) are the lovely *Preston Ponds,* which afford as good trout-fishing as is to be had in the entire region. *Mount Seward,* one of the loftiest of the group (4,348 ft.), lies 8 miles to the N. W., and *Mount Marcy,* the monarch of the region (see p. 193), may be ascended by an easy but devious path, 12 miles long. The trail to the summit leads past the exquisite *Lake Colden,* and near **Avalanche Lake,** which is one of the highest of the Adirondack lakes (2,846 ft. above the sea). The greatest attraction, however, and perhaps the finest sight in the Adirondacks, is the *****Indian Pass,** a stupendous gorge between Mts. Wallface and McIntyre, in the wildest part of that lonely and savage region which the Indians rightly named "Conyacraga," or the Dismal Wilderness, the larger part of which has never yet been visited by white men, and which still remains the secure haunt of the wolf, the panther, the great black bear, and the rarer lynx and wolverine. The springs which form the source of the Hudson are found at an elevation of more than 4,000 ft. above the sea, in rocky recesses, in whose cold depths the ice of winter never melts entirely away. Here, in the center of the pass, rise also the springs of the Ausable, which flows into Lake Champlain, and whose waters reach the Atlantic through the mouth of the St. Lawrence, several hundred miles from the mouth of the Hudson ; and yet, so close are the springs of the two rivers, that "the wild-cat, lapping the waters of the one, may bathe his hind-feet in the other ; and a rock rolling from the precipice above could scatter spray from both in the same concussion." In freshets, the waters of the two springs actually mingle. The main stream of the Ausable, however, flows from the N. E. portal of the pass ; and the main stream of the Hudson from the S. W. The latter is locally known as the Adirondack River, and after leaving the pass flows into Lakes Henderson and Sanford. The Indian Pass is reached from Adirondack by an easy and well-marked trail ; and after traversing it the visitor may descend in 10 miles by a path blazed on the trees to *N.*

Elba (see pp. 187, 194). A long and arduous trail leads from Adiron-dack to Keene Valley by way of the Ausable Ponds.

V. Schroon Lake to Elizabethtown and Keeseville.

From Pottersville (see p. 194) the Great Northern Highway runs al-most due N. to Elizabethtown (32 miles; fare, $2.50) and Keeseville (53 miles; fare, $4). Stages run on this route three times a week (Tuesdays, Thursdays, and Saturdays, returning alternate days), lead-ing for the first 10 miles along the shore of Schroon Lake, and then up the valley of Schroon River, passing for the greater part of the entire distance amid picturesque and striking scenery. Ten miles from Schroon Lake the stage stops at **Root's Inn** ($10 a week), one of the favorite resorts of sportsmen. Roads from Ticonderoga (23 miles distant) and Crown Point (18 miles distant) intersect at this point; and several of the Adirondack attractions are within easy ex-cursion distance. *Mt. Marcy* (see p. 193) is visited by a wagon-road leading in 10 miles to Mud Pond, whence a forest bridle-path leads in 9 miles to the foot of the mountain, and a well-defined trail to the summit. Beyond Root's the road traverses the beautiful Schroon Valley to its head, climbs the mountain-pass and descends into Pleas-ant Valley, passing the Split Rock Falls. *Elizabethtown* (32 miles from Schroon) is described on p. 192. Beyond Elizabethtown the road traverses the picturesque gorge of Poke-o'-Moonshine, and passes in 22 miles to *Keeseville* (see p. 192). At Elizabethtown and Keeseville con-nection is made with the usual routes into the Adirondack lake-region.

VI. Skeleton Tours or "Round Trips."

The following tour can be made in ten days or two weeks, and will embrace the most striking "sights" of the Wilderness: From Crown Point, on Lake Champlain, to *Root's Inn* (see above), 18 miles; thence to *Tahawus* (see p. 195), 20 miles; thence to *Long Lake* (see p. 190), 20 miles. From Tahawus to *Adirondack* (see p. 195), 11 miles. From Adirondack to the summit of Mount Marcy (with guides); also to the *Indian Pass*, the most majestic natural wonder, next to Niagara Falls, in the State (see p. 195). From the Indian Pass to *N. Elba*, on the Elizabethtown road (10 miles through the woods). From N. Elba to *Martin's*, on the Saranac Lake (see p. 188). From Martin's to Keeseville and the famous *Ausable Chasm* (see p. 192).

The following is a very popular "round trip" (all tramping), which embraces the "Heart of the Adirondacks": Start from Beede's, at the head of Keene Valley (see p. 193), and go by forest-path 4 miles to Lower Ausable Pond; boat through pond 2 miles; trail 1 mile to the Upper Ausable Pond; boat through Upper Pond 3 miles; trail 5 miles to summit of Mt. Marcy through Panther Gorge and past Cathedral Rocks; trail 7 miles to Lakes Colden and Avalanche, past Lake Per-kins or "Tear of the Clouds" (the highest of the Adirondack waters, 4,312 ft. above the sea) and Opalescent Flume; from Lake Colden 5

miles past Calamity Pond to Adirondack (see p. 195); thence up the
Hudson 5 miles to the Indian Pass (see p. 195); thence down the Ausable to N. Elba and John Brown's grave, 10 miles; thence to Lake
Placid, 5 miles; through Lake Placid, 5 miles; to summit of Whiteface Mt., 3½ miles; thence to Wilmington (see p. 187); and out by any
route that may be selected. This trip takes in some of the wildest and
most characteristic scenery of the Adirondacks, including the wonderful Indian Pass, the hardly less wonderful Panther Gorge on the E. of
Mt. Marcy, and that great geological curiosity, the mammoth trap dike
of Lake Avalanche. There are good lodges at Upper Ausable Pond,
Panther Gorge, Lake Perkins, near the summit of Mt. Marcy, and at
Lake Colden.

VII. Lake Pleasant.

Lake Pleasant is in Hamilton County, New York, on the borders of
the Adirondack region, and is reached from Amsterdam on the New
York Central R. R. by a stage or carriage ride of 50 miles. There are
numerous lakes in the vicinity besides Pleasant, the chief of which
are Round and Piseco; and the Saranac region is connected with
Lake Pleasant by intermediate waters and portages. Deer and other
game are abundant in the forests, and fine trout may be taken in all
the brooks and lakes. *Sageville* is a thriving little village, situated on
elevated ground between Lakes Pleasant and Round, and the Lake
Pleasant House there is a favorite resort. The Sturgis House is a large
hotel at the outlet of the lake. **Piseco Lake** is larger than Lake
Pleasant, and lies about 8 miles W. *Raquette Lake* (see p. 190) is 30
miles distant by boat on Jessup's River and Indian and Blue Mt.
Lakes. Guides and camp equipage may be obtained at the hotels.

43. Long Island.

LONG ISLAND, part of the State of New York, is 115 miles in extreme length from E. to W., with an average width of 14 miles, and
an area of 1,682 square miles. It is bounded on the N. by Long Isl-
and Sound, which separates it from Connecticut, and on the S. by the
Atlantic Ocean, while East River separates it from New York City.
The northern half of the island is agreeably diversified with hills, but
the surface is, for the most part, strikingly level. The coast is indented with numerous bays and inlets; and delicious fresh-water
ponds, fed by springs, are everywhere found on terraces of varying
elevation. These little lakes, and the varied coast-views, give Long
Island picturesque features which, if not very imposing, are certainly
of a most attractive and pleasing character, heightened by the rural
beauty of the numerous quiet little towns and charming summer villas.
Along the southern shore of the island, which is a network of shallow,
land-locked waters extending 70 miles, fine shooting and fishing may
be had. Hotel and boarding-house accommodation is ample. The
leading city of Long Island (*Brooklyn*) and the two most frequented
resorts (*Coney Island* and *Rockaway Beach*) have already been described in Routes 1 and 2.

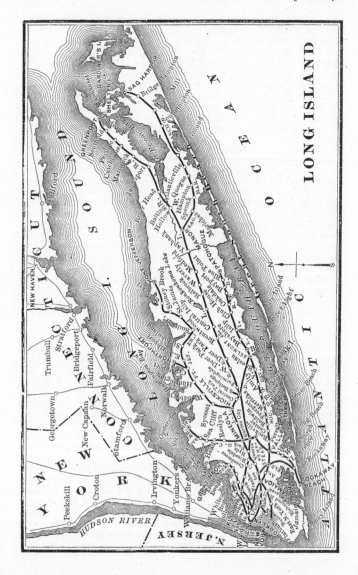

a. Long Island R. R. Main Line and Branches.

The entire railway system of Long Island is under one management, but there are three divisions so distinct that it will be convenient to follow them here. The Main Line of the Long Island R. R. extends along the central line of the island, branching at its E. end, as the island itself does. There are three depots at the W. end : one in Long Island City (Hunter's Point), reached from New York by ferries from James's Slip and from foot of E. 34th St. ; and two in Brooklyn (at the cor. of Flatbush and Atlantic Aves., and in Bushwick Ave., cor. of Montrose).

Leaving Long Island City the train passes several small suburban villages and in 10 miles reaches **Jamaica** (*Jamaica Hotel*), an interesting old town on Jamaica Bay, settled in 1656, and containing now about 4,000 inhabitants. The South Shore Division passes through the town, and it is connected with East New York and Brooklyn by the Atlantic Div., which runs frequent local trains. The hamlet of *Queens* (13 miles) is somewhat visited in summer; and, just beyond, the road branches, one branch going to *Garden City* (19 miles), the residence-city built by the late A. T. Stewart for the working people of New York, while the main line passes on to *Mineola* (19 miles), where the Glen Cove Branch crosses. There is a fine cathedral at Garden City, and the model houses are worthy of notice. Just S. of Garden City is the ancient village of *Hempstead* (21 miles), situated on the wide-spreading Hempstead Plains, whence a branch road leads S. to Rockaway Beach.

The Glen Cove Branch runs N. by Garden City and Mineola to **Roslyn** (23 miles from New York), a pretty village at the head of Hempstead Bay. Near Roslyn is *Cedarmere*, for many years the country residence of the late William Cullen Bryant. It is a spot of great though quiet picturesque beauty, overlooking the Bay and the Connecticut shore across the Sound. Bryant's grave is in the adjacent cemetery. Near Roslyn are many lovely lakelets, and a short distance S. E. is Harbor Hill, the highest land on Long Island, from the summit of which (319 ft. high) there is a pleasing view. *Glen Head*, 2 miles beyond Roslyn, is the station for **Sea Cliff**, which is 1 mile distant on a picturesque bluff overlooking the Sound, and noted for its camp meetings. The Sea Cliff House accommodates 400 guests ($8 to $15 a week), there are over 100 cottages, and the camp-meeting tabernacle seats 4,000. Four miles beyond Roslyn is **Glen Cove** (*Pavilion Hotel*), which is a highly popular resort in summer. The hotel here is excellent. Glen Cove, Sea Cliff, and Roslyn are also reached from New York by steamer from Peck Slip (Pier 24), East River (see p. 202). Two miles beyond Glen Cove is *Locust Valley*, where the road terminates, and whence stages run in 4 miles to **Oyster Bay** (also called *Syosset Bay*), a deep inlet from the Sound, which is numerously visited in summer. The *Nassau House* is a small summer hotel, and there are many farmhouses where board may be had at moderate rates.

Beyond Mineola the Main Line runs to *Westbury* (22 miles), and *Hicksville* (25 miles), which is named for Elias Hicks, the Quaker schismatic, who lived and preached in this region from 1771 to 1830, riding 10,000 miles on his missionary journeys, and preaching over 1,000 times. The Port Jefferson Branch diverges here and runs N. E. in 34 miles to Port Jefferson.

The Port Jefferson Branch (formerly called the Northport Branch) runs N. E.
from Hicksville, and in 4 miles reaches *Syosset*, whence stages run to Oyster Bay,
which is described above. From *Woodbury* (3 miles beyond Syosset), stages run
to **Cold Spring** (*Laurelton House, Forest Lawn House*), a pleasant village on
Cold Spring Harbor, which attracts many summer visitors. Three miles beyond
Woodbury is *Huntington*, a village of 2,500 inhabitants, pleasantly situated on
Huntington Harbor; and 6 miles further is **Northport** (*Northport House*), situated on another deep inlet from the Sound. Near Northport is the famous Beacon
farm, comprising 1,000 acres on the borders of the Sound. Stations, St. Johnland,
Smithtown, Stony Brook, and Setauket.   **Port Jefferson** (34 miles from Hicksville) is the terminus of the road, and is a village of 1,500 inhabitants. A steam
ferry runs across the Sound to Bridgeport, Conn. (see p. 68), twice a day.

Beyond Hicksville the Main Line runs nearly due E. to *Farming-
dale* (30 miles), *Brentwood* (41 miles), *Central Islip* (43 miles), and
Lakeland (48 miles). One mile S. of Lakeland is **Ronkonkoma
Lake,** a peculiar sheet of water about 3 miles in circumference situated nearly in the center of the island. It has neither inlet nor outlet,
and for 4 years its waters steadily fall, and then for another 4 years
gradually rise again, and this peculiarity has been noticed from the
time it was discovered. The perch-fishing in the lake is good, the
boating excellent, and near the shore are several hotels and boarding-
houses. Ten miles beyond Lakeland is *Yaphank*, whence stages run
to the pretty village of **Center Moriches** (*Moriches House, Ocean,
Long Island, Baldwin*), which is extensively visited in summer. Both
fishing and hunting are excellent, and surf-bathing may be enjoyed by
sailing across the Bay to the outer beach, where is a summer hotel
(the *Havens House*). There are many summer boarding-houses in
Moriches and also in E. Moriches, which lies across the Tenillo River.
At *Manor* (65 miles) the road forks, the Sag Harbor Branch (which
will be described below) running S. of the Great Peconic Bay to Sag
Harbor, while the Main Line runs N. E. in 29 miles to Greenport. Between Manor and Greenport are the pleasant villages of *Riverhead*
(73 miles), *Mattituck* (83 miles), *Cutchogue* (85 miles), and *Southold*
(90 miles), each of which attracts many summer visitors. **Greenport**
(*Clark House, Wyandank, Booth's*) is a lively village of 2,000 inhabitants near the E. end of the island, with a snug harbor and a large
fishing-fleet. It affords excellent still-water bathing, boating, sailing,
and fishing; and in their season wild ducks are abundant. Greenport
is also reached by steamers from New York (Peck Slip, East River),
New London, and Hartford. Daily stages run in 9 miles to *Orient
Point*, where there is a large summer hotel (300 guests), and *Orient
Village*, where there are several summer boarding-houses. Ferry-boats
connecting with every train run from Greenport to **Shelter Island,**
on which are two spacious summer hotels (the *Manhasset House* and
the *Prospect House*). The island is about 14 miles long by 4 wide,
and has a gently diversified surface, with fresh-water lakelets and
picturesque bays. It is also the site of a Methodist camp-meeting
ground, and is being rapidly improved. Eight miles E. lies *Gardiner's
Island* (3,300 acres), on which the pirate Kidd buried vast treasures,
part of which was recovered in 1699 by Gov. Bellomont, of Massachusetts.

The *Sag Harbor Branch* diverges at Manor and runs by *Moriches* (70 miles), *Speonk* (73 miles), and *W. Hampton* (75 miles) to **Quogue** (78 miles), which is another popular summer resort with several large boarding-houses. It is situated on Shinnecock Bay and the bathiṅ and fishing are good. Stations, *Southampton* (90 miles) and *Bridgehampton* (95 miles), and then, 100 miles from New York, the train stops at **Sag Harbor** (*Nassau House, American*), a prosperous village of about 2,000 inhabitants, situated at the head of the picturesque Gardiner's Bay. It was once a leading whaling station, but its maritime importance has long since ceased, though its coasting-trade is still large. A steamer runs from foot of Fulton St., North River, New York, to Sag Harbor, Greenport, and Orient, 3 times a week (Tuesday, Thursday, and Saturday), and another tri-weekly line connects Sag Harbor with New London and Hartford, Conn. Daily stages from Sag Harbor run in 7 miles to **East Hampton,** "the quietest of all quiet towns," with quaint old houses, and a street of noble elms, which were planted at the instigation of Dr. Lyman Beecher, who was pastor here from 1798 to 1810. The surf-bathing at Napeague Beach (1 mile from the village) is excellent. A short distance S. E. are several fresh-water ponds, and N. E. is the sequestered village of *Amagansett*. About 15 miles E. is *Montauk Point*, the eastern extremity of Long Island. On it is a light-house with a powerful revolving light.

b. The South Shore R. R.

The Southern Div. of the Long Island R. R. has the same terminal stations in Brooklyn and Long Island City as the main line (see p. 199). *Jamaica* (10 miles) has already been described. From *Valley Stream* 16 miles) a branch road runs N. E. to Hempstead (see p. 199), and another runs S. W. to Rockaway Beach, passing the beach-villages of *Woodsburgh* (19 miles) and *Far Rockaway* (21 miles), with their spacious ~ummer hotels and cottages. **Rockaway Beach** is described ᴏ. page 20. On the main line 20 miles from Valley Stream is the small village of **Babylon** (*Watson House, Lagrange, American*), which is much resorted to for its fishing. From Babylon a small steamer runs 8 miles across the Great South Bay to **Fire Island** (*Surf House, Old Dominy House*), which offers the attractions of surf and still-water bathing, boating and sailing, superb fishing, and cool ocean breezes, and draws many summer visitors. The beach is admirable, and occupies the W. end of a remarkable sand ridge which is only a few rods wide but runs for 40 miles along the cost to Quogue Neck, inclosing a series of broad bays and estuaries. Near the hotels are the Fire Island Light, one of the most important on the Atlantic coast, and Jesse Conklin's "Castle" on Cap Tree Island. Six miles beyond Babylon is **Islip** (*Pavilion, Lake House*) a pretty village on the Great South Bay, containing many tasteful villas. It is much visited in summer, and besides the hotels there are a number of boarding-houses. **Patchogue** (*Roe's Hotel, Eagle*) is the terminus of the Southern Div., 54 miles from New York. It is a prosperous manufacturing village of 3,000 inhabitants, about a mile from the Great South Bay. Stages

run thence in 4 miles to *Bellport*, a much visited village on Bellport
Bay.

c. The North Shore.

The North Shore Div. of the Long Island R. R. begins at Long
Island City, and its depot is reached from New York by ferries from
James Slip and E. 34th. St., and from Brooklyn by horse-cars.   Leaving Long Island City (or Hunter's Point) the train passes the pretty
suburban towns of *Woodside* (3 miles), *Winfield* (4 miles), and *Newtown*
(5 miles), and in 8 miles reaches **Flushing,** a beautiful village of
nearly 10,000 inhabitants at the head of Flushing Bay, near the entrance of Long Island Sound.   Many business men from New York
make their homes in Flushing, and the village is noted for its wealth
and culture, for its umbrageous streets and finely kept gardens, and for
its educational institutions.   One of these latter (Erasmus Hall) is the
oldest in the State.   In the N. part of the village is a neat monument
to the soldiers of the county who died in the civil war.   The extensive
nurseries of the Parsons & Sons Co. here are worth a visit, and the
drives in the vicinity are very attractive.   At Flushing the road divides, one branch running by *Bayside, Douglaston*, and *Little Neck* to
Great Neck (6 miles beyond Flushing), while the other diverges to *College Point* and *Whitestone* (3 miles beyond Flushing).   All these points
and the adjacent localities are much visited in summer, and several of
them may be reached from New York by steamer as follows: The
steamer *Seawanhaka* leaves pier 24 East River at 4 P. M. for Baylis
Dock (Fort Schuyler), Great Neck, Sea Cliff, Mott's Dock, Sands Point,
Glen Cove, Glenwood, and Roslyn, returning next morning.

The Central Div. of the Long Island R. R. runs from Long Island
City through Flushing to Garden City, Hempstead, and Babylon, all of
which have been described.   At Creedmoor, 5 miles beyond Flushing,
is the famous *Creedmoor Rifle-Range*, the most perfectly appointed in
America.

44. New York to Delaware Water Gap.

Via Morris & Essex Division of the Delaware, Lackawanna & Western R. R.   Distance, 92 miles; time, 3¼ hours; fare, $2.55.

PASSENGERS take the ferry-boat from foot of Barclay St. or Christopher St. to the station in Hoboken.   Leaving Hoboken the train
traverses the Bergen Tunnel, and passes in 9 miles to **Newark** (see
p. 25) across wide marshes.   Four miles beyond Newark is **Orange**
(*Park House, Central Hotel*), a beautiful city of 15,000 inhabitants, surrounded by lovely scenery, and a favorite suburban home of business
men from New York.   A short distance to the W. lies *Llewelyn Park*,
a small enclosure laid out in the best style of landscape gardening and
containing fine villas and mansions which have the park in common.
A little further W. is the *Orange Mountain*, the crest of which is
crowned by costly residences standing amid highly cultivated grounds.
From various points of the mountain there are remarkably fine views,

including the lake and mountain region of New Jersey and New York City and harbor. The drives about Orange are extremely picturesque and attractive.

Two miles beyond Orange the train stops at *S. Orange,* and at *Milburn,* 4 miles further, rounds the extremity of Orange Mt. a begins the steep ascent of Second Mt., on the crest of which is **Summit** (*Blackburn House, Park House*), a popular summer resort, noted for the extent and beauty of its views. At *Madison* (27 miles) the road first enters the borders of the mountain region, which continually grows more picturesque as the train proceeds westward. The Drew Theological Seminary is located at Madison, and 5 miles beyond is **Morristown** (*Mansion House, U. S. Hotel*), the capital of Morris County, beautifully situated on the Whippany River, upon a plain surrounded by hills. It is noteworthy as having been, during the Revolution, the headquarters of the American army upon two occasions. In rear of the Court-House the ruins of old Fort Nonsense may still be seen; and *Washington's Headquarters,* owned and preserved by the State, is ½ mile E. of the village. In the public square is a Soldiers' Monument, and on Pigeon Mt. is the vast and massive *State Insane Asylum,* built of granite at a cost of $3,000,000. Beyond Morristown the train crosses Morris Plains and at *Denville* (38 miles) meets the Boonton Branch.

The *Boonton Branch,* which diverges from the Morris & Essex line shortly after passing through the Bergen Tunnel, is the route taken by the through trains from New York, but is much less interesting than the one described above. The only important stations passed are **Paterson** (see p. 168) and **Boonton** (30 miles), a manufacturing town of 4,000 inhabitants on the Rockaway River and Morris Canal, in the midst of a very mountainous region. By this route *Denville* is 37 miles from New York.

Five miles beyond Denville is the prosperous little manufacturing city of **Dover** (*Mansion House*), whence a branch road runs to the pleasant village of *Chester* in 13 miles. From *Drakesville* (48 miles from New York) stages run in 4 miles to *Lake Hopatcong,* loftily situated among the Brookland Mts., 725 ft. above the sea. The lake is about 9 miles long by 4 miles wide, is dotted with islands, affords excellent fishing, and is surrounded by varied and beautiful scenery. The name (Hopatcong) means "Stone over the Water," and was given it by the Indians on account of an artificial causeway of stone which once connected one of the islands with the shore, but which is now submerged. Two small steamers ply on the lake, and there are several summer hotels (*Lake Hopatcong House, Lake View, etc.*). Near the former is *Southard's Peak,* from the summit of which the Delaware Water-Gap and the Bloomfield Mts. are both visible. Five miles beyond Drakesville is *Stanhope* (53 miles), whence stages run in 2½ miles to **Budd's Lake** (also called *Lake Senecawana*), a beautiful sheet of water nearly circular in form, 3½ miles in circumference, deep, clear, and abounding in fish, and surrounded by a picturesque country, with fine views of mountains in the distance. On the shore of the lake stands the *Forest Grove Hotel* (200 guests, $12 to $20 a week).

Schooley's Mt. is 8 miles distant, and Lake Hopatcong is easily visited from Budd's Lake. From *Hackettstown* (62 miles) stages run in 3½ miles to *Schooley's Mountain,* a favorite summer resort of New Yorkers. It is not an isolated peak, but a ridge of considerable extent, Budd's Lake being upon one part of its summit. It is about 1,200 ft. high, and even amid the "August ardors" its air is cool, pure, and bracing. Large and fine hotels are the *Heath House* ($15 to $18 per week) and *Belmont Hall* ($12 to $18 per week). The drives in the vicinity are delightful, and the scenery picturesque and pleasing. Another route from New York to Schooley's Mt. (and also to Lake Hopatcong) is *via* High Bridge Branch of the New Jersey Central R. R. (See Route 45.)

Washington (71 miles) is the junction of the Morris & Essex Div. with the Main Line of the Lackawanna & Western R. R. The Morris & Essex R. R. passes on *via* Stewartsville and Phillipsburg to *Easton, Pa.* (85 miles from New York), which is described in Route 45. Our present route takes the Del., Lack. & Western R. R. at Washington, and leads in 11 miles to *Manunka Chunk,* just before reaching which the train passes through the Manunka Chunk Mt. by the Voss Gap Tunnel, 1,000 ft. long. At Manunka Chunk the Belvidere Delaware R. R. comes in. This road, with the continuation of the present route to the Delaware Water-Gap, Scranton, Binghamton, and Oswego, is described in Route 51. **Delaware Water-Gap** (see p. 224).

45. New York to Central Pennsylvania.

By the "Allentown Line" (the Central R. R. of New Jersey, with connecting roads). Distances : to Easton, 75 miles ; to Allentown, 91 miles ; to Reading, 128 miles ; to Harrisburg, 182 miles ; to Scranton, 193 miles ; to Williamsport, 231 miles. This was formerly one of the great through routes to the West, with trains running through to Chicago without change of cars. It is now no longer so used, but is simply a local route

As far as *Bound Brook* (31 miles) this route has already been described in Route 3, *b.* Here the Raritan Valley is reached, and *Somerville* (36 miles) is a flourishing village on the Raritan River with fine views and drives in the vicinity. From *High Bridge* (54 miles) the High Bridge Branch diverges to Chester, Schooley's Mountain, Budd's Lake, and Lake Hopatcong (all described in Route 44). Here the road crosses the S. Branch of the Raritan on an embankment 1,300 ft. long and 105 ft. high, the view from which is remarkably fine. At the *Junction* (58 miles) connection is made with the Delaware, Lackawanna & Western R. R., which comes in from Philadelphia and leads N. through the Delaware Water-Gap to Scranton, Binghamton, and Oswego (see Routes 44 and 51). *Asbury* (61 miles) and *Valley* (63 miles) are small stations in the Musconetcong Valley, in the midst of exquisite scenery. Just beyond *Bloomsburg* (66 miles) the road runs along the side of the Pohatcong Mt. into the Pohatcong Valley, and passes in 7 miles to **Phillipsburg** (*Lee House, Columbia Hotel*), an important iron-manufacturing town on the Delaware River opposite Easton, Pa., with which it is connected by 3 bridges. Phillipsburg is an important railway center, and the Morris & Essex R. R. (Route 44) and the Belvidere Delaware R. R. connect here. It is also the terminus of the Morris Canal. **Eas-ton** (*United States Hotel, Franklin House*) is situated on some steep hills, at the confluence of the Delaware and Lehigh Rivers and Bushkill Creek. It is a well-built and wealthy town, with a population of 12,000, and extensive iron-works, mills, distilleries, etc. The Court-House, the County Prison, and the Opera-House are handsome buildings, and there are several fine churches. To the E. on Mt. Lafayette is * *Lafayette College*, a richly endowed institution, with 30 instructors and 350 students, an extensive library, and fine scientific collections. Pardee Hall is a handsome building, and from its tower there is a noble view. The curious *Durham Cave* is near Easton, and *Mt. Jefferson* is an abrupt peak in the center of the town. Easton is one of the great railroad centers of the country. It is the W. terminus of the Central R. R. of New Jersey, of the Morris & Essex R. R. (Route 44), and of the Morris Canal. The Lehigh Valley R. R. (Route 47) and the Lehigh Coal Navigation Co.'s Railroad and Canal extend from here to the coal regions. By the Belvidere Delaware R. R. (Route 51) it is connected with Philadelphia on the S. and with the Water-Gap and Central New York on the N.; while the present route connects it through Allentown and Harrisburg with all points West.

At Easton we take the Lehigh Valley R. R., which runs along the Lehigh River amid pleasing scenery, and in 12 miles reach **Bethlehem** (*Sun Hotel*), a town of about 10,000 inhabitants, noted as the chief seat in the United States of the Moravians, or United Brethren, who settled here under Count Zinzendorf in 1741. The old Moravian buildings for the most part still remain, and the principal ones, which are built of stone and stand in Church Row at the foot of Broad St., are in a good state of preservation. The *Moravian Church* is a spacious stone structure capable of seating 2,000 persons. Near the church is the *Moravian Boys' School* and there is also a *Moravian Female Seminary* of high repute, founded in 1749, and still flourishing. In Main St. is a *Museum* (fee, 25c.) containing many curious relics and trophies of the old days. The *Sun Hotel* was opened as an inn in 1760, and, thou ·ʰ greatly enlarged in 1851, still retains its ancient and massive walls. On a spur of the Lehigh Mts. above the town is the * *Lehigh University*, founded in 1865 and liberally endowed by the Hon! Asa Packer. It is under the control of the Protestant Episcopal church, and tuition in all branches is free. From the park around the buildings there is a view of 20 miles. Five miles beyond Bethlehem the train reaches **Allen-town** (*American House*), a thriving city of 18,000 inhabitants, built upon an eminence between Jordan Creek and Lehigh River. It is regularlʸ laid out and well built, with horse-cars on the principal streets. The County Court-House and County Prison are handsome edifices, and several of the school buildings are noteworthy. *Muhlenberg College* (Lutheran) stands amid ample grounds in the S. E. part of the city. * *Mammoth Rock*, 1,000 ft. high and commanding broad views, is near the city, as are also several mineral springs. (The continuation of the Lehigh Valley R. R. beyond Allentown is described in Route 47.)

On our present route we take at Allentown the East Pennsylvania R. R., and, passing up the valley of the Little Lehigh by several small stations, reach in 21 miles **Lyons** (*American House, Lyons Hotel*) a small village much visited in summer. Beyond Lyons the road traverses a picturesque and exceedingly fertile country, and in 15 miles reaches **Reading** (see Route 52), at the crossing of the Phila. & Reading R. R. The Schuykill River and Union Canal are now crossed, and the road traverses a mountainous country for 28 miles (several small stations *en route*) to the prosperous village of **Lebanon** (*Eagle Hotel*), situated on the Swatara River, substantially built, and having 7,000 inhabitants. Seven miles S. of the town (reached by N. Lebanon R. R.) are the *Cornwall Ore Banks*, which are three hills formed of masses of iron-ore, and called Grassy, Middle, and Big Hill. It has been estimated that Big Hill contains 40,000,000 tons of ore above the surface of the ground, yielding 70 per cent. of pure iron. Veins of copper are found among the iron, and 6 miles from Lebanon, near the Swatara River, are quarries of fine gray marble. *Hummelstown* (16 miles beyond Lebanon) is the site of a remarkable cave which is 4 miles long and filled with curious stalactites and stalagmites. **Harrisburg** (182 miles) is the end of our route. Here the traveler westward bound takes the Pennsylvania R. R. (Route 46), or if going N. or S. takes the Northern Central R. R. (Route 55). For description of Harrisburg, see page 207.

46. Philadelphia to Harrisburg and Pittsburg.

By the Pennsylvania R. R. Distances : to Downingtown, 32 miles ; to Lancaster, 69 ; to Middletown, 96 ; to Harrisburg, 105 ; to Huntingdon, 203 ; to Altoona, 237 ; to Pittsburg, 354. This was formerly the Pennsylvania Central R. R , but is now part of a vast system which includes upwards of 1,700 miles of railway under the management of one corporation. It is one of the great routes from New York to the West, and through trains, with Pullman Palace drawing-room and sleeping cars, run without change from New York via Philadelphia to Chicago, Cincinnati, St. Louis, and Louisville. The time from Phila. to Pittsburg is about 10 hours.

LEAVING the station in W. Philadelphia (cor. Market and 32d Sts.), the train passes through a pleasant suburban region and enters one of the richest agricultural districts in America, which is traversed for nearly 100 miles. The size and solidity of the houses and barns, and the perfection of the cultivation, will be apt to remind the tourist rather of the best farming districts of England than of what he usually sees in the United States. *Paoli* (19 miles) was the scene of a battle fought Sept. 20th, 1777, in which the British under Gen. Gray surprised and defeated the Americans under Gen. Wayne. The battle is commonly called the " Paoli massacre " because a large number of the Americans were killed after they had laid down their arms. A marble monument, erected in 1817, marks the site of the battle-field. Beyond Paoli the scenery grows more picturesque, and fine views are had of the beautiful Chester Valley. *Downingtown* (32 miles) is the terminus of the Chester Valley R. R., and is near the marble quarries which supplied the marble from which Girard College (in Phila.) was built. At *Coatesville* (38 miles) the W. branch of the Brandywine is crossed on a bridge 835 ft. long and 75 ft. high. *Parkesburg* (44 miles) and *Christiana* (48 miles) are busy manufacturing villages. *Gap* (51 miles) is so named because it lies in the gap through which the road passes from the Chester Valley to the Pequea Valley. The scenery in the vicinity is attractive. **Lancaster** (*Stevens House, Grape, Cooper*) is pleasantly situated near the Conestoga Creek, which is crossed in entering the city. It was incorporated in 1818, and was at one time the principal inland town of Pennsylvania, being the seat of the State government from 1799 to 1812. It is now a prosperous manufacturing city of 20,000 inhabitants, containing many fine buildings, public and private. The *Court-House* (on E. King St.) is an imposing edifice with a Corinthian portico; and the *County Prison* (also on E. King St.) is a handsome building in the Norman style. *Fulton Hall*, near the market-place, is a noteworthy structure used for public assemblies. On James St. are the substantial buildings of *Franklin and Marshall College* (Dutch Reformed), organized in 1853 by the union of Marshall with the old establishment of Franklin College, which was founded in 1787. It has a library of 13,000 volumes, and about 80 students. The oldest turnpike road in the United States terminates at Lancaster, to which it runs from Phila. Besides its extensive manufactures of locomotives, axes, carriages, etc., Lancaster derives considerable trade from the navigation of the Conestoga Creek, which descends in 18 miles by 9 locks and slack-water pools to Safe Harbor on the Susquehanna. With the help of Tidewater Canal, to Port Deposit, a navigable communication is thus opened to Baltimore.

The only station between Lancaster and Harrisburg which requires mention is *Middletown* (96 miles), an important shipping point on the Susquehanna River at the mouth of Swatara Creek. It has extensive iron-works and machine-shops, and is the terminus of the Union Canal. Nine miles beyond is **Harrisburg** (*Lochiel House, Kirkwood House, Bolton's*), the capital of the State of Pennsylvannia, beautifully situated on the E. bank of the Susquehanna River, which is here a mile wide and spanned by 2 bridges. Harrisburg was laid out by John Harris in 1785, was incorporated as a borough in 1791, became the State capital in 1812, received a city charter in 1860, and in 1875 had a population of about 25,000. The city is handsomely built, and is surrounded by magnificent scenery. The * *State House*, finely situated on an eminence near the center, is a handsome brick building 180 ft. long by 80 ft. wide, with a circular Ionic portico in front surmounted by a dome commanding a fine view. In the second story is the State Library of 30,000 volumes, with numerous portraits and cabinets of curiosities. On each side of the State House is a smaller building of similar design devoted to government uses, and in the grounds is a beautiful * monument to the soldiers who fell in the Mexican war. The *State Arsenal* is a spacious building standing a short distance to the S. The *Court-House*, in Market St., is a stately brick edifice surmounted by a dome, and the *State Lunatic Asylum* is a vast and imposing building 1½ mile N. of the city. The other principal public

buildings are the market-houses, county prison, 8 large brick school-
houses, a fine masonic hall, an opera-house, and several churches.
Front St., overlooking the river, affords the most attractive promenade
in the city, and contains many of the finest residences. *Harris Park*,
at the intersection of Front St. and Washington Ave., contains the
trunk of the tree to which John Harris, the founder of the city, was
bound by the Indians, who were about to burn him to death when a
rescuing party arrived and drove them away. *Harrisburg Cemetery*
(reached by State St.) occupies a commanding situation and affords
fine views. The iron manufactures of Harrisburg are extensive, and 6
important railways converge here.

About 5 miles above Harrisburg the railroad crosses the Susquehanna on a splendid bridge 3,670 ft. long; the view from the center of
this bridge is one of the finest on the line. Near Cove Station, 10
miles from Harrisburg, the Cove Mt. and Peter's Mt. are seen, and
from this point to within a short distance of Pittsburg the scenery is
superb, and in places grand beyond description. *Duncannon* (120
miles) is at the entrance to the beautiful Juniata Valley, which is followed for about 100 miles to the base of the Alleghany Mts. The
landscape of the Juniata is in the highest degree picturesque; the
mountain background, as continuously seen across the river from the
cars, being often strikingly bold and majestic. The passage of the
river through the Great Tuscarora Mt., 1 mile W. of *Millerstown* (138
miles), is especially fine. Four miles beyond *Mifflin* (154 miles) the
train enters the wild and romantic gorge known as the ***Long
Narrows,** which is traversed by the railway, highway, river, and
canal. *Mount Union* (191 miles) is at the entrance of the gap of
Jack's Mountain. Three miles beyond is the famous Sidling Hill, and
still farther W. the Broad Top Mountain. *Huntingdon* (203 miles) is a
flourishing village on the Juniata, finely situated and surrounded by
beautiful scenery.

The *Huntingdon & Broad Top R. R.* runs S. W. from Huntingdon to Mt. Dallas, connecting at that point with the Bedford Div. of the Pennsylvania R. R. *Bedford* (52 miles from Huntingdon) is a pretty village on the Raystown branch of the
Juniata, whence stages run in 1½ mile to the **Bedford Springs** (*Springs Hotel*).
The springs are pleasantly situated in a picturesque mountain glen, and their great
altitude and delightful summer climate, together with the beautiful mountain scenery of the neighborhood, have long made them a popular resort for pleasure-seekers
as well as invalids. The waters are saline-chalybeate, and are considered beneficial
in dyspepsia, diabetes, incipient consumption, and skin diseases.

At *Petersburg*, 7 miles W. of Huntingdon, the railroad parts company with the canal and follows the Little Juniata, which it again
leaves at *Tyrone* (223 miles) to enter the Tuckahoe Valley, famous for
its iron-ore. At the head of the Tuckahoe Valley and at the foot of
the Alleghanies is **Altoona** (*Logan House, Brant's, St. Charles*) a handsome city of 15,000 inhabitants built up since 1850, when it was a
primitive forest, by being selected as the site of the vast machine-shops
of the Pennsylvania R. R. The trains usually stop here for refreshments, and many travelers arriving here in the evening remain over
night in order to cross the Alleghanies by daylight. Just beyond Al-

toona the ascent of the Alleghanies begins, and in the course of the next 11 miles some of the finest scenery and the greatest feats of engineering on the entire line are to be seen. Within this distance the road mounts to the tunnel at the summit by so steep a grade that, while in the ascent double power is required to move the train, the entire 11 miles of descent are run without steam, the speed of the train being regulated by the "brakes." At one point there is a curve as short as the letter U, and that, too, where the grade is so steep that in looking across from side to side it seems that, were the tracks laid contiguous to each other, they would form a letter X. The road hugs the sides of the mountains, and from the windows next to the valley the traveler can look down on houses and trees dwarfed to toys, while men and animals appear like ants from the great elevation. Going W. the left-hand, and coming E. the right-hand, side of the cars is most favorable for enjoying the scenery. The summit of the mountain is pierced by a tunnel 3,612 ft. long, through which the train passes before commencing to descend the W. slope. The much-visited **Cresson Springs** are 2½ miles beyond the tunnel, 3,000 ft. above the sea. There are 7 springs here, and the waters are highly esteemed, but the place is visited rather for the delicious coolness of its summer climate than for the curative virtues of its mineral waters. The thermometer rarely reaches 75° during the hottest part of the hottest days of summer; and the nights are so cool that blankets are requisite for comfortable sleep. The hotels (of which the *Mountain House* is the principal) and the cottages accommodate about 2,000 guests. The drives in the vicinity are very attractive; and the Pennsylvania Co. runs special trains at small cost for the benefit of those who wish to view carefully the magnificent scenery along the mountain division of the road.

In descending the mountains from Cresson the remains of another railroad are constantly seen, sometimes above and sometimes below the track followed by the trains. This was the old Portage R. R. by which, in the ante-locomotive days, loaded canal-boats were carried over the mountain in sections by inclined planes and joined together at the foot. The stream which is almost continuously in sight during the descent is the Conemaugh Creek, which is crossed by a stone viaduct near *Conemaugh Station* (273 miles), the terminus of the mountain division of the road. *Johnstown* (276 miles) is a busy manufacturing borough at the confluence of the Conemaugh and Stony Creeks. The Cambria Iron-Works, seen to the right of the road, are among the most extensive in America. At *Blairsville Intersection* (300 miles) the road branches, the main line running to Pittsburg by *Latrobe* (313 miles) and *Greensburg* (323 miles); while the Western Div. runs to Allegheny City by *Blairsville* (303 miles). The scenery along both routes is pleasing but not striking.

Pittsburg.

Hotels, etc.—The *Monongahela House* ($4 a day), cor. Water and Smithfield Sts., is the principal hotel. Smaller but good houses are the *Central* ($3 a day), cor. Smithfield St. and 3d Ave., and the *St. Charles*, cor. Wood St. and 3d Ave. *Horse-cars* run on the principal streets and to the suburbs. *Reading-rooms* at the

Mercantile Library in Penn St. near 6th, and at the Y. M. C. A., cor. Penn and 6th Sts. *Post-Office* at the cor. of Smithfield St. and 5th Ave.

Pittsburg, the second city of Pennsylvania in population and importance, and one of the chief manufacturing cities in the United States, is situated at the confluence of the Alleghany and Monongahela Rivers, which here form the Ohio. The city occupies the delta between the two rivers, with several populous suburbs annexed in 1872 and 1874, and in 1875 the total population was estimated at 140,000. Pittsburg was laid out in 1565 on the site of the old French Fort du Quesne, famous in colonial annals, and on its capture by the British the name was changed to Fort Pitt, in honor of William Pitt. The city charter was granted in 1816. The city is substantially and compactly built, and contains many fine residences, particularly in the E. section. A large number of the principal avenues are graded and paved. Seven bridges span the Alleghany River and 5 the Monongahela. From its situation, Pittsburg enjoys excellent commercial facilities, and has become the center of an extensive commerce with the Western States ; while its vicinity to the inexhaustible iron and coal mines of Pennsylvania has raised it to great and merited distinction as a manufacturing center. The extent of its iron manufactures has given it the appellation of the " Iron City," while the heavy pall of smoke that constantly overhangs it, produced by burning bituminous coal in all the dwelling-houses and manufacturing establishments, has caused it to be styled the "Smoky City." The stranger will have missed the city's most characteristic sights if he fails to visit some of its great manufacturing establishments, particularly those of iron and glass. The *American Iron-Works* alone employ 2,500 hands, and cover 17 acres ; and the *Fort Pitt Works* are on a gigantic scale.

Smithfield St. is the principal business thoroughfare, and trade is very active in *Penn* and *Liberty Sts.* and *5th Ave.*, which contain many handsome retail stores. Among the public buildings are the * **Municipal Hall,** cor. Smithfield and Virgin Sts., costing $750,000, with a granite front and a massive central tower; the * **Court-House,** a solid stone edifice, cor. 5th Ave. and Grant St., with a columned portico and surmounted by a dome ; the *Custom-House* and *Post-Office,* a commodious structure of stone, cor. Smithfield St. and 5th Ave. ; and the **United States Arsenal,** a group of spacious buildings standing in the midst of ornamental grounds in the N. E. section of the city. Of the 150 churches, the most imposing is the Roman Catholic *Cathedral of St. Paul,* a large edifice of brick, with 2 spires and a dome over the choir. * **Trinity Church** (Episcopal) is a fine building in the English-Gothic style, in 6th St. near Smithfield St. *St. Peter's* (Episcopal), in Grant St., is also a handsome structure. The *First Presbyterian,* near Trinity Church, is a massive stone edifice with 2 towers. Other notable church edifices are the *First Baptist* and the *Third Presbyterian.* The spacious and handsome building of the **Mercantile Library** is in Penn St. near 6th St. ; it cost $250,000, and contains 15,000 volumes and a well-supplied reading-room. In the same building are the rooms and collections of the *Pittsburg Art Association.* The *Young Men's*

Christian Association has a good reading-room at the cor. of Penn and 6th Sts. There are in the city 2 theatres, an Opera-House, an Academy of Music, and several public halls.

The *Western University*, founded in 1819, has a handsome building in the S. E. part of the city, near the Monongahela, and has 250 students. It has a library of 2,500 volumes, extensive philosophical and chemical apparatus, and a cabinet containing over 10,000 specimens in geology, mineralogy, conchology, and zoölogy. The *Pittsburg Female College* (Methodist) is a flourishing institution. Several of the public-school buildings are large and substantial. Among the principal charitable institutions are the *Western Pennsylvania Hospital*, an immense building in Ridge Ave., with a department for the insane at Dixmont, on the Pittsburg, Fort Wayne & Chicago R. R. ; the *City General Hospital;* the *Homœopathic Hospital* and *Dispensary ;* the *Mercy Hospital*, in Stephenson St. ; the *Episcopal Church Home ;* and the Roman Catholic *Orphan Asylum*. The *Convent of the Sisters of Mercy* (Webster Ave. cor. of Chatham) is the oldest house of the order in America.

Birmingham is a flourishing suburb, lying across the Monongahela from Pittsburg (reached by bridge or ferry). It has important manufactories of glass and iron, which are worth a visit. An inclined plane R. R. (fare 6c.) leads to the summit of Mt. Oliver, 250 ft. high, which affords a fine panoramic view; and another inclined plane in the suburb of Monongahela leads to the summit of Mt. Washington (370 ft. high) whence a still better view is had. *Manchester* , now a part of Allegheny City, is 2 miles below Pittsburg, on the Ohio. Here is located the House of Refuge, incorporated in 1850; and the Passionist Monastery of St. Paul and the Franciscan Convent are near by. The United States Marine Hospital is a short distance below. *East Liberty*, 5 miles from Pittsburg, on the Pennsylvania R. R., is a thriving suburb, containing some fine residences, and affording a delightful drive to and from the city. .

Allegheny City (*Central Allegheny House*) is situated on the W. bank of the Alleghany River, opposite Pittsburg, with which it is connected by 5 bridges. Its manufacturing interests are large, and the costly residences of many Pittsburg merchants may be seen here, occupying commanding situations. In 1870 the city had a population of 53,180. The *City Hall* is on the square at the crossing of Ohio and Federal Sts., and the *Allegheny Library* is close by. The finest church in the city is * **St. Peter's** (Episcopal), which has a bas-relief of the Ascension over the entrance. The * **Western Penitentiary** is an immense stone building, in the ancient Norman style, situated on the "common." It was completed in 1827, at a cost of $183,000. Visitors are admitted from 2 to 4½ P. M. every day except Saturdays and Sundays. The *Western Theological Seminary* (Presbyterian) was established here in 1827. It is situated on a lofty, isolated ridge, 100 ft. above the river (reached by Ridge St.), and affords a magnificent prospect. The *Theological Seminary of the United Presbyterian Church*, established in 1826, and the *Allegheny Theological Institute*, organized in 1840 by the Synod of the Reformed Presbyterian Church, are also located here. The *Allegheny Observatory*, situated on an elevated site N. of the city, is a department of the Western University at Pittsburg. The *Public Park* lies around the center of the city; it contains 100 acres, and is adorned with several tiny lakelets and a monument to Humboldt. On the lofty crest near the Alleghany in the E. part of the city stands the * **Soldiers' Monument,** erected to the memory of the 4,000 men of Allegheny Co. who lost their lives in the civil war. It consists of a graceful column, surrounded at the base with statues of an infantry man, a cavalry man, an artillerist, and a sailor, and surmounted by a bronze female figure of colossal size. A fine * view is obtained from this point.

47. Philadelphia to Central New York.

Via North Pennsylvania R R. to Bethlehem, and thence *via* Lehigh Valley R. R. to Elmira, on the Erie R. R.   Distances: to Bethlehem, 54 miles ; to Allentown, 59 ; to Mauch Chunk, 83 ; to Wilkesbarre, 138 ; to Elmira, 264 ; to Buffalo, 413 ; to Niagara Falls, 435.   This route affords a great variety of scenery, and enables the tourist to visit the great iron-works of Lehigh County and some of the most interesting portions of the Pennsylvania coal-region.

THE Philadelphia depot of the N. Penn. R. R. is at the cor. of Berks and American Sts. For 6 miles the road runs through the northern suburbs of the city and then enters Montgomery County, which it traverses for many miles, entering then the rich farming and dairy region of Bucks County. *Gwynedd* (18 miles) is a Welsh village, with a population of about 2,000. Just beyond it the train runs through one of the most extensive and costly tunnels on the entire line (500 ft. long). At *Sellersville* (32 miles) the road crosses the Landis Ridge, which divides the waters of the Schuylkill and Delaware Rivers. From the summit, 1 mile W. of the station, a fine view of Limestone Valley and Quakertown is obtained. *Hellertown* (50 miles) has extensive iron works, and in the vicinity are extensive iron and zinc mines. Near here there are fine views of the hills skirting the Lehigh Valley. Four miles beyond Hellertown is **Bethlehem,** which has already been described (see p. 205). Here the Lehigh Valley R. R. is taken, which begins at Easton, 12 miles from Bethlehem. The section of this road between Easton and Allentown forms part of Route 45 and is there described. From Easton to Pittston the Lehigh Valley R. R. and the Lehigh and Susquehanna R. R. (both of which connect with the N. Penn. R. R. at Bethlehem) run parallel to each other, generally on opposite banks of the Lehigh River. **Allentown** (see p. 205). Leaving Allentown the Lehigh Valley R. R. runs by a number of huge blast-furnaces and in 3 miles reaches *Catasauqua* (62 miles from Phila.), a thriving village of 3,000 inhabitants, with vast iron-works, furnaces, and car-works. *Hokendauqua* (63 miles) and *Coplay* (64 miles) are also the site of immense iron-works. *Slatington* (76 miles) is near the most extensive slate deposits ever discovered. The slate on the Capitol at Washington, $\frac{1}{2}$ inch in thickness, came from this place. The village is charmingly situated about $\frac{1}{2}$ mile from the station, and is a pleasant summer resort. Two miles beyond Slatington is the *Lehigh Water Gap,* a picturesque gorge in which the Lehigh River flows through the Blue Mountains. Steep, forest-clad cliffs rise from the water on either side, and there is barely room in the narrow pass for the river, railroad, highway, and canal. The scenery in the vicinity is remarkably wild and impressive. *Lehighton* (85 miles) is a large village on the Lehigh River at the mouth of Mahoning Creek. The old Moravian Cemetery is on a hill from which may be had a fine view of the Mahoning Valley, and at the foot of which 12 settlers were murdered by the Indians in 1775. At *Weisseport,* on the opposite side of the river, formerly stood Fort Allen, erected by Benjamin Franklin in 1756 as a frontier defense. Its site is now occupied by the Fort Allen Hotel. At *Packerton* (88 miles) are the vast scales, 122½ ft. long with a capacity of 103 tons, which weigh loaded coal-trains while in motion, and the car shops of the Lehigh Valley R. R. Co.; and just beyond the train crosses the Lehigh River on an iron bridge, runs along the base of Bear Mt., and stops at

Mauch Chunk.

Mauch Chunk is reached from New York by Route 45 to Allentown and thence by present Route (total distance, 121 miles). The principal hotel is the *Mansion House* (300 guests, $3 a day). The *American Hotel* is good, and there are private houses where board may be had at reasonable rates.

Mauch Chunk is noted for being situated in the midst of some of the wildest and most picturesque scenery in America, the village lying in a narrow gorge between and among high mountains, its foot resting on the Lehigh River and its body lying along the hillsides. The village is but one street wide, and the valley is so narrow that the dwelling-houses usually have their gardens and outhouses perched above the roof, and there is barely room for the 2 railroads, street, river, and canal, which pass through the gorge side by side. The chief architectural feature of the village is * *St. Mark's Church* (Episcopal), a fine edifice of cream-colored stone with stained-glass windows and massive tower. *Prospect Rock* is a projecting bluff near the Mansion House, from which a pleasant view may be had; but the view from *Flag-staff Peak,* just above, is much finer and the ascent is easily made. * *Glen Onoko* is a wild and beautiful ravine in the side of Broad Mt., about 2 miles from the village. It is 900 ft. long and from 10 to 80 ft. wide, and presents a continuous succession of cascades, rapids, and pools, which afford a fine spectacle in seasons of high water. From the upper end of the Glen a path leads to the *Rock Cabin* and to *Packer's Point,* whence there is an extensive view.

Mauch Chunk lies in the very heart of the Pennsylvania coal-region, and the coal traffic sends many trains through the village every day and a constant procession of canal-boats. The coal-mines which supply this traffic are situated 9 miles back from the river, on Sharp and Black Mountains, and in Panther-Creek Valley, lying between; and the coal used to be brought this distance by the celebrated "Switch-Back" Gravity Road (now the *Mauch Chunk & Summit Hill R. R.*).

At present the coal is brought by rail through a large tunnel, thus doing away with the old route.   The "Switch-Back" is now used only
as a pleasure road.   It is run by gravity.   The cars are drawn to the
top of Mt. Pisgah by a powerful engine on the summit, whence they
descend 6 miles, by gravity, to the foot of Mt. Jefferson, where they
are again taken up by means of a plane, which ascends 462 ft. in
a length of 2,070 ft., and then run on to Summit Hill.   From that point
the cars return, all the way, by the "back-track," or gravity road, to
Mauch Chunk, landing the passengers but a short distance from the

Mauch Chunk.

spot where they commenced the ascent over Pisgah.   Several passen-
ger-trains daily run between the station at the foot of Mt. Pisgah and
the mines; and the excursion is both novel and enjoyable.   The time
required for the circuit is about 3 hours; fare, round trip, 75c., com-
mutation tickets for large parties 50 cents each for the round trip.

An omnibus, connecting with the trains, runs from the Mansion House to the foot of the inclined plane (fare, 25c.). The first plane is 2,322 ft. long, and leads to the summit of **Mt. Pisgah** (850 ft. above the river), from which a noble view is obtained. Mt. Jefferson is the highest point on the road, which descends thence on a slight grade to **Summit Hill,** on which is a mining village of 2,000 inhabitants, with a church, several hotels, and other evidences of civilization. Summit Hill is a good deal resorted to in summer. Beyond Summit Hill the center of the coal-region is reached. Visitors desirous of enjoying the experience of being "down in the mines" can do so by lying over here for a few hours. The return to Mauch Chunk is by a descending grade of 96 ft. to the mile, and the entire 9 miles is traversed in about 25 minutes.

Beyond Mauch Chunk the road passes amid wild and picturesque scenery and in 7 miles reaches *Penn Haven Junction* (95 miles) whence 3 branch roads diverge to different portions of the coal-region. Near here the road crosses the Lehigh on an iron bridge from which can be seen the tunnel of the Lehigh & Susquehanna R. R., and still following the Lehigh through rugged scenery reaches *Whitehaven* (113 miles), an important lumbering village, where large dams are thrown across the river. Here the ascent of the mountains begins with heavy grades, and at *Fairview* (127 miles) the summit is reached and the descent to the Wyoming Valley commences. *Newport* (134 miles) stands high and affords a magnificent view of the Wyoming Valley, the Susquehanna being visible for more than 20 miles from its entry through Lackawannock Gap near Pittston to its exit through Nanticoke Gap near Shickshinny. Nine miles beyond Newport, picturesquely situated on the Susquehanna River, in the center of the Wyoming Valley, is **Wilkesbarre** (*Wyoming Valley Hotel, Luzerne House, Exchange*), a prosperous city of 25,000 inhabitants, with broad, well-shaded streets, and handsome public and private buildings. The Court-House, County Prison, and Opera-House are all fine structures; and there are a good public library and several costly churches. Many fine villa residences front upon the esplanade along the river. Back of the city and about 2 miles distant is **Prospect Rock*, which is 750 ft. high and affords the best view of the entire Wyoming Valley. A small steamer runs on the Susquehanna from Wilkesbarre to Nanticoke (9 miles) and affords fine views of the lower portion of the valley, which, however, is best seen by a drive along the river-road. A bridge across the river connects Wilkesbarre with **Kingston,** 4 miles above which, near the hamlet of Troy, is the site of *Fort Forty*, where the unfortunate battle of Wyoming was fought. Near by is the * **Wyoming Monument,** a massive granite obelisk 62½ ft. high, with appropriate inscriptions. About 3 miles above Fort Forty is *Queen Esther's Rock*, so called from the half-breed Indian woman (queen of the Senecas) who there avenged her son's death by tomahawking 14 American soldiers with her own hand.

The Valley of Wyoming is about 20 miles long and 3 miles wide, being formed by two parallel ranges of mountains, averaging on the west about 800 and on the east 1,000 ft. in height. It is traversed by the Susquehanna River, which enters its upper end through a bold mountain-pass known as the Lackawannock Gap, and passes out of its lower end through another opening in the same mountain called Nanticoke Gap. The river is in most places about 200 yards wide, and from 4 to 20 ft. deep; and moves with a very gentle current, except at the rapids or when swollen with rain or melted snows. Near the center of the valley it has a rapid, called the Wyoming Falls, and another at the lower gap, called the Nanticoke Falls. Several tributary streams fall into it on each side, after traversing rocky passes, and forming beautiful cascades as they descend to the plain. Describing this valley, Dr. Silliman (the elder) says : " Its form is that of a very long oval or ellipse. It is bounded by grand mountain-barriers, and watered by a noble river and its tributaries. The first glance of a stranger entering it at either end, or crossing the mountain-ridges which divide it (like the Happy Valley of Abyssinia) from the rest of the world, fills him with peculiar pleasure, produced by a fine landscape, containing richness, beauty, and grandeur. . . . Few landscapes that I have beheld can vie with the valley of Wyoming." The Massacre of Wyoming, which has

Wyoming Valley, from Campbell's Ledge.

given the valley a melancholy prominence in history, and which forms the theme of Campbell's "Gertrude of Wyoming," occurred on July 3, 1778. The settlers, who had previously been at variance on account of being interested in charters from different authorities, had, at the outbreak of the Revolution, united in an effort to form a home-guard for self-protection. Two of the companies thus formed were ordered to join General Washington, and a third, imperfectly organized and equipped, was unequal to the terrible need that soon arose. A body of 400 British and 700 Indians, chiefly Senecas, under Colonel John Butler, entered the valley June 30, 1778; and the inhabitants, having taken refuge in Fort Forty (so called from the number in one of the bands of settlers), gave battle on the 3d of July and lost. Then followed the terrible massacre, which, though it was exaggerated at the time, has had few parallels in American history. Neither age nor sex was spared, and but few of the ill-fated people escaped by fleeing over the mountains to Stroudsburg. The village of Wilkesbarre was burnt, and its inhabitants either killed, taken prisoners, or scattered in the surrounding forests. Upward of 300 persons are estimated to have perished on that fatal day.

Nine miles beyond Wilkesbarre is **Pittston** (*Farnham, House Eagle Hotel*), situated at the head of the Wyoming Valley, on the Susquehanna, just below the mouth of Lackawanna Creek. W. of the town are the Lackawannock Mts., filled with rich coal-mines which here find an outlet. A prominent object of interest in the vicinity is *Camp-*

bell's Ledge, from which a charming view of the Valley is obtained. At Pittston the Lehigh & Susquehanna R. R., which has run parallel with the present route from Easton, diverges and runs N. E. to Scranton.

The portion of the present route beyond Pittston is much less attractive than that already traversed, though the scenery continues varied and pleasing and at times impressive. *Tunkhannock* (23 miles from Pittston and 175 from Phila.) is the capital of Wyoming County, and is picturesquely situated on the Susquehanna at the mouth of Tunkhannock Creek. From Triangle Hill, near by, there is a broad view. Still following the Susquehanna amid changing forest and hill scenery, the train passes a number of small stations and reaches **Towanda** (*Ward House, Elwell*), a busy manufacturing village of 3,000 inhabitants, situated on the river at the mouth of Towanda Creek. It is much visited in summer, and has a lucrative trade in farm and dairy produce with the surrounding region. Fifteen miles beyond Towanda is **Athens** (244 miles), a flourishing village at the confluence of the Susquehanna and Chemung Rivers. It occupies the site of the important Indian village of *Diahoga* which was the rendezvous of the Tory-Indian forces that perpetrated the massacre of Wyoming. Near by is *Spanish Hill*, on which ancient Spanish coins are said to have been found. Crossing the Chemung River at Athens the train enters the State of New York and speedily reaches *Waverly Junction* (248 miles) and **Elmira** (264 miles), where connection is made with the Erie Railway and all points E. and W. (see Route 39).

48. Philadelphia to Albany, N. Y.

By the North Pennsylvania R. R. to Bethlehem; thence by the Lehigh & Susquehanna R. R. to Green Ridge; thence by the Pennsylvania Div. of the Delaware & Hudson Co.'s R. R. to Nineveh; and thence by the Albany & Susquehanna R. R. to Albany. Distances: to Bethlehem, 54 miles; to Mauch Chunk, 88; to Wilkesbarre, 142; to Scranton, 160; to Green Ridge, 163; to Carbondale, 177; to Nineveh, 231; to Albany, 350; to Saratoga Springs, 388. This is a popular route from Philadelphia to Saratoga Springs and Montreal, and the variety of scenery which it offers makes it very attractive in summer.

As far as Bethlehem (54 miles) this route is identical with Route 47. From Bethlehem to Pittston the Lehigh & Susquehanna R. R. and the Lehigh Valley R. R. (described in Route 47) run so close together, on opposite sides of the Lehigh River, that the same description serves for both. At *Pittston* (151 miles) the Lehigh & Susquehanna R. R. diverges to the N. E. and runs in 9 miles to **Scranton** (*Wyoming House, Forest House*), a flourishing city of about 40,000 inhabitants occupying the plateau at the confluence of Roaring Brook and the Lackawanna River. It is handsomely laid out, with broad, straight streets, and contains many fine residences and public buildings, but its general appearance is somber. Its importance is due to its situation in the most northern of the anthracite basins, and to its railroad facilities. The Del., Lack. & Western R. R. (Route 51) connects here, and there are several other important lines. The trade in mining supplies is extensive, and the shipments of coal are immense. Its iron-

10

manufactures are very important, and there are vast blast-furnaces, rolling-mills, foundries, machine-shops, etc. Lackawanna, Penn, and Wyoming Aves. are the principal streets. In the suburb of Dunmore is the Forest Hill Cemetery, whence fine views are obtained; and from the N. suburbs may be seen the collieries on the opposite side of Pine Creek valley. At *Green Ridge* (2 miles beyond Scranton) the train passes on to the track of the Penn. Div. of the Delaware & Hudson Canal Co.'s R. R., and, ascending the valley of the Lackawanna amid numerous collieries and mining-villages, in 15 miles reaches **Carbondale,** a city of 7,000 inhabitants at the N. end of the anthracite-coal region, near several extremely rich coal-mines. The chief object of interest here is the *Gravity Railroad,* a series of inclined planes on which immense coal-trains are sent over the mountains to and from *Honesdale* (16 miles) on the Delaware & Hudson Canal with no impelling force but gravity, save at one point. Beyond Carbondale, the road traverses a mountainous, rugged, and sparsely-settled region, crosses the Alleghanies at an elevation of 2,500 ft., and descends amidst picturesque scenery to the valley of the Susquehanna. At *Jefferson Junction* (35 miles from Carbondale) the Erie R. R. (Route 39) is crossed near Binghamton, and the Albany train passes on by several small stations to *Nineveh* (231 miles from Phila. and 119 from Albany). Here the Albany & Susquehanna R. R. is taken, and the train passes N. E. up the smiling valley of the Susquehanna River by a number of pretty villages and hamlets. From *Afton,* 5 miles beyond Nineveh, stages run to **Vallonia Springs** (*Spring House*), a picturesque highland village 700 ft. above the river and surrounded by beautiful scenery. The waters are impregnated with sulphur, iron, and magnesia, and are beneficial in cutaneous diseases. At *Sidney Plains* (247 miles) the New York & Oswego Midland R. R. is intersected.

One mile beyond *Colliers* (75 miles from Albany and 67 from Binghamton) the Cooperstown & Susquehanna Valley R. R. diverges, and runs N. in 16 miles to **Cooperstown** (*Cooper House, Hotel Fenimore, Central*), a village of 2,000 inhabitants, at the S. end of Otsego Lake. The beautiful situation of the village, high up in the hills, with a bracing atmosphere and delightful scenery, renders it a charming summer resort, and attracts many visitors. Cooperstown was the home of J. Fenimore Cooper, the novelist, and his pen has rendered the whole region classic. "The same points still exist which Leather-Stocking saw; there is the same beauty of verdure along the hills; and the sun still glints as brightly as then the ripples of the clear water." The site of the old Cooper mansion (burned in 1854) is still pointed out; and the *Tomb of Cooper* is near Christ Church, which also contains beautiful memorial windows. The *Cooper Monument* is in Lakewood Cemetery, a mile from the village; it is of Italian marble, 25 ft. high, and is surmounted by a statue of Leather-Stocking. Two miles from the village, on the W. shore of the lake, is *Hannah's Hill* (named after Cooper's daughter), whence a fine view is obtained. On the E. shore (2 miles from the village) is *Mt. Vision,* which commands a very beautiful view of the lake and of the country adjacent. * *Rum*

Hill (7 miles distant) is said to command a prospect of over 60 miles. *Leather-Stocking's Cave* is on the E. shore, 1½ mile from the village; and the *Leather-Stocking Falls* (or Panther's Leap) are on the same side, at the head of a wild gorge. The *Mohegan Glen* is on the W. shore (3 miles from the village), and contains a series of small but picturesque cascades. There are many pleasant drives in the vicinity of Cooperstown; and highways lead to *Cherry Valley* (13 miles), to *Richfield Springs* (14 miles), and to *Sharon Springs* (20 miles). **Otsego Lake** is about 9 miles long and 1 to 1½ wide, and is described by Cooper as "a broad sheet of water, so placid and limpid that it resembles a bed of the pure mountain atmosphere compressed into a setting of hills and woods. Nothing is wanted but ruined castles and recollections, to raise it to the level of the Rhine." The shores are bold and diversified, and the clear waters teem with fish. Two small steamers ply on the lake, affording a delightful excursion, and connecting at the upper end with stages for Cherry Valley and Richfield Springs. (See p. 226).

(See p. 226).

Beyond Colliers the road passes a number of small villages, crosses the watershed between the Susquehanna and the Mohawk, and descends by gentle grades into the latter valley. At *Cobleskill* (305 miles from Phila. and 45 miles from Albany) a branch line diverges and runs N. W. in 14 miles to **Sharon Springs** (*Pavilion Hotel, Union Hall, United States, Sharon House, Mansion House, American, Frethus*), a village of Schoharie Co., New York, which is visited by more than 10,000 invalids and pleasure-seekers annually. The village is situated in a narrow valley surrounded by high hills, and is chiefly noted for its mineral springs, of which there are four: chalybeate, magnesia, white sulphur, and blue sulphur. These, together with a spring of pure water, are near each other and near a wooded bluff W. of the village, and flow into a small stream below. The waters are pure and clear, and, though they flow for ¼ mile from their source with other currents, they yet preserve their own distinct character. They tumble over a ledge of perpendicular rocks, with a descent of 65 ft., in sufficient volume and force to turn a mill. The Magnesia and White Sulphur Springs closely resemble the White Sulphur Springs of Virginia. The waters are drunk to a considerable extent, especially the Magnesia; but the specialty of the place is its baths, for which there are spacious and admirably appointed bath-houses (40c. a bath). Besides the water-baths, mud-baths are administered (in which the patient is covered with mud saturated with sulphur and heated to about 110°). These baths are considered remedial for rheumatism and kindred ailments. Other baths, prepared by mixing the magnesia-water with extract of pine from the Black Forest of Germany, are administered for pulmonary, neuralgic, and paralytic diseases. There are pleasant drives and rambles in the vicinity of the hotels, and from the summit of the hill over the village a beautiful view may be obtained, including the Mohawk Valley, the Adirondacks, and the Green Mountains of Vermont.

Sharon Springs is connected by stage (9 miles) with Palatine Bridge on the N. Y. Central R. R. (see Route 38).

Cherry Valley, a pretty little village at the head of Cherry Valley Creek, is 9 miles from Sharon Springs by railway and 7 miles by road. It is a place of great interest as the scene of one of the most atrocious massacres that have ever disgraced any war. Here, in August, 1778, the Tories and Indians fell upon the unprotected settlers, and, without making any distinction of age or sex, either killed or took captive the entire population. A monument now marks the site of the old fort and the grave of the slaughtered settlers. The valley is a popular but not fashionable summer resort, and besides the hotels (*Park Hotel* and *Palmer House*) there are numerous houses at which board may be obtained at from $7 to $12 a week. In the village is a young ladies' academy, the first principal of which was the Rev. Solomon Spaulding, whose fanciful antiquarian novel, written solely for his own amusement, was made the basis of the "Book of Mormon." Near the center of the township is *Mt. Independence*, a rocky eminence rising 2,000 ft. above the sea. On a small creek near by (2 miles from the village) are the *Tekaharawa Falls*, a picturesque cascade 160 ft. high. In the vicinity of these falls (1½ mile from the village) are the *Cherry Valley White Sulphur Springs*, which are becoming a popular resort. In the village of Salt Springsville, near by, are a number of salt-springs; and there are also chalybeate and magnesia waters in the vicinity. Cherry Valley is famous for the coolness, salubrity, and tonic effect of its summer climate.

On the main line, 6 miles beyond Cobleskill and 39 miles from Albany, is **Howe's Cave** (*Cave House*) the most remarkable cavern known, after the great Mammoth Cave of Kentucky. It was discovered in 1842 by Lester Howe, who is said to have penetrated to a distance of 12 miles, but the farthest point usually visited is about 4 miles from the entrance. The entrance is near the hotel (fee, including guide, $1.50). A stairway descends from the entrance to the Reception Room, after which follow in succession Washington Hall, the Bridal Chamber, the Chapel, Harlequin Tunnel, Cataract Hall, Ghost Room or Haunted Castle, and Music Hall. Stygian Lake is crossed in a boat, and beyond are Plymouth Rock, Devil's Gateway, Museum, Geological Rooms, Uncle Tom's Cabin, Grant's Study, Pirate's Cave, Rocky Mts., Valley of Jehoshaphat, Winding Way, and Rotunda. As far as the lake the cave is lighted with gas, and beautiful stalactites and stalagmites are everywhere seen. There are other remarkable caves in this vicinity, the most noteworthy of which is *Ball's Cave*, 4 miles E. of Schoharie.

Three miles beyond Howe's Cave is *Central Bridge*, whence a branch line runs in 5 miles to the pretty hill-village of *Schoharie ;* and 9 miles farther is *Quaker Station*, where through passengers for Saratoga and the north who wish to save the détour by Albany take a branch road which runs N. E. *via* Schenectady to **Saratoga Springs** in 37 miles. Between Quaker Station and Albany the train runs for a considerable portion of the way in sight of the far-viewing Helderberg Mountains, descends the picturesque valley of Norman's Kill, passes 5 small stations, and reaches Albany (350 miles) where connection is made with railroads leading in all directions. **Albany** is described on p. 63.

49. Philadelphia to Erie.

By the Philadelphia & Erie Division of the Pennsylvania R. R. Distances: to Harrisburg, 106 miles; to Sunbury, 163; to Williamsport, 203; to Lock Haven, 228; to Emporium, 301; to Corry, 413; to Erie, 451. Two through trains daily run on this line, making the journey in 24 hours, and this is a favorite route from Philadeladelphia to Western New York and the Oil Regions of Pennsylvania.

FROM Philadelphia to Harrisburg this route follows the Pennsylvania R. R. and has been described in Route 46. From Harrisburg to Sunbury it follows the Northern Central R. R., and this section is described in Route 55. *Sunbury* (163 miles) is pleasantly situated on the E. bank of the Susquehanna River, at the intersection of the Philadelphia & Erie and Northern Central Railways. The former road is taken here, and the train passes in 2 miles to the pleasant village of *Northumberland*, built upon a point of land formed by the confluence of the N. and W. branches of the Susquehanna. The Lackawanna & Bloomsburg R. R. connects here, and by means of it a pleasant excursion can be made to the Wyoming Valley (see p. 215). *Milton* (176 miles) is a thriving village at the junction of the present route with the Catawissa R. R. (Route 52). About 10 miles beyond Milton, the two railroads cross each other and run on nearly parallel lines to Williamsport. The scenery along this portion of the route is strikingly picturesque. **Williamsport** (*Herdic House, Hepburn House*) is a city of 18,000 inhabitants picturesquely situated on the W. Branch of the Susquehanna, surrounded by high hills and much fine scenery. The streets are wide and straight, lighted with gas, and traversed by horse-cars. The business quarter is substantially built, and numerous handsome residences and gardens make the place attractive. The suburbs of Rocktown and Duboistown lie across the river under the Bald Eagle Mts., and are connected with the city by a graceful suspension bridge. The county buildings are handsome structures, and *Trinity Church* is a very fine edifice. The *Dickinson Seminary*, with spacious buildings in Academy St., is a noted educational institution. Williamsport owes its prosperity to the lumber business, of which it is a leading mart. The great *Susquehanna Boom* extends from 3 to 4 miles up the river, has a capacity of 300,000,000 ft. of lumber, and in spring is filled with pine and hemlock logs. The annual shipments of lumber average 250,000,000 ft., and there are vast saw-mills, planing-mills, machine-shops, etc.

Leaving Williamsport the train crosses in succession the Lycoming Creek and the W. Branch, and still following the river passes in 25 miles to **Lock Haven** (*Fallon House, Irvin House*), a city of 8,000 inhabitants, also famous as a lumber-mart. Immense numbers of logs are annually received in the boom here, and furnish employment to extensive saw-mills. The charming scenery about Lock Haven,

especially that of the adjacent Bald Eagle Valley, attracts many summer visitors. Beyond Lock Haven the road runs for 27 miles through
wild scenery to **Renovo** (*Renovo Hotel*), a creation of the railroad
which here has its extensive construction-shops and foundries. The
village lies in a beautiful, mountain-surrounded valley, and the loveliness of the scenery combined with the excellent trout-fishing in the
adjacent streams has made it a popular summer resort. A few miles
beyond Renovo the railroad leaves the Susquehanna and for the next
50 miles traverses what, until its construction, was an unknown land
even to its nearest neighbors—a favorite refuge of outlawed criminals.
It is the section of country known as the *Great Horseshoe of the Alleghanies,* which encompassed and isolated it, and it is still a desolate
wilderness save where a few straggling settlements have sprung up
along the railway. *Cameron* (296 miles) is a small village near some
rich veins of bituminous coal. Five miles beyond is **Emporium**
(*Shines House*), an important lumbering town on the Driftwater, a
tributary of the Susquehanna, built in a narrow valley, the sides of which
rise abruptly to the height of 700 ft. to 1,000 ft. Valuable salt-springs
have been discovered in the vicinity, and it is expected that the manufacture of salt will prove profitable. At Emporium the Buffalo, New
York & Phila. R. R. (Route 50) diverges. Twenty-two miles beyond
Emporium is the flourishing village of **St. Mary's** (*Riley House, Franklin*) surrounded by numerous veins of the richest bituminous coal,
and near deposits of iron-ore and fire-clay, with abundance of timber
at hand. There are 2 religious houses here: St. Mary's Convent of
Benedictine Nuns and St. Mary's Priory, a Benedictine monastery.
The convent is the oldest of the order in the United States and is
called the "Mother House." *Wilcox* (347 miles) is noted as the site of
the largest tannery in the world, and *Kane* (356 miles) is where the
road leaves the *Wild-cat Country,* or "unknown land." It is situated
on the Big Level, a narrow plateau which forms the boundary from N.
to S. of the great coal and oil region of Northwestern Pennsylvania,
and is the summit whence trains descend by heavy grades to the level
of Lake Erie. *Warren* (385 miles) is an attractive town of 2,000 inhabitants at the confluence of the Conewango and Alleghany River, at
the head of navigation on the latter. It is the site of extensive tanneries, has an abundance of light sandstone for building purposes, and
lies between the coal and iron and the oil regions of Pennsylvania,
having communication with both. The Dunkirk, Warren & Pittsburg
R. R. connects here. At *Irvineton* (390 miles) the Oil Creek & Alleghany River R. R. comes in from the Oil Regions (see Route 53).
Corry (413 miles, *Downer House, St. Nicholas*) is at the junction of the
Philadelphia & Erie, Atlantic & Great Western, and Buffalo, Corry &
Pittsburg Railways. It came into existence as a result of the discovery
of oil, and prior to June, 1861, its site was covered with forest. The
first house was erected in Aug., 1861, the great Downer Oil Works
were erected shortly afterward, and the place has now a population of
about 8,000, with 8 churches, 2 banks, and 2 daily papers. Beyond
Corry are *Union* (424 miles) and *Waterford* (432 miles), and the road

traverses a pleasant farming country to its terminus at Erie (451 miles
from Phila.).

Erie (*Reed House, Morton House*) is a city and port of entry on
Lake Erie, with a population of over 26,000, a flourishing commerce,
and extensive manufactures. It stands upon an elevated bluff commanding a fine view of the lake, and is regularly laid out with broad
streets crossing each other at right angles. *The Park* is a finely shaded
inclosure in the center of the city, surrounded by handsome buildings,
and intersected by State St., which is the principal business thoroughfare.
In the Park are a *Soldiers' Monument*, with 2 bronze statues of heroic
size, and 2 handsome fountains; and near by is the *Court-House*, a neat
building in the classic style. The new *Opera-House* is a costly and
handsome edifice, and the *Custom-House* is a substantial building near
the water. The *Marine Hospital* has extensive but unused buildings
at the cor. of Ash and 2d Sts. The *Union Depot* is of brick in the
Romanesque style, 480 ft. long, 88 ft. wide, and 2 stories high, and is
surmounted by a cupola 40 ft. high. The *Erie Cemetery*, in Chestnut
St., comprises 75 acres beautifully laid out with walks and drives, and
adorned with trees, flowers, and shrubbery. The harbor is the best
on Lake Erie, being $4\frac{1}{2}$ miles long, over 1 mile wide, and 9 to 25 ft.
deep, and is inclosed by Presque Isle, lying in front of the city. At
the entrance are 3 lighthouses, and there are several large docks furnished with railroad tracks, so that the transfer of merchandise takes
place directly between the vessels and the cars. The principal articles
of shipment are lumber, coal, iron-ore, and grain. The leading manufactures are of iron-ware, machinery, cars, leather, brass, furniture, organs, boots and shoes, etc. It was from Erie that Perry's fleet sailed
on the occasion of his memorable victory, and thither he brought his
prizes. Several of his ships sank in Lawrence Bay, and the hull of
the Niagara is still visible in fair weather. At Erie the traveler can
take the Lake Shore & Michigan Southern R. R. and go E. to Buffalo
(88 miles) or W. to Chicago (451 miles).

50. Philadelphia to Buffalo.

By the Pennsylvania R. R. to Harrisburg; thence by the Northern Central R.
R. to Sunbury; thence by the Philadelphia & Erie R. R. to Emporium; and
thence by the Buffalo, New York & Philadelphia R. R. to Buffalo. Distances: to
Harrisburg, 106 miles; to Sunbury, 168; to Williamsport, 203; to Emporium, 301;
to Buffalo, 422. This is the shortest route between Philadelphia and Western New
York.

As far as **Emporium** (301 miles) this route is identical with the
preceding one. At Emporium the Buffalo, New York & Philadelphia
R. R. is taken, and the train runs N. through a sparsely-settled forest-
region to *Port Alleghany* (325 miles), a small village on the Alleghany
River. Beyond Port Alleghany the river is followed amid rugged
scenery to **Olean** (353 miles) where the Erie R. R. (Route 39) is
crossed. Olean is an important shipping-station at the head of navigation on the Alleghany River. Twelve miles beyond Olean is *Ischua*,
E. of which is the Oil Creek Reservation of the Seneca Indians. Near

Franklinville (373 miles) is the pretty Lime Lake, which may be seen from the cars on the left; and during the remaining 50 miles the road traverses a pleasant agricultural district of rolling hills and fertile intervales with small rural hamlets *en route.* **Buffalo** is described on page 160.

51. Philadelphia to Lake Ontario.

By the New York Div. of the Pennsylvania R. R. to Trenton; thence by the Belvidere Div. to Manunka Chunk; and thence by the Delaware, Lackawanna & Western R. R. to Oswego. Distances: to Trenton, 30 miles; to Manunka Chunk, 98; to Delaware Water-Gap, 108; to Scranton, 165; to Binghamton, 226; to Syracuse, 306; to Oswego, 341; to Niagara Falls, 456. This is a direct and pleasant route from Philadelphia to the Delaware Water-Gap, Schooley's Mt., Central and Western New York, Buffalo, and Niagara Falls. There is only one change of cars between Philadelphia and Oswego, at Manunka Chunk.

FROM Philadelphia to **Trenton** (30 miles) this route is described in Route 3 *a.* At Trenton the Belvidere Division is taken, and the train follows the N. bank of the Delaware River to Manunka Chunk amid varied and picturesque scenery. Four miles beyond Trenton the New Jersey Lunatic Asylum is passed, and 5 miles farther is *Washington's Crossing,* where General Washington made the celebrated passage of the Delaware, when he surprised and defeated the Hessians at Trenton (Dec. 26, 1776). *Lambertville* (46 miles) is a large manufacturing village of 3,000 inhabitants, with a fine water-power derived from a feeder of the Delaware & Raritan Canal. Beyond Lambertville the scenery is very pleasing, and 8 small stations are passed before reaching *Phillipsburg* (81 miles), where connections are made with the Morris and Essex R. R. (Route 44), and the N. J. Central R. R. (Route 45). For description of Phillipsburg, see page 204. Fourteen miles beyond Phillipsburg is *Belvidere* (American House), a pretty village situated on both sides of Pequest Creek, where it empties into the Delaware. It has a fine water-power, with considerable manufactures, and a population of about 2,500. **Manunka Chunk** (98 miles) is the junction with the Del., Lack. & Western R. R., and passengers for the north here change cars. (The Del., Lack. & Western R. R. has its E. terminus at Hoboken, and the route from New York to Manunka Chunk is described in Route 44.) *Delaware* (100 miles) is the last station in New Jersey, the train crossing the Delaware into Pennsylvania on a long bridge. All trains stop at Delaware for refreshments. Eight miles beyond Delaware station is the celebrated

Delaware Water-Gap.

Hotels, etc.—The *Kittatinny House* ($15 to $18 a week), standing on the mountain-side above the railway station, is an old and favorite resort. The *Water-Gap House* ($4 a day, $18 a week) is a spacious hotel on the summit of Sunset Hill. The *Mountain House* and the *Glenwood* are smaller ($10 to $12 a week). *Fare* from New York to the Water-Gap, $2.55. From Philadelphia, $2.95.

The Delaware Water-Gap is where the Delaware River, after a journey of about 200 miles through a wild, rugged, and romantic country, forces its way through the Kittatinny or Blue Mountains. The Gap is about 2 miles long, and is a narrow gorge between walls of rock some 1,600 ft. in height, and so near to each other at the S. E. entrance as hardly to leave room for the river and the railroad. The valley N. of the Blue Ridge and above the Gap bore the Indian name of Minnisink, or "Whence the waters are gone." "Here a vast lake once probably extended; and whether the great body of water wore its way through the mountain by a fall like Niagara, or burst through a gorge, or whether the mountains uprose in convulsion upon its margin, it is certain that the Minnisink country bears the mark of aqueous action in its diluvial soil, and in its rounded hills, built of pebbles and bowlders."

Of the two grand mountains which flank the mighty chasm of the Gap, the one on the Pennsylvania (W.) side is named *Minsi*, in memory of the Indians; that on the New Jersey (E.) side bears the name of *Tammany*, an ancient Delaware chief, who was canonized during the last century, and proclaimed the patron saint of America. Mt. Minsi is soft in outline, and densely wooded, but Tammany exhibits vast, frowning masses of naked rock. Successive ledges, or geological terraces, mark the face of Minsi, and upon the lowest of these, 200 ft. above the river, stands the old Kittatinny House. The stream that issues beneath the hotel and falls in a cascade into the river has come down the mountain-side through a dark and picturesque ravine. Far up the ascent it takes its rise in the *Hunter's Spring*, a cool and sequestered spot, reached by a path from the hotel. Under the name of *Caldeno Creek* it continues its downward course by cascade and waterfall to the river. Along the face of Minsi, about 500 ft. above the river, runs a grand horizontal plateau of red shale, extending for several miles along the mountain, and known as the *Table Rock*. Extensive views are obtained from this point, and the Caldeno flows over the ledge at an angle of 45 degrees in a charming succession of miniature falls and rapids. The rocky strata beneath are densely covered with moss, which gives the spot its name of *Moss Cataract*. Below the cataract, in a secluded, deeply-shaded glen, is the placid rock-basin known as *Diana's Bath;* and at a still lower range the stream dashes at *Caldeno Falls* over a rugged, rocky precipice. All these points are reached from the Kittatinny House by a path marked in *white* lines on rocks and trees. The summit of *Mt. Minsi* is reached from the hotel by a path 3 miles long, marked by *red* lines. The ascent is easy, and the view from the summit the finest to be obtained in this region. Paths diverging from the main path to the summit lead to various points of interest. A short distance from the hotel a path marked with *blue* lines, and turning off to the left, leads to the *Lover's Leap*, whence the best view of the Gap is obtained. Half a mile farther, a *white*-lined path to the right leads to *Hunter's Spring*, already mentioned; and still beyond a *yellow*-lined path (to the left) leads to *Prospect Rock* (2 miles from the hotel), whence another noble view is obtained. *Mt. Tammany* may be ascended from the hotels by a rugged path 2½ miles long, but it should not be undertaken except by a vigorous climber. The view from the summit is fine, but does not differ

materially from that from the summit of Mt. Minsi. On the apex of
the lofty peak is a picturesque mountain-lake, of which popular superstition declares that it has no bottom.

The best near view of the Gap is obtained by descending the river
in a boat to *Mather's Spring*, on the New Jersey shore (1½ mile from
the hotel). The *Indian Ladder Bluff*, at the foot of Mt. Tammany,
the *Cold Air Cave, Benner's Spring*, and the *Point of Rocks*, are
favorite excursion-points along the river. A few miles above the Gap
the Delaware is joined by the Bushkill Creek, upon which is one of
the most beautiful waterfalls of the district—the *Bushkill Falls*. On
a small affluent of the same stream are the *Buttermilk Falls* and the
picturesque *Marshall Falls*. All of these falls are within 7 miles of
the hotels. There is a pleasant drive from the Gap up the *Cherry Valley*.

The Water-Gap is traversed on a narrow shelf between the river
and mountain, and as the train emerges at the N. end it crosses Broad-
head Creek, and passes through a cut in Rock Difficult, so called from
the difficulty encountered in making a passage through its flinty mass.
Stroudsburg (112 miles) is the first station beyond the Gap, and is a
pleasant summer resort. At *Spragueville* (117 miles) the ascent of the
Pocono Mt., the E. slope of the Alleghanies, begins, the grade for 25
miles being at the rate of 65 ft. to the mile. Just beyond *Oakland*
(125 miles) the Pocono Tunnel is traversed near the top of the mountain, a point from which the view, extending more than 30 miles, is
most impressive. At *Tobyhanna* (138 miles) the descent of the W.
slope of the mountains begins. In the vicinity of *Moscow* (152 miles)
game and trout abound; and, just beyond, the valley of Roaring Brook
is entered, and the train descends by steep grades into the Lackawanna Valley and soon reaches **Scranton** (see p. 217). Beyond Scranton the train runs N. through a mountainous and thinly-settled region
to *Great Bend* (212 miles), a small village on the Erie R. R. and the
Susquehanna River; whence the two roads run parallel to each other
on opposite sides of the river 14 miles to **Binghamton** (see p. 171).

At Chenango Forks, 11 miles beyond Binghamton, the *Utica Division* diverges
from the main line and runs N. E. in 95 miles to **Utica** on the N. Y. Central R. R.
(see Route 38). From *Richfield Junction* (14 miles from Utica) a branch line runs
in 21 miles to **Richfield Springs**, a popular summer resort in Otsego County,
near the head of Schuyler's Lake, and within a few miles, drive of Cooperstown and
Cherry Valley (see Route 48). The village is neat, but the hotels constitute Richfield. The leading hotels are the *Spring House* ($18 to $25 a week) and the *American* ($15 to $25 a week), which face each other on opposite sides of the main street,
and accommodate each about 400 guests. Smaller houses are the *Tuller House*
($12 to $15 a week), the *National, Canadarago, Cary's, Davenport, Central*,
and others. There are 17 mineral springs near the village, the most important
being that within the grounds of the Spring House. The main constituents of its
waters are bicarbonate of magnesia and lime, sulphate of magnesia and lime, chloride of sodium and magnesia, and sulphuretted-hydrogen gas. They are considered
especially efficacious in diseases of the skin. There are delightful walks and drives
in the vicinity of the Springs, and fine boating and fishing on **Schuyler's Lake**,
which is 1 mile from the village. This lake is 3¼ miles long, and is inclosed by
gentle hills which combine with it in many attractive landscapes. The *Lake House*
is celebrated for its fish and game dinners. Stages run several times daily to
Otsego Lake, connecting with the steamers; also connecting at Springfield Center
with stages to *Cherry Valley* and *Sharon Springs*.

Leaving Binghamton the train follows the Chenango River for 10 or 12 miles, then ascends the Tioughnioga River, and then traverses a rich farming region to Syracuse on the N. Y. Central R. R.   There are numerous villages *en route*, but the only ones requiring mention are *Cortland* (269 miles), a pretty place of 3,500 inhabitants, seat of a State Normal School; and *Homer* (271 miles) a prosperous village, near the Little York Lakes.   **Syracuse** (306 miles) is described on p. 156.   Beyond Syracuse the road skirts the W. shore of Onondaga Lake, and soon reaches the Oswego River, which it follows for 17 miles to **Oswego** (*Lake Shore Hotel, Doolittle House*).   Oswego is the largest and handsomest city on Lake Ontario, with a population in 1875 of 22, 428, and extensive commerce and manufactures.   Immense quantities of grain and lumber are received and shipped here, and, with the exception of Rochester, more flour is made here than in any city in the country. *Kingsford's Oswego Starch Factory* is the largest in the world, and there are important foundries, iron-works, etc.   The city is divided into two nearly equal parts by the Oswego River, which is spanned by 3 iron drawbridges.   The streets are regularly laid out with a width of 100 ft., and contain many fine public and commercial buildings and private residences.   There are two public parks, one on each side of the river, which, as well as the residence-streets, are beautifully shaded.   The principal public buildings are the *Custom-House and Post-Office,* of Cleveland limestone, costing $120,000; the *City Hall* and the *County Court-House,* of Onondaga limestone; the *State Armory,* of brick, with stone and iron facings; and the *City Library,* costing $30,000 and containing 12,000 volumes.   There are also several handsome school-buildings, and 2 public halls.   The *Deep Rock Spring* (in First St. W.)., discovered in 1865, has attained a wide celebrity, and the spacious *Doolittle House* has been erected over it to accommodate invalids and others.   The naturally good harbor of Oswego has been artificially improved, and now has 3 miles of wharfage.   It is defended by *Fort Ontario,* a strong work on the E. shore (open to visitors). Besides the present route, Oswego is the terminus of the N. Y. & Oswego Midland R. R., of the Rome, Watertown & Oswego R. R., and of the Lake Ontario Shore R. R., which runs to Niagara Falls in 154 miles.

52. Philadelphia to Reading, Pottsville, and Williamsport.

By the Philadelphia & Reading and Catawissa Railways. Distances : to Reading, 58 miles; to Port Clinton, 78; to Pottsville, 93; to Tamaqua, 98; to Williamsport, 199.   The Phila. & Reading R. R. is the most important coal-road in the country, connecting the great anthracite coal-fields with tide-water; and vast quantities of coal are transported over it.   The road was finished in 1842 at a cost of over $16,000,000. It traverses the valley of the Schuylkill River a distance of 58 miles to Reading and thence 35 miles to Pottsville.

THE passenger station in Phila. is at the cor. of Broad and Callowhill Sts., and leaving the city the fine stone bridge over the Schuylkill is crossed in full view of Fairmount Park, Laurel Hill, and other objects

of interest mentioned in our description of Philadelphia. The Schuylkill River is now followed, and in 17 miles the train reaches *Bridgeport*,
opposite which is **Norristown** (*Montgomery House*), a handsomely built
town of 11,000 inhabitants, with a fine marble Court-House, several
handsome school-buildings, and important manufactures. The *Chester
Valley R. R.* runs in 22 miles from Bridgeport to Downingtown on the
Penn. R. R. (see p. 206). *Valley Forge* (23 miles) is memorable as the
headquarters of Gen. Washington and the American army during the
dismal winter of 1777. The building occupied by Washington is still
standing near the railroad, whence it can be seen. **Phœnixville** (27
miles) is a flourishing town of 7,000 inhabitants, noted for its rolling-
mills and furnaces. The Phœnix Iron-Works are the largest in
America, and it was here that the iron dome of the Capitol at Washington was made. Just beyond Phœnixville the train traverses a tunnel
2,000 ft. long, and passes in 12 miles to *Pottstown*, a pretty, tree-em-
bowered village of 5,000 inhabitants, surrounded by charming scenery.
The railroad passes through one of its streets and crosses the Mana-
tawny Creek on a lattice bridge 1,071 ft. long. **Reading** (*Mansion
House, American, Keystone*) is the third city of Pennsylvania in manufactures and the fourth in population, which is about 40,000. It is very
pleasantly situated on an elevated and ascending plain, backed on the
E. by Penn's Mt. and on the S. by the Neversink Mt., from both of
which flow streams of pure water, abundantly supplying the city. The
streets cross each other at right angles, and in the center of the city is
Penn Square, on which are the chief hotels and stores. The *Court-
House*, on N. 6th St., is a very handsome edifice with a fine portico
supported by 6 columns of red sandstone. The *City Hall* is at the cor.
of Franklin and S. 5th Sts., and near by is a public library with 3,000
volumes. The *County Prison* is a substantial structure in Penn St. ;
and the *Grand Opera-House* and *Mishler's Academy of Music* are fine
buildings. Of the 31 churches the most noteworthy are *Trinity* (German Lutheran) an antique building with a spire 210 ft. high, and *Christ*
(Episcopal), an imposing Gothic edifice of red sandstone in N. 5th St.,
with a spire 202 ft. high. Reading is surrounded by a rich farming
country, with which it has a lucrative trade. The inhabitants of this
district are chiefly of German origin, and a dialect of German, known as
Pennsylvania Dutch, prevails extensively among them. The city is especially noted for its manufactures, among which the production and
working of iron hold the first rank. Much of the ore is obtained from
Penn's Mt. The shops of the Phila. & Reading R. R. employ 2,800
men. The principal places of interest in the vicinity of Reading are
the *Mineral Spring*, 1½ mile E. ; *Andalusia Hall*, a spacious summer
hotel, 1 mile N. ; and the *White House Hotel*, 1½ mile S. E. on the Neversink Mt., 300 ft. above the river. *White Spot*, on Penn's Mt., 1,000
ft. above the river, is famed for its view. At Reading the present route
is intersected by the Allentown Line (see Route 45).

Beyond Reading the road still follows the Schuylkill amid picturesque mountain scenery, and in 20 miles reaches *Port Clinton* (75
miles), a pleasant place at the mouth of the Little Schuylkill. Here

the Little Schuylkill R. R. connects. From Port Clinton the Pottsville trains pass on by *Auburn* (83 miles) and *Schuylkill Haven* (89 miles) to **Pottsville** (*Pennsylvania Hall, Merchants' Hotel*), the terminus of the Phila. & Reading main line. Pottsville is situated upon the edge of the great Schuylkill coal-basin, in the gap by which the river breaks through Sharp's Mt. The annual yield of the Schuylkill coal-fields is about 5,000,000 tons, and this enormous product is conveyed to market by the Reading R. R. and the Schuylkill Canal. The city dates from 1825, and in 1875 had a population of about 15,000. The chief public buildings are the Court House, Jail, Town Hall, Union Hall, and Opera House. The coal-traffic is the principal source of the city's prosperity, but there are also extensive foundries, rolling-mills, and machine-shops. The great collieries lie to the N. and N. E., and are reached by numerous branch roads which converge upon Pottsville.

At *Port Clinton* (see above), the through trains for Williamsport take the Little Schuylkill R. R., which traverses a wild and desolate region for 20 miles to **Tamaqua** (98 miles), a prosperous town of 6,000 inhabitants, attractively situated on the Little Schuylkill, in the midst of a rich coal-region, from which it draws a large trade. At Tamaqua the Catawissa R. R. is taken, and the train traverses for 50 miles a rugged and mountainous region which is fairly gridironed with the numerous intersecting branches of the great coal-roads. The scenery of this section of the route is varied and impressive, and the Catawissa Valley, which is traversed for 30 miles, offers scenes of singular beauty. **Catawissa** (*Susquehanna House*) is 145 miles from Phila., and is picturesquely situated at the confluence of the Catawissa Creek and the Susquehanna River. The views from the surrounding hill-tops are superb. Nine miles beyond Catawissa is **Danville** (*Montour House*), a flourishing manufacturing town of 10,000 inhabitants. The Montour Iron Works here make vast quantities of railroad iron, and on a hill near by is a State Insane Asylum with extensive buildings. *Milton* (170 miles) is the junction of the present route with the Phila. & Erie R. R., which is described in Route 49. **Williamsport** (see p. 221).

53. Pittsburg to Titusville and Buffalo. The Pennsylvania Oil Regions.

By the Allegheny Valley and Buffalo, Corry & Pittsburg Railways. Distances: to Red Bank, 64 miles ; to Oil City, 132 ; to Titusville, 150 ; to Corry, 177 ; to Irvineton, 181 ; to Buffalo, 275. Through trains from Pittsburg to Buffalo *via* Oil City and Irvineton accomplish the distance in 12 hours.

PITTSBURG is described on p. 209, and the route thither from Phila. in Route 46. Leaving the Union Depot, the train passes for several miles among smoke-discolored factories and iron-works, and then reaches the Alleghany River, whose banks are followed for more than 100 miles, amid picturesque and varied scenery. *Kittaning* (44 miles) is a flourishing manufacturing borough of 2,000 inhabitants, in the midst of a rich coal-region, which is extensively worked. From *Red Bank* (64 miles) the Eastern Extension R. R. runs in 110 miles to Driftwood on the Phila. & Erie R. R. (Route 49), passing the remote forest-town of *Brookville,* which offers great attractions to the sportsman. *Brady's Bend* (68 miles) is the shipping-point for the productive Modoc Oil District, which lies near at hand. It is situated in a broad curve of the Alleghany River, and though dating only from 1869 now has a population of over 5,000. All along this section of the route the apparatus of oil-wells, some in operation and others deserted, may be seen from the cars. At *Scrubgrass* (107 miles) the trains stop for dinner, and then pass on in 16 miles to **Franklin** (*Exchange Hotel*), a city of 6,000 inhabitants, built on the site of the old French *Fort Venango*, at the confluence of French Creek and the Alleghany River. A line of small steamers plies on the river between Franklin and Pittsburg, and several railroads connect here. Nine miles beyond Franklin is **Oil City** (*Collins House, Taylor, National*), the center and headquarters of the Oil Region. It is situated on the Alleghany River at the mouth of Oil Creek, the city being built along a narrow shelf between the river and a high bluff which is crowned by residences. Oil City was founded in 1860, incorporated in 1871, and now has a population of about 2,400. It is not particularly attractive to either the eye or the nose, but it will afford the visitor in a few short rambles the best opportunity of witnessing the various operations of obtaining, refining, barreling, gauging, and shipping the precious petroleum. The wells in the vicinity yield 600 barrels daily, and about 2,000,000 barrels are annually sent thence to market. The great iron tanks for storing the oil are worth a visit.

From Oil City the through train to Buffalo runs N. E., and in 8 miles reaches *Oleopolis* (140 miles), whence a branch line runs in 7 miles to the decadent *Pithole City*, whose history is eminently characteristic of the oil regions. A well was opened here in 1864 which yielded for a time the unprecedented quantity of 7,000 barrels a day. Vast numbers flocked thither, and within 6 months Pithole City contained 15,000 inhabitants, a daily paper, 70 hotels and saloons, and 3 theatres. The well suddenly gave out, the place lost its importance, the population dwindled as rapidly as it had grown, and there are now less than 50 inhabitants in the place. At *Tidioute* (166 miles) are extensive iron-works, and at *Irvineton* (181 miles) the Phila. & Erie R. R. (see Route 49) is intersected. Beyond Irvineton the small villages of *Warren* (187 miles) and *Falconer* (210 miles) are passed, and the road traverses a sparsely populated country to **Buffalo** (see p. 160).

At Oil City the Pittsburg, Titusville & Buffalo R. R. diverges from the preceding route and passes up the valley of Oil Creek to Corry. For the first 20 miles, derricks, tanks, etc., are seen at frequent intervals, and occasional glimpses are obtained of the pumping-engines at work. *Petroleum Center* (8 miles from Oil City) is a busy place of 1,500 inhabitants, and 10 miles beyond the train reaches **Titusville** (*Parshall House, Mansion, European*), the chief place in the oil regions. It is situated on Oil Creek, in the midst of a fine dairy region, and is surrounded by hills. The streets are broad, straight, and well paved ; the business blocks are of brick ; the dwellings are of wood and brick, and are surrounded by gardens. There are extensive iron-works, foundries, and machine-shops at Titusville, but the place owes its prosperity to the petroleum wells in the vicinity. It had only 300 inhabitants in 1859 when the production was commenced, and in 1875 it had a population of 10,000. Some of the most productive oil-wells in the region are near here, and there are 7 refineries using 6,000 barrels of crude petroleum daily. The Union & Titusville R. R. runs in 25 miles from Titusville to *Union City* on the Phila. & Erie R. R. (see Route 49); and the Dunkirk, Alleghany Valley & Pittsburg R. R. runs in 90 miles to *Dunkirk* (see p. 172). The Pittsburg, Titusville & Buffalo R. R. continues for 27 miles beyond Titusville to **Corry** (see p. 222).

The first wells ever bored in order to obtain petroleum were sunk at Titusville in 1859. The occurrence of the oil about the head-waters of the Alleghany River in New York and Pennsylvania was known to early settlers, and the name Oil Creek was given to a stream in Alleghany Co., N. Y., and also to one in Venango Co., Pa. The Indians collected it on the shores of Seneca Lake, and the settlers collected it at various points, and it was long sold as a medicine by the name of Seneca or Genesee Oil. In 1854 its commercial value for illuminating purposes began to be suspected, and Col. E. L. Drake went to Titusville to see if it could be obtained in sufficient quantities. He bored the first well about 1 mile S. of Titusville, and on Aug. 26, 1859, oil was struck at a depth of 71 ft. The drill suddenly sank into a cavity of the rock, and the oil rose within 5 inches of the surface. A small pump being introduced, a supply of oil amounting to 400 gallons a day was obtained ; and with a large pump the flow was increased to 1,000 gallons a day. Though a steam-engine was applied to the work and kept in constant operation, the supply continued uninterrupted for weeks. This success gave a new value to every spot where oil had ever been found or which was thought likely to produce it. Many other wells were sunk soon after, and there began that great petroleum traffic which has since attained such vast dimensions. By the end of the year 1860 there were 2,000 wells in operation, and the production became so enormous that the price fell to 25c. a barrel. The number of wells now in operation in the Pennsylvania Oil region is about 4,000, employing about 5,000 steam-engines, representing $25,000,000 invested capital, and yielding about 400,000,000 gallons a year.

54. Harrisburg to the Cumberland Valley.

By the Cumberland Valley R. R., which runs S. W. from Harrisburg to Martinsburg on the Baltimore & Ohio R. R. Distances : to Carlisle, 18 miles ; to Shippensburg, 41 ; to Chambersburg, 52 ; to Hagerstown, 74 ; to Martinsburg, 94.

LEAVING the Harrisburg station of the Pennsylvania R. R. the train crosses the Susquehanna, and passes for several miles amid strikingly picturesque scenery. *Mechanicsburg* (8 miles) is a pretty town of 3,000 inhabitants, with several neat churches, a number of prosperous factories, and two favorably-known educational institutions—the Cumberland Valley Institute and the Irving Female College. Beyond Mechanicsburg the scenery is very pleasing, with the Kittatinny or Blue Mountains on the right and South Mountain on the left ; and in 9 miles the train reaches **Carlisle** (*Bentz House, Mansion House*), a borough of 7,500 inhabitants situated nearly in the center of the Cumberland Valley. The surrounding country is level, productive, and highly cultivated. The town is well built, with wide and well-shaded streets, and a public square on which front the county buildings and public edifices of a superior order. In the square is a handsome *Monument* erected to the memory of the soldiers of Cumberland County who fell in the civil war. *Dickinson College*, founded in 1783, and now under the care of the Methodists, is one of the oldest and most flourishing institutions in the State. It has plain buildings on Main St. W. of the public square, with valuable scientific collections and a library of 26,000 volumes. The *Carlisle Barracks* were built in 1777 by the Hessian prisoners captured at Trenton, and have accommodations for 2,000 men. Washington's headquarters were at Carlisle in 1794, at the time of the Whisky Rebellion ; and the town was shelled by the Confederates on the night of July 1, 1863, during Lee's invasion of Pennsylvania. It was captured by the Southern troops, who at the same time occupied Mechanicsburg and advanced to within 4 miles of Harrisburg. Six miles S. of Carlisle are the **Mt. Holly Springs** (*Mt. Holly Springs Hotel*), which are much patronized by families from Philadelphia, Harrisburg, and Baltimore, who find here a bracing climate, picturesque scenery, pleasant walks and drives, and good fishing in the adjacent streams. The waters are mildly sulphurous in character, tonic in effect, and recommended for chronic diseases of which general debility is a feature. At the base of Pisgah Mt., 14 miles N. of Carlisle, are the **Perry Warm Springs,** a quiet and inexpensive resort amid attractive scenery. The waters have a temperature of 70° to 72°, and when taken internally are aperient and diuretic. They are most esteemed as a bath, and employed in this way are beneficial in diseases of the skin. The Springs are also reached by stage in 12 miles from Duncannon on the Pennsylvania R. R. (see p. 208).

Eleven miles beyond Carlisle on the R. R. is *Newville*, whence stages run to the *Doubling Gap Springs*, a quiet resort. There are two mineral springs here, a sulphur and a chalybeate ; and the adjacent scenery of the Doubling Gap, where the Blue Mt. turns on itself and forms a gigantic *cul-de-sac*, is peculiarly picturesque and striking. *Shippensburg* (41 miles) is the market and shipping-point for the productive farming region of which it is the center, and has a population of about 3,000. The Cumberland Valley Normal School stands on a far-viewing hill to the N. Eleven miles beyond Shippensburg is **Chambersburg** (*Montgomery House, National*), a borough of 7,000 inhabitants pleasantly situated on the Conecocheague Creek. The surrounding country, which forms part of the great limestone valley at the S. E. base of the Blue Mts., is populous and highly cultivated. The town is well built, the houses being mostly of brick or stone ; and there are manufactories of cotton, wool, flour, paper, and iron. The *Court-House* is a handsome edifice, and *Wilson College* (for young ladies) is a flourishing institution. Chambersburg was captured and set on fire by the Confederates under Gen. Early, on July 30, 1864, during a raid into Pennsylvania. Two thirds of the town was destroyed, inflicting a loss of $2,000,000. Daily stages from Chambersburg run to Gettysburg (see p. 234).

Ascending the valley from Chambersburg, the train soon reaches the pretty village of *Greencastle* (63 miles), and 5 miles beyond crosses the famous Mason and Dixon's Line and enters the State of Maryland. Six miles beyond the line is **Hagerstown** (*Washington House*), capital of Washington County, with a population of 6,000. It is pleasantly situated on the W. bank of Antietam Creek, 22 miles above its entrance into the Potomac, at the intersection of the present route with the Western Maryland R. R. and the Washington Co. Branch of the Baltimore & Ohio R. R. The city is regularly laid out and well built, with a handsome Court-House, erected at a cost of $77,000. It is surrounded by a rich agricultural region, from which it draws considerable trade; and there are prosperous foundries and factories. About 7 miles S. of Hagerstown is the *College of St. James* (Episcopal). Hagerstown was the scene of several severe conflicts during the civil war, being captured a number of times by the Confederates and as often retaken by the National forces. *Williamsport* (81 miles) is where Lee recrossed into Virginia after the battle of Gettysburg (see p. 235). Here the train crosses the Potomac on a long bridge, enters W. Virginia, and passes in 14 miles to **Martinsburg** (*Grand Central Hotel, Continental*), a town of 6,000 inhabitants, on the Tuscarora Creek, at the junction of the present route with the Baltimore & Ohio R. R. (see Route 65). The latter road has vast machine-shops here, and there are several factories. There are here a commodious Court-House, a Town-Hall, a Market-house, and spacious agricultural fair grounds.

55. Baltimore to Niagara Falls.

By the Northern Central R. R., which traverses northern Maryland, central Pennsylvania, and western New York, intersecting all the great lines of E. and W. travel. At Harrisburg it crosses the Pennsylvania R. R.; at Williamsport, the Philadelphia & Erie; at Elmira, the Erie R. R.; and terminates at Canandaigua on the N. Y. Central R. R. It is the favorite route of travel from the South to Niagara Falls and all the great Northern resorts, and runs Pullman drawing-room and sleeping cars on all the through trains. Distances: to Hanover Junction, 46 miles; to York, 57; to Harrisburg, 85; to Sunbury, 138; to Williamsport, 178; to Ralston, 202; to Elmira, 256; to Watkins Glen, 278; to Canandaigua, 325; to Rochester, 354; to Buffalo, 422; to Niagara Falls, 431. The time from Baltimore to Canandaigua is 18 hours; to Buffalo, 23 hours; to Niagara Falls, 24 hours.

THE terminal station in Baltimore of the Northern Central R. R. is on Calvert St. near Madison. The Maryland section of the road traverses a rich but monotonous farming region, with numerous small stations *en route*, but nothing to call for special notice. Just beyond *Freelands* (35 miles) the train crosses the State line and enters Pennsylvania. From *Hanover Junction* (46 miles) a branch road diverges and runs W. in 30 miles to

Gettysburg.

From Philadelphia, Gettysburg is reached *via* Pennsylvania R. R. to Lancaster (Route 46), thence by a branch road to York, and thence by present route. Total distance, 136 miles. From New York it is reached *via* Philadelphia, or by Route 45 to Harrisburg and thence by present route. Total distance from New York, 250 miles. **Hotels.**—*Eagle Hotel, Keystone House, McClellan House.*

Gettysbur is a borough of 3,300 inhabitants, capital of Adams Co., and is pleasantly situated on a gently rolling and fertile plain, surrounded by hills, from which extensive and pleasing views are obtained. The *Court-House* and *Public Offices* are commodious brick structures, and the residences are generally neat and substantial. *Pennsylvania College*, founded in 1832, and the *Lutheran Theological Seminary*, founded in 1825, are among the institutions of the place. Both have large and beautiful buildings, and the former has a library of 18,300 volumes, and the latter a library of 10,100 volumes. One mile W. of the borough are the **Gettysburg Springs**, whose waters, denominated Katalysine, have acquired a wide reputation for their medicinal qualities. They are said to resemble the celebrated Vichy water, and are considered remedial in gout, rheumatism, dyspepsia, and affections of the kidneys. The *Springs Hotel* ($2.50 a day) accommodates the patients who resort here in large numbers during the summer.

The chief interest of Gettysburg is historic, and this it is that attracts tourists from all parts of the world. A great battle, perhaps the most important of the civil war, was fought here on the 1st, 2d, and 3d of July, 1863, between the National forces under General Meade and the Confederate army under General Lee. The battle is described below, and it is only necessary now to point out the principal objects of interest. *Cemetery Hill*, so named from having long been the site of the village cemetery, forms the central and most striking feature at Gettysburg. Here General Howard established his headquarters, and standing on its crest the visitor has the key to the position of the Union forces during those eventful three days of July. Flanking Cemetery Hill on the W., about a mile distant, is *Seminary Ridge*, on which were General Lee's headquarters and the bulk of the Confederate forces. Other spots usually visited are *Benner's Hill*, *Culp's Hill*, *Round Top*, and *Little Round Top ;* also *Willoughby Run*, where Bufford's cavalry held A. P. Hill's column in check during two critical hours. The * **National Cemetery,** containing the remains of the Union soldiers who fell in the battle of Gettysburg, occupies about 17 acres on Cemetery Hill adjacent to the village cemetery, and was dedicated with imposing ceremonies, and an impressive address by President Lincoln, Nov. 19, 1863. A * **Soldiers' Monument,** dedicated July 4, 1868, occupies the crown of the hill, is 60 ft. high, and is surmounted by a colossal marble statue of Liberty. At the base of the pedestal are 4 buttresses, bearing colossal marble statues of War, History, Peace, and Plenty. Around the monument, in semicircular slopes, are arranged the graves of the dead, the space being divided by alleys and pathways into 22 sections : one for the regular army, one for the volunteers of each State represented in the battle, and three for the unknown dead. The number of bodies interred here is 3,564, of which 994 have not been identified. Near the entrance to the cemetery is a bronze statue of Major-General Reynolds, who was killed in the battle. Opposite the cemetery, an observatory, 60 ft. high, has been erected, commanding a fine view of the entire battle-field and the surrounding country for many miles.

The **Battle of Gettysburg** was fought July 1, 2, and 3, 1863, between the Union army under General Meade, and the Confederate Army of Northern Virginia under General Lee. Having resolved upon an invasion of the North, the Confederates had early in June concentrated a force of nearly 100,000 men, including 15,000 cavalry, in the vicinity of Culpepper, Va. They moved down the valley of the Shenandoah, and on the 24th and 25th crossed the Potomac in two columns, which, uniting at Hagerstown, Md., pressed on toward Chambersburg, Pa. The Union army, having broken up its camp opposite Fredericksburg and moved N., crossed the river lower down on the 28th, on which day Hooker, having resigned the command, was succeeded by Meade. Lee's communications being threatened, he resolved to concentrate his whole force at Gettysburg, already (unknown to him) occupied by a part of the Union army under Reynolds. The first collision occurred on July 1, about 2 miles N. W. of Gettysburg, between the Confederate advance under A. P. Hill and a reconnoitering party of cavalry (afterward supported by infantry) sent out by Reynolds. The Union forces, at first superior, were soon outnumbered, and were driven back in confusion through Gettysburg, losing 5,000 prisoners and as many killed and wounded. The Confederate loss in killed and wounded was probably somewhat greater, in prisoners much less. Both sides hurried up their forces, and on the morning of the 2d the bulk of the two armies was in position, the Union on Cemetery Ridge S. of Gettysburg, and the Confederate on Seminary Ridge opposite (to the west), except Ewell's corps, which lay 2 miles distant at the foot of Culp's Hill on the Union right. The forces present or close at hand were about equal, each numbering from 70,000 to 80,000 infantry and artillery. Lee resolved to attack the Federal position. The main attack was made by Longstreet's corps on the Union left, where considerable ground was gained. On the right Ewell effected a lodgment within the Union intrenchments. The Union loss in this action was fully 10,000, half in Sickles's corps, which lost nearly half its numbers. Lee determined to continue the assault on the 3d. Early in the morning Meade took the offensive against Ewell, and forced him from the foothold which he had gained, but of this Lee was not informed. The Confederates spent the morning in preparation, and at 1 o'clock opened fire from 120 guns, which was immediately returned, though Meade, owing to the rugged nature of the ground, was able to use at once only 80 of his 200 guns. After two hours the Union fire was gradually suspended, and Lee, supposing that their batteries had been silenced and that the infantry must be demoralized, ordered the grand attack of the day, which was directed against the Union center. The attacking column numbered about 18,000, consisting of Pickett's division and Pettigrew's brigade. Though met by a terrible fire of artillery and musketry, it pressed on, Pettigrew reaching within 300 yards of Hancock's line, when he was driven back in disorder; while Pickett's division charged through Gibbon's front line among the Federal batteries, where for a quarter of an hour there was a struggle with pistols and clubbed muskets. The Union troops hurried from all sides and drove the enemy back down the slope, not one in four escaping. Meade with his right then drove back Hood from the ridge he had won the preceding day. The Confederate loss this day was about 16,000 in killed, wounded, and prisoners; the Union loss was about 3,000. Both armies remained inactive the next day, and during the night Lee began his retreat to the Potomac, which he reached on the 7th. Here he was compelled to halt by the swollen stream. On the 12th Meade came in front of the Confederate intrenchments, but an attack was postponed till the 14th, when Lee was found to be safe on the other side, having succeeded in crossing during the night. The Union loss at Gettysburg was 23,190, of whom 2,834 were killed, 13,713 wounded, and 6,643 missing. The Confederate loss has never been officially stated; but by the best estimates it was about 36,000, of whom about 5,000 were killed, 23,000 wounded, and 8,000 unwounded prisoners. The entire number of prisoners was about 14,000.—APPLETONS' CONDENSED AMERICAN CYCLOPÆDIA.

On the main line, 11 miles beyond Hanover Junction, is the ancient city of **York** (*National Hotel*), situated on Codorus Creek, and containing 14,000 inhabitants. York was settled in 1741, incorporated in 1787, and the Continental Congress sat here from Sept. 30, 1777, to July, 1778. During the Confederate invasion of Pennsylvania in 1863 it was occupied by Early, who levied a contribution of $100,000 on the citizens, but left the place unharmed. The city is

pleasantly situated in a rich agricultural region, and is regularly laid
out, with streets crossing each other at right angles. At the intersection of Main and George Sts., the leading thoroughfares, is Center
Square. The Court-House is a handsome edifice with granite front
and Corinthian columns. York contains several large car-shops, some
of the most extensive manufactories of agricultural implements in
the country, a shoe and a match factory, and the Codorus paper mills.
The train traverses the streets of York for some distance, descends
the rich Codorus Valley, and a few miles below Harrisburg reaches the
Susquehanna River, which is followed as far as Williamsport amid
extremely beautiful scenery. From *Bridgeport* (84 miles) a long bridge
crosses the river to **Harrisburg,** the capital of Pennsylvania, which is
described on page 207. The scenery along the line from Harrisburg to
Williamsport is very fine, but none of the stations possess any special
attractions for the tourist. *Sunbury* (138 miles) is at the intersection
of the present route with the Phila. & Erie R. R. (Route 49), and has
already been described on page 221. **Williamsport** (178 miles) is
the converging point of the present route, Route 49, and Route 52, and
is described on page 221.

Leaving Williamsport the train ascends the narrow valley of Lycoming Creek, and traverses for many miles a picturesque and sparsely
settled region, dear to sportsmen. The station of *Trout Run* (192
miles) is near a fish-abounding stream, and 10 miles beyond is **Ralston** (*Ralston House*), a sequestered hamlet, 1,800 ft. above the sea,
and surrounded by lofty hills covered with primeval forest. The scenery is extremely picturesque, many romantic cascades are found in the
mountain-gorges, and near by are numerous trout-streams which afford
excellent sport. The McIntire Coal-Mine is just N. of the village, and
the gravity railroad up the mountain-side is a great curiosity. *Minnequa* (220 miles) is near the **Minnequa Springs** (*Springs Hotel;* 500
guests), which have lately become popular as a summer resort. They
are situated in a lovely mountain-surrounded valley, 1,500 ft. above
the sea, with excellent trout-brooks in the vicinity, and abundance of
game in the adjacent woods. The waters contain oxide of iron, are
tonic in quality, and are said to be efficacious in dyspepsia, rheumatism,
consumption, and cutaneous diseases. *Columbia Cross Roads* (236
miles) is the last station in Pennsylvania, and a short distance beyond
the train crosses into New York and passes in 20 miles to **Elmira** (see
p. 171) at the intersection of the Erie R. R. (see Route 39). Beyond
Elmira the line traverses a quiet rural district and passes in 22 miles
to *Watkins* and the famous

Watkins Glen.

From New York, Watkins is reached either by the Erie R. R. (Route 39) to
Elmira and thence by the Northern Central R. R. (295 miles), or by the N. Y.
Central R. R. (Route 38) to Seneca Lake and thence by steamer (fare by either
route, $7.90). From Philadelphia by the North Pennsylvania and connecting roads.
or by Pennsylvania R. R. to Harrisburg, and thence by the Northern Central R. R
(fare, $8 15).

Hotels.—In the village are the *Jefferson House* and the *Fall Brook House,*

open all the year ($2 to $3 a day). On a high hill overlooking the village, and commanding a broad and lovely view, is the *Lake View Hotel* ($3.50 a day). Near the
entrance of the Glen is the *Glen Park Hotel* ($3 a day). Perched on a rocky ledge
within the Glen itself is the *Glen Mountain House* ($3 a day), connecting with a
picturesque Swiss *chalet.*

Watkins is a village of 3,000 inhabitants at the head of Seneca
Lake, and within the shadow of Glen Mt. *Franklin St.,* running parallel with the mountain-ridge, leads in ½ mile from the station to the
entrance of the * **Glen,** which is simply a vertical rift or gorge in a
rocky bluff some 700 or 800 ft. in height, through which tumbles a
roaring mountain-brook. The length of the Glen is about 3 miles, and
the cliffs at the deepest part of the gorge have an altitude of nearly
300 ft. First entering a huge amphitheatre to which there is no apparent exit, the visitor follows the path to its W. end, where he finds
that, instead of meeting, the walls of rock overlap each other, leaving
a narrow passage through and up which he passes by steep stairways,
running diagonally along the face of the wall, braced strongly to it,
and also propped firmly from beneath. This first section is called
Glen Alpha, and at its upper end are the *Minnehaha Falls,* beyond
which the path traverses the narrow gorge called the *Labyrinth* to the
Cavern Cascade and ascends the *Long Staircase,* which is flung at an
angle of 90 degrees across the tremendous chasm. From the head of
the Long Staircase a path ascends a succession of steep stairways to a
shelf of mountain on the N. side of the ravine. On this shelf is perched
the **Mountain House,** consisting of a cottage built in the style of a
Swiss *chalet,* on one side of the gorge, while on the other side (connected by a graceful iron suspension-bridge) is the main building. The
chalet is a favorite point for rest and refreshment, and is in all respects
one of the most attractive features of the Glen scenery. Its balconies
overhang the gorge, with trees jutting up above them from ledges in
the rocks below; and the visitor looks down from his advantageous
position into depths of the Glen that remain inaccessible. Close at
hand is Captain Hope's *Glen Art Gallery* (admission, 25c.), containing
upward of 100 paintings by himself, chiefly of the Glen scenery.

Leaving the Mountain House, the path descends gradually almost
to the bed of the stream, through the gloomy *Glen Obscura,* and passing the *Sylvan Rapids* enters the * **Glen Cathedral,** an enormous
amphitheatre which is considered the most imposing feature of the
wonderful gorge. It is 1,000 ft. long, with a floor as level as if paved
with human hands, and walls rising to a height of nearly 300 ft. In
the center is the lovely *Pool of the Nymphs,* and at the W. end (called
the "Chancel") the *Central Cascade* pours its waters into the gorge
over a ledge 60 ft. high. From the N. side of the Cathedral the *Grand
Staircase* leads to the *Glen of the Pools,* so named from the number of
its water-worn basins. Beyond the Glen of the Pools the *Giant's Gorge*
is reached, at the upper end of which are the exquisite * **Rainbow
Falls,** where three cascades drop from one rocky ledge to another,
foaming and seething, while to one side a thin stream, falling from a
great height, spreads itself out like a silver mist, and mingles its waters

with those in the rock-bound channel far below. The path passes behind the fall and leads up another stairway to the *Shadow Gorge*, which is narrow, rugged, and somber, the pathway being hewn out of the cliff-side, and at the head of which the **Pluto Falls** plunge over the rocky parapet into a deep black pool. Alongside the Pluto Falls, there is a rough natural stairway leading to *Glen Arcadia*, from the entrance of which there are beautiful views both up and down the gorge, and at the head of which are the *Arcadian Falls*, spanned by a bridge from which the retrospect down *Elfin Gorge* is remarkably fine. Next above is *Glen Facility*, near the head of which is the iron bridge of the Syracuse, Geneva & Corning Railway, 450 ft. long and 150 ft. above the stream; and then come *Glen Horicon*, *Glen Elysium*, with steep wooded banks 400 ft. high, and *Glen Omega*, with *Omega Falls*. The last two are little more than open forest-glades, and contain scarcely a hint of the wild scenes below.

Those who do not care to retrace their steps to the entrance, on their return (the descent of the stairs is even more trying than the ascent), can leave the Glen at the Mountain House by a path leading out to the open country and through the beautiful Glenwood cemetery.

Havana Glen, 3 miles S. of Watkins (reached by carriages), is 1¼ mile long, ascends 700 ft., and is preferred by some to the Watkins Glen. It is very picturesque, is more airy and open, and is quite easily traversed; but it is wanting in those elements of gloom, and vastness, and solemn grandeur, which are the peculiar characteristics of its better known rival. The same system of stairways and ladders prevails as at Watkins, but these aids of progress are fewer and the paths broader. (Admission, 25c.) The *Montour Glen* and the *Excelsior Glen* are also in the vicinity of Havana and Watkins, and are very striking.

Beyond Watkins the line skirts the W. shore of Seneca Lake (see p. 158) for 12 miles, and soon reaches *Penn Yan* (301 miles), a pretty village of 3,000 inhabitants at the foot of **Lake Keuka** (formerly called *Crooked Lake*), which is a beautiful sheet of water 18 miles long, 1½ mile wide at the widest part, 718 ft. above the sea, and 277 ft. above Seneca Lake, which is only 7 miles distant. At the foot or N. end it is divided by a promontory into two branches, one 5 and the other 8 miles long. The scenery along the shores is extremely picturesque, and the waters are clear and full of fish. From Penn Yan a small steamer runs twice a day to *Hammondsport*, a neat village at the head of the lake, whence a narrow-gauge railway runs to *Bath* on the Erie R. R. Hammondsport is the center of an extensive grape-growing and wine-making region, and the adjacent hill-slopes are clothed with vineyards. In the cellars of the Urbana and Pleasant Valley Wine Cos. are hundreds of thousands of bottles of Catawba, Isabella, claret, and native champagnes. The *Grove Spring House*, a well-known summer resort, is 5 miles N. of Hammondsport. Beyond Penn Yan the Northern Central R. R. passes several obscure hamlets and soon reaches its terminus at **Canandaigua** (see p. 158), on the N. Y. Central R. R.

From this point the traveler can go W. to Rochester, Buffalo, and
Niagara Falls, or E. to Albany and Troy.   The route in both directions
is described in Route 38.

56. The St. Lawrence River.

THE trip down the St. Lawrence usually begins at **Kingston**
(*British American Hotel*), a flourishing Canadian city of 13,000 inhabitants at the foot of Lake Ontario, on the line of the Grand Trunk
R. R., 172 miles from Montreal, 343 from Quebec, 392 from Detroit,
and 469 from Portland.   It is reached from New York *via* Route 38
to Rome, and thence *via* the Rome, Watertown & Ogdensburg R. R.
to *Cape Vincent* (distance 347 miles; fare $8.80).   From Cape Vin-
cent a steam-ferry connects with Kingston.   The Royal Mail steamers
of the Richelieu & Ontario Navigation Co. leave Kingston daily at 5.30
A. M., and reach Montreal at 6.45 P. M.

The Thousand Islands.

Almost immediately after leaving Kingston the steamer enters that
portion of the St. Lawrence known as the *Lake of the Thousand Islands*,
from the continuous groups of islands and islets amid which the river
threads its tortuous way toward Ogdensburg.   According to the Treaty
of Ghent these islands are 1,692 in number, and they extend for 40 miles
below Lake Ontario.   They are of every imaginable shape, size, and
appearance, some of them barely visible, others covering many acres ;
some only a few yards long, others several miles in length ; some presenting little or nothing but bare masses of rock, while others are so
thickly wooded that nothing but the most gorgeous green foliage is to
be seen in summer, while in autumn the leaves present colors of different hues hardly imaginable.   You pass close to, and near enough,
often, to cast a pebble from the deck of the steamer on to them ; cluster after cluster of circular little islands, whose trees, perpetually mois-
tened by the water, have a most luxuriant leaf, their branches overhanging the current.   The numerous lighthouses which mark out the
navigable channel are a picturesque feature, but they are drearily alike
—fragile wooden structures about 20 ft. high, uniformly whitewashed.
Many summer visitors remain at *Gananoque*, on the Canadian side of
the river, and at *Clayton* (Hubbard House), opposite ; but the ·chief
summer resort of the Thousand Islands is **Alexandria Bay** (*Thousand Islands House* and *Crossmon House*).   This is a small village on
the New York side of the river, the hotels, which are large and fine,
being the most conspicuous feature.   The *Thousand Islands House*
($17.50 per week) accommodates 600 and the *Crossmon House* 300
guests.   On the islets near the bay are numerous elegant villas, among
them one owned by Mr. Pullman, of palace-car fame.   The boating is
excellent, and the fishing in the vicinity is very fine, including pickerel,
muscalonge, black bass, and dory.   There are also myriads of wild
fowl in their season.   About 8 miles S. E. of Alexandria Bay are the

CITY OF
MONTREAL
Scale of Yards

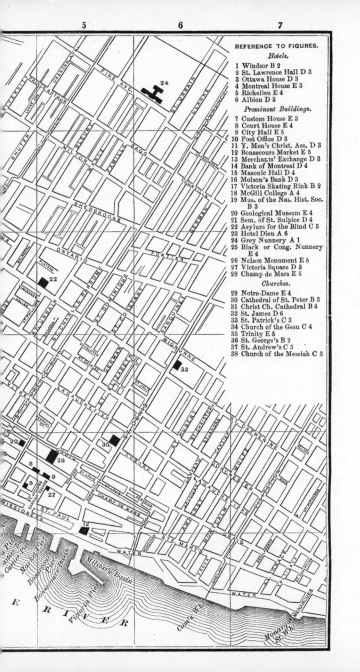

REFERENCE TO FIGURES.

Hotels.

1 Windsor B 2
2 St. Lawrence Hall D 3
3 Ottawa House D 3
4 Montreal House E 3
5 Richelieu E 4
6 Albion D 3

Prominent Buildings.

7 Custom House E 3
8 Court House E 4
9 City Hall E 5
10 Post Office D 3
11 Y. Men's Christ. Ass. D 3
12 Bonsecours Market E 5
13 Merchants' Exchange D 3
14 Bank of Montreal D 4
15 Masonic Hall D 4
16 Molson's Bank D 3
17 Victoria Skating Rink B 2
18 McGill College A 4
19 Mus. of the Nat. Hist. Soc. B 3
20 Geological Museum E 4
21 Sem. of St. Sulpice D 4
22 Asylum for the Blind C 5
23 Hotel Dieu A 6
24 Grey Nunnery A 1
25 Black or Cong. Nunnery E 4
26 Nelson Monument E 5
27 Victoria Square D 3
28 Champ de Mars E 5

Churches.

29 Notre-Dame E 4
30 Cathedral of St. Peter B 3
31 Christ Ch. Cathedral B 4
32 St. James D 6
33 St. Patrick's C 3
34 Church of the Gesu C 4
35 Trinity E 5
36 St. George's B 2
37 St. Andrew's C 3
38 Church of the Messiah C 3

romantic *Lakes of Theresa* (Clear, Crystal, Mud, Butterfield, and Lake of the North), with good fishing. and shores and islands abounding in rare minerals.   Frequent steamers ply between Cape Vincent, Clayton, and Alexandria Bay, on the arrival of trains at the two former.   *Morristown* is a post-village of New York, below Alexandria, and 14 miles from Ogdensburg.   On the Canadian shore opposite (reached by ferryboat) lies *Brockville*, an important town of nearly 6,000 inhabitants.   At this point in the river the Lake of the Thousand Islands ends, and we come somewhat unexpectedly upon the open river, 2 miles wide.   During the remainder of the great river's course the islands are large, and for the most part in the midst of the rapids.

Thirteen miles from Brockville, on the Canadian side, lies **Prescott** (*Daniel's Hotel*), and immediately opposite (connected by steam-ferry) the flourishing American city of **Ogdensburg** (*Seymour House, Johnson House*).   The city is attractively situated and handsomely built, and is connected by railroad with a number of prominent points east, west, and south.   It is the N. terminus of the Rome, Watertown & Ogdensburg R. R., and the Utica & Black River R. R. (see Route 38), and is at the W. end of the Ogdensburg & Lake Champlain R. R.   A few miles below Ogdensburg the descent of the first rapids (*Gallopes Rapids*) is made, and immediately afterward of the *Rapide de Plat*. The descent of these rapids is made with full steam on, and there is scarcely anything to indicate that the steamer is not pursuing its usual placid course.   Thirty miles below Ogdensburg is *Louisville*, whence stages run to **Massena Springs,** 7 miles distant.   These springs are on the banks of the Raquette River in New York State, and are five in number, the largest being named St. Regis, in honor of the tribe of Indians who first discovered its virtues.   They are a popular resort in summer, their attractiveness being greatly enhanced by the beautiful scenery by which they are surrounded, and by their proximity to the Long Sault Rapids, about 5 miles distant.   The *Hatfield House* and the *Harrowgate* are large and excellent hotels.   The springs are also reached by the Central Vermont R. R., with a stage-ride of either 9 miles from Brasher Falls or of 14 from Potsdam Junction.

Dickinson's Landing is at the head of the famous *** Long Sault Rapids,** which are 9 miles in length, and through which a raft will drift in 40 minutes.   Here the tourist experiences the celebrated sensation known as "shooting the Rapids."   Until 1840 this passage was considered impossible; but by watching the course of rafts down the river, a channel was discovered, and steamboats then attempted it, for the first time, under the guidance of the Indian pilot *Teronhiahéré.* Some of the pilots are still Indians, and they exhibit great skill and courage in the performance of their dangerous duties.   Yet no one need fear the undertaking, for there has never yet occurred a fatal accident in making this course.   The *Cornwall Canal*, 11 miles long, enables vessels to go round the Rapids in ascending the river.   *Cornwall* (Dominion Hotel) is a thriving town at the foot of the Rapids, opposite which is the large Indian village of *St. Regis.*   Just below this place the St. Lawrence, now entirely in Canada, expands into **Lake St. Fran-**

cis, which is 25 miles long and about 5 miles wide, and is dotted with islets, especially at the lower end. *Coteau du Lac,* 30 miles below Cornwall, is at the head of the *Coteau Rapids,* which 9 miles below take the name of the *Cedars,* and, still farther on, of the *Cascades.* At the foot of the Cascades is *Beauharnois,* at the lower end of a canal 11¼ miles long, around the Rapids. The village is prettily situated on a bay, and is a favorite resort for picnics from Montreal. The expanse of the river from this point to the head of the Lachine Rapids is called **Lake St. Louis,** which is 12 miles long by 5 wide. One of the most noticeable features of this lake is *Nun's Island,* 5 miles below Beauharnois. It was formerly an Indian burying-ground, but is now the property of the Grey Nunnery at Montreal, and in a high state of cultivation. *Lachine* is at the head of the * **Lachine Rapids,** which, though the shortest, are the most turbulent and dangerous on the river. "In the descent of these we are wrought to a feverish degree of excitement, exceeding that produced in the descent of the Long Sault. It is an intense sensation, terrible to the faint-hearted, exhilarating to the brave. As we reach calm water again, we can fairly distinguish in the growing night the prim form of the Victoria Bridge, and the spires, domes, and towers of Montreal, the commercial metropolis of British North America."

Montreal.

From New York Montreal is reached by either Route 28, or Route 29, or Route 40. From Philadelphia by Route 48. From Boston by Route 26 or Route 27. From Portland by Route 25. From Quebec by Grand Trunk R. R. or by steamer on the St. Lawrence.

Hotels.—The leading hotels are the *Windsor* in Dorchester St.; the *St. Lawrence Hall,* in Great St. James St.; the *Ottawa House,* cor. St. James and Notre-Dame Sts.; the *Montreal House,* on Custom-House Square, opposite the Custom-House; the *Richelieu Hotel,* in St. Vincent St.; and the *Albion,* in McGill St. Besides these there are numerous *cafés* and lodging-houses on a smaller scale.

Modes of Conveyance.—*Horse-cars* traverse the city in different directions, and afford easy access to principal points. *Carriages* wait at the depots and steam-boat-landings, and at various stands in the city. Their charges are: One-horse carriage for 1 or 2 persons, 25c. a course within the city limits, or 50c. an hour; for 3 or 4 persons, 40c. a course, 70c. an hour. Two-horse carriage, for 1 or 2 persons, 40c. a course, 75c. an hour; for 3 or 4 persons, 50c. a course, $1 an hour. *Stages* run to all the adjacent villages.

Montreal, the largest city and commercial metropolis of British North America, is situated on an island of the same name, at the confluence of the Ottawa and St. Lawrence Rivers, in lat. 45° 31' N. and lon. 73° 35' W. It derives its name from Mont Réal, or Mount Royal, which rises 750 ft. above the river, and closes the city in on that side. Including its suburbs, Montreal stretches along the river for 4 miles from S. E. to N. W., and for some distance extends from one to two miles inland. The houses are built of a grayish limestone from adjacent quarries, and with its tall spires and glittering roofs and domes, and the beautiful villas that stud its lofty background, the city presents as picturesque a panorama as is to be seen on the entire continent. The quays of Montreal are built of solid limestone, and, uniting with the locks and cut-stone wharves of the Lachine Canal, they present for

about 2 miles a display of continuous masonry which has few parallels.
St. Paul St., the chief commercial thoroughfare, extends along the river
the whole length of the city. Other important business streets are *St.
James*, *McGill*, *Notre-Dame*, and *Commissioner Sts.* The fashionable
promenades are *Great St. James* and *Notre-Dame Sts.* The finest private residences are in *Catherine*, *Dorchester*, and *Sherbrooke Sts.*

The settlement of Montreal dates from 1535, when it was visited by Jacques Cartier, who named its mountain. In 1542 the first European settlers arrived, and just
one century later the original Indian name (" Hochelaga ") gave place to the French
one of " Ville Marie," which in time was replaced by the present one, when the city
came into British possession in 1761. At the latter date, Montreal was well peopled
and strongly fortified ; nevertheless it was captured by the Americans under General Montgomery, in November, 1775, and held by them until the following summer.
In 1779, Montreal contained about 7,000 inhabitants. In 1861 the population had
increased to 90,323, and in 1871 to 115,926. The commerce of Montreal is very large,
as, though it is 500 miles from the sea, its advantageous position at the head of ship-
navigation on the St. Lawrence, and at the foot of the great chain of improved inland waters extending from the Lachine Canal to the western shores of Lake Superior,
has made it the chief shipping-port of the Dominion of Canada. In 1874 its imports were valued at $44,027,704, and its exports at $22,045,455. The manufactures are various and important, the principal being axes and saws, steam-engines,
printing-types, India-rubber shoes, paper, furniture, woolens, cordage, and flour.

The **Victoria Square** is a neat public ground at the intersection
of McGill and St. James Sts., containing a fountain and a bronze statue
of Queen Victoria. Fronting on the square are a number of fine buildings, including the *Albert Buildings* and the beautiful Gothic structure
of the *Young Men's Christian Association.* Of the numerous public
buildings in the city one of the handsomest is the * **Bonsecours Market,** a spacious stone edifice in the Doric style, fronting on the river
at the cor. of St. Paul and Water Sts. It is 3 stories high, and is surmounted by a dome, the view from which is extremely fine. The *Custom-House*, on the site of an old market-place between St. Paul St.
and the river, is a massive structure, with a fine tower. The *Post-
Office* is a beautiful cut-stone edifice in Great St. James St., near
the Place d'Armes. The * **Court-House**, in Notre-Dame St., is a
large and beautiful building in the Ionic style, 300 by 125 ft., erected
at a cost of over $300,000. It contains a law library of 6,000 vol-
umes. Back of it is the *Champ de Mars*, a fine military parade-
ground. The new * **City Hall** is a spacious and splendid edifice at
the head of Jacques Cartier Square ; in it are the offices of the various
civic and corporation functionaries. The *Merchants' Exchange* is a
handsome structure, in the modern Italian style, in St. Sacrament St.
It contains a large and comfortable reading-room, well supplied with
English and American newspapers and periodicals, all at the service of
the stranger when properly introduced. The handsome buildings of the
Bank of Montreal and the *City Bank* stand side by side on the Place
d'Armes. The first is a fine example of the Corinthian style. Fronting
on the same square are the *Masonic Hall*, the home of the Grand Lodge
of Masons of Canada, and several of the principal banks. In St. James St.,
E. of Victoria Square, are the elegant **Molson's Bank,** the *Merchants'
Bank*, the *Post-Office*, the principal Fire and Life Ins. Offices, and other

notable structures. The huge *Victoria Skating-Rink*, in Dominion Square, is used in summer for horticultural shows, concerts, etc. *Mechanics' Institute*, in Great St. James St., is a plain structure in the Italian style, with an elaborately decorated lecture-room. The *Windsor Hotel* is one of the finest edifices of the kind in America.

Few American cities equal Montreal in the size and magnificence of its church edifices. The Roman Catholic Cathedral of *** Notre-Dame,** fronting on the Place d'Armes, is the largest on the continent, being 241 ft. long and 135 ft. wide, and capable of seating from 10,000 to 12,000 persons. It is of stone, in the Gothic style, and has six towers, one at each corner and one in the middle of each flank. The two on the main front are 212 ft. high, and in one of them is a fine chime of bells, the largest of which (the "Gros Bourdon") weighs 29,400 pounds. The view from the tower, which is generally open to visitors, is very extensive. Even this huge structure will be surpassed in size by the new **Cathedral of St. Peter** now in course of erection at the cor. of Dorchester and Cemetery Sts., after the plan of St. Peter's, at Rome. It will be 300 ft. long by 225 ft. wide at the transepts, and is to be surmounted by 5 domes, of which the largest will be 250 ft. high, supported on 4 piers (each 36 ft. thick) and 32 Corinthian columns. The portico will be surmounted by colossal statues of the Apostles, and will afford entrance to a vestibule 200 ft. long and 30 ft. wide. The interior colonnades will support lines of rounded arches, and there are to be 20 minor chapels. *** Christ Church Cathedral** (Episcopal), in St. Catherine St., is the most perfect specimen of English-Gothic architecture in America. It is cruciform, built of rough Montreal stone with Caen-stone facings, and is surmounted by a spire 224 ft. high. The Bishop's Church (Roman Catholic), in St. Denis St., is a very elegant structure in the pointed Gothic style, known as the *St. James*. *St. Patrick's Church* (Roman Catholic) occupies a commanding position at the W. end of Lagauchetière St. It has seats for 5,000 persons, and its handsome Gothic windows are filled with stained glass. The *** Church of the Gesù** (Jesuit), in Bleury St., has the finest interior in the city. The vast nave (75 ft. high) is bordered by rich composite columns, and both walls and ceilings are beautifully painted and frescoed. Other important Roman Catholic churches are *Notre Dame de Lourdes*, in Catherine St.; the *Bonsecours*, near the great market; and *St. Ann's*, in Griffintown. There are also chapels attached to all the nunneries, in some of which excellent pictures may be seen. Besides Christ Church Cathedral, the principal Episcopal churches are *Trinity*, a fine stone edifice in the early English-Gothic style, in St. Paul St.; *St. George's*, in Dominion Square; *St. James the Apostle*, in Catherine St.; *St. Martin's*, in Upper St. Urbain St.; and *St. Stephen's*, in Griffintown. *** St. Andrew's Church** (Presbyterian), in Radegonde St., is a beautiful specimen of Gothic architecture, being a close imitation of Salisbury Cathedral, though of course on a greatly reduced scale. Near by is the *Church of the Messiah* (Unitarian), a lofty and spacious building. *Zion Church* (Independent), in Radegonde St., near Victoria Square, was the scene of the sad riot and loss of life on the occasion

CITY OF
QUEBEC

REFERENCE TO FIGURES.

Hotels.

1 St. Louis C 5
2 Russell House C 5
3 Albion B 5
4 Henchey's C 6

Prominent Buildings.

5 Custom House B 7
6 Post Office C 6
7 City Hall C 5
8 Kent Gate C 5
9 Dufferin Gate
10 Durham Terrace C 6
11 Esplanade C 5
12 Grand Battery B 6
13 Place d'Armes C 6
14 Governor's Garden C 6
15 The Citadel D 5
16 Market Square C 6
17 Basilica of Quebec C 6
18 Seminary of Quebec C 6
19 Laval University B 6
20 Morrin College C 5
21 Ursuline Convent C 5
22 Grey Nunnery B 4
23 Bishop's Palace C 6
24 Parliament House C 6
25 Music Hall C 5
26 Masonic Hall C 5
27 Champlain Steps C 6
28 Champlain Market C 6
29 Marine Hospital A 3
30 General Hospital A 2
31 Plains of Abraham E 1
32 Martello Towers C 2, C 3,
    D 3, E 3
33 Wolfe's Monument E 2

Churches.

34 Anglican Cathedral C 5
35 St. John C 3
36 Hotel Dieu B 5
37 Wesleyan C 5
38 St. Andrew's C 5
39 Notre Dame des Victoires
    C 6

of Gavazzi's lecture in 1852. The *Wesleyan Methodist*, in Dorchester St., is a graceful building in the English-Gothic style; and the same denomination has a large and handsome building in St. James St., and others in Griffintown.

First among the educational institutions is the University of **Mc-Gill College,** which is beautifully situated at the base of Mount Royal, overlooking the city. The museum of this college is one of the finest in the country. The *Museum of the Natural History Society*, another valuable collection, is at the cor. of Cathcart and University Sts., (admission, 25c.). The *Geological Museum* is in a large building fronting on St. Gabriel St. opposite the Champ de Mars. A short distance W. of McGill College, in Sherbrooke St., is the large and stately building of the ecclesiastical *Seminary of St. Sulpice*, for the education of Catholic priests. Another Seminary of St. Sulpice (founded in 1657), adjoining the Cathedral of Notre-Dame, is 132 ft. long by 29 deep, and is surrounded by spacious gardens and court-yards. The *Asylum for the Blind*, in St. Catherine St., near St. George, has a fine chapel in the Romanesque style with richly frescoed interior. The * **Hôtel Dieu,** founded in 1644 for the cure of the sick, is a vast and imposing building just outside the city limits (reached by Main St.). *St. Patrick's Hospital*, in Dorchester St., at the W. end of the town, is another spacious structure. Both of these establishments are under the charge of the Sisters of St. Joseph. The *Montreal General Hospital* and the *Deaf and Dumb Asylums* (Protestant and Catholic) are noble charities.

The * **Grey Nunnery** (founded in 1692 for the care of lunatics and children) is a vast cruciform building in Dorchester St. The *Black, or Congregational Nunnery*, in Notre-Dame St. near the Place d'Armes, dates from 1659, and is devoted to the education of young persons of the female sex. At Hochelaga (at the N. W. end of the Montreal horse-car line) is the great *Convent of the Holy Name of Mary*. The stranger desirous of visiting either of the nunneries should apply to the Lady Superior for admission, which is seldom refused.

"The lion *par excellence* of Montreal, the eighth wonder of the world," as it has been called, is the * **Victoria Bridge,** which spans the St. Lawrence, connecting the city on the island with the mainland to the S. Its length is 9,194 ft., or nearly 2 miles. It rests, in this splendid transit, upon 23 piers and 2 abutments of solid masonry, the central span being 330 ft. long. The massive iron tube through which the railway-track is laid is 22 ft. high and 16 ft. wide. The total cost of the bridge was $6,300,000. It was formally opened with great pomp and ceremony by the Prince of Wales, during his visit to America in the summer of 1860. The *Water-Works*, a mile or so above the city, are extremely interesting for their own sake, and for the delightful scenery in the vicinity. The old *Government House*, in Jacques Cartier Square, and the *Nelson Monument* near by, are objects of interest, though the monument is in a rather dilapidated condition. The *Mount Royal Cemetery* is 2 miles from the city, on the N. slope of the mountain. From the high-road round its base, a broad avenue gradually ascends to this pleasant spot. The best views of Montreal and its neighborhood are obtained by taking the famous drive "*Around the Mountain,*" 9 miles long. The * *Mt. Royal Park* should be taken *en route.* No visitor to Montreal should fail to see the **Lachine Rapids** (see p. 241). The most advantageous way of seeing them is to take the 7 A. M. train (from Bonaventure station) to Lachine, get on the steamer there, and return through the Rapids to Montreal, arriving at 9 A. M.

The Richelieu & Ontario Navigation Co. run daily steamers to Quebec and the lower river ports. Distance to Quebec, 180 miles; fare, first class (including supper and berth), $2; second class, without meals, $1. · *Varennes* (15 miles below Montreal) lies between the St. Lawrence and Richelieu Rivers. It is connected with Montreal by a steamboat line, and is coming into notice on account of its mineral springs. **Sorel** (45 miles from Montreal) is situated at the confluence of the St. Lawrence and Richelieu Rivers, and is the first point at which the through steamers for Quebec make a landing. It is a small place, but there is good fishing in the vicinity, and in the autumn excellent snipe-shooting. Five miles below Sorel, the river expands into **Lake St. Peter,** which is 25 miles long and 9 wide, and very shallow, except in the main channel, which is crooked and narrow, but which will permit the passage of the largest ships. This lake is noted for its storms, in which the immense lumber-rafts that may be constantly seen drifting down stream are sometimes wrecked. **Three Rivers** (*St. James Hotel*) is about half way between Montreal and Quebec, and is the third city in size in the E. section of the Province. It is at the mouth of the St. Maurice River, which runs through a rich lumber-district, and brings to Three Rivers large quantities of logs and manufactured lumber. The city contains about 9,000 inhabitants and several fine buildings. The **St. Leon Springs,** which are among the most famous in Canada, are reached by a stage-ride of 26 miles from Three Rivers (fare, $1.50); and the *Falls of the Shawanegan,* 30 miles up the St. Maurice River, may be visited by engaging canoes and guides for the purpose. The Falls have a sheer descent of 150 ft., and in magnitude are second only to Niagara. Below Three Rivers there is nothing worthy of notice until Quebec comes in sight, looming up majestically from the river.

Quebec.

From New York, Quebec is reached direct by Route 28. Distance, 426 miles; fare, $14.50. From Boston by Route 26, connecting with Route 28 at White River Junction; or *via* Portland. From Portland by Route 25.

Hotels.—The *St. Louis Hotel* ($2.50 to $3.50 a day), in St. Louis St. near Durham Terrace; the *Russell House* ($2.50 a day), cor. Ann and Garden Sts.; the *Albion Hotel* ($2.50 a day), in Palace St.; *Henchey's Hotel,* in St. Anne St.; and *Blanchard's,* in the Lower Town. The two latter are quiet and inexpensive.

Modes of Conveyance.—*Horse-cars* (fare, 5c.) traverse the streets along the river in the Lower Town and extend to the suburbs. *Carriages* or *calèches* may be hired at the livery-stables, and on the cab-stands near the hotels. The *calèche,* a two-wheeled one-horse apparatus, is the usual vehicle, and costs about

75c. an hour. *Ferries* connect the city with South Quebec, New Liverpool, and Point Levi, on the opposite side oi the St. Lawrence, and run three times a day to the Isle of Orleans.

Quebec, the oldest, and after Montreal the most important, city in British North America, is situated on the N. W. bank of the St. Lawrence River, at its confluence with the St. Charles, nearly 300 miles from the Gulf of St. Lawrence. The city is built on the N. extremity of an elevated tongue of land which forms the left bank of the St. Lawrence for several miles. Cape Diamond, so called from the numerous quartz crystals formerly found there, is the loftiest part of the headland, 333 ft. above the stream, and is crowned with the vast fortifications of the *Citadel.* These occupy about 40 acres, and are considered so impregnable that they have obtained for Quebec the appellation of the "Gibraltar of America." From the Citadel a line of wall runs W. toward the cliffs overhanging the valley of the St. Charles, and is thence continued around the brow of the promontory till it connects once more with Cape Diamond near the Governor's Garden. This circuit is nearly 3 miles in extent. The city is divided into the Upper and Lower Town, the ascent from the latter being by a very steep and winding street (Mountain St., or Côte de la Montagne). The Upper Town comprises the walled city with the two suburbs of St. Louis and St. John, between the walls and the Plains of Abraham. The Lower Town is built around the base of the promontory, and constitutes the business quarter. A very large part of the city within the walls, or the Upper Town proper, is taken up with the buildings and grounds of great religious corporations. Over the remaining irregular surface, not covered by fortifications, are crowded the quaint mediæval streets and dwellings, built generally of stone, two or three stories high, and roofed, like the public buildings, with shining tin. Four of the five original gates in the city wall were removed some years ago, but are now being replaced by others of a more ornamental character. *Kent Gate,* named in honor of the Duke of Kent, father of Queen Victoria, is being erected on the site of the old St. Louis Gate, and the *Dufferin Gate* is being erected on St. Patrick St. Castellated gates will be constructed on the sites of Palace and Hope Gates; and over the site of the former Prescott Gate is to be thrown a light iron bridge to extend from in front of the Parliament House to Durham Terrace.

The site of Quebec was visited by Cartier in 1534, and the city was founded by Champlain in 1608. It was taken by the English in 1629, and restored to France by the treaty of 1632. In 1690 the neighboring English colonies made an unsuccessful maritime expedition against it; and in 1711 the attempt was renewed, with no better success. In 1734 the city had, including its suburbs, 4,603 inhabitants. In 1759, during the Seven Years' War, the English, under General Wolfe, attacked the city and bombarded it. On Sept. 13th took place the first battle of the Plains of Abraham, in which both Wolfe and Montcalm, the French commander, fell, and England gained at one blow an American empire. The French, indeed, recaptured the city the next spring, but at the treaty of peace in 1763 Louis XV. ceded the whole of New France to the English. In December, 1775, a small American force, under General Montgomery, attempted its capture, but failed, after losing 700 men and their commander. The population of the city at that time was only 5,000. In 1861 it was 59,990, and in 1871 59,699, the decrease being attributed to the withdrawal of the British troops forming the garrison. Quebec has a large maritime commerce, and is one of the greatest lumber and timber markets on the American Continent. The principal articles of manufacture are ships, saw-mill products, boots and shoes, bakery products, furniture, and foundry products and machinery.

The point to which the attention of the stranger in Quebec is first directed is * **Durham Terrace,** which lies along the edge of the cliff, towering 200 ft. above the river, and overlooking the Lower Town. It occupies the site of the old Château of St. Louis, built by Champlain in 1620, and destroyed by fire in 1834. *Dufferin Terrace* has lately been added to Durham, making an unequaled promenade over ¼ mile long. The outlook from the Terrace is one of the finest in the world, and is of itself worth a trip to Quebec. The *Esplanade*, near the St. Louis Gate, is another attractive promenade; and the walk along the Ramparts, between the St. Louis Gate and St. John's Gate, affords prospects rivaled by few in America. The view from the **Grand Battery,** near the Laval University, is considered by many to be finer even than that from Durham Terrace; and that from the vast balcony of the University building is still more impressive. The *Place d'Armes*, or Parade-Ground, is a pretty little park adorned with a fine fountain, lying between Durham Terrace and the **Anglican Cathedral,** which is a plain, gray-stone edifice, surmounted by a tall spire, standing in St. Anne St. on the site to which tradition points as the spot where Champlain erected his first tent. Adjoining the Cathedral is the rectory and the pretty little *Chapel of All Saints.* Des Carrières St., running S. from the Place d'Armes, leads to the *Governor's Garden*, containing an obelisk 65 ft. high to the memory of Wolfe and Montcalm. Des Carrières St. also leads to the inner *glacis* of **The Citadel,** a powerful fortification covering 40 acres of ground on the summit of Cape Diamond.

The old *Market Square*, in the center of the Upper Town, is surrounded by more or less striking buildings. On the E. side is the * **Basilica of Quebec** (formerly the Cathedral), a spacious cutstone building, 216 ft. long and 180 ft. wide, and capable of seating 4,000 persons. The exterior of the edifice is very plain, but the interior is richly decorated, and contains several original paintings of great value by Vandyke, Caracci, Hallé, and others. In this basilica lie the remains of Champlain, the founder and first governor of the city. Adjoining the Basilica on the N., standing amid spacious and well-kept grounds, are the quaint and irregular buildings of the *Seminary of Quebec*, founded in 1663 by M. de Laval, first Bishop of Quebec. The Seminary Chapel contains some fine paintings. Adjoining the Seminary is its offshoot, the * **Laval University,** founded in 1852, and occupying three very imposing buildings. They are of cut stone, 576 ft. long (the main building being 286 ft.), five stories high, and cost $240,000. The chemical laboratory is spacious, fire-proof, and provided with complete apparatus; the geological, mineralogical, and botanical collections are very valuable; the museum of zoölogy contains upward of 1,300 different birds and 7,000 insects; and the museum of the medical department is especially complete. The *Library* numbers over 75,000 volumes, and the * *Picture Gallery* (lately thrown open to the public) is the richest in Canada, and is said to be "by far the finest N. of New York." On the W. side of Market Square is the site of the old Jesuits' College buildings, on which a Court-House is to be erected. *Morrin College* occupies the old stone prison at the cor. of St. Anne and Stanislas Sts. In one of its halls is the extensive library of the *Quebec Historical Society*, which is open to the public. The *High School* has 200 students and an excellent library.

In Garden St., S. of Market Square, is the * **Ursuline Convent,** with a striking series of buildings surrounded by extensive and beautiful grounds. This establishment was founded in 1639, and now has 40 nuns who are devoted to teaching girls, and also to painting, needle-work, etc. The parlor and chapel are open to visitors, and in the latter are some fine paintings by Vandyke, Champagne, and others. The re-mains of the Marquis de Montcalm are buried here in an excavation made by the bursting of a shell within the precincts of the convent. The *Grey Nunnery* is a spacious building on the *glacis* W. of the ram-parts, and contains about 75 Sisters. The * *Chapel* adjoining the nun-nery is a lofty and ornate Gothic edifice, with a rich interior. Near by (in St. John St. near St. Clair) is the Roman Catholic church of *St. John*, one of the largest in the city. The * **Hôtel Dieu,** with its convent and hospital, stands on Palace St., near the rampart. It was founded in 1639 by the Duchess d'Aiguillon, and in 1875 comprised 45 Sisters of the Sacred Blood of Dieppe, who minister gratuitously to 10,000 patients yearly. In the Convent Chapel are some valuable paintings. The *Black Nunnery* is in the suburbs of St. Roch. Ap-plication to the Lady Superiors will usually secure admittance to the nunneries.

The new **Post-Office** is a handsome stone edifice at the cor. of Buade and Du Fort Sts. The old Post-Office is in St. Anne St., and near by is the *Bishop's Palace*, a stately and handsome structure. The *Parliament House* is a large but plain building, to the right from Moun-tain St. just inside the ramparts. It occupies the site of Champlain's fort and the old Episcopal palace, and contains a valuable library. Other noteworthy buildings in the Upper Town are the *City Hall*, the *Quebec Music Hall*, and the *Masonic Hall*, in St. Louis St. Among noteworthy churches not already mentioned are the *Wesleyan Church* in St. Stanislas St., a fine specimen of the flamboyant Gothic style; *St. Andrew's* (Presbyterian), at the intersection of St. Anne and St. Stan-islas Sts., a spacious stone structure in the Gothic style; *St. Patrick's* (Roman Catholic), in Ste. Hélène St., and *St. Sauveur* and *St. Roch's* in the suburbs.

Just N. of Durham Terrace is the head of Mountain Hill St., which descends the steep slope of the cliff to the Lower Town. To the right, about a third of the way down, is a picturesque stairway called the * *Champlain Steps*, or Côte de la Montagne, which leads down to the venerable church of *Notre Dame des Victoires*, erected in 1690 on the site of Champlain's residence. S. of the church is the *Champlain Market*, a spacious structure on the river-bank, near the landing of the river steamers. *St. Peter St.*, running N. between the cliff and the

river, is the main business thoroughfare of this quarter, and contains
the great commercial establishments, banking-houses, wholesale stores,
etc. *St. Paul St.* stretches W. on the narrow strand between the cliff
and the St. Charles, amid breweries, distilleries, and manufactories, till
it meets, near the mouth of the St. Charles, *St. Joseph St.*, the main
artery of the large suburb of St. Roch.   On the banks of the St.
Charles are the principal ship-yards; and the numerous coves of the St.
Lawrence, from Champlain St. to Cape Rouge, are filled with acres of
vast lumber-rafts.   On the opposite shore of the St. Lawrence are the
populous towns of South Quebec, New Liverpool, and Point Levi, which
present a scene of activity scarcely surpassed by the city itself.   The
* **Custom-House** is reached from St. Peter St. by Leadenhall St., and
occupies the very apex of the point made by the confluence of the St.
Lawrence and the St. Charles Rivers.   It is an imposing Doric edifice
with a dome, and a façade of noble columns, approached by a long
flight of steps.   The **Marine Hospital,** built on the model of the
Temple of the Muses, on the banks of the Ilissus, is an imposing stone
edifice near the St. Charles River.   Close by is the *Marine and Emi-
grants' Hospital*, and ½ mile farther up the river is the **General Hospital,** an immense range of buildings.   This institution was founded
in 1693, and is under the charge of the nuns of St. Augustine.

The suburbs of St. Louis and St. John stretch S. and W. along the
plateau of the Upper Town, and are constantly encroaching on the historic Plains of Abraham.   They contain many handsome private residences, and several large conventual establishments and churches.
The best approach to the *Plains of Abraham* is by St. Louis St., which
passes the St. Louis Gate and the *Martello Towers*, four circular stone
structures erected in 1807–'12 to defend the approaches to the city.   On
the spot where Wolfe fell in the memorable battle of September 13, 1759,
stands **Wolfe's Monument,** a modest column appropriately inscribed.
A short distance to the left is the path by which his army scaled the
cliffs on the night before the battle; it is somewhat shorn of its rugged
character, but is still precipitous and forbidding.   On the Plains, near
the Ste. Foye road, stands the *Monument* commemorating the victory
won by the Chevalier de Lévis over General Murray in 1760.   It is a
handsome iron column, surmounted by a bronze statue of Bellona (presented by Prince Napoleon), and was erected in 1854.   About 3 miles
out on the St. Louis road is **Mount Hermon Cemetery,** 32 acres
in extent, beautifully laid out on irregular ground, sloping down to the
precipices which overhang the St. Lawrence.

Within excursion distance of Quebec are several points of interest
which the tourist should not fail to visit.   The *Isle of Orleans* (reached
by ferry) is a beautiful spot, and the drive around it a succession of
noble views.   There are also pleasant drives to *Spencer Wood*, the
beautiful residence of the Lieutenant-Governor of the Province, and to
Château Bigot, an antique and massive ruin, standing in solitary loneli-
ness at the foot of the Charlesbourg Mountain.   *Lorette*, an ancient
village of the Huron Indians, is reached by a 9-mile drive along the
banks of St. Charles River.   The falls near the village are very pictu-

resque, and Lake St. Charles, a famous fishing-place, is only a few miles off. The * **Falls of Montmorenci,** 8 miles below Quebec, are 250 ft. high and 50 ft. wide, and are wonderfully beautiful. A short distance above the Falls is the "Mansion House," in which the Duke of Kent passed the summer of 1791; and about 1 mile above are the curious *Natural Steps,* a succession of ledges cut by the river in the lime-

Chaudière Falls.

stone rock, each about 1 ft. high, and as regularly arranged as if they were the work of human hands. The * **Falls of the Chaudière** (10 miles) are reached *via* Point Levi on the opposite side of the St. Lawrence. The rapid river plunges in a sheet 350 ft. wide over a precipice 150 ft. high, presenting very much the look of boiling water, whence its name, *Chaudière,* or caldron.

The regular tour of the St. Lawrence usually ends at Quebec, but the Lower River is well worth visiting by all lovers of fine scenery. The excursion may be made by the steamers of the Quebec & Gulf Ports Steamship Co., one of which leaves Quebec every Tuesday, at 2 P. M., and runs to Pictou, Nova Scotia, stopping at intermediate ports. The distance to Gaspé, at the mouth of the river, is 450 miles; fare, $10 or $4; to Pictou, 1,028 miles; fare, $16 or $7.50. The steamers of the Gulf Ports line make no stoppage between Quebec and Father Point (142 miles), but the intermediate points may be reached by railway, or by local steamboat lines.

The steamers of the St. Lawrence Steam Navigation Co. leave Quebec at 7 A. M. on Tuesdays and Fridays for St. Paul's Bay, Les Éboulements, Murray Bay, Rivière du Loup (Cacouna), Tadousac, Ha! Ha! Bay, and Chicoutimi. At 7 A. M. on Wednesdays, Thursdays, and Saturdays for Murray Bay, Rivière du Loup, Tadousac, and Ha! Ha! Bay. At noon on Saturday for Murray Bay and Rivière du Loup.

The Quarantine for Quebec is at *Grosse Isle*, 30 miles down; and 6 miles below is a group of islets, of which the chief, united by a belt of lowland, are *Crane Island* and *Goose Island*. They are the resort and breeding-place of numerous ducks, geese, and teal, to say nothing of smaller game. **Château Richer** is a thriving little village on the N. shore, much resorted to by sportsmen. Ducks, partridges, and snipe abound in the vicinity, and on the streams near by good trout-fishing may be had. A few miles below Château Richer is **Ste. Anne de Beaupré**, noted for its *Church of Ste. Anne*, in which miraculous cures are said to be effected by the relics of the saint, which are exhibited at morning mass. This church contains a variety of paintings, and is well worth a visit. The celebrated **Falls of Ste. Anne** are on the Ste. Anne River, 3 or 4 miles from the village. The lower fall is 130 ft. high, and below it the water rushes down through a rugged, somber, and picturesque ravine. The *Valley of St. Féréol*, the *Seven Falls*, and *Mt. Ste. Anne* are other objects of interest in the neighborhood. Eight miles below Ste. Anne is **Cape Tourment,** a bold promontory, from the summit of which there is a superb view. A little beyond are the frowning peaks of *Cape Rouge* and *Cape Gribaune*. From Goose Island to the Saguenay River the St. Lawrence is about 20 miles wide. The water is salt, but clear and deep, and the spring-tides rise and fall 18 ft. The black seal, the white porpoise, and the black whale are sometimes seen. *St. Paul's Bay*, 55 miles from Quebec, is a popular resort, and claims to offer more attractions to the tourist, the poet, or the naturalist, than any other parish in the Province. It is surrounded by grand scenery. **Murray Bay** (82 miles below Quebec) is a popular watering-place, surrounded by wild scenery, and noted for the fine fishing in Murray River, and the Gravel and Petit Lakes. There are several hotels and large boarding-houses here, besides summer cottages, and a daily steamer from Quebec renders it easy of access. **Rivière du Loup** is a favorite summer resort on the S. shore of the river, 112 miles from Quebec. It is situated at the mouth of the Du Loup River, and commands a fine prospect of the St. Lawrence, which at this point is 20 miles wide. About a mile from the village is a * waterfall, where the Du Loup, after rushing for a while over a rocky bed, dashes in a sheet of foam over a precipice 80 ft. high. *Lake Temiscouata* is reached from Rivière du Loup by the Grand Portage Road, a distance of 36 miles. Only a few cabins dot the shores on this lovely lake, and it is just the place for the seeker after solitude and trout. **Cacouna,** 6 miles below Rivière du Loup, is the favorite summer resort of the Canadians, and is a very attractive village, combining picturesque scenery, good hotels, fine hunting and fishing, and admirable sea-bathing, for at this point the water of the St. Lawrence is almost as salt as that of the ocean. The *St. Lawrence*

Hall is a large, first-class hotel, overlooking the river (600 guests; $2.50 to $3 a day). The *Mansion House* ($2 a day) is comfortable, and there are several large summer boarding-houses. The air of Cacouna is pure and bracing, and remarkably cool in summer; and there is much pleasing scenery in the vicinity of the village. Nearly opposite Cacouna is the mouth of the **Saguenay River** (see Route 57), which is one of the most striking points on the entire river. Just below (148 miles from Quebec) is **Trois Pistoles,** at the mouth of the river of the same name, famed for its fish. There are two hotels here, and several summer cottages, and the scenery in the vicinity is very pleasing. Thirty miles below Trois Pistoles are the island promontory and harbor of *Le Bic* (the Eagle's Beak), an ancient landing-place, still honored. Near it is *L'Islet au Massacre*, remembered as the scene of the bloody massacre of all but 5 out of 200 Micmac Indians by their Iroquois foes. **Rimouski** (180 miles from Quebec) has an extensive government wharf, and contains a splendid Cathedral, a number of handsome houses, and two good hotels. This is a place at which the tourist should stop, for the scenery of the valley of the Rimouski is extremely beautiful, and the trout-fishing unrivaled. Twenty miles below Rimouski is **Metis,** the site of the largest and longest of the government wharves. It is noted as a whale-fishing station. Some 50 miles farther down, we reach the *Point de Monts*, on the N. coast, and *Cape Chatte*, a few miles above Ste. Anne, the most northerly town on the S. coast of the St. Lawrence. Here are the last approaches of the two shores. Beyond the Point de Monts the N. shore makes a sharp turn to the northward and in that direction we speedily have a sea-horizon. Rounding now the great shoulder of the Province of Quebec, we come, on the E. side, to **Cape Rosier,** passing meanwhile the S. W. half of the desert *Anticosti Island.* Here ends our present tour. Those who pursue the journey to Pictou and Halifax soon enter the region described in the chapter on the "Maritime Provinces of Canada" (Route 60).

57. The Saguenay River.

Steamers leave Quebec at 7 A. M. on Tuesdays and Fridays for Chicoutimi, at the head of navigation on the Saguenay; and on Wednesdays, Thursdays, and Saturdays for Ha! Ha! Bay. The trip from Quebec to the mouth of the Saguenay includes some of the most impressive portions of the St. Lawrence scenery, and is described in Route 56. It should be mentioned that the steamers usually make the trip *up* the Saguenay during the night, so that the best views of the river are obtained on the return-voyage next day. Distances: Quebec to Tadousac, 134 miles; Tadousac to Ste. Marguerite River, 15 miles; to St. Louis Isle, 19; to Little Saguenay River, 27; to St. John's Bay, 32; to Eternity Bay, 41; to Trinity Bay, 48; to Cape Rouge, 56; to Cape East, 63; to Cape West, 65; to St. Alphonse, 72; to Chicoutimi, 100.

THE Saguenay is the largest tributary of the St. Lawrence, and unquestionably one of the most remarkable rivers in the world. Its head-water is Lake St. John, 40 miles long and nearly as wide, which, although 11 large rivers fall into it, has no other outlet than the

Saguenay. The original name of this river was Chicoutimi, an Indian word signifying deep water ; and its present one is said to be a corruption of Saint Jean Nez. The course of the Saguenay—between lofty and precipitous cliffs and, in its upper part, amid rushing cataracts—is about 140 miles from Lake St. John to the St. Lawrence, which it enters 120 miles below Quebec. Large vessels ascend as far as Chicoutimi, 98 miles from the mouth of the river. The Saguenay is a nearly straight river, with grand precipices on either side for almost its entire length, and a peculiarly stern, somber, savage, and impressive aspect. Says Bayard Taylor : " The Saguenay is not properly a river. It is a tremendous chasm, like that of the Jordan Valley and the Dead Sea, cleft for 60 miles through the heart of a mountain wilderness. . . . Everything is hard, naked, stern, silent. Dark-gray cliffs of granite gneiss rise from the pitch-black water ; firs of gloomy green are rooted in their crevices and fringe their summits ; loftier ranges of a dull indigo hue show themselves in the background ; and over all bends a pale, cold, northern sky."

Tadousac is a small village situated a short distance above the mouth of the Saguenay, 134 miles from Quebec. Apart from its attractions as a watering-place, it is interesting as the spot on which stood the first stone-and-mortar building ever erected by Europeans on the Continent of America. The scenery here is wild and romantic in the extreme ; and the adjacent waters abound in excellent salmon and trout. The *Tadousac Hotel* ($2.50 a day) is a large and comfortable house, and there are several summer cottages. Near the hotel are the ancient buildings of the Hudson Bay Co., and just E. is the quaint old Chapel of the Jesuit Mission, erected in 1746. The steamer stops long enough at Tadousac to afford the passengers ample opportunity for seeing the sights. Just above Tadousac is the pretty little cove of *L'Anse à l'Eau*, which is a fishing-station, and here begins one of the most somber and desolate stretches of the river. The banks on either hand consist of immense perpendicular cliffs which are evidently prolonged far below the surface of the water. Now and then a massive promontory encroaches upon the channel, and at rarer intervals the river widens out into what are called bays, but would scarcely be called coves on any other stream. About 15 miles above Tadousac, after passing *Point Crêpe*, the *Ste. Marguerite River*, famous for its salmon-fisheries, comes in on the right ; and 2 miles beyond the steamer skirts the shore of the desolate *St. Louis Isle*, in whose deep waters salmon-trout abound. About 30 miles above Tadousac is **St. John's Bay,** which is 3 miles long and 2 wide, and on the shore of which is one of the few small settlements that the Saguenay can boast. Nine miles above is * **Eternity Bay,** the most striking feature of the river-scenery. It is a narrow cove, flanked at the entrance by two precipices, each rising almost perpendicularly 1,600 ft. above the water. The steepest is * **Cape Trinity,** so called because of the three distinct peaks on its N. summit ; and that on the other side is *Cape Eternity.* Speaking of these awful cliffs, Bayard Taylor says : " I doubt whether a sublimer picture of the wilderness is to be found on this continent." Farther on, *Statue Point, a grand bowlder, 1,000 ft. high, is noticeable for a cave half-way up its face, utterly inaccessible from above or below, having an orifice probably 40 ft. in diameter. Still farther above is *Le Tableau*, a lofty plateau of dark-colored granite 600 ft. high and 300 wide, smooth as though cut by the hand of art, and terminating suddenly in a single perpendicular rock, 900 ft. high. A few miles beyond is the entrance to **Ha ! Ha ! Bay,** which runs 7 miles S. W. from the Saguenay, and is a mile wide. Ha! Ha! Bay was so named because of the delightful contrast which the first French voyagers there beheld after the awful solitude of the lower river. Its upper end is surrounded by undulating meadow-lands, and on its shores are two small villages (*St. Alphonse* and *St. Alexis*), which together contain about 500 inhabitants. **Chicoutimi** (about 20 miles above Ha! Ha! Bay) is the head of navigation on the river, and is a place of considerable trade. It has 700 inhabitants, a good hotel, a cathedral and convent, and a new stone college of ambitious pretensions. The Chicoutimi River swarms with fish, and, just before it enters the Saguenay, plunges over a granite ledge 50 ft. high. Nine miles above Chicoutimi begin the *Rapids of the Saguenay*, said to be little inferior in grandeur to those of the Niagara, and a great deal longer. *Lake St. John* is 60 miles W. of Chicoutimi, and is reached by a good road.

58. Ottawa.

From Montreal Ottawa is reached by steamer up the Ottawa River (101 miles), or by Grand Trunk R. R. to Prescott, and thence by St. Lawrence & Ottawa R. R. (170 miles). From New York by Route 38 to Ogdensburg, opposite Prescott, and thence by St. Lawrence & Ottawa R. R. (447 miles). From Boston by Route 26 or 27 to Rouse's Point, thence by Ogdensburg & Lake Champlain R. R. to Ogdensburg, and thence as before. From the West *via* Detroit.

Hotels, etc.—The *Russell House* ($2.50 a day), near the Parliament Buildings; *Daniel's Hotel* ($2 a day), in the Upper Town; the *Albion*, on Court-House Square. *Horse-cars* traverse the main thoroughfares, and connect the city with towns across the river (fare 6c.).

OTTAWA, the capital of the Dominion of Canada, is situated on the S. bank of the Ottawa River, at the mouth of the Rideau. It is divided into an Upper and Lower Town by the Rideau Canal, which passes through it and connects it with Kingston, on Lake Ontario. The canal is crossed within the city limits by two bridges, one of stone and one of stone and iron, and has 8 massive locks. Bridges also connect Ottawa with the suburban towns of Hull and New Edinburgh, on the opposite side of the Ottawa River. The streets are wide and regular, the principal ones being *Sparks* and *Sussex*. The former is the popular promenade, and contains the leading retail-shops, etc. Ottawa was originally called Bytown, in honor of Colonel By, of the Royal Engineers, by whom it was laid out in 1827. It was incorporated as a city under its present name in 1854, and was selected by Queen Victoria as the seat of the Canadian Government in 1858. It has grown rapidly since the latter date, and now has a population of about 23,000. The city is the entrepot of the lumber-trade of the Ottawa and its tributaries, and

Parliament House, Ottawa, Canada.

has a number of large saw-mills, several flour-mills, and manufactories of iron-castings, mill machinery, agricultural implements, etc.

Ottawa is substantially built, containing many stone edifices, but the *** Government Buildings** are the chief feature of the city. They form three sides of a vast quadrangle on an eminence known as Barrack Hill, 150 ft. above the river, and cost nearly $4,000,000. The S. side of the quadrangle is formed by the *Parliament House*, which is 472 ft. long and 572 ft. deep from the front of the main tower to the rear of the Library, the body of the building being 40 ft. high and the central tower 180 ft. The Departmental Buildings run N. from this, forming the E. and W. sides of the quadrangle; the Eastern block is 318 ft. long by 253 ft. deep, and the Western 211 ft. long by 277 ft. deep. They contain the various Government bureaux, the *Post-Office* and the Model-Room of the *Patent-Office* being in the W. block. The buildings are in the Italian-Gothic style, of cream-colored sandstone. The arches of the doors and windows are of red Potsdam sandstone, the external ornamental work of Ohio sandstone, and the columns and arches of the legislative chambers of marble. The roofs are covered with green and purple slates, and the pinnacles are ornamented with elaborate iron trellis-work. The legislative chambers are capacious and richly furnished, and have stained-glass windows. The *Senate Hall* is reached to the right from the main entrance (which is under the central tower). The viceregal canopy and throne are at one end of this hall, and at the other are a marble statue and a portrait of Queen Victoria, together with full-length portraits of George III. and Queen Charlotte by Sir Joshua Reynolds. The *Chamber of Commons* is reached to the left from the entrance, and contains some beautiful marble columns and arches. The *Library* is a handsome polygonal structure on the N. front of the Parliament House, containing at present about 40,000 volumes. The quadrangle is neatly laid out and planted with trees, and has a massive stone wall along its front. **Rideau Hall,** the official residence of the Governor-General, is in New Edinburgh, across the Rideau River.

After the Government Buildings, the most important edifice in the city is the Roman Catholic **Cathedral of Notre-Dame,** which is a spacious stone structure, with double spires 200 ft. high. The interior is imposing and contains a painting ("The Flight into Egypt") which is attributed to Murillo. Other handsome church edifices are *St. Andrew's* (Presbyterian) and *St. Patrick's* (Roman Catholic). The *Ottawa University* (Roman Catholic) has a large building in Wilbrod St., and the *Ladies' College* (Protestant) a very handsome one in Albert St. The **Grey Nunnery** is an imposing stone structure at the cor. of Bolton and Sussex Sts. The *Black Nunnery* has several buildings just E. of Cartier Square. There are in the city two convents, two hospitals, three orphan asylums, and a Magdalen asylum. The 8 massive locks of the *Rideau Canal*, within the corporation limits, are worth a visit.

The scenery in the vicinity of Ottawa is picturesque and grand. At the W. extremity are the *** Chaudière Falls,** where the Ottawa River plunges over a ragged ledge 40 ft. high and 200 ft. wide. In the great

Chaudière (or caldron) the sounding-line has not found bottom at 300 ft. Immediately below the falls is a suspension-bridge, from which a superb view is obtained. One mile above the city are the *Little Chaudière Falls*, 13 ft. high, and 2 miles above are the rapids known as *St. Remoux*. The *Des Chênes Rapids*, 8 miles above Ottawa, have a fall of 9 ft. The **Rideau Falls,** two in number, are S. of the city on the Rideau River, and are very attractive, though eclipsed by the grandeur of the Chaudière.

The **Ottawa River,** the chief tributary of the St. Lawrence and the largest stream wholly within the Dominion, is navigable both above and below Ottawa. A morning and an evening boat runs down the river to Montreal, making the distance in about 10 hours. At *Grenville*, on this route, the traveler takes the cars around the Long Sault and Carillon Rapids to *Carillon* (12 miles), and at *Lachine* the railway is taken to Montreal. Above Ottawa the river is navigated for 188 miles by the steamers of the Union Navigation Co., but the portages are numerous and the route by no means continuous. The final stopping-place of the steamers is *Mattawa*, a remote post of the Hudson's Bay Co., beyond which is an unbroken and unexplored wilderness.

59. Toronto.

From Montreal Toronto is reached by steamer on the St. Lawrence River and Lake Ontario, or by Grand Trunk R. R. (333 miles). From New York by Route 38 or Route 39 to Lewiston and thence by steamer on Lake Ontario; or by New York Central and Great Western R. R. to Hamilton, and thence *via* Grand Trunk R. R. From Boston by Route 26 or 27 to Montreal, and thence as above.

Hotels, etc.—The *Rossin House* ($2 to $3 a day), cor. King and York Sts.; *Queen's Hotel* ($3 a day), in Front St.; *American House*, in Young St.; *Revere House* ($1.50 a day), in King St. *Horse-cars* (fare 5c.) render all parts of the city easily accessible.

TORONTO, the capital of the Province of Ontario, and next to Montreal the largest and most populous city in Canada, is situated on a beautiful circular bay on the N. W. shore of Lake Ontario, between the Don and Humber Rivers. The site of the city is low, but rises gently from the water's edge. The streets are regular and in general well paved, crossing each other at right angles. *King* and *Yonge Sts.* are the leading thoroughfares, and contain the principal retail shops, etc. Other important streets in the business quarter are Front, Queen, York, Richmond, and Bay. Many of the houses and business structures are built of light-colored brick, of a soft, pleasing tint. The growth of Toronto has been more rapid than that of any other Canadian city. It was founded in 1794 by Governor Simcoe, who gave it the name of York, changed, when it was incorporated as a city, in 1834, to Toronto— meaning, in the Indian tongue, "The place of meeting." In 1813 it was twice captured by the Americans, who destroyed the fortifications and burnt the public buildings. In 1817 the population was only 1,200 ; in 1852, it was 30,763 ; in 1861, 44,821 ; and is now upward of 80,000. The commerce of the city is very extensive. Its manufactures include iron and other foundries, flour-mills, distilleries, breweries, paper, furniture, etc.

The finest buildings in the city and among the finest of the kind in America are those of the * **University of Toronto,** standing in a

large park, and approached by College Ave., which is ½ mile long and
lined with double rows of noble trees. The buildings form three sides
of a large quadrangle. They are of grey rubble-stone, trimmed with
Ohio and Caen stone, and are admirable specimens of the pure Norman
architecture. The University library numbers 20,000 volumes, and
there is a fine Museum of Natural History. *Knox College* (Presbyterian) has a large building in the Collegiate-Gothic style a short distance
N. of the University. Adjoining the University grounds on the E. is
the * **Queen's Park,** comprising about 50 acres skillfully laid out
and pleasantly shaded. In the Park is a monument (consisting of a
brown-stone shaft surmounted by a colossal marble statue of Britannia)
to the memory of the Canadians who fell in repelling the Fenian invasion of 1866. The *Post-Office,* a handsome stone building in the Italian
style, stands at the head of Toronto St. The *City Hall,* in Front St.,
near the lake-shore, is an unpretentious structure in the Italian style,
standing in the midst of an open square. Near by is the spacious *Lawrence Market.* The *Custom-House* is a large and imposing cut-stone
building, extending from Front St. to the Esplanade; and the *Court-
House* is in Church St. **Osgoode Hall,** in Queen St., is an imposing
building of the Grecian-Ionic order, containing the provincial law courts
and an excellent law library. The *St. Lawrence Hall,* in King St., is a
stately stone structure in the Italian style, surmounted by a dome, and
containing a public hall, news-room, etc. The *Masonic Hall,* an ornate
stone building, is in Toronto St. The Young Men's Christian Association has a fine edifice at the cor. of Queen and James Sts., with the
largest hall in the city. The Grand Opera House and the Royal Opera
House each seat about 1,500 persons.

The * **Cathedral of St. James** (Episcopal), cor. King and Church
Sts., is a spacious stone edifice in the Gothic style of the thirteenth
century, with a lofty tower and spire, a clear-story, chancel, and elaborate open roof, of the perpendicular style. It is 200 by 115 ft., and
is surrounded by shady grounds. The *Cathedral of St. Michael* (Roman Catholic), in Church St. near Queen, is a lofty and spacious edifice in the decorated Gothic style, with stained-glass windows and a
spire 250 ft. high. The **Wesleyan Methodist Church,** on McGill
Square, is the finest church of the denomination in Canada. It has a
massive tower surmounted by graceful pinnacles, and a rich and tasteful interior. *Trinity* and *St. George's* (both Episcopal) are neat examples of the perpendicular Gothic style. The *Jarvis Street Baptist
Church* is in the decorated Gothic style, and one of the finest church
edifices in the Dominion. *St. Andrew's* (Presbyterian) is a massive
stone structure in the Norman style.

In Church St., near the Cathedral of St. James, is the commodious
building of the *College of Technology,* which besides the College contains the library (7,000 volumes) and reading-room of the Mechanics'
Institute. The *Normal School,* the *Model Schools,* and the *Educational
Museum* are plain buildings in the Italian style, grouped so as to produce a picturesque effect, standing amid park-like grounds in Church
St. The Museum contains some good paintings and casts, and a col-

lection of curiosities. **Trinity College,** in Queen St. west, overlooking the bay, is a spacious and picturesque building, 250 ft. long, with numerous turrets and quaint gables. It is surrounded by extensive grounds. *Upper Canada College* is a plain red-brick building fronting on King St. near John. The *Provincial Lunatic Asylum* is a large and handsome building with 200 acres of ornamental grounds W. of the city. E. of the city (Don St., near Sumach) is the fine structure of the *General Hospital.* The *Crystal Palace,* in which are held annual exhibitions of the products of the Province, is an extensive building near the Lunatic Asylum. The *Loretto Abbey,* in Wellington Place, is the principal nunnery in the city.

60. The Maritime Provinces of Canada.

To describe these Provinces in detail would require a volume of itself, and, furthermore, would be beyond the purposes of this book, as there are as yet comparatively few places that attract visitors in considerable numbers. All we shall attempt will be to give the outlines of a round trip which, with short side trips or excursions, will include the principal points of interest in New Brunswick, Nova Scotia, Cape Breton, and Prince Edward Island. This round trip *can* be made in two weeks, but at least three weeks should be assigned to it in order to make it thoroughly enjoyable. The traveler should go warmly clad. As to money, U. S. notes will be found as serviceable as anything else, but at each stopping-point they should be taken to a banker's and exchanged for as much local currency as will be needed during the sojourn.

New Brunswick.

New Brunswick, the third Province of the Dominion of Canada, lies upon the eastern boundary of the State of Maine, and is 190 miles long by 140 wide, containing an area of 27,105 square miles. The landscape is of great variety and of most picturesque beauty, the whole Province (excepting the dozen miles lying directly on the sea) being broken into attractive valleys and hills, which northward assume a very rugged character. Much of its area is covered with magnificent forests, which, as in the neighboring State of Maine, constitute its chief source of industry and wealth. Like the neighboring Province of Nova Scotia, New Brunswick so abounds in lakes and rivers that ready water access may be had, with the help of a short portage now and then, over its entire area. Thus a canoe may easily be floated from the interior to the Bay of Chaleur, the Gulf of St. Lawrence, and the ocean on the N., or to the St. John River, and thence to the Bay of Fundy on the S. All the waters of New Brunswick abound with fish of almost every variety. The fisheries of the Bay of Fundy are of immense value, and employ vast numbers of the population. The climate of New Brunswick is healthy, but subject to great extremes of heat and cold; the mercury rising sometimes to 100° in the daytime and falling to 50° at night.

St. John (*Park Hotel, Waverley House*) is the principal city of New Brunswick, and is the starting-point for our tour of the Maritime Provinces. The best way to reach it is by the steamers of the *International Steamship Co.*, which may be taken either at Boston or Portland. They leave Commercial Wharf, Boston, on Mondays, Wednesdays, and Fridays (fare from Boston to St. John, $5.50). The best railway approach is by Route 16 or Route 17 to Portland, thence by Route 23 to Bangor, and from Bangor by European & North American R. R. to St. John. The city (containing 50,000 inhabitants) is superbly situated upon a bold, rocky peninsula at the mouth of the St. John River, and presents a very imposing front to the sea. The scenery of the river is very striking in the passage immediately preceding its entrance into the harbor, and for 1½ mile above the city. It makes its impetuous way here in a chain of grand rapids, through a rugged gap 270 ft. wide and 1,200 long. The passage is navigable only during the very brief time of high and equal tides in the harbor and river; for at low water the river is about 12 ft. higher than the harbor, while at high water the harbor is 5 ft. above the river. The site of the city rises gradually from the harbor. The streets are wide and laid out at right angles; some of them are very steep, and cut through the solid rock to a depth of 30 or 40 ft. The buildings are principally of brick and stone, and there were many fine public edifices, but on June 20, 1877, a most disastrous conflagration reduced the entire business portion of the city to ashes, destroying property to the amount of about $10,000,000. The Post-Office, City Hall, Custom-House, the Wiggins Orphan Institution, the Deaf and Dumb Asylum, the Academy of Music, the Odd-Fellows' Hall, the Victoria School, all the bank buildings but one, and a number of the finest churches, were all destroyed. The fine Victoria Hotel, the Royal Hotel, Barnes's, the Acadia, and the Brunswick House were burned; and the old *Waverley House* is the only one of the old hotels that escaped. Of the buildings which remain the most noteworthy are the *Roman Catholic Cathedral* (in Waterloo Street), the largest church in the Province, the *Provincial Lunatic Asylum*, the *City Hospital* (in Waterloo Street), the *Carleton City Hall*, the *Marine Hospital*, the *Almshouse*, the *Mechanics' Institute*, the *Skating-Rink* (on the City Road), and the *Barracks*. The *Dominion Penitentiary*, a large granite building, is about a mile from the city, and 1½ mile distant is the *Rural Cemetery*, containing 110 acres. Horse-cars connect St. John with Portland and Indiantown. On the W. side of the river is a portion of the city called Carleton. Adjoining the main portion of the city, and practically part of it, is the town of Portland, containing about 12,000 inhabitants. The principal points of interest in the vicinity of St. John are *Lily Lake*, about a mile distant; *Rothesay*, a pretty village on Kennebecasis Bay, much resorted to in summer; *Loch Lomond*, 11 miles N. E., also a favorite resort; and the *Suspension Bridge*, 640 ft. long, and 100 ft. above the river. The favorite drives are on the *Marsh Road* and the *Mahogany Road*.

Several interesting excursions may be made from St. John: 1. A trip up the St. John River to Fredericton, the capital of the Province,

may be made by steamer in a day (fare, $1.50). The St. John River is
about 600 miles long, and from Grand Falls to the sea (225 miles) its
course is within British territory. The greater part of its course is
through wild forest-land, but at some points the banks rise in grand
rocky hills, forming in their lines and interlacings pictures of great
beauty. 2. To St. Stephen and Passamaquoddy Bay; by steamer
direct, or *via* Eastport, Me. Fare to St. Stephen, $1.75. This trip
gives the tourist a sight of the turbulent Bay of Fundy, and of the
picturesque scenery of Passamaquoddy Bay; it may be made in 2 days.
From *Calais* (opposite St. Stephen) a railway runs 21 miles to the
lovely and fish-abounding **Schoodic Lakes.** 3. To the Basin of
Minas by steamer, to Annapolis, and thence by Windsor & Annapolis
R. R. to Wolfville, whence a small steamer runs to Parrsboro, Kings-
port, and Windsor. The **Basin of Minas,** the E. arm of the Bay of
Fundy, penetrates 60 miles into Nova Scotia, and is remarkable for its
tremendous tides, which rise sometimes to the height of 60 or 70 ft.
Parrsboro (*Summer House*) is a pretty little town at the entrance of the
Basin, and may be made the center for many agreeable minor excursions.
Across the Basin from Parrsboro is **Grand Pré,** the land of Long-
fellow's Evangeline. The lovely and picturesque *Gaspereaux Valley*
may be visited from Wolfville. This excursion may also be made from
Halifax *via* Windsor.

The next stage in our regular round trip is from St. John to Halifax.
This may be made without change of cars *via* the Intercolonial R. R.
(distance, 276 miles; fare, $6 for 1st class, and $4 for 2d class); but
the pleasantest route in summer is by steamer to *Annapolis*, and
thence by rail (fare, $5 for 1st class, $3.50 for 2d class). By this route
the tourist obtains fine views of the picturesque scenery of **Digby
Gut,** and the lovely **Annapolis Basin.** As we have now entered
Nova Scotia, a general description of that Province is in order.

Nova Scotia.

The Province of Nova Scotia, the ancient Acadia, lies S. E. of New
Brunswick, and, besides the peninsula proper, comprises the island of
Cape Breton, from which it is separated by the narrow Gut of Canso.
Its area is 21,731 square miles, including the 4,775 of Cape Breton, and
the total population in 1871 was 387,800, of whom 75,483 resided on
Cape Breton. The surface of the peninsula is undulating, and though
there are no mountains there are several ranges of hills, most of which
traverse the country in an E. and W. direction. The shores are indented with a great number of excellent bays and harbors, and there
are numerous small rivers, mostly navigable by coasting vessels for
short distances. The surface is dotted with many lakes and ponds,
the largest being Lake Rossignol in the S. W., 15 miles long by about 5
wide. In the N. E. part of the Province, in the vicinity of the St.
Mary's River, moose or elk abound, and are hunted successfully in the
autumn and early winter. The black bear is also occasionally found,
while partridge, plover, and wild fowl are shot in enormous numbers.

In the St. Mary's and other rivers large numbers of salmon are speared and caught in their season ; and the hunter or angler can hardly miss finding his prey in any portion of the country.

Halifax (*Halifax Hotel, International, Carlton*), the capital of Nova Scotia, is situated near the middle of the S. E. coast of the Province, on the W. side of a deep inlet of the Atlantic called Chebucto Bay or Halifax Harbor. Besides the routes mentioned above, it is reached direct from Boston by steamer (fare, $8), from Portland (fare, $7 and $5), and from Norfolk or Baltimore ($20 and $12). The city is built on the declivity of a hill rising 236 ft. above the level of the harbor, and had a population in 1871 of 29,582. Its plan is regular, most of the streets crossing each other at right angles ; many of them are spacious and handsome. The lower part of the city is occupied by wharves and warehouses, above which rise the dwelling-houses and public buildings, while the summit of the eminence is crowned by the granite bastions of the Citadel. The * **Provincial Building,** in which are the Government offices, the Post-Office, and the City Library, is in Hollis St., and is 140 ft. long by 70 broad, with an Ionic colonnade. On the third floor is the Provincial Museum, containing specimens of the various natural products of the Province and a number of curiosities. West of the Provincial Building is the *Parliament Building*, a plain gray-stone edifice surrounded by pleasantly shaded grounds. In the Legislative Chamber are some fine portraits. Near by is the handsome building of the Young Men's Christian Association, containing a free reading-room. The *Court-House* is a spacious free-stone structure on the Spring Garden Road. Just below it is the fine Roman Catholic *Cathedral of St. Mary*, with a lofty spire. The *Government House*, in Pleasant St., is a solid but gloomy structure, and is the official residence of the Lieutenant-Governor of Nova Scotia. The *Wellington Barracks*, which comprises two long ranges of substantial stone and brick buildings, is the most extensive and costly establishment of the kind in America. The *Admiralty House, Dalhousie College, Military Hospital, Lunatic Asylum* (in Dartmouth), *Workhouse, Jail, Penitentiary*, the *Exchange*, and some of the public schools, are the other most prominent buildings. The * **Citadel** occupies the summit of the heights commanding the town, and is a mile in circumference. It is a costly work, and, after that of Quebec, is the strongest fortress in British North America. The *Queen's Dockyard* covers 14 acres in the northern portion of the city, and is said to be inferior in equipment to few except those of England. The harbor is over a mile wide opposite the city, but about a mile above it narrows to $\frac{1}{4}$ of a mile, and then expands into *Bedford Basin*, which has a surface of 10 square miles and is completely land-locked. The road to *Point Pleasant* is a favorite promenade. The *Dartmouth Lakes*, entered on the opposite side of the harbor, afford a pleasing excursion.

Three interesting minor excursions may be made from Halifax : 1. To the Basin of Minas and Grand Pré *via* railway to Windsor and thence by steamer to Parrsboro. This has the same objective as excursion 3 from St. John (see p. 261). 2. To Yarmouth and the Tusket

Lakes. The trip from Halifax to Yarmouth may be made by railway to Annapolis, and thence by stage; or by steamer from Annapolis to Digby, and thence by stage (70 miles; fare, $4); or by steamer leaving Halifax every Tuesday at 6 A. M., and running all the way to Yarmouth (fare, $6). This latter gives the tourist an opportunity of seeing the richly beautiful scenery of the Atlantic coast of Nova Scotia. **Yarmouth** (*U. S. Hotel, American*) is a flourishing seaport on the south-west coast of Nova Scotia, containing 5,335 inhabitants. The picturesque **Tusket Lakes** are entered by way of *Tusket* (10 miles from Yarmouth) or *Lake George* (12 miles from Yarmouth). They afford excellent fishing, and the surrounding forests are full of game.   3. To the **Liverpool Lakes** by stage from Annapolis to *Greenfield* (50 miles), or by preceding steamer route to *Liverpool*, and thence by stage to Greenfield, or by stage *via* Mahone Bay (109 miles) to Liverpool. A road through the forest leads from Greenfield to the Indian village on *Ponhook Lake*, where guides may be procured. From Ponhook 12 lakes may be entered without making a single portage, including *Lake Rossignol*, the largest and finest in Nova Scotia. These lakes and the region around them are the paradise of sportsmen, affording a greater variety of game than perhaps any other of equal extent in America.

From Halifax, the next and final stage in our regular round trip is to Cape Breton and the famous Bras d'Or Lakes. There are three principal routes by which this excursion may be made: 1. From Halifax *via* the Pictou Branch R. R., which diverges from the Intercolonial R. R. at Truro, to *New Glasgow;* thence by stage to *Port Hawkesbury*, crossing the Gut of Canso; and from Port Hawkesbury by stage to *Sydney, Arichat*, or *West Bay* on the Bras d'Or. Fare from Halifax to Port Hawkesbury, $7.25; to Sydney, $12.   2. By steamer on alternate Tuesdays and Saturdays, direct to Sydney. The fare by Saturday steamers is $10 (with meals); by the Tuesday steamers, $8 (without meals).   3. By Pictou Branch R. R. to *Pictou*, thence by steamer to Port Hawkesbury, thence by stage to West Bay, and thence by steamer on the Bras d'Or to Sydney. Fare, $8. The best way to make the round trip is to take route 1 or 2 to Sydney, and route 3 for the return. In this way the sail on the lakes will be made during the day.

Cape Breton.

The Island of Cape Breton is separated from Nova Scotia by the Gut of Canso, a narrow strait from 1 to 1½ mile wide. Its greatest length is 100 miles, and its greatest breadth 85 miles, with an area of 4,775 square miles and a population of 75,483. The island is very irregular in shape, and is nearly divided into two parts by the **Bras d'Or,** which is not a lake, but a great inland sea with a narrow outlet. At the entrance lies Boularderie Island, between which and the main island on the S. is *Little Bras d'Or.* The Bras d'Or is 55 miles long and 20 miles wide, and varies in depth from 70 to 300 ft. The coast is for the most part rocky and elevated, and indented by numerous bays and inlets. There are several fresh-water lakes, the principal of

which are *Lake Margarie*, in the N. W. division, 40 miles in circumference, and *Grand Lake* and *Miré Lake* in the S. division.   Miré Lake
receives the Salmon River, which flows from the W.

The chief town on the island is **Sydney** (*Archibald's Hotel, International*), which is reached from Halifax or St. John as explained above.
It has 2,900 inhabitants, and one of the finest harbors on the Atlantic
coast.   An interesting excursion from Sydney is a stage-ride of 24 miles
to the ruins of the once famous fortress of **Louisburg,** now a small
fishing-hamlet.   The steamer which leaves Sydney twice a week (Tuesdays and Thursdays) for West Bay traverses the entire length of the
Bras d'Or, and affords the best opportunity for seeing that remarkable
water.   It stops at **Baddeck** (whose name Mr. Charles Dudley Warner
has rendered familiar), and at *West Bay* connects with stages and
wagons which convey passengers 13 miles to *Port Hawkesbury*, where
they may take stages or steamers to Halifax and St. John, or to Prince
Edward Island.

Prince Edward Island.

Prince Edward Island lies in the Gulf of St. Lawrence, 9 miles from
New Brunswick, 15 miles from Nova Scotia, and 30 miles from Cape
Breton Island.   Its extreme length is 140 miles and greatest
breadth 40 miles, and it has an area of 2,173 square miles and a population of 94,021.   The surface is generally flat, but rises here and there
to a moderate height, without being anywhere too broken for agriculture.   The coasts are bold, and are lined with red cliffs ranging from 20
to 100 ft. in height, and deeply indented by bays, with numerous projecting headlands.   Fires, lumbering, and cultivation have made large
inroads upon the original forest which once covered the entire island,
but a considerable portion still remains.   The climate is salubrious,
and is milder than that of the adjacent continent.   The winters are
long and cold; the summers are warm, but not oppressive.   Prince
Edward Island offers fewer attractions to the tourists than either of
the Provinces previously described, presenting fewer picturesque
features to the sight-seer and a more contracted field to the sportsman.

Charlottetown (*St. Lawrence Hotel, Revere House*) is the capital,
chief commercial center, and only city.   It has about 9,000 inhabitants, is regularly laid out, and fronts on a good harbor.   The only
handsome buildings in the city are the *Colonial Building*, containing the
offices and Legislative Chambers of the Provincial Government, and the
Post-Office.   During the season of navigation a line of steamers runs 4
times a week from Charlottetown to Pictou, Nova Scotia (fare, $2),
where connection is made with railway to Halifax; and to Shediac,
New Brunswick (fare, $3), where connection is made with railway to
St. John.   Weekly lines connect with Quebec, and with Halifax and
Boston (fare to Halifax, $4, $5, and $6; to Boston, $5.50, $7.50, and
$9).   The Prince Edward Island R. R. traverses the entire length of
the island, connecting Charlottetown with *Tignish* (117 miles), with
Georgetown (46 miles), with *Summerside* (49 miles), and with *Souris*
(60 miles).   This railroad affords access to any part of the island.

INDEX.

12

INDEX.

INDEX.

THE MASSASOIT HOUSE,

SPRINGFIELD, MASS.

M. & E. S. CHAPIN, PROPRIETORS.

The Massasoit House, near the Railroad Stations, was established in 1843. It has been twice enlarged, making it three times its original size, and thoroughly remodeled and refurnished. The large, airy sleeping-rooms, furnished with hot and cold water, are excelled by none in the country. Special attention paid to ventilation and all sanitary improvements. The proprietors are determined that the world-wide reputation of the Massasoit shall be maintained in all respects.

MOSELEY'S NEW HAVEN HOUSE,

Fronting the Park opposite Yale College,

Is one of the most comfortable and home-like hotels in the country. It has reduced its price to $3.50 per day, and at the same time improved upon its former high standard of excellence. All the furnishings which add to the comfort of guests have been improved, and 600 yards of new carpets laid. Families seeking change or rest can arrange for permanent board at very reasonable prices. Mr. Moseley also has the Restaurant at the Railway Station, which is the best eating-place for passengers between New York and Boston. All express trains stop ten minutes at New Haven.   S. H. MOSELEY,
Formerly of the Massasoit House, Springfield, and for five years partner of the charming Brevoort House, N. Y.

CATSKILL MOUNTAIN HOUSE.

APPLETONS'

EUROPEAN GUIDE-BOOK.

Containing Maps of the various Political Divisions, and Plans of the Principal Cities.

===

BEING A COMPLETE GUIDE TO THE CONTINENT OF EUROPE, EGYPT, ALGERIA, AND THE HOLY LAND.

===

To which are appended a Vocabulary of Travel-talk, in English, German, French, and Italian; an Hotel Appendix, and Specialties of European Cities.

SPRING EDITION, 1879.

Completely revised and corrected up to date. Handsomely bound in two volumes, in red morocco, gilt edges. Price, $5.00.

*** Sent free by mail to any address, on receipt of the price.

D. APPLETON & CO., Publishers,

549 & 551 BROADWAY, NEW YORK.

Cozzens's West Point Hotel.

OPEN FROM MAY TO OCTOBER.

Forty-eight miles from New York. 200 Rooms. 555 feet of Piazza. For particulars, address *GOODSELL BROS., West Point, N. Y.*

NOW READY.

NEW YORK ILLUSTRATED.

With 102 Illustrations and a Map of the City. The illustrations and text fully delineating the Elevated Railway system, Post-Office, and other Public Buildings, Churches, etc., etc. Cover printed in colors. **Price, 60 cents.**

THE HUDSON RIVER ILLUSTRATED.

A Guide for Tourists. With 60 Illustrations. 50 cents. An indispensable work to those who desire to view the glorious beauties of the grand old Hudson.

SCENERY OF THE PACIFIC RAILWAYS AND COLORADO.

Illustrated with Maps, and 71 Illustrations. One of the most beautifully illustrated Guide-Books ever issued. Paper cover, 75 cents; cloth, $1.25.

APPLETONS' RAILWAY GUIDE.

Paper cover, 25 cents. Published monthly. Always revised and corrected up to date.

D. APPLETON & CO., 549 & 551 Broadway, New York.

"THE ARLINGTON,"

WASHINGTON, D. C.

T. ROESSLE & SON, PROPRIETORS.

Also of the FORT WILLIAM HENRY HOTEL, Lake George, New York.

THE WEST POINT HOTEL,

AT WEST POINT, NEW YORK.

THE ONLY HOTEL ON THE POST.

ALBERT H. CRANEY.

COLONNADE HOTEL,

CHESTNUT STREET, Cor. 15th, PHILADELPHIA.

Most desirably located and adapted in all respects to requirements of the best class of the traveling public.

H. J. & G. R. CRUMP.

APPLETONS' GUIDE-BOOKS.

Appletons' Illustrated Hand-book of Summer Resorts.

Revised each summer to date, with Maps and Illustrations.   Large 12mo.
Paper, 50 cents ; cloth, 75 cents.

Appletons' Illustrated Hand-book of Winter Resorts.

For Tourists and Invalids.   New edition, revised.   Large 12mo.
Paper, 50 cents ; cloth, 75 cents.

Appletons' Hand-book of American Cities.

With numerous Illustrations, and Principal Routes of Travel.   Large 12mo.
Paper, 50 cents; cloth, 75 cents.

TO TOURISTS AND TRAVELERS.

G̲o̲ ̲t̲o̲ ̲t̲h̲e̲ Grand Trunk Railway Ticket-Office,

No. 285 BROADWAY, NEW YORK,

AND GET RATES OF FARE AND ROUTES

FOR THE

EXCURSION SEASON, 1879,

From NEW YORK via

NIAGARA FALLS, LAKE ONTARIO, THE THOUSAND ISLANDS, AND RAPIDS OF THE ST. LAWRENCE,

To Montreal, Quebec, River Saguenay, Cacouna, White Mountains, Lake Champlain, Lake George, Saratoga, Portland, Profile House, Crawford House, Lake Memphremagog, Boston, Newport, New York, etc., etc.,

VIA GRAND TRUNK RAILWAY AND ROYAL MAIL LINE STEAMERS.

THE GRAND TRUNK RAILWAY

AND THE

Richelieu & Ontario Navigation Co.'s Royal Mail Line of Steamers

ON LAKE ONTARIO AND RIVER ST. LAWRENCE

Offer better inducements to the Traveling Public than ever before.

The Grand Trunk Railway has been relaid with "steel rails," and been equipped with new locomotives and first-class cars. Pullman's Palace Drawing-room and Sleeping Cars are run on all Day and Night Trains.

The favorite Steamers of the Richelieu and Ontario Navigation Co.'s Royal Mail Line have been thoroughly overhauled, refitted, and refurnished, and an addition of several new composite Steamers have been added to the Line.

Tickets for sale at GREATLY REDUCED RATES at the General Agency, 285 Broadway, New York.

ALEX. MILLOY, TRAFFIC MANAGER, *Royal Mail Line, Montreal.*

W. WAINWRIGHT, GEN. PASS. AGENT, *Grand Trunk Railway, Montreal.*

E. P. BEACH, General Agent, 285 Broadway, New York.

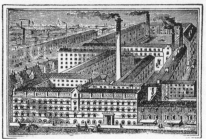

APPLETONS'

GENERAL GUIDE

TO THE

UNITED STATES

AND

CANADA.

WITH RAILWAY MAPS, PLANS OF CITIES, AND ILLUSTRATIONS.

PART II.

𝔚𝔢𝔰𝔱𝔢𝔯𝔫 𝔞𝔫𝔡 𝔖𝔬𝔲𝔱𝔥𝔢𝔯𝔫 𝔖𝔱𝔞𝔱𝔢𝔰.

NEW REVISED EDITION.

NEW YORK:

D. APPLETON AND COMPANY,

1, 3, AND 5 BOND STREET.

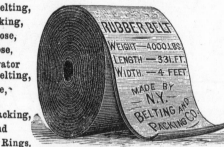

MORTON, BLISS & CO.,

BANKERS,

No. 25 Nassau Street (cor. Cedar), New York,

ISSUE

CIRCULAR NOTES,

AND

Letters of Credit for Travelers;

ALSO,

COMMERCIAL CREDITS,

Available in all parts of the World;

Negotiate first-class Railway, City, and State Loans;

MAKE

TELEGRAPHIC TRANSFERS OF MONEY,

AND DRAW EXCHANGE ON

Morton, Rose & Co., London;
Hottinger & Co.,
Credit Lyonnais, } Paris;
Amsterdamsche Bank, Amsterdam.

THE MASSASOIT HOUSE,

SPRINGFIELD, MASS.

M. & E. S. CHAPIN, PROPRIETORS.

The Massasoit House, near the Railroad Stations, was established in 1843. It has been twice enlarged, making it three times its original size, and thoroughly remodeled and refurnished. The large, airy sleeping-rooms, furnished with hot and cold water, are excelled by none in the country. Special attention paid to ventilation and all sanitary improvements. The proprietors are determined that the world-wide reputation of the Massasoit shall be maintained in all respects.

THE GREAT LAKE ROUTE.

LAKE SUPERIOR TRANSIT COMPANY.

Buffalo, Erie, Cleveland, Detroit, and Port Huron, to Sault Ste. Marie, Marquette, Houghton, Hancock, Bayfield, Ashland, and Duluth, connecting at Duluth with St. Paul & Duluth and Northern Pacific Railroads.

Ten magnificent steamers, unequaled in size and elegance of appointment, are now running in this service.

For time-tables, illustrated Tourist Guides, and other information, address

T. P. CARPENTER,
Gen. Passenger Agt.,
Atlantic Dock, BUFFALO, N. Y.

KOUNTZE BROTHERS,

BANKERS,

120 Broadway, New York,   (Equitable Building),

ISSUE

Circular Notes and Letters of Credit,

Payable in American Funds, and available in all parts of the
United States and Canada.

ALSO ISSUE

Circular Notes and Letters of Credit on the Union Bank of London,

Payable in Sterling, and available in all parts of the World.

---

*Make Cable Transfers to and from London, San Francisco,
and other Cities.*

Execute Orders for the Purchase and Sale of Bonds,
and all Investment Securities.

---

*MAKE LOANS TO CLIENTS ON APPROVED COLLATERAL,
AND UNDERTAKE THE BUSINESS OF COLLECTING
COUPONS, DIVIDENDS, AND OTHER PAPER.*

CARDS OF LEADING HOTELS.

By referring to the advertising pages of these Guides, the traveler will find advertisements giving full information of many of the leading Hotels, as also Bankers and others.

BOSTON, MASS.

AMERICAN HOUSE,
Hanover Street. Prices reduced to $3 and $3.50 per day.
LEWIS RICE & SON, Proprietors.

REVERE HOUSE,
Bowdoin Square. The Prince of Wales, the Duke Alexis, King Kalikau, Dom Pedro, Jenny Lind, Christina Nilsson, and hosts of other celebrities, have made the Revere House their home while in Boston. The best people of both Europe and America are its patrons. Horse-cars to all the depots pass the door.
CHAS. B. FERRIN, Proprietor.

ST. JAMES,
Franklin Square. Largest Hotel in Boston. Accessible by street-cars from all railway stations.
DOYLE & MEAD, Proprietors.

UNITED STATES HOTEL.
Directly opposite the Boston and Albany, and only one block from the Old Colony and Fall River Lines, three blocks only from the New York and New England and Providence and Stonington Stations, and connecting directly by horse-cars, every five minutes, with all the Northern and Eastern Railroads and Steamboats, giving guests every possible facility and convenience of rapid and economical transfer from all points. Unequaled by any Hotel in Boston.
TILLY HAYNES, Proprietor.
ISAAC N. ANDREWS, Manager.

CAPE MAY.

CONGRESS HALL,
Rebuilt and reopened in 1879, will be open this season, June 26th.
H. J. & G. R. CRUMP,
(*of Colonnade Hotel, Phil.*), } Proprietors.
EDWARD A. GILLETT, }

CATSKILL, N. Y.

PROSPECT PARK HOTEL.
First-class new Summer Hotel. A well-situated, well-arranged, and well-conducted place of resort, of easy access, on the banks of the Hudson River, with all the latest improvements.
PROSPECT PARK HOTEL COMPANY.

CATSKILL MOUNTAIN HOUSE.
57th Season. 1824-1880. This famous Summer Hotel is situated on the Catskill Mountains, *eight miles west of the Hudson River*, and *twelve miles* from the village of Catskill, N. Y. Open June 1st to October 1st. *Great reduction in rates.* Send for circular.
C. L. BEACH, Prop'r, Catskill, N. Y.

LAKE GEORGE, N. Y.

FORT WILLIAM HENRY HOTEL.
This magnificent hotel has accommodations for 900 guests. $3 per day.
T. ROESSLE & SON, Proprietors.

NEW YORK.

HOFFMAN HOUSE AND RESTAURANT, Madison Square—said by all travelers to be the best hotel in the world; its restaurant can not be surpassed.
C. H. READ, Proprietor.

GRAND UNION HOTEL.
When you visit or leave New York City, save Baggage Expressage and Carriage-Hire, and stop at *Grand Union Hotel*, nearly opposite Grand Central Depot. European plan. 350 elegant rooms reduced to $1 and upward per day. Elevator. Restaurant supplied with the best. Horse-cars, Stages, and Elevated Railroad to all depots. ☞ Be careful and see that *Grand Union Hotel* is on the sign when you enter.
W. D. GARRISON, Manager.

NIAGARA FALLS (Canada Side).

THE PROSPECT HOUSE.
The nearest and best located at the Falls. Rates, $2.50 to $3.50.
D. ISAACS, Proprietor.

GUION LINE.

United States Mail Steamers.

ARIZONA	5,500 Tons.	WISCONSIN	3,720 Tons.
WYOMING	3,716 "	ALASKA (Building)	5,500 "
NEVADA	3,350 "	OREGON "	3,500 "

☞ These Steamers are built of iron, in water-tight compartments, and are furnished with every requisite to make the passage across the Atlantic both safe and agreeable, having Bath-room, Smoking-room, Drawing-room, Piano, and Library ; also, experienced Surgeon, Stewardess, and Caterer, on each Steamer.

The State-rooms are all on Upper Deck, thus insuring those greatest of all luxuries at sea, perfect Ventilation and Light.

SAILING FROM

NEW YORK EVERY TUESDAY.
LIVERPOOL EVERY SATURDAY.

For Cabin, Intermediate, or Steerage Passage at Lowest Rates, apply to GUION & CO., 25 Water Street, Liverpool, or 5 Waterloo Place, Pall Mall, London; J. M. CURRIE, Paris and Havre; WM. LANGTRY, Belfast; D. R. DAWSON, Dundee; JAS. SCOTT & Co., Queenstown; J. S. BAGSHAW, Manchester; WILLIAMS & GUION, New York; also to authorized agents in all the principal cities in the United States.

PREFACE.

THE leading idea which has governed the preparation of the following work has been to combine fullness and precision of information with the utmost attainable economy of space; to present the information in such a manner as to be most easy of use; to furnish such a Handbook for the traveler as will supply the place of a guide in a land where *couriers* or professional guides are unknown. All the important cities and great routes of travel in the United States and Canada are carefully and minutely described in it, and also every locality which is sufficiently visited for its own sake to entitle it to a place in such a work. At the same time it is believed that the book will be not less useful for what it excludes than for what it includes. Most previous guides have been either too sketchy and incomplete to be of any practical use, or have usurped the functions of a gazetteer—obtruding upon the traveler's attention multitudes of places and facts which can not possibly be either useful or interesting to him, and furnishing him with no test by which to discriminate between the noteworthy and the unimportant. In the present work the gazetteer plan has been deliberately discarded, and mention is made only of those places, facts, and items which are considered in some way interesting and worthy of attention.

The Editor desires particularly that his method in this respect shall be clearly understood. Small stations *en route* are often mentioned in order to indicate distances and rate of progress—in itself, frequently, a highly interesting item of information; but, as a general rule, not only are merely local lines of travel and off-route places (unless attractive for special reasons) omitted entirely, but the tourist's attention is invited only to such things as are really worth attention, and the Editor has been much more anxious in describing a route to indicate the characteristic features of the country traversed, and where fine views may be obtained, than to enumerate and describe all the little stations at which the train may happen to pause. Nor has he scrupled to devote more space to a famous mountain-view, to a bit of grand or exquisite scenery, to a great achievement of nature or art, than to many cities which are important as regards population, commerce, and industry, but which possess no special interest for the traveler. In short, the standpoint is not that of a gazetteer, but of the tourist, who cares little for statistical or geographical data, but wishes to see and learn about whatever is novel, picturesque, beautiful, memorable, striking, or curious.

The plan of the book, its arrangement and classification of matter, and the system of treatment, are based on the famous Baedeker Handbooks, which are conceded to possess in a preëminent degree the grand desiderata of compactness, portability, and facility of consultation. As much aid as possible is afforded to the eye by printing the names of places and objects either in italics, or, where they are of sufficient importance, in bold-faced **black type.** Objects worthy of special attention are further distinguished by asterisks (*).

The Plans of Cities also follow the excellent Baedeker system of numbered and lettered squares, with figures corresponding to similar figures prefixed to lists of the principal public buildings, hotels, churches, and objects of interest. This system will be found to add very materially to the usefulness of the maps. The Illustrations afford a trustworthy idea of American architecture, and in a less degree of American scenery.

Great care has been taken to make the GUIDE accurate and fully up to date in its information ; in most cases the descriptions of important places have been submitted to the revision of a resident. Nevertheless, in dealing with so many and diverse facts it is probable that some errors have crept in and that there are some omissions. The book will be subjected to a thorough annual revision, and the Editor will be grateful for any corrections and suggestions.

CONTENTS.

CONTENTS. vii

MAPS.

PLANS OF CITIES.

*** This volume forms the second part of " Appletons' General Guide to the United States and Canada," of which the first part, comprising 60 Routes and 264 pages, is devoted to the New England and Middle States and Canada. Though paged consecutively with the preceding part, the present volume is complete in itself and for the field it covers. Both parts are also bound together in one compact and handy volume of about 520 pages.

THEODORE B. STARR,

(Of late firm STARR & MARCUS,)

206 Fifth Avenue, Madison Square,
NEW YORK,

Importer of Diamonds, Pearls, and other Precious Stones, and Manufacturer of Rich Jewelry. Entire originality and artistic beauty of design, with the most skillful workmanship in the production of every article, is one of the leading aims of this establishment. Visitors, whether with or without intention to purchase, are always welcomed to an inspection of a stock which is one of the largest to be found in the United States, and at moderate prices.

KOUNTZE BROTHERS,

BANKERS,

120 Broadway, New York,   **(Equitable Building),**

ISSUE

Circular Notes and Letters of Credit,

Payable in American Funds, and available in all parts of the
United States and Canada.

ALSO ISSUE

Circular Notes and Letters of Credit on the Union Bank of London,

Payable in Sterling, and available in all parts of the World.

---

*Make Cable Transfers to and from London, San Francisco,
and other Cities.*

Execute Orders for the Purchase and Sale of Bonds,
and all Investment Securities.

---

*MAKE LOANS TO CLIENTS ON APPROVED COLLATERAL,
AND UNDERTAKE THE BUSINESS OF COLLECTING
COUPONS, DIVIDENDS, AND OTHER PAPER.*

INTRODUCTION.

I. Passports, Customs Duties, etc.

PASSPORTS are not required in the United States. The examinations of baggage at the ocean ports and the Canadian frontier are usually conducted in a courteous manner, but are at times very rigid; and the visitor from abroad will do well to include in his luggage only such articles as can be strictly regarded as of necessary personal use. The articles most watched for and guarded against by the customs authorities are clothing (new and in undue quantity), silks, linens, laces, cigars, watches, jewelry, and precious stones. In case of any portion of the luggage being found "dutiable," it is best to pay the charges promptly (under protest), and forward complaint to the Treasury Department at Washington.

II. Currency.

The present currency of the United States consists of gold and silver coin, and of U. S. Treasury notes (called "greenbacks") and national-bank bills redeemable in coin at par. In California gold alone is the standard of value, and silver is taken only at a discount. The fractional currency (which includes all sums below a dollar) is of silver, with nickel five-cent pieces, and copper pieces of the value of one and two cents. In Canada the currency is coin, or the notes of the local banks, which are at par. Foreign money is not current in the United States, but may be exchanged for the usual currency at the brokers' offices at fixed rates. For practical purposes, a pound sterling may be rated as equivalent to five dollars of American money, and a shilling as equivalent to twenty-five cents, or a "quarter." A franc is equivalent to about twenty cents of American money; five francs to a dollar.

III. Hotels.

The hotels of the United States have the reputation of being among the largest, finest, and best conducted in the world. In the larger cities there are two kinds: those conducted on what is called the American plan, by which a fixed charge includes lodgings and the usual meals at *table d'hôte;* and those conducted on the European plan, where the charge is made for lodgings alone, and the meals are taken *à la carte* in the hotel or elsewhere. At a few hotels the two plans are combined, and the traveler has his choice between them. The charge at first-class hotels (on the American plan) is from $3 to $5 a day; but good accommodations may be had at houses of the second class for $2 to $3 a day. A considerable reduction is usually made on board by the week. The charge for rooms at hotels on the European plan ranges from $1 to $3 a day. The "extras" and "sundries" which make European hotel-bills so exasperating are unknown in America; and the practice of feeing servants, though it has some slight and irregular observance, has never attained the force of custom. The best hotels at the various points are designated at their proper places in the body of the GUIDE; they are named in what the Editor believes to be the order of their reputation. At the larger hotels, besides a reading-room for the use of guests, there will nearly always be found a letter-box, a telegraph-office, and an office for the sale of railroad tickets.

IV. Conveyances.

The average cost of travel by *Railroad* is two to three cents per mile in the Middle States and New England, and from three to five cents in the Western and Southern States. Children between the ages of five and twelve are generally charged half price; those under five are passed free. Between distant places which may be reached by competing lines there are usually what are called "through tickets," costing much less than regular mileage rates. These tickets are good only for the day and train for which they were purchased, and, if the traveler wishes to stop at any intermediate point, he must notify the conductor and get a "stop-over check." Attached to all "through trains" on the longer routes are Palace or Parlor cars, which are richly finished and furnished, provided with easy-chairs, tables, mirrors, etc., and, being mounted on twelve wheels, run much easier than the ordinary coaches. Those attached to the night-trains are so arranged as to be ingeniously converted into sleeping-berths, and are provided with lavatories in addition to the usual conveniences. From $2 to $3 a day in addition to the regular fare is charged for a seat or berth in these palace-cars, or a whole "section" may be secured at double rates. On a few of the more important lines have been placed what are called "hotel or dining cars" (on the same plan as the palace-cars), where meals are served *en route* in first-class restaurant style. The average speed on express-trains is 30 miles an hour.

Travel by *Steamboats* is somewhat less expensive and less expeditious than by rail. The ticket (in case of a night-passage) gives the right to a sleeping-berth in the lower saloon; but the extra cost of a state-room (usually $2 per night) is more than compensated by the greater comfort and privacy. On the much-traveled lines, state-rooms should be secured a day or two in advance, and, if possible, in the out-side tier. Meals are usually an extra on steamboats, and will cost about $1 each when the service is not *à la carte*.

The vast extension of the railway system has nearly superseded the old *Stages* and *Coaches*, but a few lines still run among the mountains and in remote rural districts. Where the object is not merely to get quickly from point to point, this is perhaps the most enjoyable mode of travel, and, in pleasant weather, the traveler should try to get an out-side seat. The charges for stage-travel are relatively high—often as much as 10c. or 15c. a mile.

In all the cities and larger towns there are *Omnibuses* at the station on the arrival of every train, which connect directly with the principal hotels; a small charge (usually 50c.) is made for this conveyance.

V. Baggage—The Check System.

It is the custom in America to deliver baggage to a person known as the baggage-master, who will in return give a small numbered brass plate (called a " check ") for each piece, on presentation of which the baggage is delivered. Baggage may be " checked" over long routes in this way, and the traveler, no matter how many times he changes cars or vehicles, has no concern about it. The railroad company are responsible if the baggage should be injured or lost, the " check " being evidence of delivery into their hands. The traveler, arrived at the station or depot, should first procure his ticket at the ticket-office, and then, proceeding to the baggage-room or proper station of the bag-gage-master, have his trunks checked to the point to which he wishes them sent. (The baggage-master usually requires the traveler to ex-hibit his ticket before he will check the trunks.) Arriving at his des-tination, the checks may be handed to the hotel-porter, always in wait-ing, who will procure the various articles and have them sent to the hotel. Should the owner be delayed on the route, the baggage is stored safely at its destined station until he calls or sends for it (of course presenting the check). Beyond a certain weight (usually 80 or 100 lbs.) for each ticket bought, baggage is charged for extra; and this may become a serious item where the distances are great. Be-fore arriving at the principal cities a baggage- or express-man gen-erally passes through the cars and gives receipts (in exchange for checks) for delivering baggage at any point desired.

VI. Round-trip Excursions.

Every summer the leading railway companies issue excursion-tickets at greatly reduced prices. These excursions embrace the principal places of interest throughout the country, and are arranged in a graded series, so that the tourist may have choice of a number of round trips of a day or two to popular resorts near by, or may make one of the grand tours to distant points affording thousands of miles of travel. As the tickets are good for thirty, sixty, and ninety days, the traveler can consult his convenience *en route*, lingering or hastening on as he may happen to choose. Lists of these excursions and such information about them as may be required can be obtained at the central offices of the various companies in the larger cities, either by personal application or by letter.—Messrs. Thomas Cook & Son (with central office in New York) also issue excursion-tickets, the difference between their plan and that of the railway companies being that they arrange the tour to suit the wishes of the individual traveler. There is no affinity between this plan and the " personally conducted tours " which have made " Cook's Tourists " a by-word throughout the world; it is, in fact, little more than an arrangement for enabling the economically minded traveler to save money on his railway-tickets and hotel-bills.

VII. Climate and Dress.

Of course in a country so extensive as the United States the differences of climate are very great, New England and the Middle States being frequently buried in snow at the very moment when the Southern States are enjoying their most genial season, while California has but two seasons (the wet and the dry) instead of the four seasons of the temperate zone. It is true of the country as a whole, however, that the summers are hotter and the winters colder than those of Europe; and that there is greater liability to sudden changes from heat to cold, or from cold to heat. For this reason it is highly important that the traveler should be dressed with sufficient warmth; it will be better for him to suffer at noonday from too much clothing than to expose himself at night, in storms, or to sudden changes of temperature, with too little. Woolen underclothing should be worn both summer and winter, and a shawl or extra wrap should always be on hand. At the same time, exposure to the vertical rays of the sun in summer must be carefully avoided; sunstroke being by no means unusual even in the Northern cities.

WESTERN AND SOUTHERN STATES.

61. New York to Chicago via Suspension Bridge and Detroit.

By the New York Central and Hudson River R. R., the Great Western R. R. cf Canada, and the Michigan Central R. R. The distance from New York to Chicago by this Route is 978 miles, and the time of the fast express trains is about 34 hours. Drawing-room cars are attached to all the day trains, and Palace Sleeping-cars to all the night trains, and there is no change of cars between New York and Chicago. Distances : New York to Albany, 143 miles; to Utica, 238; to Rome, 252; to Syracuse, 291 ; to Rochester, 373 ; to Suspension Bridge, 447 ; to Hamilton, 491 ; to London, 576; to Detroit, 677; to Chicago, 978.

LEAVING the Grand Central Depot in New York, the train passes to Albany amid the picturesque scenery of the Hudson River.* The Hudson River R. R. runs along the E. bank of the river all the way to Albany, and though the view from the cars is restricted to the other and least attractive side of the river, the journey is nevertheless a most agreeable one. Going N. the traveler should secure a seat on the left-hand side of the car, and going S. on the right-hand side. The lower Hudson, emptying into New York Bay, is like a huge arm of the sea, and, as we ascend, preserves its noble width, occasionally expanding into lakes, while at several places among the Highlands the mountains approach so close on either side as to reduce the river to a contracted and tortuous channel. The railroad runs close along the bank of the river, in sight of its waters almost continuously, making occasional short cuts from point to point, and ever and anon crossing wide bays and the mouths of tributary streams.

Passing beneath the upper part of New York City through long tunnels, the train crosses the Harlem River, and then, turning to the left, follows the Spuyten Duyvel Creek to the Hudson. On reaching the river the traveler's attention is at once caught by the * **Palisades,** a series of grand precipices rising in many places to the height of 300 ft. and stretching in an unbroken line along the W. river-bank for

* Our description of this route as far as Suspension Bridge is a mere outline or summary, designed to furnish such cursory information about the places and scenery *en route* as may meet the wants of through passengers to the West. Those who desire a more detailed description will find it in the section of the work devoted to the New England and Middle States (Routes 9 and 38).

more than 20 miles. The rock is trap, columnar in formation, and the summit is thickly wooded. In striking contrast with the desolate and lonely appearance of these cliffs, the E. bank presents a continuous succession of beautiful villas standing amid picturesque and exquisite-ly-kept grounds, with a frequent sprinkling of villages and hamlets. *Yonkers* (17 miles) is a fashionable suburban town beautifully situated at the mouth of the Neperan or Saw-Mill River. *Piermont* (22 miles) is on the opposite side of the river at the end of the Palisades, and takes its name from a mile-long pier which extends from the shore to deep water. Here begins the * **Tappan Zee,** a lake-like expansion of the river, 10 miles long and 3 miles wide at the widest part, surrounded by beautiful scenery. *Tarrytown*, immortalized by Washington Irving, and *Sing Sing*, the site of one of the most important of the State Prisons, are on the E. shore of the Tappan Zee; and the pretty little town of *Nyack* is on the W. shore. Croton Point divides the Tappan Zee from *Haverstraw Bay*, another lake-like widening of the river, at the upper end of which stands *Peekskill* (43 miles), at the gate of the * **Highlands,** as the mountains through which the Hudson forces its way are called. The scenery for the next 16 miles is unsurpassed in the world, but a very imperfect idea of it is obtained from the cars. The first seen of the Highland group is *Dunderberg Mt.*, which looms up grandly across the river. Nearly opposite is *Anthony's Nose*, whose base is tunneled by the railway a length of 200 ft. In the river, under Dunderberg, is the pretty *Iona Island*, noted for its vineyards. In the heart of the Highland Pass, a beautiful view is obtained of * **West Point,** the seat of the U. S. Military Academy, with fine buildings on a broad plateau 157 ft. above the river. *Garrison's* (51 miles) is a station on the R. R. nearly opposite West Point. Just above West Point, on the same side, is *Cro' Nest*, one of the loftiest of the High-land group, and then comes *Storm King*, the last of the range on the W. On the E. side, scarcely visible from the cars, are *Mt. Taurus, Breakneck*, and *Beacon Hill*, which are among the most commanding features of the river scenery. At the end of the Highlands the river again expands into the broad *Newburg Bay*, on the W. shore of which is **Newburg,** a beautifully-situated city of 18,000 inhabitants. **Poughkeepsie** (75 miles) is on the railway, and is the largest city between New York and Albany. It contains 23,000 inhabitants, and is the site of Vassar College and other famous educational institutions. Above Poughkeepsie on either bank are many pleasant towns and fine country-seats, but the river-banks are for the most part low and unin-teresting. Just before reaching Hudson the noble range of the Cats-kill Mountains is seen along the W. horizon. *Catskill*, whence these are visited, offers a pleasant view across the river, with the spacious *Prospect Park Hotel* on an elevated plateau above the landing. **Hud-son** (115 miles) is a flourishing city of 13,000 inhabitants, at the head of ship-navigation on the river. The heights back of the city com-mand majestic views of the Catskills. Between Hudson and Albany there is nothing to call for special mention. **Albany** (143 miles) is the capital of New York State, and is a city of 80,000 inhabitants, beautifully situated on the W. bank of the Hudson near the head of tide-water. It contains many features of interest, and the tourist who has time to stop over will find them all described on page 63.

The through trains make but a short pause at Albany, and then take the tracks of the N. Y. Central R. R., which traverses from E. to W. the entire length of New York State, passing through the rich and populous midland counties. The scenery along this portion of the route is mostly of a pastoral character, with nothing bold or striking, but with much that is pleasing. The famous valley of the Mohawk is first traversed. The river, now quiet, now rushing along its rocky bed, is continually in sight, the hills bounding the valley adding to the picturesqueness of the view, and the many villages clustering along the line giving evidence of solid prosperity. The great Erie Canal traverses the State from Albany to Buffalo, nearly on the same line with the railroad. *Schenectady* (160 miles) is one of the oldest towns in the State, and is distinguished as the site of Union College. Just beyond Schenectady the train crosses the Mohawk and the Erie Canal on a bridge 1,000 ft. long. *Little Falls* (217 miles) is remarkable for a bold passage of the river and canal through a wild and most picturesque defile. **Utica** (238 miles) is a handsome manufacturing city of 35,000 inhabitants, on the S. bank of the Mohawk, nearly in the center of New York State. The *State Lunatic Asylum* here holds high rank among institutions of the kind. **Rome** (252 miles) is a flourishing city of 11,000 inhabitants, with several fine buildings, of which the handsomest is the Seminary. **Syracuse** (291 miles) is the next important city on the line of the road, and is famed for its salt-springs, and for being the place at which the political conventions of the State are usually held. The restaurant in the depot at Syracuse is of noteworthy excellence. Next comes **Rochester** (373 miles), the metropolis of Central New York, with a population of 82,000, and the site of the celebrated Genesee Falls. The train passes about 100 rods S. of the most southerly fall, so that passengers in crossing lose the view. At *Lockport* (428 miles) the wonderful system of locks by which the Erie Canal descends from the level of Lake Erie to the Genesee level is visible from the windows of the cars. At *** Suspension Bridge** (447 miles) the train crosses the Niagara River, in view of the Falls and of the rapids rushing to the whirlpool below. The bridge itself is worth attention as one of the achievements of modern engineering. It is 800 ft. long from tower to tower, is 258 ft. above the water, and was finished in 1855 at a cost of $500,000.

From Suspension Bridge to Detroit the route runs through Canada, and is most uninteresting, though the road (the Great Western R. R.) is an admirable one. In the neighborhood of *St. Catherine's* (458 miles), noted for its mineral springs, and *Hamilton* (491 miles) there is some attractive scenery; but with these exceptions everything is dull, flat, and monotonous, and the traveler will be glad when, emerging from a deep cut, he suddenly comes upon the bank of the Detroit River at *Windsor* (676 miles), opposite Detroit. Here the train is transferred to the other side of the river on a steam ferry-boat, and the route is resumed on the line of the Michigan Central R. R.

Detroit.

Hotels, etc.—The leading hotels are the *Russell House*, fronting on the Campus Martius, the *Biddle House*, the *Michigan Exchange*, and the *Brunswick*. Eight lines of *horse-cars* intersect the city, and three lines of *ferry-boats* ply across the river to Windsor on the Canadian side. There are 7 steamboat lines with numerous boats running to various points on the lakes.

Detroit, the chief city of Michigan, is situated on the S. bank of the Detroit River, a noble stream 20 miles long, connecting Lakes Erie and St. Clair. The city extends along the bank for about 7 miles, and is built up for about 2½ miles from the water. For at least 6 miles, the river-front is lined with mills, dry-docks, ship-yards, foundries, grain-elevators, railway-depots, and warehouses. For a short distance from the river-bank the ground rises gradually, and then becomes perfectly level, furnishing an admirable site for a large city. Detroit is laid out upon two plans: the one that of a circle with avenues radiating from the Grand Circus as a center; the other that of streets crossing each other at right angles. The result is a slight degree of intricacy in certain localities, which inconvenience is more than compensated by a number of little triangular parks which diversify and ornament the place. The avenues are from 100 to 200 ft. wide; the streets vary in width from 50 to 100 ft., and are generally shaded by an abundance of trees.

The site of Detroit was visited by the French as early as 1610; but no permanent settlement was made until 1701, when Fort Pontchartrain was built. In 1760 it passed into the hands of the English, and in 1763 was besieged for 11 months by Pontiac in his attempt to expel the whites from that region. In 1783 Detroit was ceded to the United States, but the Americans did not take possession of it till 1796. During the war of 1812 it fell into the hands of the British, but was recaptured in 1813. It was incorporated as a city in 1824, when its population was less than 2,000, and in 1876 had 103,000 inhabitants. The manufactures of the city are numerous and important, including extensive iron-works and machine-shops, railroad-car factories, flour-mills, breweries, and immense tobacco and cigar factories. The shipping interests are also large, while pork and fish packing employ numerous hands.

The principal streets of the city are *Jefferson Ave.*, parallel with the river; **Woodward Ave.,** which crosses the former at right angles, and divides the city into two nearly equal parts; and *Fort St.*, *Michigan Ave.*, *Grand River Ave.*, and *Gratiot St.* at various angles with Woodward Ave. **West Fort St.** is a broad and beautiful street, lined with handsome residences; and *Lafayette Ave.* is a fashionable street. *Griswold St.* is the Wall St. of the city. The **Grand Circus,** the principal park, ½ mile back from the river, is semicircular in form, and is divided by Woodward Ave. into two quadrants, each containing a fountain. About half way between the river and the Grand Circus is the *Campus Martius*, an open space 600 ft. long and 250 ft. wide, which is crossed by Woodward and Michigan Avenues, and from which radiate Monroe Ave. and Fort St. Facing the Campus Martius on the W. is the * **City Hall,** a handsome structure in the Italian style, 200 ft. long, 90 ft. wide, and 180 ft. high to the top of the tower, completed in 1871, at a cost of $600,000. In front of

the City Hall is a fine * *Soldiers' Monument*, erected in memory of the
Michigan soldiers who fell in the civil war. Facing the Campus Martius on the N. is the *Opera House ;* and in Fort St. is **Whitney's
Opera House,** one of the finest in the country. The *Custom-House*,
which also contains the *Post-Office*, is a large stone building in Griswold
St. The new *Board of Trade Building*, cor. Jefferson Ave. and Griswold St., is spacious and ornate. The * **Freight Depot** of the Michigan Central R. R. is one of the most noteworthy structures in the city.
It stands on the wharf, and consists of a single room, 1,250 ft. long
and 102 ft. wide, covered by a self-sustaining roof of corrugated iron.
In the immediate vicinity are the great *Wheat-Elevators* of the company,
from the cupola of which a superb view of the city, river, and Lakes
St. Clair and Erie may be had. Besides the Opera-Houses, there are
the German *Stadt Theatre*, and several large public halls. The *Y. M. C.
A.* has a large building in Farmer St., with library, gymnasium, restaurant, public hall, etc.

The churches of Detroit are noted for their number and beauty. *St.
Anne's* (Roman Catholic), Larned St. cor. of Bates, is the oldest church
in the city, and is noted for its fine choir. The * **Cathedral of St.
Peter and St. Paul** (Roman Catholic), Jefferson Ave. cor. of St. Antoine St., is the largest church-edifice in the State, and has an imposing interior. *St. Joseph's* (Roman Catholic) is a very handsome building. * **St. Paul's** (Episcopal), cor. Congress and Shelby Sts., is the
parent church of the diocese, and is famous for its beautiful roof, which
is self-sustaining. Other handsome Episcopal churches are *Christ's*, in
Jefferson Ave. above Hastings St., *St. John's*, in Woodward Ave., and
Grace, in Fort St. The **Fort St. Presbyterian** (Fort St. cor. 3d)
has the handsomest front of any church in the city and a beautiful interior. The **Central Church** (Methodist), in Woodward Ave. above the
Grand Circus, has a richly-decorated interior. The *First Presbyterian*,
in State St., the *Jefferson Ave. Presbyterian*, above Rivard St., and the
First Congregational, Fort St. cor. Wayne, are all fine edifices. There
are several libraries in the city, of which the principal are the *Public
Library*, containing 37,000 volumes, and that of the *Young Men's Society*,
containing 14,000. The * **Convent of the Sacred Heart,** in Jefferson Ave. near St. Antoine St., is a large and beautiful building. The
House of Correction, in the N. portion of the city, is used for the confinement of petty criminals. Directly opposite is a home for discharged female prisoners, who are received here and furnished with work until
places can be found for them out of the reach of the influences previously
surrounding them. The *U. S. Marine Hospital*, on the bank of the river,
just above the city, commands a fine view of the Canada shore. *Elmwood Cemetery* is a beautiful burying-ground within the city limits
(reached by horse-cars). *Woodmere Cemetery*, on high ground, 4 miles
W. of the city, is of recent origin. *Fort Wayne* is a bastioned redoubt,
about 3 miles below the Michigan Central Depot, standing upon the
bank of the river and completely commanding the channel. The Fort
St. and Elmwood horse-cars run within half a mile of it, and it is also
a favorite point to which rides and drives are taken. *Belle Ile*, an isl.

and in the river opposite the upper limit of the city, is a favorite resort for picnics. *Grosse Point*, projecting into Lake St. Clair, 7 miles above the city, is at the end of a beautiful drive.

———

From Detroit the route is *via* the Michigan Central R. R., which traverses a fine agricultural country, the general aspect of which is pleasing, especially in spring and summer, but which is not of a striking or picturesque character. In many places it passes through dense virgin woods, and in others across and along the winding rivers which abundantly water this section of Michigan. *Ypsilanti* (30 miles from Detroit) is a thriving city of 6,000 inhabitants, on the Huron River, which furnishes water-power for several flour-mills, paper-mills, and other factories. The State Normal School is located here. Beyond Ypsilanti the train follows the Huron River and passes in 8 miles to **Ann Arbor** (*Cook's Hotel, Gregory House*), a city of 8,000 inhabitants lying on both sides of the Huron River, chiefly known as the seat of the *University of Michigan,* one of the noblest insti-

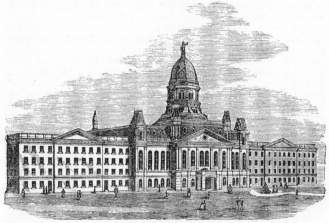

University Hall.

tutions of learning in America. With fees little more than nominal, and a high standard of scholarship, the University attracts students from all parts of the world, and is open to females as well as males. The University buildings stand in the midst of grounds comprising 44½ acres, and thickly planted with trees. *University Hall* is 347 ft. long and 140 ft. deep, and is devoted to the uses of the department of literature, science, and art. There are also buildings for the departments of law, medicine, and dentistry, a hospital, a chemical laboratory, and a residence for the president, but no dormitories. The *Observatory* is on a hill about a mile from the other buildings. The libraries of the University contain 30,000 volumes, and the museums are large and valuable. The building of the *Union School* at Ann Arbor is one of the finest in the State, accommodating 1,000 pupils. There are 5 mineral springs in the city (over one of which has been erected a large water-cure establishment), an Opera House, and several fine churches. **Jackson** (*Hibbard House, Hurd*) is 753 miles from New York, and is a busy manufacturing city of 12,000 inhabitants on the Grand River, at the intersection of 6 railroads. It lies on the edge of the coal-deposits of the State, and the mines can be seen from the cars. The city is regularly laid out and substantially built. Several of the churches and the two Union school-houses are handsome edifices. The *Michigan State Penitentiary*, with spacious stone buildings, is located here, and the *Passenger Depot* of the Michigan Central R. R. is the finest in the State. The manufactures are extensive and various. At *Parma*, 11 miles beyond Jackson, the road reaches the Kalamazoo River, which it follows to Kalamazoo, passing through a fertile country noted for its wheat. *Marshall* (785 miles) is a very pretty town of 5,000 inhabitants, noted for its flour; and *Battle Creek* (798 miles) is a milling city of 6,000 inhabitants, at the confluence of Battle Creek and the Kalamazoo River. Twenty-three miles beyond Battle Creek is **Kalamazoo** (*Burdick House, Kalamazoo*), the largest village in Michigan, with a population of about 10,000. It is regularly laid out, with broad well-shaded streets, and contains many fine business structures and costly residences. The buildings of the *State Lunatic Asylum* are spacious and imposing; and *Kalamazoo College* (Baptist) and the *Michigan Female Seminary* are flourishing institutions. The manufactories are numerous and varied. *Niles* (868 miles) is a handsome and well-built city of 5,000 inhabitants on the St. Joseph's River, in the midst of a rich agricultural region. The remaining stations are unimportant, being chiefly junctions with connecting railways. **Chicago** (see p. 291).

The **Canada Southern R. R.**, connecting with the N. Y. Central at Buffalo or Suspension Bridge, and with the Michigan Central at Detroit, offers another through route from East to West. Except for the interval between Buffalo and Detroit, this route is, of course, the same as that described above. The distance is slightly greater (980 miles) from New York to Chicago), but the time of through trains is the same. As for the route traversed between Buffalo and Detroit, it is, if possible, less interesting than that of the Great Western R. R., having no important cities along the line; but the road is excellently constructed and admirably equipped. Perhaps the most interesting feature of the route is the great * *International Bridge* by which the train crosses the Niagara River from Black Rock in the United States to Fort Erie in Canada.

62. New York to Chicago via Buffalo and Cleveland.

By the New York Central & Hudson River R. R. to Buffalo, and thence by the Lake Shore & Michigan Southern R. R. Through trains, with Wagner Drawing-room and Sleeping-cars attached, run through without change of cars on this route, making the journey in about 34 hours. Distances: New York to Albany, 143 miles; to Utica, 238; to Rome, 252; to Syracuse, 291; to Rochester, 373; to Buffalo, 440 ; to Dunkirk, 480; to Erie, 528; to Cleveland, 623 ; to Toledo, 736 ; to Elkhart, 879 ; to Chicago, 979. The Erie R. R. also sells tickets by the L. S. & M. S. R. R., with which it connects (with change of cars) at Buffalo and Dunkirk.

From New York to Rochester this route is the same as Route 61. Leaving Rochester, the train runs W. to Buffalo, passing several small towns, of which the only one requiring notice is *Batavia*, which contains 4,000 inhabitants, and is laid out in broad streets, beautifully shaded. The N. Y. Institution for the Blind, one of the finest structures of the kind in the country, is located here. **Buffalo** (440 miles) is the third city in size of New York State (with a population in 1875 of 134,557), and is situated at the E. end of Lake Erie at the head of Niagara River. The great New York Central and Erie Railways, with many less important lines, terminate here, and the famous Erie Canal extends E. to the Hudson River at Albany, giving the city a commerce which surpasses that of many important maritime cities. The manufactures also are varied and extensive, and few places of its size give a better idea of the characteristic American energy and enterprise. Buffalo possesses many features which will interest the tourist if he can stay for a day or two—in which case he should consult the detailed description of the city and its environs given in Route 38.

The through train makes a short stop in the Union Depot at Buffalo, and then passes out on the tracks of the Lake Shore & Michigan Southern R. R., skirting the S. shore of Lake Erie, and in 40 miles reaching *Dunkirk* (480 miles from New York), where close connection is made with the Erie R. R. (see Route 63). Just beyond Dunkirk the road leaves New York State and crosses the upper corner of Pennsylvania to **Erie** (528 miles), an old, pleasant, and important lake city, with 20,000 inhabitants and extensive commerce and manufactures (fully described on p. 233). *Conneaut* (556 miles) is the first station in Ohio, and is noted as the landing-place of the party who first settled N. W. Ohio. *Painesville* (585 miles) is charmingly situated on Grand River, 3 miles from and about 100 ft. above Lake Erie. The valley through which the river runs is deep and picturesque, and the R. R. crosses it on a stone bridge more than 800 ft. long. Twenty-eight miles beyond Painesville the train reaches

Cleveland.

Hotels, etc.—The best hotels are the *Kennard House*, cor. St. Clair and Bank, the *Weddell House*, cor. Superior and Bank Sts., and the *Forest City House*, cor. Superior St. and Public Square. There are numerous smaller houses, some of them well kept. Several *Bridges* cross the Cuyahoga, connecting the different portions of the city, and there are 13 *horse-car* lines, intersecting the city in all directions. *Reading-rooms* at the Public Library (10,000 volumes), and at the rooms of the Cleveland Library Association, in Case Hall.

Cleveland, the second city in size and importance in Ohio, is situated on the S. shore of Lake Erie, at the mouth of the Cuyahoga River. Originally the town was confined to the E. bank of the river, but subsequently Brooklyn, or Ohio City, sprung up on the opposite side, and both parts are now united under one corporation. The greater portion of the city stands on a gravelly plain, elevated about 100 ft. above the lake. The river passes through it in a winding course, affording an excellent harbor, which has been improved by dredging out a commodious ship-channel (branching from the river near its mouth), and by the erection of 2 piers 200 ft. apart, stretching several hundred feet into the lake. On each pier is a lighthouse, and another stands on the cliff above. The city is laid out with much taste, chiefly in squares, the streets being remarkably wide and well paved. The abundance of shade-trees, chiefly elms, has given it the title of the "Forest City." The business blocks are mostly of brick and stone, from 3 to 5 stories high, and a large proportion of the dwellings are constructed of the same materials. The great stone * **Viaduct** which spans the river-valley between the two divisions of the city, on a level with the plateau, was completed in 1878, and is justly reckoned among the triumphs of American engineering. It extends from the foot of Superior St. to the junction of Pearl and Detroit Sts., is 3,211 ft. long, and cost $2,200,000.

The growth of Cleveland has been very rapid. It was laid out in 1796, but in 1830 contained only 1,000 inhabitants. It received its first impetus from the completion in 1834 of the Ohio Canal, which connects Lake Erie at this point with the Ohio River at Portsmouth. A further stimulus was given after 1850 by the development of the railroad system, and since 1860 its prosperity has been greatly increased by the rapid extension of manufacturing industry. In 1870 the population was 92,829, but it is now estimated at more than 160,000. The commerce of the city is very large, especially with Canada and the mining regions of Lake Superior. The most important manufactures are of iron and coal-oil; in the production of refined petroleum Cleveland is the first city in the world. Other important products are sulphuric acid, wooden-ware, agricultural implements, marble and stone, railroad-cars, and white lead. Pork-packing is also carried on to some extent.

The main business thoroughfare of the city is *Superior St.*, on which are the larger retail stores, banks, and hotels. Other important business streets are *Ontario*, *Water*, *Euclid Ave.*, *Merwin*, and *River* on the E. side, and *Detroit*, *Pearl*, and *Lorain* on the W. side. After leaving the business portion, which extends from the park to Erie St., **Euclid Ave.** is lined with costly residences, each surrounded by ample grounds, and is considered the handsomest street in the country. *Prospect St.*, parallel to the avenue, ranks next in beauty. * **Monumental Park** is a square of 10 acres in the centre of the city, at the intersection of Ontario and Superior Sts., which divide it into 4 smaller squares. It is shaded with fine trees, and is admirably kept. In the S. E. quarter stands a statue of Commodore Perry, the hero of the battle of Lake Erie, erected in 1860 at a cost of $8,000. The pedestal is of Rhode Island granite, 12 ft. high; the statue itself is of Italian marble and is 8 ft. 2 in. high. In front of the pedestal is a marble medallion representing the passage of Perry in a small boat from the Lawrence to the Niagara during the heat of the battle. In the N. W. corner of the park there is a handsome fountain; and in the S. W. a pool and cascade. W. of the river is another park, called the *Circle*, which has a fountain in the centre, and is finely adorned with shade-trees. The United States building, fronting on the park, containing the *Custom-House*, *Post-Office*, and Federal courts, is a fine stone structure, as is also the *County Court-House*, which also fronts on the park. The *City Hall*, on Superior St., E. of Monumental Park, is a magnificent six-story building—200 × 100 ft.—with stores underneath. **＊Case Hall,** a beautiful edifice near the park, contains, besides the rooms of the Cleveland Library Association, which has a library of 15,000 volumes and a reading-room, a fine hall capable of seating 1,500 persons, and used for lectures, concerts, etc. The principal place for dramatic entertainments is the Euclid Ave. **Opera House,** a new and very handsome building, besides which there are the *Academy of Music*, the *Globe Theatre*, a Bohemian theatre, a German theatre, a Theatre Comique, and several public halls for lectures, etc. The **Union Depot,** built in 1866, is a massive stone structure, one of the largest of its kind in the world. On the keystone over the main entrance is a bas-relief portrait of Mr. Amasa Stone, under whose supervision the depot was built. There are similar portraits of Grant and Lincoln, and various symbolical designs upon keystones at either end of the building. The *Water-Works* stand near the lake, W. of the river. By means of a tunnel extending 6,600 ft. under the lake, pure water is obtained, which is forced by two powerful engines into a large reservoir, occupying the highest point W. of the river, whence it is distributed through the city. The ＊ **Reservoir** is a popular resort, and affords a broad and beautiful view over the city, lake, and surrounding country.

Of the 96 churches in the city, the most noteworthy are *St. Paul's* (Episcopal), cor. Case and Euclid Aves., the *Second Presbyterian*, cor. Prospect St. and Sterling Ave., and the *Methodist Church*, cor. Erie St. and Euclid Ave., all of stone in the Gothic style. The *Roman Catholic Cathedral* is a large and handsome building; and *Trinity Church* (Episcopal) is an imposing edifice, also in the Gothic style. The *First* and *Third Presbyterian* churches are fine structures. Among the educational institutions, the *Cleveland Medical College*, founded in 1843, is the most important. It occupies an imposing structure at the corner of Erie and St. Clair Sts. The *Cleveland Female Seminary*, in Woodland Ave., is a fine building; and the two High-School buildings are handsome edifices of brick and stone. The *Public Library*, opened in 1869, contains about 10,000 volumes. It is free, and is supported by an annual tax upon the citizens of one-tenth of a mill, which produced in 1870 a revenue of $4,000.

On the shore of the lake, near the Medical College, stands the extensive building of the *U. S. Marine Hospital*. The *Charity Hospital*, in Perry St., was established partly by the city and partly by private subscriptions, and is attended by the Sisters of Charity. The *Homœopathic Hospital* has a large and handsome building on Huron St. Connected with it is a Homœopathic College, which is a flourishing institution, admitting female students. The *Work House*, on the E. outskirts of the city, is a large and handsome structure, for the confinement and utilizing of city offenders. The *City Infirmary*, to which the sick and homeless poor are taken, has attached to it a good farm, which is worked by the inmates of the institution.

Cleveland has four beautiful cemeteries. *City Cemetery*, in Erie St., is laid out with rectangular walks shaded with trees, and contains many fine monuments. *Woodland Cemetery*, more recently opened, is in the E. part of the city. It is prettily laid out with paths winding amid noble trees and abundant shrubbery, and is rich in monuments and statuary. *Lake View Cemetery*, containing 300 acres, is in Euclid Ave., about 5 miles from the city. It is 250 ft. above the level of the lake, commands extensive views, and, though only opened in 1870, has already been greatly beautified and adorned. *Riverside Cemetery* on the S. side has a picturesque location.

Leaving Cleveland the train passes the pretty villages of *Berea* and *Elyria*, and in 30 miles reaches *Oberlin* (653 miles from New York), noted as the seat of Oberlin College, from which no person is excluded on account of sex or color. This college, founded in 1834, combines manual labor with study, inculcates entire social equality between whites and blacks, and has had a prosperous career. The next important station is **Toledo** (*Boody House, Oliver House, Island*), which within a few years has developed from an inconsiderable village into a large and rapidly-growing city. In 1850 the population was 3,820; in 1870 it was 31,693, and is now estimated at 50,000. It is situated on the Maumee River, 4 miles from a broad and beautiful bay, and 12 miles from Lake Erie, of which it is regarded as one of the ports. Its commerce is very large, consisting chiefly of the handling of grain; and its manufactures are numerous and important, including car-factories, iron-works, locomotive-shops, furniture-factories, flour-mills, and breweries. The city is regularly laid out, having wide streets that give an easy ascent from the harbor to the table-land on which most of the houses are built. It has large and handsome public buildings, several neat parks, street railroads, and costly water-works. Toledo communicates with Cincinnati by the Miami & Erie Canal, and is the converging point of 13 railroad lines. Six of these lines concentrate at the *Union Depot*, an immense and imposing structure. The *Public Library* contains 10,000 volumes, and there are several handsome churches. The principal charitable institutions are the City Hospital, St. Vincent's Hospital, House of Refuge and Correction, Home for Friendless Women, and 3 orphan asylums.

At Toledo the road branches, one branch running through Indiana and known as the Air Line Div., and the other running through Southern Michigan and known as the Michigan Southern Div. The former is the one followed by the through trains, and the same rich agricultural country, numerously sprinkled with small towns, is traversed by both. **Adrian** (769 miles, *Lawrence Hotel*) is the largest city in Southern Michigan, with a population in 1870 of 8,438. It is well built, and has prosperous manufactures. There is a fine Soldiers' Monument to the 77 citizens of Adrian who fell in the civil war, and the Central Union School-building is one of the finest in the West. At *Elkhart* (879 miles) the two divisions of the road unite again; and the route from there to Chicago is through a level prairie-country which has been well described as having "a face but no features." **South Bend** (894 miles, *Grand Central Hotel, Dwight House*) is a busy manufacturing city of 11,000 inhabitants, one of the chief places in northern Indiana, situated in a great bend of the St. Joseph River, which is navigable to this point and affords a good water-power. The Court-House here is one of the finest buildings in the State, and the University of Notre Dame is a Roman Catholic institution of some note. **La Porte** (921 miles, *Tea-garden House, Myers*) is a city of 7,000 inhabitants, situated on the edge of the prairie of the same name, and surrounded by an exceedingly rich agricultural country. A chain of several beautiful lakes runs N. of the city, which from their facilities for boating and bathing are a favorite summer resort. **Chicago** (see p. 291).

63. New York to Chicago via Erie Railway and Connecting Lines.

By the Erie R. R., the Atlantic and Great Western R. R., and the Pittsburg, Fort Wayne & Chicago R. R. Through trains on this route, with Pullman Parlor, Drawing-room, and Sleeping-cars attached, run without change of cars from New York to Chicago in about 36 hours. Distances : to Paterson, 17 miles ; to Turner's, 48 ; to Port Jervis, 88 ; to Susquehanna, 193 ; to Binghamton, 215 ; to Elmira, 274 ; to Hornellsville, 331 (to Buffalo, 423 ; to Dunkirk, 460) ; to Salamanca, 413 ; to Corry, 474 ; to Meadville, 515 (to Cleveland, 626) ; to Akron, 615 ; to Mansfield, 682 ; to Fort Wayne, 826 ; to Chicago, 974.

The Erie R. R. also sells through tickets to Chicago *via* the Lake Shore & Michigan Southern R. R. (with which it connects at Buffalo and Dunkirk), *via* the Canada Southern (with which it connects at Buffalo), and *via* the Great Western R. R. (with which it connects at Suspension Bridge). All these roads are described in Routes 61 and 62.

The Erie Railway, which forms the first section of this through route to the West, is one of the greatest achievements of engineering skill in this or any other country, and affords some of the grandest and most varied scenery to be found E. of the Rocky Mountains. Portions of the line were considered impassable to any other than a winged creature, yet mountains were scaled or pierced, and river-cañons passed, by blasting a path from the face of stupendous precipices ; gorges of fearful depth were spanned by bridges swung into the air ; and broad, deep valleys crossed by massive viaducts. When first completed in 1851, the road, except at a few points, lay through an almost unknown country—a country which was looked upon then pretty much as the Adirondack wilderness is now. Numerous towns and villages have since grown up along the line, but there is no such chain of populous cities as that along the N. Y. Central R. R. The great charm of the Erie route lies in its romantic and picturesque scenery.*

For the first 31 miles the road traverses the State of New Jersey,

* Our description of this route as far as Salamanca is a mere outline or summary, designed to furnish such cursory information about the places and scenery *en route* as may meet the wants of through passengers to the West. Those who desire a more detailed description will find it in the section of the work devoted to the New England and Middle States (Route 39).

passing through the great manufacturing city of *Paterson* (17 miles), famed for the beautiful falls of the Passaic. Just this side of *Sufferns Station*, it crosses the line and enters the State of New York, commencing the ascent of the famous Ramapo Valley, which is followed for 18 miles. At *Sloatsburg* (36 miles) the road passes near Greenwood Lake, a noted summer resort, around which are a number of pretty little lakes. *Turner's* (48 miles) is the most picturesque station on this portion of the line. The view from the hill N. of the station is superb, the Hudson River, with Fishkill and Newburg, being in sight. On approaching *Otisville* (76 miles), the eye is attracted by the bold flanks of the Shawangunk Mountain, the passage of which great barrier (once deemed insurmountable) is a miracle of engineering skill. A mile beyond Otisville, after traversing an ascending grade of 40 ft. to the mile, the road runs through a rock-cutting 50 ft. deep and 2,500 ft. long. This passed, the summit of the ascent is reached, and thence we go down the mountain's side many sloping miles to the valley beneath, through the midst of grand and picturesque scenery. Onward the way increases in interest, until it opens in a glimpse, away over the valley, of the mountain-spur known as the *Cuddeback*; and at its base the glittering water is seen, now for the first time, of the Delaware & Hudson Canal. Eight miles beyond Otisville we are imprisoned in a deep cut for nearly a mile, and, on emerging from it, there lies spread before us (on the right) the rich and lovely valley and waters of the *Neversink*. Beyond sweeps a chain of blue hills, and at their feet, terraced high, gleam the roofs and spires of the town of *Port Jervis* (88 miles); while to the S. the eye rests upon the waters of the Delaware, along the banks of which the line runs for the next 90 miles. Three miles beyond Port Jervis the train crosses the Delaware into the State of Pennsylvania, which it traverses for 26 m. to Delaware Bridge, where it again enters New York. Near *Shohola* (107 miles) some of the greatest obstacles of the entire route were encountered, and for several miles the roadway was hewed out of the solid cliff-side at a cost of $100,000 a mile. *Lackawaxen* (111 miles) is a pretty village at the confluence of the Lackawaxen Creek and Delaware River. Here the Delaware is spanned by an iron suspension bridge supporting the aqueduct by which the D. & H. Canal crosses the river. The country around *Narrowsburg* (123 miles) was the theatre of the stirring incidents of Cooper's novel, "The Last of the Mohicans." Beyond Narrowsburg for some miles the scenery is uninteresting and the stations unimportant.

At *Deposit* (177 miles) the valley of the Delaware is left, and we begin the ascent of the high mountain-ridge which separates it from the lovely valley of the Susquehanna. As the train descends into the latter valley, there opens suddenly on the right a picture of bewitching beauty. This first glimpse of the *Susquehanna* is esteemed one of the finest points of the varied scenery of the Erie route. A short distance below, we cross the great *Starucca Viaduct*, 1,200 ft. long and 110 ft. high, constructed at a cost of $320,000. From the vicinity of *Susquehanna*, the next station (193 miles), the viaduct itself makes a most effective feature of the valley views. For a few miles beyond Susque-

hanna the route still lies amid mountain-ridges, but these are soon left
behind, and we enter upon a beautiful hilly and rolling country, thickly
dotted with villages and towns. **Binghamton** (215 miles) is a flourishing city of 16,000 inhabitants, an important railroad center, and
the site of the Asylum for Chronic Insane. Twenty-two miles farther is
Owego, a large and prosperous manufacturing town, and then comes
Elmira (274 miles), the most important city on the road, with a population of 15,863. At *Hornellsville* (332 miles) we reach the last and
least interesting division of the road, and soon after begin to descend
to the Lake Erie level, passing through a wild and desolate region,
with few marks of human habitation. At *Salamanca* (413 miles) the
train takes the track of the Atlantic & Great Western R. R.

Passengers holding through tickets *via* Buffalo take the Buffalo Div. of the Erie
R. R. at Hornellsville, and pass in 92 miles to Buffalo. The scenery at **Portage** on
this division is considered by many the finest on the entire road, but the traveler
must leave the cars and visit the Falls in order to enjoy it. The famous * Portage
Bridge, by which the train crosses the Genesee River, is worthy of attention. At
Buffalo the passenger for Chicago takes either of the routes mentioned at the head
of this route. Passengers holding tickets *via* Dunkirk continue on the Erie main
line from Salamanca, traversing a dreary and uninteresting wilderness. At Dunkirk, connection is made with the Lake Shore and Michigan Southern R. R. (see
Route 62).

From Salamanca the Atlantic and Great Western R. R. runs S. W.
along the forest-clad valley of the Allegany River, enters the Conewango Valley, and in 34 miles reaches **Jamestown** (*Weeks House,
Jamestown*), a popular summer resort on the Chautauqua Outlet. **Chautauqua Lake** is the farthest W. of all the New York lakes, being
bounded on two sides by Pennsylvania. It is 18 miles long and 1 to 3
wide, and is said to be the highest navigable water on the continent,
being 730 ft. above Lake Erie and 1,291 ft. above the sea. A steamer
runs twice a day from Jamestown in 22 miles to **Mayville** (*Chautauqua House, Mayville House*), another popular summer resort at the
N. end of the lake. The lake is surrounded by hills 500 to 600 ft.
high, and affords some attractive scenery. Passing S. W. from Jamestown, the train soon crosses the line and enters Pennsylvania. **Corry**
(474 miles) is a city of 7,000 inhabitants which has sprung up since
1861 as the product of the oil business. It lies at the entrance of the
Pennsylvania Oil-Regions (see Route 53), and is at the intersection of
several important railways which have given it its prosperity. Beyond
Corry the road descends the valley of French Creek, along the banks
of which are several of the principal wells in the oil region. *Venango*
(505 miles) is in this valley. Ten miles beyond Venango is **Meadville**
(*Commercial Hotel, McHenry House*), a city of 8,000 inhabitants, with
important manufactures and an extensive trade with the oil regions.
It lies on the E. bank of French Creek, and is one of the oldest towns
W. of the Alleghanies. The business portion of the city is compactly
built, and there are a handsome Court House, a State Arsenal, an Opera
House, and a Public Library with 3,000 volumes. *Allegheny College*
(Methodist) occupies 3 buildings on a hill N. of the city. It was founded
in 1817, and has libraries with 12,000 volumes. The *Meadville Theo-*

logical School (Unitarian) was established in 1844, and has a library of 12,000 volumes. *Greendale Cemetery*, in the suburbs, is well laid out, and tastefully adorned.

A short distance beyond Meadville the road leaves the French Creek, and, passing several small stations, enters the State of Ohio near *Orangeville* (554 miles), which is the first station in Ohio. From *Leavittsbury* (578 miles) the Mahoning Div. diverges, and runs in 49 miles to **Cleveland** (see p. 273). *Ravenna* (598 miles) is a flourishing manufacturing town on the Pennsylvania & Ohio Canal, which affords a good water-power. It is also the point of shipment for large quantities of cheese, butter, grain, and wool. Seventeen miles beyond Ravenna is **Akron** (*Sumner House, Empire Hotel*), a city of 10,000 inhabitants at the intersection of the Penn. & Ohio and Ohio & Erie canals. The canals and the Little Cuyahoga River furnish ample water-power for numerous mills, factories, etc. The chief articles of manufacture are flour and woolen goods. The city is 400 ft. above Lake Erie, being the highest ground on the line of the canal between the lake and the Ohio River. In the vicinity are immense beds of mineral fire-proof paint, which is exported to all parts of the country. Beyond Akron the road traverses a rich agricultural country, passing 6 or 8 small towns, and soon reaches **Mansfield** (*St. James Hotel, Wiler*), a city of 8,000 inhabitants, compactly built on a beautiful and commanding elevation in the midst of a fertile and populous region. It has a number of handsome public buildings, including several of the churches and schoolhouses, and the *Court House*, which cost $227,000. Many of the residences are costly, and surrounded by spacious ornamental grounds. The principal manufactures are of threshing machines, machinery, woolens, paper, furniture, and flour.

At Mansfield the Atlantic & Great Western R. R. is intersected by the Pittsburg, Fort Wayne & Chicago R. R., which is followed by the through trains to Chicago. *Crestline* (695 miles) is at the crossing of the Cleveland, Columbus, Cincinnati & Indianapolis R. R. (Route 67). *Bucyrus* (707 miles) is a thriving village on the Sandusky River, with several mineral springs and a well of inflammable gas in the vicinity. An excellent specimen of a mastodon was found in a marsh near here in 1838. *Forest* (734 miles) is at the crossing of the Cincinnati, Sandusky & Cleveland R. R., and *Lima* (765 miles) is at the crossing of the Cincinnati, Hamilton & Dayton R. R. Some manufacturing is done at Lima, and the Union School building is a handsome edifice. **Fort Wayne** (*Aveline House, Mayer*) is known as the "Summit City," from the fact that it is on the watershed from which the streams run E. and W. It is situated at the point where the Maumee River is formed by the confluence of the St. Joseph and the St. Mary's, and takes its name from an old frontier fort which was built here in 1794, and which was retained as a military station until 1819. It is one of the chief cities of Indiana, with a population of 30,000, and extensive manufactures, the water-power for which is furnished by the river and by the Wabash & Erie Canal. The vast machine-shops of the Pittsburg, Fort Wayne & Chicago R. R. and of the Toledo, Wabash &

Western R. R. are located here. The former cover 6 acres. The city is well built, most of the business blocks and many of the residences being of brick. Among the public buildings are the *Court House,* which cost $80,000, and the *County Jail.* Prominent educational institutions are the *Concordia College* (Lutheran) and the *Fort Wayne College* (Methodist). There are 3 public parks, and W. of the city is a trotting-park. Of the 5 cemeteries, the largest and handsomest is *Linden-wood* 1½ mile W. of the city. *Warsaw* (864 miles) is a thriving town, pleasantly situated on the Tippecanoe River. At *Plymouth* (888 miles) the present route is intersected by the Indianapolis, Peru & Chicago R. R., and at *Wanatah* (919 miles) by the Louisville, New Albany & Chicago R. R. **Chicago** (see p. 291).

64. New York to Chicago via Philadelphia and Pittsburg.

By the Pennsylvania R. R. and the Pittsburg, Fort Wayne & Chicago R. R. The Pennsylvania R. R., formerly a merely local line between Philadelphia and Pittsburg, is now a vast corporation, including upward of 1,700 miles of track under a single management. It is one of the great highways of traffic and travel between the Atlantic coast and the Western States, and through trains, with Pullman Palace Drawing-room and Sleeping-cars attached, run through without change of cars from New York via Philadelphia to Chicago, Cincinnati, St. Louis, and Louisville. The time from New York to Chicago is 34 to 36 hours. Distances : to Newark, 9 miles ; to New Brunswick, 31 ; to Trenton, 57 ; to Philadelphia, 90; to Lancaster, 158 ; to Harrisburg, 195 ; to Altoona, 327 ; to Cresson, 342 ; to Johnstown, 365 ; to Pittsburg, 444 ; to Mansfield, 620 ; to Fort Wayne, 764 ; to Chicago, 913.

The station in Jersey City is reached by ferries from the foot of Desbrosses and Cortlandt Sts. The route across New Jersey is through a flat and featureless country, which would be monotonous but for the numerous cities and towns along the line.* **Newark** (9 miles) contains 100,000 inhabitants, and is the largest city and chief manufacturing center of New Jersey, but offers few attractions to the tourist. The *Passaic Flour Mills* turn out 2,000 barrels of flour daily, and there are large manufactories of india-rubber goods, boots and shoes, carriages, paper, and jewelry. *Broad St.* is the principal thoroughfare, and the *U. S. Custom House* and *Post Office,* the *City Hall,* the *Court House,* the *Newark Academy,* and several of the churches, are fine buildings. **Elizabeth** (15 miles) is the handsomest city in New Jersey, and contains many fine residences of New York business men, a few of which are visible from the cars. **New Brunswick** (31 miles) is a city of 20,000 inhabitants at the head of navigation on the Raritan River, and is noted for possessing the most extensive india-rubber factories in the United States, and as the site of *Rutgers College,* an ancient and flourishing institution. *Princeton* (48 miles) is

---

* Our description of this route as far as Pittsburg is a mere outline or summary, designed to furnish such cursory information about the places and scenery *en route* as may meet the wants of through passengers to the West. Those who desire a more detailed description will find it in the section of the work devoted to the New England and Middle States (Routes 3 and 46).

chiefly known as the seat of **Princeton College,** one of the oldest and most famous institutions of learning in America. Several of the college buildings are very costly and handsome structures, standing amid ample, well-shaded grounds. **Trenton** (57 miles), the capital of New Jersey, is pleasantly situated at the head of navigation on the Delaware River, and contains some fine public buildings. The *State House* is a picturesque old building, occupying a commanding site near the river. The *U. S. Post Office*, the *State Lunatic Asylum*, the *State Penitentiary*, and the *State Arsenal*, are among the other edifices worthy of notice. On leaving Trenton the train crosses the Delaware on a bridge 1,100 ft. long, and follows the right bank of the river to *Frankford*, where it turns W. and swings round the N. portion of the great city of **Philadelphia,** the second in size in the United States, to the station in W. Philadelphia (32d and Market Sts). The city of Philadelphia is fully described in Route 4.

Leaving the station in W. Philadelphia, the train passes in sight of Fairmount Park, traverses a pleasant suburban region, and enters one of the richest agricultural districts in America, which is traversed for nearly 100 miles. The size and solidity of the houses and barns, and the perfection of the cultivation, will be apt to remind the tourist rather of the best farming districts of England than of what he usually sees in the United States. *Paoli* (109 miles) was the scene of a battle fought Sept. 20, 1777, in which the British under General Gray surprised and defeated the Americans under Gen. Wayne. The battle is commonly called the "Paoli massacre" because a large number of the Americans were killed after they had laid down their arms. A marble monument, erected in 1817, marks the site of the battle-field. Beyond Paoli the scenery grows more picturesque, and fine views are had of the beautiful Chester Valley. *Downington* (122 miles) is the terminus of the Chester Valley R. R., and is near the marble quarries which supplied the marble from which Girard College (in Phila.) was built. At *Coatesville* (128 miles) the W. branch of the Brandywine is crossed on a bridge 850 ft. long and 75 ft. high. *Gap* (141 miles) is so named because it lies in the gap by which the road passes from the Chester Valley to the Pequea Valley. The scenery in the vicinity is attractive. **Lancaster** (158 miles) is pleasantly situated near the Conestoga Creek, which is crossed in entering the city. It was incorporated in 1818, and was at one time the principal inland town of Pennsylvania, being the seat of the State government from 1799 to 1812. It is now a prosperous manufacturing city of 20,000 inhabitants, containing many fine public buildings, among which are the *Court House*, the *County Prison*, *Fulton Hall*, and *Franklin and Marshall College* (Dutch Reformed). Lancaster has extensive manufactures of locomotives, axes, carriages, etc., and has navigable communication by canal and river with Baltimore. The only station between Lancaster and Harrisburg which requires mention is *Middletown* (186 miles), an important shipping-point on the Susquehanna River at the mouth of Swatara Creek. It has extensive iron-works and machine-shops, and is the terminus of the Union Canal. Nine miles beyond is **Harrisburg** (195 miles), the capital of the State of Pennsylvania, beautifully situated on the E. bank of the Susquehanna River, which is here a mile wide and spanned by 2 bridges. The city is handsomely built, and is surrounded by beautiful scenery. The *State House*, finely situated on an eminence near the center, is a spacious brick building in the classic style, and is plainly visible from the cars. The other important public buildings are the *State Arsenal*, the *Court House*, the *State Lunatic Asylum*, the *County Prison*, the market houses, the school houses, and several handsome churches. The iron-manufactures of Harrisburg are extensive, and 6 important railways converge here.

About 5 miles above Harrisburg the railroad crosses the Susquehanna on a splendid bridge, 3,670 ft. long; the * view from the center of this bridge is one of the finest on the line. Near *Cove Station* (10 miles from Harrisburg) the Cove Mt. and Peter's Mt. are seen, and from this point to within a short distance of Pittsburg the scenery is superb, and in places grand beyond description. *Duncannon* (210 miles) is at the entrance of the beautiful Juniata Valley, which is followed for about 100 miles to the base of the Alleghany Mts. The landscape of the Juniata is in the highest degree picturesque; the mountain background, as continuously seen across the river from the cars, being often strikingly bold and majestic. The passage of the river through the Great Tuscarora Mt., 1 mile W. of *Millerstown* (228 miles), is especially fine. Four miles beyond *Mifflin* (244 miles) the train enters the wild and romantic gorge known as the ***Long Narrows,** which is traversed by the railway, highway, river, and canal. *Mount Union* (281 miles) is at the entrance of the gap of Jack's Mountain, and 3 miles beyond is the famous Sidling Hill and still further W. the Broad Top Mountain. *Huntingdon* (293 miles) is a flourishing village on the Juniata, finely situated, and surrounded by beautiful scenery.

At *Petersburg* (300 miles) the railroad parts company with the canal and follows the Little Juniata, which it again leaves at *Tyrone* (313 miles) to enter the Tuckahoe Valley, famous for its iron ore. At the head of the Tuckahoe Valley and at the foot of the Alleghanies is **Altoona** (327 miles), a handsome city of 15,000 inhabitants, built up since 1850, when it was a primitive forest, by being selected as the site of the vast machine shops of the Pennsylvania R. R. All the trains stop here for meals, and many travelers arriving here in the evening remain over night in order to cross the Alleghanies by daylight. Just beyond Altoona the ascent of the Alleghanies begins, and in the course of the next 11 miles some of the finest scenery and the greatest feats of engineering on the entire line are to be seen. Within this distance the road mounts to the tunnel at the summit by so steep a grade that, while in the ascent, double power is required to move the train. The entire 11 miles of descent are run without steam, the speed of the train being regulated by the "brakes." At one point there is a curve as short as the letter U, and that, too, where the grade is so steep that in looking across from side to side it seems that, were the tracks laid contiguous to each other, they would form a letter X. The road hugs the sides of the mountains, and from the windows next to the valley the traveler can look down on houses and trees dwarfed to toys, while men and animals appear like ants from the great elevation. Going W., the left-hand, and coming E. the right-hand, side of the cars is most favorable for enjoying the scenery. The summit of the mountain is pierced by a tunnel 3,670 ft. long, through which the train passes before commencing to descend the W. slope. The much-visited **Cresson Springs** are 2¼ miles beyond the tunnel, 3,000 ft. above the sea. There are 7 mineral springs here, and the hotels and cottages, accommodating about 2,000 guests, are apt to be thronged in summer. In descending the mountains from Cresson the remains of another railroad are constantly seen, sometimes above and sometimes below the track followed by the trains. This was the old Portage R. R., by which, in the ante-locomotive days, loaded canal-boats were carried over the mountains in sections by inclined planes and joined together at the foot. The stream which is almost continuously in sight during the descent is the Conemaugh Creek, which is crossed by a stone viaduct near *Conemaugh Station* (363 miles), the terminus of the mountain division of the road.

From the foot of the mountains to Pittsburg the road traverses a rich farming region, the scenery of which, though pleasing, will be apt to seem somewhat tame after the magnificent panorama of the Alleghanies. *Johnstown* (365 miles) is a busy manufacturing borough at the confluence of the Conemaugh with Stony Creek. The Cambria Iron-Works, seen to the right of the road, are among the most extensive in America. At *Blairsville Intersection* (390 miles) the road branches, the main line running to Pittsburg by *Latrobe* (403 miles) and *Greensburg* (413 miles); while the Western Div. runs to Allegheny City by *Blairsville* (393 miles). The former is the route followed by the through trains. **Pittsburg** (444 miles) is the second city of Pennsylvania in population and importance, and one of the chief manufacturing cities of the United States. It occupies the delta at the confluence of the Alleghany and Monongahela Rivers, with several populous suburbs on the opposite banks, and in 1875 had an estimated population of 140,000. **Allegheny City,** with a population of 55,000, lies just across the Alleghany River, and contains many costly residences of Pittsburg merchants. In both cities are numerous places of interest, in seeing which two or three days may be pleasantly and profitably spent, and such tourists as can spare the requisite time should consult the detailed description of the two cities given in Route 46. Such glimpses of Pittsburg as are obtained from the cars are not prepossessing, and the heavy pall of smoke that constantly overhangs it and renders the atmosphere murky will be apt to be the most prominent impression left in the mind of the passing tourist.

After a short stop in the great Union Depot at Pittsburg, the train passes out on the tracks of the Pittsburg, Fort Wayne & Chicago R. R., crosses the Alleghany River in full view of several handsome bridges, runs through the heart of Allegheny City, and sweeps past a number of small suburban villages to *Rochester* (26 miles from Pittsburg, 470 from New York), at the confluence of the Ohio and Beaver Rivers. From Rochester the train runs N. up the Beaver River, passing the busy manufacturing towns of *New Brighton* and *Beaver Falls*, and at *Homewood* (479 miles) turns W., and in about 15 miles enters the State of Ohio. *Salem* (514 miles) is the first important station in Ohio, and is a neat manufacturing village, surrounded by a very rich and highly-cultivated farming country. At *Alliance* (528 miles) the through cars for Cleveland take the track of the Cleveland & Pittsburg R. R., and run in 3½ hours to **Cleveland** (see p. 273). The Chicago train passes on to **Canton** (546 miles, *St. Cloud Hotel*), a city of 9,000 inhabitants, beautifully situated on Nimishillen Creek, and surrounded by a fertile farming country, which enjoys the distinction of sending more wheat to market than any other portion of the State. Bituminous coal and limestone are found in the vicinity, and considerable manufacturing is carried on. **Massillon** (554 miles, *American House*) is a flourishing manufacturing city of 7,000 inhabitants, situated on the Tuscarawas River and the Ohio Canal, by which it has water communication with Lake Erie. It is regularly laid out, is substantially and compactly built, and contains many handsome residences and an Opera House costing $100,000. It is surrounded by one of the most productive coal-fields of the State, and the coal obtained here has a wide reputation. The Massillon white sandstone, which is largely quarried, is shipped to all parts of the country. Large shipments of iron-ore, wool, flour, and grain are also made, and the manufactures are varied and important. Several small stations are now passed, of which the principal is *Wooster* (579 miles), and then comes **Mansfield** (620 miles), which has already been described (see p. 279). From this point to Chicago the route is the same as in Route 63.

65. Baltimore to Chicago and Cincinnati.

By the Baltimore and Ohio R. R., which forms one of the great through routes between the Atlantic seaboard and the Western States. With its various branch lines it controls 1,820 miles of road, and has for its western termini the principal cities of the interior. Through trains, with Pullman Palace Parlor and Sleeping-cars attached, run through without change from Baltimore to Chicago, Columbus, Cincinnati, and St. Louis. The time to Chicago is 36 hours, to Cincinnati, about 24 hours, to St. Louis, 38 hours. Distances: to Relay Station, 9 miles; to Washington, 40; to Point of Rocks, 69; to Harper's Ferry, 81; to Martinsburg, 100; to Cumberland, 178; to Grafton, 280; (to Parkersburg, 384; to Chillicothe, 481; to Cincinnati, 589; to Louisville, 696; to St. Louis, 929;) to Bellaire, 376; (to Wheeling, 379); to Zanesville, 454; to Newark, 480; (to Columbus, 513); to Mansfield, 542; to Chicago Junction, 568; to Chicago, 839.

THE grandeur of the scenery along the line of the Baltimore & Ohio R. R. makes it one of the most attractive routes that tourists can take, and it possesses the additional interest of having been the theatre of some of the most exciting scenes in the late civil war, during which it suffered severely by the destruction of its track, bridges, and rolling-stock. The terminal station in Baltimore is in Camden St. near Howard, and in leaving the city the train no sooner emerges from the dingy suburbs than the pleasures of the trip commence. The first object of interest is the *Carrollton Viaduct*, a fine bridge of dressed granite, with

an arch of 80 ft. span, over Gwinn's Falls, beyond which the road soon
enters the long and deep excavation under the Washington turnpike.
Less than a mile farther the "deep cut" is encountered, famous for its
difficulties in the early history of the road. It is 76 ft. deep, and nearly
½ mile long. Beyond this the road crosses the deep ravine of Robert's
Run, and, skirting the ore-banks of the old Baltimore Iron Company,
now covered by a dense forest of cedar-trees, comes to the long and
deep embankment over the valley of Gadsby's Run, and the heavy cut
through Vinegar Hill immediately following it. At the *Relay Station*
(9 miles) the road branches, the main line striking westward through
Ellicott City (14 miles), *Elysville* (20 miles), *Mount Airy* (42 miles), and
Monocacy (58 miles); while the Washington Branch diverges to Washington City. The latter route is the one taken by the through-trains.
Just beyond Relay Station the famous * *Washington Viaduct* is crossed,
a magnificent piece of masonry whose arches rest on seven lofty piers.
The scenery in this vicinity is very attractive, and a fine summer hotel
has been erected on the E. side of the river. *Elk Ridge* (10 miles) is
a small manufacturing village on the Patapsco; and *Hanover* (12 miles)
is near the iron-mines which supply the Avalon Furnaces. At *Annapolis
Junction* (19½ miles) the Annapolis & Elk Ridge R. R. diverges to Annapolis, the capital of Maryland, which is worth a visit if the traveler
have time. From *Alexandria Junction* (34 miles) a branch-road diverges
to Shepherd, opposite Alexandria, and 5 miles beyond the train enters
Washington City, the capital of the Republic. The first view of the
Capitol in approaching the city from this direction is exceedingly fine,
and should not be lost—the dome presents "such majesty and whiteness as you never saw elsewhere." Owing to the number and magnificence of its public buildings Washington is one of the most interesting
cities in America, and no tourist should pass through without stopping
at least long enough to visit its principal places of interest. A detailed
description of the city and its environs, with illustrative cuts, will be
found in the portion of the book devoted to the New England and Middle States (Route 8).

From Washington to Point of Rocks (where the main line is again
reached) the road traverses a beautiful champaign country extending to
the Catoctin Mountains, a continuation of the Blue Ridge. *Point of
Rocks* (69 miles) takes its name from a bold promontory, which is
formed by the profile of the Catoctin Mountain, against the base of
which the Potomac River runs on the Maryland side, the mountain
towering up on the opposite (Virginia) shore, forming the other barrier
to the pass. The railroad passes the Point by a tunnel, 1,500 ft. long,
cut through the solid rock. Beyond, the ground becomes comparatively
smooth, and the railroad, leaving the immediate margin of the river to
the Chesapeake & Ohio Canal, runs along the base of gently-sloping
hills, passing the villages of Berlin and Knoxville, and reaching the
Weverton Factories, in the pass to the *South Mountain*, near which was
fought the desperate battle of South Mountain (Sept. 14, 1862). From
South Mountain to Harper's Ferry the road lies along the foot of a
precipice for the greater part of the distance of 3 miles, the last of

which is immediately under the rocky cliffs of Elk Mountain, forming the N. side of this noted pass. The Shenandoah River enters the Potomac just below the bridge over the latter, and their united currents rush rapidly over the broad ledges of rock which stretch across their bed. The length of the bridge, over river and canal, is about 900 ft., and at its W. end it bifurcates, the left-hand branch connecting with the Valley Branch of the B. & O. R. R., which passes directly up the Shenandoah, and the right-hand carrying the main road, by a strong curve in that direction, up the Potomac. **Harper's Ferry** (81 miles) is delightfully situated in Jefferson Co., W. Virginia, at the confluence of the Potomac and Shenandoah Rivers, the town itself being compactly but irregularly built around the base of a hill. Before the civil war it was the seat of an extensive and important United States armory and arsenal; but these were destroyed during the war, and have not been rebuilt. The scenery around Harper's Ferry is wonderfully picturesque. Thomas Jefferson pronounced the passage of the Potomac through the Blue Ridge "one of the most stupendous scenes in Nature, and well worth a voyage across the Atlantic to witness." The tourist should stop here for at least one day, and climb either Maryland Heights (across the Potomac) or Bolivar Heights (above the town). Apart from its scenery, the chief interest pertaining to Harper's Ferry (which is now a decadent village of about 1,200 inhabitants) is historical. It was the scene of the exploits which in October, 1859, rendered the name of John Brown, of Ossawattomie-Kansas notoriety, still more notorious; and Charlestown, the county-seat where Brown and his followers were tried and executed, is only 7 miles distant on the road to Winchester. During the civil war Harper's Ferry was alternately in the hands of the Federals and Confederates, and a detailed narrative of its changing fortunes would reflect with fidelity the vicissitudes of the war itself.

A short distance beyond Harper's Ferry the road leaves the Potomac and passes up the ravine of Elk Branch, which, at first narrow and serpentine, widens gradually until it almost loses itself in the rolling table-land which characterizes the "Valley of Virginia." The head of Elk Branch is reached in about 9 miles, and thence the line descends gradually over an undulating country to the crossing of Opequan Creek. Beyond the crossing, the road enters the open valley of Tuscarora Creek, which it crosses twice and follows to **Martinsburg** (100 miles), where the railroad company have built extensive shops. The town contains about 5,000 inhabitants, and is pleasantly situated on an elevated plateau above Tuscarora Creek, which affords a fine water-power. Much fighting occurred in this vicinity during the civil war, and in June, 1861, the Confederates destroyed 87 locomotives and 400 cars belonging to the B. & O. R. R. The Cumberland Valley R. R. (Route 54) runs from Martinsburg to Harrisburg in 94 miles. Seven miles beyond Martinsburg the road crosses North Mountain by a long excavation, and enters a poor and thinly-settled district covered chiefly with a forest in which stunted pine prevails. The Potomac is again reached at a point opposite the ruins of Fort Frederick, on the Maryland side. *Sir John's Run* (128

Harper's Ferry.

miles) is but a few miles from **Berkeley Springs** (see Route 118), and just beyond the station the track sweeps around the Cacapon Mountain, opposite the remarkable insulated hill called " Round Top." The next point of interest is the *Doe Gulley Tunnel* (1,200 ft. long), the approaches to which are very imposing. The *Paw-Paw Tunnel* is next reached, and, after passing through some 20 miles of rugged and impressive scenery, the train crosses the N. branch of the Potomac by a viaduct 700 ft. long and enters Maryland. **Cumberland** (*Queen City Hotel*) is in the mountain-region of the narrow strip which forms the W. part of Maryland, and in point of population and commerce is its second city. The entrance to the city is beautiful, and displays the noble amphitheatre in which it lies to great advantage. The city itself has a population of about 8,000, and is the site of the great rolling mills of the R. R. Co. for the manufacture of steel rails. A few miles W. of Cumberland, upon the summit of the Alleghanies, begins the district known as the Cumberland coal-region, which extends W. to the Ohio River. Vast quantities of this coal are sent E. by the railroad and by the Chesapeake & Ohio Canal, which has its W. terminus at Cumberland and runs to tide-water at Georgetown. At Cumberland the Pittsburg Div. diverges, and runs in 150 miles to **Pittsburg** (see p. 209). From Cumberland to Piedmont (28 miles) the scenery is remarkably picturesque. For the first 22 miles to the mouth of New Creek, the Knobly Mountain bounds the valleys of the N. branch of the Potomac on the left, and Will's and Dan's Mountains on the right; thence to Piedmont, the river lies in the gap which it has cut through the latter mountain. The crossing of the Potomac from Maryland to W. Virginia is 21 miles from Cumberland, and the view from the bridge, both up and down the river, is very fine. At *Piedmont* (206 miles) the ascent of the Alleghanies is commenced, and *Altamont* (223 miles) is upon the extreme summit of the range 2,720 ft. above the sea. From Altamont westward for nearly 20 miles are beautiful natural meadows (known as the "Glades") lying along the upper waters of the Youghiogheny River, and its numerous tributaries, divided by ridges of moderate elevation and gentle slope, with fine ranges of mountains in the background. Three miles beyond Altamont is the *Deer Park Hotel*, a first-class summer hotel, built and managed by the railroad company. It is 2,800 ft. above the sea, and is surrounded by grand scenery. At *Oakland* (6 miles beyond Deer Park) is the spacious *Glades Hotel*, near which are some excellent trout streams, and game in the adjacent forests. The descent from the summit plateau to Cheat River presents a succession of very heavy excavations, embankments, and tunnels, and at the foot the famous **Cheat River Valley** is crossed, with fine views on either side. For several miles on this part of the line the road runs along the steep mountain-side, presenting a succession of magnificent landscapes. Descending from Cassidy's Ridge, which forms the W. boundary of Cheat River Valley, the train soon reaches the great *Kingwood Tunnel*, which is 4,100 ft. long and cost $1,000,000; and, 2 miles beyond, *Murray's Tunnel*, 250 ft. long. **Grafton** (280 miles) is at the end of the mountain section of the road, and is a village of 2,000 inhabitants picturesquely situated on the Tygart's Valley River.

At Grafton the Parkersburg Div. diverges to Parkersburg and Cincinnati, and is described on page 290. The Chicago train runs N. W. down the Tygart's River Valley, amid a variety of pleasing scenery, and in 20 miles reaches *Fairmont*, at the head of navigation on the Monongahela River, which is here spanned by a fine suspension bridge 1,000 ft. in length, connecting Fairmont with the village of Palatine. Just beyond Fairmont the road leaves the valley of the Monongahela, and ascends the winding and picturesque ravine of Buffalo Creek. At the head of the valley, 23 miles from Fairmont, the road passes the ridge by deep cuts and a tunnel 350 ft. long, and descends the other side by the valley of Church's Fork of Fish Creek, through many windings and tunnels. Just beyond *Littleton* (337 miles) the road passes through *Board-Tree Tunnel* under a great hill which was originally crossed on a zigzag track with seven angles representing seven V's, and enters the Pan-Handle of West Virginia. *Moundsville* (368 miles) is one of two villages on the Ohio at the mouth of Grave Creek, the other being *Elizabethtown*. The approach to the Ohio at this point is very beautiful. The line, emerging from the defile of Grave Creek, passes straight over the "flats" that border the river, forming a vast rolling plain, in the middle of which looms up the great *Indian Mound*, a relic of the prehistoric inhabitants of America, 80 ft. high and 200 ft. broad at the base. About 3 miles up the river from Moundsville the "flats" terminate; and the road passes for a mile along rocky narrows washed by the river, after which it runs over wide, rich, and beautiful bottom-lands all the way to *Benwood* (375 miles), where the river is crossed and connection made with the Central Ohio Division. Four miles from Benwood, on the same side, is **Wheeling** (*McLure House*), the capital of West Virginia and a flourishing city of about 30,000 inhabitants. It has a large commerce on the Ohio River, and its manufacturing interests are extensive, including iron and nail mills, glass-works, and foundries and machine-shops. The National Road crosses the Ohio here by a graceful suspension-bridge 1,010 ft. long, and the railroad-bridge (below the city) is one of the finest in the country. The *Custom House*, of stone, also contains the Post-Office and U. S. Court room, and a new Capitol is in course of erection. There are an Odd Fellows' Hall, a Public Library with 5,000 volumes, and an Opera House. Near the city is an extensive Fair Ground, with a trotting-course.

At Benwood the Chicago train crosses the Ohio River to *Bellaire* (376 miles), whence the Central Ohio Div. runs in about 100 miles to Newark, through a productive and populous country. The principal station on this portion of the line is **Zanesville** (*Zane House, Clarendon Hotel*), a city of 21,000 inhabitants situated on both sides of the Muskingum River at the mouth of Licking River. The Muskingum is here crossed by an iron railroad bridge 538 ft. long, and by 3 other bridges. The city is well built, with wide, regular streets, lighted with gas, and has water-works costing over $500,000, street railroads, and

REFERENCES TO FIGURES.

Hotels.
1 Palmer House H 9
2 Grand Pacific G 9
3 Sherman House H 10
4 Tremont House H 10
5 Burdick House H 9
6 Metropolitan H 9

Prominent Buildings.
7 City Hall & County Court House G 10
8 Custom H. & Post O. H 9
9 Chamber of Commerce G 9
10 Chicago Tribune H 9
11 Exposition Building H 9
12 Public Library H 10
13 Academy of Sciences H 6
14 University of Chicago I 3
15 Baptist Theol'gic'l Sem. I 3
16 St. Ignatius College E 7
17 Rush Medical College H 11
18 Chicago Med College I 4
19 Cook County Hospital G 4
20 Mercy Hospital I 4
21 Home for the Fr'ndl'ss H 6
22 Prot'st'nt Orph'n Asyl. H 6
23 Water Works H 11
24 Union Depot G 9
25 Central Depot H 10
26 Wells St. Depot G 10

27 Kinzie St. Depot G 10
28 P., Ft. W. & Chi. Dep. G

Churches.
29 Unity H 12
30 Second Presbyterian H 6
31 Michigan Avenue H 5
32 Grace H 7
33 St. James H 11
34 Union Park D 10
35 Second Baptist E 9
36 Twelfth St. F 7
37 Cathedral H 11

Theatres.
38 McVicker's H 9
39 Hooley's Opera House G 10
40 Metropolitan H 10
41 Havely's H 9
42 Hamlin's H 10
43 Academy of Music F 9

Parks.
44 Lincoln H 14
45 Humboldt A 13
46 Central A 9
47 Douglas A 7
48 Union D 10
49 Lake H 9
50 Jefferson E 9

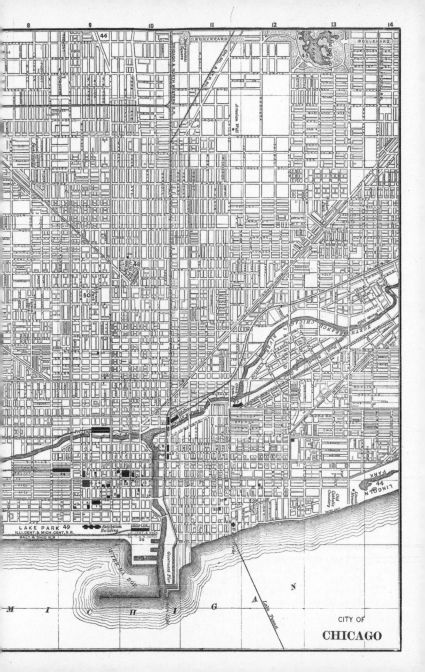

CITY OF

CHICAGO

a stone *Court-House* costing $300,000. Several of the school-build-
ings are remarkably handsome, and the *Zanesville Athenæum* has a
reading-room and a library of 5,500 volumes. The country around
Zanesville is fertile and is the source of a profitable trade ; but the
chief interest is manufacturing, for which facilities are afforded by the
water-power in the rivers and the bituminous coal, iron-ore, limestone,
and clays of the adjacent region. The Muskingum River is navigable
to *Dresden,* 17 miles above the city. **Newark** (480 miles) is at the
crossing of the Pittsburg, Cincinnati & St. Louis R. R. (Route 68), and
is described on page 301. From Newark the Central Ohio Div. passes
W. in 33 miles to **Columbus** (see p. 301). The Lake Erie Div. of the
B. & O. R. R. runs N. W. through a rich agricultural region, by numerous small towns to **Mansfield** (542 miles), which is at the junction of Routes 63 and 64, and which has already been described on
page 279. *Shelby Junction* (554 miles) is at the crossing of Route 67.
From *Chicago Junction* (568 miles) the Lake Erie Div. continues N.
to **Sandusky** (596 miles) on Lake Erie, while the Chicago Div. diverges and runs W. across northern Ohio and Indiana. This section
of the line is new, the towns *en route* are for the most part small,
and the country traversed, though extremely fertile and productive,
offers few picturesque features. *Defiance* (656 miles) is at the crossing of the Toledo, Wabash & Western R. R. (Route 74). At *Garrett*
(696 miles) most of the trains stop for meals, and between this place
and Chicago there is little to attract attention except the numerous
railways that are intersected. **Chicago** (see p. 291).

From Grafton to Cincinnati.

At Grafton, as already mentioned (see p. 288), the Parkersburg Div.
diverges from the main line and runs W. to the Ohio River. It passes
through a country which is well wooded, and rich in coal and petroleum, but without interest for the tourist, though some rugged mountain scenery is occasionally seen from the cars. *Clarksburg* (302 miles
from Baltimore) is the first station of any consequence, and is situated
on a high table-land on the W. bank of the Monongahela River, surrounded by hills. It has about 2,000 inhabitants, and in the vicinity
there are valuable mines of bituminous coal. *Petroleum* (362 miles) is
in the rich oil-regions of West Virginia, and from *Laurel Fork Junction* (364 miles), a branch road leads N. to *Volcano*, the most important place in the oil-region. At *Claysville* (377 miles) the Little Kanawha River is reached, and the train follows it for 7 miles to **Parkersburg** (*Central Hotel, Hill's*), a city of about 6,000 inhabitants with a
large trade in petroleum. Here the train crosses the Ohio River to
Belpré on a splendid bridge 1½ mile long, with 6 spans over the river
and 43 approaching spans, completed in 1871 at a cost of over $1,000,-
000. At Belpré the train passes on to the tracks of the Marietta &
Cincinnati R. R., and in 37 miles reaches **Athens** (*Warren House,
Cornell*), one of the largest towns of S. Ohio, with a population of
about 5,000, and considerable trade with the surrounding country. It

is pleasantly situated on the Hocking River, and is the seat of the *Ohio University*, founded in 1804, and the oldest college in the State. One of the *State Lunatic Asylums* is also located here, and in the vicinity are several Indian mounds similar to the one at Moundsville (see p. 289). Several small stations are now passed, and then comes the flourishing city of **Chillicothe** (*Warren House, Emmitt*), beautifully situated on a hill-environed plateau through which flows the Scioto River. Chillicothe was settled in 1796, and from 1800 to 1810 was the seat of the State government, which was afterward removed to Zanesville and then to Columbus. It now has a population of about 10,000, and is the center of nearly all the trade of the rich farming country bordering on the Scioto, one of the finest agricultural districts in the United States. Its manufactures are also important, including carriage and wagon factories, flour-mills, machine-shops, a paper-mill, etc. The city is regularly laid out, the principal avenues following the course of the river, and being intersected at right angles by others, all lighted with gas. The two main streets, which cross each other in the center of the city, are each 99 ft. wide; Water St., facing the river, is 81½ ft. wide; and the width of the others is 66 ft. There are many handsome public buildings, including 13 churches, 4 brick schoolhouses, and a *Court-House*, built of stone at a cost of over $100,000. The Ohio & Erie Canal passes through the city. Between Chillicothe and Cincinnati there is no place requiring mention, though the traveler through this portion of Ohio can not but be struck with the neatness of the villages, the fertility of the land, and the high state of cultivation to which it has been brought. **Cincinnati** (see p. 305).

66. Chicago.

Hotels.—Most of the old and well-known hotels of Chicago perished in the great fire of 1871, but those which have taken their places are probably unequaled in the world. The *Palmer House* ($3 to $5 a day) is an immense fire-proof structure of sandstone, occupying the entire block in State St., between Wabash Ave. and Monroe St. The building is one of the most imposing in the city, and its interior decorations are very fine. The *Grand Pacific Hotel* ($3 to $3 50 a day) is in no respect inferior to the preceding. It occupies half the block bounded by Jackson, Clark, Adams, and La Salle Sts., is of stone, six stories high, and is richly decorated and sumptuously furnished. The *Sherman House* ($2.50 to $4 a day), cor. Randolph and Clark Sts., is near the business center of the city. The *Tremont House* ($2.50 to $4.50 a day), cor. Lake and Dearborn Sts., is one of the finest of the new buildings. Good hotels on a more modest scale are: the *Burdick House* ($2.50 a day), cor. Wabash Ave. and Adams St.; the *Gardner House* ($3 a day), cor. Michigan Ave. and Jackson St.; the *Briggs House* ($2 a day), cor. Randolph and Wells Sts.; the *Atlantic* ($2 a day), cor. Van Buren and Sherman Sts.; and the *Commercial*, cor. Lake and Dearborn Sts. There are also good hotels on the European plan, prominent among which are *Burke's*, the *Windsor*, and the *Brevoort*.

Restaurants.—The principal restaurants are the *Palmer House* (in connection with the hotel), cor. State and Monroe Sts.; *Chapin & Gore*, in Monroe St.; *Race Bros.*, in Madison St.; *Burke's*, 140 and 142 Madison St.; *Thomson's*, Tribune Block, Dearborn St.; *Kingsley's*, 66 Washington St.; the *Vienna Bakery*, 36 Washington St.; and the *Brevoort*, 145 Madison St.

Modes of Conveyance.—*Horse-cars* (fare 5c.) traverse the city in all directions, affording cheap and easy communication. The great center of the horse-car routes is at the intersection of State and Randolph Sts. *Parmelee's omnibuses* are in waiting at the depots, and convey passengers to hotels or to other depots (fare, 50c.). There are also lines of *omnibuses* running south on Wabash Ave., and north to Lincoln Park (fare, 5c.). *Hackney-carriages* are in waiting at the depots and steamboat-landings, as well as at hotels, and around Court-House Square. The legal rates of fare are as follows : For 1 passenger from one depot to another, 50c.; for 1 passenger 1 m. or less, 50c.; over 1 m. and less than 2 m., $1; over 2 m., $1.50; each additional passenger, 50c.; children between 5 and 14 years of age, half-rates. By the hour, $2 for the first hour and $1 for each additional hour. Between midnight and 7 A. M., each trip (without regard to distance or number of passengers), $2. In case of disagreement, call for a policeman or drive to a police-station.

Railroad Depots.—The *Union Depot*, in Van Buren St. at the head of La Salle, is one of the largest and finest in the country. It is of stone, and is used by the Chicago, Rock Island & Pacific R. R., and by the Lake Shore & Michigan Southern R. R. The *Central Depot*, at the foot of Lake St., is used by the Illinois Central, Michigan Central, and the Burlington & Quincy Railroads. The *Wells Street Depot*, cor. N. Wells and Kinzie Sts., is used by the Galena Division of the Chicago & Northwestern R. R.; the *Kinzie Street Depot*, cor. Canal and West Kinzie Sts., is used by the Milwaukee and Wisconsin Divisions of the same road. The Passenger Depot of the *Pittsburg, Fort Wayne & Chicago R. R.*, and of the *Chicago & Alton R. R.*, is at the cor. of Canal and Madison Sts.; that of the *Baltimore & Ohio R. R.* at the N. end of the Exposition Building.

Theatres and Amusements.—*McVicker's Theatre*, in Madison St. near State, has a fairly good company. *Hooley's Opera House* is just W. of the Sherman House. The *Olympic Theatre* is on Clark St. opposite the Sherman House, and *Haverly's Theatre* is at the cor. of Monroe and Dearborn Sts. *Hamlin's Theatre* is at 87 Clark St., opposite the Court-House, and the *Academy of Music* is on the W. side at 88 S. Halsted St. A number of other theatres are in contemplation. The Shooting Club has a park near the Union Stock Yards (see p. 298), and in the season keeps about 25,000 pigeons in cages and houses for practice and matches.

Reading-Rooms.—At all the leading hotels there are reading-rooms for the use of guests, well supplied with newspapers. The *Public Library*, with rooms in the building cor. Dearborn and Lake Sts., contains 60,000 volumes, has an excellent reading-room, and is open from 9 A. M. to 9 P. M. The *Chicago Athenæum*, 63 and 65 Washington St., is open from 9 A. M. to 10 P. M. The *Young Men's Christian Association* has a library and reading-room at 148 Madison St., to which all are welcome (open from 8 A. M. to 10 P. M.). The *Academy of Sciences*, in Wabash Ave. near Van Buren St., has a small library and a museum. *Cobb's Library*, 173 Wabash Ave., contains 20,000 volumes, the charge for using which is 8c. a day per volume.

Clubs.—The *Chicago Club* has a handsome building in Monroe St. opposite the Palmer House. The *Union Club* is at the cor. of Chicago Ave. and State St.; the *Owl Club* is in Madison St. near State; the *Standard*, cor. Michigan Ave. and 13th St.; and the *Calumet*, cor. Michigan Ave. and 18th St. Admission to the privileges of any of these clubs is obtained only on introduction by a member.

Post-Office.—The General Post-Office is on the block bounded by Adams, Jackson, Dearborn, and Clark Sts. It is open from 8 A. M. to 7 P. M. There are, besides, 5 sub-post-offices or stations in different portions of the city. Letters may be posted in the lamp-post boxes, whence they are collected at frequent intervals by the letter-carriers.

CHICAGO, the principal city of Illinois, has within 40 years grown from a small Indian trading station to the position of the metropolis of the Northwest, and the greatest railway center on the continent. It is situated on the W. shore of Lake Michigan, at the mouth of the Chicago River, in lat. about 41° 50' N., and lon. 10° 33' W. from Washington. The site of the business portion is 14 ft. above the lake; it was originally much lower, but has been built up from 3 to 9 ft. since 1856. It is an inclined plane, rising toward the W. to the height of 28 ft., giving slow but sufficient drainage. The city stands on the dividing ridge between the basins of the Mississippi and St. Lawrence, and is surrounded by a prairie stretching several hundred miles S. and W.　One eighth of a mile N. of the Court-House a bayou, called the Chicago River, extends W. a little more than half a mile, and then divides into the North and South branches, which run

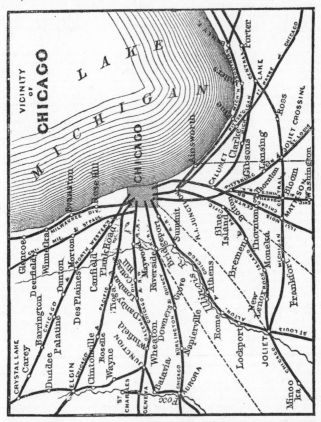

nearly parallel with the lake-shore, about 2 miles in each direction. The river and its branches, with numerous slips, afford a water front-age of 38 miles, of which 24 miles are improved, without including the lake front, on which an outer harbor is now in process of construction. Connected with the S. branch is the terminus of the Illinois & Michi-

gan Canal, which extends to the Illinois River at La Salle. The city
extends N. and S. along the lake about 8 miles, and W. from the lake
about 5 miles, embracing an area of nearly 35 sq. m. The river
divides the city into three distinct parts, known as the North, South,
and West Divisions, which are connected by 33 bridges and 2 brick
tunnels under the river-bed. The city is regularly laid out, with
streets generally 80 ft. wide, and many of them from 3 to 7 miles in
length, crossing each other at right angles. The principal thoroughfares run N. and S.

The first white visitors to the site of Chicago were Joliet and Marquette, who
arrived in August, 1673. The first permanent settlement was made in 1804, during
which year Fort Dearborn was built by the U. S. Government. The fort stood
near the head of Michigan Ave., below its intersection with Lake St. It was
abandoned in 1812, rebuilt in 1816, and finally demolished in 1856. At the close of
1830, Chicago contained 12 houses and 3 "country" residences in Madison St., with
a population (composed of whites, half-breeds, and blacks) of about 100. The town
was organized in 1833, and incorporated as a city in 1837. The first frame building
was erected in 1832, and the first brick house in 1833. The first vessel entered
the harbor June 11, 1834; and at the first official census, taken July 1, 1837, the
entire population was found to be 4,170. In 1850, the population had increased to
29,963; in 1860, to 112,172; and in 1870, to 298,977. Local estimates placed the
population in 1878 at 550,000. In October, 1871, Chicago was the scene of one of
the most destructive conflagrations of modern times. The fire originated on Sunday evening, October 8th, in a small barn in De Koven St., in the S. part of the
West Division, from the upsetting, as is supposed, of a lighted kerosene-lamp.
The buildings in that quarter were mostly of wood, and there were several lumber-yards along the margin of the river. Through these the flames swept with
resistless fury, and were carried across the South branch by the strong westerly
wind then prevailing, and thence spread into the South Division, which was closely
built up with stores, warehouses, and public buildings of stone, brick, and iron,
many of them supposed to be fire-proof. The fire raged all day Monday, and
crossed the main channel of the Chicago River, sweeping all before it in the Northern District, which was occupied mostly by dwelling-houses. The last house was
not reached till Tuesday morning, and many of the ruins were still burning several
months afterward. The total area burned over, including streets, was nearly 3½ sq.
m. The number of buildings destroyed was 17,450; persons rendered homeless,
98,500; persons killed, about 200. Not including depreciation of real estate or loss
of business, it is estimated that the total loss occasioned by the fire was $190,000,000,
of which about $30,000,000 was recovered on insurance, though one of the first
results of the fire was to bankrupt many of the insurance companies all over the
country. The business of the city was interrupted but a short time, however. Before winter many of the merchants were doing business in extemporized wooden
structures, and the rest in private dwellings. In a year after the fire, a large part
of the burnt district had been rebuilt, and at present there is scarcely a trace of
the terrible disaster save in the improved character of the new buildings over those
destroyed. On July 14, 1874, still another great fire swept over the devoted city,
destroying 18 blocks or 60 acres in the heart of the city, and about $4,000,000 worth
of property. Chicago ranks next in commercial importance to New York among
the cities of the United States. As early as 1854 it had become the greatest pri-
mary depot for grain in the world; and since then it has also become the greatest
grain market in the world. Chicago is also the most important market for live
stock in the United States. During the year ending March 1, 1879, 4,911,913
hogs were packed, and about 65,000 cattle. The lumber-trade is a very important
item of the city's commerce. The manufactures of Chicago are already extensive and important, employing about 50,000 persons, and including iron and steel
works, flour-mills, cotton-factories, boot and shoe factories, and tanneries.

State St., in the South Division, is the Broadway of Chicago, and
on it or near it are the finest commercial structures, hotels, retail
stores, and the like. Other important business streets are *Lake, Clark,*

La Salle, Randolph, Dearborn, Adams, Monroe, Madison, and *Washington.* In fact, there is scarcely a street in the South or business district which does not contain some notably fine buildings. The finest residences are in *Wabash, Prairie,* and *Michigan Avenues,* which are of a semi-suburban character, adorned with rows of trees, and bordered by villas surrounded with beautifully ornamented grounds. Scarcely inferior are *Indiana, Calumet,* and *South Park Avenues, West Washington St.,* and *North Dearborn St.* The favorite drives are out Wabash and Michigan Avenues; through the parks and boulevards, especially to *South Park,* which extends along the lake shore; and to *Lake View,* on the N. side, beyond Lincoln Park.

Most of the public buildings of Chicago were burned down in the great fire, and have not been replaced as rapidly as the business structures destroyed at the same time. A new *City Hall and County Court-House,* estimated to cost $5,000,000, is going up on the square bounded by Clark, Washington, La Salle, and Randolph Sts. It occupies the entire block and will be a magnificent structure. A new *** U. S. Custom-House and Post-Office** has been erected on the square bounded by Clark, Adams, Jackson, and Dearborn Sts. It is one of the finest public buildings in the country, occupying an entire block 342 by 210 ft., and costing upward of $5,000,000. The *County Jail and Criminal Court Building* is a massive edifice at the cor. of N. Dearborn and Michigan Sts., comprising three detached buildings. The *** Chamber of Commerce** is a spacious and imposing building, at the cor. of Washington and La Salle Sts., opposite City Hall Square. Its interior decorations are very elaborate. The Board of Trade meets here, and strangers will find it interesting to visit the ladies' gallery during the daily session (from 11 A. M. to 1 P. M.); or any gentleman is admitted to the floor on introduction by a member. The great hall in which the Board of Trade meets is 142 ft. long, 87 ft. wide, and 45 ft. high. The ceiling is elaborately frescoed with allegorical pictures representing the trade of the city, the great fire, and the rebuilding. The new hotels, already enumerated at the head of this article, are among the finest buildings in the city; as is also the *Union Depot,* in Van Buren St. at the head of La Salle. The new and handsome brown-stone building of the "Chicago Tribune," cor. Dearborn and Madison Sts., is worthy of notice. Other representative structures are the American Express Co's. building in Monroe St. near State; *Portland Block,* at the cor. of Dearborn and Washington Sts.; and the *Honore Block,* cor. Dearborn and Adams Sts. The *** Exposition Building** is a vast and ornate structure of iron and glass, fronting on Michigan Ave. between Monroe and Jackson Sts. It is 800 ft. long and 200 ft. deep, and the center is surmounted by a dome 60 ft. in diameter and 160 ft. high. An exhibition of art and industrial products is held here every autumn.

There are about 300 church edifices in Chicago, including those untouched by the fire and those which have since been rebuilt. Among them are a few which deserve special mention. The *** Unity Church** (Unitarian), in Dearborn Ave. cor. Lafayette Place, is a light-stone structure, in the modern Gothic style, with double spires. The *Second Presbyterian*, cor. Michigan Ave. and 18th St., is a large and imposing stone structure. The *Michigan Avenue Baptist Church*, in Michigan Ave. near 24th St., is of stone, in the Gothic style, with a graceful tower and spire. *Grace Church* (Episcopal), in Wabash Ave. near 14th St., is a handsome stone edifice in the Gothic style, with open timber roof and a richly decorated interior. *St. James's* (Episcopal), cor. Cass and Huron Sts., is large and massive, with a square flanking tower. The *Union Park Congregational*, cor. Ashland Ave. and Washington St., has a lofty spire, and is quite ornate in style. The *Second Baptist*, cor. Monroe and Morgan Sts., is a plain edifice in the Italian style, with a most peculiar spire. The *Twelfth St. Church* (Roman Catholic) is pure Gothic in style, and has an extremely rich and noble interior. The Roman Catholic *Cathedral* is also a fine building. The great *Tabernacle*, on Monroe St., where Messrs. Moody and Sankey held their meetings, will seat 10,000 persons, and is used for sacred concerts and other religious gatherings.

Among the literary and educational institutions of Chicago a foremost place must be assigned to the *Public Library,* the nucleus of which was contributed by English authors and publishers in 1872, and which now numbers 60,000 volumes, including many German, French, Dutch, Norse, Swedish, and Bohemian books. Its rooms are at the cor. of Dearborn and Lake Sts. The *Academy of Sciences*, established in 1857, lost a valuable collection of 38,000 specimens in the fire, but has erected a new building on the old site (in Wabash Ave. near Van Buren St.), and is slowly gathering a new museum and library. The *Academy of Design* (cor. State and Monroe Sts.) is a school of art established in 1869. The *University of Chicago,* founded by the late Stephen A. Douglas, occupies a beautiful site, overlooking Lake Michigan, near Cottage Grove Ave., 4 miles S. of City Hall Square (take Cottage Grove Ave. cars). The main building, 136 by 172 feet, was completed in 1866, at a cost of $110,000. *Dearborn Observatory*, adjoining the University on the W., contains a Clark refracting telescope, which is one of the largest and best in the world. It has 23 feet focal length and 18½ inches aperture. The *Baptist Theological Seminary* has a large and handsome building in rear of the University. The *Chicago Theological Seminary* has a fine stone building in the Norman style on the W. side of Union Park, at the intersection of Ashland Ave. and Warren St. The *Presbyterian Theological Seminary* has a fine edifice at the cor. of Fullerton Ave. and Halstead St. It is 5 stories high, and contains a good library. The *St. Ignatius College* (Roman Catholic) has an ornate and costly building, No. 413 W. 12th St. There are 6 medical colleges in the city, of which the most noteworthy is the *Rush Medical College*, founded in 1842, and with a new and stately building at the cor. of N. Dearborn and Indiana Sts. The *Chicago Medical College* has a large structure at the cor. of Prairie Ave. and 26th St. The *Hahnemann College* (homœopathic) is at the cor. of Cottage Grove Ave and 28th St.

The *Cook County Hospital* comprises several spacious buildings at

the cor. of 18th and Arnold Sts. ***Mercy Hospital** is a vast and
ornate structure at the cor. of Calumet Ave. and 26th St., well worth
visiting (take Indiana Ave. cars). Other important charitable institutions are the *Magdalen Asylum*, in N. Market St. ; the *Home for the
Friendless*, No. 911 Wabash Ave. ; the *Protestant Orphan Asylum*, cor.
Michigan Ave. and 22d St. ; and *St. Joseph's* (male) and *St. Mary's*
(female) *Orphan Asylums*, in N. State St. cor. Superior St. The two
last named are under the charge of the Sisters of Mercy. The ***U. S.
Marine Hospital,** situated at Lake View, a little beyond Lincoln
Park, is one of the largest and costliest in the country. It is built of
Joliet stone, is 340 ft. long, and cost $371,132.

Chicago has a magnificent system of public parks, authorized in
1869, and partially improved previous to the fire, since which the work
has proceeded more slowly. There are six parks, aggregating nearly
1,900 acres, which are connected by a cordon of boulevards 200 ft.
wide, extending around the three land-sides of the city, with a drive
on the lake-shore. These give 33 miles of drives, besides those around
the parks. ***Lincoln Park,** on the lake-shore, in the N. Division,
contains about 230 acres, and has five miles of drives and walks, fine
trees, artificial hills and mounds, miniature lakes and streams, sum-
mer-houses, rustic bridges, and shady rambles. Open-air concerts are
given here on Saturday afternoons in summer. From the N. end of
Lincoln Park a boulevard, 3½ miles long, extends W. to *Humboldt
Park*, which contains 193½ acres, and is only partially improved. On
the upper terrace stands a statue of Baron von Humboldt. About 2
miles S. of Humboldt Park, with which it is connected by a similar
boulevard, is *Central Park*, an irregular tract of land nearly a mile
long from N. to S., and containing 171 acres, the middle line of which
lies on Madison St., 4 miles from the Court-House. From this park
the Douglas Boulevard runs 1½ mile S. E. to *Douglas Park*, which also
contains 171 acres. From this another boulevard runs S. 4½ miles,
thence E. 4¼ miles to the two *South Parks*, containing 1,055 acres,
which are tastefully laid out. The most southerly extends upward of
1¼ mile along the shore of the Lake. Two boulevards run thence to
the well-paved streets that connect with the business portion of the
city. ***Union Park** (reached by Madison and Randolph St. cars) is
located in the very center of the residence portion of the W. Division.
Though containing only 23 acres, the judicious expenditure of $100,000
on lakelets, drives, hills, pagodas, zoölogical gardens, and skillful land-
scape-gardening, has rendered its apparent size much greater. There
are open-air concerts here every Wednesday evening in summer. *Lake
Park*, on the S. side, running about 1 mile on the lake-shore, is ornamented by the elegant Michigan Ave. residences, and is a favorite
promenade on summer evenings. ***Jefferson Park,** one of the
smaller public squares, contains a handsome fountain, and is one of the
most frequented in the city.

Of the cemeteries, *Graceland, Rose-Hill,* and *Calvary*, in the North
Division, are the most interesting. The last two are on the line of the
Chicago & Northwestern R. R. *Oakwood*, on the Vincennes road, 3

miles S. of the city limits, is a pretty rural spot. This cemetery can be reached by horse-cars and dummy, or by a pleasant drive through the boulevards.

The system by which Chicago is supplied with water has been called one of the wonders of the world. The * **Water-Works** are situated on the lake-shore in the North Division (take N. Clark St. cars and get off at Chicago Ave.), and may be inspected on application to the engineer in charge. They comprise a stone water-tower, 160 ft. high, up which the water is forced by 4 engines, having a pumping capacity of 74,500,000 gallons daily, and flows thence through pipes to every part of the city. A very fine * view of the city, lake, and surrounding country may be obtained from the top of the tower, which is reached by a spiral staircase. From this tower a nearly cylindrical brick tunnel, 62 inches high and 60 wide, extends 2 miles under the lake, lying 66 to 70 ft. below the lake-surface. The water enters the tunnel through a grated cylinder, inclosed in an immense crib, on which are a lighthouse and dwelling. The tunnel was begun in 1864 and finished in 1866, at a cost of $550,000. Another tunnel, 7 ft. in diameter, was completed in 1874 at a cost of $957,622, which also connects with the crib, and, through independent pumping-works, supplies the S. W. section of the city. Another abundant source of water-supply has been recently developed in the *Artesian Wells*, of which there are about 40. The first two sunk are situated at the intersection of Chicago and Western Avenues (reached by W. Randolph St. cars), are respectively 911 and 694 ft. deep, and flow about 1,200,000 gallons daily. The stock-yards, the west-side parks, and numerous manufacturing establishments are supplied from artesian wells.

Until recently intercourse between the three divisions of the city was effected only by 33 bridges, which span the river at intervals of two squares, and swing on central pivots to admit the passage of vessels. These bridges, however, are a serious impediment to navigation, as well as to vehicles and pedestrians; and, in order to obviate the inconvenience, a * **Tunnel** was constructed in 1868 under the South Branch at Washington St. It is 1,608 ft. long, with a descent of 45 ft., has a double roadway for vehicles and a separate passage for pedestrians, and cost $512,707. In 1870 another similar tunnel, with a total length of 1,854 ft., including approaches, was constructed under the main river on the line of La Salle St., connecting the North and South Divisions (cost $549,000).

No visitor to Chicago should fail to inspect the * **Union Stock-Yards,** where the vast live-stock trade of the city is transacted (reached by State St. cars, or by trains every few minutes). The yards comprise 345 acres, of which 146 are in pens, and have 32 miles of drainage, 8 miles of streets and alleys, 2,300 gates, and cost $1,675,-000. They have capacity for 25,000 cattle, 100,000 hogs, 22,000 sheep, and 1,200 horses. There is a large and handsome brick hotel connected with the yards; also a Bank and a Board of Trade. Quite a large town (5,000 inhabitants) has sprung up in the immediate vicinity, with post-office, telegraph-office, churches, schools, etc. The scene is very animated and interesting during the day. The *Grain-Elevators* are also a very interesting feature, and should be visited, in order to obtain an idea of the manner in which the immense grain-trade of Chicago is carried on. There are 19 of these buildings, all situated on the banks of the river, and connected with the railroads by side-tracks. They have an aggregate storage capacity of 15,600,000 bushels, and receive and discharge grain with almost incredible dispatch. *Pork-packing* is a highly interesting process. The hogs are driven up an inclined plane to a pen in the upper part of the packing-house. A chain or cord attached to a pulley in a sliding frame near the ceiling is slipped over one leg, the hog is jerked up, his throat cut, the body lowered into a long vat of boiling water, lifted out, scraped, disemboweled, and hung up to cool. When cooled, the bodies are cut up into " meats," salted, and packed. The largest houses are in the vicinity of the Stock-Yards, and are usually open to the inspection of visitors.

67. New York to Cincinnati via Buffalo and Cleveland.

By the N. Y. Central & Hudson River R. R. (Route 62) or the Erie R. R. (Route 63) to Buffalo; thence by Lake Shore R. R. (Route 62) to Cleveland; and from Cleveland by the Cleveland, Columbus, Cincinnati & Indianapolis R. R. No through cars are run on this route, but close connection is made at Cleveland. The time from New York to Cincinnati is about 30 hours. Distances: New York to Cleveland, 623 miles; to Crestline, 698; to Delaware, 737; (to Columbus, 761); to Springfield, 787; to Dayton, 811; to Cincinnati, 867.

THE portion of this route between New York and Cleveland is described in Routes 61 and 62, or, if the Erie R. R. be taken, in Route 63. Leaving Cleveland by the C. C. C. & I. R. R. (better known as the " Bee Line "), the train passes in quick succession a number of small towns, which please by their neatness and air of prosperity, but which do not require special mention. *Shelby* (67 miles from Cleveland, 690 from New York) is a busy village at the crossing of the Lake Erie Div. of the Baltimore & Ohio R. R. (Route 65), and *Crestline* (698 miles) is at the intersection of the Pittsburg, Fort Wayne & Chicago R. R. (Route 64). *Galion* (703 miles), *Gilead* (716 miles), and *Cardington* (720 miles) are small villages. **Delaware** (737 miles; *American House, St. Charles*) is a thriving town of 6,000 inhabitants on the right bank of the Olentangy River. It is pleasantly situated on rolling ground and is neatly built. In 1842 the *Ohio Wesleyan University* was founded here, and the *Ohio Wesleyan Female College* in 1863. Both are prosperous institutions, and the former has a library of 13,000 volumes. There is also here a medicinal spring which is much resorted to. At Delaware a branch line diverges and runs in 24 miles to **Columbus** (see p. 301). Beyond Delaware several small stations are passed, and in 50 miles the train reaches **Springfield** (*Lagonda House, St. James*), one of the most beautiful cities in Ohio, pleasantly situated at the confluence of the Lagonda Creek and Mad River, both of which furnish excellent water-power, which is utilized in numerous manufactures. It is in the heart of one of the richest and most populous agricultural regions in the Union, and has a large trade in wheat, flour, Indian corn, and other produce. The city is well laid out and handsomely built, with 6 large public-school buildings, including a fine edifice for the High School, several costly churches, and many fine residences. The *Springfield Seminary* is a flourishing institution; and *Wittenberg College* (Lutheran), founded in 1845, has 160 students and a library of 6,000 volumes. The *Public Library* contains 4,000 volumes. Springfield has an extensive reputation for the manufacture of agricultural implements, 30,000 mowers and reapers being produced annually. Six lines of railway intersect here. Twenty-four miles beyond Springfield the train reaches **Dayton** (*Beckel House, Phillips*), a beautiful city of 35,000 inhabitants, on the E. bank of the Great Miami River at the mouth of Mad River. It is regularly laid out, with broad, well-shaded streets crossing each other at right angles, and lined with tasteful private residences, surrounded by fine gardens. The public buildings are unusually fine. The * *County Court-House*, planned after the model of the Parthenon, is an imposing white marble edifice, 127 ft. long by 62 ft. wide, with a stone roof and doors of solid iron. One of the market-houses, 400 ft. long and paved with blocks of limestone, has accommodations for the municipal offices in the second story. There is a large water-power within the city limits, obtained from an hydraulic canal, and Dayton is a place of great industrial activity. It is especially noted for its manufactures of agricultural machinery, steam engines and boilers, railroad-cars, stoves, paper, and hollow ware, which amount annually to over $15,000,000. The public schools are of a high character, and the *Public School Library* contains 10,-000 volumes. *Miss Westfall's* and the *Cooper Seminaries* are flourishing institutions for the superior instruction of females. The principal charitable institutions are the City Orphan Asylum, the County Almshouse, and the Southern Lunatic Asylum of Ohio. To the tourist the most interesting feature of Dayton is the * *Central National Soldiers' Home*, situated on a picturesque elevation, 4 miles from the city, and reached by horse-cars. The Home is an extensive group of fine, large buildings, over 40 in number, including a handsome church, built of native white limestone, and a splendid hospital, said to be the best adapted to its purpose of any in the United States. The latter is of red brick, with freestone facings and trimmings, and accommodates 300 patients. The principal other buildings are a brick dining-hall, capable of seating 1,100 persons, a fine library, a music-hall, billiard-room, bowling-alley, headquarters building, and several barracks for the men. The grounds embrace an area of 640 acres, well shaded with natural forest-trees, and are handsomely laid out, with winding avenues, a deer-park stocked from Lookout Mountain, a beautiful artificial lake, a natural grotto, hot-houses, and flower-beds. Between Dayton and Cincinnati there are no stations requiring mention, but the country *en route* is fertile, populous, and pleasing. **Cincinnati** (see p. 305).

68. New York to Cincinnati via Philadelphia, Pittsburg, and Columbus.

By the " Pan-Handle Route," consisting of the Pennsylvania R. R. to Pittsburg, and the Pittsburg, Cincinnati & St. Louis R. R. from Pittsburg to Cincinnati. Through trains, with Pullman palace drawing-room and sleeping cars attached, run through without change of cars in 28 hours. Distances : to Philadelphia, 90 miles ; to Harrisburg, 195 ; to Pittsburg, 444 ; to Steubenville, 487 ; to Newark, 604 ; to Columbus, 637 ; to Xenia, 692 ; to Cincinnati, 757.

As far as **Pittsburg** (444 miles), this route is the same as Route 64.   Shortly beyond Pittsburg the train enters and crosses that narrow arm of West Virginia (the " Pan-Handle ") which is thrust up between Pennsylvania and Ohio, and then crosses the Ohio River into the State of Ohio. The first station of importance in Ohio is **Steubenville** (*U. S. Hotel, Imperial*), a city of 15,000 inhabitants, pleasantly situated on the W. bank of the Ohio River, which is here $\frac{1}{4}$ mile wide. The city is well laid out and substantially built, is surrounded by a rich farming and stock-growing country, and is the center of an important trade. There are also a number of foundries, rolling-mills, machine-shops, flour-mills, etc. Abundance of excellent coal is found in the neighborhood, and there are 8 shafts within the city limits. The * *County Court-House* is the finest in E. Ohio, and there are several very handsome churches and school-buildings. Among the educational institutions are an academy for boys and a noted female seminary, the latter delightfully situated on the bank of the river. The scenery in the vicinity of Steubenville is very attractive. Beyond Steubenville a number of small towns are passed, of which the principal is *Coshocton* (568 miles), the capital of the county of the same name, picturesquely built on 4 natural terraces rising above the Muskingum River. The Ohio Canal, connecting the Ohio River with Lake Erie, passes through the village and furnishes a good water-power. *Dresden* (582 miles) is another busy village on the Muskingum River, and 22 miles beyond is **Newark** (*Park House, American*), a flourishing city of 7,000 inhabitants, situated on a level plain at the confluence of three branches of the Licking River. It is a handsome place, the streets being wide and regular, and the churches, stores, and private residences well built. The surrounding country is very productive, and in the vicinity are quarries of sandstone, an extensive coal mine, and several coal-oil factories. The Ohio Canal passes through the city. The next important station after leaving Newark is

Columbus.

Hotels, etc.—The leading hotels are the *Neil House* ($3 a day), cor. High and Capitol Sts. ; *Park Hotel* ($3 a day), cor. High and Goodale Sts. ; *American House* ($2.50 a day), cor. High and State Sts. ; *St. Charles* ($2 a day), cor. High and Gay Sts. ; *U. S. Hotel* ($2 a day), cor. High and Town Sts. *Horse-cars* (fare 5c.) reach all parts of the city, and there are six bridges across the Scioto River.

Columbus, the capital of Ohio, and one of the largest cities in the State, is situated on the E. bank of the Scioto River, 100 miles N. E.

of Cincinnati. It was laid out in 1812, became the seat of the State government in 1816, and was incorporated as a city in 1834, when its population was less than 4,000. The population in 1870 was 31,274, and is now estimated at nearly 50,000. The commercial interests of the city are large, and its manufactures numerous and important; but its growth and wealth are chiefly due to the concentration there of the State institutions, and the liberal expenditure of public money. The streets are very wide and are regularly laid out in squares. **Broad St.** is 120 ft. wide for a distance of more than 2 miles. It has a double avenue (4 rows) of trees, alternate maple and elm, and is one of the most beautiful streets in the country. The finest residences in the city are on this and *Town St.* The principal business thoroughfare is *High St.*, which is 100 ft. wide, and paved with the asphalt pavement. In the center of the city, occupying the square of 10 acres between High and Third and Broad and State Sts., is *** Capitol Square,** surrounded by majestic elms and beautifully laid out. It is proposed to make it a complete *arboretum* of Ohio trees, of which many varieties are already represented.

The most interesting feature of Columbus to the stranger is its public buildings and institutions, in which it is not excelled by any city in the United States except Washington, and much surpasses any other of the Western capitals. The State has concentrated here nearly all the public buildings devoted to its business, benevolence, or justice. The *** Capitol,** which stands in Capitol Square, is one of the largest and finest in the United States. It is constructed of fine gray limestone, resembling marble, in the Doric style of architecture, of which it is a noble specimen. It is 304 ft. long and 184 ft. wide, and is surmounted by a dome 64 ft. in diameter and 157 ft. high. The interior is elegantly finished. The hall of the House of Representatives is 84 ft. long by 72½ ft. wide, and the Senate Chamber is 56 by 72½ ft. There are also rooms for all the State officers, besides 26 committee rooms. The *** State Penitentiary** is another very striking building. It is of hewn limestone, in the castellated style, and with its yards and shops covers 30 acres of ground on the E. bank of the Scioto, just below the mouth of the Olentangy. The **Central Ohio Lunatic Asylum** has a series of spacious buildings standing amid 300 acres of elevated ground W. of the city. These buildings are in the Franco-Italian style, with a frontage of about 1,200 ft., a depth of 300 ft., a central tower 165 ft. high, and a capacity for 600 patients. The *Idiot Asylum*, a plain Gothic structure, 272 by 198 ft., occupies grounds 123 acres in extent, adjoining those of the Lunatic Asylum. The *Blind Asylum*, in the E. part of the city, on the grounds of the old one, is a stone structure, 340 by 270 ft., in the Gothic style of the Tudor period. The *** Deaf and Dumb Asylum,** centrally located in extensive and handsome grounds on Town St., cor. Washington Av., is built in the Franco-Italian style, with Mansard roof. The building is 400 ft. long and 380 deep, and has numerous towers, the central one of which is 140 ft. high. The *** U. S. Barracks** is located in the midst of spacious and handsome grounds, beautifully wooded, in the N. E. suburb of the city. It comprises, besides an immense central structure, numerous other buildings, used for offices, quarters, storehouses, etc. There is a fine drive to the Barracks, and beautiful drives are laid out through and around the grounds. The State has also a large and well-built Arsenal. The *City Hall*, facing Capitol Square on the S. side of State St., is a handsome Gothic structure, 187½ ft. by 80, with a small central tower 138 ft. high. In the third story is a large audience-chamber, capable of seating 2,830 persons. The *High School* (on Broad St.) is a fine building in the simple Norman or church style of architecture. The *Holly Water-Works* occupy a large building near the junction of the Scioto and Olentangy Rivers. The machinery is on a massive scale. The *Odd-Fellows' Hall*, in High St., near Rich St., is a fine specimen of classic Italian, and opposite is *Opera-House Block*, a beautiful specimen of American street architecture, in the florid Italian style. The Opera-House in this block is one of the handsomest in the country. The *Union Depot* is a spacious and handsome structure.

There are about 50 churches in the city, and some are fine examples of the decorative period of Gothic architecture. Most notable among them are *Trinity Church* (Episcopal), cor. Broad and 3d Sts.; *St. Joseph's Cathedral* (Roman Catholic), cor. Broad and 5th Sts.; the *Second Presbyterian*, cor. Third and Chapel Sts.; and *St. Paul's* (German Lutheran), cor. High and Mound Sts. The latter is surmounted by a graceful spire 216 ft. high, and in the tower is a clock. The *State Library*, in the Capitol, contains over 46,400 volumes. *** Starling Medical College,** cor. State and 6th Sts., is a very noble building in the Norman castellated style. It is of brick trimmed with whitish limestone. *Capital University* (Lutheran) is an unpretentious building in the Italian style, surrounded by beautiful grounds, in the E. part of the city. The handsome building of the female seminary of *St. Mary's of the Springs* adjoins the city on the E., and near by is the *Water-Cure*. The Ohio *State University*, endowed with the Congressional land-grant, was opened in 1873. Of the charitable institutions, the *Hare Orphans' Home*, the *Hannah Neil Mission*, and the *Lying-in Hospital* may be mentioned. The *Catholic Asylum* for the reclamation of fallen women is W. of the city, and the Sisters of Mercy have a fine Hospital in the city, in the Starling Medical College Building. A convent of the Sisters of the Good Shepherd has been established at West Columbus, a suburban town.

* Goodale Park, presented to the city by Dr. Lincoln Goodale, is at the N. end of the city, and comprises about 40 acres of native forest, beautifully improved and well kept. *City Park*, at the S. end of the city, is of about the same size as Goodale Park and resembles it in many respects. The grounds of the **Franklin County Agricultural Society,** 83 acres in extent, on the E. border of the city, are the finest in the State. In the immediate vicinity are the gardens of the *Columbus Horticultural Society*, occupying 10 acres. **Green Lawn** is the most beautiful of the five cemeteries of Columbus.

CITY OF
CINCINNATI

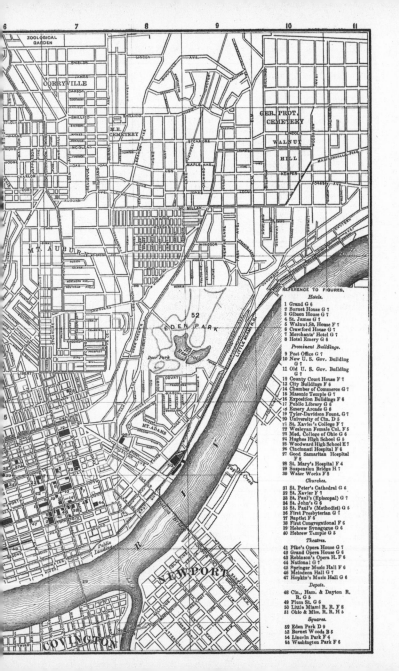

REFERENCE TO FIGURES.

Hotels.

1 Grand G 6
2 Burnet House G 7
3 Gibson House G 7
4 St. James G 7
5 Walnut St. House F 7
6 Crawford House G 7
7 Merchants' Hotel G 7
8 Hotel Emery G 6

Prominent Buildings.

9 Post Office G 7
10 New U. S. Gov. Building G 7
11 Old U. S. Building G 7
12 County Court House F 7
13 City Buildings F 6
14 Chamber of Commerce G 7
15 Masonic Temple G 7
16 Exposition Buildings F 6
17 Public Library G 6
18 Emery Arcade G 6
19 Tyler-Davidson Fount. G 7
20 University of Cin. D 5
21 St. Xavier's College F 7
22 Wesleyan Female Col. F 5
23 Med. College of Ohio G 6
24 Hughes High School E 3
25 Woodward High School E 7
26 Cincinnati Hospital F 6
27 Good Samaritan Hospital F 8
28 St. Mary's Hospital F 4
29 Suspension Bridge H 7
30 Water Works F 8

Churches.

31 St. Peter's Cathedral G 6
32 St. Xavier F 7
33 St. Paul's (Episcopal) G 7
34 St. John's G 8
35 St. Paul's (Methodist) G 5
36 First Presbyterian G 7
37 Baptist F 6
38 First Congregational F 6
39 Hebrew Synagogue G 6
40 Hebrew Temple G 5

Theatres.

41 Pike's Opera House G 7
42 Grand Opera House G 6
43 Robinson's Opera H. F 6
44 National G 7
45 Springer Music Hall F 6
46 Melodeon Hall G 7
47 Hopkin's Music Hall G 6

Depots.

48 Cin., Ham. & Dayton R. R. G 5
49 Plum St. G 6
50 Little Miami R. R. F 8
51 Ohio & Miss. R. R. H 5

Squares.

52 Eden Park D 9
53 Burnet Woods B 5
54 Lincoln Park F 4
55 Washington Park F 6

Leaving Columbus the train soon reaches *London* (662 miles), a pretty town, capital of Madison County, and containing a fine Union school-house, and then passes on in 30 miles to **Xenia** (*St. George Hotel, Ohmer*), a city of 9,000 inhabitants, with an important trade and extensive manufactures. The streets of the city are well paved and beautifully shaded, and there are many substantial business blocks and costly residences. The chief public buildings are the *Court-House*, one of the finest in the State, in a large and handsome park in the center of the city; the *City Hall*, containing a fine public hall, and the *Jail*. Besides the flourishing public schools, Xenia is the seat of several important educational institutions. *Xenia College* (Methodist) admits both sexes, and has two fine buildings in a large wooded park in the E. part of the city. *Wilberforce University*, established in 1863 for the higher education of colored youth of both sexes, is a short distance outside the city limits, and has a library of 4,000 volumes. The *Theological Seminary* (Presbyterian) dates from 1794, and has a library of 3,500 volumes. The *Ohio Soldiers' and Sailors' Orphans' Home* has about 30 buildings, accommodating 700 inmates, surrounded by very attractive grounds 200 acres in extent. The country between Xenia and Cincinnati is undulating, fertile, and highly cultivated, but presents nothing calling for special mention. *Morrow* (721 miles) is a thriving village at the junction with the Cincinnati & Muskingum Valley R. R., and *Loveland* (734 miles) is at the crossing of the Marietta & Cincinnati R. R. (Route 65). *Milford* (743 miles) is a flourishing village on the opposite side of the Little Miami River, and connected with the R. R. station by a bridge. **Cincinnati** (see p. 305).

69. New York to Cincinnati via Erie Railway and Connecting Lines.

By the Erie R. R. and the Atlantic & Great Western R. R. Through trains, with Pullman palace drawing-room and sleeping cars attached, run through on this route without change of cars in about 35 hours. (The Erie R. R. also sells through tickets to Cincinnati *via* Buffalo and Cleveland, as explained at the head of Route 67). Distances : to Port Jervis, 88 miles ; to Susquehanna, 193 ; to Binghamton, 214 ; to Elmira, 273 ; to Hornellsville, 331 ; to Salamanca, 413 ; to Meadville, 515 ; to Akron, 615 ; to Mansfield, 682 ; to Marion, 717 ; to Urbana, 766 ; to Springfield, 781 ; to Dayton, 801 ; to Hamilton, 836 ; to Cincinnati, 861.

As far as Mansfield (682 miles) this route is described in Route 63. **Mansfield** (see p. 279) is at the junction of the present route with Routes 63, 64, and 65. From Mansfield to Dayton the Atlantic & Great Western R. R. closely follows the line of the Cleveland, Columbus & Cincinnati R. R. (Route 67), touching the same places at frequent intervals. *Galion* (697 miles) is a station on both roads, and *Marion* (717 miles) is a prosperous village at the crossing of the Indianapolis Div. of the C. C. C. & I. R. R. **Urbana** (766 miles, *Weaver House*) is a handsomely built city of 7,000 inhabitants, capital of Champaign County. The trade with the fertile surrounding country is large, and there are several important manufactories, of which the chief is the U. S. Rolling-Stock Co., which employs 500 hands. *Urbana University* (Swedenborgian) was founded in 1851, and has a library of 5,000 volumes. The High School building cost $90,000, and accommodates 400 pupils. There is also a free public library. **Springfield** (781 miles) has already been described on page 299, and **Dayton** (801 miles) on page 300. At Dayton the train passes on to the track of the Cincinnati, Hamilton & Dayton R. R., and soon reaches **Hamilton** (*Phillips House, Straub House*), a city of 12,000 inhabitants, situated on both sides of the Miami River, and on the Miami Canal. Hamilton is surrounded by a rich and populous district, and is extensively engaged in manufactures, of which the most important are machinery, agricultural implements, paper, woolen goods, flour, carriages and wagons, boots and shoes, etc. Abundant water-power is supplied by a hydraulic canal, which gives a fall of 28 ft. There are a number of handsome churches and school buildings in Hamilton, and the free Public Library contains 2,000 volumes. **Cincinnati** (see below).

70. Cincinnati.

Hotels.—The *Grand Hotel* ($3 to $4 a day) is a handsome structure, cor. 4th St. and Central Ave. The *Burnet House* ($2.50 to $3 a day), cor. 3d and Vine Sts., has been for more than a quarter of a century the principal hotel of Cincinnati. The *Gibson House* ($2.50 to $3 a day), at the cor. of 4th and Walnut Sts., is large and centrally located. Other good hotels are the *St. James* ($2.50 a day), in E. 4th St. between Main and Sycamore; *Walnut Street House* ($2.50 a day), in Walnut between 6th and 7th Sts.; *Crawford House* ($2.50 a day), cor. 6th and Walnut Sts.; *Merchants' Hotel* ($2.50 a day), in 5th St. between Main and Sycamore; and the *Galt House* ($2 a day), cor. 6th and Main Sts. Good hotels on the European plan are the *St. Nicholas*, cor. 4th and Race Sts., and *Keppler's Hotel*, in 4th St. between Plum St. and Central Ave. (rooms $1 to $3 a day). The *Hotel Emery*, in the Arcade, is a first-class house, conducted on both the American and European plans ($3 per day).

Restaurants.—The best restaurants for ladies and gentlemen are *Keppler's*, in 4th St., between Plum St. and Central Ave.; the *St. Nicholas*, cor. 4th and Race Sts.; *Schmidt's*, cor. 7th and Race Sts.; *Brock's*, in Mound St. near 6th; *Hunt's*, in Vine St. near 4th; and *Hotel Emery*, in the Arcade. At the head of each of the 4 inclined planes leading to the tops of the hills surrounding the city is an extensive beer-garden.

Modes of Conveyance.—*Horse-cars* (fare, 5c.) run to all parts of the city and suburbs, and to Covington and Newport, Ky. *Omnibuses* run from all the depots and steamboat-landings to the hotels (fare, 50c.). *Hacks* are in waiting at the depots, steamboat-landings, and at various other points in the city. Their legal rates are: For 1 or 2 persons to any point within the city, $1; 3 or more persons, 50c. each; large baggage, extra; by the hour, $2 for the first hour and $1.50 for each additional hour. These rates are seldom observed, however, and to avoid imposition a bargain should be made with the driver before starting. *Ferries* to Covington from foot of Central Ave.; to Newport from foot of Pike St.; to Ludlow from foot of 5th St.

Railroad Depots.—The Depot of the *Cincinnati, Hamilton & Dayton R. R.* is a spacious and ornate structure at the cor. of 5th and Hoadley Sts. The *Plum St. Depot*, cor. Plum St. and Pearl, is a large building, 400 by 64 ft. The *Little Miami R. R. Depot* is cor. Kilgour and Front Sts. The *Ohio & Mississippi Depot* is cor. W. Front and Mill Sts. The *Kentucky Central Depot* is in Covington. *Cincin. Southern R. R. Depot* at foot of Gest St.

Theatres and Amusements.—*Pike's Opera-House*, in 4th St., between Vine and Walnut, is one of the most imposing structures of the kind in the United States. It is of fine sandstone, in the Elizabethan style, and the interior is elaborately painted and frescoed. The *Grand Opera-House*, cor. Vine and Longworth Sts., is the old Mozart Hall, remodeled and fitted up as a regular theatre. It will seat 2,000 persons. At *Robinson's Opera-House*, cor. 9th and Plum Sts., German opera and drama are given, varied by an occasional concert. The *National Theatre* (Varieties) is in Sycamore St., between 3d and 4th. The new *Springer Music Hall*, in Elm St., is one of the finest in America, and contains one of the largest organs in the world. Concerts and lectures are given at *Hopkins's Music Hall*, cor. 4th and Elm Sts.; at *Melodeon Hall*, cor. 4th and Walnut Sts.; at *College Hall*, in College Building, in Walnut St., near 4th; and at *Greenwood Hall*, in the Mechanics' Institute, cor. 6th and Vine Sts. The large German halls "over the Rhine" are noticed further on. The *Gymnasium*, in 4th St., between Race and Vine, is one of the most perfect in the country (open from 8 A. M. to 10 P. M.). The *Floating Bath* is moored at the foot of Broadway (single bath, 15c.). A favorite place of resort outside of the city is the *Zoölogical Gardens*, which are located N. of the city near Avondale. The buildings are substantial and the grounds beautifully laid out, and the collection of birds and animals is one of the best in the country. Admission, 25c. Reached by either Main St. or Elm St. cars *via* Inclined Planes.

Reading-Rooms.—In the leading hotels are reading-rooms for the use of guests, well supplied with newspapers, etc. The *Public Library*, in Vine St. between 6th and 7th, contains 90,000 volumes, and a well-supplied reading-room (open from 8 A. M. to 10 P. M.). The *Young Men's Mercantile Library* is in the 2d story of the College Building, in Walnut St. between 4th and 5th, and contains 37,000 volumes. The library of the *Philosophical and Historical Society* is also in the College Building, and numbers 5,000 bound volumes and 12,000 pamphlets. The *Law Library*, in the Court-House, has 7,600 volumes. The *Mechanics' Institute Library*, cor. 6th and Vine Sts., has 6,500 volumes, and a reading-room.

Clubs.—The *Queen City Club*, organized in 1874, has a commodious and handsome building at the corner of 7th and Elm Sts. The *Phœnix Club* has a fine building richly furnished at the cor. of Central Ave. and Court St. The *Allemania Club* also has a fine building at the cor. of 4th St. and Central Ave., with billiard-rooms, ball-rooms, supper-rooms, etc. The *Eureka Club* has rooms at the cor. of Walnut and 9th Sts. The *Cuvier Club* has rooms at 200 W. 4th St. Introduction by a member secures the privileges of any of these clubs.

Post-Office.—The general Post-Office is at the cor. of 4th and Vine Sts., and is open from 6 A. M. to 10 P. M. There are also sub-stations in different parts of the city, and letters may be mailed in the numerous lamp-post boxes.

CINCINNATI, the chief city of Ohio, is situated on the N. bank of the Ohio River, in lat. 39° 6′ N. and lon. 84° 27′ W. It has a frontage of 10 miles on the river, and extends back about 3 miles, occupying half of a valley bisected by the river, on the opposite side of which are the cities of Covington and Newport, Ky. It is surrounded by hills from 400 to 465 ft. in height, forming one of the most beautiful amphitheatres on the continent, from whose hilltops may be seen the splendid panorama of the cities below, and the winding Ohio. Cincinnati is principally built upon two terraces, the first 60 and the second 112 ft. above the river. The latter has been graded to an easy slope, terminating at the base of the hills. The streets are laid out with great regularity, crossing each other at right angles, are broad and well paved, and for the most part beautifully shaded. The business portion of the city is compactly built, a fine drab freestone being the material chiefly used. The outer highland belt of the city is beautified by costly residences which stand in the midst of extensive and neatly adorned grounds. Here the favorite building material is blue limestone. The names of the suburbs on the hilltops are Clifton, Avondale, Mt. Auburn, Price's Hill, and Walnut Hills.

Cincinnati was settled in 1788, but for a number of years a continual series of difficulties with the Indians retarded the progress of the town. In 1800 it had grown to 750 inhabitants, and in 1814 it was incorporated as a city. About 1830 the Miami Canal was built, and during the next 10 years the population increased 85 per cent. In 1840 the Little Miami, the first of the many railroads now centering at Cincinnati, was finished, and in 1850 the population had increased to 115,436. In 1860 it was 161,044, and in 1870, 216,239. The central position of Cincinnati in relation to extensive producing regions and to leading channels of commerce has

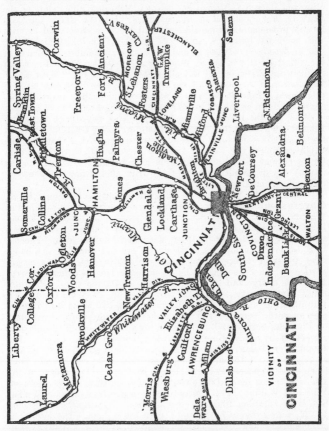

rendered it one of the most important commercial centers of the West; but manufactures constitute its chief interest. In 1875 there were 4,469 manufacturing establishments whose products were valued at $144,000,000. Iron, furniture, boots and shoes, beer and whisky, machinery and steamboats, are leading items in the product; but pork-packing is the principal industry. In this branch Cincinnati ranks next to Chicago, 563,359 hogs having been packed in 1875-'6.

There is no one among the streets of Cincinnati which has the same preëminence over the others as Broadway in New York, or even as Chestnut St. in Philadelphia. Of the business streets, *Pearl St.*, which contains nearly all the wholesale boot and shoe and dry-goods Houses, is noted for its splendid row of lofty, uniform stone fronts between Vine and Race Sts. *Third St.*, between Main and Vine, contains the banking, brokerage, and insurance offices. **Fourth St.** is the fashionable promenade and most select retail business street, and is lined with handsome buildings. In *Pike St.*, in *4th St.* from Pike to Broadway, and in *Broadway* between 3d and 5th Sts., are the finest residences of the "East End"; in *4th St.* W. of Smith, in *Dayton St.*, and in *Court St.* between Freeman and Baymiller Sts., those of the "West End." The portion of *Freeman St.* lying along the Lincoln Park is a favorite promenade. *Pike St.*, from 3d to 5th, along the old Longworth homestead, is known as the "Lover's Walk." Along Front St., at the foot of Main, lies the *Public Landing*, an open area, paved with bowlders, 1,000 ft. long and 425 feet wide. There are many beautiful drives in the vicinity of Cincinnati. One of the most attractive is that from the Brighton House, cor. Central Ave. and Freeman St., to Spring Grove Cemetery, and thence around Clifton and Avondale, returning to the city by way of Mount Auburn. This drive affords fine views of the city and surrounding country.

Of the public buildings, the finest in the city is the new * **U. S. Government Building** occupying the square bounded by Main and Walnut and 5th and 6th Sts., designed to accommodate the Custom-House, Post-Office, and U. S. Courts. It is of granite in the Renaissance style, 354 ft. long by 164 ft. deep, and 4 stories high. The old U. S. Government building, at the cor. of 4th and Vine Sts., is a handsome freestone edifice in the Roman-Corinthian style, with a classic portico on 4th St. supported by 6 columns. The * **County Court-House** is a large and imposing structure of Dayton stone, in the Roman-Corinthian style, in Main St., near Court St. The front has a porch with 6 Corinthian columns. With the *County Jail* in its rear, it occupies an entire square. The *City Buildings* occupy the entire square on Plum St., between 8th and 9th. They are large and handsome, and are set off by a trim little park, with a fountain in the center. The *Chamber of Commerce* is in 4th St., between Main and Walnut, but will shortly remove to the site of the present Post-Office, cor. 4th and Vine. Open every business-day from 11 A. M. to 1 P. M. The rooms of the *Board of Trade* are in Pike's magnificent building in 4th St., between Vine and Walnut. The * **Masonic Temple,** cor. 3d and Walnut Sts., is an imposing freestone structure in the Byzantine style, 195 by 100 ft., with 2 towers 140 ft. and a spire 180 ft. high. The interior is elaborately ornamented. Visitors admitted at 10 A. M. daily. *Odd-Fellows' Hall* is a spacious and handsomely furnished building, cor. 4th and Home Sts. Fine blocks of commercial buildings may be found in Pearl, Third, Fourth, Main, Walnut, and Vine Sts. The *Exposition Buildings*, in Elm St., fronting Washington Park, cover 3½ acres of ground, and have 7 acres' space for exhibiting. The Exposition opens annually during the first week in September, and closes the first week in October, and is always largely attended (admission, 25c.; children, 15c.). Adjoining the Exposition Buildings is the new ***Springer Music Hall,** a beautiful building in the modified Gothic style, 178 ft. wide, 293 ft. deep, and 150 ft. high from the side-walk to the pinnacles of the front gable. The auditorium seats 5,000 persons, the interior decorations are extremely rich, and the great organ is one of the largest in the world, having more pipes, but fewer speaking stops, than the famous Boston Music Hall organ. The carving on the case of the organ is worth attention. *Pike's Opera-House*, in 4th St., between Vine and Walnut, is one of the most imposing structures of the kind in the United States. It is of sandstone, in the Elizabethan style, and the interior is elaborately painted and frescoed. The *Public Library* building, in Vine St., between 6th and 7th, is one of the finest and largest in the city. It is of stone and brick, in the Romanesque style, is fire-proof, and will afford shelf-room for 300,000 volumes. The library now contains 110,000 volumes and a well-supplied reading-room (open from 8 A. M. to 10 P. M.). The ***Emery Arcade,** said to be the larges

in the world, extends from Vine to Race St. between 4th and 5th. The roof is of glass; it is well protected from the weather, and in it are shops of various kinds, and the Hotel Emery.

There is no public art-gallery in Cincinnati, but the private collections are numerous and valuable, especially those of Henry Probasco, on Clinton Heights, and Joseph Longworth, on Walnut Hills. (Visitors are always politely received.) The most notable work of art in the city is the ****Tyler-**

Tyler-Davidson Fountain.

Davidson Fountain, in 5th St., between Vine and Walnut. It stands on a freestone esplanade, 400 ft. long and 60 ft. wide. In the center of a porphyry-rimmed basin 40 ft. in diameter is the quatrefoil Saxon porphyry base supporting the bronze-work, whose base is 12 ft. square and 6 ft. high, with infant figures at each corner representing the delights of children in water. Bas-relief figures around the base represent the various uses of water to mankind. From the upper part of the bronze base extend 4 great basins, and from the center rises a column, up whose sides vines ascend and branch at the top in palm-like frondage. Around this column are groups of statuary; and on its summit stands a gigantic female figure, with outstretched arms, the water raining down in fine spray from her fingers. The work was cast in Munich, and cost nearly $200,000. It plays during warm days from morning till midnight.

The finest church edifice in the city is * St. Peter's Cathedral (Roman Catholic), in Plum St., between 7th and 8th. It is of Dayton limestone, in pure Grecian style, 200 by 80 ft., with a stone spire 224 ft. high, and a portico supported by 10 sandstone columns. The altar, of Carrara marble, was made in Genoa; and the altar-piece, "St. Peter Delivered," by Murillo, is one of the chief glories of art in America. *St. Xavier Church* (Roman Catholic), in Sycamore St., between 6th and 7th, is a fine specimen of the pointed Gothic style, with a spire 350 ft. high. *St. Paul's* (Episcopal), in 4th St., between Main and Walnut, is a quaint structure in the Norman-Gothic style, and has fine music. *St. John's* (Episcopal), cor. 7th and Plum Sts., is of stone and stuccoed brick, in the Norman style, notable for its square towers, rough ashlar gable, and deep and lofty Norman door. * St. Paul's (Methodist), cor. 7th and Smith Sts., of blue limestone, in cruciform style, has a fine interior and a spire 200 ft. high. The *First Presbyterian*, in 4th St., between Main and Walnut, is noted for its huge tower surmounted by a spire 270 ft. high, terminating in a gilded hand, the finger pointing upward. The *Baptist Church*, in 9th St., between Vine and Race, is a handsome building with massive clock-tower. The *First Congrega- tional*, cor. Plum and 8th Sts., is surmounted by a dome and lighted from the roof. Some of the German churches "over the Rhine" are very large, and the music excellent. The * Hebrew Synagogue, in Plum St., opposite the Cathedral, is of brick, profusely ornamented with stone in the Moorish style, and has one of the most brilliant interiors in the city. The *Hebrew Temple*, cor. 8th and Mound Sts., is in the Gothic style, with double spires, and the interior is gorgeously frescoed.

The educational and charitable institutions of Cincinnati are numerous and important. The * University of Cincinnati, founded and endowed by the late Charles McMicken, has an imposing building at the cor. of Hamilton Road and Elm St. Connected with the University are the *School of Design* and the *Law School*, both of which are in the College Building, in Walnut St., between 4th and 5th. * St. Xavier's College (Jesuit), cor. Sycamore and 7th Sts., is a splendid building in the Romanesque style, of brick, profusely ornamented with stone. The college possesses a library of 12,000 volumes, valuable chemical and philosophical apparatus, a museum, and a large mineralogical and geological collection. The *Wesleyan Female College* is a prosperous institution, with a spacious and handsome building in Wesley Ave., between Court and Clark Sts. The *Seminary of Mount St. Mary's* is a famous Roman Catholic college, beautifully situated on Western Hills, which command extensive views. *Lane Theological Seminary* (Presbyterian) is situated on E. Walnut Hills, and possesses a library of 12,000 volumes. The *Medical College of Ohio* is one of the most famous in the West, and has a very fine building in 6th St., between Vine and Race. The *Miami Medical College*, in 12th St., near the Hospital, is another famous institution. The *Chickering Classical and Scientific Institute* in George St., between Smith and John, is the largest private school for boys in the West. The *Hughes High School*, in 5th St., at the head of the Mound, is an imposing edifice in the Gothic style, with octagon towers at the corners. The *Woodward High School* is an ornate building in Franklin St., between Sycamore and Broadway. The *Mechanics' Institute* is a commodious building, cor. 6th and Vine Sts., containing a library of 6,500 volumes and a reading-room.

In 12th St., between Central Ave. and Plum St., occupying a square of 4 acres, stands the * **Cincinnati Hospital,** said to be the largest and best appointed institution of its kind in the country. It consists of eight distinct buildings arranged *en échelon* round a central court, and connected by corridors. The central building, through which is the main entrance, is surmounted by a dome and spire 110 ft. high. The *Good Samaritan Hospital* is a fine, large, red-brick building, situated on a grassy hill at the cor. of 6th and Locke Sts. *St. Mary's Hospital,* cor. Baymiller and Betts Sts., is also a fine and spacious building. The * **Longview Asylum for the Insane**, at Carthage, 10 miles N. of the city, is of brick, in the Italian style, 612 ft. long and 3 and 4 stories high. Its grounds are laid out in beautiful lawns, walks, and parks, with greenhouses. There are no bars to the windows, and everything prison-like is avoided. The *House of Refuge* is situated in Mill Creek Valley, 1 mile N. of the city limits. The buildings are of blue limestone trimmed with white Dayton stone, and are surrounded by 6 acres of ground. The *City Workhouse* is near the House of Refuge. The main building is 510 ft. long, and is one of the most imposing edifices about the city. The *Cincinnati Orphan Asylum* is a spacious brick edifice at Mount Auburn, comprising ample grounds which command extensive views.

The chief public park of Cincinnati is * **Eden Park,** situated on a hill in the E. district, and commanding magnificent views of the city, the valley of the Ohio, and the surrounding country. It contains 216 acres, beautifully laid out and adorned; and in it are the two new city reservoirs, which look like natural lakes. *Burnet Woods*, on a hill N. of the city, contains 170 acres, nearly all forest. *Lincoln Park*, in Freeman St., between Betts and Hopkins, contains only 18 acres, but is admirably adorned and finely shaded. *Washington Park*, one of the oldest pleasure-grounds in the city, formerly a cemetery, is in 12th St., between Race St. and the Miami Canal. It comprises 10 acres. *Hopkins's Park* is a small lawn with shubbery on Mount Auburn, N. of the

city.   * **Spring Grove Cemetery,** one of the most beautiful in the
West, lies 5 miles N. W. of the city, in the valley of Mill Creek, and is
approached by an attractive avenue 100 ft. wide.   It contains 600 acres
well wooded and picturesquely laid out, and many fine monuments.
The entrance-buildings are in the Norman-Gothic style, and cost $50,-
000.   The chief attractions are the Dexter mausoleum, representing a
Gothic chapel, and a * bronze statue of a soldier, cast in Munich, erected in 1864 to the memory of the Ohio volunteers who died during the war.

More than a third of the residents of Cincinnati are Germans or of
German parentage.   They occupy the large section of the city N. of the
Miami Canal, which they have named " the Rhine."   The visitor finds
himself in an entirely different country " *over the Rhine,*" for he hears
no language but German, and all the signs and placards are in German.
The business, dwellings, theatres, halls, churches, and especially the
beer-gardens, all remind the European tourist of Germany.   Strangers
should visit the Great Arbeiter and Turner Halls, in Walnut St., Heuck's
Opera House, cor. Vine and 13th Sts., and some one of the vast beer-
cellars, which can be found almost anywhere "over the Rhine."   The
* **Suspension-Bridge** over the Ohio, connecting the city with Covington, Ky., is the pride of Cincinnati.   From tower to tower it is
1,057 ft. long; the entire length is 2,252 ft., and its height over the
water 100 ft.   There is another handsome suspension-bridge over the
Licking River, connecting the cities of Covington and Newport.   By
taking the horse-cars at Front St., in an hour's ride one may cross both
these bridges, and return to the starting-point, having been in two
States and three cities, and having crossed two navigable rivers.   There
are also two pier railroad-bridges across the Ohio at Cincinnati.   The
Water-Works, in E. Front St., near the Little Miami Depot, are well worth
a visit.   There are 4 pumping-engines with a capacity of 30,000,000 gallons a day.   Well worth visiting are the *United Railroads Stock Yards,*
comprising 50 acres on Spring Grove Ave., built at a cost of $750,000, and
with accommodations for 25,000 hogs, 10,000 sheep, and 5,000 cattle.
There are 4 *Inclined Planes,* leading from the terrace on which the
business portion of the city is built to the top of the surrounding hills.
At the head of each is an extensive Beer-Garden, viz., Mt. Adams,
Highland House; Mt. Auburn, Lookout House; head of Elm St., Bellevue House; and Price's Hill.   No one should miss the views from
Price's Hill and from the * Lookout House, Mt. Auburn (reached by
horse-cars from cor. Main and 5th Sts.).

71. Cincinnati to Louisville.

Besides the routes described below, Louisville may be reached from Cincinnati
by steamer on the Ohio River.   There are two or three steamers daily, and in summer the trip is a very pleasant one.   The scenery along the river is both varied and
attractive (see Route 119).

a. Via Louisville, Cincinnati & Lexington R. R.   Distance, 110 *miles.*

LEAVING Cincinnati by this route the train at once crosses the
Ohio River on a long and lofty pier-bridge to **Newport,** a very

handsome city of Kentucky, with a population of 15,000. It is built on an elevated plain commanding a fine view, and is ornamented and made attractive by numerous shade-trees. In the city and its suburbs are a large number of fine residences, and the schools are noted for their excellence. As already mentioned in the description of Cincinnati, a graceful suspension-bridge across the Licking River connects Newport with **Covington,** which in turn is connected with Cincinnati by the famous suspension-bridge across the Ohio. Covington is a city of 25,000 inhabitants, the largest in Kentucky after Louisville, but is substantially a suburb of Cincinnati, whose business men have here many costly residences. It is built upon a beautiful plain several miles in extent, and includes within its corporate limits over 1,350 acres. The combined *Court-House* and *City Hall* is a handsome edifice ; and the *U. S. Post-Office* and Court building cost $150,000. There is a public library with 5,000 volumes, and several flourishing educational institutions. The *Hospital of St. Elizabeth* (Roman Catholic) occupies a commodious building, with ample grounds adorned with shrubbery, in the center of the city, and has a foundling asylum connected with it. Beyond Newport, the Louisville train crosses the Licking River, passes in rear of Covington, and traverses a rich but uninteresting agricultural region. The stations passed are small. From *Walton* (21 miles) stages run to Williamstown, and at *Lagrange* (83 miles) a branch road diverges to Frankfort and Lexington.

　　　b. Via Ohio & Mississippi R. R.　　Distance, 127 miles.

As far as *N. Vernon* (73 miles) this route is described in Route 73. From N. Vernon the road runs S. through one of the most productive and populous sections of southern Indiana, which, however, offers little to attract the eye of the traveler. The numerous stations *en route* are mostly small villages, none of which require special mention. At *Jeffersonville* (126 miles) the train crosses the Ohio River on a magnificent bridge which is described in connection with Louisville.

72. Louisville.

Hotels.—The *Galt House* ($3 to $4 a day), a massive stone structure in the English style, has long been celebrated as one of the best hotels in the United States. The *Louisville Hotel* ($3 to $3.50 a day), in Main St., between 6th and 7th, and the *Willard Hotel* ($3 a day), in Jefferson, between 5th and 6th Sts., are both commodious and well-kept houses.

Modes of Conveyance.—The *Horse-car* system is excellent, affording easy access to all parts of the city (fare 5c.). *Carriages* are in waiting at the depots and steamboat-landings, and in the vicinity of the hotels. Their charges are regulated by law, and are as follows : Per hour, $2 for the first hour, and $1 for each subsequent hour ; from depots and steamboat-landings, 50c. for each person. There are two *Ferries*, one to Jeffersonville from the foot of First St., and one to New Albany from Portland (foot of Ferry St.).

Railroad Depots.—The depot of the *Louisville, Cincinnati & Lexington R. R.* is on Jefferson St., cor. Brook ; that of the *Louisville, Nashville & Great Southern R. R.*, on Maple St., cor. 10th ; the *Louisville, Paducah & Southwestern R. R.*, the *Jeffersonville, Madison & Indianapolis R. R.*, the *Ohio & Mississippi R. R.*, and the *Louisville, New Albany & Chicago R. R.*, cor. Main and 14th

14

St.; the *Louisville, Harrod's Creek & Westport R. R.* (narrow gauge), on First St., near the river.

Theatres and Amusements.—*Macauley's Theatre*, in Walnut St., near 4th, is the most fashionable place of amusement, and is fitted up in handsome style. *Library Hall*, 4th St., between Green and Walnut, *Liederkranz Hall*, Market St., near 2d, and *Masonic Temple*, cor. Jefferson and 4th Sts., are tasteful and commodious buildings. *Central* and *Floral Parks*, in the S. part of the city (reached by the 4th St. and 6th St. cars), are noted places of summer resort.

Reading-Rooms.—In the leading hotels are reading-rooms, provided with newspapers, etc., for the use of guests. The *Public Library*, on 4th Ave. bet. Green and Walnut Sts., has 30,000 volumes, a natural history museum with 100,-000 specimens, and a reading-room (open from 9 A. M. to 10 P. M.). The *Louisville Library Association*, cor. 5th and Walnut Sts., has a library of 7,000 volumes and a well-supplied reading-room.

Post-Office.—The Post-Office is at the cor. of Green and Third Sts. It is open on secular days from 7 A. M. to 6 P. M.; on Sundays from 8 to 9 A. M. Letters may also be mailed in the lamp-post boxes, whence they are collected several times a day.

LOUISVILLE, the chief city of Kentucky, and one of the most im portant in the country, is situated at the Falls of the Ohio, where Beargrass Creek enters that river. Its site is one of peculiar excellence. The hills which line the river through the greater part of its course recede just above the city, and do not approach it again for more than 20 miles, leaving an almost level plain about 6 miles wide, and elevated about 70 ft. above low-water mark. The Falls, which are quite picturesque, may be seen from the town. In high stages of the water they disappear almost entirely, and steamboats pass over them; but, when the water is low, the whole width of the river has the appearance of a great many broken cascades of foam making their way over the rapids. To obviate the obstruction to navigation caused by the falls, a canal, 2½ miles long, has been cut around them to a place called Shippingport. It was a work of vast labor, being for the greater part of its course cut through the solid rock, and cost nearly $1,000,000. The city extends about 3 miles along the river and about 4 miles inland, embracing an area of 13 square miles.

The first settlement of Louisville was made by 13 families, who accompanied Colonel George Rogers Clarke on his expedition down the Ohio in 1778. The town was established in 1780, and called Louisville, in honor of Louis XVI. of France, whose troops were then aiding the Americans in their struggle for independence. It was incorporated as a city in 1828, when its population was about 10,000. In 1850 the population had increased to 43,194; in 1860 to 68,033; and in 1870 to 100,-753. The trade of Louisville is immense. It is one of the largest leaf-tobacco markets in the world, the sales of this one article amounting to over $5,000,000 annually. The trade in provisions aggregates from $11,000,000 to $15,000,000 annually; and the city is rapidly becoming one of the most important markets for live-stock in the country. Pork-packing is extensively carried on, and the sugar-curing of hams is a special feature of the business. The annual product of iron foots up $5,-000,000. Louisville is the great distributing market for the fine whiskies made by the Kentucky distilleries. The manufacture of beer has also become a very important interest. Leather, cement, agricultural implements, furniture, and iron pipes for water and gas mains, are the other leading manufactures.

The city is regularly laid out, with wide, well-paved streets, and large squares, which are bisected each way by paved alleys 20 ft. wide. The beauty of the residences is a notable feature of the city; most of them are set back from the street, leaving lawns in front, which are planted with flowers and shrubbery, and the streets are lined with shade-trees. The business portion is compactly built, and contains many fine edifices. *Main, Market, Jefferson,* and *Fourth,* are the principal streets in this section.

The public buildings of Louisville are not fine architecturally, but are of a solid and substantial character. The ***Court-House**, in Jefferson St., between 5th and 6th, is a large granite structure, with Doric portico and columns, and cost over $1,000,000. The ***City Hall** is the most ambitious edifice in the city, and is much admired.

Louisville City Hall.

It is of stone, in the Composite style, with a square clock-tower at one corner, and cost $500,000. The Council-room is very fine. The *Custom-House,* which also contains the *Post-Office,* is a plain but substantial building at the corner of Green and 3d Sts. The *Masonic Temple,* corner 4th and Green Sts., is a handsome structure, with tasteful interior decorations. The *Industrial Exposition Building,* located in 4th St.

between Walnut and Chestnut, is spacious and graceful in design, and in summer, when the Exhibition is in progress, presents an attractive and characteristic spectacle. The new * building of the *Courier-Journal*, cor. 4th and Green Sts., is by far the handsomest in the city, and is one of the most completely appointed newspaper offices in America.

Of the numerous church edifices which adorn the city, the most noteworthy are the *Cathedral* (Roman Catholic), on 5th St., near Walnut; the *Second Presbyterian*, cor. Broadway and 2d; *College Street Presbyterian*, cor. College and 2d; the *Church of the Messiah* (Unitarian), cor. 4th and York; the *Temple Adas Israel*, cor. Broadway and 6th; and *Broadway Church* (Baptist), Broadway, between Brook and Floyd. These are all fine edifices, of imposing appearance, and exhibiting much architectural beauty.

The * **Public Library** occupies a commodious edifice on 4th Ave. between Green and Walnut Sts. The library numbers 30,000 volumes, and connected with it is a museum and natural history department, with 100,000 specimens. The celebrated Troost collection of minerals, one of the largest in the United States, is included in it. Louisville being the center of one of the finest fossiliferous regions in the world, there are numerous private collections, containing many excellent specimens elsewhere rare. The *Louisville University Medical College* is a flourishing institution, and has one of the finest buildings in the city, at the corner of 9th and Chestnut Sts. The *Louisville Medical College* and *Hospital College of Medicine* are prosperous institutions of learning. The two *High Schools* (male and female) are large and handsome brick structures. The *Colored Normal School*, dedicated in 1873, is probably the finest public-school edifice designed for the instruction of negroes in the country.

The * **State Blind School,** on the Lexington Turnpike, E. of the city, is a massive and imposing structure, one of the finest of its kind in the Southwest. In the same building is the *American Printing House for the Blind*, established in 1858 and endowed by Act of Congress in 1879 with $250,000, the interest of which is to be used in manufacturing embossed books and apparatus for all the schools for the blind in the United States. The *Almshouse* is a large building in the midst of ample grounds near the W. limits of the city (reached by Park St.). The *City Hospital* is a plain but spacious edifice in Preston St., between Madison and Chestnut. Other important charitable institutions are the *House of Refuge for Boys*, the *House of Refuge for Girls*, the *Eruptive Hospital*, and the *St. Vincent Orphan Asylum* (Roman Catholic), in Jefferson St., near Wenzell.

Strangers should visit * **Cave Hill Cemetery,** if for nothing else, to see the monument of George D. Prentice, the poet, journalist, and politician. The monument consists of a Grecian canopy, of marble, resting on four columns, with an urn in the center, and on the top a lyre with a broken string. The cemetery is situated just E. of the city limits, and contains other noteworthy monuments. *Silver Creek*, 4 miles below the city, on the Indiana side, is a beautiful rocky stream, and a favorite fishing and picnic place for the citizens. *Harrod's Creek*, 8 miles up the Ohio, *Riverside*, *Smyser's*, and the *Water-Works Grounds* afford pleasant excursions. The *Lexington* and *Bardstown* turnpikes afford enjoyable drives through a picturesque and well-cultivated country. *Jeffersonville*, a flourishing town on the Indiana shore, opposite Louisville, and connected with it by ferry and bridge, is situated on an elevation from which a fine view of Louisville may be obtained. The great railroad-bridge across the Ohio at this point is 5,219 ft. long, divided into 25 spans, supported by 24 stone piers, and cost $2,016,819. **New Albany,** opposite the W. end of Louisville, is a finely-situated and handsomely-built city of 25,000 inhabitants, with wide and delightfully-shaded streets, fine churches and public buildings, and handsome private residences. "From the hills back of New Albany," says Mr. Edward King, "one may look down on the huge extent of Louisville, half hidden beneath the foliage which surrounds so many of its houses; can note the steamers slowly winding about the bends in the Ohio, or carefully working their way up to the broad levees, can see the trains crawling like serpents over the high suspended bridge, and the church spires and towers gleaming under the mellow sunlight."

73. Cincinnati to St. Louis.

By the Ohio & Mississippi R. R. Through trains from Baltimore to St. Louis *via* Baltimore & Ohio R. R. (Route 65) run on this line. Close connection is made with the trains of the various routes from New York to Cincinnati. Another way of reaching St. Louis from Cincinnati is by steamer on the Ohio River and Mississippi River. This latter is a pleasant route in summer. *Stations on the Ohio & Mississippi R. R.:* North Bend, 15 miles; Lawrenceburg, 20; Aurora, 24; Osgood, 52; Nebraska, 62; N. Vernon, 73; Seymour, 87; Medora, 106; Washington, 173; Vincennes, 192; Olney, 223; Clay City, 238; Xenia, 254; Salem, 271; Odin, 276; Sandoval, 280; Lebanon, 317; Caseyville, 331; St. Louis, 340.

THIS route traverses from side to side the great States of Indiana and Illinois, passing through an extremely rich agricultural country which is for the most part under fine cultivation. The numerous towns and villages *en route* are neat and attractive, with that air of busy prosperity about them which is eminently characteristic of the West; but, like the stretches of country between them, they are curiously alike, and few present any features requiring special notice. For 25 miles after leaving Cincinnati the train runs nearly parallel with the Ohio River. *North Bend* (15 miles) is a pretty village on the river, noted as the residence of General William Henry Harrison, President of the United States. His tomb, a modest brick structure, stands on a commanding hill, whence there is a fine view, including portions of Ohio, Indiana, and Kentucky. Three miles beyond N. Bend, the train crosses the Great Miami River and enters Indiana, speedily reaching *Lawrenceburg* (20 miles), a city of 3,500 inhabitants, on the Ohio River at the end of the Whitewater Canal, which affords a good water-power for several factories. The Indianapolis, Cincinnati & Lafayette R. R. connects here. Four miles beyond Lawrenceburg, also on the river, is the beautiful little city of **Aurora** (*Indiana House, Eagle Hotel*), with 5,000 inhabitants, and a large trade derived from the rich farming country of which it is the shipping port. A number of small stations are now passed. From *N. Vernon* (73 miles) the Louisville branch diverges and runs S. in 54 miles to **Louisville** (see p. 313). *Seymour* (87 miles) is a thriving village at the intersection of the Jeffersonville, Madison & Indianapolis R. R.; and *Mitchell* (127 miles) is at the crossing of the Louisville, New Albany & Chicago R. R. *Washington* (173 miles) is a small town, capital of Daviess County, and 19 miles beyond is **Vincennes** (*Laplant House, Grand Hotel*) a flourishing city of 8,500 inhabitants on the E. bank of the Wabash River, which is here navigable by steamboats. Vincennes is the oldest town in the State, having been settled by the French Canadians, who established a mission here in 1702, and a few years later built a fort. It became the capital of the territory of Indiana upon its organization in 1800 and so remained until 1814. The surrounding country is fertile and abounds in coal, and the city enjoys good manufacturing facilities. The leading establishments are the flouring-mills and the extensive machine-shops of the O. & M. R. R. The public schools are excellent, and there are 10 churches and 4 libraries. *Vincennes University*, chartered in 1807, is conducted as a high school.

Leaving Vincennes, the train crosses the Wabash River and enters the State of Illinois, passing at frequent intervals a number of small stations. *Olney* (223 miles) is the capital of Richland County, the general character of which is suggested by its name. It is one of the most prosperous places on the line of the road, and boasts of a school-house which cost $80,000. *Clay City* (238 miles), *Xenia* (254 miles), and *Salem* (271 miles) are neat and thriving villages. *Odin* (276 miles) is at the crossing of the Chicago Branch of the Illinois Central R. R. (Route 79), and *Sandoval* (280 miles) is at the crossing of the Main Line of the Illinois Central R. R. Sandoval is a prosperous place, in the midst of a fine fruit-growing region, and has an engine-house and large repair-shops of the O. & M. R. R. *Carlyle* (293 miles) is situated on the Kaskaskia River, on the margin of a fine prairie, and is a lumber-market of some importance, logs being floated to this point, where they are made into lumber and sent to St. Louis. *Lebanon* (317 miles) is a beautifully-situated and well-built village, with a handsome Union school-house, and the seat of McKendree College. At *Caseyville* (331 miles) the train first enters the great American Bottom, or Valley of the Mississippi. The village is built just at the foot of the bluff, and is one of the principal points from which St. Louis is supplied with coal; the bluffs being underlain for many miles by inexhaustible deposits. At *E. St. Louis* (339 miles) the train crosses the Mississippi on the splendid bridge which is described in connection with St. Louis. **St. Louis** (see p. 323).

74. New York to St. Louis via Cleveland and Indianapolis.

By the N. Y. Central R. R. and the Lake Shore & Michigan Southern R. R. (Route 62) to Cleveland; and thence by the Cleveland, Columbus, Cincinnati & Indianapolis R. R. (commonly called the "Bee Line"). Through trains, with Drawing-room and Sleeping cars attached, run through from New York to St. Louis on this route, without change of cars, in 38 hours. Distances : New York to Cleveland, 623 miles; to Crestline, 698; to Galion, 703; to Bellefontaine, 764; to Indianapolis, 906; to Terre Haute, 978; to Mattoon, 1,034; to Alton Junction, 1,146; to St. Louis, 1,167.

FROM New York to **Cleveland** (623 miles) this route is described in Route 62. From Cleveland to *Galion* (703 miles) it is described in Route 67. At Galion the Indianapolis Div. of the C., C., C. & I. R. R. diverges from the main line, and runs nearly due W. through one of the richest sections of Ohio. *Marion* (724 miles) is at the intersection of the Atlantic & Great Western R. R. (see Route 69). *Bellefontaine* (764 miles) is a flourishing town of about 4,000 inhabitants, so named from the numerous fine springs in the neighborhood. It is surrounded by a productive and populous agricultural country, and has a large trade. There are also several manufactories, and the County buildings are located here, Bellefontaine being the capital of Logan County. *Sidney* (787 miles) is a neat village, built upon an elevated plateau on the W. bank of the Great Miami River, which affords a fine water-power. A navigable feeder of the Miami Canal also passes through the place. In the center of the village is a neat public square, around which are the principal buildings. *Union* (820 miles) is situated directly on the boundary-line, and is partly in Ohio and partly in Indiana. It is a flourishing place, and an important railroad centre. *Winchester* (831 miles) and *Muncie* (853 miles) are pretty towns. *Anderson* (870 miles) is picturesquely situated on a high bluff on the left bank of White River, in the midst of a very fertile region. A few miles above the village is a dam by which a fall of 34 ft. is obtained, the extensive water-power being used in numerous manufacturing establishments. *Pendleton* (878 miles) is a thriving village on Fall Creek, which affords a good water-power. In the vicinity are quarries of limestone. *Fortville* (886 miles) is a small station, 20 miles beyond which the train reaches

Indianapolis.

Hotels, etc.—The leading hotels are the *Grand Hotel* ($3 a day); the *Bates House* ($2.50 a day); the *Occidental* ($3 a day); the *Remy House* ($2.50 a day); and the *Sherman House* ($2 a day). *Horse-cars* render all parts of the city easily accessible, and there are 9 bridges across the river (three of them for railroad purposes). The *Post-Office* is at the cor. of Pennsylvania and Market Sts.

Indianapolis, the capital and largest city of Indiana, is situated near the center of the State, on the W. fork of White River, 110 miles N. W. of Cincinnati, and 165 miles S. E. of Chicago. The city is built in the midst of a fertile plain, chiefly on the E. bank of the river, which is crossed by 9 bridges. The streets are 90 ft. wide (except Washington St., which has a width of 120 ft.), and cross each other at right angles; but there are four long avenues radiating from a central square (the Circle) and traversing the city diagonally. Indianapolis was first settled in 1819, became the seat of the State government in 1825, was incorporated in 1836, and received a city charter in 1847. In 1840 it had a population of only 2,692; in 1850, 8,091; in 1860, 18,611; in 1870, 48,244; and in 1876, upward of 90,000. Its trade has kept pace with the growth of its population, and its manufactures are varied and important, the principal industries being pork-packing, and the manufacture of machinery, agricultural implements, cars, carriages, furniture, and flour. No less than 12 completed railways converge here, making it one of the great railway centers of the West.

Washington St. is the principal thoroughfare, and many business houses are clustered on *South Meridian, Pennsylvania,* and *Illinois Sts.* The most prominent public building is the * **State House,** now in course of erection. It will occupy two entire squares, and is estimated to cost about $2,000,000. The * **Court-House,** completed in 1876 at a cost of $1,200,000, is an imposing structure. The *State Institute for the Blind,* in North St., between Illinois and Meridian, was built in 1847, at a cost of $300,000, and is surrounded by 8 acres of grounds. The main building has a front of 150 ft., and is five stories high, consisting of a center and two wings, each surmounted by a Corinthian cupola, the center also having an Ionic portico. The *State Lunatic Asylum,* 1½ mile W. of the city limits, is a fine group of buildings, surrounded by 160 acres of grounds, a portion of which is handsomely laid out and adorned. The *State Institute for the Deaf and Dumb,* just E. of the city limits, was erected in 1848 at a cost of $220,000. The grounds comprise 105 acres, handsomely laid out and adorned with trees and shrubbery. The *U. S. Arsenal,* 1 mile E. of the city, is a handsome building, and is surrounded by 75 acres of grounds. The **Union Passenger Depot** (in Louisiana St., between Illinois and Meridian) is 420 ft. long, and is one of the most spacious and convenient structures of the kind in the country. Other prominent public buildings are the *Post-Office,* cor. Pennsylvania and Market Sts.; the *City Hall, County Jail,* and *City Prison;* the *Masonic Hall,* cor. Washington and Tennessee Sts.; and the *Odd-Fellows' Hall,* cor. Washington and Pennsylvania Sts. Of the churches, the most noteworthy are *Christ* and *St. Paul's,* Episcopal; *Meridian St.* and *Roberts Park,* Methodist; *First* and *Second,* Presbyterian; *First,* Baptist; *Plymouth,* Congregational; the Roman Catholic *Cathedral;* and the Jewish *Synagogue.* The *Butler University,* founded in 1850, occupies a handsome Gothic building 4 miles E. of the city; it admits both sexes, and has a library of 5,000 volumes. The *State Library* contains 15,000 volumes, and there is a *Free City Library* with 30,000 volumes. The principal charitable institutions are two *Asylums for Orphans,* the *German Orphan Asylum,* the Catholic *Female Reformatory and Asylum,* the Catholic *Infirmary,* and a *City Hospital.*

There are 6 public parks in the city, viz.: the *Circle,* in the center, containing 4 acres, and ornamented with shade trees; the *Military Park,* 18 acres; *University Park,* 4 acres; the *Trotting Park,* with a course of one mile, 86 acres ; a park in the N. portion of the city, embracing 100 acres ; and the *State-Fair Grounds*, with Exposition Building, containing 40 acres. *Greenbaum Cemetery* is within the city limits, and is coeval with the city itself; 2 miles N. of the city is **Crown Hill,** which is handsomely laid out and tastefully adorned; and the *Catholic Cemetery* is just S. of the city limits.

At Indianapolis the train makes a short pause, and then, taking the track of the Indianapolis & St. Louis R. R., resumes the journey to St. Louis. *Danville* (20 miles from Indianapolis, 926 from New York) is a pretty village, with county buildings which cost $180,000. **Greencastle** (944 miles, *Grand Central Hotel*) is a handsome little academic city of 4,000 inhabitants, pleasantly situated on a high table-land, in the midst of a rich farming and extensive stock-raising region. It contains a Court-House, a Jail, a large rolling mill and nail factory, 7 public schools, including a High School, and several churches. The *Indiana Asbury University* (Methodist), founded in 1835, is open to both sexes, and has nearly 500 students. The Whitcomb and the college circulating libraries contain 9,000 volumes. There is also in the city a flourishing Presbyterian female college. The Vandalia line to St. Louis (see Route 75) touches Greencastle, and runs nearly parallel with the present line to **Terre Haute** (*Terre Haute House, National*). Terre Haute is a city of about 25,000 inhabitants, beautifully situated on an elevated plateau on the E. bank of the Wabash River, which is here spanned by 3 bridges. It is regularly laid out and well built, and its broad streets, crossing each other at right angles, are ornamented with shade trees. It contains a commodious Market-House and City Hall, a good Opera-House, two Orphan Asylums, 8 fine public school buildings, several private schools and academies, 2 public libraries, and 20 churches. The State Normal School is a spacious edifice erected at a cost of $230,000. Terre Haute is the center of trade for a rich and populous region, abounding in coal, and has extensive manufactures, including blast furnaces, glass and iron works, and machine-shops. It is also an important railroad center, being the point of intersection of 7 lines, and the Wabash River is navigable for steamboats during a portion of the year.

Leaving Terre Haute the train crosses the Wabash River into the State of Illinois, passes several small stations, of which *Paris* (997 miles) and *Charleston* (1,023 miles) are the principal, and soon reaches *Mattoon* (1,034 miles), one of the principal towns between Terre Haute and St. Louis. The Chicago Branch of the Illinois Central R. R. (Route 79) crosses here, and here are the machine-shops, round house, and car-works of this division of the road. *Pana* (1,073 miles) is a prosperous little city at the crossing of the Northern Div. of the Illinois Central R. R. It is surrounded by a rich agricultural region with which it does a large trade. *Litchfield* (1,112 miles) is another busy little city, situated on a high and fertile prairie, with coal-mines in the neighborhood which afford an abundant supply of fuel. There are several grain-elevators here; and besides several steam-mills it contains

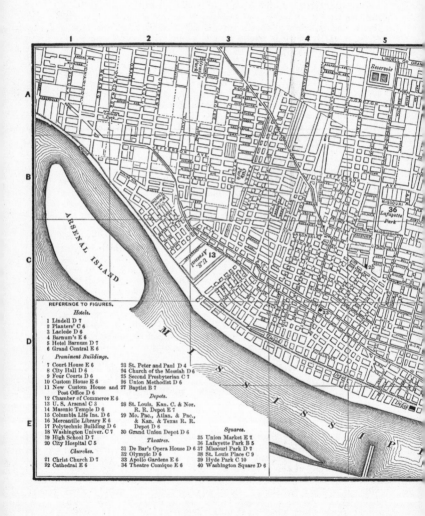

REFERENCE TO FIGURES.

Hotels.

1 Lindell D 7
2 Planters' C 6
3 Laclede D 6
4 Barnum's E 6
5 Hotel Barnum D 7
6 Grand Central E 6

Prominent Buildings.

7 Court House E 6
8 City Hall D 6
9 Four Courts D 6
10 Custom House E 6
11 New Custom House and Post Office D 6
12 Chamber of Commerce E 6
13 U. S. Arsenal C 3
14 Masonic Temple D 6
15 Columbia Life Ins. D 6
16 Mercantile Library E 6
17 Polytechnic Building D 6
18 Washington Univer. C 7
19 High School D 7
20 City Hospital C 5

Churches.

21 Christ Church D 7
22 Cathedral E 6
23 St. Peter and Paul D 4
24 Church of the Messiah D 6
25 Second Presbyterian C 7
26 Union Methodist D 6
27 Baptist B 7

Depots.

28 St. Louis, Kan. C. & Nor. R. R. Depot E 7
29 Mo. Pac., Atlan. & Pac., & Kan. & Texas R. R. Depot D 6
30 Grand Union Depot D 6

Theatres.

31 De Bar's Opera House D 6
32 Olympic D 6
33 Apollo Gardens E 6
34 Theatre Comique E 6

Squares.

35 Union Market E 7
36 Lafayette Park B 5
37 Missouri Park D 7
38 St. Louis Place C 7
39 Hyde Park C 10
40 Washington Square D 6

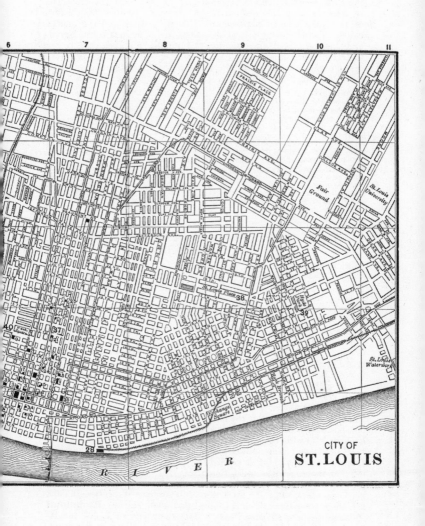

CITY OF
ST. LOUIS

the R. R. construction and repair-shops. At *Bethalto* (1,142 miles) the road leaves the prairie and enters the "American Bottom", as the strip of rich alluvial land between the Mississippi River and the bluffs is called; scattered over it in all directions are numerous lakes, bayous, and sloughs. From *Alton Junction* (1,146 miles) a branch line diverges to **Alton** (see Route 80). At *E. St. Louis* (1,166 miles) the train crosses the Mississippi on the noble bridge described in connection with St. Louis. **St. Louis** (see p. 323).

Wabash Line.—Another favorite route from New York to St. Louis, though no through trains are run on it, is *via* the Wabash R. R., which runs from *Toledo, Ohio*, across northern Ohio, northern Indiana, and central Illinois, to *St. Louis*. Toledo is reached from New York *via* N. Y. Central and Lake Shore R. R. (Route 62); also *via* Erie R. R. (Route 63) and the Canada Southern R. R. (see p. 271). Close connection is made at Toledo with trains on both these routes; and there is no change of cars between Toledo and St. Louis. At *Fort Wayne*, the Wabash R. R. connects with Route 64 from New York; so that the "Wabash Line" may be combined with either of the great routes from the seaboard to the far West. The Wabash R. R. runs nearly parallel to and a little N. of the route described above, and through a very similar section of country. The principal cities and towns on the line are *Fort Wayne*, *Wabash*, *Peru*, *Logansport*, and *Lafayette*, in Indiana; and *Danville*, *Tolono*, and *Decatur*, in Illinois. It intersects Route 74 at Litchfield (55 miles from St. Louis). The time from New York to St. Louis by the "Wabash Line" is 38 to 40 hours.

75. New York to St. Louis via Philadelphia, Pittsburg, and Indianapolis.

By the Pennsylvania R. R., the Pittsburg, Cincinnati, & St. Louis R. R., and the St. Louis, Vandalia, Terre Haute & Indianapolis R. R. This is commonly called the "Pan Handle" and "Vandalia" Line. Through trains, with Pullman Palace drawing-room and sleeping cars attached, run through from New York to St. Louis, without change of cars, in about 36 hours. Distances: to Columbus, 637 miles; to Urbana, 684; to Piqua, 710; to Richmond, 757; to Indianapolis, 825; to Terre Haute, 898; to Vandalia, 996; to St. Louis, 1,063.

As far as **Columbus** (637 miles) this route is the same as Route 68. *Milford* (665 miles) is at the crossing of the Springfield Branch of the C., C., C. & I. R. R. (Route 67), and *Urbana* (684 miles) is at the crossing of the Atlantic & Great Western R. R. (Route 69). Urbana is described on page 304. Twenty-six miles beyond Urbana the train reaches **Piqua** (*City Hotel, Leland*), a city of 8,000 inhabitants, charmingly situated on the W. bank of the Great Miami River, just at a bend which leaves a level plateau between the city and the water's edge, while on the opposite side the bank rises boldly. The city is regularly laid out with wide streets, and is substantially built. A large business is carried on with the surrounding country, which is rich in agricultural products. Water-power is supplied by the Miami Canal, and considerable manufacturing is carried on, the principal establishments being car-shops, woolen mills, foundries, etc. At *Bradford Junction* (720 miles) the road branches; one division running N. W. to Chicago via Logansport, while the present route continues W., enters Indiana a little beyond *Greenville* (721 miles), and soon reaches **Richmond** (*Githens House, Arlington Hotel*), a flourishing city of 12,000 inhabitants, situated on the E. fork of the Whitewater River, in the center of a fertile agricultural district from which it derives an important trade. It has an abundant water-power, and is the seat of numerous mills and factories, the chief articles of manufacture being agricultural machinery and implements. The city is handsomely built, contains many costly residences, and has 2 theatres, a Public Library of 10,000 volumes, and 20 churches. The Quakers form a large element in the population of Richmond, and they have here two important educational institutions: the *Friends' Academy* and *Earlham College*, which was founded in 1859, admits both sexes, and has a library of 3,500 volumes. The college buildings are about ½ mile W. of the city. In the N. E. corner of the city are Fair Grounds 33 acres in extent. Four railroads intersect at Richmond, and horse-cars traverse the principal streets. *Cambridge City* (772 miles) and *Knightstown* (791 miles) are thriving towns. Near the latter is a Soldiers' Home for the disabled soldiers of Indiana, and for the indigent widows and orphans of the soldiers from Indiana who fell in the civil war. The next important station on the line is **Indianapolis,** the capital of Indiana, which has already been described on page 319.

From Indianapolis to Terre Haute the present route and Route 74 run close beside each other, touching at *Greencastle* (see p. 321) and at **Terre Haute** (see p. 321). Between Terre Haute and St. Louis the present route makes a gain in distance of 24 miles, but traverses a newer and more thinly-settled region, though the stations along either route are not of much importance. *Effingham* (965 miles) is at the intersection of the Chicago Branch of the Illinois Central R. R. (Route 79). It is situated near the Little Wabash River, and has considerable trade and manufactures, with a population of about 3,000. *Vandalia* (996 miles) is a town of 2,000 inhabitants on the W. bank of the Kaskaskia River. From 1818 to 1836 it was the capital of Illinois, and was then a very prosperous place. After the removal of the capital to Springfield, it became rapidly decadent, but is reviving now under its railroad advantages, and promises to become an important manufacturing center. *Greenville* (1,014 miles) is the highest point on the line between Terre Haute and St. Louis, and is a flourishing town of 2,500 inhabitants on the E. bank of Shoal Creek. To the S. is a fine prairie. *Highland* (1,034 miles) is a busy manufacturing town with 3,000 inhabitants, mainly Germans. It is pleasantly situated and well built. At *E. St. Louis* (1,062 miles) the train crosses the Mississippi on the magnificent bridge which is described in connection with St. Louis.

76. St. Louis.

Hotels.—The *Lindell Hotel* ($3 to $4 a day), in Washington Ave., between 7th and 8th Sts., is a vast and magnificent building of bluish-gray sandstone. It is six stories high, cost $800,000, and is sumptuously furnished. The *Planters' Hotel* ($2.50 to $3.50 a day) is a very large and fine hotel, occupying the entire block in 4th St. between Pine and Chestnut. The *Laclede Hotel* ($2.50 to $3 a day) is a well-kept house centrally located at the cor. of 5th and Chestnut Sts. *Barnum's Hotel* ($2 to $2.50 a day) is a large brick building at the cor. of Walnut and 2d Sts., near the river. Other good houses, on a smaller scale, are the *Everett House, St. Nicholas, Olive St. Hotel,* and *Broadway Hotel*. The *Hotel Barnum*, cor. 6th

St. and Washington Ave., and the *Grand Central* in Pine St., between 4th and 5th, are on the European plan (rooms $1 to $1.50 a day). The *Southern Hotel*, one of the largest and finest in the Mississippi Valley, was burned down in 1877, and has not yet been rebuilt.

Restaurants.—The most popular restaurant in the city for ladies and gentlemen is *French's*, at the cor. of 5th and Pine Sts., or No. 201 N. 5th St. *Porcher's*, 900 Olive St., is famous for its dinners and suppers and for the excellence of its wines. Other good restaurants are *Sincler & Beer's*, No. 910 Olive St.; *Garne's*, cor. 9th and Olive Sts.; *Cafferetta*, No. 101 N. 12th St.; *Lamon Pezotte*, No. 200 N. 5th St.; *Nicholas Cantine*, No. 408 Washington Ave.; the *Vienna Café*, cor. 5th and Olive Sts. and the *Hotel-Garni Restaurant*, cor. 4th and Elm Sts. The cookery and service of many of these restaurants are in genuine French style.

Modes of Conveyance.—*Horse-cars* traverse the city in every direction and render all parts easily accessible (fare 7c.; 5 tickets for 25c.). The cars on 4th and 5th Sts. run nearly the entire length of the city from N. to S.; those on Market, Pine, Olive, Locust, Washington Ave. and Franklin Ave., run E. and W. *Carriages* are in waiting at the depots and steamboat-landings, and at stands in different parts of the city. The rates established by law are: For conveying 1 or more persons a distance of 1 m. or less, $1; more than 1 m. and less than 2 m., $1.50, and 50c. for each additional mile. By the hour, $2 for the first hour, and $1.50 for each additional hour. In case of disagreement as to distance or fare, call a policeman, or complain at the City Hall. *Ferries* to East St. Louis from foot of Spruce St. and from foot of Cary St.

Railroad Depots.—The depot of the *St. Louis, Kansas City & Northern R. R.* is at the foot of Biddle St., 12 blocks N. of Market St. The depot of the *Missouri Pacific*, of the *Atlantic & Pacific*, and of the *Kansas & Texas Railroads*, is at the cor. of Poplar and 7th Sts., 6 blocks S. of Market St. The depot of the *Iron Mountain R. R.* is at the foot of Plum St., 7 blocks below Market. All roads entering the city from the N. and E., over the bridge, use the **Grand Union Depot**, an immense edifice in Poplar St., between 11th and 12th Sts. (accessible by the Pine St. cars).

Theatres and Amusements.—The leading theatre is *De Bar's Opera-House*, in Market St., between 5th and 6th; but there is no well-organized theatrical company in the city. The *Olympic Theatre*, in 5th, between Walnut and Elm Sts., has a fine auditorium. The *Apollo Gardens* is a German theatre at the cor. of 4th and Poplar Sts., where the new and old operas may be heard throughout the season. The singing is usually very good, and between the acts the audience refreshes itself with beer and soda-water. The *Théâtre Comique*, in Pine St., between 3d and 4th, is a favorite resort for gentlemen. There are numerous German beer-gardens, at the more aristocratic of which, such as *Uhrig's* and *Schneider's*, really fine music may be heard. Ladies and gentlemen resort to the gardens just as do the citizens of Berlin and Dresden.

Reading-Rooms.—At all the principal hotels there are reading-rooms for the use of guests, well supplied with newspapers, etc. The *Mercantile Library*, cor. 5th and Locust Sts., has a library of 50,000 volumes and a reading-room, both of which are free to strangers (open from 9 A. M. to 10 P. M.). Besides the library, the hall contains paintings, statuary, coins, etc. The *Public-School Library*, on the 2d floor of the Polytechnic Building cor. Chestnut and 7th Sts., contains 38,000 volumes and a good reading-room, both of which are open to the public (from 10 A. M. to 10 P. M.). *St. John's Circulating Library* numbers 27,000 volumes, and the *Law Library*, in the Court-House, 7,100. The *Academy of Science*, founded in 1856, has a large museum and a library of 3,000 volumes. The *Missouri Historical Society*, founded in 1865, has a large historical collection. Both the preceding have rooms on the 3d floor of the Polytechnic Building cor. Chestnut and 7th Sts.

Clubs.—The *Germania Club* has a fine building at the cor. of 8th and Gratiot Sts., with first-class restaurant, billiard-rooms and rooms for other games, and a spacious ball-room. The *University Club* has a large and handsomely-furnished building. The privileges of either of these may be obtained on introduction by a member. There are other club-houses of less note.

Post-Office.—The general Post-Office is at the cor. of Olive and 3d Sts. It is open on secular days from 7¼ A. M. to 6 P. M. On Sundays from 12 M. to 1 P. M. There are also sub-stations in different parts of the city, and letters may be mailed in the lamp-post boxes, whence they are collected at frequent intervals by the carriers.

Sᴛ. Lᴏᴜɪs is situated geographically almost in the center of the great valley of the Mississippi, or basin of the continent, on the W. bank of the Mississippi River, 20 miles below the entrance of the Missouri, about 175 miles above the mouth of the Ohio, and 1,170 miles above New Orleans, in lat. 38° 37′ N. and lon. 90° 15′ W.   The city

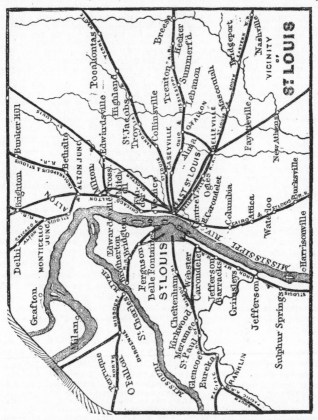

is perched high above the surface of the river.   It is built on three terraces, the first rising gently from the river-bank for about 1 mile to 17th St., where the elevation is 150 ft. above the stream.   The ground then gently declines, rises in a second terrace to 25th St., again falls, and subsequently rises in a third terrace to a height of 200 ft. at

Côte Brillante or Wilson's Hill, 4 miles W. of the river. The surface
here spreads out into a broad and beautiful plain. The corporate
limits extend 11 miles along the river and about 3 miles back from it,
embracing an area of nearly 21 square miles. The densely-built portion is comprised in a district of about 6 miles along the river and 2
miles in width.

In 1762 a grant was made by the Governor-General of Louisiana, then a French
province, to Pierre Liguest Laclede and his partners, comprising the "Louisiana
Fur Company," to establish trading-posts on the Mississippi; and on February 15,
1764, the principal one was established where the city now stands, and named St.
Louis. In 1803 all the territory then known as Louisiana was ceded to the United
States. In 1812 that portion lying N. of the 33d degree of latitude was organized
as Missouri Territory. In 1822 St. Louis was incorporated as a city. The first
census was taken in 1764, and the population was then 120. In 1811 it was only
1,400; in 1850 it had increased to 74,439; in 1860 to 160,773; and in 1870 to 310,-
864. In 1878 the local authorities estimated it at 560,000, which would make St.
Louis the third city in the United States in population. As the natural commercial
entrepot of the vast Mississippi Valley, the commerce of St. Louis is immense; the
chief articles of receipt and shipment being breadstuffs, live-stock, provisions, cotton, lead (from the Missouri mines), hay, salt, wool, hides and pelts, lumber, tobacco, and groceries. St. Louis is the first city of the Union in the manufacture
of flour. There were 24 mills in operation in 1874, which produced 1,573,202 barrels. The number of hogs packed during the season of 1873-'74 was 463,793. Vast
as are its commercial interests, however, the prosperity of the city is chiefly due
to its manufactures, in which it is surpassed only by New York and Philadelphia.
The number of establishments in the county (mostly within the city limits) in 1870
was 4,579, employing 40,856 hands, and turning out products valued, in 1874, at
nearly $240,000,000.

The city is, for the most part, regularly laid out, the streets near
the river running parallel with its curve, while farther back they are
generally at right angles with those running W. from the river-bank.
From the Levee, or river-front, the streets running N. and S. are named
numerically, beginning with Main or 1st St., 2d St., 3d St., etc. The
notable exceptions to this are Carondelet Ave., which is a continuation
of 4th and 5th Sts. southward; Broadway, a continuation of the same
Sts. northward; and Jefferson Ave., corresponding in part with 29th
St. Streets running E. and W. are named arbitrarily or from some
historical association. The houses are numbered on the "Philadelphia
system," all streets running parallel to the river being numbered N.
and S. from Market St.; while on all streets running E. and W. the
numbering begins at the Levee. *Front St.*, which is 100 ft. wide, extends along the levee, and is built up with massive stone warehouses.
This street, with *Main* and *Second*, is the location of the principal
wholesale trade. **Fourth St.** is the fashionable promenade, and contains the leading retail stores. *Grand Ave.* is 12 miles long, running
parallel with the river on the W. boundary of the city. *Washington
Ave.* is one of the widest and handsomest in the city. The finest residences are on **Lucas Place,** in *Pine, Olive,* and *Locust Sts.,* in *Washington Ave. W.,* of 27th St., and in *Chouteau Ave.* The favorite drives
are through the parks and boulevards, to be described further on.

The city is remarkably well built, stone and brick being the chief
materials used, and the architecture being more substantial than
showy. The finest public building in the city, and one of the finest of

its kind in the United States, is the *** Court-House,** occupying the square bounded by 4th, 5th, Chestnut, and Market Sts. It is built of Genevieve limestone, in the form of a Greek cross, with a lofty iron dome surmounting its center, and cost $1,200,000. The fronts are adorned with beautiful porticoes, and from the cupola of the dome

St. Louis Court-House.

(which is accessible to all) there is a fine view of the city and its surroundings. The *City Hall*, cor. Market and 10th Sts., is a plain brick structure occupying half a square. The *** Four Courts** is a spacious and handsome limestone building, in Clark Ave. between 11th and 12th

Sts., erected at a cost of $1,000,000. In the rear is an iron jail, semi-circular in form, and so constructed that all the cells are under the observation of a single watchman at once. (Strangers admitted on Mondays, Wednesdays, and Fridays, from 8 to 9 A. M., and from 3 to 4 P. M.) The *Custom-House*, which also contains the *Post-Office*, is a large and substantial edifice of Missouri marble, at the cor. of 3d and Olive Sts. A new Custom-House and Post-office is in course of construction at the cor. of Olive and 8th Sts. It will occupy an entire block, will be of Maine granite with rose-colored granite trimmings, will be three stories high, with a French roof and louver dome, and is estimated to cost $5,000,000. The *U. S. Arsenal*, situated in the extreme S. limits of the city, immediately on the river, is a beautiful spot (reached by 5th St. cars). The *** Chamber of Commerce,** in 3d St., between Pine and Chestnut, is the great commercial mart of the city, and is claimed to be the finest edifice of the kind in the country. It is 233 ft. long by 187 ft. deep, is solidly built of gray limestone, is five stories high, and cost $800,000. The main hall or "Exchange" is a magnificent room, over 200 ft. long, 100 ft. wide, and 70 ft. high. The sessions of the Exchange are from 11 A. M. to 1 P. M. Strangers are admitted to the floor on introduction by a member; the galleries are free to all. The *** Masonic Temple,** cor. Market and 7th Sts., is a very fine edifice, with richly-decorated interior. The *** Columbia Life-Insurance Building,** cor. 6th and Locust Sts., is the most ornate and showy in the city. It is of rose-colored granite, in the Renaissance style, four stories high, with a massive cornice on the roof upon which are mythological figures in stone. From the roof (reached by elevator) a fine view is obtained. The *Republican Building*, cor. 3d and Chestnut, is one of the most complete and admirably-appointed newspaper offices in the world. The *Union Market* occupies the square bounded by 5th, 6th, Greene, and Morgan Sts., and is well worth a visit. So is the *St. Louis Elevator*, on the Levee at the foot of Ashley St. It has a capacity of 2,000,000 bushels, and is one of the largest in the country. The *Levee* should also be visited.

The most imposing church edifice in the city is *** Christ Church** (Episcopal), cor. 13th and Locust Sts. It is of stone, in cathedral-Gothic style, with stained-glass windows and lofty nave. The *** Cathedral** (Roman Catholic), in Walnut St. between 2d and 3d, is a splendid edifice, with a front of polished freestone, ornamented by a Doric portico. It is surmounted by a lofty spire in which is a fine chime of bells. Other fine Roman Catholic churches are *St. Alphonsus*, on Grand Ave., and *St. Peter and Paul*, cor. 7th St. and Allen Ave. The *Church of the Messiah* (Unitarian), cor. Olive and 9th Sts., is a fine Gothic structure; and the *Second Presbyterian*, cor. 17th St. and Lucas Place, is another noble specimen of the Gothic style. *St. George's* (Episcopal), cor. Locust and 7th Sts., is a handsome building. The *** First Presbyterian,** cor. 14th St. and Lucas Place, is a large and costly structure in the English-Gothic style, with richly-decorated interior, and a peculiarly graceful and elegant spire. The *Union Church* (Methodist), cor. 11th and Locust Sts., is a good model of an old Lombard church, believed to be the only structure of the kind in the country. The *Baptist Church*, cor. Beaumont and Locust Sts., is a stone structure of handsome design. The following are also notably fine buildings: the *Congregational Church*, in Locust St. between 10th and 11th Sts.; the *Lutheran Church*, cor. 8th and Walnut Sts.; the *First Methodist*, cor. 8th St. and Washington Ave.; and the *Presbyterian Churches*, cor. 11th and Pine and 16th and Walnut Sts. The * **Jewish Temple,** cor. 17th and Pine Sts., is one of the finest ecclesiastical structures in the city.

Of the literary and educational institutions the most interesting is the * **Mercantile Library,** which has a large and handsome brick building at the cor. of 5th and Locust Sts. The library and reading-room are in the 2d story, and both are free to strangers (open from 9 A. M. to 10 P. M.). The library numbers 50,000 volumes, and the hall contains paintings, coins, and statuary, among which may be mentioned Miss Hosmer's life-size statues of Beatrice Cenci and * Œnone; a bronze copy of the Venus de' Medici; marble busts of Thomas H. Benton and Robert Burns; and a sculptured slab from the ruins of Nineveh. The reading-room is tastefully fitted up and well supplied with newspapers and magazines. The *Polytechnic Building* is a commodious edifice at the cor. of Chestnut and 7th Sts. On the 2d floor is the Public-School Library, with 38,000 volumes and a good reading-room. On the 3d floor are the rooms of the *Academy of Science,* which was founded in 1856 and has a large museum and a library of 3,000 volumes; and of the *Missouri Historical Society,* which was founded in 1865, and has a valuable historical collection. The *St. Louis University* (Jesuit), cor. 9th St. and Washington Ave., is the oldest educational institution in St. Louis, having been founded in 1829. It has a valuable museum, very complete philosophical and chemical apparatus, and a library of 17,000 volumes, among which are some rare specimens of early printing. It has about 25 instructors and 350 students. * **Washington University** is a large and substantial building, cor. Pine and 16th Sts. The university was organized in 1853, and is intended to embrace the whole range of university studies, except theological. Connected with it are the *Mary Institute,* for the education of women; the *Polytechnic School,* which has the handsome building mentioned above; and the *St. Louis Law School.* It has about 60 instructors connected with the different departments, and 700 students. The *College of the Christian Brothers* (Roman Catholic), cor. 8th and Gratiot Sts., is a flourishing institution with about 400 students, and a library of 10,000 volumes. *Concordia College* (German Lutheran) was established in 1839, and has a library of 4,500 volumes. The public-school system of St. Louis is one of the best in the country, and the school-houses are exceptionally fine. The *High School,* cor. 15th and Olive Sts., is a beautiful building in the castellated Norman style. The Roman Catholics have about 100 parochial, private, and conventual schools.

The * **County Insane Asylum,** on the Arsenal road, 4½ miles from the Court-House, is an immense brick and stone structure, occu-

pying about 40 acres of ground, beautifully laid out.   On the premises
is an artesian well, 3,843 ft. deep.   The Asylum is open to visitors from
10 A. M. to 12 M., and from 2 to 5 P. M.   The *Poor-House* and the *House
of Industry* are just beyond, on the Arsenal road, and are spacious brick
buildings.   The *Workhouse* and the *House of Refuge* are 4 miles S. of
the Court-House (reached by the 5th St. line of cars).   The *City Hospital*, cor. Lafayette Ave. and Linn St., is a handsome building, situated
in the midst of pleasant grounds (reached by 4th St. cars ; open to visitors from 2 to 3 P. M.).   The *St. Louis Hospital*, cor. Montgomery and
Bacon Sts., is conducted by the Sisters of Charity, and accommodates
400 patients.   The *U. S. Marine Hospital* is in Carondelet Ave., 3 miles
from the Court-House.   The *Convent of the Good Shepherd*, for the re-
formation of fallen women, is at the cor. of Chestnut and 7th Sts.   The
Deaf and Dumb Asylum (Roman Catholic) is at the cor. of 26th St.
and Christy Ave.   St. Louis is famous for the number of its charitable
institutions, of which we have found space to enumerate only a few.

The public squares and parks of St. Louis embrace in the aggregate
about 2,000 acres.   The most beautiful is **∗ Lafayette Park,** which
embraces about 30 acres in the S. portion of the city (reached by Chouteau Ave. cars running on 4th St.).   It is for pedestrians only, is admirably laid out and adorned, and is surrounded by costly residences.
In it are a bronze statue of Senator Benton, by Harriet Hosmer, and a
bronze statue of Washington.   Band concerts are given here on Thursday afternoons in summer.   *Missouri Park* is a pretty little park of 4
acres, at the foot of Lucas Place, the 5th Avenue of St. Louis.   In the
center is a handsome fountain.   *St. Louis Place* and *Hyde Park*, in the
N. part of the city, are attractive places of resort, the former containing 16 and the latter 12 acres.   *Washington Square* (16 acres) lies on
12th St. and Clarke Ave., and is tastefully improved.   *Northern Park*
(180 acres), on the bluffs in the N. portion, is noted for its fine trees.
Forest Park contains 1,350 acres, and lies 4 miles W. of the Court-House.
It is still mostly covered with primitive trees, and the Des Peres River
meanders through it.   Lindell Boulevard (194 ft. wide) and Forest Park
Boulevard (150 ft. wide) extend from it toward the heart of the city.
Lindell Park (60 acres), on the line of Forest Park Boulevard, is tastefully laid out and filled with native forest-trees.   **∗ Tower Grove
Park,** embracing 277 acres, lies in the S. W. part of the city (reached
by Gravois Railway line, from 4th and Pine Sts.).   It is beautifully laid
out, with green lawns and shrubbery, and offers the pleasantest drives
of any park in the city.

Adjoining Tower Grove Park is **∗ Shaw's Garden,** owned by Mr.
Henry Shaw, who has opened it to the public, and intends it as a gift
to the city.   The garden contains 109 acres, and is divided into three
sections.   The Herbaceous and Flower Garden, embracing 10 acres, contains almost every flower that can be grown in this latitude ; and there
are several greenhouses, in which are thousands of exotic and tropical
plants.   In the Fruticetum, comprising 6 acres, are fruits of all kinds.
The Arboretum is 25 acres in extent, and contains all kinds of ornamental and fruit trees that will grow in this climate.   The Labyrinth is

an intricate, hedge-bordered pathway, leading to a summer-house in the center. A brick building near Mr. Shaw's residence contains a museum and botanical library. On Sundays the garden is open only to strangers, who may procure tickets at the leading hotels. The * **Fair Grounds** of the St. Louis Agricultural and Mechanical Association embrace 85 acres, 3 miles N. W. of the Court-House, are handsomely laid out and ornamented, and contain extensive buildings. The Amphitheatre will seat 40,000 persons. "Fair-week," which is usually the first week in October, is the gala-season in St. Louis, and the stranger will be fortunate if he happens there at that time. The grounds are reached by cars on Franklin Ave. and 4th St.

* **Bellefontaine Cemetery,** the most beautiful in the West, is situated in the N. part of the city, about 4½ miles from the Court-House (reached by 5th St. cars). It embraces 350 acres, is tastefully decorated with trees and shrubbery, and contains some fine monuments. *Calvary Cemetery* lies a short distance N. of Bellefontaine, and is little inferior, either in size or beauty.

The great * **St. Louis Bridge** across the Mississippi, from the foot of Washington St. to a corresponding point in East St. Louis, is regarded as one of the greatest triumphs of American engineering. It was designed by James B. Eads, and was begun in 1869 and completed in 1874. It consists of three spans resting on four piers. The piers are composed of granite and limestone, and rest on the bed-rock of the river, to which they were sunk through the sand from 90 to 120 ft. by the use of wrought-iron caissons and atmospheric pressure. The center span is 520 ft. and the side ones are each 500 ft. in the clear ; each of them is formed of four ribbed arches, made of cast steel. The rise of the arches is 60 ft., sufficiently high to permit the passage of steamboats at all stages of the water. The bridge is built in two stories ; the lower one containing a double car track and the upper one two carriage-ways, two horse-car tracks, and two footways. It passes over a viaduct of five arches (27 ft. span' each) into Washington Ave., where the lower roadway runs into a tunnel 4,800 ft. long, which passes under a large part of the city, terminating near 11th St. The total cost of bridge and tunnel was over $10,000,000. The city *Water-works* are situated at Bissell's Point, on the bank of the river, 3½ miles N. of the Court-House (reached by 5th St. cars). The buildings are substantial, and the two-pumping-engines, each with a capacity of 17,000,000 gallons a day, are worth seeing. The engine-rooms are open to visitors at all times.

77. Chicago to Cincinnati.

a. By the Cin., Richmond & Chicago R. R. and the Pittsburg, Cin. & St. Louis R. R.   Distance, 294 miles.

LEAVING Chicago by this route the train runs S. E. by the small stations of *Dalton* (20 miles), *Crown Point* (41 miles), and *Hebron* (51 miles), to *La Crosse* (67 miles), a small village at the intersection of the Louisville, New Albany & Chicago R. R. *Winamac* (91 miles) is the capital of Pulaski County, Ind., and is pleasantly situated on the Tippecanoe River. Twenty-six miles beyond Winamac the train reaches the flourishing city of **Logansport** (*Murdock Hotel, Windsor*), situated on the Wabash River at its confluence with Eel River, and on the Wabash & Erie Canal. It has a population of 14,000, and is at the intersection of four important railroads, including the Wabash Line described on page 322. The iron bridge by which this road crosses the Wabash at Logansport is a noteworthy structure. The city is surrounded by a rich agricultural country, and has an important trade, considerable quantities of poplar and black walnut lumber being shipped. Water-power is abundant and is used to some extent in manufactures. The principal industrial establishment is the car-works of the Pittsburg, Cincinnati & St. Louis R. R., which cover 25 acres and employ 600 workmen. Three cars per day can be turned out at these shops. The *Court-House*, one of the finest in the State, is built of cut stone ; and several of the churches and other buildings are also of stone. Beyond Logansport the train traverses a rich agricultural district, and soon reaches *Kokomo* (139 miles), a pretty village on Wild-Cat Creek, noted as the site of the State Normal School, which has a fine building. Connection is made here with the Indianapolis, Peru & Chicago R. R. **Anderson** (see p. 319) is at the crossing of the C., C., C. & I. R. R. (see Route 74). *Newcastle* (197 miles) is situated on the Blue River, which furnishes a fine water-power. The Fort Wayne, Muncie & Cin. R. R. connects here. *Hagerstown* (208 miles) is a prosperous town on a branch of the Whitewater River, at the terminus of the Whitewater Canal. The present route is intersected here by the Indianapolis, Cin. & Lafayette R. R. **Richmond** (224 miles) is described on page 322. *Eaton* (241 miles) is a pretty and thriving village on Seven-Mile Creek, which supplies a good water-power. It is about a mile E. of the site of old Fort St. Clair, which was built in the winter of 1791–'92, General Harrison, then an ensign and afterward President of the United States, commanding the guard. *Camden* (250 miles) is a pleasant village, surrounded by a fine farming country. **Hamilton** (269 miles) and the route thence to Cincinnati are described in Route 69.

b. Via Chicago & Cincinnati Through Line.   Distance, 310 miles.

This route is composed of three distinct railroads : the Illinois Central from Chicago to Kankakee ; the Cin., Lafayette & Chicago R. R. from Kankakee to Lafayette; and the Indianapolis, Cin. & Lafayette R. R. from Lafayette to Cincinnati. Two trains daily run through both ways without change of cars. As far as *Kankakee* (56 miles) this route is described in Route 79. From Kankakee the train runs S. E. by a number of small stations to **Lafayette** (*Lahr House, St. Nicholas*), one of the principal cities of Indiana, with a population of about 25,000, a flourishing trade with the surrounding country, and a number of important manufactories, embracing foundries and machine-shops, marble works, flouring mills, woolen mills, breweries, etc. The city is

situated at the head of navigation on the Wabash River, is on the line
of the Wabash & Erie Canal, and is the point of intersection of 5 lines
of railway, including the great Wabash Line to the West (see p. 322). It
is built on rising ground, enclosed in the rear by hills of easy ascent,
commanding a fine view of the river valley. The streets are paved,
and lighted with gas, and there are many handsome buildings, among
them the *County Jail*, erected in 1869 at a cost of $95,000, and an
Opera-House which cost $62,000. Lafayette is the seat of *Purdue
University*, a richly endowed institution, with which is associated the
State College of Agriculture and the Mechanic Arts. The University
Building proper is a fine edifice, and there are 8 other buildings with
grounds 184 acres in extent. *St. Mary's Academy* (Roman Catholic)
has about 300 pupils. Of the 5 public school buildings, *Ford's School-
house*, erected in 1869 at a cost of $85,000, is the finest. The *Y. M. C. A.*
has a free reading-room and library. Near the center of the city is
a public square containing an artesian well 230 ft. deep, from which
issues sulphur-water possessing curative properties. To the N. and
N. E. are Greenbush and Springvale Cemeteries, handsomely situated
and adorned with trees; and just S. of the city limits are the Agricultural Fair Grounds of the county. The battle-ground of Tippecanoe,
where Gen. Harrison defeated the Indians Nov. 7, 1811, is 7 miles N.
of the city.

Beyond Lafayette the train passes the small villages of *Colfax*,
Thorntown, and *Lebanon*, and in 64 miles reaches the city of **Indianapolis** (195 miles from Chicago) which has been described on page
319. Between Indianapolis and Cincinnati there are many pretty towns
and villages, but few that present any noteworthy features. *Shelbyville*
(232 miles) is situated on the left bank of Blue River, and is the seat
of a large seminary. *Greensburg* (251 miles) attracts attention by its
air of neatness and busy thrift. At *Lawrenceburg* (see p. 317) the road
turns E. and follows the bank of the Ohio River to Cincinnati.

78. Chicago to Louisville.

By the Michigan Central R. R. and the Louisville, New Albany & Chicago R. R.
Distances : to Michigan City, 56 miles; to La Crosse, 84; to Lafayette, 147; to
Crawfordsville, 174; to Greencastle, 205; to Bloomington, 248; to Mitchell, 283;
to New Albany, 344; to Louisville, 345.

FROM Chicago to *Michigan City* (56 miles) this route is the same
as Route 61, taken in reverse. During the entire distance, the road
skirts the S. shore of Lake Michigan, affording occasional picturesque
glimpses of its blue waters. At Michigan City the traveler takes the
Louisville, New Albany & Chicago R. R., which runs almost due S.
from end to end of Indiana, intersecting every one of the great routes
to the West that have been described in preceding pages. *La Croix*
(65 miles) is at the crossing of Route 62; *Wanatah* (77 miles) is at
the crossing of Routes 63 and 64; and *La Crosse* (84 miles) is at the
crossing of Route 77a. The first important station on the line is

Lafayette (147 miles), which has already been described on page 332. Twenty-seven miles beyond Lafayette is **Crawfordsville** (*Nutt Hotel, St. James*), a city of 5,000 inhabitants, beautifully situated on Sugar Creek, in the midst of a fertile and well-wooded farming country, in which coal is abundant. *Wabash College* (Presbyterian) has nearly 250 students and a library of 12,000 volumes. The public schools are excellent. **Greencastle** (205 miles) is at the crossing of Routes 74 and 75, and is described on page 321. *Gosport* (231 miles) is a thriving village on the W. Fork of White River, at the intersection of the Indianapolis & Vincennes R. R. Seventeen miles beyond Gosport is **Bloomington** (*Orchard House, National*), a village of about 1,200 inhabitants, chiefly noted as the seat of the *State University*, which admits both sexes, has about 300 students, and a library of 5,000 volumes. The Law School attached to the University is of considerable reputation. *Mitchell* (283 miles) is at the crossing of Route 73. *Salem* (306 miles) is a pretty village, capital of Washington County. *Lost River*, which rises in this county, is an interesting stream. At one point it sinks into the earth and runs in a subterranean channel for 11 miles, and then rises to the surface and unites with Lick Creek, a tributary of White River. **New Albany** is described in connection with Louisville. **Louisville** (see p. 313).

79. Chicago to Cairo.

By the Chicago Division of the Illinois Central R. R. This road traverses Illinois from end to end, nearly in the center of the State. It passes through one of the most productive and populous sections of the Great West, but, important as it is from a commercial point of view, it offers very little *en route* to challenge the attention of the tourist. Distances: Chicago to Kankakee, 56 miles; to Gilman, 81; to Paxton, 103; to Mattoon, 173; to Effingham, 199; to Centralia, 253; to Du Quoin, 289; to Carbondale, 308; to Jonesboro, 329; to Cairo, 365.

LEAVING Chicago by this route, the train passes several pretty suburban villages, and in 14 miles reaches *Calumet*, at the crossing of the Michigan Central R. R. (Route 61). *Monee* (84 miles) is the highest point on the entire line, being upon the dividing ridge between Lake Michigan and the Mississippi. *Kankakee* (56 miles) is upon the river of the same name, which is one of the principal tributaries of the Illinois. When the railroad was begun, a forest stood upon the site of this now important town. In the immediate neighborhood of Kankakee are quarries of a superior kind of limestone. *Clifton* (69 miles) is supplied with water by artesian wells, a constant supply being obtained at a depth of 80 to 100 ft. The streets of the village are regularly laid out and planted with shade-trees. At *Gilman* (81 miles) the Springfield Division of the Illinois Central R. R. diverges, and runs S. W. in 111 miles to **Springfield** (see p. 337). *Onarga* (85 miles) lies in the midst of a famous fruit-growing region. It is the seat of the Onarga Institution and the Grand Prairie Seminary, both of which are flourishing institutions. *Loda* (99 miles), beautifully situated on undulating ground in the center of Grand Prairie, is the market for the agricultural products of the surrounding country. *Paxton* (103 miles) is the seat of a Swedish college named the *Augustina College of North America*, which has in its library 5,000 volumes presented by the King of Sweden. The public schools of Paxton are noted for their excellence. Twenty-five miles beyond Paxton is **Champaign** (*Doane House, Moore*), a rapidly growing city of 5,000 inhabitants at the intersection of the Indianapolis, Bloomington & Western R. R. It has a female academy, a public library, and 3 newspapers, and its schools are large and well conducted. *Tolono* (137 miles) is a thriving village at the crossing of the Wabash R. R. (see Route 74). *Tuscola* (150 miles) and *Arcola* (158 miles) are prosperous and rapidly growing towns. **Mattoon** (173 miles) is at the crossing of Route 74, and is described on page 321. *Effingham* (199 miles) is at the crossing of Route 75, and is described on page 323.

We have now entered the great fruit-growing region of Central Illinois, and for many miles the road traverses a country of wide-spreading and prolific orchards. *Kinmunday* (229 miles) is noted for the particularly fine fruit raised in its neighborhood, and in which it does a large trade. *Odin* (244 miles) is a very prosperous place at the crossing of Route 73. It is described on page 318. Nine miles beyond Odin is **Centralia** (*Central House*), a busy little city of 4,000 inhabitants, with a coal mine and various manufactories. The cultivation of fruit is extensively carried on in the neighborhood, and vast quantities of peaches are shipped annually to Chicago. Centralia is the point of junction of the Chicago Div. and the Northern Div. of the Illinois Central R. R., which continues thence in a single line to Cairo. *Ashley* (266 miles) is a pretty village, attractively situated on a rolling and well watered prairie. *Tamaroa* (280 miles) is another place which derives great prosperity from being the market of a rich fruit-growing region. It also has a large coal-shipping trade, coal of a superior quality being found in the vicinity. Nine miles beyond Tamaroa is **Du Quoin** (*City Hotel, Planter's*), a thriving city of about 5,000 inhabitants, surrounded by highly productive prairie-land. Fruit-raising, tobacco and cotton growing, and general agriculture, are important sources of the city's prosperity; but the principal business is coal-mining, about a dozen companies being in active operation. At Du Quoin connection is made with the St. Louis & Cairo Short Line R. R. (see Route 115). *Carbondale* (308 miles) is a busy town, with a number of cotton-gins, mills, etc., the leading productions of the adjacent plantations being cotton and tobacco. About one fourth of all the tobacco grown in Illinois is sent to market from this place. **Jonesboro** (329 miles) is the principal town of the great fruit-region of Southern Illinois, and is also the mart of large crops of cotton. It is pleasantly situated in a hilly country, about 4 miles from the Mississippi River. Limestone crops out among the hills, fine building-stone abounds, and iron-ore is found in the vicinity. The *Southern State Insane Asylum* is located here, and is a handsome stone structure. Near the village are some remarkable springs and caves, and 5 miles N. is *Bold Knob*, the highest point of land in the State. *Villa Ridge*

(353 miles) is at the commencement of a series of ridges or terraces, rising from the Mississippi River and extending to and along the Ohio. Twelve miles beyond, the terminus of the road is reached at **Cairo** (*St. Charles, Planter's, Arlington*), a city of 7,000 inhabitants built on a low point of land at the confluence of the Ohio and Mississippi Rivers, forming the southernmost point of the State. It is connected by steam-ferry with Columbus, Ky., the N. terminus of the Mobile & Ohio R. R.; and is the point of connection with the Chicago, St. Louis & New Orleans R. R., which forms the "Great Jackson Route" from Chicago and St. Louis to New Orleans (see Route 115). Steamers upon the Ohio and Mississippi make this one of their stopping points. Cairo was founded with the expectation that it would become a great commercial city, and large sums of money were expended in improvements, chiefly in the construction of levees to protect it from inundation. During the civil war it was an important depot of supplies, and enjoyed great prosperity, but is now somewhat decadent. The *County Buildings* are large and handsome; the *U. S. Custom-House* is of cut stone, and cost $200,000.

The *Northern Division* or Main Line of the Illinois Central R. R. runs N. from Centralia in 345 miles to Dubuque, on the Mississippi River; and from Dubuque the *Iowa Division* runs W. in 326 miles more to Sioux City, on the Missouri River. The principal places on the Northern Division are Vandalia, Pana, Decatur, Bloomington, Mendota, Dixon, Freeport, and Galena. Most of these are described in connection with other routes (see Index). **Dubuque** is one of the chief cities of Iowa (see Route 120), and **Sioux City** is an important railway center.

80. Chicago to St. Louis.

By the Chicago & Alton R. R. Distances : Chicago to Lockport, 33 miles; to Joliet, 38 ; to Normal, 124; to Bloomington, 127; to Springfield, 185; to Alton, 257; to St. Louis, 283.

THIS road runs S. W. through the rich prairie-lands of Central Illinois, which roll off as far as the eye can reach on either hand. The scenery is somewhat monotonous, and, since the country has become thickly settled, has lost the distinctive prairie character which is now seen to perfection only in the W. part of Iowa and on the plains be yond the Missouri. In leaving Chicago a number of pretty suburban villages are passed in quick succession, and in 33 miles the train reaches *Lockport*, a prosperous town on the Des Plaines River and on the Illinois & Michigan Canal, from which it derives a fine water-power. In the vicinity are some valuable stone-quarries. Four miles beyond Lockport is **Joliet** (*Robertson House, St. Nicholas*), a city of 8,000 inhabitants, situated on both sides of the Des Plaines River, and on the Illinois & Michigan Canal, at the intersection of the present route and the Chicago, Rock Island & Pacific R. R. (Route 84). It is well built, and lighted with gas. The *City Hall* is a large and imposing edifice; and the * *State Penitentiary*, one of the finest buildings of the kind in the United States, cost over $1,000,000. The surrounding country is extremely productive, and Joliet is its principal mart and shipping-

point. The canal and river furnish good water power, and there are
several flour-mills, manufactories of agricultural implements, etc. Near
the city are extensive quarries of a fine blue and white limestone which
is much used for building purposes throughout the Northwest. Beyond
Joliet numerous small stations are passed, of which the principal are
Wilmington (53 miles), *Pontiac* (92 miles), and *Chenoa* (103 miles).
Normal (124 miles) is a prosperous place at the crossing of the Northern Div. of the Illinois Central R. R. It is surrounded by the largest
nurseries in the State, and by farms devoted to the cultivation of hedge-
plants. Coal-mines are also worked in the vicinity. The State Normal
School and the Soldiers' Orphans' Home are located in the city. Two
miles beyond is **Bloomington** (*Ashly House, Phœnix Hotel*), one of
the principal cities of Illinois, an important railway center, and the
seat of large shipping and manufacturing interests. The city contains
about 20,000 inhabitants, is handsomely built, has street railways and
steam fire-engines, and is the seat of several important educational institutions. *Durley Hall*, the *Opera House*, and the *Court House* are
large and handsome buildings, and several of the churches and school-
houses are fine edifices. The *Illinois Wesleyan University* (Methodist)
is a flourishing institution, with 200 students and a library of 15,000
volumes. The *Major Female College* has a high reputation, and there
is a female seminary. The construction and repair shops of the Chicago & Alton R. R. are built of stone, and with the yards attached
cover 13 acres of ground.

The *Jacksonville Division* diverges at Bloomington, and is looped up to the
main line again at Godfrey. The distance from Chicago to St. Louis by this route
is 308 miles. Numerous small towns and villages are passed *en route*, but the
only important place on the line is **Jacksonville** (*Park House*), a busy city of
10,000 inhabitants, attractively situated in the midst of an undulating and fertile
prairie, at the intersection of several railroads, of which the Wabash Line (see p.
322) is one. The streets are wide and adorned with shade-trees; the houses are
for the most part well built, and surrounded with flower-gardens and shrubbery.
Jacksonville is the seat of the State Institution for the Education of the Deaf and
Dumb; of the State Institution for the Blind; of a State Hospital for the Insane;
of the State Institution for the Education of Feeble-Minded Children; and of a
private Asylum for the Insane. All these have handsome buildings. The *Illinois
College* (Congregational) and the *Illinois Female College* (Methodist) are flourishing institutions. The former has a library of 10,000 volumes, and the latter of 2,000,
and there is a free public library of 1,600 volumes.

Beyond Bloomington on the main line six or eight small stations
are passed, and in 58 miles the train reaches **Springfield** (*Leland
House, St. Nicholas*), the capital of the State, a city of 30,000 inhabitants, built on a beautiful prairie, 5 miles S. of the Sangamon
River. Its streets are broad, intersect each other at right angles, and
are tastefully adorned with shade trees. From the beauty of the place
and its surroundings, Springfield has been called the "Flower City."
The * *State Capitol*, now nearly completed, is one of the finest buildings
of the kind in America. Other noteworthy buildings are the *U. S.
Building* (containing the Court-House, Custom-House, and Post-Office),
the *County Court-House*, the *State Arsenal*, the *High School*, and several
handsome churches. There are a theatre and a commodious concert

15

The State Capitol.

and lecture hall.   Two miles N. of the city is *Oak Ridge Cemetery*, a
picturesque and well kept burying-ground of 72 acres, containing the
remains of President Lincoln and the noble * monument erected to his
memory by the Lincoln Monument Association.   The monument cost
$206,550, and was dedicated on Oct. 15, 1874.   There are vast coal mines
in the vicinity of Springfield, the surrounding country is very productive, and the trade of the city is extensive.   The principal manufacturing establishments are flouring mills, foundries and machine shops,
rolling mills, woolen mills, breweries, and a watch factory.   The extensive shops of the Wabash R. R. are worth visiting.   *Godfrey* (251
miles) is at the junction of the main line with the Jacksonville Div.
described above ; and 6 miles beyond is **Alton** (*Brent House, Depot
Hotel*), a prosperous city of 10,000 inhabitants, built upon a high
limestone bluff, overlooking the Mississippi River.   It is the center of
a rich farming country, and besides the river navigation, 3 railroads
connect it with all parts of the country.   The manufactures are varied
and extensive, and lime and building stone are largely exported.
There are 11 churches, among them a large Roman Catholic Cathedral,
Alton having been made a bishopric in 1868.   The State Penitentiary,
established here in 1827, was removed several years since to Joliet.
The buildings are still standing, and were used during the civil war as
a government prison.   At Upper Alton, 1½ mile E. of the city, is
Shurtleff College, an important Baptist institution.   Three miles below
Alton is the confluence of the Missouri and Mississippi Rivers.   At *E.
St. Louis* (281 miles) the train crosses the Mississippi on the magnifi-
cent bridge described on p. 331.   **St. Louis** (see p. 323).

81. Chicago to Milwaukee.

a. Via Milwaukee Div. of Chicago & Northwestern R. R.   85 miles.

THIS road runs along the W. shore of Lake Michigan through a rich farming region, well cultivated and populous. The first 8 or 10 stations after leaving Chicago are neat suburban villages. *Waukegan* (36 miles) is a flourishing town, with a large export business in grain, wool, and butter. Its site is high, and it is becoming a summer resort. A few miles beyond Waukegan the train crosses the boundary line and enters Wisconsin, soon reaching **Kenosha** (*Grant House*), a city of 5,000 inhabitants, built on a bluff, and possessed of a good harbor with piers extending into the lake. The manufactures are important, and the city has an extensive trade in the products of the surrounding country. Eleven miles beyond Kenosha is the academic city of **Racine** (*Congress Hall, Commercial Hotel*), which is the second city of Wisconsin in population and commerce. It is pleasantly situated at the mouth of Root River, on a plateau projecting about 5 miles into Lake Michigan and elevated about 40 ft. above its level. Its harbor is one of the best on the lake, and its commerce is very large; but manufactures are the chief source of the city's wealth and prosperity, and these are varied and extensive. The city is regularly laid out, with wide, well shaded streets. *Main St.* is the business thoroughfare, and its upper portion is lined with fine residences. *Racine College* (Episcopal) is one of the most prominent educational institutions in the West, and has commodious buildings in grounds 10 acres in extent at the upper end of Main St. The public schools are excellent, and the Roman Catholics have a flourishing academy. Of the 24 churches, several are handsome edifices. Racine was settled in 1834, was incorporated as a city in 1848, and in 1875 had a population of 13,282. Between Racine and Milwaukee there are no important stations.

b. Via Chicago Div. of the Milwaukee & St. Paul R. R.   85 miles.

This route runs nearly parallel with the preceding, a little further inland. There are no important places *en route*, the busy lake-ports being on the other line. The country traversed is fertile and highly cultivated, and the scenery is pleasing.

Milwaukee.

Hotels, etc.— The *Plankinton House* ($4 a day) is one of the finest hotels in the Northwest. The *Newhall House* and the *Kirby House* are large and well kept. All these houses are convenient to the business portion of the city. *Horse-cars* render all parts of the city easily accessible. *Post-Office* at the cor. of Wisconsin and Milwaukee Sts.

Milwaukee, the commercial capital of Wisconsin, and, next to Chicago, the largest city in the Northwest, is situated on the W. shore of Lake Michigan, at the mouth of Milwaukee River. This river flows through the city, and with the Menomonee, with which it forms a junction, divides it into three nearly equal districts, which are severally known as the East, West, and South Divisions. The river has been rendered navigable to the heart of the city by vessels of any tonnage used on the lakes, and is regarded as the best harbor on the S. or W. shore of Lake Michigan. The climate of Milwaukee is peculiarly bracing and healthful, and the atmosphere remarkably clear and pure. The city embraces an area of 17 square miles, and is regularly laid out. The center, near the Milwaukee and Menomonee Rivers, is the business quarter; and the E. and W. parts, the former of which is built upon a high bluff overlooking the lake, while the latter is still more elevated, are occupied by residences. The peculiar cream-color of the "Milwaukee brick," of which many of the buildings are constructed, gives the city a unique and pretty appearance, and has earned for it the name of the "Cream City of the Lakes." A delightful drive is over the White-Fish Bay road, extending 5 miles along the high bluffs bordering the lake.

Milwaukee was settled in 1835, and incorporated as a city in 1846. Its population in 1840 was 1,712; in 1860, 45,246; in 1870, 71,440; and in 1878 the local authorities estimated it at about 150,000. The Germans constitute nearly one half the entire population, and their influence upon the social life of the inhabitants is everywhere seen. Breweries and lager-bier saloons, gardens, gasthausen, music-halls, and restaurants abound; and on the street one hears German spoken quite as often as English. The commerce of Milwaukee is very large, wheat and flour being the most important items. The storage accommodations for grain comprise six elevators, with a combined capacity of 2,450,000 bushels; and the flour-mills are on an immense scale. Butter, wool, hides, and lumber are also important articles of trade. The manufactures are extensive, and embrace lager-bier (which is highly esteemed and widely exported), pig-iron and iron castings, leather, machinery, agricultural implements, steam-boilers, car-wheels, furniture, and tobacco and cigars. Pork-packing is extensively carried on.

The streets of Milwaukee, except those in the commercial quarter, are generally well shaded. *East Water St.*, *Wisconsin St.*, and *Grand Ave.* are very wide and handsome thoroughfares, and on them are the principal hotels and retail stores. Among the public buildings, the finest is the * **U. S. Custom-House,** which also contains the *Post-Office* and the U. S. Courts. It is of Athens stone, and stands on the cor. of Wisconsin and Milwaukee Sts. The * **County Court-House** is a large and handsome edifice. The *Academy of Music* has an elegant auditorium, with sittings for 2,300 persons. It was erected in 1864, at a cost of $65,000, and is owned by the German Musical Society. The *Opera-House* is a fine building, and is used for theatrical performances. There are several banking-houses which have large and imposing buildings. The finest church-edifice in the city is the *Immanuel Presbyterian Church.* The *Roman Catholic Cathedral of St. John* and the new *Baptist Church* are also handsome structures. Of the literary institutions the most prominent is the *Milwaukee Female College*, which, in 1873, had 6 instructors and 118 students. The *Free Public Library* has a library of 14,000 volumes, and a well supplied reading-room. The * **Northwestern National Asylum** (for disabled soldiers) is an immense brick building, about 3 miles from the city, having accommodations for 700 or 800 inmates. The institution has a reading-room, and a library of 2,500 volumes. The grounds embrace 425 acres, more than half of which is under cultivation, the residue being laid out as a park. In the city there are three orphan asylums, a Home for the Friendless, and two hospitals. Several of the industrial establishments are well worth a visit, especially the * **Grain-Elevator** of the Milwaukee & St. Paul R. R. This immense structure has a storage capacity of 1,500,000 bushels, and is one of the largest on the continent. The flour-mill of E. Sanderson & Co. has a capacity for producing 1,000 barrels of flour daily; and the rolling-mill of the North Chicago Rolling-Mill Co. is one of the most extensive in the West.

82. Milwaukee to St. Paul.

a. Via the La Crosse and St. Paul Divisions of the Milwaukee & St. Paul R. R. Distance, 341 miles. Time, about 17 hours.

Two through trains run daily each way on this route. *Brookfield* (13 miles) is at the junction with the Prairie du Chien Div. *Watertown* (43 miles) is a small village on the Rock River. Connection is made here with the Wisconsin Division of the Chicago & Northwestern R. R. From *Watertown Junction* (44 miles) a branch road runs W. in 37 miles to **Madison** (see p. 343); while the present route continues N. W. and soon reaches *Columbus* (63 miles), a pleasant village of about 2,000 inhabitants, on the Crawfish River. Twenty-eight miles beyond Columbus is **Portage City** (*Corning House, Ender's*), situated at the head of navigation on the Wisconsin River, and on the canal connecting the Fox and the Wisconsin, at the junction of three divisions of the Milwaukee & St. Paul R. R. It has a population of 4,000, does a large trade with the surrounding country, and the water-power furnished by the canal is extensively used in manufactures. The R. R. Co. has repair-shops here, and there are 8 churches, a fine Court-House and Jail, and a handsome High-School building. *Tomah* (153 miles) is a growing village at the crossing of the Wisconsin Valley Railroad; and *Sparta* (170 miles) is situated on the La Crosse River, in a very fertile valley. Twenty-five miles beyond Sparta, the train reaches **La Crosse** (*International Hotel, Robbins*), a city of 13,000 inhabitants on the E. bank of the Mississippi River at the mouth of the Black and La Crosse Rivers. It is finely situated on a level prairie, and has many handsome buildings, including the Court-House, which cost $40,000, the Post-Office, an Opera House, and the High-School building. There are flourishing graded schools, a Young Men's Library of 2,400 volumes, and 17 churches. The city has an extensive trade in lumber, and contains 9 saw-mills, 3 foundries and machine-shops, a large manufactory of saddlery and harness, and various other establishments.

At La Crosse, the train crosses the Mississippi and follows its W. bank all the way to St. Paul, amid remarkably picturesque scenery. On the bank of the river, 28 miles from La Crosse, is the prosperous little city of **Winona** (*Huff House, Jewell House*), charmingly situated on a plain which commands a fine view of the river for several miles. Being somewhat sheltered by the high bluffs which line the river above and below, it is thought to offer conditions favorable to consumptives, and has some reputation as a winter resort. The streets of the city are wide, and the business portion is compactly built of brick and stone. The *First State Normal School* is located here, and has a fine building which cost $145,000. The High School building cost $55,000, and there are several handsome churches. Winona is one of the most important lumber-distributing points on the Upper Mississippi, and as a grain-shipping point it ranks among the first in the Northwest. Two railroads converge here, and manufacturing is extensively carried on. The population of the city in 1875 was 10,737. *Wabasha* (256 miles) does a large grain-shipping business with the productive Chippewa Valley. *Reed's Landing* (262 miles) is at the foot of the beautiful expansion of the river known as Lake Pepin. *Lake City* (268 miles) stands upon a level plain at the foot of high bluffs, and is the port of a rich farming district. It has a population of 2,500 and is growing rapidly. **Frontenac** (279 miles) lies in the center of the lake region, and is a favorite resort in summer on account of its fine scenery, and the hunting, bathing, fishing, and sailing which it affords. Besides the sport furnished by Lake Pepin, there are fine trout-fishing in the streams and deer-hunting in the woods of Wisconsin, on the opposite side of the river, while prairie-chickens are found in abundance in the country back of the village. At the head of Lake Pepin, 6 miles beyond Frontenac, is **Red Wing** (*St. James Hotel*), a well built city of 4,000 inhabitants, beautifully situated on a broad level plain, which extends to the foot of some majestic bluffs. It is a favorite summer resort, and, being thoroughly protected by high hills, is also a desirable winter residence for consumptives. It is the port and market of a fertile region, and considerable manufacturing is done here. Twenty-one miles beyond Red Wing is the thriving city of **Hastings** (*Foster House, Tremont House*), situated at the mouth of the Vermilion River, which here falls 110 ft. in $\frac{1}{2}$ mile and furnishes abundant water-power. The population is about 4,000, and the principal manufactories are 4 flour-mills, a saw-mill, and a shingle-mill. The Central School House is a fine building, there are 2 Catholic schools, and 8 churches. The train again crosses the river at Hastings, and passes in 20 miles to St. Paul.

b. Via the Prairie du Chien Div. of the Milwaukee & St. Paul R. R.
  Distance, 410 *miles.   Time,* 22 *hours.*

One through train runs daily each way on this route. *Brookfield* (14 miles) is at the junction with the La Crosse Div. described above. *Waukesha* (21 miles) is a thriving village on the Fox River, built on the edge of a beautiful prairie. The Court House and Jail are constructed of a superior quality of limestone, found in abundance in the immediate vicinity. *Whitewater* (51 miles) is another busy village, situated in the midst of a rich farming region, and actively engaged in man-

ufactures. At *Milton Junction* (64 miles) a branch line diverges to
Monroe, while the St. Paul train passes on in 32 miles to

Madison.

Hotels, etc.—The *Park Hotel* ($3 a day), near the State Capitol, is a first-class
house. The *Vilas House* ($2.50 a day), also near the Capitol, and the *Capital
House* ($1.50 a day), are smaller but comfortable. There are also several large sum-
mer boarding-houses.

Madison, with a population of about 10,000, enjoys the rare distinction of being at once a State capital, a flourishing commercial center,
and a popular summer resort. It lies in the very heart of the "Four-
Lake Country," so called from a chain of beautiful lakes which extend
over a distance of 16 miles, and discharge their surplus waters into
Yahara or Catfish River, a tributary of Rock River. *Mendota* or *Fourth
Lake*, the uppermost and largest, is 9 miles long, 6 miles wide, and from
50 to 70 ft. deep in some places. It is fed chiefly by springs ; and has
beautiful white gravelly shores and pure cold water. *Monona* or *Third
Lake* is 5½ miles long and 2 miles wide ; and Lakes *Waubesa* and *Keg-
onsa* are each about 3 miles long by 2 in width. The city of Madison
occupies an undulating isthmus between Lakes Mendota and Monona,
and in point of situation and scenery is the most beautiful city in the
West. It is about 3 miles in length by 1 mile in breadth, and has wide,
straight, and regular streets, with many fine buildings. The *State
Capitol* stands in the center of a square park of 14 acres wooded with
native trees, is built of limestone, and commands a noble view. It has
recently been enlarged and improved at a cost of about $550,000. The
Court-House and *Jail* are situated near the S. corner of the park ; and
on an adjacent street is a United States *Post-Office* and *Court-House*,
which cost about $400,000. The *University of Wisconsin*, with four
elegant buildings, stands on a picturesque eminence called College Hill,
about a mile W. of the Capitol, and 125 ft. above the lakes. The views
from this point are extremely fine. The *Soldiers' Orphans' Home*
stands on the shore of Lake Monona, about a mile from the park. The
State Hospital for the Insane, on the shore of Lake Mendota, 4 miles N.
of the Capitol, is a vast and massive building, surrounded by grounds
containing 393 acres, partly wood and farming land, and partly laid
out and adorned. The *Wisconsin Historical Society* has an interesting
collection of curiosities and relics in a wing of the Capitol, and a valuable library of 58,000 volumes. The *State Library* contains 7,500 volumes. There are several handsome churches in the city, and some
fine villa residences in the outskirts. Small steamers ply on Lakes
Mendota and Monona, and afford agreeable excursions. *Lake Monona*
is the most beautiful of the lakes, and from its surface the finest views
of the city are obtained. The climate of Madison is delightfully cool
and invigorating in summer, and is thought to be especially beneficial
to those suffering from pulmonary complaints.

Beyond Madison the St. Paul train passes a number of small stations, but none requiring mention until **Prairie du Chien** (194 miles ;
Railway House, Mondell's) is reached. Prairie du Chien is a town of

about 3,000 inhabitants, situated on the E. bank of the Mississippi
River, 2 miles above the mouth of the Wisconsin, on a beautiful prairie which is 9 miles long and 1 mile wide, bordered on the E. by high
bluffs.   It is an important local shipping-point, and has varied and important manufactures.   *St. John's College* and *St. Mary's Female Institute*
are under the control of the Roman Catholics.   The public schools are
well conducted.   Leaving Prairie du Chien, the train crosses the river
to *McGregor, Iowa,* a flourishing town, and runs W. by several small
villages.   *Calmar* (238 miles) is a village of 1,000 inhabitants at the
junction with the Iowa & Dakota Div.   Turning now to the N., the
road soon enters Minnesota and reaches *Austin* (306 miles), a prosperous village, pleasantly situated on Red Cedar River.   *Ramsey* (309
miles) is at the junction with the Minnesota R. R., and *Owatonna* (339
miles) is at the crossing of the Chicago & Northwestern R. R.   Fifteen
miles beyond Owatonna is **Faribault** (*Barron House, Arlington*), one
of the most populous and prosperous interior towns in the State.   In
1853 it was the site of Alexander Faribault's trading-post; since 1857
its growth has been rapid, and the present population is estimated at
5,000.   It is the seat of the State Asylum for the Deaf and Dumb and
Blind, and of an Episcopal academy, and contains several other schools,
6 or 8 churches, 2 weekly newspapers, 2 national banks, and several
flour-mills, saw-mills, foundries, etc.   Between Faribault and St. Paul
the only important station is *Northfield,* where are located Carlton College (Congregational) and St. Olaf's College (Lutheran).

St. Paul.

Hotels, etc.—The leading hotels are the *Metropolitan* ($3 a day), in Third
St.; the *Merchants' Hotel* ($3 a day), near the center of the business quarter; and
the *Windsor* ($2 a day), centrally located near the parks and public buildings.   There
are two lines of *Horse-cars* connecting all parts of the city, and two bridges across
the river.   The *Post-Office* is in the Custom-House building.

St. Paul, the capital of Minnesota, is a beautiful city of about
50,000 inhabitants, situated on both banks of the Mississippi River, 2,200 miles from its mouth.   It was formerly confined to the
left bank, the site embracing four distinct terraces, forming a natural amphitheatre with a southern exposure, and conforming to the
curve of the river.   The city is built principally upon the second and
third terraces, which widen into level, semicircular plains, the last,
about 90 ft. above the river, being underlaid with a stratum of blue
limestone from 12 to 20 ft. thick, of which many of the buildings are
constructed.   The original town is regularly laid out, but the newer
portions are irregular.

The first recorded visit to the site of St. Paul was made by Father Hennepin, a
Jesuit missionary, in 1680.   Eighty-six years afterward, Jonathan Carver came
there and made a treaty with the Dakota Indians, in what is now known as
Carver's Cave.   The first treaty of the United States with the Sioux, throwing
their lands open to settlement, was made in 1837, and the first claim was entered
by Pierre Parent, a Canadian *voyageur*, who sold it in 1839 for $30.   It is the
present site of the principal part of the city.   The first building was erected in
1838, and for several years thereafter it was simply an Indian trading-post.   It was

laid out into village streets in 1847, and a city government was obtained in 1854, when the place contained about 3,000 inhabitants. It derives its name from that of a log chapel dedicated to St. Paul by a Jesuit missionary in 1841.

The streets of St. Paul are well graded and partially paved, are lighted with gas, and a system of sewerage is in progress. The principal public buildings are the *State Capitol*, a plain brick structure situated on high ground and occupying an entire square, and the *U. S. Custom-House*, which also contains the Post Office. The principal place of amusement is the *Opera-House* in Wabashaw Street, near Third, a large and handsome building, with a fine auditorium seating about 1,200 persons. There are about 40 churches of all denominations in the city, some of them large and handsomely finished. There are 4 public and as many private circulating libraries, the former including the State Law Library, and those of the Historical Society and Library Association, comprising together about 24,000 volumes. The *Academy of Sciences* contains about 126,000 specimens in natural history. The public and private schools are noted for their excellence, the latter including several female seminaries of a high grade. There are three free hospitals, managed by the county and church organizations, and a Protestant and a Roman Catholic orphan asylum. * *Carver's Cave* is a great natural curiosity, near the river, in Dayton's Bluff, on the E. side of the city. It was named after Jonathan Carver, who, on May 1, 1767, made a treaty with the Indians, by which they ceded him a large tract of land. There is a lake in the cave, which may be crossed in a boat. *Fountain Cave*, about 2 miles above the city, was apparently hollowed out of the rock by a stream which flows through it. It contains several chambers, the largest being 100 feet long, 25 wide, and 20 high; and it has been explored for 1,000 feet without the termination being reached.

There are some beautiful drives in and around St. Paul, and many places in the neighborhood of the city which can be reached either by carriage or by rail. Of these the most popular is *White Bear Lake*, 12 miles distant, on the St. Paul & Duluth R. R. It is about 9 miles in circumference, with picturesque shores and an island in its center. The lake affords excellent boating, fishing, and bathing. *Bald-Eagle Lake*, a mile beyond White Bear Lake, is noted for its fishing and picturesque scenery, and is a popular resort for picnic-parties. * *Minnehaha Falls*, immortalized by Longfellow, are reached by a delightful drive past Fort Snelling. The Falls are picturesquely situated, but they hardly merit the prominence that Mr. Longfellow's poem has obtained for them. *Lake Como* is reached by a pleasant drive of 2 miles from the center of the city. The boating and fishing here are excellent, and the city park, comprising several hundred acres, is located on its shores.

No visitor to St. Paul should fail to visit the twin city of **Minneapolis and St. Anthony,** situated on both sides of the Mississippi River, 10 miles above St. Paul, with which it is connected by 3 lines of railway. It is built on a broad esplanade overlooking the famous Falls of St. Anthony and the river, which is bordered at various points

by picturesque bluffs. The city is regularly laid out, with avenues
running E. and W., and streets crossing them N. and S. They are
generally 80 ft. wide, with 20 ft. sidewalks, and two rows of trees on
each side. There are many substantial business blocks and elegant
residences. The *Court-House, City Hall, Academy of Music, Opera-
House,* and *Athenæum* are noticeable structures; as are also the
Nicollet House and the *First National Hotel.* The Athenæum Library
contains 8,000 volumes, and that of the University of Minnesota about
13,000. Besides the University, there are several other important educational institutions, and the public schools are numerous and good.
The number of churches is 65, including all the denominations, and
some of the church-edifices are elegant and imposing. A large part
of the business prosperity of Minneapolis and St. Anthony is owing to
the * *Falls of St. Anthony,* which afford abundant water-power for
manufacturing purposes. The fall is 18 ft. perpendicular, with a rapid
descent of 82 ft. within 2 miles. The rapids above the cataract are
very fine, in fact much finer than the fall itself, the picturesqueness of
which has been destroyed by the wooden "curtain" erected to prevent the wearing away of the ledge. The falls can be seen with about
equal advantage from either shore, but the best view is from the
center of the suspension-bridge which spans the river above the falls.
Minneapolis is the center of immense lumber and flouring interests,
and has a population of about 50,000.

83. Chicago to St. Paul.

By the Chicago & St. Paul Div. of the Chicago & Northwestern R. R. Two
through trains daily, with Pullman Palace cars attached, run on this line, making
the journey in 18 to 20 hours. Distances: Chicago to Montrose, 8 miles; to Crystal
Lake, 43; to Beloit, 90; to Madison, 138; to Elroy, 212; to Black River Falls, 265;
to Eau Claire, 321; to Menomonee, 344; to Hudson, 390; to St. Paul, 410.

LEAVING the Chicago depot (cor. Canal and Kinzie Sts.), the train
passes in 8 miles to the pretty suburban village of *Montrose,* and soon
reaches *Crystal Lake* (43 miles), a neat village picturesquely situated
on a small lake of the same name. The first important station on the
line is **Beloit** (90 miles; *Goodwin House, Salisbury*), a flourishing city
of 5,000 inhabitants, situated on both sides of Rock River, at the mouth
of Turtle Creek. It is built on a beautiful plain, from which the ground
rises abruptly to a height of 50 to 60 ft., affording excellent sites for
residences. The city is noted for its broad, beautifully shaded streets,
and for its fine churches; the *First Congregational Church,* constructed
of gray limestone, is one of the largest and handsomest in the State.
Beloit College (Congregational), founded in 1847, is a flourishing institution with about 200 students and a library of 7,200 volumes. Beloit
is surrounded by a fine prairie country, which is dotted with numerous
groves of timber. A fertile prairie, the largest in the State, lies on the
E. side of Rock River. The city is well supplied with water-power, and
has several flouring mills, several manufactories of woolen goods, reapers,
scales, and carriages, and an iron foundry and machine-shop. The

Western Union R. R. intersects here. The small stations of *Hanover* (104 miles) and *Evansville* (116 miles) are now passed, and the train speedily reaches **Madison** (138 miles), the capital of Wisconsin, which has already been described (see p. 343).

Beyond Madison the train runs N. W. by a number of unimportant villages to *Elroy* (212 miles). From Elroy the Madison Div. runs W. to La Crosse and Winona (both described in Route 82), while the present route traverses a more thinly settled portion of Wisconsin, which has only recently been rendered accessible by railway. *Black River Falls* (265 miles) and *Augusta* (299 miles) are rapidly-growing villages, near extensive pine forests. *Eau Claire* (321 miles), the capital of Eau Claire County, is a township of 2,000 inhabitants, on the Chippewa River. It has an important trade in lumber, and several large saw-mills are in operation. *Menomonee* (344 miles) is another busy lumbering village on the Menomonee River, down which are floated immense numbers of logs from the vast forests above. The great saw-mill of Wilson & Co., one of the largest in the country, is located at Menomonee. Forty-six miles beyond Menomonee is **Hudson** (*Baldwin House*), the most important place on this section of the road. It is a flourishing village of 2,500 inhabitants on the E. shore of Lake St. Croix, with a lucrative trade with the fertile surrounding country, and a large flour-mill, saw-mills, etc. Its situation is very attractive. Twenty miles beyond Hudson the train reaches **St. Paul** (see p. 344).

84. Chicago to Omaha.

a. Via Chicago & Northwestern R. R.   Distance, 492 miles.

Two through trains daily, with Pullman Palace hotel and sleeping cars attached, run each way on this route. The road traverses for the larger portion of the way the great prairie-region of the West, which fifty years ago was almost uninhabited, save by the Indian and the trapper; but which now teems with an industrious and thriving population. Many of the towns and cities *en route* exhibit the unmistakable symptoms of wealth and prosperity, but there are very few which possess any features of special interest to the tourist. *Geneva* (35 miles) and *Dixon* (99 miles) are pleasant villages with a large trade and important manufactures. From Dixon the train follows the Rock River for 10 miles to **Sterling** (*Galt House*), a city of 6,000 inhabitants, attractively situated on the N. bank. The river at this point is spanned by a dam of solid masonry, 1,100 ft. long and 7 ft. high, which with the 9 ft. natural fall of the rapids above affords an immense water-power. The city is chiefly devoted to manufacturing, and the articles produced are remarkably varied and valuable. The Rockford, Rock Island & St. Louis R. R. begins here. *Fulton* (135 miles) is the last station in Illinois; and here the train crosses the Mississippi River on a magnificent iron * bridge 4,100 ft. long, with a draw 300 ft. long. From the center of the bridge, looking up the river, there is a fine view, taking in three towns. At the Iowa end of the bridge is the

prosperous city of **Clinton** (*Revere House, Central*), with a population of 8,000, the extensive repair-shops of the C. & N. R. R., and a
large number of saw-mills, one of which is capable of producing
200,000 ft. of lumber a day.   From Clinton to Cedar Rapids the
road traverses a rolling prairie, dotted with a succession of small but
thriving towns, and relieved from monotony by numerous plantations
of trees.   **Cedar Rapids** (219 miles, *Grand Hotel, Northwestern*)
is a rapidly growing city of 10,000 inhabitants on the Red Cedar River
at the intersection of several important railways.   Its trade with the
surrounding country is large, and there are a number of manufactories
and pork-packing establishments.   The city is regularly laid out and
well built, and promises to become one of the most important in Iowa.

Beyond Cedar Rapids, a fertile but more thinly-peopled agricultural
region is traversed, with a number of small stations at frequent intervals along the line.   *Boone* (340 miles) is a thriving village, surrounded
by a rich and productive farming country.   Soon after leaving Boone,
the train begins the descent into the valley of the Des Moines River,
amid extremely rugged and picturesque scenery, and with very heavy
grades, in some places of 80 ft. to the mile.   The Des Moines River,
which is the largest river in Iowa, is crossed on a fine bridge.   For
many miles after leaving the Des Moines Valley the road traverses a
superb prairie, which, except for the villages that have sprung up
around the few stations since 1866, remains in its primitive condition.   *Arcadia* (405 miles) is the highest point in Iowa, being 870 ft.
above the level of Lake Michigan.   In spring and summer the surrounding prairie is rich in long grass and beautiful flowers, but in
winter snow-drifts 20 ft. deep are not uncommon.   *Denison* (424
miles) is a promising young town.   At this point the train enters the
Boyer Valley, the scenery of which furnishes a pleasing contrast to
that of the prairie.   *Dunlap* (441 miles) is a growing town, containing
one of the R. R. engine-houses.   *Missouri Valley Junction* (467 miles)
is at the junction of the Sioux City and Pacific R. R.   Here the
descent into the Missouri Valley begins, and a full view of the
"bluffs" is obtained for the first time.   The road, turning S. W.,
almost skirts those on the Iowa side, while those of Nebraska loom
up on the opposite side of the broad river-bottom.   At the foot of
the bluffs, which are here high and precipitous, 3 miles E. of the Missouri River, is the important city of **Council Bluffs** (*Ogden House,
Pacific*), with a population of about 15,000.   It is the converging point
of all the railroads from the East which connect with the Union Pacific,
and communicates by horse-cars and steam-railroad with Omaha, on
the opposite river-bank, 4 miles distant.   The great * **Missouri River
Bridge,** which connects the two cities, is 2,750 ft. long, has 11 spans,
and cost over $1,000,000.   It rests on piers, each consisting of two
hollow columns of wrought iron $1\frac{3}{4}$ inch thick and $8\frac{1}{2}$ ft. in diameter,
which are sunk to the bed-rock of the river and filled with concrete
and masonry.   The bridge is fifty feet above high-water mark, and
its entire length, including the necessary approaches on either side,
is 9,950 ft.   Council Bluffs is well laid out, with streets crossing

each other at right angles, and the principal edifices are of brick. The most important public buildings are the *County Court-House,* which cost $50,000; the *City Hall ;* two public halls; the *High School,* which cost $50,000; and 6 ward school-houses. The *State Institute for the Deaf and Dumb* is in the vicinity. There are in the city 9 churches, a library association, and a Young Men's Christian Association, with reading-room. The views from the bluffs above the city are very fine. It has been decided by the U. S. Supreme Court that Council Bluffs is the E. terminus of the Union Pacific R. R.   **Omaha** (see p. 353).

b. Via Chicago, Rock Island & Pacific R. R.   Distance, 501 miles.

Two through trains daily, with restaurant and sleeping-cars attached, run each way on this route. The country traversed is very similar in character to that along the preceding route, and might be described in the same general terms (see above). The first important place on the line is **Joliet** (40 miles), which has already been described on page 336. *Morris* (61 miles) is a busy little city of 3,000 inhabitants on the Illinois & Michigan Canal, with an important trade in grain and a Roman Catholic female seminary of some note. Twenty-three miles beyond Morris is **Ottawa** (*Clifton Hotel, White's*), a flourishing city of about 12,000 inhabitants on the Illinois River, just below the mouth of the Fox, and on the Illinois & Michigan Canal. It is lighted with gas, and contains many handsome residences. The chief public buildings are the Court-House in which the Supreme Court for the N. division of the State is held, and the County Court-House and Jail. The surrounding country is fertile and abounds in coal. The Fox River has here a fall of 29 ft., affording an immense water-power which is extensively used in manufactures. There are several grain elevators, and large quantities of wheat are shipped from this point.   **La Salle** (99 miles) is a busy manufacturing city on the Illinois River, at the terminus of the Illinois & Michigan Canal, 100 miles long, which connects it with Chicago. It also connects with the Illinois Central R. R., and with steamer to St. Louis. It is the center of extensive mines of bituminous coal, of which large quantities are shipped. *Pond Creek* (128 miles) is at the intersection of the Chicago, Burlington & Quincy R. R.   *Geneseo* (159 miles) is in the heart of one of the finest agricultural districts in the State; and 20 miles beyond is **Moline** (*Keator House, Gault*), a city of 7,000 inhabitants on the E. bank of the Mississippi River, 3 miles above **Rock Island** (*Harper House, Rock Island*), which is another flourishing city on the E. bank of the river, with a population of about 12,000. The river is here divided by the island of Rock Island, which is 3 miles long; and from 16 miles above Moline to 3 miles below are the Upper Rapids. By means of a dam at Moline an immense water-power, said to nearly equal the combined water-power of all New England, is obtained, and employed in various manufactories, constantly increasing in number and importance. The scenery about Moline is highly picturesque, and the surrounding country is rich in coal. The city of Rock Island is at the foot of the rapids, opposite the W. extremity of Rock Island, from which it takes its name. It is an important railroad center, is the shipping-point for the productive country adjacent, and has numerous and varied manufactures. The island of * **Rock Island** is the property of the U. S. Government and the site of the great Rock Island Arsenal and Armory, intended to be the central United States armory. The design embraces 10 vast stone workshops, with a storehouse in the rear of each, besides officers' quarters, magazines, offices, etc. Several of the shops are already completed. The shops will be supplied with motive-power by the Moline water-power, three-fourths of which is owned by the Government. The island (which comprises 960 acres) resembles West Point in the manner in which it has been improved and in its buildings. There are 20 miles of splendid roadways running in every direction; drives, walks, promenades, and paths; delightful shade, and magnificent prospects from numerous points of view.

Opposite Rock Island, on the Iowa side of the river, is the city of **Davenport** (*Burtis House, Newcomb*), and the train crosses the river between them on the magnificent railroad and wagon * bridge built by the Government in connection with the armory at a cost of $1,000,000. Davenport is the second city of Iowa in size, has about 25,000 inhabitants, and is the great grain depot of the upper Mississippi. It is also an important manufacturing center, and is situated in the heart of extensive bituminous coal-fields. The city is built at the foot and along the slope and summit of a bluff 3½ miles long, rising gradually from the river, and enclosed on the land side by an amphitheatre of hills half a mile in the rear. It is regularly laid out and handsomely built, and horse-cars traverse the principal streets. The County buildings are substantial structures, the *City Hall* is an imposing edifice, and the *Opera House* is one of the finest in the West. Several of the churches and school-houses are handsome buildings. *Griswold College* (Episcopal) is a flourishing institution, with a library of 4,000 volumes, and the *Academy of the Immaculate Conception* (Roman Catholic) is of high standing. The *Library Association* has a library of about 5,000 volumes, and there are an *Academy of Natural Sciences*, two medical societies, and the Iowa Orphans' Home.

Beyond Davenport several small stations are passed, including *Wilton* (208 miles), whence a branch road runs S. W. to Leavenworth and Atchison, on the Missouri River. On the main line, 29 miles beyond Wilton, is **Iowa City** (*St. James Hotel, Pinney House*), formerly the State capital, and now the seat of the *State University*, which has an attendance of 600 students; an extensive laboratory, and a library of 6,500 volumes. The University occupies 4 buildings, of which the largest, formerly the Capitol, is a fine edifice in the Doric style, 120 by 60 ft. The *Mercy Hospital* is connected with the medical department of the University. The County Offices and the Court House are the other principal public buildings. The *State Historical Society* has a library of 3,500 volumes. The Iowa River, which is navigable to this point, furnishes water-power for various factories and flour-mills. The city contains 9,000 inhabitants, and is built upon the highest of three plateaus, 150 ft. above the river. It is embowered amid trees, and is surrounded by a fertile farming country. *Grinnell* (302 miles) is the seat of *Iowa College*, which was removed here from Davenport. **Des Moines** (357 miles, *Aborn House, Morgan*) is the present capital of Iowa, and is situated at the head of navigation on the Des Moines River, at its confluence with the Raccoon. The city, which contains 23,800 inhabitants, is laid out in quadrilateral form, extending 4 miles E. and W. and 2 miles N. and S., and is intersected by both rivers, which are spanned by 6 bridges. The business quarter lies near the rivers, and the finest residences are on the higher ground beyond. The old *Capitol* is a plain building erected in 1856 at a cost of $60,-000. A new capitol, to cost $3,000,000, is in process of construction. The *Post-Office*, which also accommodates the U. S. Courts and other federal offices, cost over $200,000. There are 15 churches, 9 public school-houses, and a Baptist college with a spacious building on an eminence commanding a fine view. The *State Library* contains 15,000 volumes, and there is a *Public Library* with about 3,000 volumes. In the N. W. part of the city is a public park of 40 acres, and, in a bend of the Raccoon River, spacious Fair Grounds, with a race-course.

Beyond Des Moines the road traverses a fine prairie country, dotted with neat villages, descends the bluffs into the Missouri Bottom, and soon reaches **Council Bluffs** (498 miles), which has been described on page 348.

c. *Via Chicago, Burlington & Quincy R. R. Distance, 502 miles.*

Two through trains daily, with Pullman Palace hotel and sleeping cars attached, run each way on this route. The Chicago, Burlington & Quincy R. R. passes through some of the most fertile farming lands of Illinois, crossing the State diagonally from Lake Michigan to the Mississippi River. It then crosses Southern Iowa, a section teeming with agricultural wealth, and better cultivated than some other portions of the State. The country as a whole does not differ greatly from that traversed by the two preceding routes, but there are fewer important cities along the line. The first place requiring mention is **Aurora** (39 miles, *Fitch House, Tremont*), a city of 12,000 inhabitants situated upon Fox River, which furnishes the power for numerous important manufactories. It contains a handsome City Hall, a college, 14 churches, and many fine stores and dwellings. The construction and repair-shops of the R. R., situated here, employ 700 men. **Mendota** (84 miles, *Passenger House, Warner*) is a rapidly growing city of 6,000 inhabitants at the intersection of the Northern Div. of the Illinois Central R. R. (Route 79). It is surrounded by a rich farming region; and coal being abundant, manufactures are extensive and varied. *Mendota College* and a *Wesleyan Seminary* are located here, and some of the churches are handsome edifices. **Galesburg** (164 miles, *Union Hotel, Brown's*) is a city of 12,000 inhabitants noted for its educational advantages, being the seat of *Knox College* (Congregational), with 330 students and a library of 6,200 volumes, and of *Lombard University* (Universalist), with 165 students and a library of 3,500 volumes. Both institutions admit females. The *City Library* contains 6,500 volumes, and that of the *Young Men's Library Association* 4,000 volumes. Galesburg is surrounded by a rich farming country, and has several manufactories, including the machine-shops of the R. R. Co. Thirteen miles beyond Galesburg is **Monmouth** (*Commercial Hotel, Baldwin*), a city of 5,000 inhabitants situated on a rich and beautiful prairie. It is the seat of *Monmouth College*, established in 1856, and of the *Theological Seminary of the Northwest*, established in 1839, both under the control of the United Presbyterians. At *E. Burlington* (206 miles) the train crosses the Mississippi to **Burlington** (*Barrett House, Gorham*), which, after Dubuque and Davenport, is the largest city in Iowa, with a population of about 20,000, and a place of great commercial importance. The business portion of the city is built upon low ground along the river, while the residences upon the high bluffs command extended views of the fine river scenery. The river at this point is a broad, deep, and beautiful stream, and upon the bluffs between which it passes are extensive orchards and vineyards. The city is regularly laid out and well built, the houses being chiefly of brick. It contains *Burlington University* (Baptist), a business college, a public library, and several handsome churches. Four railroads converge at Burlington, and it is connected with all the river ports by regular lines of steamers.

From Burlington to Council Bluffs the road traverses wide-stretching prairie-lands, which rise gradually to *Creston* (397 miles), and then descend more rapidly to the Missouri Bottom. **Mount Pleasant** (235 miles, *Harlem House, Brazelton*) is a city of 5,000 inhabitants, built on an elevated prairie, nearly inclosed in a bend of Big Creek. It contains *Iowa Wesleyan University* and *German College*, both under the control of the Methodists. The former has 200 students and a library of 3,000 volumes. Near the village, and in full view from the cars, is the spacious building of the *State Hospital for the Insane.* The next important station is *Fairfield* (257 miles), picturesquely situated on Big Cedar Creek. The surrounding country is rolling prairie, diversified with forests of hard wood. **Ottumwa** (285 miles, *Planters' House*), is the largest city on this line between the Mississippi and the Missouri, and has a population of about 7,000. It is situated on the Des Moines River, which is here spanned by a bridge, is surrounded by a fertile country, has a good water-power which is extensively used in manufactures, and does a trade amounting to $6,000,000 annually. *Albia* (307 miles), *Chariton* (337 miles), and *Osceola* (363 miles) are small but prosperous places. *Creston* (397 miles) is on the dividing ridge between the Mississippi and Missouri Rivers, 800 ft. above their level. The engine-houses and repair-shops of this division of the road are located here. The stations between Creston and Council Bluffs are small. **Council Bluffs** (see p. 348).

Omaha.

Hotels, etc.—The *Grand Central Hotel*, the finest between Chicago and San Francisco. was burned down in 1878, but is expected to be rebuilt. Other hotels are the *Withnell House* and *Metropolitan*. *Horse-cars* traverse the city in various directions. The *Post-Office* is at the cor. of 15th and Dodge Sts.

Omaha, the largest city of Nebraska, is situated on the Missouri River, opposite Council Bluffs, with which it is connected by the magnificent railroad bridge described on page 348. It occupies a beautiful plateau, rising gradually into bluffs, and in 1875 had a population of 20,000. The streets are broad, cross each other at right angles, and are lighted with gas. The level portion is chiefly devoted to business purposes, and contains many substantial commercial blocks and buildings. The bluffs are occupied by handsome residences with ornamental grounds. The * *U. S. Post-Office and Court-House* is a fine building of Cincinnati freestone, 122 by 66 ft., and 4 stories high, costing $350,000. The * *High-School Building* cost $250,000, and is one of the finest of the kind in the country. It crowns a far-viewing hill, and has a spire 185 ft. high, from which there is a noble outlook. Several of the churches are costly and elegant structures. The *Union Pacific R. R. Depot* is a spacious and ornate edifice. The prosperity of Omaha is due chiefly to its having been for 15 years the E. terminus of the Union Pacific R. R. Since the completion of that road in May, 1869, its growth has been extremely rapid, and it now has an immense trade and numerous important manufactories. Of the latter, the principal are the *Omaha Smelting-Works*, said to be the largest in America, several large breweries and distilleries, extensive linseed-oil works, steam-engine works, 4 brick-yards, extensive stock-yards and pork-packing establishments, and the vast machine-shops, car-works, and foundry of the Union Pacific R. R. The latter occupy about 30 acres on the bottom adjoining the table land upon which most of the city proper is built.

85. Omaha to San Francisco.

By the Union Pacific and Central Pacific Railways. Distance, 1,916 miles. Time, 4¼ days. Fare, $100. The Pacific Railroads occupy so peculiar a position among achievements of the kind that a brief outline of their history will perhaps prove interesting. The project of a railway across the continent was publicly advocated as early as 1846 by Asa Whitney, and in 1853 Congress passed an act providing for surveys by the corps of topographical engineers. Further acts were passed in 1862 and 1864 providing for a subsidy in United States 6 per cent. gold bonds at specified rates per mile. The same acts also gave to the companies undertaking the work 20 sections (12,800 acres) of land for each mile of railroad built, or about 25,000,000 acres in all. The railroad was built from Omaha, Neb., to Ogden, Utah, 1,033 miles, by the Union Pacific Company, and from San Francisco to Ogden, 883 miles, by the Central Pacific Company. Work was begun in 1863; the first 40 miles from Omaha to Fremont were completed in 1865; and on May 12, 1869, the railroad communication from the Atlantic to the Pacific ocean was opened. The route crosses 9 mountain-ranges, the highest being the Black Hills, at an elevation of 8,242 ft. above the sea, and the lowest Promontory Mountain, W. of Great Salt Lake, 4,889 ft. The aggregate length of the tunnels, of which there are 15, all occurring in the Sierra Nevada or its spurs, is 6,600 ft. The gradients do not often exceed 80 ft. to the mile, though in one instance they reach 90 ft. and in another 116 ft. to the mile. The cost of the Union Pacific road was reported to the Secretary of the Interior at $112,-

259,360; but the liabilities of the Company at the date of the completion of the road were $116,730,052. In 1868 Jesse L. Williams, a civil engineer and one of the government directors, reported the approximate cost of the Union Pacific road in cash at $38,824,821; and this was probably not far from correct. The cost of the Central Pacific road and branches (1,222 miles) in liabilities of every sort was reported in 1874 at $139,746,311.

Stations.—*Union Pacific R. R.*: Omaha to Gilman, 10 miles; Papilion, 15; Millard, 21; Elkhorn, 29; Waterloo, 31; Valley, 35; Riverside, 42; Fremont, 47; North Bend, 62; Schuyler, 76; Richland, 84; Columbus, 92; Jackson, 99; Silver Creek, 109; Clark, 121; Lone Tree, 132; Chapman, 142; Lockwood, 148; Grand Island, 154; Alda, 162; Wood River, 170; Shelton, 178; Gibbon, 183; Kearny, 191; Stevenson, 201; Elm Creek, 212; Overton, 221; Josselyn, 225; Plum Creek, 230; Coyote, 239; Cozad, 245; Willow Island, 250; Warren, 260; Brady Island, 268; McPherson, 278; Gannett, 285; North Platte, 291; Nichols, 299; O'Fallon's, 308; Dexter, 315; Alkali, 322; Roscoe, 332; Ogalalla, 342; Brule, 351; Big Spring, 361; Barton, 369; Julesburg, 377; Chappell, 387; Lodge Pole, 397; Colton, 407; Sidney, 414; Brownson, 423; Potter, 433; Bennett, 442; Antelope, 451; Adams, 457; Bushnell, 463; Pine Bluff, 473; Tracy, 479; Egbert, 484; Burns, 490; Hillsdale, 496; Atkins, 502; Archer, 508; Cheyenne, 516; Granite Cañon, 535; Sherman, 549; Laramie, 573; Lookout, 608; Medicine Bow, 647; Carbon, 657; Percy, 668; Fort Steele, 695; Rawlins, 711; Creston, 739; Red Desert, 763; Table Rock, 776; Bitter Creek, 786; Black Buttes, 796; Hallville, 801; Rock Springs, 832; Green River, 847; Bryan, 860; Church Buttes, 888; Carter, 905; Piedmont, 929; Evanston, 957; Wahsatch, 968; Castle Rock, 977; Echo, 993; Weber, 1,009; Peterson, 1,017; Uintah, 1,026; Ogden, 1,023. *Central Pacific R. R.*—Corinne, 1,053; Promontory Point, 1,082; Kelton, 1,123; Terrace, 1,153; Toano, 1,214; Pequop, 1,224; Otego, 1,230; Wells, 1,250; Elko, 1,307; Carlin, 1,330; Palisade, 1,339; Winnemucca, 1,451; Mill City, 1,479; Humboldt, 1,493; Hot Springs, 1,569; Wadsworth, 1,588; Reno, 1,622; Truckee, 1,656; Summit, 1,671; Emigrant Gap, 1,692; Blue Cañon, 1,698; Dutch Flat, 1,709; Colfax, 1,722; Auburn, 1,740; Rocklin, 1,754; Sacramento, 1,777; Brighton, 1,782; Galt, 1,804; Stockton, 1,825; Lathrop, 1,833; Tracy, 1,844; Antioch, 1,872; San Pablo, 1,906; Oakland Wharf, 1,913; San Francisco, 1,916.

THE journey from Omaha to San Francisco, by reason of its great length and the time which it takes, will be in many respects a new experience to the traveler, no matter how extended his previous journeyings may have been. It is more like a sea-voyage than the ordinary rushing from point to point by rail, and, as on a sea-voyage, one ceases to care about time-tables and connections, and makes himself comfortable. Says Mr. Charles Nordhoff, whose "California, for Health, Pleasure, and Residence," will prove a useful companion for the journey: "Until you have undertaken this journey, you will never know how great a difference it makes to your comfort whether your train goes at the rate of 40 or at 22 miles an hour. This last is the pace of the iron horse between Omaha and San Francisco; and it is to the fierce and rapid rush of an Eastern lightning-express what a gentle and easy amble is to a rough and jolting trot. Certainly a lightning-express rushing through from Chicago to San Francisco would not carry any one, except an expressman, a second time. At 40 or 45 miles per hour, the country you pass through is a blur; one hardly sees between the telegraph-poles; pleasure and ease are alike out of the question; reading tires your eyes, writing is impossible, conversation impracticable, except at the auctioneer pitch, and the motion is wearing and tiresome. But, at 22 miles per hour, travel by rail is a different affair; and having unpacked your books, and unstrapped your wraps, in your

Pullman or Central Pacific Palace-car, you may pursue all the sedentary avocations and amusements of a parlor at home; and as your housekeeping is done—and admirably done—for you by alert and experienced servants; as you may lie down at full length, or sit up, sleep or wake, at your choice; as your dinner is sure to be abundant, very tolerably cooked, and not hurried; as you are pretty certain to make acquaintances on the car; and as the country through which you pass is strange, and abounds in curious and interesting sights, and the air is fresh and exhilarating—you soon fall into the ways of the voyage; and if you are a tired business man, or a wearied housekeeper, your careless ease will be such a rest as certainly most busy and overworked Americans know how to enjoy."

In order to secure the comfort thus described, it will be necessary to engage a berth in the Pullman Palace-cars to Ogden, and in the Silver Palace-cars beyond Ogden. The cost of these is $8 from Omaha to Ogden, and $6 from Ogden to San Francisco, in addition to the cost of the regular ticket; but no more fruitful outlay could be made. One person alone is not allowed to take an entire section, and passengers are obliged to take such berths as are assigned; but by stopping over a day at Omaha a choice of berths can be obtained. Good eating-stations are placed at proper intervals, and the train stops long enough for a meal to be eaten with reasonable deliberation.

As there are nearly 250 stations on the line, only the more important are included in the list given above, and the information there conveyed (names and distances) is all that the traveler will care to have about most of them. In such a case as this the only method of description not likely to prove tedious will be to direct attention in a general way to the characteristic features of the different sections of the route. *

During the first day out from Omaha, the road traverses vast prairies, which the tourist now sees for the first time in something like their primitive nakedness and solitude. Settlements and farms are still seen, but, unlike those in the more populous States E. of the Mississippi, they appear to be swallowed up in the immensity of the interminable levels which roll off to the horizon like the sea. On the left is the Platte River, through whose valley, entered at *Elkhorn* (29 miles), the road runs for nearly 400 miles. *North Platte* (291 miles) is the principal station on this section of the line, and contains a fine hotel, round-house, and machine-shop belonging to the railway company. Its population is about 2,000, and it boasts of a brick Court House, a brick school house, and several churches. Shortly beyond North Platte the rich farming-lands of Nebraska are left behind, and the road enters a vast grazing country, which extends to the base of the Rocky Mountains, and is covered summer and winter with nutritious grasses. Herds of antelope are seen feeding quietly on the verdurous slopes, and villages of prairie-dogs break the monotony of the level. *Sidney* (414 miles) is

* A more detailed description will be found in "Scenery of the Pacific Railways and Colorado. With Map and 71 Illustrations." Published by D. Appleton & Co.

the largest place between North Platte and Cheyenne, and is quite a prosperous village, with round-house, repair-shops, hotel, and eating-house. It is the nearest railroad station to the Black Hills, and daily stages run thence to the mining town of Deadwood. Just before reaching *Archer* (508 miles), the first glimpse is obtained of the Rocky Mountains, whose snow-clad tops are at first mistaken for clouds. * Long's Peak, 14,000 ft. high, soon becomes plainly visible, and the Spanish Peaks are seen in the dim distance; while away to the N., as far as the eye can reach, the dark line of the Black Hills leans against the horizon. **Cheyenne** (516 miles) is one of the largest towns on the entire road, though settled only in 1867. It now has a population of 4,000, is the point of junction with the Denver Pacific Railway (see Route 93), and has an extensive round-house and shops. The R. R. hotel here is excellent and the meals well cooked and served. The town is substantially built, largely of brick, and contains a fine Court House and Jail, a neat City Hall, a large public school building, and a brick opera-house. Cheyenne is another point of departure for the Black Hills, and daily stages run to Deadwood in 48 hours.

A few miles beyond Cheyenne the ascent of the Rocky Mountains (Black Hills) is begun, and for 30 miles the road climbs rugged granite hills, winding in and out of interminable snow-sheds. *Sherman* (549 miles) is one of the highest R. R. stations in the world (8,235 ft.) and affords grand views. Here commences the descent to the Laramie Plains, which are about 40 miles wide on the average and 100 miles long, bounded by the Black Hills and the Medicine Bow Mountains. They are overrun by enormous flocks of sheep, and are said to afford the best grazing in the United States. In the adjacent hills there is abundance of game, such as mountain-sheep, antelopes, and bears. **Laramie City** (572 miles) is situated on the Laramie River, in the midst of the Laramie Plains, and has a population of about 3,000 which is rapidly increasing. It is the end of a division of the R. R., and has large machine and repair-shops, and the rolling-mills of the company. The streets are regularly laid out at right angles with the railway, and there are many handsome buildings of brick and stone. Within 30 miles of Laramie there are deposits of antimony, cinnabar, gold, silver, lead, plumbago, and several other minerals; and it is expected that the place will become an important manufacturing center. Beyond Laramie the road traverses the Plains for many miles, crosses a region of rugged hills, and descends once more into the valley of the North Platte. Near *Miser* (616 miles) there are fine views from the cars of Laramie Peak on the right and Elk Mountain on the left. *Rock Creek* (625 miles) is a regular eating-station, and ranks among the best on the line. The North Platte is reached at *Fort Fred Steele* (695 miles), and then another steep ascent is begun. *Creston* (737 miles) is upon the dividing ridge of the continent, from which water flows each way; E. to the Atlantic and W. to the Pacific. At *Green River Station* (845 miles) the train emerges from the desolate plains, and enters a mountain-region, which affords some fine views. Utah Territory is entered at *Granger* (876 miles). Within this region, between Green River and Salt

Lake Valley, five tunnels are traversed, aggregating nearly 2,000 ft. and cut through solid rock, which never crumbles, and consequently does not require to be arched with brick. *Castle Rock* (975 miles) is a station at the head of Echo Cañon, and we there enter a region whose grand and beautiful scenery has been often described. * *Echo Cañon* and the celebrated * *Weber Cañon* offer the most magnificent sights on the whole Pacific route, and the tourist will be fortunate if he passes them by daylight. The road winds through all the devious turns of these cañons, while rock-ribbed mountains, bare of foliage except a stunted pine, and snow-capped, rise to an awful height on either hand. Emerging from these grim battlements of rock, the train enters the Salt Lake Valley and soon reaches **Ogden** (1,033 miles), the point of junction between the Union Pacific and Central Pacific Railways, and of the Utah Central R. R., which extends to Salt Lake City, and the Utah & Northern R. R. Ogden is a flourishing city of 6,000 inhabitants, situated on a high mountain-environed plateau, and remarkably well built. Its streets are broad, with running streams of water in nearly all of them, and it contains a brick Court-House, 3 churches and a Mormon tabernacle, many tasteful residences, and two hotels (the *Utah Hotel* and the *Beardsley House*), besides the excellent railroad hotel at the depot. The machine- and repair-shops of the Central Pacific R. R. are located here. Ogden is the regular supper and breakfast station of both Pacific railroads, and here cars are changed. Passengers are allowed one hour in which to get their meals, look about, and secure new berths in the palace-cars.

The Utah Central R. R. connects with the Union and Central Pacific at Ogden, and the *détour* to Salt Lake City (37 miles from Ogden, fare $2) may be made in one day. The country between Ogden and Salt Lake City is quite thickly settled, except within the first 7 miles, and stoppages are made at four Mormon villages, with nothing in particular to characterize them except the coöperative stores, with an open eye and the legend "Holiness to the Lord" printed over the doorways.

Salt Lake City.

Hotels, etc. The best hotels are the *Walker House*, in Main St., and the *Townsend House*, at the cor. of W. Temple and S. 2nd Sts. *Horse-cars* run on the principal streets and render all parts of the city easily accessible. The population of Salt Lake City is about 25,000, of whom about one third are Gentiles and apostate Mormons.

Salt Lake City, the capital of Utah Territory, is situated at the W. base of a spur of the Wahsatch Mts., about 12 miles from the S. E. extremity of the Great Salt Lake. It lies in a great valley, extending close up to the base of the mountains on the N., with an expansive view to the S. of more than 100 miles of plains, beyond which in the distance rise, clear cut and grand in the extreme, the gray and rugged mountains whose peaks are covered with perpetual snow. Great care was displayed in selecting the site and in laying out the city. The streets are 128 ft. wide, and cross each other at right angles. There are 260 blocks each ⅛ of a mile square and containing 10 acres. Each block is divided into 8 lots, 10 by 20 rods, and containing 1¼ acre. Several of the blocks in the business quarter have been cut by cross streets laid out since the founding of the city. Shade trees and ditches filled with running water line both sides of every street, while almost every lot has an orchard of pear, apricot, plum, peach, and apple trees. The city is divided into 20 wards, nearly every one of which has a public square. The dwellings and business structures are built principally of adobe (sun-dried bricks); but a few of the newer stores are built of stone, and are very handsome and commodious structures. The dwellings are generally small and of one story, with separate entrances where the proprietor has a plurality of wives.

The chief business thoroughfares are *Main St.* and *Temple St.* On the latter is the great * **Tabernacle,** which is the first object to attract the eye as one approaches the city, although destitute of any architectural beauty. It is of wood, except the 46 huge sandstone pillars which support the immense dome-like roof, is oval in shape inside and out, and will seat 15,000 persons. It is used for worship, lectures, and debates. The Tabernacle organ is one of the largest in America. A little E. of the Tabernacle, and enclosed within the same high wall, are the foundations of the new *Temple*, estimated to cost $10,000,000, but which will probably never be finished. Within the same walls is the famous *Endowment House*, in which the various Mormon rites and mysteries are performed, and which no Gentile is permitted to enter. It is an inferior-looking adobe building. On S. Temple St., E. of Temple Block, is *Brigham's Block*, enclosed by a high stone wall, and containing the Tithing House, the Beehive House, the Lion House, the office of the *Deseret News*, and various other offices, shops, dwellings, etc. Here was the residence of the late Brigham Young, and 18 or 20 of his wives lived in the Beehive and the Lion House. Nearly opposite is a large and handsome house supposed to belong to the Prophet's favorite wife, and known familiarly as *Amelia Palace*. On S. Temple St., opposite the Tabernacle, is *The Museum* (small admission fee), where may be seen the various products of Mormon industry, specimen ores from the mines, precious stones from the desert, specimen birds of Utah, and various Indian relics, and curiosities. The *Theatre* is a vast building, gloomy-looking from the street, but with a very ornate interior. The *City Hall* cost $60,000, and is used as the territorial capitol. The *City Prison* is in the rear. Other handsome buildings are those of the *Deseret National Bank*, at the cor. of E. Temple and S. 1st Sts., and the *Coöperative Store* in E. Temple St. About 2 miles E. of the city is * **Camp Douglas,** beautifully situated on an elevated plateau, overlooking the city, and commanding a fine view.

Most visitors to Salt Lake City will as a matter of course wish to see the * **Great Salt Lake** from which it takes its name, and which is one of the greatest natural curiosities of the West. It is most easily reached *via* Utah Western R. R. to *Lake Point* (20 miles), where there is a large hotel and bath-house, and whence a steamer crosses the lake (fare, round trip, $1.50, which includes a ride on the lake-steamer and the privilege of a bath). Great Salt Lake is 75 miles long and about 30 miles broad, is 4,200 ft. above the sea, and contains six islands, of which Church Island is the largest. Several rivers flow into it, but it has no outlet. The water is shallow, the depth in many extensive parts being not more than 2 or 3 ft. The floods of spring spread the lake over large tracts, from which it recedes as summer advances. It was evidently once vastly more extensive than at present. Its water is transparent, but excessively salt, and so buoyant that a man may float in it at full length upon his back, having his head and neck, his legs to the knee, and both arms to the elbow entirely out of the water. If he assumes a sitting posture, with the arms extended, his shoulders will rise above the water. Swimming, however, is difficult from the tendency of the lower extremities to rise above the surface; and the brine is so strong that it cannot be swallowed without danger of strangulation, while a particle of it in the eye causes intense pain. A bath in it is refreshing and invigorating, though the body requires to be washed afterward in fresh water.

Leaving Ogden, the westward-bound train passes two small stations, and in 25 miles reaches **Corinne** (*Central Hotel*), the largest Gentile town in Utah, having a large trade with the mining-regions of eastern Idaho and Montana. Beyond Corinne the train winds among the Promontory Mts., and skirts the N. shore of the Great Salt Lake, while the Mormon City lies near the S. end of it. *Promontory Point* (1,082 miles) is interesting as the spot where the two companies building the Pacific Railroad joined their tracks on May 10, 1869. The last tie was made of California laurel trimmed with silver, and the last four spikes were of solid silver and gold. Beyond this the road enters upon an extended plateau, about 60 miles long and of the same width, known as the *Great American Desert.* Its whole surface is covered with a sapless weed 5 or 6 inches high, and never grows any green thing that could sustain animal life. The only living things found upon it are lizards and jackass-rabbits; and the only landscape feature is dry, brown, and bare mountains. "The earth is alkaline and fine, and is whirled up by the least wind in blinding clouds of dust. Rivers disappear in it, and it yields no lovelier vegetation in return than the pallid artemisia or sage-brush. It seems to have been desolated by a fire, which has left it red and crisp; the blight which oppresses it is indescribable. The towns along the railway do not enliven the prospect. A disproportionate number of the buildings are devoted to liquor-selling, and a disproportionate number of the inhabitants are loafers. The phase of civilization presented makes one doubt whether such civilization is preferable to the barbarism of the Piute and Shoshone Indians, who swarm near the depots, and whose numerous encampments dot the plain." At *Humboldt Wells* (1,250 miles) are some 30 springs in a low basin about ½ mile W. of the station. Some of these springs have been sounded to a depth of 1,700 feet without revealing a bottom, and it is supposed that the whole series form the outlets of a subterranean lake. The most important station on this portion of the line is **Elko** (1,307 miles), which has a population of 1,200, a large brick court-house and jail, a church and a public school, and the State University, founded in 1875. Several important mining districts are tributary to Elko, and secure it a large trade. About 1½ mile W. is a group of mineral springs which are achieving a good deal of local reputation. Elko is the regular breakfast and supper station of the R. R., and meals are well served. *Winnemucca* (1,451 miles) is another prosperous town with a large mining trade; and *Humboldt* (1,493 miles) affords a grateful if momentary relief to the now wearied eye of the tourist. "The desert extends from Humboldt in every direction—a pallid, lifeless waste, that gives emphasis to the word desolation; mountains break the level, and from the foot to the crest they are devoid of vegetation and other color than a maroon or leaden gray; the earth is loose and sandy; Sahara itself could not surpass the landscape in its woe-begone infertility; but here at Humboldt a little intelligence, expenditure, and taste have, by the magic of irrigation, compelled the soil to yield flowers, grass, fruit, and shrubbery."

At *Wadsworth* (1,588 miles) the ascent of the Sierra Nevada is begun. The wearying sight of plains covered with alkali and sage-brush is exchanged for picturesque views of mountain-slopes, adorned with branching pine-trees, and diversified with foaming torrents. The ascent soon becomes so steep that two locomotives are required to draw the train. At short intervals there are strong wooden snow-sheds, erected to guard the line against destruction by snow-slides. These sheds, which are very much like tunnels, interrupt the views of some of the most romantic scenery on the line.

Reno (1,622 miles) is a busy town of 2,000 inhabitants situated on the Truckee River about 5 miles from the base of the Sierra. It has an immense trade with the mining-districts, and contains the grounds of the State Agricultural Society, a Young Ladies' Seminary, and several factories. It was exceptionally well built, but a disastrous fire on March 2, 1879, swept away the entire business portion of the place, with nearly all the finest buildings.

The Virginia & Truckee R. R. runs from Reno to Carson and Virginia City, in the great Nevada mining-region, and affords the opportunity for an excursion which the tourist should certainly make if he have time. **Carson** (31 miles from Reno) is the capital of Nevada, and is a thriving city of 4,000 inhabitants, containing the Capitol, the U. S. Mint, a Court House, 4 churches, the best schoolhouse in the State, and many handsome residences. The State Prison, 2½ miles distant, is a massive building yet unfinished. From Carson daily stages run in 15 miles (fare $3) to * **Lake Tahoe,** one of the loveliest bodies of water in the world. It is about 22 miles long and 10 miles wide, is 6,000 ft. above the sea, is surrounded by snow-capped mountain-peaks, and has marvellously clear water which has been sounded to a depth of over 1,600 ft. Small steamers circumnavigate the lake (fare across $2.50; round trip, $5), and enable its exquisite scenery to be viewed to great advantage.—Twenty-one miles beyond Carson is **Virginia City** (*International Hotel*), built half way up a steep mountain-side, completely environed by mountains, and containing 25,000 inhabitants, about one-third of whom are usually under ground. The pitch of the ground is such that what is the first story of a house in front becomes the second or third story in the rear, and in looking in any direction the eye meets an unvaried prospect of chain after chain of interlocked peaks. On Oct. 26, 1875, the city was almost entirely destroyed by fire, but it has been rebuilt more handsomely than ever, and a similar catastrophe provided against with characteristic energy by the construction of water-works costing over $2,000,000. . "The people," says a recent visitor, "are ultra-Californian in their nature and habits, excessively fond of display, lavishly hospitable, impetuous in business, and irrepressible in speculativeness. What is most surprising to the stranger is the proportions of the constant rushing crowd on C Street, the principal thoroughfare, and the cosmopolitan character of its elements. Piute and Washoe Indians in picturesque rags, Chinamen in blue-and black blouses, brawny Cornishmen, vehement Mexicans, and many other people from far-apart countries, mingle and surge along in the stream." Virginia City stands directly over the famous Comstock Lode, and near by are the celebrated *Consolidated Virginia Mine* and the *Big Bonanza Mine*, said to be the richest in the world. There are numerous other mines, and a visit to any one of them will be a most fascinating experience. (An excellent way to make the excursion described above will be to go direct from Reno to Virginia City, then return to Carson and take the stage for Lake Tahoe, cross the lake to Tahoe City, and take the stage thence to Truckee on the C. P. R. R.)

Truckee (1,656 miles) is the first important station in California, and is a handsomely-built town of 2,000 inhabitants, perched high up amid the Sierras. Three miles from the town is the lovely *Donner Lake, embosomed in the lap of towering hills; and daily stages (fare $2) run to Tahoe City on Lake Tahoe (see above). *Summit* (1,671 miles) is the highest point on the Central Pacific road (7,042 ft.), and the scenery around the station is indescribably beautiful and impressive. "A grander or more exhilarating ride than that from Summit to Colfax," says Mr. Nordhoff, "you can not find in the world. The scenery is various, novel, magnificent. You sit in an open car at the end of the train, and the roar of the wind, the rush and vehement impetus of the train, and the whirl around curves, past the edge of deep chasms, among forests of magnificent trees, fill you with excitement, wonder, and delight. . . . The entrance to California is as wonderful and charming as though it were the gate to a veritable fairy land. All its sights are peculiar and striking: as you pass down from Summit the very color of the soil seems different from and richer than that you are accustomed to at home; the farmhouses, with their broad piazzas, speak of a summer climate; the flowers, brilliant at the roadside, are new to Eastern eyes; and at every turn of the road new surprises await you." From Summit to Sacramento is a distance of 106 miles, and between these places the descent from a height nearly half as great as that of Mont Blanc to 56 ft. above the sea-level has to be made. The line is carried along the edge of precipices plunging downward for 2,000 or 3,000 ft., and in some parts upon a narrow ledge excavated from the mountain-side by men swung down in baskets. It is thus at * *Cape Horn*, a point grand and imposing in the extreme, which is passed just before reaching *Colfax* (1,722 miles). **Sacramento** (*Capitol House, Golden Eagle, Grand*,) is the capital of California, and the third city of the State in size, having a population of about 20,000. It is built on an extensive plain on the E. bank of the Sacramento River, immediately S. of the mouth of the American River. Its site is very low, having originally been only 15 ft. above low-water, and the city formerly suffered greatly from inundations; but the business portion has been artificially raised 8 ft. above the original level, and the exposed portions surrounded by a great levee. Sacramento is a very attractive city. The streets are straight and wide, and cross each other at right angles; the shops and stores are mostly of brick; the dwellings mostly of wood, and surrounded by gardens. Shade-trees are abundant, and a luxuriant growth of flowers and shrubs may be seen in the open air at all seasons of the year. The only important public building is the * State Capitol, but this is one of the finest structures of the kind in the United States. It is situated almost in the heart of the city, and the grounds cover eighteen blocks, beautifully laid out with trees,

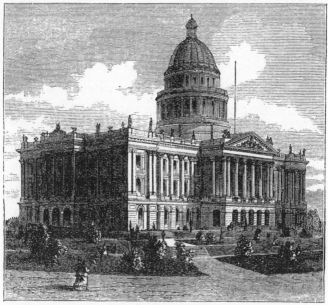

State Capitol of California.

shrubs, and flowers. The *State Library*, in the Capitol, has upward of 35,000 volumes; and the *Sacramento Library*, in a fine building belonging to the association, about 7,000 volumes. The *State Agricultural Society* has ample accommodations for the exhibition of stock, and one of the finest race-courses in the world. It holds a fair annually, about the middle of September. There are a number of fine church edifices in the city, many schools, charitable institutions, a convent, and vast manufactories and machine-shops. Sacramento is a great railroad and steamboat center, and connects directly with all parts of the State.

The journey from Sacramento to San Francisco is very pleasant, but without special interest, being for the most part through the highly-cultivated valley of the Sacramento and San Joaquin.* Fifty-four miles beyond Sacramento is **Stockton** (*Yosemite House, Mansion, Grand*), containing 15,000 inhabitants, and situated at the head of tide-navigation on the San Joaquin River. It occupies a level site, and is substantially and compactly built, with handsome, wide streets, and public buildings that indicate enterprise and taste. The *Court House* and *City Hall*, near the center of the city, is surrounded with choice shade-trees and shrubbery, as are also many of the residences. The business-blocks are principally of brick, and there are several handsome churches and school-houses. The *State Lunatic Asylum* is located here, and its spacious buildings are seen just before the train enters the city.

The * **Calaveras Grove of Big Trees** is best visited from Stockton, *via* the Stockton & Copperopolis R.R. to *Milton*, and thence by stage 25 miles to *Murphy's*. It is usual to stay over night at Murphy's, and take the stage in the morning for the Big Trees, 16 miles distant. There is a good hotel at the grove. The grove occupies a belt 3,200 ft. long by 700 ft. broad, in a depression between two slopes, through which meanders a small brook that dries up in summer. There are 93 trees of large size in the grove, and a considerable number of smaller ones, chiefly on the outskirts. Several have fallen since the grove was first discovered, one has been cut down, and one has had the bark stripped from it up to the height of 116 ft. above the ground. The tallest now standing is the *Keystone State*, which is 325 ft. high, and 45 ft. in circumference: and the largest and finest is the *Empire State*. There are 4 trees over 300 ft. high, and from 40 to 61 ft. in circumference. Their age is supposed to be about 1,500 years. The tree which was cut down occupied 5 men 22 days, pump-augers being used for boring through the tree. After the trunk was severed from the stump, it took 5 men 3 days, with ponderous wedges, to topple it over. The bark was 18 inches thick.—The **Stanislaus Grove** (or *South Grove*) is situated on Beaver Creek, 5 miles S. E. of the Calaveras Grove. There are 700 or 800 trees in this grove; several of them being very fine specimens, and in excellent condition. The grove is often visited by tourists, who ride over from the hotel in the other grove, where horses and guides are furnished.

At *Lathrop* (1,833 miles) the Visalia Div. of the Central Pacific R. R. diverges, and constitutes the favorite route to the **Yosemite Valley** (see Route 87). Beyond Lathrop, on the main line, a number of small stations are passed, and the train soon reaches **Oakland** (*Tubb's Hotel, Grand Central*), a beautiful city of 35,000 inhabitants, situated on the E. shore of San Francisco Bay, nearly opposite San Francisco, of which it is practically a suburb. It is a favorite residence of persons doing business in San Francisco, and is much resorted to from that city for its drives and fine scenery. Oakland is luxuriantly shaded, live-oak being the favorite tree, is remarkably well built, and has a delightful climate. At Berkeley, 4 miles N., is the *State University*, which is open to both sexes, and whose tuition is free. The train passes around the city to Oakland Point, where the company has built an immense pier 2¼ miles into the bay. From this pier (which is well worth notice) a ferry-boat conveys the passengers and freight to San Francisco, 3 miles distant.

* The route for through trains between Sacramento and San Francisco has been changed from the one above described *via* Stockton to the new and shorter way *via* Benicia, crossing the Straits of Carquinez on a mammoth ferry-steamer which transports the entire train. Beyond Benicia the route is through Oakland as before.

REFERENCE TO FIGURES.

Hotels.

1 Palace D 8
2 Baldwin House E 7
3 Grand D 8
4 Occidental D 8
5 Lick House D 8
6 Russ House D 8

Prominent Buildings.

7 City Hall E 6
8 Old City Hall C 7
9 Custom H. & Post O. C 8
10 U. S. Branch Mint E 7
11 Merchants' Exchange D 8
12 Nevada Bank D 8
13 Bank of California D 8
14 Anglo-California Bank
15 Mercantile Library D 8
16 Odd Fellows Hall D 8
17 California Market D 8
18 Center Market D 7

Churches.

19 St. Patrick's E 8
20 St. Mary's Cathedral D 7
21 St. Francis's C 7

22 St. Joseph's F 6
23 Grace D 7
24 Trinity D 7
25 Calvary Presbyterian D 7
26 First Unitarian D 7
27 First Methodist C 7
28 First Congregational D 7
29 Emanu-El D 7
30 Sherith-Israel D 7
31 Chinese Mission House C 7
32 Mission Dolores H 4

Theatres.

33 California D 7
34 Grand Opera House C 8
35 Wade's Opera House E 8
36 Baldwin's Acad. of Music
    E 7
37 Adelphi
38 Alhambra D 8
39 Woodward's Gardens G 5

Squares.

40 Golden Gate Park F 1
41 Lone Mt. Cemetery E 3

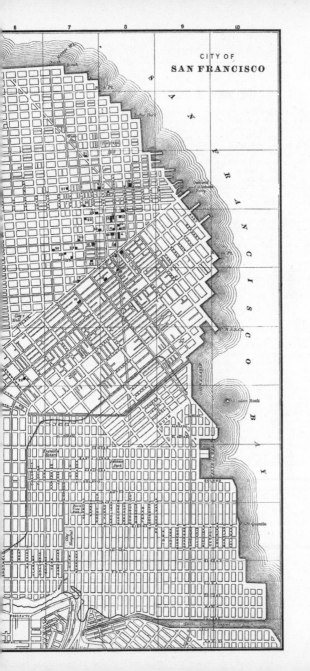

86. San Francisco.

Hotels.—The *Palace Hotel* ($3 to $4.50 a day), the largest building of its kind in the world, can accommodate about 1,200 guests, and cost with land and furniture $3,250,000. The *Baldwin House* ($3 to $4.50 a day), though somewhat smaller than the Palace, is of still greater magnificence, and cost $3,500,000. The *Grand Hotel* ($3 to $4 a day), cor. Market and New Montgomery Sts., is a large and well-kept house. Other first-class hotels are the *Occidental* ($3 a day), in Montgomery St., extending from Bush to Sutter; and the *Lick House* ($3 a day), in Montgomery St., between Post and Sutter. The *Russ House* ($2.50 a day) is an old-established hotel, cor. Montgomery and Bush Sts.; and the *Cosmopolitan* ($3 a day), cor. Bush and Sansome Sts. Good accommodations at from $1.75 to $2.50 a day can be obtained at the *American Exchange*, 319 Sansome St.; the *Brooklyn Hotel*, 210 Bush St.; and the *International Hotel*, 824 Kearney St. There are many cheap lodging-houses, where comfortable rooms may be had at from 25c. to 50c. per night; the most frequented of these is the *What Cheer*, 529 Sacramento St.

Restaurants.—Restaurants, chop-houses, *rôtisseries*, abound in every quarter of San Francisco. A great many are first class, and so nearly on a par that it is difficult to make a selection. Chop-houses and *rôtisseries* differ from restaurants, in that the cooking-furnaces are arranged on one side of the room, and each person can select the raw food and have it cooked right before his eyes. There are also numerous *tables-d'hôte*, where, by paying from 50c. to $1, one can sit at the table and call for anything he likes, provided it is on the bill of fare, including wines. *Martin's*, in Commercial St., near Montgomery, is noted for its excellent suppers.

Modes of Conveyance.—Horse-cars (fare, 5c.) intersect the city in every direction. "Endless wire cable" roads are much in vogue. *Omnibuses* run out on the Point Lobos Road to the Cliff House. *Hackney-carriages* are in waiting at the steamer-landings and at various stands in the city (they may be found at all hours at the Plaza, opposite the City Hall, Kearney St.). The legal charges are: For a carriage drawn by more than 1 horse, for 1 person, not exceeding 1 mile, $1.50; for more than 1 person, not exceeding 1 mile, $2.50; for each additional mile, for each passenger, 50c. By the hour, $3 for the first hour, and $2 for each subsequent hour. For a carriage drawn by 1 horse, for 1 person, not exceeding 1 mile, $1; for more than 1 person, not exceeding 1 mile, $1.50; for each passenger, for each additional mile, 25c. By the hour (for 2 persons), $1.50 for the first hour, and $1 for each subsequent hour. No extra charge is allowed for ordinary baggage.

Ferries.—All the ferries, viz., to Oakland, Alameda, Saucelito, San Quentin, Berkeley, and San Rafael, run from the foot of Market St.

Theatres and Amusements.—The largest and finest theatre in the city, and one of the finest in the United States, is the *Grand Opera House*, cor. Mission and 3d Sts., seating 3,500 persons. The *California Theatre*, 414 Bush St., ranks next, and is devoted to the legitimate drama and star performances. *Baldwin's Academy of Music*, under the new Baldwin House (936 Market St.), is spacious and tastefully decorated. The *Adelphi Theatre* is at 607 California St.; the *Bella Union Theatre* at 805 Kearney St.; and the *Standard Theatre* at 318 Bush St. The *Bush St. Theatre*, in Bush St., between Montgomery and Kearney, is devoted to varieties and negro minstrelsy. *Woodward's Gardens*, in Mission St., between 13th and 14th Sts., is the Barnum's of San Francisco. It contains a Museum of Curiosities, an Art Gallery, and a Menagerie : and the grounds are tastefully laid out (admission 25c.). The *City Gardens*, in Folsom St., between 12th and 13th, are a popular resort. There are two *Chinese Theatres*, one at 618 Jackson Street, and the other at 623¼ Jackson Street. The principal *Race-course* is near Golden Gate Park.

Reading-Rooms.—In all the leading hotels there are reading-rooms for the use of the guests, supplied with newspapers, etc. The *Mercantile Library*, 216 Bush St., has a well-supplied reading-room and extensive chess-rooms (open from 7.30 A. M. to 10 P. M.). The *Mechanics' Institute Library*, 27 Post St., has a library of 32,000 volumes and a reading-room (open from 9 A. M. to 10 P. M.). The *Law Library*, in Montgomery Block, has 16,000 volumes and is open from 9 A. M. to 10 P. M. The *Young Men's Christian Association*, 232 Sutter St., has a library of 8,500 volumes and a reading-room (open from 9 A. M. to 10 P. M.).

Clubs.—The *Union Club* has a handsome building at the cor. of Montgomery and California Sts. The stone of which it is constructed was quarried and cut in China. The *Olympic Club* has a fine building (with extensive gymnasium) in Post St. above Kearney. The *California Dramatic Ass.* has elegant rooms on Kearney St. The *Bohemian Club*, an association of gentlemen connected professionally with literature, art, the drama, and music, has rooms at 430 Pine St. The *San Francisco Verein*, 219 Sutter St., has a library of 6,000 volumes and a reading-room. The *Pacific Turner Bund*, for the cultivation of gymnastic exercises, has rooms at 323 Turk St. Introduction by a member secures the privileges of these clubs.

Post-Office.—The Post-Office is at the cor. of Washington and Battery Sts. Open from 8 A. M. to 8 P. M. on secular days, and on Sundays from 9 to 10 A. M. Letters are collected 6 times daily from the street-boxes (205 in number).

SAN FRANCISCO, the chief city of California and commercial metropolis of the Pacific coast, is situated at the N. end of a peninsula which is 30 miles long and 6 miles across at the city, and separates San Francisco Bay from the Pacific Ocean, in lat. 37° 46′ N. and lon. 122° 46′ W. The city stands on the E. or inner slope of the peninsula and at the base of high hills. In 1846 these hills were steep and cut up by numerous gullies, and the low ground at their base was narrow, save in what is now the S. part of the city, where there was a succession of ridges of loose, barren sand, impassable for loaded wagons. The sand-ridges have been leveled, the gullies and hollows filled up, and the hills cut down; and where large ships rode at anchor in 1849 there are now paved streets. The greater part of the peninsula is hilly, bare of trees, and unfit for cultivation; and there is but one road leading out of the city. The business streets are built up densely, but beyond that the houses are scattered at considerable intervals, and the settled part of the city may be said to cover an area of 9 square miles. In the N. E. corner of the city is Telegraph Hill, 294 ft. high; in the S. E. corner Rincon Hill, 120 ft. high; and on the W. side Russian Hill, 360 ft. high. The densely-populated quarters are in the amphitheatre formed by the three hills.

The history of San Francisco is interesting on account of the rapid growth of the place. The first house was built in 1835, when the village was called Yerba Buena, which in Spanish means "good herb," so named from a medicinal plant growing in abundance in the vicinity. In 1847 this was changed to San Francisco, and in 1848, the year that gold was first discovered in California by the white settlers, the population had increased to 1,000. The influx from the East then commenced, and in December, 1850, the population was about 25,000. In 1860 it was 56,802; in 1870, 149,473; and in 1878, the number was estimated by local authorities at 300,000. The city was incorporated in 1850, and the city and county were consolidated in 1856. In 1851 and 1856, in consequence of bad municipal government and corrupt administration of the criminal laws, the people organized Vigilance Committees, and summarily executed several criminals and banished others. This rough but wholesome discipline had its effect, and the city is now one of the most orderly in the country. The commerce of San Francisco is very large, the chief articles of export being the precious metals, breadstuffs, wines, and wool; and of import, lumber, coal, coffee, tea, rice, and sugar. The manufactures are important, including woolen and silk mills, and manufactories of watches, carriages, boots, furniture, candles, acids, wire-work, castings of iron and brass, and silver-ware.

The city is regularly laid out, though not on a uniform plan. The streets are broad and cross each other at right angles. The business streets are generally paved with Belgian blocks or cobble-stones, and most of the residence streets are planked. The leading thoroughfare (like Broadway in New York) is *Montgomery St.*, which is broad and lined with handsome buildings. At its N. end it extends to the top of a hill, which is so precipitous that carriages can not ascend it. A flight of steps enables pedestrians to mount with comparative ease; and from the top there is a fine view over the city and bay. *Kearney St.* and *Market St.* are the fashionable promenades, and contain some of the principal retail shops. In *California St.* the principal banks and brokers' and insurance offices are located. The importers and jobbers are in *Front, Sansome,* and *Battery Sts.* The handsomest private residences are on Van Ness Ave., Clay St. Hill, Pine St. Hill, and Taylor, Bush, Sutter, Leavenworth, and Folsom Sts. Especially worth seeing are the Hopkins Mansion, cor. Mason and California Sts., and the residence of Governor Stanford, at the cor. of Powell and California Sts. The "Chinese Quarter" comprises portions of Sacramento, Commercial, Dupont, Pacific, and Jackson Sts.

A stranger's first impression of San Francisco is that there are no public buildings, though the new **City Hall,** in process of erection in Yerba Buena Park, bounded by Market, MacAllister, and Larkin Sts., will be a fine structure, surpassed by few in the United States. The *U. S. Appraiser's Store* is a spacious four-story structure in Sansome St., extending from Jackson to Washington Sts. The *Custom-House,* which also contains the *Post-Office,* is a plain but substantial building at the cor. of Battery and Washington Sts. The *** U. S. Branch Mint** is a massive stone structure in the Doric-Ionic style at the cor. of 5th and Mission Sts. The machinery here is believed to be unapproached in perfection and efficiency (visitors are admitted from 10 A. M. to 12 M.). The *U. S. Treasury* is located in Commercial St. (office-hours from 10 A. M. to 3 P. M.). The *San Francisco Stock Exchange* is a splendid six-story granite and marble edifice in Pine St., surmounted by a handsome tower. The *** Merchants' Exchange,** on the S. side of California St., between Montgomery and Sansome, is one of the most costly and spacious buildings in the city. The Exchange is a splendid room in the first story, with lofty ceiling, and is well supplied with the leading papers and magazines, home and foreign. In the tower over the building is a fine clock. Other notable commercial buildings are those of the ** Bank of California,* the *Safe-Deposit Bank,* in California St., the *Nevada Bank,* cor. Montgomery and Pine, and the *Anglo-Californian,* 422 California St. Much the most imposing edifices in the city are the new hotels. The *** Palace Hotel** is a vast and ornate building at the cor. of Market and New Montgomery Sts., 275 by 350 ft., 9 stories, erected at a cost (including furniture) of $3,250,000. It is entered by a grand court-yard surrounded by colonnades, and from the roof (reached by elevator) a bird's-eye view of the whole city can be obtained. Another palatial structure is *** Baldwin's Hotel,** at the cor. of Market and Powell Sts., which though smaller than the Palace cost still more ($3,500,000). It is finished, furnished, and decorated in a style which may fairly be called magnificent. The building of the *** Mercantile Library** in Bush St., between Montgomery and Sansome, is large and fine, of brick and brown-stone, 4 stories high. The library contains 50,000 volumes, and there are several reading-rooms, chess-rooms, and an unusually fine collection of pictures. The *Odd-Fellows' Hall*, 325 and 327 Montgomery St., is commodious and contains a library numbering 34,000 volumes. The *Mechanics' Institute* is a substantial building in Post St., between Montgomery and Kearney, with a library of 23,000 volumes. The * **California Market** for fruits, vegetables, meat, and produce of all kinds is one of the sights of San Francisco. It is between Kearney and Montgomery Sts., extending through from Pine to California. The *Center Market*, at the cor. of Sutter and Dupont Sts., is also well worth visiting.

The largest and finest church-edifice on the Pacific Coast is that of * **St. Ignatius** (Roman Catholic) in MacAllister St. It has two lofty towers. The finest interior is that of * **St. Patrick's** (Roman Catholic), in Mission St., between 3d and 4th. *St. Mary's Cathedral* (Roman Catholic), cor. California and Dupont Sts., is a noble building in the Gothic style, with a spire 200 ft. high. *St. Francis's* (Roman Catholic), in Vallejo St., between Dupont and Stockton, is a large brick structure, in the Gothic style. *St. Joseph's* (Roman Catholic), in 10th St., between Folsom and Howard, is in the cruciform Gothic style, with richly-decorated interior. * *Grace Church* (Episcopal), cor. California and Stockton Sts., is a stone building with stained-glass windows. * **Trinity Church** (Episcopal), cor. Post and Powell Sts., has a lofty tower and spire, and a fine interior. The *Calvary Presbyterian*, cor. Geary and Powell Sts., is a large and costly edifice, in the Composite style, with 10 small towers rising above the roof. The * **First Unitarian** (Horatio Stebbins, pastor), in Geary St., between Dupont and Stockton, is one of the finest churches in the city, remarkable for the purity of its architectural design, and the elegance of its interior finish. The *First Methodist*, in Powell St., between Washington and Jackson, was founded in 1849, and is the oldest of the denomination in the city. The *First Baptist* is in Eddy St., between Jones and Leavenworth Sts. ; the *Columbia Square Baptist*, in Russ St., between Howard and Folsom ; and the * *First Congregational*, cor. Post and Mason Sts. The Jewish synagogue of * **Emanu-El**, in Sutter St., between Stockton and Powell, is a large, elegant, and substantial structure, with 2 lofty towers, and richly-decorated interior. That of the *Sherith-Israel*, cor. Post and Taylor Sts., is an imposing structure ; the lofty ceiling, arched and frescoed in imitation of the sky at night, is much admired. The *Chinese Mission House*, cor. Stockton and Sacramento Sts., will prove interesting to strangers.

The most important educational institution near San Francisco is the *University of California*, at Berkeley (see p. 363). In the city are an excellent *School of Design*, two Medical Colleges, and three Academies. Among the charitable institutions the principal are the *United States Marine Hospital*, in extensive and handsome new buildings on the Presidio Reservation, W. of the city ; the *New City Hospital*, in the S. part of the city ; *St. Mary's Hospital* (Roman Catholic), cor. Bryant and 1st Sts. ; the *State Woman's Hospital*, cor. 12th and Howard Sts. ; the *Almshouse*, on the San Miguel Road, in the suburbs ; the Protestant

Orphan Asylum, in Laguna St., near Haight ; and the *Roman Catholic Orphan Asylum*, in S. San Francisco. The *Alameda Park Asylum for the Insane* is situated on the Encinal, Alameda. The fine building of the *State Asylum for the Deaf, Dumb, and Blind*, near Oakland, was burned in 1875.

The * **Golden Gate Park,** W. of the city, comprises 1,043 acres beautifully laid out in walks, drives, lawns, etc. *Portsmouth Square*, commonly called the *Plaza* (W. side Kearney St. from Washington to Clay Sts.), is inclosed with a handsome iron railing, is tastefully improved with gravel-walks, trees, shrubs, and grass-plats, and has a fountain in the center. *Washington Square, Union Square,* and *Columbia Square* have also been neatly laid out and planted with trees and shrubbery. * **Laurel Hill Cemetery** is in many respects unsurpassed. It lies 2½ miles W. of the principal hotels (reached by horse-cars). Within the inclosure of the cemetery is a singular mountain, of conical shape, which rises up singly and alone to a considerable height above the surrounding country, which is tolerably level. On its summit is a large wooden cross ; and both mountain and cross are very conspicuous, and may be seen from almost any part of the city. There are several fine monuments in the cemetery, that of Senator Broderick and Ralston's (modeled after the Pantheon at Rome) being especially noteworthy ; but the great feature is Lone Mountain, with its unrivaled outlook, embracing views of the city, bay, ocean, Mount Diablo, and the Coast Range. There are several other cemeteries, among which are the *Calvary* (Catholic), the *Masonic*, and the *Odd-Fellows'*.

There are about 20,000 Chinese in San Francisco, and the " Chinese Quarter " has already been defined as comprising portions of Sacramento, Commercial, Dupont, Pacific, and Jackson Sts.   Here they hold undisputed possession of several blocks, and the houses are crammed from sub-cellar to attic. No stranger in San Francisco, who has leisure, should fail to visit one of the two *Chinese Theatres* (see p. 364). He will find the entire audience, even the ladies, who have a compartment to themselves, smoking either tobacco or opium, and the performance is carried on amid the clashing of cymbals, the beating of drums and gongs, the blowing of trumpets, and other hideous kinds of noise. A visit to the *Gambling-houses* and *Opium-cellars* will repay the curious tourist ; but it had better be made in company with a policeman.   The Chinese are probably the most inveterate gamblers in the world, and they all gamble. In a cellar, greasy and dirty and filled with smoke, eighty or a hundred will be found sitting around tables betting. Their mode of gambling is simple : some one throws a handful of copper coins on the table, and after putting up stakes they bet whether the number of coins is odd or even ; then they count them and declare the result. Often in a single night they will gamble away several months' earnings. The opium-cellars are fitted up with benches or shelves, on each of which will be found a couple of Chinamen lying on the boards with a wooden box for a pillow. They smoke in pairs : while one smokes and prepares the opium, the other is dozing in a half-drunken sleep. There are three *Temples*, and at all times the visitor will find them open and joss-sticks smoking in front of the favorite gods.

The point of chief interest in the vicinity of San Francisco is the **Cliff House,** a low, rambling building, set on the edge of some cliffs rising sharply from the ocean and facing west. It is 6 miles from the city, and is reached by the Point Lobos Road, a fine, admirably-kept boulevard, on which riders and vehicles of every description are met, especially Saturday afternoon, the half-holiday of business men. The restaurant attached to the house is famous for its excellence, and it is a delightful experience to drive down in the early morning, before the summer northers begin to blow, and breakfast there. *Seal Rock* is close by the hotel, and the greatest charm of the place is to lounge on the wide, shady piazza and watch the seals basking in the sun or wriggling over the rocks, barking so noisily as to be heard above the roar of the breakers. Northward lies the *Golden Gate,* the beautiful entrance to San Francisco Bay. Southward is the beach, upon which the waves beat ceaselessly, and beyond, a rocky shore whose outlines melt in the blue distance. In front is the vast Pacific ocean, on whose distant horizon on a clear day the peaks of the *Farallone Islands* are visible. The road passes beyond the hotel to a broad, beautiful beach several miles long, over which at low tide one can drive to the *Ocean House* at its extreme end, and return to the city by a road behind the Mission hills. Another popular drive is through Golden Gate Park to the beach near the Cliff House. At *Hunter's Point,* 4½ miles S. E. of the City Hall, is a Dry Dock, cut out of the solid rock, and said to be one of the finest in the world. The drive to it is across an arm of the bay, and affords varied and pleasant views. The *Mission Dolores,* the old mission of San Francisco, lies in the S. W. part of the city (reached by Market St. cars and also by omnibus). It is an adobe building of the old Spanish style, built in 1778. Adjoining it is the cemetery, with its well-worn paths and fantastic monuments. *Alameda, Saucelito,* and *Oakland,* across the Bay (reached by ferry), are beautiful towns with fine public gardens.

87. The Yosemite Valley.

THERE are now four stage-routes to the valley: 1. By the Visalia Div. of the Central Pacific R. R. which diverges from the main line at *Lathrop* (see p. 363), to *Madera* (185 miles from San Francisco), and thence *via* Clark's and Inspiration Point. There are 90 miles of staging on this route, and it is popular because it affords an opportunity for visiting *en route* the **Mariposa Grove of Big Trees,** which is only 3½ miles from Clark's. The Mariposa Grove is part of a grant made by Congress to be set apart for "public use, resort, and recreation" for ever. The area covered by the grant is 2 miles square, and embraces two distinct groves which are about ⅓ mile apart. The Upper Grove contains 365 trees of a diameter of one foot and over, besides a great number of smaller ones. The average height of the Mariposa trees is less than that of the Calaveras (see p. 363), the highest of the former (272 ft.) being 53 ft. less than the tallest of the latter; but their average size is greater. The largest tree in the grove is the *Grizzly Giant* (Lower Grove), which is still 94 ft. in circumference, and 31 in diameter, though much decreased in size by burning. The first branch is nearly 200 ft. from the ground, and is 6 ft. in diameter. The remains of a prostrate tree, now nearly consumed by fire, indicate that it must have reached a diameter of about 40 ft., and a height of 400. The trunk is hollow, and will admit of the passage of three horsemen riding abreast. There are about 125 trees over 40 ft. in circumference. The *Fresno Grove* is also directly on the line of this route, and contains over 800 trees spread over an area 2½ miles long and 1 to 2 broad. The largest is 95 ft. in circumference at 3 ft. from the ground.

2. The second route is to *Merced*, on the Visalia Div. of the Central Pacific R. R. (151 miles from San Francisco) and thence by stage *via* Snelling and Coulterville. The staging on this route is over 100 miles. The *Tuolumne Grove of Big Trees*, containing about 30 trees widely scattered, and none of them very large, is near Crane Flat on this route.

3. The third route is to *Merced*, on the Visalia Div. of the Central Pacific R. R., 151 miles from San Francisco, and thence by stage to Clark's, whence the route is the same as in the first route. The staging on this route is 95 miles, and by stopping over at Clark's the tourist can visit the Fresno and Mariposa Groves of Big Trees.

4. The fourth route is from Stockton on the C. P. R. R. (see p. 363) *via* Stockton and Copperopolis R. R. to *Milton* (133 miles from San Francisco), and thence by stage. There are 147 miles of staging on this route, and it is only taken by those who wish to visit the *Calaveras Grove of Big Trees* (see p. 363). The best plan for the tourist is to enter the valley by the 1st or 3d route and return by the 2d route.

Yosemite Valley.

Hotels, etc.—There are three hotels in the valley—Leydig's, Black's, and Walsh & Coulter's. The sleeping-accommodations are good, and the table fairly provided, considering the distance of the locality from the ordinary markets. Board, $3.50 a day. *Guides*, including their horses, will usually cost $5 a day.

The Yosemite Valley is situated on the Merced River, in the S. portion of the county of Mariposa, California, 140 miles a little S. of E. from San Francisco, but over 220 miles from that city by any of the usually-traveled routes. It is on the western slope of the Sierra Nevada, midway between its E. and W. base, and nearly in the center of the State, measuring N. and S. The valley is a nearly level area, about six miles in length, and from a half to a mile in width, and almost a mile in perpendicular depth below the general level of the adjacent region, and inclosed in frowning granite walls rising with almost unbroken and perpendicular faces to the dizzy height of from 3,000 to 6,000 ft. From the brow of the precipices in several places spring streams of water which, in seasons of rains and melted snow, form cataracts of a beauty and magnificence surpassing anything known in mountain scenery. "The principal features of the Yosemite," says Professor J. D. Whitney, in his excellent "Yosemite Guide-Book," "and those by which it is distinguished from all other known valleys,

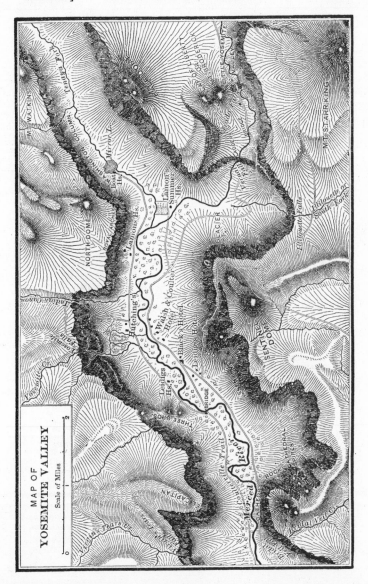

MAP OF
YOSEMITE VALLEY
Scale of Miles

are: 1. The near approach to verticality of its walls; 2. Their great height, not only absolutely, but as compared with the width of the valley itself; and 3. The very small amount of *débris* at the base of these gigantic cliffs. These are the great characteristics of the Yosemite region, throughout its whole length; but, besides these, there are many other striking peculiarities and features, both of sublimity and beauty,

The Yosemite Valley.

which can hardly be surpassed, if equaled, by those of any mountain valleys in the world. Either the domes or the waterfalls of the Yosemite, or any single one of them even, would be sufficient, in any European country, to attract travelers from far and wide in all directions. Waterfalls in the vicinity of the Yosemite, surpassing in beauty many of the best known and most visited in Europe, are actually left entirely unnoticed by travelers, because there are so many other objects of interest to be visited that it is impossible to find time for them all." The valley is almost one vast flower-garden. Plants, shrubs, and flowers of every hue cover the ground like a carpet; the eye is dazzled by the brilliancy of the color, and the air is heavy with the fragrance of a million blossoms. Trees of several centuries' growth raise their tall heads heavenward, yet, beside and in comparison with the vast perpendicular clefts of rocks, they look like daisies beside a tall pine. On every side are seen the beautiful and many-colored manzanita and madrone, and trees of such shape and variety as are never seen in the Atlantic States. The Yosemite was discovered in the spring of 1851 by a party under the command of Captain Boling, in pursuit of a band of predatory Indians, who made it their stronghold, considering it inaccessible to the whites. By an act of Congress passed in 1864, the Yosemite Valley and the Mariposa Grove of Big Trees were granted to the State of California upon the express condition that they shall be kept "for public use, resort, and recreation," and shall be "inalienable for all time." The Indian residents of the valley had a name for each of the prominent cliffs and waterfalls, but these are difficult of pronunciation, and have all been discarded except the name of the valley itself (which means "Large Grizzly Bear").

The most striking feature of the valley scenery is *** El Capitan.** Although not so high by several thousand feet as some of its giant neighbors, yet its isolation, its breadth, its perpendicular sides, and its prominence as it projects like a great rock promontory into the valley, make it, as its name indicates, the Great Chief of the Valley. It is 3,300 ft. high, and the sides or walls of the mass are bare, smooth, and entirely destitute of vegetation. "It is doubtful," says Prof. Whitney, "if anywhere in the world there is presented so squarely-cut, so lofty, and so imposing a face of rock." On the opposite side of the valley is the beautiful *** Bridal-Veil Fall,** where the creek of the same name leaps over a cliff 900 ft. high into the valley below. The water, long ere it reaches its rocky bed, is converted into mist, and descends in a white sheet of spray. The *Virgin's Tears Creek*, on the other side of the valley, directly opposite the Bridal Veil, makes a fine fall over 1,000 ft. high, inclosed in a deep recess of the rock near the lower corner of El Capitan. This is a beautiful fall while it lasts, but the stream which produces it dries up early in the season. On the same side as the Bridal Veil, and a little above it, is *Cathedral Rock*, a massively sculptured pile of granite, 2,660 ft. high, with nearly vertical sides, bare of vegetation. Just beyond are *The Spires*, two graceful columns of granite standing out from, but connected at the base with, the walls of the valley. From one point of view these spires appear symmetrical and of equal height, and rise above the edge of the cliff exactly like the towers of a Gothic cathedral. Farther up the valley, on the opposite side, is the triple group of rocks known as the *Three Brothers*. The peculiar outline of these rocks, as seen from below, resembling three frogs sitting with their heads turned in one direction, is supposed to have suggested the Indian name Pompompasus, which means "Leaping-Frog Rocks." The highest of the peaks is 3,830 ft. high, and from its summit there is a superb view of the valley and its surroundings. Nearly opposite the Three Brothers is a point of rocks projecting into the valley, the termination of which is a slender obelisk of granite, which, from its peculiar position, or from its resemblance to a gigantic watch-tower, is called *Sentinel Rock (3,043 ft. high). This is one of the grandest masses of rock in the Yosemite. Directly across the valley are the *Yosemite Falls, which are justly regarded as the most wonderful feature of the Yosemite scenery. The fall has a total height of 2,600 ft., which, however, is not all perpendicular. There is first a vertical leap of 1,500 ft., then a series of cascades down a descent equal to 626 ft. perpendicular, and then a final plunge of 400 ft. to the rocks at the base of the precipice. The rumble and roar of the falls are heard at all times, but, in the quiet of the evening, they are so great that it seems as if the very earth were shaking. No falls in the known world can be compared with these in height and romantic grandeur. The renowned Staubbach of Switzerland is greatly inferior, both in height and volume. The best time to see the falls is in May, June, and July; by August or September both the Yosemite and Bridal Veil have shrunk almost to nothing. The cliff a little to the east of the Yosemite Fall rises in a bold peak to the height of 3,030 ft. above the valley, and affords a magnificent view of the entire region. Its summit is easily reached by a trail leading up Indian Cañon.

About 2 miles above the Yosemite Falls the main valley ends, and branches out in three distinct but much narrower cañons. Through the middle one of these the Merced River comes down; in the left-hand or N. W. one the Tenaya Fork of the Merced flows in; and in the right-hand or S. W. one, the South Fork or Illilouette. At the angle where the Yosemite branches is the rounded columnar mass called *Washington Column*, and immediately to the left of it the immense arched cavity known as the *Royal Arches*. Above these the symmetrical form of the *North Dome* looms up to the height of 3,568 ft. The *Half Dome, on the opposite side of the Tenaya Cañon, is the loftiest and most imposing mountain of those considered as part of the Yosemite. It is a crest of granite, rising to the height of 4,737 ft. above the valley, and was long considered perfectly inaccessible, but in 1879 certain improvements were made by which tourists were enabled and will in future be enabled to reach this commanding point. Lying in perfect quiet and seclusion at the foot of and between the North and Half Domes is the exquisite little *Mirror Lake, an expansion of the Tenaya Fork. It is frequently visited (and best early in the morning) for the purpose of getting the reflection upon its mirror-like surface of an overhanging mass of rock to which the name of *Mt. Watkins* has been given. In the middle cañon the Merced River comes down from the plateau above in a series of noble cascades and two grand cataracts, which are among the chief attractions of the Yosemite. The first fall reached in ascending the cañon is the Vernal Fall, which has a vertical height of about

400 ft. The ledge over which the fall descends is surmounted by a steep but not difficult path, and the view down the cañon from the summit is extremely fine. "From the Vernal Fall up-stream," to quote Prof. Whitney again, "for the distance of about a mile, the river may be followed, and it presents a succession of cascades and rapids of great beauty. As we approach the Nevada Fall, the last great one of the Merced, we have at every step something new and impressive. On the left hand, or N. side of the river, is the **Cap of Liberty,** a stupendous mass of rock, isolated and nearly perpendicular on all sides, rising perhaps 2,000 ft. above its base, and little inferior to the Half Dome in grandeur. It has been frequently climbed, and without difficulty, although appearing so inaccessible from the cañon of the Merced. The * **Nevada Fall** is in every respect one of the grandest waterfalls in the world, whether we consider its vertical height, the purity and volume of the river which forms it, or the stupendous scenery by which it is environed. The fall is not quite perpendicular, as there is near the summit a ledge of rock which receives a portion of the water and throws it off with a peculiar twist, adding considerably to the general picturesque effect." The height of the fall is about 600 ft. In the cañon of the South Fork, or Illilouette, there is a fine fall estimated at 600 ft. high. It is visible from a point on the trail from the hotel to Mirror Lake, but is seldom visited by travelers, as the cañon is rough and difficult to climb.

Several small encampments of Digger Indians are generally to be found in the valley; and, if not delighted, the visitor will certainly be amused, by the primitive mode of living of these "children of Nature." Professor Whitney warmly recommends tourists visiting the Yosemite to make an excursion round the valley on the outside. Such an excursion can be made mostly on beaten trails without the slightest difficulty or danger, will occupy but a few days, and will afford as grand panoramic views of mountain and valley as can be found in Switzerland itself. Those who cannot make this tour should at least make excursions to *Inspiration Point,* on the Mariposa trail, and to *Glacier Point* (3½ miles), on the McCauley trail. The view from either is indescribably grand.

88. California Resorts.

AN easy and popular excursion from San Francisco is by steamer from foot of Market St. to *San Quentin* (11 miles), and thence by narrow-gauge R. R. in 3 miles to **San Rafael,** a remarkably pretty town near the W. shore of San Pablo Bay, built on the site of the old Jesuit mission of San Rafael. It is sheltered on the N. and W. by mountains, and is something of a *sanitarium* for those who find the ocean-winds and fogs that prevail at San Francisco too trying. The scenery in the vicinity of San Rafael is extremely picturesque, and there are many charming drives, but the chief attraction is the ascent of * **Mt. Tamalpais** (12 miles distant). The W. summit of the mountain is 2,606 ft. high, and the view from it embraces the cities of San Francisco and

Oakland, numerous towns and villages, the bay and the Golden Gate, and the illimitable ocean beyond.—Another favorite excursion is to **Pescadero** (*Swanton's Hotel*), which is reached by stage from San Mateo or Redwood City on the Southern Pacific R. R. The stage-ride of 30 miles over the Contra Costa Range affords some noble views. Pescadero is a thriving town, beautifully situated in a remarkably productive valley, on both sides of Pescadero Creek, near its confluence with the Butano, about a mile from the sea-shore. The new San Francisco Water Company takes its supply from the head of the creek. Near the town is the famous *Pebble Beach*, where agates, opals, jaspers, carnelians, and other siliceous stones, of almost every conceivable variety of color, are found in great abundance, with a natural polish imparted by the action of the waves and the smooth sea-sand.—Tri-weekly stages run along the coast from Pescadero to **Santa Cruz,** the principal watering-place of California. (Santa Cruz is also reached direct from San Francisco *via* Southern Pacific R. R. to *Pajaro*, and thence by the Santa Cruz R. R.). Santa Cruz is attractively situated on the N. side of Monterey Bay, and near by are *Aptos* and *Soquel*, popular seaside resorts. Bathing, fishing, and hunting may be enjoyed here to the full, and in the vicinity there are charming drives.—Opposite Santa Cruz, at the S. extremity of the bay, is the historic city of **Monterey** (reached from San Francisco by steamer, or *via* Southern Pacific R. R. to Salinas and thence by the Monterey & Salinas Valley R. R.). Until 1847 this town was the seat of government and principal port on the California coast; but since the rise of San Francisco its commerce and business have dwindled away, and it is now one of the quietest places in the State. Within the past two or three years, however, it has begun to attract attention as a health-resort; its climate being warm in winter, cool in summer, and dry all the year round. The Southern Pacific R. R. Co. have erected a fine hotel here, and extensive improvements have been begun with the design of making Monterey a great health and pleasure resort.

One of the excursions most frequently recommended to the stranger in San Francisco is that to San José and the Santa Clara Valley (*via* Southern Pacific R. R.). The *Santa Clara Valley* lies between the Coast and Santa Cruz Mts., and is about 100 miles in length; it is watered by the Coyote and Guadalupe Rivers and by artesian wells, and claims to be the most fertile in the world. Vineyards covering hundreds of acres, vast wheat-fields one and two miles in length, stately trees, forests of live-oak, and finely-cultivated farms, are to be seen on every hand; and the vegetation is of tropical luxuriance and beauty. In the heart of the valley, 40 miles S. E. of San Francisco and 8 miles from the head of San Francisco Bay, is the city of **San José** (*Auzerais House, St. James*), with a population of about 15,000. The main portion of the city occupies a gently-rising plateau between the Coyote and Guadalupe Rivers, here 1½ miles apart, with suburbs extending beyond them. The principal public buildings are the * *Court-House*, a massive Corinthian structure, costing $200,000, with a dome commanding a fine view; the *Jail*, adjoining it, the finest in the State, costing $80,000;

the *City Hall ;* two *markets,* costing more than $40,000 each ; 8 pub-
lic-school buildings ; and 10 churches, of which the largest and most
expensive is an unfinished edifice belonging to the Roman Catholics.
The city is noted for its educational institutions.   Besides the public
schools, there are the *College of Notre Dame* (Roman Catholic), a day
and boarding school for girls ; the *San José Institute,* a day and boarding school for both sexes; the *University of the Pacific* (Methodist),
connected with which is a young ladies' seminary ; and the *State Normal School,* whose building, erected at a cost of $275,000, is the finest
of the kind on the Pacific Coast.   The library of the *San José Library
Association* contains 4,000 volumes.   There is an *Opera-House,* seating
1,200 persons, and an elegant and commodious *Music-Hall.*   The city
has three public parks, containing 2, 8, and 30 acres respectively, and
owns a tract of 400 acres in Penitencia Cañon, 7 miles E., reserved for
a public park, containing a wild rocky gorge with a mountain-stream
and a variety of mineral springs.   The surrounding country yields
grain and fruits abundantly, and in the vicinity are some of the finest
vineyards in California.   There are many fine drives in the neighborhood of San José, notably one to the *Lick Observatory* (in course of
erection) on the summit of Mt. Hamilton, 12 miles distant. This mountain is 4,443 ft. high, and affords a magnificent view of the Santa Clara
Valley.   The famous *Almaden Quicksilver Mines* are about 14 miles
from San José, and may be reached by a pleasant two-hours' ride in a
stage-coach.   They are well worth a visit.   Three miles W. of San
José is the picturesque village of **Santa Clara,** with a population of
about 4,000.   Horse-cars connect the two, running along the * *Alameda,*
a beautiful avenue bordered by fine residences, and rows of superb
trees planted by the Jesuit fathers in 1777.   Santa Clara contains several fine churches, and is the site of the Santa Clara College (Jesuit),
which occupies a number of handsome buildings in an inclosure of about
12 acres.   Included in this institution is the Old Mission, founded by
the Spanish missionaries in early times, and the orchards planted by
them may still be seen.   Stages run from the depot at Santa Clara to
the **Pacific Congress Springs** (10 miles S. W.).   These waters contain carbonate and sulphate of soda, chloride of sodium, lime, iron,
silicate of alumina, and magnesia, and are recommended for rheumatism.

    Still another favorite excursion from San Francisco is to Calistoga
and the Geysers.   Steamers from the foot of Market St. convey the
tourist to *South Vallejo* (26 miles), where the California Pacific R. R. is
taken.   **Napa City** (41 miles from San Francisco) is a thrifty place
of about 4,000 inhabitants, surrounded by a highly productive agricultural region, rich in fruits of all kinds, and in vast fields of grain that
stretch away in every direction.   There are many beautiful drives in
the vicinity, one of the most attractive of which is that to Santa Rosa,
taking in the famous wine-cellars of Sonoma.   The highly-esteemed
Napa Soda Springs are situated in the foot-hills about 5 miles N. E. of
the town.   **Calistoga** (*Magnolia Hotel, Cosmopolitan*), the terminus
of the Napa Valley branch of the California Pacific R. R., is a pretty
town, lying in a valley a mile in width, and encircled by forest-clad

hills and mountains. It is supplied with pure water from a reservoir on the adjacent mountain-side, and there are several bath-houses, supplied with water from neighboring springs. The public warm swimming-bath, 40 ft. square, is one of the features of the place. The scenery is exceedingly picturesque, the well-cultivated fields, green lawns, sunny slopes, and shaded villas contrasting pleasantly with the wild grandeur of the rugged mountains. There are numerous mineral springs in the vicinity, the most noted of which are *Harbin's* (20 miles N. of Calistoga), and the *White Sulphur Springs*, situated in a deep and picturesque gorge of the mountains, which rise on either side to a height of about 1,000 ft. About 5 miles S. E. of Calistoga is the * **Petrified Forest,** which is justly regarded as one of the great natural wonders of California. Portions of nearly 100 distinct trees, of great size, prostrate and scattered over a tract 3 or 4 miles in extent, have been found, some on the surface and others projecting from the mountain-side. They are supposed to have been silicified by an eruption of the neighboring Mount St. Helena, which discharged hot alkaline waters containing silica in solution. Daily stages run from Calistoga to the famous * **Geyser Springs,** which are situated in Sonoma County, in a lateral gorge of the Napa Valley, called the "Devil's Cañon," near the Pluton River. The approaches to the springs are very impressive, the scenery being finer, according to Bayard Taylor, than anything in the Lower Alps. The narrow Geyser ravine, which is always filled with vapor, is shut in by steep hills, the sides of which, marked with evidences of volcanic action, are smoking with heat and bare of vegetation. A multitude of springs gush out at the base of these rocks. Hot and cold springs, boiling springs, and quiet springs lie within a few feet of each other. They differ also in color, smell, and taste. Some are clear and transparent, others white, yellow, or red with ochre, while still others are of an inky blackness. Some are sulphurous and fetid in odor, and some are charged with alum and salt. The surface of the ground about the springs, which is too hot to walk upon with thin shoes, is covered with the minerals deposited by the waters, among which are sulphur, sulphate of magnesia, sulphate of aluminum, and various salts of iron. A properly directed course of these waters is said to afford an almost certain cure for rheumatism, gout, and skin-diseases; but persons suffering from throat or pulmonary affections should not reside in the neighborhood.

The Geysers may also be reached from San Francisco *via* steamer twice daily to *Donahue* (34 miles), where connection is made with the North Pacific R. R. From *Cloverdale* on this road (90 miles from San Francisco) stages run in 12 miles (fare for the round trip, $4.50) to the Geysers over an excellent road. A good plan for the tourist is to go by one route and return by the other.

Among the health-resorts of Southern California,* the most frequented is **Santa Barbara** (*Arlington Hotel, Occidental*), lying in a sheltered nook of the shore of the Pacific, 275 miles S. S. E. of San

* Full particulars concerning these health-resorts, with details as to climate, changes of temperature, relative dryness, etc., etc., will be found in *Appletons' Illustrated Handbook of American Winter Resorts.*

Francisco (from which it is reached by steamer, and also *via* Southern Pacific R. R. to *Newhall* [438 miles] and thence by stage). It is completely protected on the N. by several ranges of mountains, and its climate is extremely equable and mild, the mean temperature for summer being 69.58° and for winter 53.33°, while the variations are very slight. The air too is not only warm, but remarkably *dry ;* and the days are nearly always brilliantly bright and sunny. The town has grown out of an old Spanish mission which was founded in 1780, and which gradually drew around it the native cultivators of the adjacent lands. Its present population is about 6,000, half of whom are Americans that have come here in search of health from the New England and Middle States ; and, as most of these latter belong to what are called the "better classes," the society of the place is exceptionally pleasant and refined. There are 2 banks, a college, good public schools, 3 daily and 2 weekly newspapers, and 7 churches. The town contains a "Spanish quarter" and a " Chinese quarter," both of which will prove interesting to strangers by their tumble-down picturesqueness ; but the new or American part of the town, and especially the suburbs, are handsomely built and tastefully adorned. Every plot of ground, no matter how small, has its row of orange-trees, its exotics, and its bed of native perennials. Roses abound summer and winter. The verbena-beds are cut down like grass thrice yearly and spring up again stronger than ever. Vines of every sort flourish luxuriantly, heliotrope climbs 20 ft. high, cacti of the rarest and most curious sort grow freely, and a little shoot of the Australian blue-gum (*Eucalyptus globulus*) becomes in 2 years a shade-tree 15 or 20 ft. high. *Montecito* is a suburb 2 or 3 miles from the town, near which are the *Hot Sulphur Springs*, some containing sulphur and sulphuretted hydrogen, and others containing iron, alumina, and potash. Horseback-riding is the chief recreation at Santa Barbara, and horses can be bought for from $20 to $50, and kept for very little.

San Diego (*Horton House*), another favorite resort of health-seekers, lies on the N. E. shore of a bay of the same name, about 460 miles S. E. of San Francisco and 15 miles N. of the Mexican border (in lat. 32° 44' 41"). Its harbor is, next to that of San Francisco, the best on the California coast. The town is more than 100 years old, having been founded by the Roman Catholic missionaries in 1769. Its growth during the last few years has been rapid, and it now has 4 churches, 2 academies, 2 daily and 2 weekly newspapers, two banks, a fine courthouse, an excellent hotel, several large boarding-houses, and a population estimated at 5,000. The climate of San Diego is remarkably equable and salubrious, the thermometer seldom rising to 80°, or sinking to the freezing point, and the usual mean being 62°. The winter days are as sunny and inviting as those of June in the Eastern States, and an out-door life is possible to all save the feeblest invalids. There is no fog, as in Santa Barbara and more northern latitudes, and very little moisture in the air. For consumptives and asthmatics, San Diego is probably as healthful a place of residence as any in Europe or America ; but rheumatism is said to be more or less prevalent in winter, and malarious diseases in summer. San Diego has been fixed by act of Congress as the W. terminus of the Texas & Pacific R. R.; but its present connection with San Francisco is by steamer along the coast, or by the Southern Pacific R. R. to Los Angeles, thence by the San Diego Div. to *Santa Ana*, and from Santa Ana by stage (103 miles, fare $10).—The **Paso-Robles Hot Springs** lie on the line of the stage-route between Santa Ana and San Diego, but the easiest way of reaching them from San Francisco is *via* steamer to San Luis Obispo, and thence by a pleasant stage-ride of 28 miles. They are situated on the great Paso-Robles ranch, and contain sulphuretted hydrogen, carbonic acid, soda, magnesia, potassa, iron, bromine, iodine, alumina, and sulphuric acid. The waters are taken chiefly in the form of baths, at the natural temperature, and are considered among the most valuable in America for rheumatism, gout, and chronic diseases of the skin. There are good accommodations for visitors at the springs, and the climate has the mildness and salubrity common to all Southern California.

Los Angeles (*Pico House, St. Charles*), the largest city in Southern California, is situated on the W. bank of the Los Angeles River, a small stream, 30 miles above its entrance into the Pacific, and 350 miles S. S. E. of San Francisco. A railroad 18 miles long connects it with Santa Monica on the coast, whence it has connection with San Francisco by steamer; and it may also be reached from San Francisco *via* the Los Angeles Div. of the Southern Pacific R. R. (482 miles). The city was settled by the Spaniards in 1780, and was called Pueblo de los Angeles (" town of the angels "), from the excellence of its climate and the beauty of its surroundings. Its present population is about 16,000, and the adobe buildings of which it was originally composed are fast giving way to larger and more imposing structures. In the N. W. portion is a hill 60 ft. high, commanding a fine view of the city, which lies in a sheltered valley, bounded on the W. by low hills, that extend from the Santa Monica Mountains, 40 miles distant, and on the E. by the San Gabriel plateau. The climate of Los Angeles is almost as mild as that of San Diego, and some invalids prefer it, because here they escape the winds, which blow all along the coast. The nights, however, are chilly, and it is not considered a desirable residence for persons affected with throat diseases. Along both banks of the river below the city extends a fertile plain, planted with vineyards and orange-groves, and there are also large vineyards within the city limits. Los Angeles is the center of the orange-growing business of California, and lemons, olives, and other tropical fruits are cultivated in the vicinity.

About 60 miles E. of Los Angeles (reached by a stage-ride of 10 hours) is **San Bernardino** (*Starke's Hotel*), the most frequented of the inland resorts. It lies in a beautiful valley, with picturesque mountains on three sides of it, and contains about 4,000 inhabitants. It is supplied with water by artesian wells, and all parts of the town are embowered in fruit and ornamental trees. Fruits of all kinds are grown here, and oranges and lemons are produced in great abundance. The view of Mt. San Bernardino, the loftiest peak of the Coast Range, is exceedingly grand. The air of San Bernardino is drier than that of points nearer the coast, and for this reason is preferable for some consumptives. Little rain falls during the year, malaria is unknown, and the climate is a perpetual invitation to an open-air life. Many invalids find a residence in *Old San Bernardino* (which lies higher than the new town), or in *Riverside*, more beneficial than one in the town proper ; but the entire valley is remarkably salubrious. About 4 miles distant, near Mt. San Bernardino, are some *hot springs*, containing lime, soda, iron, and alumina ; their medicinal properties have not been fully ascertained, and the waters should be taken with caution. Horses may be bought at from $20 to $50 each at San Bernardino ; their keep costs very little, and many attractive excursions may be made—to the San Gorgonio Pass, the Great Yuma Desert, the San Jacinto tin mines, or the placer gold diggings.

89. San Francisco to Portland, Oregon.

Besides the overland route described below there are several lines of coast-steamers from San Francisco to Portland, Victoria, and intervening ports. The Pacific Coast Steamship Co. runs semi-weekly steamers, and the voyage from San Francisco to Portland occupies about 3 days. Fare to Portland, $30 for cabin passage ; $15 for steerage.

THE starting-point for the overland trip to Northern California and Oregon is **Sacramento** (see p. 361). Here the Oregon Div. of the Central Pacific R. R. diverges from the main line and extends to Redding (170 miles), whence stages convey the traveler to Roseburg, the terminus of the Oregon and California R. R. The total distance from San Francisco to Portland by this route is 784 miles, and the fare $55.

Leaving Sacramento, the R. R. follows the Sacramento River in a general northern direction. The country traversed is one of the most productive wheat-growing sections of the State, and the grazing which it affords is unsurpassed. The first important station is **Marysville** (52 miles, *Western Hotel*), a flourishing town of 5,000 inhabitants at the confluence of the Yuba and Feather Rivers, at the head of navigation on the latter. It is well built, has several foundries and machine-shops, and contains an abundance of choice fruit and shade trees, including oranges and lemons. From Marysville a fine view is obtained of the *Marysville Buttes*, an isolated chain of mountains which rise from the plain of the Sacramento Valley to the height of 1,200 ft. and extend for some 8 miles in length, forming a remarkable feature of the scenery. Beyond Marysville the Feather River is crossed, and the train traverses the upper Sacramento Valley, which is one vast wheat-field. **Chico** (96 miles, *Chico House*) is another thriving town of 5,000 inhabitants, situated on the Chico Creek near its junction with the Sacramento River. Just N. of the town is the magnificent estate of General Bidwell, which comprises 32,000 acres of the richest land in one tract. The orchard is filled with oranges, lemons, figs, walnuts, almonds, and other choice fruits ; and the vegetable and flower gardens are said to be unsurpassed in Northern California. Near *Tehama* (123 miles) the

Sacramento River is crossed, and the train passes several small stations to *Redding* (170 miles), the present terminus of the railroad.

At Redding the stages of the California & Oregon Stage Co. are taken, and for 275 miles the route lies amid wild and picturesque scenery. Just beyond Redding the Sacramento Valley is left behind, though the river is ascended for about 80 miles amid the foot-hills. The N. extremity of the Sierra Nevada range is then climbed and crossed, and the road strikes the Pitt and McCloud Rivers, the main affluents of the upper Sacramento. "Near the crossing of the McCloud," says Mr. Williams in his "Pacific Tourist," "is the U. S. fish-hatching establishment. All these rivers abound in trout and salmon, but the best place on them for trout-fishing is the upper waters of the McCloud. The valley of the Sacramento grows narrower as one goes N., and at last is almost a cañon. Just beyond *Campbell's Soda Springs* (69 miles N. of Redding) the road ascends from the river to an extensive mountain-basin, walled in by yet loftier mountains—a sort of semicircular wall from Scott's Mt. on the N. to Trinity on the W. and Castle Rock on the S. E. On the E. side of the road, and in this great basin, Mt. Shasta rears its lofty head into the dark, deep blue of heaven." The ascent of ** **Mt. Shasta** is made from *Sisson's* (77 miles from Redding), and though tedious is not dangerous. The trip will take about 36 hours, and the cost, including horses, guides, provisions, etc., will be $15 to $20 for each person, according to the size of the party. Shasta from Sisson's is a broad triple mountain, the central summit (14,442 ft. high) being flanked on the W. by a large and quite perfect crater whose rim is 12,000 ft. high. As a whole, Shasta is the cone of an immense extinct volcano, which rises from its base 11,000 ft. in one sweep.

"There is no reason why any one of sound wind and limb should not, after a little mountaineering practice, be able to make the Shasta climb. There is nowhere the shadow of danger and never a real piece of mountain climbing—climbing, I mean, with hands and feet—no scaling of walls or labor involving other qualities than simple muscular endurance. The fact that two young girls have made the ascent proves it a comparatively easy one. Indeed, I have never reached a corresponding altitude with so little labor and difficulty. Whoever visits California, and wishes to depart from the beaten track of Yosemite scenes, could not do better than come to Strawberry Valley and get Mr. Sisson to pilot him up Shasta. When I ask myself to-day what were the sensations on Shasta, they render themselves into three—geography, shadows, and uplifted isolation. . . . A singularly transparent air revealed every plain and peak until the earth's curve rolled them under remote horizons. The whole great disk of world outspread beneath wore an aspect of glorious cheerfulness. The Cascade range, a roll of blue forest land, stretched northward, surmounted at intervals by volcanoes ; the lower, like symmetrical Mount Pitt, bare and warm with rosy lava colors; those farther N. lifting against the pale horizon-blue solid white cones upon which strong light rested with brilliance. It seemed incredible that we could see so far toward the Columbia River, almost across the State of Oregon, but there stood Pitt, Jefferson, and the Three Sisters in unmistakable plainness. N. E. and E. spread those great plains out of which rise low lava chains, and a few small, burned-out volcanoes, and there, too, were the group of Klamath and Goose Lakes lying in mid plain, glassing the deep upper violet. Farther and farther from our mountain base in that direction the greenness of forest and meadow fades out into rich mellow brown, with warm cloudings of sienna over bare lava hills, and shades, as you reach the E. limit, in pale ash and lavender and buff, where stretches of level land slope down over Madelin plains into Nevada deserts. . . . S. E. the mountain spurs are smoothed into a broad glacis, densely overgrown with chapparal, and ending in open groves around plains of yellow grass. A little farther begin the wild, cañon-carved piles of green mountains which represent the Sierras, and afar, towering over them, eighty miles away, the lava dome of Lassen's Peak standing up bold and fine. S. the Sacramento cañon cuts down to unseen depths, its deep trough opening a view of the California plain, a brown, sunny expanse, over which loom in vanishing perspective the Coast Range peaks. W. of us, and quite around the semicircle of view, stretches a vast sea of ridges, chains, peaks, and sharp walls of cañons, as wild and tumultuous as an ocean storm. Here and there above the blue billows rise snow-crests and shaggy rock-chains, but the topography is indistinguishable. . . . Whichever way we turned the great cone fell off from our feet in dizzying abruptness. We looked down steep slopes of *névé*, on over shattered ice-wreck, where glaciers roll over cliffs, and around the whole broad massive base curved deeply through its lava crusts in straight cañons."—*Mountaineering in the Sierra Nevada, by* CLARENCE KING.

Beyond Sisson's several fine views of Shasta are obtained from various points on the road, the best being from the summit of Scott Mt., which is crossed at an elevation of 5,000 ft. above the sea. Another fine distant view is obtained from a ridge just E. of *Yreka* (115 miles from Redding). Beyond Yreka the road climbs the Siskiyou Mt., and descends to *Jacksonville* (177 miles from Redding), the principal town of Southern Oregon, picturesquely situated in the fertile Rogue River Valley. At *Roseburg* (275 miles from Redding) the stages connect with the Oregon & California R. R., whose route of 200 miles is through the beautiful and productive Willamette Valley. Many pretty towns cluster along the railway, but none require special mention until **Salem,** the capital of Oregon, is reached, 53 miles from Portland. Salem is a city of about 6,000 inhabitants, beautifully situated on the E. bank of the Willamette River, and surrounded by a fertile prairie. Mill Creek enters the river at this point, and its rapid fall affords a good water-power, which is extensively used in manufacturing. Here are Willamette University and three State institutions, the Penitentiary, the Deaf-Mute School, and the Institute for the Blind. Thirty-seven miles beyond Salem, at the Falls of the Willamette, is **Oregon City** (*Cliff House*), with a population of 3,000, and several large flouring and woolen mills. The falls have a descent of 38 ft., and constitute one of the finest water-powers in the world. Sixteen miles beyond Oregon City the train reaches **Portland** (*Clarendon Hotel, St. Charles*), the chief city of Oregon, with a population of about 12,000. It is situated at the head of navigation on the Willamette River, 12 miles above its mouth in the Columbia, and is built on a plateau rising gradually from the river. A range of fir-covered hills surrounds it in a semicircle on the W., and commands fine views of the Willamette Valley, with the Cascade Mts. in the distance. The streets are regularly laid out, well paved, lighted with gas, and, except in the business portion, shaded with maples. A park 300 ft. wide extends almost the entire length of the city, and there are many handsome residences and substantial business structures. The chief public buildings are the Custom-House, the Masonic and Odd Fellows' Halls, the Market, and the County buildings. The Library Association has a reading-room and a library of 6,000 volumes, and there are several flourishing educational institutions.

Several very agreeable excursions may be made from Portland, of which the easiest and most attractive is that up the Columbia River. Steamers run daily to the *Dalles* (120 miles, fare $5), and tri-weekly to *Wallula* (245 miles, fare $12). The scenery all the way is grand and impressive beyond description, especially at the Cascades and the Dalles. Another pleasant excursion is to Puget Sound, and may be made in two ways : 1. *via* daily steamer to Kalama (50 miles, fare $1), where connection is made with the Northern Pacific R. R. for various points on the Sound ; 2. *via* semi-weekly steamers to Victoria, the capital of British Columbia. *Puget Sound* is one of the most picturesque bodies of water in the world, and the stopping-places of the steamers are all pretty and prosperous towns. A third excursion is to *Astoria*, near the mouth of the Columbia, and thence across the promontory to * *Clatsop Beach*, the great watering-place of Oregon.

90. St. Louis to Denver.

FROM St. Louis to Kansas City two routes are available : The Missouri Pacific R. R. (distance, 282 miles) ; and the St. Louis, Kansas City & Northern R. R. (distance, 275 miles). Both routes traverse a rich and productive section of Missouri, but the St. Louis, Kansas City & Northern R. R. has been more recently constructed, and has fewer important towns and cities along the line. The principal stations on this route are *St. Charles* (22 miles), where the Missouri River is crossed on a magnificent iron bridge, *Warrenton* (58 miles), *Montgomery* (82 miles), *Centralia* (122 miles), *Moberly* (146 miles), *Salisbury* (167 miles), *Miami* (196 miles), *Carrollton* (209 miles), and *Missouri City* (254 miles).

The Missouri Pacific R. R. has a considerable number of large towns *en route*, but very few of them possess any features which will prove of special interest to the tourist. *Kirkwood* (13 miles) is a beautiful suburban town with many fine villas of St. Louis merchants. *Pacific* (37 miles), *Washington* (54 miles), and *Hermann* (81 miles) are prosperous and handsome towns. **Jefferson City** (125 miles ; *McCarty House, Madison Hotel*) is the capital of the State of Missouri, and is beautifully situated on high bluffs which overlook the Missouri River for many miles. It is well built, and has a population of about 8,000. The *State House* is a handsome stone edifice ; the *State Penitentiary* is massive and spacious ; there are 8 churches of various denominations ; the State Library contains 12,000 volumes ; and there are numerous flour mills and factories. **Sedalia** (188 miles ; *Sichers Hotel, Garrison*) is a busy manufacturing town and railroad center, built on one of the highest swells of a rolling prairie, and containing about 10,000 inhabitants. The principal street is 120 ft. wide, is finely shaded, and has many handsome buildings. The shops of two R. R. companies are located here, and there are extensive mills, foundries, machine-shops, etc. The Missouri, Kansas & Texas R. R. (Route 95) intersects here. *Warrensburg* (218 miles), *Holden* (232 miles), *Pleasant Hill* (248 miles), and *Independence* (272 miles) are all neat and thriving towns, with much business activity. **Kansas City** (*Coates House, St. James Hotel*) is the second city of Missouri in size and importance, has a population of about 40,000, and is situated on the S. bank of the Missouri River, just below the mouth of the Kansas River, and near the Kansas border. It is somewhat irregularly laid out, but is well built, chiefly of brick, and contains many handsome business blocks and private residences. Its manufacturing interests are comparatively unimportant, but it has an immense and increasing trade which is brought to it by the 12 important railroads which converge here, and by the steamboat traffic on the river. The first bridge ever built across the Missouri is located at Kansas City; it is 1,387 ft. long and cost over $1,000,000. The *Opera House* is a tasteful structure, and the *Union Depot* of the Kansas Pacific R. R. is one of the finest of the kind in the West. Four lines of street railroad run to various parts of the city, and to the suburbs of Wyandotte, Kan., and Westport.

Kansas City to Denver via Kansas Pacific R. R.

On this route there is one through train daily, with Pullman palace drawing-room and sleeping-cars attached, which runs from Kansas City to Denver without change in about 30 hours. It traverses the central portion of Kansas, linking together the principal cities and towns of the State, and affording the opportunity to view its famous wheat- and corn-fields and immense cattle-ranges. Striking the Kansas (or Kaw) River at Kansas City, the route follows the windings of this beautiful stream for nearly 200 miles amid extremely pleasing scenery, and as it approaches the Rocky Mountains commands some grand views. Leaving Kansas City, the train passes in 38 miles to **Lawrence** (*Ludington House*), a beautiful city of 10,000 inhabitants situated on both sides of the Kansas River, which is here spanned by two bridges. It is built on a rolling slope, and is regularly laid out, with wide streets, partly shaded by trees, and many handsome buildings. Massachusetts St., the principal business thoroughfare, is built up for nearly a mile with blocks of brick and stone. The *State University*, a large and handsome structure, stands upon a bluff called Mt. Oread in the S. W. part of the city. The trade of Lawrence is very large, and a substantial dam across the river furnishes water-power for numerous mills and factories. Thirty miles beyond Lawrence the train reaches **Topeka** (*Tefft House, Fifth Ave.*), the capital of Kansas, situated on both sides of the Kansas River, which is here spanned by a fine iron bridge. The city contains about 7,500 inhabitants, and is remarkably well built. The *State House* cost $400,000, and is one of the finest in the West. A site has been purchased by the U. S. Government for a public building, and a spacious State Asylum for the Insane is in course of construction about 2 miles W. of the State House. There are several important educational institutions, besides the excellent public schools, and the Topeka Library Association has about 2,000 volumes. The river affords a good water-power, and the surrounding country is very fertile and contains deposits of coal. *Wamego* (103 miles), *St. George* (110 miles), *Manhattan* (118 miles), and *Ogden* (129 miles) are busy and rapidly-growing towns. At *Junction City* (138 miles) connection is made with the Neosho Div. of the Missouri, Kansas & Texas R. R. (Route 95). A highly productive agricultural region is next traversed, with

17

numerous thriving villages *en route*. *Brookville* (200 miles) is at the end of the second division of the Kansas Pacific R. R. and has a fine depot. *Ellsworth* (223 miles) is situated on the Smoky Hill River in a fine stock-raising country. *Fort Hays* (288 miles) is one of the handsomest military posts in the West, situated on a commanding elevation overlooking the plains. Opposite, upon Big Creek, is Hays City, once the center of the buffalo range. *Fort Wallace* (420 miles) is another important military post, situated near the W. boundary-line of Kansas, and just beyond the train enters Colorado. The first noteworthy station in Colorado is *Kit Carson* (487 miles), named after the great "Pathfinder" and situated on Sand Creek about 20 miles above the spot where Colonel Chivington's Indian massacre took place. The Arkansas Valley Branch to Las Animas (56 miles) diverges here. Between Kit Carson and Denver there are only "station towns," but the country along the line is rapidly filling up. At * *First View* (472 miles) the first view is obtained of the Rocky Mountains. "Towering against the western sky, more than 150 miles away, is Pike's Peak, standing out in this rarefied atmosphere with a clearness which deludes the tourist, if it be his first experience, into a belief that he is already in close proximity to the mountains. Henceforth you feel, in the presence of the mighty peaks which disclose themselves one after another, that you have entered a new world—a land of unapproachable beauty and grandeur—and you reach Denver having before you an unobstructed panorama of mountains, snow-clad peaks, and plain, more than 300 miles in length."

Kansas City or Atchison to Denver via Atchison, Topeka & Santa Fé R. R.

The Atchison, Topeka & Santa Fé R. R. has two termini, one at Kansas City, and one at Atchison, at both of which close connections are made with the through routes from the East. One daily express train, with Pullman palace drawing-room and sleeping cars attached, runs on this route from Atchison and Kansas City to Pueblo, where passengers for Denver change cars and take the Denver & Rio Grande R. R. (total distance from Kansas City, 753 miles; time, about 33 hours). By this route Denver is approached from the S., taking *en route* Colorado Springs, Manitou, Pike's Peak, Garden of the Gods, Monument Park, and others of the most famous Colorado resorts. The country traversed, though sparsely settled, is for the most part extraordinarily fertile and productive, and affords a charming variety of pleasing views, which, as the mountains are approached, become magnificent in the extreme.

A **Topeka** (60 miles from Kansas City, and 50 miles from Atchison) the two branches of the road unite. Topeka is the capital of Kansas, and has already been described on page 385. Beyond Topeka a number of thriving towns are passed, of which *Burlingame* (93 miles), *Osage City* (101 miles), *Emporia* (127 miles), *Cottonwood* (147 miles), and *Florence* (172 miles) are the most important. At Florence a

branch road diverges from the main line and runs in 30 miles to El-
dorado, and at *Newton* (201 miles) another branch diverges to Wichita
(27 miles).   From Newton to Pueblo, a distance of 433 miles, the road
follows the fertile valley of the Arkansas River, through one of the
finest agricultural and stock-raising regions in America.   The principal
towns on this portion of the route are *Hutchinson* (234 miles), *Sterling*
(253 miles), *Great Bend* (285 miles), *Larned* (307 miles), *Dodge City*
(368 miles), *Granada* (497 miles), and *Las Animas* (547 miles); but
these are simply small "settlements," and there is still "ample room
and verge enough" in the teeming valley for many thousands of emi-
grants.   Just before reaching Las Animas the first glimpse is caught
of the Rocky Mountains, still 90 miles distant.   Soon Pike's Peak
looms up on the remote horizon; then the Spanish Peaks reveal their
snowy crowns; and finally, as Pueblo is neared, the splendid mountain
panorama gradually unfolds itself before the straining vision.   **Pueblo** (*Lindell Hotel, Commercial*) is the chief city of Southern Colorado,
and is situated at the confluence of Arkansas River and Fontaine
Creek.   It is the center of a vast and rich agricultural and grazing
region, does a very large trade, and has a population of about 4,000.
It is built in a broad, nearly level, sandy basin, and is regularly laid
out, but the houses are for the most part small and unpretentious.   In
the Union Depot at Pueblo, connection is made with a train of the
Denver & Rio Grande R. R., which conveys passengers to Denver in
119 miles, passing *Colorado Springs* and *Monument*, whose attractions
are described in Route 91.   The points of interest in Southern Colorado
which can be visited from Pueblo are described in Route 92.

Denver.

Hotels, etc.—The leading hotels are the *Grand Central* ($3 a day); the
American ($3 a day), the *Inter-Ocean* ($3 a day), the *Wentworth* ($2 a day), and
the *Alvord* ($2 to $3 a day).   The *State Library* contains over 2,500 volumes.

Denver, the capital and largest city of Colorado, is situated on the
S. bank of the South Platte River, at the junction of Cherry Creek, 15
miles from the E. base of the Rocky Mountains, and about 500 miles
W. of the Missouri River.   It occupies a series of plateaus, facing the
mountains, and commanding a grand and beautiful view.   Through
the clear mountain atmosphere may be seen Pike's and Long's Peaks,
and the snow-capped range extending more than 200 miles, its rich
purple streaked with dazzling white, and here and there draped in
soft, transparent haze.   The city is the commercial center of Colorado,
and is compactly built, chiefly of brick manufactured in the vicinity.
Its trade is very large, and five railroads radiate from it, which, with
their stage connections, afford access to all parts of the State.   There
are upward of 30 hotels, numerous handsome commercial buildings, a
U. S. Branch Mint, several fine churches and school-houses, a theatre,
large manufactories and breweries, and some elegant private residences.
The Mint is employed in the melting and assaying of bullion, which is
returned to depositors in the form of bars with the weight and fineness
stamped upon them.   The Denver Smelting and Refining Works occupy

a building 55 by 200 ft., with capacity for 40 tons of ore per day.   The
population of the city is estimated at 20,000, and it is annually visited
by large numbers of tourists.   Whatever places in Colorado the tourist
may wish to visit, Denver will be his natural starting-point.

91.   Colorado Springs and Vicinity.

COLORADO SPRINGS (76 miles from Denver *via* the Denver & Rio
Grande Narrow-Gauge R. R.) is an important center for the tourist, being situated in close proximity to various points of interest; but its
name is misleading, the springs being 5 miles distant, and bearing
another name.   Colorado Springs is a flourishing village, situated on
the plains, with a fine view of the mountains, and with pleasantly-sha-
ded streets.   The following table of distances will show how conveniently it is situated for tourists bent on sight-seeing : To Manitou Springs,
5 miles ; to Garden of the Gods, 4 miles ; to Glen Eyrie, 5 miles ; to
Monument Park, 8 miles ; to Cheyenne Cañon, 5 miles ; and to the
summit of Pike's Peak, 16 miles.   Guides are at hand for the more
distant points, and horses, etc., are easily procured.

The * **Manitou Springs** are 5 miles from Colorado Springs, with
which they connect by stages on the arrival of every train, and are so
much resorted to as to be known as the "Saratoga of Colorado."   They
are situated among the foot-hills at the base of Pike's Peak, on the
banks of the beautiful Fontaine Creek.   The waters contain sulphur,
soda, and iron, and are recommended for their tonic effects in all diseases of which general debility is a feature.   Asthmatics and consumptives are usually benefited by a residence at Manitou ; the former
always.   There are several hotels, of which the most prominent are the
Manitou House and the *Beebe House ;* and the adjacent grounds are
beautifully laid out and adorned.   Within easy walking-distance of the
hotel is the picturesque and romantic *Ute Pass*, through which a road
runs to the South Park.   A short distance above the mouth of the Pass
are the *Ute Falls*, where the creek descends in an unbroken sheet over
a precipice 50 ft. high.   The road runs close to the edge of this precipice, while on the other hand the rocks tower above to an immense
height.   In this vicinity is the picturesque *Williams Cañon*, 15 miles
long, with walls of rock rising 600 or 800 ft. above a very narrow pass
below.   Manitou is on the trail to * **Pike's Peak,** the summit of
which is only 11 miles distant, and may be reached on horseback.
This peak stands on the outer edge of the great mountain-range, and
the view from its summit (14,300 ft. high) is magnificent, embracing
many thousand square miles of mountain and plain.   Here is a station
of the Weather-Signal Bureau, which is occupied winter and summer.

* **Garden of the Gods** is the fanciful title of a little mountain-
valley lying 4 miles N. W. of Colorado Springs.   The road enters it
through the "Beautiful Gate," a narrow passage-way between two towering but narrow ledges of cliffs, which is still further narrowed by a
rock-pillar, 30 ft. high, standing nearly in the center.   The Garden con-

sists of a tract of land less than 500 acres in extent, hemmed in by
mountains on the W. and N., bordered by ravines on the S., and by
old red sandstone-cliffs on the E., which shut it in entirely from the
plains. Its features are a number of isolated rocks, upheaved into perpendicular positions, some of them rising to a height of 350 ft. The

Eroded Sandstones, Monument Park.

rocks are mainly of a very soft, brilliantly-red sandstone, although several ridges of cliffs are of a white sandstone. The foot-hills in the
vicinity are many of them capped by similar upheavals, while all about
the main cliff in the valley are numerous separate, spire-like columns.
At the entrance to **Glen Eyrie** (1 mile from the Garden, and 5 miles
from Colorado Springs) are similar formations, one of which the *Major
Domo*, rises to a height of 120 ft., while at its base it is not over 10 ft.
in diameter. Glen Eyrie is a most picturesque mountain-gorge, closed
in on either hand by frowning cliffs, and with a purling mountain-brook
traversing it from end to end. Within it is the elegant summer-villa
of General Palmer, President of the Denver & Rio Grande R. R., and
the natural attractions of the place have been enhanced by art. Up
the rugged *Queen's Cañon* is the Devil's Punch-Bowl, and a succession
of picturesque rapids and cascades. The road to the Glen from Colorado Springs offers a succession of noble views.

Cheyenne Cañon, 5 miles from Colorado Springs, is a sequestered
mountain-gorge, in which are some striking rock-formations and picturesque cascades. A tortuous trail leads from the mouth of the cañon
in 3 miles to the first fall, which is 30 ft. high, and extremely fine.
From the ledge above the fall there is a view of a succession of falls, 6

in all, rising one above another at almost regular intervals, the remotest and highest being several miles away.

    * **Monument Park,** perhaps the most visited spot in Colorado, is 8 miles from Colorado Springs, and still nearer to *Monument,* a station on the railway above the Springs. The Park is very striking. "It is filled with fantastic groups of eroded sandstone, perhaps the most unique in the Western country, where there are so many evidences of Nature's curious whims. If one should imagine a great number of gigantic sugar-loaves, quite irregular in shape, but all showing the tapering form, varying in height from 6 feet to nearly 50, with each loaf capped by a dark, flat stone, not unlike in shape to a college-student's hat, he would have a very clear idea of the columns in Monument Park. They are for the most part ranged along the low hills on each side of the park, which is probably a mile wide, but here and there one stands out in the open plain. On one or two little knolls, apart from the hills, numbers of these columns are grouped, producing the exact effect of cemeteries with their white-marble columns." The stone is very light in color.

92. Southern Colorado.

    THE Denver & Rio Grande R. R. (narrow gauge) runs S. from Denver to the southern part of the State, and is being rapidly extended toward New Mexico and Arizona. As far as **Pueblo** (119 miles from Denver) it has been described in Routes 90 and 91. Pueblo is a center from which several very attractive excursions may be made. The one we shall first describe is that to **Cañon City** (*McClure House, Sanderson*), which is reached by a branch road from Pueblo in 40 miles. Cañon City is a flourishing mining-town, lying at the foot of the mountains and, besides mines, has in its vicinity coal-deposits, oil-wells, and mineral springs that are prized for their medicinal qualities. Its attraction for the tourist, however, lies in its proximity to much superb scenery. Twelve miles above the town the Arkansas River makes its exit from the mountains through the * **Grand Cañon of the Arkansas,** a wild gorge 3,000 ft. deep and of inconceivable majesty and grandeur. It can only be viewed from the top, and is seen to best advantage from a point called Royal Gorge. Other attractive excursions from Cañon City are to * *Grape Creek Cañon* (9 miles), taking in *Temple Cañon* on the way; to *Marble Cave* through the romantic *Oil Creek Cañon* (11 miles); to *Oak Creek Cañon* (15 miles); and to *Talbott Hill,* where Professor Marsh is excavating the bones of huge prehistoric animals which he declares to be seven million years old. The Denver & Rio Grande R. R. is rapidly extending its line beyond Cañon City to **Leadville,** a city of 25,000 inhabitants, in the heart of the new silver El Dorado whose fabulous richness was discovered in 1878.

    The most impressive of the Southern Colorado "sights" is the * **La Veta Pass,** by which the San Juan branch of the Denver & Rio Grande R. R. crosses the Sangre di Cristo range. It is about 80 miles S. W. of Pueblo, and the scenery amid which the road winds up for 14 miles is of unsurpassed sublimity and magnificence. The road itself is a stupendous feat of engineering, ascending at the average grade of 213 ft. to the mile, doubling on itself in curves in comparison with which the famous Horseshoe Bend on the Pennsylvania R. R. is broad and easy, and crossing the mountain-crest at a height of 9,486 ft., the highest point reached by a railroad on this continent. Descending the W. slope of the mountain, the road passes on to *Garland City* and *Alamosa* (130 miles from Pueblo). Alamosa is the nearest point to the San Juan mining district reached by rail, and stages run daily to *Del Norte* (34 miles) and *Lake City* (115 miles). Del Norte is a prosperous town of 2,000 inhabitants situated on the W. border of the San Luis Park, distant 80 miles from the Lake Silver Mining District and 100 miles from *Silverton*, the heart of the great San Juan Silver Mines. Stages run to all these points, and in 31 miles to the famous * Wagon-Wheel Gap, where the Rio Grande River flows through a most romantic and picturesque gorge. Near the entrance is the *Hot Springs Valley*, said to contain hot springs which rival those of Arkansas in medicinal value.

93. The Colorado Central Railway.

THIS road is now completed from Denver to Cheyenne, on the Union Pacific R. R. (131 miles), and a branch line extends from Golden to Georgetown (20 miles). Both routes traverse exceedingly picturesque regions and afford some of the finest scenery to be enjoyed in all Colorado. *Golden* (16 miles from Denver) is situated near the line of the foot-hills of the mountains, between two picturesque hills and the North and South Table Mountains. It is the center of an extensive mining-region, and is the point of departure for the celebrated *Bear Creek Cañon* (6 miles distant by wagon-road).

At Golden the mountain division of the road diverges from the main line, and passing up * Clear Creek Cañon, follows the windings of the Creek through one of the wildest and most picturesque localities on the continent. The cañon is very narrow, and the irregular walls of rock rise to a height of from 1,000 to 2,000 ft. Every turn of the road shows a new and often startling picture—piles of Titanic rocks, ponderous masses that seem to threaten instant downfall into the stream below. In order to see the splendid scenery to advantage, a seat should be secured in the "observation car," which is usually attached to every passenger-train. It is claimed by some that no railroad ride in the country equals this in all the conditions of wild and wonderful scenery. *Black Hawk* (37 miles from Denver) is built irregularly along the gulches and mountain-sides, and is one of the busiest mining-towns in the State. Professor Hill's reduction works, the most extensive in Colorado, and numerous stamp-mills and foundries, are located here. A mile from Black Hawk is *Central City*, a flourishing mining-town of 2,500 inhabitants, very picturesquely situated on the mountain-slopes, at an elevation of 8,300 ft. There are a number of quartz-mills here, and the town has a U. S. land office and an assay office. Being in the center of an exceedingly rich gold-mining region, it is at once a depot of supply and a point of shipment, and business is very active. *James Peak* may be ascended from Central City and affords a wide-extended view. The Georgetown Branch diverges at *Forks Creek* (29 miles from Golden) and runs in 9 miles to **Idaho Springs** (*Beebe House*), a quiet little village, beautifully situated in a lovely valley nestling among lofty mountain-ranges at an elevation of 7,800 ft. above the sea. The air is remarkably dry, pure, and invigorating, and the surrounding scenery is charming ; but the chief attraction of the place is its hot and cold mineral springs. The waters contain soda, magnesia, iron, and lime, have fine tonic properties, and are considered remedial in rheumatism and paralysis. They are used chiefly for bathing, and there are extensive bathing establishments and swimming-baths, in which baths may be had at the natural heat of the water as it bubbles from the ground, or at a lower temperature. During the summer the little town is thronged with tourists, and its sheltered position makes it a desirable resort in winter. It is a favorite rendezvous for excursion parties, and full outfits of carriages, horses, and guides are here furnished to those desiring to visit Middle Park, the Chicago Lakes, Green Lake, the Old Chief, or the mining regions. The most popular excursions are to *Fall River* (2½ miles), and to the lofty-lying ***Chicago Lakes** (15 miles by trail). These lakes are the most picturesque sheets of water in Colorado, and are embosomed on the slopes of Mt. Rosalie at a height of 11,995 ft. above the sea. Georgetown and Idaho Springs are equidistant from them, and though the trail by which they are approached is rough, they are visited by many tourists during the summer months. Twelve miles beyond Idaho Springs is **Georgetown** (*Barton House, Ennis House*), an important mining town with a population of 3,500, situated on S. Clear Creek, at an altitude of 8,412 ft.—the highest town in the world, 5,000 ft. higher than the glacier-walled valley of Chamounix, higher even than the famous hospice of St. Bernard. It is enclosed in a perfect amphitheatre of hills and mountains and cliffs, is laid out with broad streets, and is divided by the creek which winds through it in a silvery current. There are many romantic spots in the neighborhood. Just above the town is the *Devil's Gate*, a profound chasm through which a branch of Clear Creek foams and leaps. About 2½ miles distant is *Green Lake*, with clear waters of a bright green color produced by a coppery sediment on the rocks at the bottom. Many mountaineering tourists make Georgetown their base of operations during the season, and complete outfits and guides may easily be procured. The distance to the Hot Springs in Middle Park (see p. 394) is 45 miles. Georgetown is also the starting point for ***Gray's Peak,** which every one who can should ascend. It is only 15 miles to the summit (14,251 ft. above the sea), and the trip there and back can be made in a day. The mountain-view from Gray's Peak, except that it lacks the picturesqueness of the glaciers, has all the beauties of Alpine scenery.

The main line of the Colorado Central R. R. runs N. W. from Golden, and in 24 miles reaches *Boulder*, a mining town whose proximity to the famous * **Boulder Canon** makes it interesting to tourists. A wagon-road leads up the cañon, which is a stupendous mountain-gorge, 17 miles long, with walls of solid rock that rise precipitously to a height of 3,000 ft. in many places. A brawling stream rushes down the center of the ravine, broken in its course by clumsy-looking rocks, and the fallen trunks of trees that have been wrenched from the sparse soil and moss in the crevices. About 8 miles from Boulder are the *Falls of Boulder Creek*, and at the head of the cañon is a mining settlement. *Longmont* (13 miles beyond Boulder) is the starting-point for a delightful excursion through the lovely **Estes Park** to the summit of *Long's Peak* (36 miles). Estes Park affords some beautiful views and excellent trout-fishing. Long's Peak is 14,088 ft. high, and affords one of the grandest views to be obtained in Colorado. The ascent is tedious, but not difficult. Beyond Longmont the railway gradually nears the mountains, crosses the beautiful and productive Cache la Poudre Valley at *Fort Collins*, and for the last 50 miles runs at the base of the Rocky Mountains, affording magnificent panoramic views of their snow-capped summits. **Cheyenne** (131 miles from Denver) is described on p. 356.

The *Denver Pacific Railroad* also runs from Denver to Cheyenne. The distance by this route is 106 miles, and the country traversed is for the most part a vast level plain covered only with the short gray buffalo grass. The road runs nearly parallel with the principal range of the Rocky Mts., and 20 to 30 miles from their E. base. The only noteworthy town *en route* is Greeley (51 miles from Denver), which is a flourishing little town of 2,000 inhabitants situated on the banks of the Cache La Poudre River, and named after the founder of the *N. Y. Tribune*. It is watered by an excellent system of irrigation, and is well wooded. No intoxicating liquors are sold within its limits.

94. The Great Natural Parks.

THE surface of Colorado is generally mountainous, but in the E. and N. W. portions are elevated plains, and the spurs or branches of the Rocky Mountains inclose large fertile valleys. These valleys are known as the North Park, Middle Park, South Park, and San Luis Park, and are perhaps the most characteristic feature of Colorado. **North Park,** lying in the extreme northern part of the State, has been less explored and settled than the rest, owing to its remote situation and colder climate. It offers, for these reasons, the greatest attractions for the sportsman and adventurer; its streams are stocked with fish, and its forests and hill-sides abound with deer, antelopes, wolves, and bears. The park embraces an area of about 2,500 square miles, and has an elevation of about 8,000 ft. above the sea. Guides and outfit may be procured at Georgetown.

Middle Park lies directly S. of North Park, from which it is separated by one of the cross-chains of the great mountain labyrinth. The snow-range, or continental divide, sweeps around on its E. side, and it is completely encircled by majestic mountains. Long's Peak, Gray's

Peak, and Mount Lincoln, from 13,000 to 14,500 ft. high, stand sentinels around it. It embraces an area of about 3,000 square miles, extending about 65 miles N. and S. and 45 miles E. and W., and is about
7,500 ft. above the sea. It is drained by Blue River and the head-
waters of Grand River, flowing westward to the Colorado. The portions
of the park not covered by forest expand into broad, open meadows, the
grasses of which are interspersed with wild-flowers of every hue. There
is game in abundance, including deer, mountain-sheep, elk, bears, and
antelopes, and the waters teem with fish. The climate, notwithstand-
ing the great elevation, is remarkably mild and equable, with cool
nights in summer and warm days in winter. No one, of course, should
attempt to winter here who can not safely be cut off from many of the
comforts and conveniences of life; but those who are able and willing
to "rough it" will hardly find a place where they can do so under more
favorable conditions. The usual objective point of tourists who go to
the Middle Park is the **Hot Sulphur Springs,** which may be reached
from Georgetown by the Berthoud Pass (45 miles); from Central City
by the James's Peak trail (60 miles); and from South Bowlder. The
Colorado Company's fine stages leave the Barton House, Georgetown,
every other day for the Springs. A pleasant way of making the journey is on horseback *via* the first-mentioned route. The Springs are
situated on a tributary of Grand River, about 12 miles from the S.
boundary of the park. The waters are used chiefly in the form of
baths, and have been found highly beneficial in cases of rheumatism,
neuralgia, chronic diseases of the skin, and general debility. The accommodations for invalids are not first-rate as yet, but sufficient, perhaps, for those who ought to venture upon the journey thither over the
mountains. A small town is gradually growing up in the vicinity. One
of the pleasantest excursions in Middle Park is up the valley, 27 miles
from the Springs, by a good road to *Grand Lake,* the source of the
main fork of Grand River. The lake nestles close to the base of the
mountains, precipitous cliffs hang frowning over its waters on three
sides, tall pines come almost down to the white sand-beach, and its
translucent depths are thronged with trout and other fish.

South Park, the best known and most beautiful of all the parks,
lies next below Middle Park, from which it is separated by a branch of
the Park range. It is 60 miles long and 30 wide, with an area of about
2,200 square miles, and, like the Middle Park, is surrounded on all sides
by gigantic ranges of mountains, whose culminating crests tower above
the region of perpetual snow. The maximum elevation of the park
above the sea is 10,000 ft., while the average elevation is about 9,000
ft., and nearly all the land which it contains is well adapted to agriculture. The streams, which are supplied by melting snows from the surrounding mountains, are tributaries of the South Platte, and flow E.
through the park to the plains. The climate of the South Park is milder than that of either North or Middle Park, and its greater accessibility
gives it peculiar advantages for such tourists and invalids as can not
endure much fatigue. *Fairplay* is the chief town of the region, and the
best center for excursions. It is reached by stage, or wagon, or horse-

back, from Denver *via* Turkey Creek Cañon (95 miles); from Colorado
Springs *via* Ute Pass (75 miles); and from Cañon City, at the end of the
Denver & Rio Grande R. R. (75 miles). The scenery afforded by any or
all of these routes is of incomparable grandeur and beauty. The visitor to
Fairplay in summer should not fail to ascend * **Mount Lincoln,** which
is one of the highest of the Colorado peaks (14,296 ft.) and which affords a view that Professor Whitney declares to be unequaled by any in
Switzerland for its reach or the magnificence of the included heights.
The ascent may be made nearly all the way by wagon or carriage, and
presents no difficulty. Another pleasant excursion from Fairplay is to
the beautiful *Twin Lakes* (35 miles). The *Denver & South Park R. R.*
is building from Denver S. W. through South Park to *Leadville* (see p.
390), and will be finished probably during 1880.

San Luis Park is larger than the other three combined, embracing
an area of nearly 18,000 square miles—about twice the size of New
Hampshire. It lies S. of South Park, from which it is separated by the
main range, which forms its N. and E. boundary, while its W. boundary
is formed by the Sierra San Juan. It is watered by 35 streams descending from the encircling snow-crests. Nineteen of these streams flow
into *San Luis Lake,* a beautiful sheet of water near the center of the
parks, and the others discharge their waters into the Rio del Norte, in
its course to the Gulf of Mexico. On the flanks of the great mountain,
dense forests of pine, spruce, fir, aspen, hemlock, oak, cedar, and piñon
alternate with broad, natural meadows, producing a luxuriant growth of
nutritious grasses, upon which cattle subsist throughout the year, without any other food, and requiring no shelter. The highest elevation in
the park does not exceed 7,000 ft. above the sea, and this, together
with its southern and sheltered location, gives it a wonderfully mild,
genial, and equable climate. Thermal springs abound here, as in other
parts of Colorado, generally charged with medicinal properties. The
San Juan branch of the Denver & Rio Grande R. R. (see Route 92) is
rendering this vast and attractive region more accessible.

95. St. Louis to Texas.

a. *Via Missouri, Kansas & Texas R. R.*

THE Missouri, Kansas & Texas R. R. has two termini at its northern
end: one at *Hannibal* on the Mississippi River, where close connection
is made with the Chicago, Burlington & Quincy and other important
railroads (see Route 120); and the other at St. Louis, where also
connections are made with the railways which converge there from
the East. The two branches unite at **Sedalia,** which is 143 miles
from Hannibal and 188 miles from St. Louis. Two express trains
daily, with Pullman palace sleeping-cars, run from both Hannibal and
St. Louis to the principal points in Texas. The Missouri, Kansas &
Texas R. R. brings the rich agricultural and cattle-raising districts
of Texas within 3 or 4 days' time of the Northern markets. It is
this which gives the road its importance, and except for this it pre-

sents little of interest to the traveler, traversing as it does a region which is for the most part unsettled, barren, and destitute of picturesque features. From St. Louis to Sedalia the route (*via* Missouri Pacific R. R.) is described in Route 90, and Sedalia is described on page 384. At *Fort Scott* (298 miles from St. Louis) it enters Kansas, and just beyond *Chetopa* (370 miles) it enters the Indian Territory, which it crosses in a nearly straight line from N. to S. If the tourist desires to visit the great Indian Reservations, this is the road which he should take, as it carries him directly into their midst ; otherwise he will find but little to claim his attention in the long journey of nearly a thousand miles.

The principal stations on the northern section of the line are Fort Scott (298 miles) and Parsons (347 miles), both in Kansas. **Fort Scott** (*Gulf House, Wilder*) is a city of about 6,000 inhabitants, situated on the Marmiton River, a branch of the Osage. It was established as a military post in 1842, and incorporated as a town in 1855, and is now rapidly growing. Bituminous coal is abundant in the surrounding country, and the manufacturing interests promise to become important. **Parsons** (*St. James Hotel*) is a flourishing little city of 3,500 inhabitants at the junction of the Neosho Div. of the M. K. & T. R. R. with the main line. It is the site of the R. R. construction- and repairshops, and is built on a high rolling prairie between and near the confluence of the Big and Little Labette Rivers. *Vinita* (399 miles) is the first station in the Indian Territory, which is traversed to *Durant* (600 miles). The first important station in Texas is **Denison** (621 miles, *Alamo Hotel, Planters'*) which is the S. terminus of the M. K. & T. R. R. and which is becoming an important railroad center. It dates only from 1872, and in 1878 had a population estimated at 6,000, with several important flour-mills and factories. At Denison the train passes to the tracks of the Houston & Texas Central R. R. which traverses the "garden district" of Texas. Nine miles beyond Denison is **Sherman** (*Binkley House*), a city of 8,000 inhabitants at the intersection of the Transcontinental branch of the Texas & Pacific R. R. It is substantially built, largely of stone, and has a handsome stone Court-House, with excellent schools and churches. Its trade with the surrounding country is large, and its manufactures are varied and important. Thirty-six miles beyond Sherman is **Dallas** (*Grand Windsor Hotel, Lamar*), the commercial capital of Northern Texas, with a population of 15,000, an extensive trade with the surrounding country, and numerous manufacturing establishments. It is well built for so young a city (its population in 1872 was but 1,500), and has 22 churches, 19 schools, street railways, fire companies, gas-, and water-works. The *Court-House* is a neat building, as are also the Catholic and Episcopal Churches, and the Dallas Female College (Methodist) and Male and Female College (Baptist). Dallas is on the main line of the Texas & Pacific R. R., which is completed from Shreveport, Louisiana, to Fort Worth, Texas, 254 miles. *Corsicana* (748 miles) and *Mexia* (778 miles) are thriving towns. At *Bremond* (816 miles from St. Louis and 143 from Houston) a branch line known as the Waco Tap diverges and runs in 45 miles to **Waco**

(*McClelland House, Central City Hotel*), a rapidly-growing city of 9,000 inhabitants, situated nearly in the center of the State, on both sides of the Brazos River, which is spanned by a handsome suspension bridge. The city is regularly laid out and remarkably well built, and contains a substantial stone Court-House, 9 churches, and a number of flourishing educational institutions, of which *Waco University* is the principal. Waco is the commercial center of a rich and fertile country, which is rapidly filling up with immigrants, and has a number of prosperous manufacturing establishments.

On the main line, 22 miles S. of Bremond, is *Hearne*, where the International & Great Northern R. R. intersects the present route. From *Hempstead* (51 miles from Houston) the Western Div. diverges and runs in 115 miles to **Austin** (*Raymond House, Avenue*), the capital of Texas, a city of 16,000 inhabitants, beautifully situated on the N. bank of the Colorado River, 160 miles from its mouth. The city is built on an amphitheatre of hills, and overlooks the valley of the Colorado and the rich prairies beyond. The public buildings are constructed of a white limestone called marble, but too soft to admit of polish. *Capitol Square* contains 20 acres on a gentle elevation in the center of the city, upon the summit of which the *Capitol* is situated. In the square are the Supreme Court and Treasury buildings, and on the E. side is the *General Land Office*, which is a handsome edifice. Other noteworthy buildings are the *County Court-House*, the *County Jail*, the *Deaf and Dumb*, *Blind*, and *Lunatic Asylums*, and the *Market House*, in the 2nd story of which are the municipal offices. An artesian well has been sunk just N. of the capitol, to the depth of 1,300 ft., from which a small stream constantly flows. The water is impregnated with lime, and has some medicinal qualities. A substantial truss bridge, 900 ft. long, spans the Colorado River, which is navigable to this point in winter by steamboats. (Austin is also reached by a branch of the International & Great Northern R. R.)

Houston (*Barnes House, Hutchins House*), the second city of Texas in population and commerce and the first in manufactures, is situated at the head of tide-water on Buffalo Bayou, 45 miles above its mouth in Galveston Bay, and 819 miles from St. Louis. It is built on the left bank of the bayou, which is spanned by several bridges, embraces an area of 9 square miles, and has a population of about 25,000. Its manufactures are varied and extensive; and it is the center of the railroad system of the State, with 9 diverging railways, which bring to it the products of a rich grazing and agricultural region. An extensive lumber trade is also carried on with the Louisiana and Florida coasts. · The principal public building is the * *City Hall and Market House* constructed of brick at a cost of $400,000. It is 272 ft. long by 146 ft. wide, and, besides the city offices, contains a hall 70 by 110 ft. fitted up for public entertainments and capable of seating 1,300 persons. From the top of the main tower, 128 ft. high, there is a fine view. The *Masonic Temple* is a spacious and ornate structure costing $200,000. The city is lighted with gas, and horse-cars run on the principal streets. Everywhere is the shade of beau-

tiful trees. The bayou is navigable by vessels drawing 9 ft. of water,
and the Morgan Line of Steamships affords connections with Galveston and New Orleans. From Houston the Galveston, Houston &
Henderson R. R. runs S. E. in 50 miles to **Galveston** (*Tremont House,
Girardin*), the largest city and commercial metropolis of Texas, situated at the N. E. extremity of Galveston Island, at the mouth of the bay
of the same name. The city is laid out with wide and straight streets,
bordered by numerous flower-gardens, and contains about 35,000 inhabitants. Besides the churches, of which several are handsome edifices, the public buildings include the Custom House, Post-Office, U. S.
Court-House, County Court-House, City Hall, Opera-House, 2 theatres,
several public halls, and 3 market houses. In the business portion of
the city are numerous handsome commercial buildings, and there are
many fine residences. The *University of St. Mary* (Roman Catholic)
and the *Galveston Medical College* are flourishing institutions. The
Ursuline Convent contains 25 nuns and has a female academy connected
with it. The *Mercantile Library* contains about 9,000 volumes and has
a reading-room. *Oleander Park* comprises 80 acres and the *City Park*
25 acres. *Magnolia Grove Cemetery* embraces 100 acres neatly laid
out. The *Island of Galveston* is about 28 miles long and $1\frac{1}{2}$ to $3\frac{1}{2}$ wide,
and is bordered throughout its whole length by a smooth hard beach
which affords a pleasant drive and promenade. The harbor is the best
in the State, and the commerce of the city is very extensive, the chief
business being the shipment of cotton.

There is a daily line of steamers (the Morgan Line) from Galveston to New Orleans, and another to Indianola and Corpus Christi; a weekly line (the Mallory Line)
to New York (starting-point in New York, Pier 20 East River), and another to
Havana ; and a semi-monthly line to Liverpool. There is also a line plying along
the coast to the Rio Grande, and another through Buffalo Bayou to Houston.

From *Harrisburg* (a station on the Galveston, Houston & Henderson
R. R., 44 miles from Galveston and 6 miles from Houston) the Galveston,
Harrisburg & San Antonio R. R. runs W. 205 miles through a rather
sparsely settled country to **San Antonio** (*Menger Hotel, Hord House,
Central*), the chief city of Western Texas, with a population of about
20,000, one third of whom are of German and one third of Mexican
origin. It is situated on the San Antonio and San Pedro Rivers, and is
divided into three "quarters": San Antonio proper, between the two
streams; Alamo, E. of the San Antonio ; and Chihuahua, W. of the San
Pedro. The former is the business quarter, and has been almost entirely
rebuilt since 1860. The two principal streets are Commerce and Market,
running parallel with each other from the main plaza. Separated from
the main plaza by a fine Catholic church is the *Plaza de las Armas.*
Chihuahua is almost exclusively Mexican in character and population ;
its houses are one story high, built partly of stone and partly of upright
logs with cane roofs. Alamo is considerably higher than the other two
sections of the city, and is mostly inhabited by Germans. In the N.
part, on the Alamo Plaza, is the famous * *Fort Alamo,* where in March,
1836, a garrison of Texans, attacked by an overwhelming Mexican force,
perished to a man rather than yield. Missions San José, San Juan, and

Concepçion, built by the Spaniards, who founded San Antonio in 1714, are interesting objects; and the market-places and street-scenes will amuse the visitor. Owing to its remarkably mild and dry climate, San Antonio is rapidly becoming popular as a winter resort.

b. Via St. Louis, Iron Mountain & Southern R. R.

This route is nearly 100 miles shorter than the previous one, and extends S. W. through Eastern Missouri and Central Arkansas, connecting at Longview with the International & Great Northern R. R. One train daily, with Pullman palace sleeping-cars attached, runs through without change of cars to Houston, where close connections are made for Galveston and San Antonio. For about 25 miles from St. Louis the W. bank of the Mississippi River is followed, and afterward the road traverses a rich and highly cultivated agricultural region, and the great mineral fields of Missouri, including the famous Iron Mountain and Pilot Knob. At *Bismarck* (75 miles) the road branches: one line running S. E. to Belmont, on the Mississippi, opposite Columbus, Ky., where connection is made with the railway system of the Southern States E. of the Mississippi River; while the Texas line passes S. W. and crosses the State of Arkansas in a diagonal direction. The only important place on this section of the line is **Little Rock** (*Capital Hotel, Robinson House*), the capital and chief city of Arkansas, with a population of about 20,000, built upon the first bed of rocks that is met with in ascending the Arkansas River. Its elevation is not more than 40 or 50 ft.; but about 2 miles above, on the opposite bank, is a precipitous range of cliffs, 400 to 500 ft. high, known as Big Rock. The name Little Rock is antithetical to this. The city is regularly laid out, with wide streets lighted with gas and traversed by horse-cars. The business blocks are mainly of brick, and the residences are surrounded by gardens adorned with shade trees and shrubberies, presenting a handsome appearance. The principal public buildings are the *State House* and *St. John's College* (a military institute), of brick; but several of the churches and school-houses are handsome structures. Little Rock is the seat of a U. S. Arsenal and Land Office, of the State Penitentiary, and of the State Institutions for deaf mutes and the blind. The *State Library* contains 12,500 volumes and the *Mercantile Library* 1,800. The Arkansas is navigable to Little Rock at all times by steamers, and several important railways converge here. From *Malvern* (42 miles S. of Little Rock) the Hot Springs R. R. diverges and runs in 25 miles to the famous **Hot Springs** (numerous hotels and boarding-houses), one of the most frequented health-resorts in America. The town, which is simply an appendage of the sanitarium, contains about 5,000 inhabitants, and is built principally in the narrow valley of Hot Springs Creek, which runs N. and S. amid the Ozark Mts. The valley is about 1½ mile long, is 1,500 ft. above the sea, and is very rugged and picturesque. The springs (66 in number) issue from the W. slope of Hot Springs Mountain, vary in temperature from 93° to 160° Fahr., and discharge into the creek about 500,000 gallons a day. The waters are taken both internally and externally (but chiefly in the form of baths), and are remedial in rheuma-

tism, rheumatic gout, malarial fevers, scrofula, and diseases of the skin.
The air being warm and moist is bad for consumptives. At *Texarkana*
(491 miles from St. Louis) Texas is entered, and connections are made
with the Texas & Pacific R. R., by which *Marshall* (566 miles), *Sherman*
(see p. 396), *Dallas* (see p. 396), and *Fort Worth* (743 miles) are reached.
At *Longview* (587 miles) the train passes on to the track of the International & Great Northern R. R., which runs S. to *Palestine* (765 miles),
and there branches, one line leading to **Austin** (see p. 397) and the
other to **Houston** (see p. 397).

96. The Great Lakes.

LAKES Ontario, Erie, Huron, Michigan, and Superior are known as
the "Great Lakes," and are the largest bodies of fresh water in the
world.   They are part of one great system of continental drainage,
and are connected in such a manner that one and the same boat can
traverse them almost from end to end.   **Lake Ontario,** however, is
cut off from the others by the Falls of Niagara, and, being the least attractive of the five, is seldom included in the regular routes of summer
travel.   The tour of the lake may be made in connection with the tour
of the St. Lawrence by taking the Royal Mail Steamers of the Canadian
Navigation Co. at *Hamilton* instead of at Kingston (see Route 56).   A
steamer leaves Hamilton daily at 9 A. M., stopping at Toronto, Port
Hope, and Cobourg, and reaching Kingston, at the E. end of the lake,
at 5.30 o'clock next morning.   Lakes Erie, Huron, and Superior may
be included in a single tour, and afford one of the most delightful trips
that can be taken in this country during the summer.   The steamers
of the Lake Superior Transit Co. are swift, strong, commodious, and
handsomely furnished.   These steamers leave Buffalo, Erie, Cleveland,
and Detroit.   They may be taken at any one of these places, or at Port
Huron or Sault Ste. Marie.   In the following description of the route
we shall suppose ourselves to be starting from Buffalo, at the E. end of
Lake Erie, which is fully described on p. 160.   Excursion steamers
leave Buffalo on Mondays, Tuesdays, Thursdays, and Saturdays for Lake
Superior, making the round trip in two weeks (fare, $50).

Lake Erie.

"Among the five great lakes of the Western Chain," says a writer
in "Picturesque America," "Erie occupies the fourth place as regards
size, the last place in point of beauty, and no place at all in romance."
For the rest, the lake is 250 miles long, 60 wide, less than 90 ft. in
average depth, and 564 ft. above the level of the sea.   It is the shal-
lowest and most dangerous of the entire chain of the Great Lakes.   It
can be avoided at the cost of a 10 or 12 hours' railway journey, but
then the tourist loses the pleasure of the Detroit River trip.

After leaving Buffalo, the scenery for a time is uninteresting, as the
steamer does not approach near enough to the land to enable us to see
anything, except when entering and leaving port, and many of the

steamers make no stops until reaching Detroit. For the convenience of the traveler who may be upon a boat making all the landings, brief mention will be made of the principal ones on the S. shore of the lake. *Dunkirk* (42 miles from Buffalo) has a good harbor, and is described on p. 172. **Erie** (90 miles) is situated on "that sturdy little elbow which Pennsylvania has pushed up to the lake-shore, as if determined to have a port somewhere, on fresh water if not on salt." It is the terminus of the Philadelphia & Erie R. R. (Route 49), and has a very large and beautiful harbor, formed by what was once a long, narrow peninsula, but is now an island. The bar at the mouth has been dredged away so as to afford a good channel, and Erie is a United States naval station. It was here that Commodore Perry built his fleet, and here he brought his prizes after the battle of Lake Erie, in September, 1813. On the bank above, the embankments of the old French fort Presque Isle can be traced. For description of the city see page 223. Dotted along the coast of the lake are numerous lighthouses, standing on lonely islets and rocky ledges, wherever they can command a wide sweep of the horizon. To the traveler they appear both picturesque and friendly. There is almost always one in view; and, a pillar of cloud by day and of fire by night, they greet the voyager as he journeys, one fading astern as the next shines out ahead. The light at Erie is visible for a distance of 20 miles. **Cleveland** (185 miles) is universally considered the most beautiful city on the Great Lakes. It stands upon a high bluff, and a good view of it is had from the water; though it is so embowered in trees that little save the spires of the churches can be seen through the green. Steamers usually make a stay of several hours at Cleveland, and give passengers an opportunity of seeing the city. It is fully described on page 272. W. of Cleveland the coast grows more picturesque; the shore is high and precipitous, and the streams come rushing down in falls and rapids. Seven miles from the city is *Rocky River*, which flows through a deep gorge between perpendicular cliffs that jut boldly into the lake and command a wide prospect. "Here is the most extensive and unbroken view of Lake Erie; Black River Point is seen on the W., and the spires of Cleveland shine out against the green curve of the E. shore; but far away toward the N. stretches the unbroken expanse of water, and one can see on the horizon-line distant sails, which are still only in mid-lake, with miles of blue waves beyond." W. of Rocky River, the Black, Vermilion, and Huron rivers flow into the lake through ravines of wild beauty; and then, after a long stretch of dreary coast, the steamer approaches **Sandusky** (*West House, Colton*), with its beautiful bay, which is 20 miles long and 5 or 6 wide. Sandusky is handsomely built on ground rising gradually from the shore, and commands a·fine view of the bay and lake. Beneath its site is an inexhaustible bed of excellent limestone, which is extensively employed in building and in the manufacture of lime. The city is celebrated for its manufacture of articles of wood, of which handles, spokes, and hubs, "bent work" for carriages, and carpenters' tools are the most important; and fresh and salt fish, ice, and lumber are extensively exported. It is also the center of one of the most important vine-growing

402 THE GREAT LAKES. [Route 96.

districts in the United States. The Lake Erie Div. of the Baltimore & Ohio R. R. (see Route 65) terminates here, and there are two other railroads.

After leaving Sandusky, the steamer speedily reaches the * **Put-in- Bay Islands,** a beautiful group, 15 or more in number, lying in the S. W. corner of Lake Erie, near the mouth of the Detroit River. Within a few years past these islands have become a favorite summer resort, as they combine all the advantages of pure air, bathing, fishing, boating, and convenience of access from any of the lake-cities. From Detroit there is a daily steamer to *Kelly's Island*, the largest of the group. *Put-in-Bay Island* has a large summer hotel (the *Beebe House*), and roses are said to bloom in its gardens in December. The islands are noted for their vineyards and the superior quality of the wine produced; but some of them are still wild and uninhabited. Shortly after passing the islands the steamer enters the Detroit River.

The Detroit and St. Clair Rivers.

There are 15 islands within the first 12 miles of the Detroit River. Father Hennepin, who passed up the river in 1679, enthusiastically writes: "The islands are the finest in the world; the strait is finer than Niagara; the banks are vast meadows; and the prospect is terminated with some hills crowned with vineyards, trees bearing good fruit, groves and forests so well disposed that one would think that Nature alone could not have made, without the help of art, so charming a prospect." Since that day, "art" has done something to mar the freshness of the scene; but the strait still affords some of the loveliest river scenery in America. The river is broad, varying from 3 miles at the mouth to a mile in width at the city of Detroit; the Canadian shore rising abruptly from the water to a height of from 20 to 25 ft., the American shore being low, and in some places marshy. The only island calling for special mention is *Grosse Ile*, which is a favorite summer resort for Detroiters, who find here, within 20 miles of their homes, a delightful retreat from the heat and dust of the city. The island divides the river into two channels, which are known as American and Canadian; the latter, being the deepest, is used by the through-boats, none passing on the American side except to touch at *Trenton* or *Gibraltar*, the former of which is a flourishing place noted for its shipbuilding. *Wyandotte, Mich.* (15 miles below Detroit), is the site of extensive rolling-mills, which may be said to have created the town. Three miles below the steamboat-landing at **Detroit,** the river makes a sudden turn, and the city comes into full view. On the right hand is the village of *Windsor*, in Canada, and directly opposite is *Fort Wayne*, a bastioned redoubt, mounted with heavy ordnance. For at least 6 miles above the fort the river-front is lined with mills, dry-docks, ship-yards, foundries, grain-elevators, railway-depots, and warehouses; and, on the level plateau above, the city extends inland for 2½ miles. The steamers generally stop at Detroit several hours, and the tourist should improve this opportunity for seeing the city, which is described on page 268.

Beyond Detroit, the steamer passes *Belle Isle,* a small island at the head of the river, and enters **Lake St. Clair,** which is 25 miles long and about the same distance from shore to shore. It is shallow, and at the upper end, where the river St. Clair comes in, large deposits of sand have been made, known as "The Flats." These for a long time greatly impeded navigation, but the difficulty has been lately overcome by the construction of a ship-canal, which is justly regarded as a triumph of engineering skill. Around the shores of the lake are large fields of wild rice. Here immense flocks of wild ducks swarm, geese are found in the shooting-season, and the waters teem with fish. *Ile la Pêche* (commonly known as "Peach Island"), near the lower end of the lake, belongs to Canada. It was at one time the summer home of the celebrated Indian chief Pontiac. The **St. Clair River** is really a strait through which the waters of Lake Huron take their way toward the Atlantic Ocean. It is 48 miles long, and has a descent in that distance of 15 ft., which gives a current of 3½ to 4 miles an hour. The scenery along the St. Clair is beautiful, the banks on either side being well cultivated or covered with a thick forest-growth. There are several small towns along the river, but none of much importance (except *St. Clair, Mich.*) until we reach **Port Huron** (*Huron House*), a port of entry at the mouth of Black River, which runs through a rich pine-region, and down which is floated the lumber that supplies the numerous saw-mills at this point. The trade in fish is important, and there are 3 ship-yards and 2 dry docks. During the season of navigation Port Huron is connected by daily lines of steamers with Detroit, Saginaw, and the principal lake and river ports. **Port Sarnia,** a Canadian port of entry opposite Port Huron (connected by ferry), is a place of active business, being the terminus of the main line of the Grand Trunk R. R., and of a branch of the Great Western R. R. Two miles above Port Huron, between *Fort Gratiot,* a United States military post, and *Point Edward,* the river narrows until it is less than 1,000 ft. wide, the increased velocity of the current being so noticeable that the descent of the water can be seen from the wharves on either side. Here the Grand Trunk R. R. crosses the St. Clair River on a handsome bridge, passing which the steamer enters

Lake Huron.

Lake Huron lies between the 43d and 46th degrees of north latitude, is 250 miles in length from the head of the St. Clair River to the Straits of Mackinaw, and 100 miles wide. It is 574 ft. above the level of the ocean, and varies in depth from 100 to 750 ft. *Georgian Bay,* at the N. E. side of the lake, is very large, and lies entirely within the Dominion of Canada ; *Saginaw Bay,* on the S. W., being within the limits of the State of Michigan. *Tawas Bay* is a good harbor on the S. W. side of Saginaw Bay. *Thunder Bay* is farther N., and has the *Thunder Bay Islands* at its mouth. The stormiest part of the lake is between the Saginaw and Georgian Bays, where the wind often sweeps with terrific violence. But few islands are seen, and the traveler who has never been at sea can form some idea of what the ocean is, for during a portion of the voyage no land can be seen even from the mast-head ; the boundless expanse of water, dotted here and there with a distant sail, stretching on every side.

Mackinaw Island.

Except on special excursion-trips, the regular Lake Superior steamers do not touch at Mackinaw, but there are many of these excursions in the course of the summer, and it will be easy for the tourist to secure passage on one of the excursion-boats. There is also a daily line of steamers between *Collingwood*, on Georgian Bay, one of the termini of the Grand Trunk R. R., and *Chicago*, touching at Mackinaw ; and a mail-boat three times a week from Port Sarnia.

Mackinaw (also called Mackinac, and formerly Michilimackinac) is an island in the Strait of Mackinaw, which connects Lake Michigan and Huron, 260 miles N. W. of Detroit, and about 300 N. of Chicago. It is about 3 miles long and 2 wide, is rough and rocky, and has 800 inhabitants. It is an old military post of the United States, as well as a delightful and popular place of summer resort. The waters surrounding the island are wonderfully clear and pellucid, and teem with fish of delicious flavor. The fisherman sees the fish toying with his bait, and the active little Indian boys on the piers are always ready to dive for any coins the visitor may throw into the water for them. The inhabitants of the decayed and antiquated village at the foot of the cliff are mainly dependent on their seines and fishing-nets for support, and upon the money spent every summer by tourists, there being 4 good hotels and several stores where Indian curiosities, agates, photographs, and other mementoes of the place are offered for sale. Boats for pleasure-excursions may always be had ; and the usual accessories of a summer resort, such as bowling-alleys, billiard-rooms, etc., are provided at the best hotels (the *Mission House, Island House,* and *St. Cloud*) On the cliff over the village (reached by a steep road) is *Fort Mackinaw,* 200 ft. above the level of the lake, and overlooking the village- and beautiful harbor. In rear of and about 100 ft. above this fort are the ruins of old *Fort Holmes,* and in their immediate neighborhood, 320 ft. above the lake, the highest point on the island, stands a signal-station. The view from this elevation is very fine.

" The natural scenery of Mackinaw," says a writer whom we have already several times quoted, " is charming. The geologist finds mysteries in the masses of calcareous rock dipping at unexpected angles ; the antiquarian feasts his eyes on the Druidical circles of the ancient stones ; the invalid sits on the cliff's edge in the vivid sunshine, and breathes in the buoyant air with delight, or rides slowly over the old military roads, with the spicery of cedars and juniper alternating with the fresh forest-odors of young maples and beeches. The haunted birches abound, and on the crags grow the weird larches beckoning with their long fingers, the most human tree of all. Bluebells on their hair-like stems swing from the rocks, fading at a touch, and in the deep woods are the Indian pipes, but the ordinary wild flowers are not to be found. Over toward the British landing stand the Gothic spires of the blue-green spruces, and now and then an Indian trail crosses the road, worn deep by the feet of the red men, when the Fairy Island was their favorite and sacred resort." Chief among the curiosities of the island is * **Arched Rock,** on the E. side, a natural bridge 145 ft. high by less than 3 ft. wide, excavated in a projecting angle of the limestone cliff. The beds forming the summit of the arch are cut off from direct connection with the main rock by a narrow gorge of no great depth. The portion supporting the arch on the N. side, and the curve of the arch itself, are comparatively fragile, and can not long resist the action of rain and frosts, which, in this latitude, and on a rock thus constituted, produce great ravages every season. *Fairy Arch* is of similar formation to Arched Rock, and lifts from the sands with a grace and beauty that justify the name bestowed upon it. The *Lover's Leap* is a rock about a mile W. of the village, having a vertical height of 145 ft. The Indian legend to which the rock owes its name is that a young squaw, standing on this point waiting for the return of her lover from battle, saw the warriors carrying his dead body to the island, and in her grief threw herself into the lake. *Robinson's Folly* is a precipitous cliff E. of the village, 128 ft. high. It is named after a Scotchman, who, delighted with the situation, built himself a small house on its verge. One night the house was blown over the edge, and Mr. Robinson, being within, paid for his folly with his life. The *Sugar-Loaf* is a solitary conical rock, rising 134 ft. from the plateau upon which it stands, and 284 ft. above the lake. The *Devil's Kitchen* is a curious cave. The *British Landing* is a favorite resort for picnics, and received its name from being the point where the British landed when they captured the island in 1812. There are other places of interest on the island, and many pleasant excursions may be made to fishing and hunting grounds in the vicinity.

The regular lake-steamers pass a considerable distance to the E. of Mackinaw Island, and enter the **St. Mary's River,** a remarkably beautiful stream, 62 miles long, and forming the only outlet to Lake Superior. It is a succession of expansions into lakes and contractions into rivers, and is dotted with beautiful forest-clad islands, while a few small towns are scattered along either shore. The *Ste. Marie Rapids* are avoided by a ship-canal, and 6 miles beyond the steamer traverses the picturesque *Waiska Bay*, and passing between Iroquois Point, on the American, and Gros Cap, on the Canadian side, enters the vast reaches of

Lake Superior.

Lake Superior, the largest body of fresh water in the world, is 360 miles long and 140 miles wide in its widest part, having an average width of 85 miles, a circuit of 1,500 miles, and an estimated area of 32,000 square miles. It is 800 ft. deep in its deepest portion—the bottom there being 200 ft. below the level of the ocean. It receives its waters from about 200 rivers and streams draining an area of 100,000 square miles. It contains a number of islands in the E. and W. portions, but very few in the central. The most important of these are Ile Royal, The Apostles, and Grand Island, belonging to the United States, and Michipicoton, Ile St. Ignace, and Pie Islands, belonging to Canada. The early French Jesuit fathers, who first explored and described this great lake, and published an account of it in Paris in 1636, speak of its shores as resembling a bended bow, the N. shore being the arc, the S. shore the cord, and Keweenaw Point, projecting from the S. shore to near the middle of the lake, the arrow. The coast of Lake Superior is mostly formed of rocks of various kinds, and of different geological groups. With the exception of sandy bars at the mouth of some of the rivers and small streams, the whole coast of the lake is rock-bound ; and in some places, but more particularly on the N. shore, mountain-masses of considerable elevation rear themselves from the water's edge, while mural precipices and beetling crags oppose themselves to the surges of this mighty lake, and threaten the unfortunate mariner who may be caught in a storm upon a lee-shore with almost inevitable destruction. The waters are of surprising clearness, are very cold, and filled with the most delicious fish.

Once having passed *White-Fish Point*, with its " sand dunes" or hills, and its tall lighthouse, the steamer usually takes a course for *Point au Sable*, 50 miles beyond, keeping in sight of the Michigan shore, which here presents a succession of desolate sand-hills, varying from 300 to 500 ft. in height. Twenty miles beyond the Point are the famous **Pictured Rocks,** a wonderful exhibition of the denuding effect of water, combined with the stains imparted by certain minerals. They extend for a distance of about 5 miles, rising in most places vertically from the water's edge to a height of from 50 to 200 ft., there being no beach whatever. When the weather permits, the steamers run near enough to give passengers a cursory view of these great curiosities ; but, in order to be able to appreciate their extraordinary character, the tourist should leave the steamer at *Munesing*, and visit them in a small boat. As we cannot spare the space required for such a detailed description of these rocks as they deserve, we must content ourselves with briefly mentioning the more conspicuous features in order from E. to W. (the visitor from Munesing approaches them in the opposite direction). The *Chapel* is a vaulted apartment in the rock, 30 or 40 ft. above the level of the lake. An arched roof of sandstone rests on 4 columns of rock so as to leave an apartment about 40 ft. in diameter and the same in height. Within are a pulpit and altar, perfect as if fashioned by the hand of man. A little to the west of the Chapel, Chapel River falls into the lake over a rocky ledge 15 ft. high. The **Grand Portal,** which appears next, is the most imposing feature of the series. It is 100 ft. high by 168 broad at the water-level, and the cliff in which it is cut rises above the arch, making the whole height 185 ft. The great cave, whose door is the portal, extends back in the shape of a vaulted room, the arches of the roof built of yellow limestone, and the sides fretted into fantastic shapes by the waves

driving in during storms, and dashing a hundred feet toward the rever-
berating roof. Within this cave there is a remarkably clear echo. *Sail
Rock* is about a mile W. of the Grand Portal, and consists of a group
of detached rocks, bearing a resemblance to the jib and mainsail of a
sloop when spread; so much so that, when viewed from a distance,
with a full glare of light upon it, while the cliff in the rear is left in
the shade, the illusion is perfect. The height of the block is about 40
ft. Passing to the westward, we skirt the cliffs worn into thousands
of strange forms, colored deep brown, yellow, and gray, bright blue,
and green. They are arranged in vertical and parallel bands, extending
to the water's edge, and are brightest when the streams are full of water.
Miner's Castle, 5 miles W. of the Chapel, and just W. of the mouth of
Miner's River, is the western end of the Pictured Rocks. It resembles
an old turreted castle with an arched portal. The height of the advanced mass in which the Gothic gateway may be recognized is about
70 ft., that of the main wall forming the background being 140 ft. The
coast of Pictures is not yet half explored, nor its beauties half discovered. " In one place there stands a majestic profile looking toward
the north—a woman's face, the *Empress of the Lake.* It is the pleasure of her royal highness to visit the rock only by night, a Diana of
the New World. In the daytime, search is vain; she will not reveal
herself; but when the low-down moon shines across the water, behold,
she appears! She looks to the north, not sadly, not sternly, like the
Old Man of the White Mountains, but benign of aspect, and so beautiful in her rounded, womanly curves, that the late watcher on the
beach falls into the dream of Endymion; but when he wakes in the
gray dawn he finds her gone, and only a shapeless rock glistens in the
rays of the rising sun."

Leaving Munesing and the Pictures, and going westward past the
Temples of Au Train and the *Laughing-Fish Point*, the city of **Marquette** (*Cozzens Hotel, Northwestern*), the entrepot of the Marquette
Iron Region, comes into view. It has a large and picturesque harbor,
is well built, and has a population of about 6,000. It is the chief depot of supplies for the iron mines of the Upper Peninsula, and the
principal point of shipment for the ore. There are 3 blast-furnaces
and a rolling-mill within the city limits, and several furnaces in the
vicinity. The place has great attractions for the invalid and tourist, in
its healthy, invigorating atmosphere, beautiful walks and drives, fine
scenery, boating, and fishing. Persons spending several weeks at Marquette can pass the time very agreeably in making excursions to *Grand
Island* and the *Pictured Rocks*, to *Carp River*, *Dead River*, and *Choco-
lat River*, all of which offer fine trout-fishing. Another excursion is by
the Marquette, Houghton & Ontonagon R. R. to *Champion* on Lake
Michigami (32 miles), where there are good boating, hunting, and fishing, but poor accommodations for travelers. A visit may also be made
to the iron-regions. Beyond Marquette the steamer makes no stops
until it reaches *Portage Lake*, passing on the way *Granite Island*
(12 miles from Marquette); *Stanard's Rock*, a very dangerous granite ledge; the *Huron Islands*, a picturesque group; *Huron Bay* and

Point Abbeye ; and crossing *Keweenaw Bay* to *Portage Entry.* The Entry was originally a narrow, crooked channel, leading from Keweenaw Bay into Portage Lake, and very difficult of navigation; but the channel has been artificially deepened, and in conjunction with the Portage Lake ship-canal saves the tedious and dangerous circuit of 120 miles around Keweenaw Point. In digging the canal indubitable evidences were found that Portage Lake was once an arm of Lake Superior, cutting off Keweenaw Point, which was then a large island. The lake is about 20 miles long, and from ½ to 2 miles in width. On either side the banks are covered with dense forests, a farmhouse with wide clearings and a wood-dock occasionally varying the scene. *Ontonagon* (400 miles from Sault Ste. Marie) is a small village at the mouth of a river of the same name, and is connected with Marquette by railway. Twenty miles beyond, the *Porcupine Mountain,* 1,300 ft. high, is a conspicuous object; and 70 miles from Ontonagon are the *** Twelve Apostles' Islands,** a large and beautiful group, 27 in number. The clay and sandstone cliffs have been worn into strange shapes by the action of the water, and the islands are covered with fine forest-trees. At *Bayfield,* a Wisconsin town on the mainland opposite, is the United States agency for the Chippewa Indians, who come here from all quarters to receive their annual payment. At the head of Lake Superior the *St. Louis River* comes in, and on the lake-shore near its mouth is **Duluth** (1,235 miles from Buffalo). Duluth is a lively town of some 5,000 inhabitants, and has considerable commercial importance as the extreme western link of the Great Chain of Lakes, and as the terminus of the Northern Pacific R. R. and of the St. Paul & Duluth R. R., which runs S. to St. Paul. It is well built, has a fine hotel (the *Clark House*), and from the hill above the town there is a beautiful view over the lake.

The *Northern Pacific R. R.,* which when completed will form another great highway across the continent, is now finished from Duluth to *Bismark,* at the crossing of the Missouri River (465 miles). It strikes directly across the center of Minnesota and Dakota, and traverses the richest portions, which are fast filling up with settlers. For the first 24 miles, from Duluth to the *Junction,* it is identical with the *St. Paul & Duluth R. R.,* which extends from Duluth to St. Paul (156 miles). About 20 miles from Duluth on this route are the *** Dalles of the St. Louis River,** a series of cascades and rapids, by which the river descends 400 ft. in about 4 miles. The Dalles are advantageously seen from the cars, and are justly regarded as among the wonders of American scenery. Also worthy of notice on this section of the line are the lofty trestle-bridges by which the railroad crosses several deep ravines.

The **North Shore of Lake Superior** is comparatively an unknown region, traversed only by the hunters, trappers, and *voyageurs* of the Hudson Bay Company, who own more than half its length. The easiest way of seeing it is by taking the steamers of the Lake Superior Transit Co. to Sault Ste. Marie, whence the Canadian steamers may be taken to the more important points; but, if the tourist desires to visit any number of the many places of interest, he must hire a small boat and 2 or 3 experienced men as a crew. N. of Duluth, the shore rises into grand cliffs of greenstone and porphyry, 800 to 1,000 ft. in height. The *** Pali-**

sades (58 miles from Duluth) are a remarkable rock formation, pre.
senting vertical columns from 60 to 100 ft. high, and from 1 to 6 ft. in
diameter.   Near by, *Baptism River* comes dashing down to the lake in
a series of wild waterfalls.   *Pigeon River* (113 miles) is the boundary-
line between the United States and Canada ; and here begins the " Grand
Portage," by which, through a series of lakes and streams, the very
names of which have a wild sound (Rainy Lake, Lake of the Woods,
and Winnipeg), the *voyageurs* are enabled, with short portages, to take
their canoes through to the Saskatchewan and Manitoba.   The whole
Canadian coast is grandly beautiful in every variety of point, bay, island,
and isolated cliff.   Passing *Fort William* (143 miles), an important post
of the Hudson Bay Company, *Thunder Cape* is seen, a basaltic cliff 1,350
ft. high, on whose summit is the crater of an extinct volcano.   At the
foot of this cliff, near the shore, is *Silver Island*, the tales of whose
productiveness read like pages of " Monte Cristo."   Here are extensive
quartz-mills and a busy mining settlement.   W. of the Cape is Thunder Bay, on the shore of which stands the rising village of *Prince Arthur's Landing*, with a population of about 1,000.   This is the E. terminus of the " Dawson Route " to Manitoba (see Route 98) and also of
the projected railway to Winnipeg.   *Neepigon Bay* (203 miles) is 40
miles long by 15 wide, and contains a number of beautiful islands.
Beyond Neepigon Bay eastward, the coast, studded with waterfalls,
stretches for miles, entirely uninhabited save by a few Indians.   Hunt-
ing-parties from the lower lake towns camp along the beach occasionally
during the summer months ; but the region is as wild as in the days before Columbus.   At *Pic River* (276 miles) is a post of the Hudson Bay
Company, and here the shore-line bends to the S. and the lake begins to
narrow toward the Sault.   At *Otter Head* (30 miles S. of Pic River) the
cliff rises in a sheer precipice 1,000 ft. from the water, and on its summit stands a rock like a monument, which on one side shows the profile
of a man, and on the other the distinct outline of an otter's head.   The
Indians never passed this point without stopping to make their offerings
to its manitou.   Still farther S. is the broad bay of Michipicoten, or the
" Bay of Hills " ; and here is another post of the Hudson Bay Company.
There are many islands in this portion of the lake, among the most important of which are *Isle Royale* (45 miles long and 8 to 12 wide), *Saint
Ignace*, and *Michipicoten Island*, the latter of which will probably become
a favorite place of summer resort.

97. The Yellowstone Park.

How to Reach.—The usual starting-points for tourists visiting the Yellowstone Park are *Virginia City*, a mining town of about 1,500 inhabitants, situated in
Madison County, Montana, on Alder Gulch ; and *Bozeman*, a small mining town, 60
miles W. of Virginia City, at the head of Gallatin Valley. Either of these places may
be reached from the East as follows : (1) *Via* Union Pacific R. R. (see Route 85) to
Ogden, Utah ; thence *via* Utah & Northern R. R. to terminus of road ; and thence
via overland stage to Virginia City or Bozeman. The fare from Omaha to Virginia City by this route is $100 ; from New York, $136. The rapid extension
of the Utah & Northern Railroad has lately brought the Park within one day's
stage-ride of the railroad. (2) *Via* the Missouri River. Here the tourist has choice
18

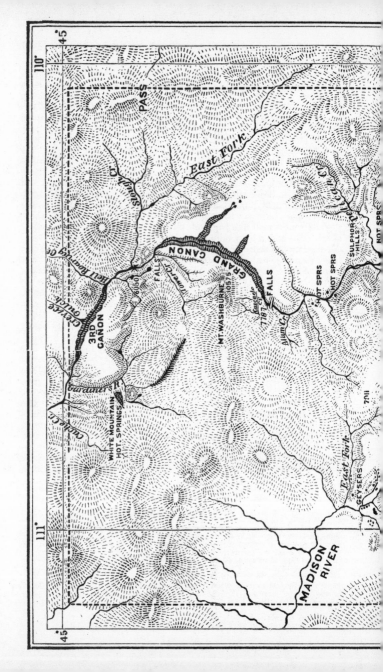

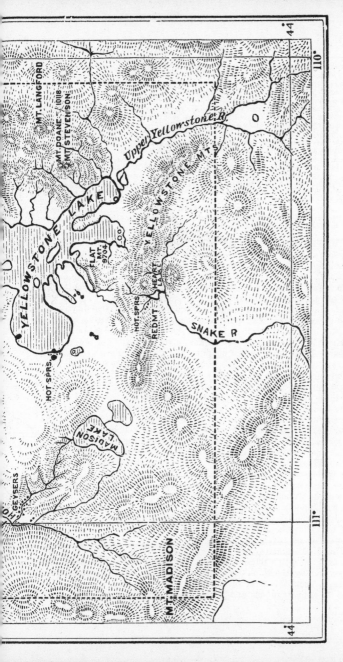

MAP OF YELLOWSTONE PARK.

of two routes. He can go all the way by steamer from Yankton to Fort Benton (1,508 miles). A quicker way is to go from St. Paul (see p. 344) or Duluth (see p. 408) *via* Northern Pacific R. R. to Bismark; thence by steamer (several first-class lines) to Fort Benton; and thence by stage (140 miles) to Helena, the capital of Montana. Distance from St. Paul to Helena by this route 1,628 miles; time about 13 days; fare, 1st class, $75; 2nd class, $55. From Helena stages run to Bozeman (110 miles, fare $12) and to Virginia City (120 miles, fare $15). (3) To Bismark as above and then ce*via* steamer on Yellowstone River to Miles City, or Fort Keogh, 2 miles W. From Miles City tri-weekly stages run to Bozeman up the Yellowstone Valley (335 miles). At either Bozeman or Virginia City guides, camp equipage, pack-mules, and all the requirements of the Yellowstone tour can be procured. From Bozeman the tourist can cross the divide, descend Trail Creek to the Yellowstone, and ascend that river to the White Mountain Hot Springs—about 75 miles—in wagon or carriage. From Virginia City the route is up Madison River to the Lower Geyser Basin (about 100 miles). Within the Park the various points of interest may be visited on horseback without danger or difficulty. Bridle-paths are so numerous and so well traveled that guides are not strictly necessary. Parties entering *via* Bozeman usually come out *via* Virginia City, and *vice versa*. The best time to visit the Park is in August and September. Either before or after that time snow is liable to be encountered and the roads are not good.

THE Yellowstone National Park, which Congress has "dedicated and set apart as a public park or pleasuring ground for the benefit and enjoyment of the people," lies partly in Wyoming and partly in Montana Territory. It is 65 miles N. and S. by 55 miles E. and W., comprises 3,575 square miles, and is all more than 6,000 ft. above the sea. Yellowstone Lake has an altitude of 7,788 ft., and the mountain ranges that hem in the valleys on every side rise to the height of 10,000 and 12,000 ft., and are covered with perpetual snow. The entire region was at a comparatively recent geological period the scene of remarkable volcanic activity, the last stages of which are still visible in the hot springs and geysers. In the number and magnitude of these the Park surpasses all the rest of the world. There are probably 50 geysers that throw a column of water to a height of from 50 to 200 ft., and from 5,000 to 10,000 springs, chiefly of two kinds, those depositing lime and those depositing silica. There is every variety of beautiful color, and the deposits form around their border the most elaborate ornamentation. The temperature of the calcareous springs is from 160° to 170°; that of the others rises to 200° or more. The principal collections are the upper and lower geyser basins of the Madison River and the calcareous springs on Gardiner's River. The Park is also one of the most interesting geographical localities in North America, having within its limits or in its vicinity the sources of vast rivers flowing in various directions. On the N. are the sources of the Yellowstone; on the W. those of the principal forks of the Missouri; on the S. W. and S. those of Snake River, flowing into the Columbia and through it into the Pacific Ocean, and those of Green River, a branch of the great Colorado, which empties into the Gulf of California; while on the S. E. side are the numerous head waters of Wind River.

The **Yellowstone River,** which is a tributary of the Missouri, is without exception the most extraordinary river on the continent. Its source is near the S. E. corner of the Park, in the ***Yellowstone Lake,** a beautiful sheet of water 22 miles long and 10 to 15 wide, 7,788 ft. above the sea, and nearly enclosed by snow-clad mountains rising 3,000 to 5,000 ft. higher. Its waters are exquisitely clear and cool, are 300 ft. deep at the deepest part, and abound in salmon-trout. Its shores are rugged but extremely picturesque, and on the S. W. arm is a belt of hot springs 3 miles long and ½ mile wide, some of which extend into the lake itself. The Upper Yellowstone, the ultimate source of the river, flows into the lake from the S. E. after a course of 25 miles ; and from its N. end the Yellowstone River emerges on its course of 1,300 miles to the Missouri. About 15 miles below the lake are the *Upper Falls,* where the river, after passing through a series of rapids, makes an abrupt descent of 140 ft. ; and about ¼ mile farther down are the majestic *** Lower Falls,** which are 360 ft. high. Below the Lower Falls the river flows for 20 miles through the *** * Grand Canon,** whose perpendicular sides, from 200 to 500 yards apart, rise to the height of 1,200 to 1,500 ft.

In Professor F. V. Hayden's report to Congress on the explorations which he conducted, to which we are indebted for nearly all the authentic knowledge we have of the Yellowstone region, he says : " No language can do justice to the wonderful grandeur and beauty of the cañon below the Lower Falls : the very nearly vertical walls, slightly sloping down to the water's edge on either side, so that from the summit the river appears like a thread of silver foaming over its rocky bottom ; the variegated colors of the sides, yellow, red, brown, white, all intermixed and shading into each other ; the Gothic columns of every form, standing out from the sides of the walls with greater variety and more striking colors than ever adorned a work of human art. The margins of the canon on either side are beautifully fringed with pines. . . . The decomposition and the colors of the rocks must have been due largely to hot water from the springs, which has percolated all through, giving to them their present variegated and unique appearance. Standing near the margin of the Lower Falls, and looking down the cañon, which looks like an immense chasm or cleft in the basalt, with its sides 1,200 to 1,500 ft. high, and decorated with the most brilliant colors that the human eye ever saw, with the rocks weathered into an almost unlimited variety of forms, with here and there a pine sending its roots into the clefts on the sides as if struggling with a sort of uncertain success to maintain an existence—the whole presents a picture that it would be difficult to surpass in Nature. Mr. Thomas Moran, a celebrated artist, and noted for his skill as a colorist, exclaimed, with a kind of regretful enthusiasm, that these beautiful tints were beyond the reach of human art. It is not the depth alone that gives such an impression of grandeur to the mind, but it is also the picturesque forms and coloring. After the waters of the Yellowstone roll over the upper descent, they flow with great rapidity over the apparently flat, rocky bottom, which spreads out to nearly double its width above the falls, and continues thus until near the Lower Falls, when the channel again contracts, and the waters seem, as it were, to gather themselves into one compact mass, and plunge over the descent of 350 ft. in detached drops of foam as white as snow ; some of the large globules of water shoot down like the contents of an exploded rocket. It is a sight far more beautiful than, though not so grand or impressive as, that of Niagara Falls. A heavy mist always rises from the water at the foot of the falls, so dense that one can not approach within 200 or 300 ft., and even then the clothes will be drenched in a few moments. Upon the yellow, nearly vertical wall of the W. side, the mist mostly falls ; and for 300 ft. from the bottom the wall is covered with a thick matting of mosses, sedges, grasses, and other vegetation of the most vivid green, which have sent their small roots into the softened rocks, and are nourished by the ever-ascending spray."

Just below the Grand Cañon, the river receives Tower Creek, which flows for 10 miles through a deep and gloomy cañon known as the *Devil's Den.* About 200 yards above its mouth the creek pours over an abrupt descent of 156 ft., "forming," as Professor Hayden says, " one of the most beautiful and picturesque falls to be found in any country." Below the mountains the course of the Yellowstone lies through a wide open valley bounded by high rolling hills.

As already mentioned, there are immense numbers of hot springs in the Yellowstone Basin, some dead and others evidently dying. A very interesting group is on the E. side of Mt. Washburn, covering an area of 10 or 15 square miles, and there are other extensive groups on both sides of the Yellowstone Lake and also at various points on the river (see map). But the most remarkable group, not only in the Yellowstone region but in the world, is the *White Mountain Hot Springs, which are situated on the W. side of Gardiner's River, on the slope of White Mountain. Many of the springs are dead, but the calcareous deposits from them cover an area of about 2 miles square. The active springs extend from the margin of the river to an elevation nearly 1,000 ft. above.

"After ascending the side of the mountain," says Professor Hayden, "about a mile above the channel of Gardiner's River we suddenly came in full view of one of the finest displays of Nature's architectural skill the world can produce. The snowy whiteness of the deposit at once suggested the name of White Mountain Hot Spring. It had the appearance of a frozen cascade. If a group of springs near the summit of a mountain were to distribute their waters down the irregular declivities, and they were slowly congealed, the picture would bear some resemblance in form. We pitched our camp at the foot of the principal mountain, by the side of the stream that contained the aggregated waters of the hot springs above, which, by the time they reached our camp, were sufficiently cooled for our use. Before us was a hill 200 ft. high, composed of the calcareous deposit of the hot springs, with a system of step-like terraces, which would defy any description in words. The steep sides of the hills were ornamented with a series of semicircular basins, with margins varying in height from a few inches to 6 or 8 ft., and so beautifully scalloped and adorned with a kind of bead-work that the beholder stands amazed at this marvel of Nature's handiwork. Add to this a snow-white ground, with every variety of shade of scarlet, green, and yellow, as brilliant as the brightest of our aniline dyes. The pools or basins are of all sizes, from a few inches to 6 or 8 ft. in diameter, and from 2 inches to 2 ft. deep. As the water flows from the spring over the mountain-side from one basin to another, it loses continually a portion of its heat, and the bather can find any desired temperature. At the top of the hill there is a broad, flat terrace, covered more or less with these basins, 150 to 200 yards in diameter, and many of them going to decay. Here we find the largest, finest, and most active spring of the group at the present time. The largest spring is very near the outer margin of the terrace, and is 25 by 40 ft. in diameter, the water so perfectly transparent that one can look down into the beautiful ultramarine depth to the bottom of the basin. The sides of the basin are ornamented with coral-like forms, with a great variety of shades, from pure white to a bright cream-yellow, and the blue sky, reflected in the transparent waters, gives an azure tint to the whole which surpasses all art. Underneath the sides of many of these pools are rows of stalactites, of all sizes, many of them exquisitely ornamented, formed by the dripping of the water over the margin of the basin."

On the W. side of the Yellowstone River, about 10 miles from the falls, is the *Sulphur Mountain*, rising to a height of 150 ft. from an almost level plain and perforated with numerous fissures and "craters" from which sulphurous vapor pours forth in great abundance. The fissures are lined with sulphur-crystals, and the ground is hot and parched with internal fires. Close by are some boiling *Mud Springs*, and there is another remarkable group of them about 2 miles S. E. on the bank of the river. A few miles above Sulphur Mountain is the *Mud Volcano, which has broken out from the side of a well-timbered hill. The crater is 25 ft. across at the top and about 30 ft. deep. The surface of the bottom is in a constant state of ebullition, puffing and throwing up masses of boiling mud, and sending forth dense columns of steam which rise several hundred ft. and can be seen for many miles in all directions. Close by are three large hot springs, one of which is a geyser having periods of active eruption about every 6 hours.

The great **Geysers** of the Yellowstone region are situated on the Fire-Hole River, the middle fork of the Madison, in the W. portion of the Park. They lie in two large groups, in what are called the Upper and Lower Geyser Basins. The *Lower Basin*, beginning near the junction of the East and Middle Forks of the Madison, comprises an area of about 30 square miles, and contains uncounted numbers of geysers and springs which are distributed in 7 groups. The most interesting of these is the second group, which lies near the center of the basin, and which is said to resemble a factory village, the steam rising in jets from more than 100 orifices. The principal geyser of this group, situated on the side of a hill, is about 20 ft. in diameter, and throws a column to the height of 50 ft. Another is named the *Thud Geyser*, from the dull, suppressed sound given off as the water rises and recedes. It has a beautiful scalloped rim, with small basins around it. The *Upper Basin* lies in the valley of the same river, about 8 miles S. of the Lower

The Giantess.

Basin. It is not so large as the latter, covering an area of only 3 square miles, and there are fewer springs; but the phenomena exhibited are far more remarkable. Most of the springs and geysers are near the river extending along on both branches about 3 miles. Their average temperature is over 170 °, that of the air being 67 °. At the head of the valley, near its S. extremity, stands * **Old Faithful,** a geyser so called for its regularity; it spouts at intervals of about an hour, throwing a column of water 6 ft. in diameter to a maximum height of 130 ft., and holding it up by a succession of impulses from 4 to 6 minutes. When the action ceases, the water recedes out of sight and nothing but the occasional hiss of steam is heard until the time approaches for another eruption. On the opposite side of the river is the *Beehive,* which once in 24 hours throws a column of water 3 ft. in diameter to a height of from 100 to 220 ft. The eruption lasts from 5 to 15 minutes. About 200 yards from the Beehive is * **The Giantess,** one of the largest of the geysers. It has an oval aperture 18 by 25 ft. in diameter, the inside of which is corrugated and covered with a whitish silicious deposit. When not in action, no water can be seen in its basin, alt'   'i its sides are visible to the depth of 100 ft., but a gurgling sound can be heard at a great distance below. When an eruption is about to take place, the water rises in the tube with much sputtering and hissing, sending off vast clouds of steam. When it finally bursts forth, it throws up a column of water the full size of its aperture, to the height of 60 ft., and through this rise 5 or 6 smaller jets, varying from 6 to 15 inches in diameter, to the height of 250 ft. The eruption, which takes place at irregular intervals, continues for about 20 minutes. Farther down the river, on the same side, is the *Sawmill Geyser,* which throws a small stream 10 or 15 ft. high almost uninterruptedly. Near it is the * **Grand Geyser,** one of the most powerful in the basin. Its orifice is 2½ by 4 ft., and when not in eruption the water is quiet and clear as crystal. An eruption (which occurs at irregular intervals) is preceded by a rumbling and shaking of the ground, followed by a column of steam shooting up from the crater, immediately after which the water bursts forth in a succession of jets, apparently 6 ft. in diameter at the bottom and tapering to a point at the top, to a height of from 175 to 200 ft., while the steam ascends to 1,000 ft. or more. This immense body of water is kept up to this height for about 20 minutes, when it gradually recedes and again becomes quiescent. Only 20 ft. from the Grand Geyser, and in the same basin, but apparently having no connection with it, is *Turban Geyser,* with an orifice 3 by 4 ft., which is never wholly quiet, and as often as once in 20 minutes throws its water to the height of from 15 to 25 ft. The * **Giant Geyser** has a rugged crater, like a broken horn, 10 ft. in height, 25 ft. in diameter at the base and about 8 ft. at the top. The cone is open on one side, having a ragged aperture from the ground upward. Its discharges are irregular and continue for irregular periods. When Prof. Hayden saw it in 1871, it played an hour and 20 minutes, throwing the water 140 ft.; but Lieut. Doane, who visited it the year before, states that it played 3½ hours at one time, to a height varying from 90 to 200 ft.

The *Castle*, the *Grotto*, the *Punch Bowl*, the *Riverside*, the *Soda*, and the *Fan Geysers*, and numerous others which have not yet even been named, are worthy of notice.

98. Manitoba.

How to reach.—(1) In summer the cheapest and pleasantest way to reach Manitoba is by the Lake steamers (which may be taken at Buffalo [see Route 96] Toronto, Detroit, Collingswood, Windsor, Sarnia, or Southampton) to *Duluth*, at the W. end of Lake Superior (see p. 408); thence by the Northern Pacific R. R. to *Glyndon* (223 miles); and from Glyndon by the St. Paul, Minneapolis & Manitoba R. R. and the Pembina Branch of the Canada Pacific Railway, which runs down the E. bank of the Red River of the North, to St. Boniface, opposite the city of Winnipeg. (2) Another route (and the only one available in winter) is by Route 82 or 83 to St. Paul, thence *via* the St. Paul, Minneapolis & Manitoba and the Pembina Branch of the Canada Pacific Railway, as before. (3) A very romantic and picturesque route for those who have the time is the "Dawson Route" from *Prince Arthur's Landing*, on the N. shore of Lake Superior (see p. 409), partly by boat and partly by stage to Winnipeg (477 miles, fare, $10). This route being chiefly by water, it is available only during the season of navigation (May to November). The Canadian Pacific Railway is under construction from Winnipeg to Lake Superior, and when completed will form a new and popular route from the East to Manitoba.

MANITOBA, a province of the Dominion of Canada, lies just N. of Minnesota and Dakota, and is in the form of a parallelogram, 135 miles long E. and W. by 104 miles in breadth; area, 14,340 square miles; population about 25,000, of whom nearly half are half-breeds. These half-breeds include all having any intermixture of Indian blood, and are the descendants of Indian mothers and French-Canadian, English, and Scotch fathers. Since 1870, a considerable immigration from the Eastern Provinces and from Europe has set in, and the whites are rapidly becoming the dominant element in the population, which, besides the half-breeds, comprises about 600 Indians.

The general surface of Manitoba is a level prairie 80 ft. above Lake Winnipeg and 700 ft. above the sea. It is broken by the Big Ridge and Pembina Mountain, ancient beaches of that vast lake which is supposed at one time to have covered this entire region. The only important lakes at present are Winnipeg and Manitoba, from the latter of which the province derives its name. *Lake Winnipeg* is of irregular shape, being about 260 miles in length and from 6 to 60 miles wide. It is 628 ft. above the sea, contains many islands, and does not exceed 12 fathoms in depth. Ice forms frequently to a thickness of 5 ft., and does not leave the upper part of the lake before the 10th of June. The name Winnipeg in Algonquin signifies "dirty water." *Lake Manitoba* lies about 60 miles S. of Lake Winnipeg, into which it discharges through the Little Saskatchewan or Dauphin River, and is 120 miles long and 25 wide at the widest part. It abounds in fish. The name signifies "supernatural strait," the Indians attributing the peculiar agitation of the water in a portion of the lake to the presence of a spirit. The principal stream in Manitoba is the Red River of the North, which, rising in Minnesota, flows for 140 miles through the province and empties into Lake Winnipeg. Its chief affluent, the Assiniboin, joins it about 50 miles above Lake Winnipeg.

The climate is healthy, but exhibits great extremes of temperature, the thermometer falling in winter to 40° below zero, and in summer rising as high as 100°. Owing to the dryness of the atmosphere, however, the cold is not severely felt, and horses winter on the prairies without shelter, fattening on the grasses which they dig from beneath the snow, which is seldom very deep. The rainfall in summer is ample for agricultural purposes, and vegetation comes rapidly to maturity. Winter sets in early in November, and lasts until the middle of April. Frosts are liable to occur until the end of May, and cold nights begin toward the end of August. The soil is very fertile.

To the sportsman, Manitoba, being a comparatively virgin field, offers unrivaled attractions. The rivers and lakes abound in white-fish, sturgeon, trout, cat-fish, pike, perch, and gold-eyes. Ducks, geese, cranes, swans, snipe, prairie-hens, and other birds swarm in countless numbers; and among the wild animals are elks, black bears, rabbits, squirrels, and badgers. The great buffalo-ranges, visited by the half-breed and Indian hunters, lie to the W. and S. W. of the province.

The capital and chief city of Manitoba is **Winnipeg** (*Grand Central Hotel, Exchange*), near *Fort Garry,* situated at the confluence of the Red River of the North with the Assiniboin, 50 miles S. of Lake Winnipeg. It covers an area of 3 square miles, is regularly laid out, and contains about 8,000 inhabitants. The chief public buildings are the *Governor's Residence,* the *Court-House,* the *City Hall,* the *Post-Office,* the *Custom-House,* and the *Dominion Land-Office ;* these, with the *Merchants' Bank, Ontario Bank, Hudson Bay Company's Office,* and many warehouses, are large and handsome structures of white brick manufactured in the vicinity. Winnipeg is the headquarters of the Dominion bureaus relating to the Northwest Territories, and in America of the Hudson Bay Co. Opposite, on the E. bank of the river (reached by ferry), is *St. Boniface,* which is the northern terminus of the Pembina Branch of the Canada Pacific Railway. The trade of Winnipeg is important, and consists chiefly in jobbing to the traders on the plains of the Saskatchewan, Bow, Mackenzie, and Peace Rivers, and in furnishing supplies to the new settlements and arriving immigrants. The exports consist chiefly of furs. The principal settlements in Manitoba besides Winnipeg are on both banks of the Red River, from about 20 miles N. to 15 miles S. of that city, and along the Assiniboin for about 20 miles W.; but the province is rapidly filling up by immigration, and each year sees marked changes.

Manitoba forms part of the territory granted in 1670 by Charles II. to the Hudson Bay Co., which in 1811 sold a tract, including what is now the province, to Thomas Douglas, Earl of Selkirk. Under his auspices a colony was established, which was sometimes called the Selkirk Settlement, but more commonly the Red River Settlement. In 1835 the Hudson Bay Co. bought back this tract, and in 1870 Manitoba became a province of Canada, upon the annexation of the Hudson Bay territory to the Dominion. A previous attempt of the Dominion authorities to take possession of the country led to organized resistance on the part of the French half-breeds under the lead of Louis Riel, who formed a provisional government, adopted a bill of rights, and held possession of the province from about Oct. 20, 1869, to Aug. 24, 1870, when a force under Col. (now Gen. Sir Garnet) Wolseley entered Winnipeg and reinstated the regular authorities, Riel having previously vacated the place.

99. Baltimore to Richmond and the South.

Via Steamer on Chesapeake Bay and Connecting Railways.

THE trip down the Chesapeake Bay from Baltimore to Portsmouth or Richmond, if made in pleasant weather, is delightful. The fine steamers of the *Bay Line* make daily trips from Baltimore (Union Dock, foot of Mill St.) to Portsmouth, running through in about 12 hours, and connecting at the latter point with the Seaboard & Roanoke R. R. for the South-Atlantic States. The principal points of interest seen in the passage of the Bay are the mouth of the Patapsco River and the battle-ground of North Point near Baltimore, referred to in the description of that city (see p. 40); the Bodkin, 3 miles distant; and the harbor of Annapolis, 15 miles below, with a distant view of the great dome of the Capitol at Washington. At the lower end of the Bay are the famous fortifications of * **Fortress Monroe** and the *Rip Raps*, protecting the entrance to Hampton Roads and James River. At the head of the steamboat landing at Old Point Comfort, within 100 yards of the Fortress, stands the spacious and elegant *Hygeia Hotel*, which accommodates 500 guests, and is open all the year. Fortress Monroe, the largest in America, is always open to visitors, and presents many features of interest. **Norfolk** (*Atlantic Hotel, Purcell House*), whose harbor is defended by the above-mentioned forts, is pleasantly situated on the N. bank of the Elizabeth River, 8 miles from Hampton Roads and 32 miles from the ocean. After Richmond, it is the most populous city of Virginia, with about 25,000 inhabitants, and has an extensive trade. Large quantities of oysters and early fruits and vegetables are brought thither by the railways and canals and shipped to Northern ports. The city is irregularly laid out, but the streets are generally wide, and the houses well built of brick and stone. The *Custom-House and Post-Office*, on Main St., is a handsome edifice erected at a cost of $228,505; and the *City Hall* has a granite front and a cupola 110 ft. high. The *Norfolk Academy*, the *Masonic Temple, Mechanics' Hall*, and several of the banks, are handsome structures; and the Baptist Church, on Freemason St., has a fine steeple. There are two cemeteries tastefully laid out and adorned with cypress-trees. Norfolk was founded in 1805, burned by the British in 1776, severely visited by the yellow fever in 1855, and played a prominent part in the first year of the civil war, when it was captured by the Virginians and became the chief naval depot of the Confederacy. Off Norfolk, on March 8, 1862, was fought the memorable engagement between the Confederate iron-clad Virginia and the Federal iron-clad Monitor, which marks one of the most notable epochs in naval warfare and changed the course of naval construction throughout the world. From Norfolk Richmond is reached by steamer on the James River. The boats of the *Va. Steamboat Co.* make the trip in 10 hours, passing amid much pleasing scenery and by many localities of great historical interest. Directly opposite Norfolk, with which it is connected by ferry, is **Portsmouth** (*American House, Crawford*), a city of 15,000 inhabitants, regularly laid out on level ground, and well built. Its harbor is one of the best on the Atlantic coast, and is accessible by the largest vessels. At Gosport, the S. extremity of the city, is a *U. S. Navy Yard,* which contains a Dry Dock constructed of granite at a cost of $974,536. Near by is the *U. S. Naval Hospital,* a spacious brick edifice on the bank of the river. At the time of the secession of Virginia (April 18, 1861) nearly 1,000 men were employed at the Navy Yard. Two days afterward it was destroyed by fire, with property valued at several million dollars, including 11 vessels of war. At Portsmouth, the Bay steamers connect with the Seaboard & Roanoke R. R., which runs in 80 miles to *Weldon,* where connection is made with through routes to the South (see p. 423).

Daily steamers run from Baltimore (Pier 10, Light St.) to *West Point,* at the head of navigation on York River, whence the Richmond, York River & Chesapeake R. R. runs in 88 miles to Richmond. **Yorktown,** a small village on the right bank of York River, 10 miles above its mouth, is memorable as the scene of that decisive event in the American Revolution, the surrender of the British army under Lord Cornwallis, Oct. 19, 1781. The precise spot where the surrender took place will be pointed out to the inquiring visitor. Remains of the British intrenchments may still be seen, and the country around bears abundant evidences of the operations conducted there by McClellan in 1862. The railway between West Point and Richmond traverses a section of country remarkable as the scene of many important events during the late civil war. A short distance from the point where the railway crosses the Chickahominy River are *Powhite Creek* and *Cold Harbor,* famous as the localities of the great struggles of 1862 and 1864. *Fair Oaks Station* (7 miles from Richmond) was the scene of the bloody but indecisive *Battle of Seven Pines,* fought May 31, 1862, between McClellan and Johnston. **Richmond** (see p. 419).

100. Washington to Richmond.

a. Via Baltimore & Potomac R. R.   Distance, 116 miles.

THE City of Washington is fully described in Route 8. The Richmond train leaves the depot in Washington at the cor. of 6th and B Sts., crosses the Long Bridge into Virginia, and runs down parallel with the Potomac 7 miles to **Alexandria,** which is described on page 58. Beyond Alexandria it still follows the Potomac for 27 miles to *Quantico,* a small station and steamer-landing, where connection is made with the steamers from Washington. Here the train takes the track of the Richmond, Fredericksburg & Potomac R. R., which runs S. E. across a broken and desolate-looking region, part of which is known as "The Wilderness" and is famous as the scene of the great combats of 1863 and 1864. Twenty-one miles beyond Quantico is **Fredericksburg,** a quaint and venerable old city on the S. bank of the Rappahannock River. It was founded in 1727, contains about 6,000 inhabitants, and is notable as the scene of one of the severest battles of the civil war, fought Dec. 13, 1862, in which Gen. Burnside was defeated by Gen. Lee. Many traces of the conflict still remain and may be seen from the cars. In the vicinity are a National and a Confederate cemetery, the latter being adorned with a monument. Eleven miles W. of Fredericksburg, on the E. edge of "The Wilderness," the *Battle of Chancellorsville*, in which "Stonewall" Jackson lost his life, was fought, May 2–4, 1863. Southward from Chancellorsville is *Spottsylvania Court-House*, where, in May, 1864, were fought some of the bloodiest battles of Grant's campaign on his way to Richmond. Just outside the limits of Fredericksburg an unfinished monument, begun in 1833, marks the tomb of the mother of Washington, who died here in 1789. It was in the vicinity of Fredericksburg that Washington himself was born, and here he passed his early years. Leaving Fredericksburg the train crosses the Rappahannock and passes directly over the ground where Gen. Meade's charge was made in the battle of Fredericksburg, already referred to. *Guinney's* (12 miles beyond Fredericksburg) was the scene of the death of Stonewall Jackson. He was wounded May 2, 1863, and died at the house of William Chandler, May 10, exclaiming, " Let us cross over the river and rest under the shade of the trees." At *Hanover Junction* (37 miles from Fredericksburg) another battle was fought between Generals Grant and Lee in May, 1864. Remains of the works occupied by the two armies may still be seen. *Ashland* is a favorite residence of many citizens of Richmond, from which it is only 16 miles distant. Near here Henry Clay was born.

b. By Steamer to Quantico and thence by Railway.

This is a pleasant way of reaching Richmond from Washington when a few hours more or less are of no importance to the traveler. The trip down the Potomac is made by day, and affords good views of the river scenery and the various places of interest on its banks—Alexandria, Arlington, and Mount Vernon. In passing Mount Vernon the bell of the boat is always tolled. At *Quantico* (about 45 miles) the steamer connects with the Richmond, Fredericksburg & Potomac R. R., which is described in the foregoing route. (Passengers can use the same ticket on either of these routes.)

Richmond.

Hotels, etc.—The leading hotels are the *Exchange* and the *Ballard House*, facing and connected with each other on Franklin St. below the Capitol ($3 a day). *Ford's*, the *St. James*, and the *American* are smaller but good houses. *Horse-cars* (fare 10c.) traverse the main thoroughfares. *Garber's* omnibuses and hacks are in waiting at the depots and steamboat landings, and at stands in the city. Fare from depot or landing to any point in the city, 50c. Hacks by the hour, $1.50 for 1st hour and $1 for each additional hour. *Post-Office* in Main St., between 10th and 11th.

Richmond, the capital and largest city of Virginia, is situated on the N. bank of the James River, about 100 miles (by water) from Chesapeake Bay. It is built on several eminences, the principal of which are Richmond and Shockoe Hills, which are separated by Shockoe Creek, and is surrounded by beautiful scenery. It is regularly laid out and well built; the streets, which are lighted with gas, cross each other at right angles. In the business quarter are many substantial and handsome buildings, and nearly all the residences have grass and flower plots in front.

Richmond was founded in 1737, was incorporated in 1742, and became the State capital in 1779, at which period it was a small village. The city was, in turn, the scene of the conventions of 1788, to ratify the Federal Constitution, those of 1829, 1850, and 1861, and other important political gatherings, which largely shaped the destinies of the Commonwealth. In 1861 still greater prominence was given to it as the capital of the Southern Confederacy; and one of the great aims of the Federal authorities, throughout the war, was to reduce it into their possession. The obstinacy with which the Confederates defended it was a proof of the great importance which they attached to its retention. To effect this, strong lines of earthworks were drawn around the place, and may still be seen as memorials of the great struggle. When General Lee evacuated Petersburg, April 2, 1865, the troops defending Richmond on the E. were withdrawn, and, to prevent the tobacco warehouses and public stores from falling into the hands of the Federal forces, the buildings—together with the bridges over James River—were fired. This resulted in the destruction of a large part of the business section of the city, the number of buildings destroyed having been estimated at 1,000, and the loss at $8,000,000. With the cessation of hostilities, Richmond set to work to rebuild her blackened quarters, which she has now almost wholly accomplished, and the city is rapidly surpassing its former prosperity. The population in 1870 was 51,038, and in 1878 was estimated at 77,500. The commerce is large, the chief articles of export being tobacco and flour. The manufactures include iron-works, machine-shops, foundries, sugar-refineries, cigar-factories, coach and wagon factories, furniture, sheetings and shirtings, and stoneware. Five lines of railroad intersect at Richmond, and regular lines of steamers run to Norfolk, Baltimore, Philadelphia, and New York.

The most prominent public building of Richmond, and by far the most conspicuous object in the city, or from its approaches, is the *State Capitol, standing in the center of a park of 8 acres, on the summit of Shockoe Hill. It is a Græco-Composite building, adorned with a portico of Ionic columns, the plan having been furnished by Thomas Jefferson after that of the *Maison carrée* at Nismes, in France. The view from the platform on the roof is extensive and beautiful. In the center of the building is a square hall surmounted by a dome, beneath which stands *Houdon's celebrated statue of Washington. It is of marble, of the size of life, and represents Washington as clad in the uniform worn by an American general during the Revolution. Near by, in a niche in the wall, is a marble bust of Lafayette. The *State Library* contains 40,000 volumes and many portraits of historical personages. On the esplanade leading from the Governor's house to the W. gate of the Capitol Square, and near the latter, is Crawford's equestrian **Statue of Washington, consisting of a bronze horse and rider, of colossal size, rising from a massive granite pedestal, and surrounded by bronze figures of Patrick Henry, Thomas Jefferson, John Marshall, George Mason, Thomas Nelson, and Andrew Lewis. The horse is half thrown upon its haunches, and is thought to be one of the finest bronzes in the world. A life-size marble statue of Henry Clay (near the W. corner), and Foley's statue of *General "Stonewall" Jackson*, of heroic size, on a granite pedestal (N. of the Capitol), complete the decorations of the Capitol Square. The *Governor's House* is a plain building on the N. E. corner of Capitol Square. The *Custom-House, which also contains the *Post-Office*, is a handsome structure of granite, in the Italian style, in Main St., between 10th and 11th. The **Medical College, in rear of the Monumental Church, is a fine specimen of the Egyptian style of architecture. In the vicinity is the *Brockenbrough House*, which was the residence of Jefferson Davis,

President of the Southern Confederacy; it is now used as a school-house. The *Almshouse* is one of the finest edifices in the city, and the *State Penitentiary*, a vast brick building, is in the W. suburbs. *Libby*

Statue of Washington

Prison, Castle Thunder, and *Belle Isle* retain some interest from their celebrity as military prisons during the civil war; the two former are now used as tobacco warehouses.

The churches of Richmond are numerous, and several of them are some specimens of architecture. Those with historic associations are St. John's and the Monumental. *** St. John's** (Episcopal) is a plain edifice with a modern spire, on Church Hill, cor. Broad and 24th Sts. It is of ante-Revolutionary origin, and in it was held (in 1775) the Virginia Convention to decide the action of the colony, on which occasion Patrick Henry made his celebrated speech containing the words, "Give me liberty or give me death!" St. John's Church was subsequently, in 1788, the scene of the meeting of the convention to determine whether Virginia would ratify the Federal Constitution. The

* **Monumental Church** (Episcopal), cor. Broad and 13th Sts., is a handsome edifice, with a dome, standing on the spot formerly occupied by the Richmond Theatre. In 1811, during the performance of a piece called "The Bleeding Nun," the theatre caught fire, and, in the terror and confusion of the crowd rushing to the doors, 69 persons, including the Governor of Virginia and some of the most eminent men and beautiful women of the State, were crushed or burned to death. The church was erected as a memorial of the event, the remains of the victims being interred beneath a mural tablet in the vestibule. Of the more modern structures, * **St. Paul's** (Episcopal), cor. Grace and 9th Sts., is the most imposing. In it Jefferson Davis was seated when a messenger brought him the fatal news that Lee was about to evacuate Petersburg. The old *African Church* is a long, low building in Broad St., near Monumental Church, famous as a place of political meetings before and during the war.

Of the several cemeteries of Richmond, * **Hollywood** (reached by horse-cars) is the principal. It is a spot of great natural beauty, in the W. limits of the city, above James River, and embraces an extensive tract, alternately hill and dale, the whole ornamented with venerable trees, shrubs, and flowers. On the hill at the S. extremity, a monument marks the resting-place of President Monroe. Other persons of note are buried here, among them General J. E. B. Stuart, commander of Lee's cavalry. In the soldiers' section are the graves of hundreds of Confederate dead, from the midst of which rises a monumental pyramid of rough stone. *Monroe Park* is near the W. and *Marshall Park* (Libby Hill) near the E. end of the city. From the latter a fine river view may be had. Five bridges across the river connect Richmond with Spring Hill and *Manchester*, the latter a pretty town with two fine cotton-mills. The *Tredegar Iron-Works*, which were the great cannon manufactory of the Confederacy, are worth a visit. The buildings cover 15 acres of ground. The *Gallego* and *Haxall Flour-Mills* are among the largest in the world. A carriage may be taken and within a few hours' ride from the city several battle-fields and National Cemeteries visited.

101. Richmond to Charleston.
a. By "Atlantic Coast Line."

The "**Atlantic Coast Line**," a combination of nineteen different roads, is the fast mail and passenger route to the South. It runs two fast express trains daily, with Pullman palace cars attached, from Boston to Charleston and Savannah, without change of cars. The route from Boston to New York is *via* Route 13; from New York to Philadelphia *via* Route 3 *a;* from Philadelphia to Baltimore *via* Route 5; from Baltimore to Washington *via* Route 7; from Washington to Richmond *via* Route 100 *a;* from Richmond to Charleston as described below; and from Richmond to Savannah *via* Route 102 *a.* The schedule time from New York to Charleston is 33 hours; to Savannah, 39 hours.

LEAVING Richmond the train crosses the James River on a handsome bridge and runs in 23 miles to **Petersburg** (*Jarratt's Hotel, Bollingbrook*), a well-built city of about 25,000 inhabitants, situated at the head of navigation on the Appomattox River, 12 miles above its entrance into the James. Its trade is large, the handling of tobacco and cotton, with wheat, corn, and general country produce, being the chief business. The principal buildings are the Custom-House and Post-Office, the Court-House, two market-houses, and the Theatre. There is a public park called Poplar Lawn. Petersburg was the scene of the last great struggles during the late civil war. Since the war, the place has prospered, and the marks of the conflict are rapidly disappearing; but the fortifications are still distinctly traceable, and the chief battlefields, etc., are easily found. *Weldon* (86 miles) is a thriving post-village in North Carolina, at the head of steamboat navigation on Roanoke River. Here the Seaboard & Roanoke R. R. (see Route 99) from Portsmouth and Norfolk connects. Beyond Weldon the country is flat and uninteresting, the road traversing for many miles the great pine belt which extends from Virginia to Florida. **Goldsboro** (164 miles, *Gregory House*) is a prosperous town of 5,000 inhabitants, near the Neuse River, at the head of navigation, and at the intersection of the Atlantic & North Carolina R. R. Eighty-four miles beyond, passing many small stations *en route*, the train reaches **Wilmington** (*Purcell House, National Hotel*), the largest city of North Carolina, situated in the S. E. corner of the State, upon the Cape Fear River, 20 miles from the sea. Wilmington has an extensive commerce, both coastwise and foreign, and has long been the leading market for naval stores in the world. There are regular lines of steamers to Baltimore, Philadelphia, and New York. The principal articles of shipment are lumber, turpentine, rosin, tar, pitch, shingles, and cotton. The population of the city is about 18,000. Street cars run through the principal streets to *Oakdale Cemetery* and to the R. R. depots. *The Sound*, a place of summer resort, is 7 miles distant; and *Fort Fisher*, which played so conspicuous a part in the civil war, is 20 miles below, at the mouth of the river. From Wilmington to Florence (108 miles) the country is of the same featureless and monotonous character, the route now being through South Carolina. *Florence* (356 miles) is a place of considerable commercial importance by reason of its railroad facilities, and is the point of shipment for most of the cotton of the adjacent country. Here the Charleston train takes the track of the Northeastern R. R. which runs to Charleston in 102 miles, through an uninteresting region. **Charleston** (458 miles) is described on page 426.

b. Via Charlotte and Columbia.

From Richmond to Charlotte this route is by the Piedmont Air Line R. R. (which comprises the Richmond & Danville and North Carolina Railways). Crossing the James River on a substantial covered bridge, the train passes through the populous suburb of *Manchester*, and runs S. W. through a famous tobacco-growing region to *Burkeville* (53 miles), situated at the intersection of the Atlantic, Mississippi and Ohio R. R., formerly the *South Side Railway*, which played so prominent a part in the siege of Petersburg.

In April, 1865, Burkeville became a place of critical importance. General Lee, having evacuated Petersburg on the night of April 2d, retreated up the N. bank of the Appomattox, and, recrossing, reached Amelia Court-House, from which it was

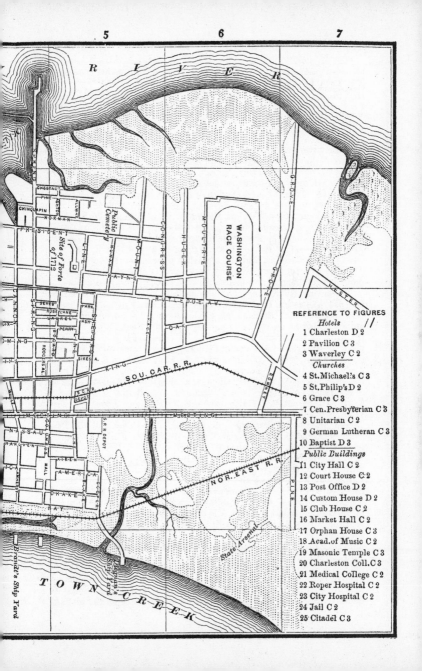

REFERENCE TO FIGURES

Hotels
1 Charleston D 2
2 Pavilion C 3
3 Waverley C 2

Churches
4 St. Michael's C 3
5 St. Philip's D 2
6 Grace C 3
7 Cen. Presbyterian C 3
8 Unitarian C 2
9 German Lutheran C 3
10 Baptist D 3

Public Buildings
11 City Hall C 2
12 Court House C 2
13 Post Office D 2
14 Custom House D 2
15 Club House C 2
16 Market Hall C 2
17 Orphan House C 3
18 Acad. of Music C 2
19 Masonic Temple C 3
20 Charleston Coll. C 3
21 Medical College C 2
22 Roper Hospital C 2
23 City Hospital C 2
24 Jail C 2
25 Citadel C 3

his design to advance to Burkeville Junction. General Grant moved more rapidly toward the same point from Petersburg, and, having a shorter distance to pass over, reached the place before Lee, who was forced to halt at Amelia Court-House to obtain rations. The presence of General Grant at Burkeville induced Lee to alter his line of march and retire toward Lynchburg, which resulted, April 9, 1865, in the surrender of the Confederate forces at Appomattox Court-House. The scene of the surrender was near *Appomattox*, a station on the Atlantic, Mississippi & Ohio R. R., 48 miles W. of Burkeville and 23 miles E. of Lynchburg

Thirty-two miles beyond Burkeville is *Roanoke*, the name of which will recall the famous orator "John Randolph of Roanoke," who passed almost his entire life in this region. *Danville* (140 miles) is a town of 3,500 inhabitants, pleasantly situated at the head of navigation on the Dan River. It is the market town of the best tobacco-growing section of Virginia, and has an active trade. Connection is made here with the Washington City, Virginia Midland & Great Southern R. R., which forms with the present line a popular through route (known as the "Virginia Midland") from Washington *via* Lynchburg to the South-Atlantic States (see Route 113). Five miles beyond Danville the train enters North Carolina, and soon reaches *Greensboro* (McAdoo House), a rapidly growing town, situated in the midst of a rich tobacco-producing region, and near valuable deposits of coal, iron, and copper.

From Greensboro a branch line runs S. E. in 130 miles to *Goldsboro* (see p. 423), passing **Raleigh** (*Yarborough House, National*), the capital of North Carolina. Raleigh is a city of about 8,000 inhabitants, pleasantly situated on an elevation 6 miles W. of the Neuse River and a little N. E. of the center of the State. It is regularly laid out, with a park of 10 acres in the center (*Union Square*), from which extend 4 streets, dividing the city into 4 parts, in each of which is a square of 4 acres. In Union Square is the beautiful * *State House*, built of granite, after the model of the Parthenon, at a cost of $531,000. The old State House, containing Cánova's statue of Washington, was burned in 1831. Other public buildings are the *U. S. Custom-House and Post-Office*, a fine granite structure, the *State Geological Museum*, the *State Insane Asylum*, the *Institution for the Deaf and Dumb*, and the *Penitentiary*. Raleigh is also reached from *Weldon* (see p. 423) by the Raleigh & Gaston R. R. (distance, 97 miles).

The next important station S. of Greensboro on the main line is *Salisbury* (238 miles), where connection is made with the Western North Carolina R. R., by which the tourist may reach the Mountain Region (see Route 118). Forty-four miles beyond is **Charlotte** (*Central Hotel*), a busy little city of 5,000 inhabitants, on Sugar Creek, at the junction of several important railways. It is situated on the gold range of the Atlantic States, and its prosperity is chiefly owing to the working of the mines in its vicinity. A U. S. Assay Office (formerly a branch mint) is located here. A plank road 120 miles long connects Charlotte with Fayetteville. From Charlotte the route is *via* the Charlotte, Columbia & Augusta R. R., which runs S. through a pleasant and productive farming region, and in 110 miles (392 miles from Richmond) reaches **Columbia** (*Wright's Hotel, Wheeler House*), the capital of South Carolina. Columbia is a beautiful city, situated on the bluffs of the Congaree, a few miles below the charming falls of that river. It was famous for its delightfully shaded streets and its wonderful flower-gardens, but the aspect of the city was greatly changed by the unfortunate conflagration which destroyed so large a part of it during its occupation by General Sherman's forces, in Feb., 1865. The streets, however, are still abundantly shaded, and there are many attractive drives in the vicinity. The view from *Arsenal Hill* is the most beautiful in this portion of South Carolina. The *State House*, when completed, will be one of the handsomest public buildings in the United States; it has cost $3,000,000, and about $1,000,000 more will be required to finish it. The *Executive Mansion* has grounds laid out in walks, gardens, and drives, and commands a picturesque view of the Congaree Valley. The *State Penitentiary* is a vast structure situated in a plot of 20 acres at the junction of the Broad and Saluda Rivers, within the city limits. The *Lunatic Asylum* occupies a group of spacious buildings in the N. E. part of the city. The grounds, 4 acres in extent, are surrounded by an inclosure and beautified with gardens, hot-houses, and walks. Other noteworthy public buildings are the U. S. Court-House and Post-Office, the City-Hall, and the Market-House. There are several important educational institutions, of which the principal are the *University of South Carolina*, which has substantial brick buildings in grounds 12 acres in extent, with a library of 27,000 volumes; the *Presbyterian Theological Seminary*, with a library of 18,340 volumes; the *Lutheran Theological Seminary*, with 4,000 volumes; and the *Columbia Male Academy*, founded in 1785. The car-shops of C. C. & A. R. R. occupy 4 acres of ground, and there are other large manufacturing establishments. The * *Fair Grounds* of the South Carolina Agricultural and Mechanical Society, in the N. W. suburbs, contain about 30 acres, with spacious buildings, and are well supplied with fountains, fish-ponds, a race-course, etc. *Sydney Park* contains about 25 acres tastefully laid out and adorned with trees and shrubbery.

From Columbia to Charleston (*via* South Carolina R. R.), the journey will give the traveler some inkling of the lowland features of Southern landscape, though not in its most interesting character, since the country is level, and most of the way is through extensive pine-forests. The only station on the line requiring mention is *Summerville* (22 miles from Charleston), a small village situated on a pine-clad ridge which extends across from the Cooper to the Ashley River. Its climate is remarkably agreeable, and the place is attracting attention as a winter-resort.

Charleston.

Hotels, etc.—The best hotels are the *Charleston Hotel* ($2.50 to $4 a day), in Meeting St. between Hayne and Pinckney Sts.; the *Pavilion Hotel* ($2 to $2.50 a day), cor. Meeting and Hasel Sts.; and the *Waverley House* ($2 a day), in King St. near Hasel. *Horse-cars* (fare 5c.) traverse the city and afford easy access to the chief points of interest. *Omnibuses* are in waiting at the depots and landings on the arrival of trains and steamers, and convey passengers to any portion of the city (fare 50c.). Besides the rail-routes described above Charleston is reached from New York by *Steamers* (" New York & Charleston Line ") leaving Pier 27 North River

at 3 P. M. on Wednesdays and Saturdays. Time, about 3 days; fare (cabin), $20.
Also from Philadelphia by weekly steamers (fare $15), and from Baltimore every 5
days.

Charleston, the chief commercial city of South Carolina, is picturesquely situated at the confluence of the Ashley and Cooper Rivers, in
lat. 32° 45' N., and lon. 79° 57' W. The rivers run a parallel course
for nearly 6 miles, widening as they approach the sea, and thus gradually narrowing the site of the city to a peninsula. The corporate limits
of the city extend from Battery or White Point, on the extreme S.
verge of the city, to an arbitrary line on the N. about 3 miles above.
Within this area the city is laid out with tolerable regularity, the streets
generally crossing each other at right angles. The houses are mostly
of brick or wood, and have large open grounds around them, ornamented
with trees and shrubbery. The two principal streets are King and
Meeting, which run N. and S., nearly parallel, the whole length of the
city, but converge to intersection near the northern limits. *King St.*
contains the leading retail stores, and is the fashionable promenade.
The jobbing and wholesale stores are chiefly in *Meeting St.* ; and the
banks, and brokers' and insurance offices, are in *Broad St.* The
* **Battery** is a popular promenade, lying near the water's edge, and
commanding an extensive view of the Bay; it is surrounded by fine
private residences. Fine residences are also found in Meeting St. below Broad, in Rutledge St. and Ave., and at the W. end of Wentworth
St. The roads leading out of the city along the Ashley and Cooper
Rivers are singularly beautiful, and afford interesting drives. They are
all embowered in loveliest foliage; pines, oaks, magnolias, myrtles, and
jasmines vying with each other in tropical luxuriance and splendor.
There are also fine drives on Sullivan's Island (reached by ferry).

Charleston was settled in 1679 by an English colony under William Sayle, who
became the first Governor. It played a conspicuous part in the Revolution, having
been the first among the chief places of the South to assert a common cause with
and for the colonies. It was thrice assaulted by the British, and only yielded to a
six weeks' siege by an overwhelming force, May 12, 1780. It was the leading city,
both in the nullification movement during Jackson's administration and in the incipient stages of Southern secession. Open hostilities in the civil war began at
Charleston, with the bombardment of Fort Sumter on April 12, 1861; and for the
next four years it was one of the chief points of Federal attack, without being lost
by the Confederates, however, until Sherman's capture of Columbia on February 17,
1865. During the war many buildings were destroyed, and the towers and steeples
of churches riddled with shot and shell. Since its close rapid progress has been
made in the work of rebuilding, and Charleston is now more prosperous than ever.
The growth of population has been as follows : In 1800 it was 18,711; in 1850, 42,-
985; in 1860, 40,519 ; and in 1870, 48,956. The commerce of the city is large, the
chief exports being cotton (for which it is one of the chief shipping-ports), rice,
naval stores, and fertilizers. The manufacture of fertilizers from the valuable beds
of marl and phosphate, discovered in 1868, is now one of the principal industries;
but there are also flour and rice mills, bakeries, carriage and wagon factories, and
machine-shops.

Of the public buildings of Charleston, several of the most important
are clustered at the intersection of Broad and Meeting Sts. On the N.
E. corner is the * **City Hall,** an imposing building, entered by a
double flight of marble steps, and standing in an open square. The
Council-Chamber is handsomely furnished, and contains some interest-

ing portraits. On the N. W. corner is the *Court-House*, a substantial structure of brick, faced so as to resemble stone. On the S. W. corner is the *Guardhouse*, or Police Headquarters, a plain brick building, with a colonnade extending over the sidewalk in Broad St.; and on the S. E. corner stands the venerable * **St. Michael's Church** (Episcopal), built in 1752, it is said from designs by a pupil of Sir Christopher Wren. The tower is considered very fine, and the situation of the church makes the spire a conspicuous object far out at sea. Its chimes are celebrated for their age and sweetness. The * view from the belfry is very fine, embracing the far stretch of sea and shore, the fortresses in the harbor, the shipping, and nearer at hand buildings as ancient as the church itself. At the foot of Broad St. stands the *Post-Office*, a venerable structure, dating from the colonial period, the original material having been brought from England in 1761. It was much battered during the war, but has since been renovated. The new * **U. S. Custom-House,** which has been building for several years and is still unfinished, is situated just S. of the Market-wharf, on Cooper River. It is of white marble, in the Roman-Corinthian style, and will be the finest edifice in the city. A noble view is obtained from its graceful Corinthian portico. The *U. S. Court-House* (formerly the Charleston Club-House) is a neat building, in Meeting St. between Broad and Tradd, with a pretty garden in front. The *Chamber of Commerce* occupies the 2d and 3d floors of a handsome building at the cor. of Broad and E. Bay Sts.; it has a good reading-room and a restaurant for the use of the members. The *Academy of Music*, cor. King and Market Sts., is one of the finest theatres in the South. It is 60 by 231 ft., and cost $160,000. Besides the theatre, with accommodations for 1,200, it contains two large halls for concerts, lectures, etc. The *Masonic Temple* is a large but fantastic building, at the cor. of King and Wentworth Sts. The old * **Orphan-House,** standing in the midst of spacious grounds, between Calhoun and Vanderhorst Sts., is the most imposing edifice in the city, and one of the most famous institutions of the kind in the country. John C. Fremont, once a candidate for the presidency, and C. C. Memminger, Confederate Secretary of the Treasury, were educated there. A statue of William Pitt, erected during the Revolution, stands in the center of the grounds. The *College of Charleston*, founded in 1788, has spacious buildings, located in the square bounded by George, Green, College, and St. Philip Sts. It has a library of about 6,000 volumes, and a valuable museum of natural history. The *Medical College*, cor. Queen and Franklin Sts., and *Roper Hospital*, cor. Queen and Logan Sts., are large and handsome buildings, the latter especially so. On the same square with these two are the *City Hospital* and *County Jail*. The *Workhouse*, near by, in Magazine St., is a spacious castellated structure in the Norman style. The *Charleston Library*, founded in 1748, has a plain but commodious building at the cor. of Broad and Church Sts. It lost heavily in the fire of 1861, but now contains about 17,000 volumes. The *South Carolina Society Hall*, in Meeting St. near St. Michael's Church, is a substantial structure, with colonnade and portico, and a fine interior

* **Market Hall,** in Meeting St. near the Bay, is a fine building, in temple form, standing on a high, open basement, having a lofty portico in front, reached by a double flight of stone steps. In rear of this building are the markets, consisting of a row of low sheds supported by brick arches, and extending to E. Bay St. Between 6 and 9 A. M. these markets present one of the most characteristic sights that the stranger can see in Charleston.

After St. Michael's (already described) the most interesting church edifice in Charleston is * **St. Philip's** (Episcopal), in Church St. near Queen. It was the first church establishment in Charleston ; but the present structure, although of venerable age, is yet not quite so old as St. Michael's. The view from the steeple is fine ; but there is a keener interest in the graveyard than even in the old church itself, for here lie South Carolina's most illustrious dead. In the portion of the grave-yard that lies across the street is the tomb of John C. Calhoun. It consists of a plain granite slab, supported by walls of brick, and for inscription has simply the name of " CALHOUN." *St. Finbar's Cathedral*, (Roman Catholic), or rather the ruins of it (for the building was destroyed in the great fire of 1861), is at the cor. of Broad and Friend Sts. It was one of the costliest edifices in Charleston, and the walls, turrets, and niches, still standing, are highly picturesque. The *Citadel Square Baptist Church*, cor. Meeting and Henrietta Sts., is a fine building, in the Norman style, with a spire 220 ft. high. The *Central Presbyterian*, in Meeting St. near Society, has an elegant Corinthian portico with 8 columns. The *Unitarian Church*, in Archdale St. near Queen, is a fine specimen of the perpendicular Gothic style, and has a very rich interior. The new *German Lutheran Church*, in King St. opposite the Citadel, is a handsome building, in the Gothic style, with lofty and ornate spire. *Grace Church* (Episcopal), in Wentworth St., is the most fashionable in the city. The old *Huguenot Church*, cor. Church and Queen Sts., is worthy of a visit, if for no other purpose, to see the quaint and elegant mural entablatures with which its walls are lined.

Just outside of the city, on the N. boundary, is * **Magnolia Cemetery** (reached by horse-cars). It is embowered in magnolias and live-oaks, is tastefully laid out, and contains some fine monuments, of which the most noteworthy are those to Colonel Wm. Washington, of Revolutionary fame, Hugh Legaré, and W. Gilmore Simms, the novelist. Perhaps the most interesting spot in the neighborhood of Charleston is the old * **Church of St. James,** on Goose Creek (reached by carriage, or by Northeastern R. R. to Porcher's Station, 15 miles). It is situated in the very heart of a forest, is approached by a road little better than a bridle-path, and is entirely isolated from habitations of any sort. The church was built in 1711, and was saved from destruction during the Revolutionary War by the royal arms of England that are emblazoned over the pulpit. The floor is of stone, the pews are square and high, the altar, reading-desk, and pulpit are so small as to seem like miniatures of ordinary church-fixtures, and on the walls and altar are tablets in memory of the early members of the congregation. One dates from 1711 and two from 1717.—A short distance from the church, on the other side of the main road, is a farm known as *The Oaks*, from the magnificent avenue of those trees by which it is approached. The trees are believed to be nearly 200 years old; they have attained great size, and for nearly ¼ mile form a continuous arch over the broad road.

The harbor of Charleston is a large estuary, extending about 7 miles to the Atlantic, with an average width of 2 miles. It is landlocked on all sides except an entrance about a mile in width. The passage to the inner harbor is defended by four fortresses. On the right at the entrance is *Fort Moultrie*, on Sullivan's Island, occupying the site of the fort which, on June 28, 1776, beat off the British fleet of Sir Peter Parker. On the left, raised upon a shoal in the harbor and directly covering the channel, is * **Fort Sumter,** rendered famous by the part which it played in the opening scene of the civil war. Immediately in front of the city, and but 1 mile from it, is *Castle Pinckney*, covering the crest of a mud-shoal, and facing the entrance. A fine view of the city is obtained in entering the harbor from the sea; and, as it is built on low and level land, it seems to rise from the water as we approach, whence it has been called the "American Venice." *Sullivan's Island* is fast becoming the "Long Branch" of South Carolina, and contains many handsome cottages and some attractive drives. A steamboat plies regularly every hour between the city, Sullivan's Island, and *Mount Pleasant;* the latter being a popular picnic resort.

102. Richmond to Savannah.
a. By "Atlantic Coast Line."

THE Savannah through cars of the "Atlantic Coast Line" run by way of Charleston; and the route from Richmond to Charleston has been described in Route 101 *a*. From Charleston to Savannah the route is *via* Savannah & Charleston R. R. (distance, 115 miles), which runs within a few miles of the Atlantic coast line, though never in sight of the ocean. For miles the rails are laid on piles, passing through marsh and morass, and crossing swift-rushing, dirty streams, dignified by the name of rivers, and baptized with unpronounceable Indian names. There are no towns of importance on the line, but the scenery is wild and rich. Extensive pine-forests, lofty cypresses, wreathed in garlands of pendent moss, the bay and the laurel, draped with the vines of the wild grape and of ivy, and huge oaks that have stood the wear and tear of centuries, line the road on either side. Noble avenues are created by these forest giants, and pendent from their stalwart limbs hang long festoons of moss and vine, dimly veiling the vista beyond. At *Yemassee* (61 miles) the Savannah & Charleston R. R. is intersected by the Port Royal R. R., which extends from Augusta to *Beaufort* and *Port Royal* (112 miles). **Savannah** (see p. 431).

b. Via Charlotte, Columbia, and Augusta (609 *miles*).

As far as **Columbia** (see p. 425) this route is the same as Route 101 *b*. Beyond Columbia the Charlotte, Columbia & Augusta R. R.

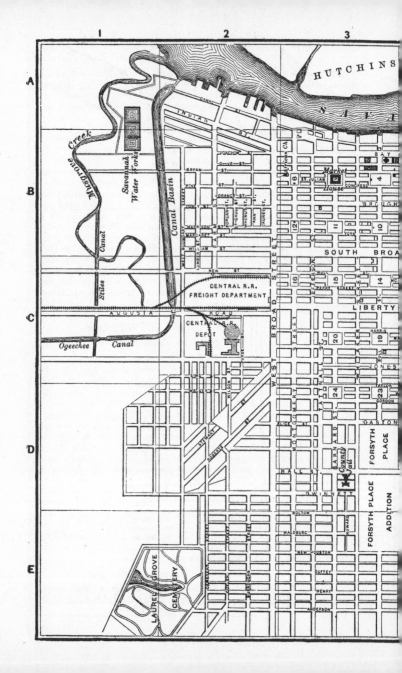

REFERENCE TO SQUARES

1 Washington Square
2 Warren
3 Reynolds
4 Johnson
5 Ellis
6 Franklin
7 Green
8 Columbia
9 Oglethorpe
10 Wright
11 St. James
12 Liberty
13 Crawford
14 Chippewa
15 Orleans
16 Elbert
17 Troup
18 La Fayette
19 Madison
20 Pulaski
21 Whitefield
22 Calhoun
23 Monterey
24 Chatham

CITY OF
SAVANNAH

Scale of Yards

0   440   880

continues on through a level, wooded region, unmarked by any striking features.   *Graniteville* (511 miles) is a busy manufacturing town,
with several large granite cotton-mills, giving employment to several
hundred operatives who constitute the bulk of the population.   Here
connection is made with the South Carolina R. R., and on this railway,
6 miles from Graniteville, is **Aiken** (*Highland Park Hotel, Aiken,
Clarendon*), the most famous and frequented winter-resort in America.*
The land upon which it lies is an elevated plateau, some 600 or 700 ft.
above the sea.   The soil is an almost unmixed sand, covered by a
scanty crust of alluvium which is so thin that a carriage-wheel easily
breaks through.   It bears but little grass and hardly any of the minor
natural plants; but the great southern pine finds here a congenial
habitat, and vast forests of it encircle the town on all sides.   The
streets of the town are remarkably wide, the main avenue being 205
ft. wide, and the cross-streets 150 ft.   The houses are generally large
and pleasant, and very far apart.   Within the town, the natural bar-
renness of the soil has been overcome by careful culture and a liberal
use of fertilizers; and every house has its garden full of trees and
Southern plants.   Inside the white palings are dense thickets of yellow
jasmine, rose bushes, orange, wild-olive, and fig trees, bamboo, Spanish
bayonet, and numberless sorts of vines and creepers, to say nothing of
the low bush and surface flowers that are common in the North.   But,
without the palings, the sand is as dry and white as it is upon the sea-
shore.   The air of Aiken is remarkably pure and dry, and the balsamic
odors of the pines endow it with a peculiar healing power.   The winter
climate is wonderfully mild and genial, consisting, as some one has described it, of "four months of June."   From observations recorded
during the year 1870, it was found that the mean temperature of Aiken
in spring is 63·4°; in summer, 79·1°; in autumn, 63·7°; in winter, 46·4°;
for the year, 63·1½°.   The average rainfall during the same period was,
spring, 11·97 inches; summer, 13·89; autumn, 7·34; winter, 7·16; for
the year, 40·36.   The climate is as beneficial to rheumatic and gouty patients as to consumptives; and many visit Aiken who, without being
sick, desire to escape the rigors of a Northern winter.

Eleven miles beyond Graniteville the Savannah train reaches **Augusta** (*Central Hotel, Planter's, Globe*), the third city of Georgia in
population (about 30,000), and one of the most beautiful in the South.
It is situated at the head of navigation on the Savannah River, and
embraces an area of about 2 miles in length and a mile in breadth.   It
is regularly laid out, with broad streets crossing each other at right
angles, and many of them beautifully shaded.   *Broad St.* is the main
thoroughfare of the city, and is 165 ft. wide and 2 miles long.   On
it are the principal banks, hotels, and shops; and in the center of it
is the * *Confederate Monument* (the finest in the South), consisting of
an obelisk 80 ft. high, surmounted by a statue of a soldier, and with 4
portrait statues (including Lee and Jackson) on the corner pedestals.

---

* For full and minute description of Aiken, giving tables of comparative temperature, relative dryness (or humidity), etc., see APPLETONS' ILLUSTRATED HAND-
BOOK OF AMERICAN WINTER RESORTS.

* *Greene St.* is 168 ft. wide and lined with handsome residences; tall, spreading trees not only grace the sidewalks, but a double row, with grassy spaces between, runs down the center of the ample roadway. Of the public buildings, the * *City Hall*, completed in 1824 at a cost of $100,000, and set in an ample green amid tall trees, is the most attractive. In front of it stands a granite monument erected by the city in 1849 to the memory of the Georgian signers of the Declaration of Independence. The *Masonic Hall*, the *Odd-Fellows' Hall*, the new *Orphan Asylum*, and the *Opera House* are handsome edifices. The commerce of Augusta is very prosperous, and the fine water-power secured by means of the *Augusta Canal*, 9 miles long, which brings the upper waters of the Savannah River to the city at an elevation of 40 ft., is enriching it with extensive manufactures. Just outside of the city, and E. of the *City Cemetery*, are the * *Fair Grounds* of the Cotton States Mechanics' and Agricultural Fair Association, comprising 47 acres, laid out in attractive walks and drives. A most charming view of Augusta and its environs may be had from **Summerville,** a suburban town of handsome villas situated on high hills about 3 miles from the city (reached by horse-cars). Among the objects of interest at Summerville are the *U. S. Arsenal*, built in 1827, and the range of workshops, 500 ft. in length, built and used by the Confederates during the war. Across the river from Augusta at Hamburg there are some beautiful wooded and grassy terraces, known as *Schultz's Hill*, and much resorted to as a picnic-ground.

From Augusta to Savannah (132 miles), the route is *via* the Central R. R. of Georgia, which passes through one of the most productive and populous sections of the State. There are no points, however, of special interest on the line, all the towns being small and of merely local importance. At *Millen* (53 miles from Augusta), the road forks, one branch going to Macon and the other to Savannah.

Savannah.

Hotels, etc.—The leading hotels are the *Screven House*, ($2.50 to $3.50 a day), on Johnson Square; the *Pulaski House* ($2.50 to $3.50 a day), in Bryan St., Johnson Square; and the *Marshall House*, ($3 a day), in Broughton St. Besides the routes described above, Savannah is reached from New York by *Steamers* leaving Pier 35 North River, at 3 P. M., on Wednesdays and Saturdays. Time, about 3 days; fare (cabin). $20. There are also steamers to Savannah from Philadelphia every Saturday at noon, and from Boston and Baltimore once a week. Savannah is also reached from Charleston by steamer (fare $4).

Savannah, the chief city and commercial metropolis of Georgia, is situated on the S. bank of the Savannah River, 18 miles from its mouth. The site was selected by General Oglethorpe, the founder of the colony of Georgia, who made his first settlement at this point in Feb., 1733. The city occupies a bold bluff, about 40 ft. high, extending along the river-bank for a mile, and backward, widening as it recedes, about 6 miles. The river making a gentle curve around Hutchinson's Island, the water-front of the city is in the shape of an elongated crescent about 3 miles in length. The corporate limits extend back on the elevated plateau about 1½ mile, the total area of the city being 3⅓ sq. m. In

its general plan, Savannah is universally conceded to be one of the
handsomest of American cities. Its streets are broad and beautifully
shaded, they cross each other at right angles, and at many of the principal crossings are small public squares or parks from 1½ to 3 acres in
extent. These parks, 24 in number, located at equal distances through
the city, neatly enclosed, laid out in walks, and planted with the evergreen and ornamental trees of the South, are among the most characteristic features of Savannah ; and, in the spring and summer months,
when they are carpeted with grass, and the trees and shrubbery are in
full foliage, afford delightful shady walks, and playgrounds for the children, while they are not only ornamental, but conducive to the general
health by the free ventilation which they afford. The residences are
mostly surrounded by flower-gardens, which bloom throughout the year ;
and among the shrubbery, in which the city is literally embowered, are
the orange-tree, the banana, the magnolia, the bay, the laurel, the cape-
myrtle, the stately palmetto, the olive, the flowering oleander, and the
pomegranate.

Savannah was founded by Gen. Oglethorpe in 1733. In 1776 the British attacked
it and were repulsed ; but on December 29, 1779, they reappeared in overwhelming
force and took possession of the city. In October, 1779, the combined French and
Americans attempted to recapture it, but were unsuccessful, and Count Pulaski fell
in the engagement. Savannah received a city charter in 1789. In 1850 it had 15,312
inhabitants ; in 1860, 22,292; and in 1870, 28,235. In 1878 its population was locally estimated at 40,000. The chief business of the place is the receipt and shipment of cotton, though the trade in lumber is also considerable. As a cotton port
it ranks second in the United States. It recovered rapidly from the effect of the civil
war, and its commerce has since about doubled. The chief manufacturing establishments are planing-mills, foundries, and flouring and grist mills.

The great warehouses of the city are located on a narrow street at
the foot of the steep bluff ; they open below on the level of the piers,
and from the uppermost story on the other side upon a sandy area 200
ft. wide and divided by rows of trees. This is called the **Bay,** and is
the great commercial mart of Savannah. The principal business streets
are *Bull, Drayton,* and *Broad* Sts., and the favorite promenade is out
Bull St. to Forsyth Park. Among the noteworthy public buildings are
the granite * **Custom-House,** which also contains the *Post-Office,*
cor. Bull and Bay Sts. ; the *City Exchange,* in front of which General
Sherman reviewed his army, January 7, 1865 ; the *Court-House,* the
U. S. Barracks, the *Police Barracks, Artillery Armory,* and *Jail.* The
Chatham Academy and *St. Andrew's Hall* are conspicuous buildings.
From the tower of the Exchange the best * view of the city and neighborhood is to be had. The building on the N. E. cor. of Bull and
Broughton Sts., known as the *Masonic Hall,* is interesting as the place
where the Ordinance of Secession was passed, Jan. 21, 1861. Four
years later (Dec. 28, 1864), a meeting of citizens was held in the same
apartment to commemorate the triumph of the Union arms. The
* *Market* presents an animated and characteristic spectacle in the early
morning. The *Georgia Historical Society* has a large and beautiful
hall, in which are a fine library and some interesting relics. Of the
church edifices the Episcopal Churches of *St. John's* and *Christ's* are
the most striking. The former is in the Gothic, the latter in the Ionic

style. The lofty spire of the *Independent Presbyterian Church* is much admired. This church is built of Quincy granite, and cost $130,000.

Presbyterian Church.

Trinity Church is in Johnson Square, near the spot where Wesley delivered his famous sermons. The new Roman Catholic *Cathedral* is a fine edifice.

The most attractive place of public resort is * **Forsyth Park,** an inclosure of 30 acres in the S. part of the city. It is shaded by some venerable old trees, is laid out in serpentine walks, and ornamented with evergreen and flowering trees and shrubs. In the center is a handsome fountain, after the model of that in the Place de la Concorde, Paris, and a stately *Confederate Monument* stands in the new portion. In Johnson or *Monument Square*, near the center of the city, is a fine Doric obelisk, erected to the memory of General Greene and Count Pulaski, the corner-stone of which was laid by Lafayette, during his visit in 1825. The * **Pulaski Monument** stands in Monterey Square, and is one of the most chaste and perfect specimens of monumental architecture in the United States. The steps are plinths of granite;

the shaft is of purest marble, 55 ft. high, and is surmounted by an exquisitely-carved statue of Liberty, holding the national banner. The monument appropriately covers the spot where Pulaski fell, during an attack upon the city while it was occupied by the British, in 1779.

Though built upon a sandy plain, Savannah is not without suburban attractions, there being several places in its vicinity whose sylvan character and picturesque beauty are in keeping with the "Forest City" itself. Thunderbolt, Isle of Hope, Beaulieu, Montgomery, and White Bluff, are all rural retreats on "The Salts," within short driving-distance of the city, where, in the summer months, bracing sea-breezes and salt-water bathing may be enjoyed. The great drive is to * **Bonaventure Cemetery,** which is situated on Warsaw River, a branch of the Savannah, about 4 miles from the city. The scenery of Bonaventure has long been renowned for its Arcadian beauty; for its broad avenues of live-oaks draped in pendant gray moss. *Laurel Grove,* the municipal cemetery, lies N. W. of the city, near Forsyth Park. *Thunderbolt,* a popular drive and summer-resort, is on the Warsaw River, 1 mile beyond Bonaventure. According to local tradition, this place received its name from the fall of a thunderbolt. A spring of water which issued from the spot upon that event has continued to flow ever since. *Jasper Spring,* 2½ miles W. of the city, is the scene of the famous Revolutionary exploit of Sergeant Jasper, who, with only one companion, successfully assailed a British guard of eight men and released a party of American prisoners. *White Bluff,* 10 miles out, is another favorite resort of the Savannah people, and the road to it is one of the most fashionable drives.

103. Charleston or Savannah to Jacksonville, Florida.

Steamer Routes.—(1) A steamer of the Florida line leaves Charleston every Tuesday and Saturday (on the arrival of New York steamer), and runs *via* Savannah to Fernandina, Jacksonville, and up the St. John's River to Pilatka, stopping at the principal landings. The steamer leaving Charleston on Saturday morning reaches Savannah Saturday afternoon, Jacksonville Sunday morning, and Pilatka Sunday afternoon. Fare, Charleston to Jacksonville, $14; to Pilatka, $16. (2) The "*Inside Line*" of steamers (running behind the fringe of islands that lines the coast) leaves Savannah on Mondays, Tuesdays, Thursdays, and Saturdays at 5 P. M., and reaches Jacksonville the next day (fare, $10).

The all-rail route from Savannah to Jacksonville is *via* Atlantic & Gulf R. R. to *Dupont* (130 miles), thence *via* Florida Div. to *Live Oak* (179 miles), and thence *via* Jacksonville, Pensacola & Mobile R. R. to *Jacksonville* (total distance to Jacksonville, 261 miles; fare, $8.40). The Atlantic and Gulf R. R. is the great connecting link between the railways from the North (*via* Savannah) and Southern Georgia and Florida. The main line runs S. W. from Savannah to *Bainbridge* on the Flint River (236 miles). Numerous small towns are clustered along the line, but the only one that need be mentioned is **Thomasville** (200 miles from Savannah), which has lately begun to attract attention as a winter resort. It is a pretty town of about 4,000 inhabitants, situated at the N. verge of the great pine-forest which stretches across Southern Georgia from E. to W. in a belt 75 miles wide. It stands on the highest ground between the Savannah and Flint Rivers, 300 ft. above the sea, and has the dry pure atmosphere, laden only with the odors of pine-forests, which consumptives highly prize. The streets of the town are broad and shady, and in the surrounding country, besides corn and cotton, grapes are produced in abundance. An excellent hotel (the *Mitchell House*), owned and conducted by Northern men, has been opened here.

Diverging from the main line at Dupont, the Florida Div. runs S. in 49 miles to *Live Oak*, which derives its importance from being situated at the junction with the Jacksonville, Pensacola & Mobile R. R. Eleven miles beyond Live Oak is the village of **Wellborn** (several boarding-houses), pleasantly situated, and a favorite resort for invalids. In the neighborhood are *Lake Wellborn* and other lakes, well stocked with fish. Eight miles distant are the *Suwanee White Sulphur Springs*, situated upon the beautiful banks of the Suwanee River. The *Upper White Sulphur Springs* are a few miles farther up the river. The waters of both springs are said to be a valuable cure in cases of rheumatism and dyspepsia. Twelve miles beyond Wellborn is **Lake City** (*Thrasher House, Central*), the most important place in this portion of Florida, with about 2,500 inhabitants. Within the city limits are Lakes Isabella, De Soto, and Hamburg, and Indian or Alligator Lake is only half a mile away. The climate of Lake City is very similar to that of Jacksonville, but the air is thought to be somewhat drier, while the rich balsamic odors from the surrounding forests endow it with exceptional curative and healing power, and render the neighborhood remarkably beneficial to consumptives in the more advanced stages of the disease. *Olustee* (12 miles beyond Lake City) is noted as the site of a battle between the Federal and Confederate forces, fought in Feb., 1864, in which the former were defeated. *Baldwin* is a small station at the crossing of the Fernandina and Cedar Keys R. R. (Route 108).

Jacksonville.

Hotels, etc.—The principal hotels are the *St. James* ($4 a day), the *Carlton* ($3 a day), the *Windsor* ($3 a day), the *Nicholls House* ($3 a day), the *Metropolitan* ($2 to $2.50 a day), the *Moncrieff House* ($1 to $2 a day), and the *St. John's* ($1.50 to $2). There are said to be upward of a hundred boarding-houses, at which the prices range from $8 to $20 per week. Good furnished rooms, including lights, fuel, and attendance, may be had in private houses for from $4 to $6 per week, and board without rooms is $11 per week at the hotels, and less at the boarding-houses. Unfurnished cottages can be hired at from $20 to $30 per month.

Jacksonville, the largest city in Florida, is situated on the right bank of the St. John's River, about 25 miles from its mouth. It was named after General Andrew Jackson, was laid out as a town in 1822, had a population of 1,045 in 1850, and of 6,912 in 1870. Its resident population is now about 14,000, which is largely increased during the winter months by transient visitors. The city is regularly laid out, with streets crossing each other at right angles and shaded with trees. The principal thoroughfare is *Bay St.*, and on this are situated the leading hotels and stores. On the N. W. side of the city is a picturesque bluff, covered with fine residences, and commanding a beautiful view of the river. There are several suburban villages (East Jacksonville, Springfield, Brooklyn, River Side, Arlington, St. Nicholas, South Shore, and Alexandria), and those on the other side of the river are connected with the city by ferry. Besides several good schools, Jacksonville contains Catholic, Episcopal, Presbyterian, Methodist, and Baptist churches ; a circulating library and a free reading-room ; half a dozen newspapers ; banks, public halls, and telegraphic connections with all parts of the United States. The commerce of the city is extensive, the chief business being the cutting and shipment of lumber ; cotton, sugar, fruit, fish, and early vegetables are also shipped to Northern and foreign ports. Jacksonville is much resorted to by invalids on account of its mild and salubrious climate ; and many prefer remaining here to going farther into the interior, on account of the superior accommodations which it offers, and its social advantages. The mean temperature of Jacksonville, as reported by the chief signal-officer of the United States, is 69·6° ; of the coldest month (January) 52·7° ; of the hottest month (July) 83·4°. Frost is unknown in Southern Florida, and is comparatively light even in the N. part of the State. It occurs oftenest between November and March, being most frequent in December and January, and rarely showing itself in October and April as far north as Jacksonville. As a general thing no frost occurs throughout the year below lat. 28° N. Summer being the rainy season in Florida, the winters are usually clear and dry. By observations taken for a period of 22 years at Jacksonville it was found that January averaged 20 clear days ; February, 19 ; March, 20 ; April, 25 ; May, 22 ; June, 17 ; July, 18 ; August, 19 ; September, 17 ; October, 19 ; November, 20 ; and December, 20. It must not be inferred, moreover, that rain fell on all the days which could not be registered as clear ; it may be said in general terms that from October to May there are not more than four or five rainy days in a month. Among the amusements at Jacksonville are excursions on the river and drives on the excellent shell-roads which lead out of the city. A favorite drive is to *Moncrief's Spring* (4 miles), whose waters are said to cure malarial diseases. There are bath-houses here, a restaurant, a bowling-alley, a dancing-pavilion, and a race-course.

104. Jacksonville to St. Augustine.

St. Augustine is reached from Jacksonville by daily steamer to Tocoi on the St. John's River (57 miles), and thence by railway (15 miles). Fare from Jacksonville, $4. The steamboat journey is over one of the most attractive reaches of the river (see Route 105), and from the car the traveler has an excellent chance to see some characteristic Florida scenery. The entrance to the city is exceedingly picturesque, and should be noted by the traveler.

St. Augustine.

Hotels, etc.—The principal hotels are the *St. Augustine* ($4 a day), fronting on the Plaza and Charlotte St. ; the *Magnolia* ($4 a day), in St. George St. near the Plaza ; and the *Florida House* ($4 a day), cor. St. George and Treasury Sts. There are also numerous boarding-houses, at which board may be had for from $10 to $15 a week. Two lines of sailing packets ply between St. Augustine and New York.

St. Augustine is situated on the Atlantic coast of Florida, about 40 miles S. of the mouth of the St. John's River, and 33 S. E. of Jacksonville. It occupies a narrow peninsula formed by the Matanzas River on the E., and the St. Sebastian on the S. and W., the site being a flat, sandy level, encompassed for miles around by a tangled undergrowth of low palmettos and bushes of various descriptions. Directly in front lies Anastasia Island, forming a natural breakwater, and almost entirely cutting off the sea-view. On the N. end of the island is a lighthouse with a revolving light, situated in lat. 29° 53′ N., and lon. 81° 16′ W. *St. George St.* is the Fifth Avenue of the place, and the other principal streets are *Tolomato St., Charlotte St.,* and *Bay St.* The latter commands a fine view of the harbor, Anastasia Island, and the ocean. All the streets are extremely narrow, the thoroughfares being only 12 or 15 ft. wide, while the cross-streets are narrower still. An advantage of these narrow streets in this warm climate is that they give shade, and increase the draught of air through them as through a flue. The principal streets were formerly paved with shell-concrete, portions of which are still to be seen above the shifting sand; and this flooring was so carefully swept that the dark-eyed maidens of Old Castile who once led society here could pass and repass without soiling their satin slippers. No rumbling wheels were permitted to crush the firm road-bed, or to whirl the dust into the airy verandas. All the old Spanish residences are built of coquina-stone, which is first stuccoed and then whitewashed. Many of them have hanging balconies along their second stories, which in the narrow streets seem almost to touch, and from which their respective occupants can chat confidentially and even shake hands. It must not be supposed, however, that St. Augustine is built wholly of coquina and in the Spanish style; there are many fine residences there in the American style, and in a few years St. Augustine will rival Newport in the number of its villas. A profusion of oranges, lemons, bananas, figs, date-palms, and all manner of tropical flowers and shrubs, ornament their grounds. A charming drive is out St. George St., through the City Gate to the beach of the San Sebastian.

The most interesting feature of St. Augustine is the old * **Fort of San Marco** (now *Fort Marion*), which is built of coquina, a unique conglomerate of fine shells and sand found in large quantities on Anastasia Island, at the entrance of the harbor, and quarried with great ease, though it becomes hard by exposure to the air. The fort stands on the sea-front at the N. E. end of the town. It was 100 years in building, and was completed in 1756, as is attested by the following inscription, which may still be seen over the gateway, together with the arms of Spain, handsomely carved in stone: " Don Fernando being King of Spain, and the Field-Marshal Don Alonzo Fernando Herida being governor and captain-general of this place, St. Augustine of Florida and its provinces, this fort was finished in the year 1756. The works were directed by the Captain-Engineer Don Pedro de Brazos y Gareny." While owned by the British, this was said to be the prettiest fort in the king's dominions. Its castellated batttlements; its formidable bastions, with their frowning guns; its lofty and imposing sally-port, surrounded by the royal Spanish arms; its portcullis, moat, and drawbridge; its circular and ornate sentry-boxes at each principal parapet-angle; its commanding lookout tower; and its stained and moss-grown massive walls—impress the external observer as a relic of the distant past; while a ramble through its heavy casemates—its crumbling Romish chapel, with elaborate portico and inner altar and holy-water niches; its dark passages, gloomy vaults, and more recent-ly-discovered dungeons—bring you to ready credence of its many tra-ditions of inquisitorial tortures; of decaying skeletons, found in the latest opened chambers, chained to the rusty ring-bolts, and of alleged subterranean passages to the neighboring convent. Next to the fort the great attraction is the * **Sea-Wall,** which, beginning at the water-battery of the fort, extends S. for nearly a mile, protecting the entire ocean-front of the city. It is built of coquina, with a granite coping 4 ft. wide, and furnishes a delightful promenade of a moonlight evening. Near the S. end of the wall are the *U. S. Barracks*, which are among the finest and most complete in the country. The building was formerly a Franciscan monastery, but has undergone extensive modifications and repairs. The old Spanish wall, which extended across the penin-sula from shore to shore and protected the city on the N., has crum-bled down or been removed, but the * **City Gate,** which originally formed a part of it, still stands at the head of St. George St. It is a picturesque and imposing structure, with lofty ornamented towers and loop-holes and sentry-boxes in a fair state of preservation.

In the center of the town is the *Plaza de la Constitucion*, nearly in the center of which stands a monument, about 20 ft. high, erected in 1812 in commemoration of the Spanish Liberal Constitution. Fronting on the Plaza are several imposing buildings, the most striking of which is the old * **Catholic Cathedral,** erected in 1793 at a cost of $17,-000. Its quaint Moorish belfry, with four bells set in separate niches, together with the clock, form a perfect cross. One of the bells bears the date of 1682. A neat Episcopal church also fronts on the Plaza, and there are Methodist, Baptist, and Presbyterian churches in the city. The old *Convent of St. Mary's* is an interesting building in St. George St., just W. of the Cathedral. In its rear is a more modern structure designated as the Bishop's Palace. The new *Convent of the Sisters of St. Joseph* is a tasteful coquina building on St. George St., S. of the Plaza; the old convent of this sisterhood is on Charlotte St., N. of the Barracks. The nuns are mainly occupied in teaching young girls, but they also manufacture lace of a very fine quality, and excel-lent palmetto hats. After the Cathedral, the most imposing edifice on the Plaza is the *Governor's Palace*, formerly the residence of the Span-ish Governors, but now used as Post-Office, City Clerk's Office, and Public Library. The old **Huguenot Burying-Ground,** on King Street near the City Gate, is a spot of much interest; and so is the *Military Burying-Ground* (just S. of the Barracks), where rest the re-mains of those who fell near here during the prolonged Seminole War. The *Soldiers' Monument*, erected in 1871, in honor of the Confederate dead, is located on St. George St., just S. of Bridge St.

Although the severe frost of 1835 killed all the trees and nearly put a stop to the culture of the orange in this part of Florida, there are many fine orange-groves in the environs of St. Augustine, and visits to them are among the unfailing delights of visitors. The harbor affords excellent opportunities for boating, and numerous points of interest attract excursion-parties. Among the most popular of these are those to the *North Beach*, one of the finest on the coast, affording an admirable view of the ocean; to the *South Beach ;* to the sand-hills, where General Oglethorpe planted his guns and laid siege to Fort Marion; to *Fish's Island ;* and to the light-houses and coquina-quarries on Anastasia Island. A pleasant trip is to *Matanzas*, where are the ruins of a fortress more ancient than any structure in the city itself; and *Matanzas Inlet* affords excellent camping-places for hunting and fishing parties. About 2½ miles off Matanzas an immense *Sulphur Spring* boils up out of the ocean where the water is 132 ft. deep, and is well worth a visit. Salt-water bathing may be practiced at St. Augustine in suitable bathing-houses, but the sharks render open sea-bathing dangerous.

St. Augustine is the oldest European settlement in the United States, having been founded by the Spaniards under Menendez in 1565, more than half a century before the landing of the Pilgrims at Plymouth. It experienced many vicissitudes; was several times attacked by the French, English, and Indians; and was twice assailed by expeditions from the neighboring English colonies of South Carolina and Georgia. With the rest of Florida it came into the possession of the English by the treaty of 1763, was ceded to Spain in 1783, and was transferred to the United States in 1819. During the civil war it changed masters three times. The resident population at the present time is about 2,200; but this is increased by from 7,000 to 10,000 visitors during the winter, and St. Augustine is then one of the gayest places in the South. The *climate* of St. Augustine is singularly equable both winter and summer, the mean annual temperature being 70°. The mean temperature for winter is 58·08°; for spring, 68·54°; for summer, 80·27°; and for autumn, 71·73°. Frosts seldom occur even in mid-winter, and the sea-breezes temper the heats of summer so that they are quite endurable.

105. The St. John's River.

The steamers of the Florida line from Charleston and Savannah (see Route 103) run up the St. John's as far as Pilatka. The steamer "Hampton" leaves Jacksonville daily (except Sundays) at 9 A. M. for Pilatka, stopping at principal landings and returning the same day. Fare to Green Cove Springs, $1; to Pilatka, $2; to Enterprise, $9. Other steamers running all the way to Enterprise leave Jacksonville 4 times a week. The following list of principal places on the St. John's may prove useful to the tourist: Riverside, 3 miles from Jacksonville; Black Point, 10; Mulberry Grove, 11; Mandarin, 15; Fruit Cove, 18; Hibernia, 22; Remington Park, 25; Magnolia, 28; Green Cove Springs. 31; Hogarth's Landing, 36; Picolata, 45; Tocoi, 52; Federal Point, 60; Orange Mills. 64; Dancy's Wharf, 65; Whitestone, 66; Russell's Landing, 69; Pilatka, 75; Rawlestown, 77; San Mateo, 80; Buffalo Bluff. 88; Ocklawaha River, 100; Welaka, 100; Beecher, 101; Orange Point, 103; Mount Royal, 109; Fort Gates, 110; Georgetown, 117; Lake View, 132; Volusia, 137; Orange Bluff, 140; Hawkinsville, 160; Cabbage Bluff, 162; Lake Beresford, 165; Blue Spring, 172; Emanuel, 184; Shell Bank, 193; Sanford, 199; Mellonville, 200; Enterprise, 205; Cook's Ferry and King Philip's Town, 224; Lake Harney, 225; Sallie's Camp; 229; Salt Lake, 270.

THE St. John's River has its sources in a vast elevated savanna midway down the peninsula, flows almost directly N. for 300 miles to

Jacksonville, and then turning E. empties into the Atlantic. Its whole course, which lies through an extremely level region, is about 400 miles, and throughout the last 150 miles it is little more than a succession of lakes, expanding in width from 1½ mile to 6 miles and having at no point a width of less than ½ mile. Its banks are lined with a luxuriant tropical vegetation, handsome shade-trees and orange-groves, and here and there are picturesque villages. "The banks are low and flat," says Edward King, "but bordered with a wealth of exquisite foliage to be seen nowhere else upon this continent. One passes for hundreds of miles through a grand forest of cypresses robed in moss and mistletoe; of palms towering gracefully far above the surrounding trees, of palmettos, whose rich trunks gleam in the sun; of swamp, white and black ash, of magnolia, of water-oak, of poplar and plane-trees; and, where the hammocks rise a few feet above the water-level, the sweet bay, the olive, the cotton-tree, the juniper, the red cedar, the sweet gum, the live oak, shoot up their splendid stems; while among the shrubbery and inferior growths one may note the azalea, the sumach, the sensitive plant, the agave, the poppy, the mallow, and the nettle. The vines run not in these thickets, but over them. The fox-grape clambers along the branches, and the woodbine and bignonia escalade the haughtiest forest-monarchs. When the steamer nears the shore, one can see far through the tangled thickets the gleaming water, out of which rise thousands of 'cypress-knees,' looking exactly like so many champagne bottles set into the current to cool. The heron and the crane saucily watch the shadow which the approaching boat throws near their retreat. The wary monster-turtle gazes for an instant, with his black head cocked knowingly on one side, then disappears with a gentle slide and a splash. An alligator grins familiarly as a dozen revolvers are pointed at him over the boat's side, suddenly 'winks with his tail,' and vanishes! as the bullet meant for his tough hide skims harmlessly over the ripples left above him. . . . For its whole length of 400 miles, the river affords glimpses of perfect beauty. One ceases to regret hills and mountains, and can hardly imagine ever having thought them necessary, so much do these visions surpass them. It is not grandeur which one finds on the banks of the great stream, it is Nature run riot. The very irregularity is delightful, the decay is charming, the solitude is picturesque."

A highly attractive excursion point from Jacksonville is *Mulberry Grove*, a beautiful grove on the W. bank of the river. Four miles above, on the E. bank, is *Mandarin*, one of the oldest settlements on the St. John's. It is a village of about 250 inhabitants, and is the winter-home of Mrs. Harriet Beecher Stowe, whose cottage is situated near the river, a few rods to the left of the shore-end of the pier. She owns about 40 acres of land, three or four of which are planted with orange-trees. Seven miles above Mandarin, on an island near the opposite bank, is *Hibernia* (22 miles from Jacksonville). This is a popular resort for invalids, and Mrs. Fleming keeps a large and excellent boarding-house (terms, $12 a week). **Magnolia** (*Magnolia Hotel*, $4 a day) is situated on the W. bank, and is considered one of the most desirable resorts in Florida for consumptives. It has a sandy soil, covered with beautiful groves of pine and orange trees, and there are no dangerous hammock-lands near by. In the vicinity is *Magnolia Point*, one of the highest points of land extending into the river between Jacksonville and Pilatka. A little to the N. of the point, Black Creek, a navigable stream, up which small steamers make weekly trips as far as *Middleburg*, empties into the St. John's. The banks swarm with alligators, which are apt to be mistaken at times for logs which are floated down this stream in large quantities to market. Three miles above Magnolia are the **Green Cove Springs** (*Clarendon Hotel, San Marco*), one of the favorite resorts on the river. The place takes its name from a sulphur-spring, situated about 100 yards from the landing amid a grove of great water-oaks, covered with hanging festoons of gray moss and misletoe. The spring discharges about 3,000 gallons a minute and fills a pool some 30 ft. in diameter with greenish-hued crystal-clear water. The water has a temperature of 78° Fahr.; contains sulphates of magnesia and lime, chlorides of sodium and iron, and sulphuretted hydrogen; is used both for bathing and drinking; and is considered beneficial for rheumatism, gouty affections, and Bright's disease of the kidneys. *Picolata* is the site of an ancient Spanish settlement, of which no traces now remain. On the opposite side of the river are the ruins of a great earthwork fort of the time of the Spanish occupation. **Tocoi** is of some importance as the point where connection is made with St. John's R. R. to St. Augustine, 15 miles distant. (See Route 104.) Passing *Federal Point*, a wood-station, *Orange Mills* (64 miles), and *Dancy's Wharf* (65 miles)—the two latter noted for their fine orange-groves—the steamer stops at **Pilatka** (*Putnam House, Larkin House, St. John's*), the largest town on the river above Jacksonville. It has a population of about 1,500, and is admirably situated on high ground on the W. bank of the river, where the surface-land is for the most part sandy. The wonderful blandness of its climate renders Pilatka peculiarly favorable to consumptives, and it offers advantages in the way of churches, schools, postal and telegraphic facilities, etc., not possessed by many of the interior resorts. Pilatka is the steamboat headquarters for the Upper St. John's and its tributaries; and the steamers *en route* for Enterprise lie here overnight to discharge and receive freight, affording passengers an opportunity to spend a few hours ashore. Steamers run from Pilatka up the Ocklawaha River to Silver Spring, Ocala, and the head of navigation (see Route 106). Another line runs *via* Deep River to *Crescent City*, on Lake Crescent, 25 miles S. of Pilatka. Stages run from Crescent City to New Britain and Daytona (see Route 107).

Above Pilatka the vegetation becomes more characteristically tropical, and the river narrows down to a moderate-sized stream, widening out at last only to be merged in grand Lake George, Dexter's Lake, and Lake Monroe, at Enterprise. The steamers make the run from Pilatka to Enterprise in about 12 hours. Five miles above Pilatka, on the opposite bank, is *San Mateo* (Riverdale House), a thriving settlement situated on a high ridge overlooking the river. **Welaka** (25 miles above Pilatka) is opposite the mouth of the Ocklawaha River, and is the site of what was originally an Indian village, and afterward a flourishing Spanish settlement. Just above Welaka the river widens into *Little Lake George*, 4 miles wide and 7 miles long, and then into **Lake George**, 12 miles wide and 18 miles long. This is one of the most beautiful sheets of water in the world, being considered by many tourists equal in attractions to its namesake in the State of New York. Among the many lovely islands which dot its surface is one called *Rembert*, which is 1,700 acres in extent, and contains one of the largest orange-groves on the river. All along the lake the eye is delighted and the ear charmed by the brilliant plumage and sweet song of the southern birds. One finds here the heron, the crane, the white curlew, the pelican, the loon, and the paroquet; and there are many varieties of fish. *Volusia* (5 miles above Lake George) is a wood-station, with a settlement of considerable size back from the river. An ancient Spanish town used to stand here, this formerly being the principal point on the line of travel between St. Augustine and the Mosquito Inlet country. *Orange Grove* and *Hawkinsville* are simply wood-landings, but 35 miles above Volusia is *Blue Spring*, one of the largest mineral springs in the State. It is 500 yards from the St. John's, but the stream flowing from it is large enough at its confluence with the river for the steamers to float in it. Pursuing its voyage to the south, and passing several unimportant landings, the steamer speedily enters *Lake Monroe*, a sheet of water 12 miles long by 5 miles wide, teeming with fish and wild-fowl. On the south side of the lake is **Mellonville** (*Mellonville House*), formerly the site of Fort Mellon, erected during the Indian wars, and now an attractive resort for invalids and sportsmen, and a center of extensive orange plantations. About a mile N. of Mellonville is **Sanford,** a new resort, whose excellent hotel (the *Sanford House*) is attracting many visitors; and in the vicinity are Eureka, Eauclair, Wekiva, Lake Jennie, Lake Maitland, Lake Conway, Fort Reid, and other settlements, at most of which good boardinghouses or hotels may be found. On the opposite side of the lake from Mellonville is **Enterprise** (*Brock House*, $2.50 to $3.00 a day), the head of regular steamboat navigation, and one of the most popular resorts in Southern Florida for invalids, especially for those suffering from rheumatism. The climate is rather warmer than that of Jacksonville and Magnolia, but it is said to have special invigorating qualities which speedily convert invalids into successful fishermen and hunters. About a mile N. of the town is the *Green Sulphur Spring*, with water of a pale-green hue but quite transparent. It is nearly 80 ft. in diameter, and about 100 ft. deep.

Although Enterprise is the terminus of regular navigation on the St. John's, there is for the sportsman still another hundred miles of narrow river, deep lagoons, gloomy bayous, and wild, untrodden land; where all sorts of game, such as bears, wild turkeys, deer, and ducks are plentiful, while the waters teem with innumerable varieties of fish. Small steamers run during the winter through Lake Harney to *Salt Lake*, the nearest point to the Indian River from St. John's; and a small steamboat makes frequent excursions through *Lake Jessup* to *Lake Harney*, for the benefit of those who wish to try their hand at the exciting sport of alligator-shooting, or of those who wish simply to enjoy the charming scenery.　The trip to Lake Harney and back is made in 12

Post-Office, Ocklawaha River.

hours.　Lake Jessup is near Lake Harney: it is 17 miles long and 5 miles wide, but is so shallow that it can not be entered by a boat drawing more than 3 ft. of water.　The St. John's rises in the elevated savannah before mentioned, fully 120 miles S. of Enterprise, but tourists seldom ascend farther than Lake Harney. About 20 miles S. E. of Enterprise (reached by stage) is the ancient town of *New Smyrna* (see p. 445).

106. The Ocklawaha River.

THE Ocklawaha empties into the St. John's about 25 miles south of Pilatka, opposite the small town of Welaka (see p. 441), after flowing for nearly 300 miles through Putnam and Marion Counties. The channel possesses no banks, being simply a navigable passage through a succession of small lakes and cypress-swamps; but small steamers ascend it for a distance of nearly 200 miles. An excursion up the Ocklawaha to Silver Spring (109 miles) is perhaps the most unique experience of the tourist in Florida; and every one who can should make it. Alligators of immense size are numerous, and birds of the most curious forms and brilliant plumage may be everywhere seen. Steamers leave Jacksonville every Thursday at 9 A. M. for Silver Spring *via* Pilatka; and every Sunday at 8 A. M. for Okahumkee. From Pilatka another line runs to Silver Spring every Monday and Thursday, on the arrival of the Charleston and Savannah steamers.

The principal landing on the Ocklawaha is **Silver Spring,** the largest and most beautiful of the springs of Florida, navigable by steamers of several tons' burden. This spring is said to be the traditional "fountain of youth" of which Ponce de Leon heard, and for which he so vainly searched. The clearness of its waters is wonderful; they seem more transparent than air. "You see on the bottom, 80 ft. below, the shadow of your boat, and the exact form of the smallest pebble; the prismatic colors of the rainbow are beautifully reflected, and you can see the fissure in the rocky bottom through which the water pours upward like an inverted cataract." A deep river, 100 ft. wide, is formed by the water of this spring, which in the course of 7 miles forms a junction with the Ocklawaha. *Ocala* is only 5 miles distant.

Silver Spring was once considered the head of navigation in this direction, but small steamers now run far beyond it on the Ocklawaha, through Lakes Griffin, Eustis, Harris, and Dora, to *Leesburg* (182 miles from the mouth of the St. John's), *Pendryville* (215 miles), *Yalaha* (227 miles), and *Okahumkee*, a little settlement in the remote wilderness.

107. The Indian River Country.

INDIAN RIVER is a long lagoon or arm of the sea, beginning near the lower end of Mosquito Inlet (with which it is connected by a short canal), and extending S. along the E. side of the peninsula for a distance of nearly 150 miles. It is separated from the Atlantic by a narrow strip of sand, through which it communicates with the open water by the Indian River Inlet (latitude 27° 30' N.) and by Jupiter Inlet; and for more than thirty miles of its northern course the St. John's River flows parallel with it, at an average distance of not more than 10 miles. The water of the lagoon is salt, though it receives a considerable body of fresh water through Santa Lucia River, an outlet of the Everglades; there are no marshes in the vicinity; the adjacent lands are for the most part remarkably fertile, producing abundantly oranges, lemons, limes, bananas, pineapples, guavas, grapes, sugar-cane, strawberries, blackberries, and all varieties of garden vegetables; and the river itself teems to an almost incredible degree with fish of every kind, including the pompano, the mullet, the sheepshead, turtles, and oysters of the most delicious flavor. Along the shore of the lagoon toward the Atlantic is a belt of thick, evergreen woods, which, breaking the force of the chilling east winds that sometimes visit these latitudes in winter, renders the climate of the Indian River country peculiarly favorable to consumptives. "The sportsman who pitches his tent for a few days on the splendid camping-ground of the W. shore will see the pelican, the cormorant, the sea-gull, and gigantic turtles, many of them weighing 500 pounds; may see the bears exploring the nests for turtles' eggs; may 'fire-hunt' the deer in the forests; chase the alligator to his lair; shoot at the 'raft-duck'; and fish from the salt-ponds all the finny monsters that be. Hardly a thousand miles from New York one may find the most delicate and delightful tropical scenery, and may dwell in a climate which neither Hawaii nor Southern Italy can excel. Settlements throughout this section are few and far between. The mail is carried down the great silent coast by a foot-messenger; for there is a stretch of nearly 100 miles along which there is not a drop of fresh water for a horse to drink."

At its N. end, as already mentioned, the Indian River connects by a canal with the Mosquito Lagoon, which is also known as the Hillsboro' River; and at the N. end of Mosquito Lagoon the Halifax River comes in, which begins about 40 miles south of St. Augustine. The principal settlements are *New Britain, Daytona,* and *Port Orange,* on the Halifax River; *New Smyrna,* on the Hillsboro' River, 3 miles S. of Mosquito Inlet, near the coast; and *Titusville* (formerly Sand Point), on the W. bank of the Indian River, 35 miles S. of Mosquito Inlet. Titusville is the terminus of the St. John's & Indian River R. R., which is to run to Salt Lake (8 miles) and Lake Harney (21 miles).

The routes to the Indian River country are as follows: (1) By steamer on the St. John's to Enterprise, as described in Route 105; thence by stage to New Smyrna (20 mi'es); and from New Smyrna to other localities by boat. (2) By steamer from Jacksonville or Pilatka to Crescent City (see p. 441), and thence by stage to New Britain and Daytona. (3) By steamer from Jacksonville ("outside route") to New Smyrna. These steamers stop at St. Augustine *en route.*—When the St. John's & Indian River R. R. is completed, an easy route will be by steamer from Jacksonville *via* Enterprise to Lake Harney, and thence by rail to Titusville.

108. Fernandina to Cedar Keys.

FERNANDINA (*Egmont Hotel, Mansion House*) is an interesting old seaport town, situated on the W. shore of Amelia Island, at the mouth of Amelia River, 50 miles N. of Jacksonville. It is reached by rail from Jacksonville; by steamer, direct from New York (leaving Pier

27 North River every Thursday at 3 P. M.); and by steamers from Charleston and Savannah (see Route 103). Fernandina was founded by the Spaniards in 1632, and at the present time has a population of about 1,500, which is largely increased during the winter season. Its harbor is the finest on the coast S. of Chesapeake Bay, being land-locked and of such capacity that, during the War of 1812, when the town was Spanish and neutral, more than 300 square-rigged vessels rode at anchor in it at one time. It has an important trade in lumber; possesses a large cotton-ginning establishment and a manufactory of cotton-seed oil; and it is in the neighborhood of numerous sugar, cotton, and orange plantations. The *climate* of Fernandina is very similar to that of St. Augustine; mild and equable in winter, and in summer tempered by the cool sea-breezes. The town, which is the seat of the Episcopal bishopric of Florida, contains 7 churches, a flourishing young ladies' seminary, under the charge of the bishop, and a weekly newspaper. Fernandina possesses other attractions for visitors besides its delightful climate. There is, for instance, a fine shell-road, 2 miles long, leading to the ocean-beach, which affords a remarkably hard and level drive of nearly 20 miles. A favorite excursion is to *Dungeness*, the home of the Revolutionary hero, General Nathaniel Greene. This estate, of about 10,000 acres of choice land, was the gift of the people of Georgia to the general, in recognition of his services as commander of the Southern provincial army. The grounds are beautifully laid out, and are embellished with flower-gardens, and handsome groves and avenues of olive-trees, and live oaks draped with long festoons of the graceful Spanish moss. On the beach, about half a mile from the Dungeness mansion, is the grave of another Revolutionary hero, General Henry Lee, marked by a headstone erected by his son, General Robert E. Lee.

Beginning at Fernandina, the Atlantic, Gulf & West India Transit R. R. extends directly across the State to Cedar Keys, on the Gulf coast (155 miles) passing through some of the most picturesque scenery in Florida. There are a number of small stations on the line, but few requiring mention. *Baldwin* is at the crossing of the Jacksonville, Pensacola & Mobile R. R. (see Route 103). The next noteworthy town is **Waldo** (84 miles, *Waldo House*), at the junction of the railroad constructing to Tampa Bay. The climate here is dry and the air balsamic, and the region is regarded as particularly favorable to invalids suffering from lung-diseases. The woods in the vicinity of the village abound in deer, ducks, quail, etc.; and about 2 miles distant is *Santa Fé Lake*, which is 9 miles long and 4 wide, and affords good facilities for boating and fishing. The streams in the neighborhood are filled with trout and perch. The Santa Fé River disappears underground a few miles from Waldo, and after running underground for two miles rises and continues to its discharge into the Suwanee River. **Gainesville** (*Arlington House, Oak Hall House*) is the principal town on the line of the road (98 miles from Fernandina). It has 1,500 inhabitants, 4 churches, and 2 newspapers. Owing to its favorable situation in the center of the peninsula and in the midst of the pine-forests, which clothe this portion of Florida, Gainesville is much frequented by consumptives and other invalids. Tri-weekly stages run between Gainesville and Tampa (see p. 449) on the Gulf of Mexico. **Cedar Keys** (*Gulf House, Island House*), the Gulf terminus of the railway, is a village of about 700 inhabitants, pleasantly situated on a large bay, which affords excellent facilities for bathing, boating, and fishing. The chief commerce of the place is in cedar and pine wood, turtles, fish, and sponges, the sponging-grounds being about 60 miles distant. The climate of Cedar Keys is blander than that of Jacksonville, and is beneficial to rheumatism as well as consumption. Sportsmen will find unlimited occupation for both rod and gun. Eighteen miles W. of Cedar Keys, the *Suwanee River*, navigable to Ellaville, enters the Gulf; and the *Withlacoochee River*, 18 miles south. The steamers of the New Orleans, Florida & Havana Steamship Co. leave every Saturday for Havana, New Orleans, and Key West. A semi-weekly line runs to Tampa, Charlotte Harbor, Manatee, Key West, etc. (see Route 110).

109. Middle Florida.

THAT portion of Florida known as "Middle Florida" (in the midst of which Tallahassee lies) differs from the rest of the State in that its surface is more broken and undulating, reaching here and there an elevation of from 300 to 400 ft. The hills are singularly graceful in outline, and the soil is exceedingly fertile, producing all the characteristic products of the Southern States, including tobacco and early garden vegetables. The vegetation is less tropical in character than that of Eastern and Southern Florida, but it is very profuse and comprises many beautiful evergreens. **Tallahassee** (*City Hotel*), the capital of the State and county-seat of Leon County, is situated on the Jacksonville, Pensacola & Mobile R. R., 155 miles west of Jacksonville and 21 miles north of the Gulf of Mexico. It is beautifully located on high ground, and is regularly laid out in a plot a mile square, with broad streets and several public squares, shaded with evergreens and oaks. The abundance and variety of the shrubs and flowers give it the appearance of a garden. The business portion of the city is of brick. The public buildings are the *Capitol* (commenced in 1826), a large three-story brick edifice, with pillared entrances opening east and west; the *Court-House*, a substantial two-story brick structure; and the *West Florida Seminary*, a large two-story brick building, on a hill commanding a view of the entire city. The climate is delightful, the heat of summer and the cold of winter being tempered by the breezes from the Gulf; but consumptives should bear in mind that, as the site is higher than that of Jacksonville, the air is more likely to prove trying to weak lungs, unless proper precautions are taken as to clothing, etc. In the immediate neighborhood of Tallahassee are *Lake Bradford, Lake Jackson* (17 miles long), and *Lake Lafayette* (6 miles long). During the winter months these lakes swarm with ducks and brant; and to the angler Lake Jackson presents many attractions, as it is well stocked with bass and bream. Quail are also very abundant. About 15

miles from Tallahassee is the famous * **Wakulla Spring,** which is
reckoned among the chief wonders of Florida. It is an immense limestone basin, 106 ft. deep, and with waters so crystalline clear that the
fish near its bottom can be seen as plainly as though they were in the
air, and so copious that a river is formed at the very start.

Along the line of railway on which Tallahassee is situated (the
Jacksonville, Pensacola & Mobile) there are several towns which offer
great attractions to invalids, tourists, and sportsmen. **Quincy** (24
miles W. of Tallahassee) is a prosperous village of about 1,000 inhabitants, the county-seat of Gadsden County. Its climatic characteristics are the same as those of Tallahassee, and there is a similar abundance of game in the vicinity. Board may be had at the *Stockton
House* and at private boarding-houses. **Monticello** (33 miles E. of
Tallahassee) is an important town of about 2,000 inhabitants, and the
terminus of a branch road 4½ miles in length. It contains Baptist,
Episcopalian, Methodist, and Presbyterian churches, several schools,
and a weekly newspaper. The *Monticello Hotel* and the *Florida House*
are good houses, and board may be had in private families. In the
vicinity of Monticello is *Lake Miccosukie,* whose banks are noted as
the camping-ground of De Soto, and as the field of a bloody battle
between General Jackson and the Miccosukie Indians. At its S. end
the lake contracts to a creek and disappears underground. Near Monticello is the Lipona plantation, where Murat resided for some time
while in Florida.

110. The Gulf Coast and Key West.

MUCH the larger part of the coast-line of Florida is washed by the
Gulf of Mexico; but this immense stretch of sea-front is almost inac-
cessible on account of shallow soundings, and has few good harbors.
The principal place in this part of the State is **Pensacola** (*City Hotel,
European*), a city of about 5,000 inhabitants, situated on the N. W.
side of the bay of the same name, 10 miles from the Gulf of Mexico.
Its commerce is extensive and its lumber-business important. The
Pensacola R. R. (45 miles long) connects with the Mobile & Montgomery R. R. (see Route 111), and brings Pensacola into connection with
the general railway system of the country. The Perdido R. R. runs
in 9 miles to *Millview,* on Perdido Bay, where there are extensive lumbering establishments. The principal public buildings of Pensacola
are a Custom-House and several churches. The remains of the old
Spanish forts, San Miguel and St. Bernard, may be seen in rear of the
city. A weekly line of steamers was established in 1878 to ply between Pensacola and Tampa, calling at Cedar Keys. **Appalachicola**
is a decadent city of about 1,000 inhabitants attractively situated at
the entrance of the river of the same name into the Gulf of Mexico,
through Appalachicola Bay. It is connected with Columbus, Georgia
(see p. 453) by steamers on the Appalachicola and Chattahoochee Rivers. **Cedar Keys** has already been described on page 447. Semi-
weekly steamers run down the coast from Cedar Keys to Tampa, Charlotte Harbor, Manatee, Key West, etc.

Tampa (*Orange Grove Hotel, Tampa*), the first noteworthy point below Cedar Keys, is situated near the center of the W. coast, at the head of the beautiful Tampa Bay (formerly Espíritu Santo Bay). The bay is about 40 miles long, is dotted with islands, and forms a splendid harbor for the largest vessels. Its waters swarm with fish and turtle, and there is an abundance of sea-fowl, including the beautiful flamingo. Deer swarm on the islands. The surrounding country is sandy, and for miles along the shore there is a luxuriant tropical vegetation. Large groves of orange, lemon, and pine trees are everywhere to be seen. The village contains about 500 inhabitants, and is probably destined to become one of the chief health-resorts of Florida. Tampa has regular mail communication (by stage) with Gainesville (see p. 446). The projected railway to Waldo, on the Cedar Keys & Fernandina R. R., when completed, will make Tampa one of the principal ports on the Gulf. *Manatee* is a small village situated on the Manatee River about 8 miles from its mouth. There are two or three boarding-houses here where fair accommodations may be had at $2 a day or $40 a month. *Charlotte Harbor* is about 25 miles long and from 8 to 10 miles wide, and is sheltered from the sea by several islands. The fisheries in and around the harbor are very valuable, the oysters gathered here being remarkably fine and abundant. On one of the islands in Charlotte Harbor there are a number of Indian shell-mounds, from one of which some curious Indian relics have been dug. *Punta Rassa* is a small hamlet near the mouth of the Caloosahatchie River, chiefly noteworthy as the point where the Cuban telegraph-line lands and as a U. S. Signal-Service station. The thermometrical observations recorded here are interesting as indicating the climate of all this portion of the coast. In 1874 the range was as follows : January, highest 79°, lowest 42°; February, highest 84°, lowest 50°; March, highest 85°, lowest 55°; April, highest 87°, lowest 55°; May, highest 90°, lowest 59°; June, highest 91°, lowest 70°; July, highest 91°, lowest 70°; August, highest 91°, lowest 70°; September, highest 91°, lowest 67°; October, highest 85°, lowest 64°; November, highest 82°, lowest 50°; December, highest 80°, lowest 49°.

Key West (*Russell House*), the largest city of Florida, next to Jacksonville, is situated upon an island of the same name off the S. extremity of the peninsula, and occupies the important post of key to the Gulf passage. The island is 7 miles long by from 1 to 2 miles wide, and is 11 ft. above the sea. It is of coral formation, and has a shallow soil, consisting of disintegrated coral, with a slight admixture of decayed vegetable matter. There are no springs, and the inhabitants are dependent on rain or distillation for water. The natural growth is a dense, stunted chaparral, in which various species of cactus are a prominent feature. Tropical fruits are cultivated to some extent, the chief varieties being cocoanuts, bananas, pineapples, guavas, sapodillas, and a few oranges. The air is pure and the climate healthy. The thermometer seldom rises above 90°, and never falls to freezing-point, rarely standing as low as 50°. The mean temperature, as ascertained by 14 years' observations, is, for spring, 75·79°; for

summer, 82·51° ; for autumn, 78·23° ; for winter, 69·58°. The city
has a population of about 7,000, a large portion of whom are Cubans
and natives of the Bahama Islands. They are a hardy and adventurous race, remarkable for their skill in diving. The language commonly spoken is Spanish, or a *patois* of that tongue. The streets of the
town are broad, and for the most part are laid out at right angles with
each other. The residences are shaded with tropical trees, and embowered in perennial flowers and shrubbery, giving the place a very
picturesque appearance. The buildings, however, are mostly small,
and are constructed of wood, except the Western Union telegraph-
office, those belonging to the U. S. Government, and one other, which
are of brick. Key West has a fine harbor, and being the key to the best
entrance to the Gulf of Mexico it is strongly fortified. The principal
work of defense is **Fort Taylor,** built on an artificial island within
the main entrance to the harbor, and mounting about 200 guns.
Among the principal industries of Key West are turtling, sponging,
and the catching of mullet and other fish for the Cuban market. Upward of 30 vessels, with an aggregate of 250 men, are engaged in
wrecking on the Florida Reef, and the island profits by this industry to
the amount of $200,000 annually. The manufacture of cigars employs
about 800 hands, chiefly Cubans, and 25,000,000 cigars are turned out
yearly. There are a number of charming drives on the island, and the
fishing and boating are unsurpassed. (From New York Key West is
reached *via* New York and New Orleans steamers leaving Pier 36 North
River every Saturday at 3 P. M. ; also *via* New York and Galveston
steamers leaving Pier 20 East River every Saturday at 3 P. M. From
Baltimore by semi-monthly steamers. Through tickets by rail from
New York to Cedar Keys and thence by steamer, $45).

111. Richmond to Mobile.

a. Via Charlotte, Atlanta, and Montgomery.

As far as *Charlotte* (282 miles) this route has been described in
Route 101 *b.* At Charlotte the Atlanta & Charlotte Air-Line R. R. is
taken. This road runs S. W. through South Carolina and Georgia,
reaching Atlanta in 267 miles. The country traversed is for the most
part rolling and hilly, being on the border of the picturesque mountain-
region of both States. Numerous small towns are passed *en route*, but
most of them are mere railroad stations, and only three or four present
features worthy of notice. The first of these is *King's Mountain* (35
miles from Charlotte), near an eminence of the same name which was
the scene of a battle, Oct. 7, 1780, between the British and the patriot
forces, in which the former were defeated and their entire detachment
captured. Near *Cowpens* (67 miles) is the memorable Revolutionary
battle-field of the Cowpens, situated on the hill-range called the Thickety
Mountain. The battle was fought Jan. 17, 1781, and resulted in the
defeat of the British under Tarleton. In the olden time the cattle were

allowed to graze on the scene of the conflict—whence the name. Ten miles beyond Cowpens is **Spartanburg** (*Palmetto Hotel, Piedmont House*), the most important town in this portion of South Carolina. It is pleasantly situated in the midst of a region famous for its gold and iron, and is much resorted to in summer by people from Charleston and the lowlands. Near Spartanburg are the *Glenn Springs*, whose waters are strongly impregnated with sulphur, and recommended for rheumatism and dyspepsia; and the *Limestone Spring*, a chalybeate possessing valuable tonic properties. The Spartanburg, Union & Columbia R. R. connects Spartanburg with Columbia. Thirty-two miles beyond Spartanburg is **Greenville** (*Commercial Hotel, Mansion House*), a city of 6,000 inhabitants, beautifully situated on Reedy River, near its source, and at the foot of Saluda Mountain. It is one of the most popular resorts in the up-country of the State, lying as it does at the threshold of the chief beauties of the mountain region of South Carolina (see Route 118). The Greenville & Columbia R. R. runs S. E. in 143 miles to Columbia. At *Seneca City* (148 miles from Charlotte) connection is made with the Blue Ridge R. R., and a short distance beyond, the road crosses the Savannah River and enters the State of Georgia. *Toccoa* (176 miles) and *Mount Airy* (189 miles) are convenient entrances to the mountain region of Georgia (see Route 118). From *Lulu* (203 miles) the Northeastern R. R. runs in 39 miles to the collegiate town of *Athens*, on the Georgia R. R. The principal place on this portion of the line is **Gainesville** (216 miles, *Richmond House*), a town of 2,500 inhabitants, which has grown wonderfully since the completion of the railway. One mile from Gainesville (reached by horse-cars) is the *Gower Springs Hotel*, and 2 miles E. are the *New Holland Springs*, a favorite resort. The *Porter Springs* are 28 miles N., attractively situated among the mountains. Just before reaching Atlanta, Stone Mountain comes into view far away on the left, and shortly afterward the train crosses Peach Tree Creek, the scene (lower down) of the bloody conflict of July 22, 1864. **Atlanta** (*Kimball House, Markham*) is the capital of Georgia, and, next to Savannah, the largest and most important city in the State (with a population estimated in 1878 at 38,000). It is the outgrowth of the railroad-system centering there, and is rather Northern than Southern in character. The city is picturesquely situated upon hilly ground 1,100 ft. above the sea, and is laid out in the form of a circle about 3 miles in diameter, the Union Passenger Depot occupying the center. The most noteworthy buildings are the * *State House* (from the cupola of which a fine view is obtained), the *City Hall* (beautifully located), the *First Methodist Church* (South), the *Union Passenger Depot*, the *Opera-House*, and the *Kimball House*, one of the largest and finest hotels in the South. The *State Library* contains about 16,000 volumes; the *Young Men's Library* about 5,000; and *Oglethorpe College* about 5,000. * *Oglethorpe Park*, at the head of Marietta St. about 2 miles from the depot, contains fine drives, lakes, etc. The chief interest which Atlanta possesses for the tourist is the memorable siege with which it is inseparably associated. Its position made it of vital importance to the Southern

cause, and with its capture by Sherman, Sept. 2, 1864, the doom of the
Confederacy was sealed. Before abandoning the city, to fall back upon
Macon, Gen. Hood set fire to all the machinery, stores, and munitions
of war which he could not remove, and in the conflagration which resulted the greater part of the city was reduced to ashes. Atlanta
became the State capital in 1868.

From Atlanta the route is *via* the Atlanta & West Point R. R.,
which runs S. W. through a prosperous agricultural region, and in 87
miles reaches West Point, on the Alabama border. The principal
towns *en route* are *Newnan* (40 miles), where connection is made with
the Savannah, Griffin & North Alabama R. R., and *La Grange* (72
miles), which is noted throughout the State for the excellence of its
educational establishments. *West Point* is a thriving town of 1,500
inhabitants on both sides of the Chattahoochee River, with an active
trade in cotton, and several cotton-factories. At West Point the
Western R. R. of Alabama is taken, which runs W. in 88 miles to
Montgomery. *Opelika* (22 miles) is a flourishing village at the junction
of the branch line from Columbus, Georgia, 29 miles distant (see p. 453).
Montgomery (*Exchange Hotel, Central*) is the capital of Alabama,
and the second city of the State in size and commercial importance.
It is situated on a high bluff on the left bank of the Alabama River,
was founded in 1817, named after the lamented Gen. Richard Montgomery, who fell at Quebec, had a population of 10,588 in 1870, and
has a sort of fame as the first capital of the Confederate States (from
Feb. to May, 1861). The principal public building is the * *State House*,
which though small, is an imposing structure. It is situated on Capitol Hill, at the head of Market St., and from its dome there is a fine
view. Other noteworthy buildings are the *City Hall*, a fine edifice containing a market and rooms for the fire department, the *Court House*,
several of the churches and the *Theatre*. The Alabama River is navigable to Montgomery by steamers at all seasons, and 4 important railroads converge here. From Montgomery to Mobile the route is *via* the
Mobile & Montgomery R. R., which extends S. W. through one of the
most productive portions of Alabama (distance 180 miles). The most
important town *en route* is *Greenville* (44 miles from Montgomery),
with a population of about 1,200. **Mobile** (see p. 454). The total distance from Richmond to Mobile by this route is 904 miles.

b. Via Augusta, Macon, and Columbus.

Between Richmond and *Augusta* (477 miles) the tourist may take
either of the routes described in Route 102. In Route 102 *a* the Wilmington, Columbia & Augusta R. R. is followed to Columbia, whence
the route is the same as in *b*. From Augusta to Macon there are two
routes: the Georgia R. R. and the Central R. R. of Georgia. The
principal towns on the Georgia R. R. are *Camak* (47 miles from Augusta), whence a branch line runs in 124 miles to **Atlanta** (see p. 451) ;
Warrenton (51 miles) and *Sparta* (71 miles), both pretty towns ; and
Milledgeville (93 miles), the former capital of the State, and the site of

the State Penitentiary and of the Georgia Asylum for the Insane. The most important places on the Central R. R. of Georgia are *Millen* (53 miles from Augusta), where the road forks, one branch going to Savannah (see Route 102 *b*); and *Gordon* (144 miles), whence a branch line runs to Milledgeville (see above) and *Eatonton*, a pleasant town with excellent schools. The former route is the shorter, but, owing to an advantage in connections, the latter is the route usually followed by through travel.—**Macon** (*Lanier House, Brown's Hotel*) is one of the most populous and prosperous cities of Georgia, and is picturesquely situated at the head of steamboat navigation on the Ocmulgee River, which is here crossed by a bridge. It contains about 11,000 inhabitants, is the site of several important iron-foundries, machine-shops, and flour-mills, is regularly laid out and well built, and is embowered in trees and shrubbery. The * *Central City Park*, combining pleasure and fair grounds, possesses great beauty; and * *Rose Hill Cemetery*, comprising 50 acres on the Ocmulgee, ½ mile below the city, is one of the most beautiful burial-grounds in the United States. Macon is the seat of the *State Academy for the Blind*, which occupies an imposing brick edifice 4 stories high, and has a library of 2,000 volumes. *Mercer University* (Baptist) is a prosperous institution, with a library of 9,000 volumes; and the *Wesleyan Female College* has a wide reputation. The *Pio Nono College* (Roman Catholic) has a spacious and handsome building. *Vineland* is a lovely suburban village, about a mile from the city. Four railroads center at Macon, and secure it an extensive trade.

From Macon the route is *via* the Southwestern R. R., which runs in 100 miles to Columbus, through a level, sandy, and unpicturesque region. The most important place on the line is *Fort Valley* (29 miles from Macon), an attractive village of about 1,500 inhabitants, situated at the junction of two important branches of the Southwestern R. R. **Columbus** (*Rankin House, Central Hotel*) is situated on the E. bank of the Chattahoochee River, and is the fifth city of Georgia in population (about 15,000), and the chief manufacturing center in the South. Opposite the city the river rushes over huge, rugged rocks, forming a water-power which has been greatly improved by a dam 500 ft. long, and which is extensively utilized in manufactures. There are 6 cotton-factories, 4 run by water-power and 2 by steam; one of them (the Eagle and Phœnix mill) is the largest ever established in the South. There are also 6 flour and grist-mills, and machine-shops, iron founderies, saw-mills, planing-mills, etc. The Chattahoochee is navigable from Columbus to the Gulf of Mexico during 8 months of the year; and from the end of October to the 1st of July its waters are traversed by numerous steamboats laden with cotton. The city is regularly laid out, with streets from 99 to 165 ft. wide, and residences surrounded by ample gardens. The most noteworthy buildings are the *Court-House*, the *Presbyterian Church, Temperance Hall*, the *Springer Opera-House*, the *Georgia Home Insurance Co.*, and the *Bank of Columbus*. A handsome bridge connects Columbus with the village of *Girard*, in Alabama. From Columbus the route is *via* the Columbus branch of the

Western R. R. of Alabama, which connects with the main line at
Opelika (29 miles). Beyond Opelika the route is the same as that
described in the foregoing route (see p. 452). By this route the total
distance from Richmond to Mobile is 1,006 miles.

Mobile.

Hotels, etc.—The *Battle House* ($3 a day), cor. Royal and St. Francis Sts.,
and the *St. James* are the leading hotels. *Horse-cars* traverse the city from end to
end, and make all points easily accessible. Besides the routes described above,
Mobile is reached from the North by Route 112, and from the West by Louisville,
Nashville & Gt. Southern line (Route 114) and by Mobile & Ohio R. R. The Route
from Mobile to New Orleans is described in Route 112. *Steamers* ply between
Mobile and the interior by way of the Alabama, Tombigbee, and other Rivers.

Mobile, the largest city and only seaport of Alabama, is situated on
the W. side of Mobile River, immediately above its entrance into Mobile
Bay, 30 miles from the Gulf of Mexico in lat. 30° 42′ N. and lon. 88°
W. Its site is a sandy plain, rising as it recedes from the river, and
bounded, at a distance of a few miles, by high and beautiful hills.
The corporate limits of the city extend 6 miles N. and S. and 2 or 3
miles W. from the river. The thickly-inhabited part extends for about
a mile along the river, and nearly the same distance back toward the
hills. It is laid out with considerable regularity, and the streets are
generally well-paved and delightfully shaded. *Fort Morgan* (formerly
Fort Bowyer), on Mobile Point, and *Fort Gaines*, on the E. extremity
of Dauphine Island, command the entrance to the harbor, which is
about 30 miles below the city. On Mobile Point is also a lighthouse,
the lantern of which is 55 ft. above the sea-level. The remains of
several batteries erected during the war may be seen in and about the
harbor; and on the E. side of Tensas River are the ruins of *Spanish
Fort* and *Fort Blakely*.

Mobile was the original seat of French colonization in the Southwest, and for
many years the capital of the colony of Louisiana. Historians differ as to the precise
date of its foundation, though it is known that a settlement was made a little above
the present site of the city at least as early as 1702. Many of the first settlers were
Canadians. In 1723 the seat of the colonial government was transferred to New
Orleans. In 1763, Mobile, with all that portion of Louisiana lying E. of the Mississippi and N. of Bayou Iberville, Lakes Maurepas and Pontchartrain, passed into the
possession of Great Britain. In 1780 England surrendered it to Spain, and that Government made it over to the United States in 1813. It was incorporated as a city in
1819, the population being then about 800. Mobile was one of the last points in the
Confederacy occupied by the Union forces during the late war, and was not finally
reduced until April 12, 1865, three days after the surrender of General Lee. On
August 5, 1864, the harbor fortifications were attacked by Admiral Farragut, who
ran his fleet past the forts, and closed the harbor against blockade-runners, though
he failed to capture the city itself. The trade of Mobile is much hindered by the
shallowness of its harbor. Vessels drawing more than 8 or 10 ft. are obliged to
anchor in the bay, 25 miles or more from the city; but improvements are now in
progress which it is hoped will enable vessels of 13 ft. of water to reach the wharves.
The chief business is the receipt and shipment of cotton. The manufactures include
carriages and furniture, paper, foundries and machine shops, and a brewery.

Government St. is the finest avenue and favorite promenade of the
city. It is shaded by superb oak-trees, and is bordered by fine residences surrounded by luxuriant gardens. *Bienville Park*, between

Dauphin and St. Francis Sts., is also a place of much resort. It is adorned with live oaks and other shade-trees. The * **Custom-House,** which also contains the *Post-Office,* at the cor. of Royal and St. Francis Sts., is the finest, largest, and most costly public edifice in the city. It is built of granite, and cost $250,000. The *Theatre* and the *Market-House,* with rooms in the upper story for the municipal officers, are in Royal St. The *Battle House* presents an imposing façade of painted brick, immediately opposite the Custom-House. *Odd Fellows' Hall,* in Royal St., and *Temperance Hall,* cor. St. Michael and St. Joseph Sts., are conspicuous buildings. Adjoining Odd-Fellows' Hall is the *Bank of Mobile,* with a stately colonnade and portico. * **Barton Academy,** in Government St., is a large and handsome building surmounted by a dome. Of the church edifices the most notable are the *Cathedral of the Immaculate Conception* (Roman Catholic), in Claiborne St., between Dauphin and Conti ; *Christ Church* (Episcopal), cor. Church and St. Emanuel Sts. ; *Trinity* (Episcopal) with massive campanile and belfry ; and the *First Presbyterian,* cor. Government and Jackson Sts. The principal charitable institutions are the *City Hospital,* the *United States Marine Hospital,* four Orphan Asylums, and the *Providence Infirmary.* The *Medical College* is also a prosperous institution.

Spring Hill is a pleasant suburban retreat 6 miles W. of the city (reached by the St. Francis St. cars). The *College of St. Joseph,* a Jesuit institution, is located here. It was founded in 1832 by Bishop Portier, and has a fine building 375 ft. long surmounted by a tower from which noble views may be obtained. The college has a library of 8,000 volumes and a valuable collection of scientific apparatus. A statue of the Virgin Mary brought from Toulouse, France, stands in rear of the building. The **Gulf Shell Road** affords a delightful drive, 9 miles in length, along the shore of the bay.

112. Richmond to New Orleans via Mobile.

BETWEEN Richmond and Mobile either of the routes described in Route 111 may be taken. From Mobile the route is *via* the New Orleans, Mobile & Texas R. R. (distance 141 miles). There are no important stations on the line, but the journey is one of great interest from a scenic point of view. "Nothing in lowland scenery," says Mr. Edward King, in his "Great South," "could be more picturesque than that afforded by the ride from New Orleans to Mobile, over the Mobile & Texas R. R., which stretches along the Gulf line of Louisiana, Mississippi, and Alabama. It runs through savannahs and brakes, skirts the borders of grand forests, offers here a glimpse of a lake and there a peep at the blue waters of the noble Gulf; now clambers over miles of trestle-work, as at *Bay St. Louis, Biloxi* (the old fortress of Bienville's time) and *Pascagoula ;* and now plunges into the very heart of pine-woods, where the foresters are busily building little towns and felling giant trees, and where the revivifying aroma of the forest is mingled with the fresh breezes from the sea." **New Orleans** (see p. 465).

113. Washington to Mobile and New Orleans.

a. Via "*Great Southern Mail and Kennesaw Routes.*"

THE first section of this route, between Washington and Lynchburg, is *via* the Washington City, Virginia Midland & Great Southern R. R., which traverses a portion of Virginia full of memorials, both of the Revolutionary era and of the late civil war. Leaving *Alexandria* (7 miles), which has been described on page 58, the trains pass amid the scenes of the earliest struggles of the war, the outposts of the opposing armies occupying this ground for a large part of the time. **Manassas** (34 miles) was the scene of the first great battle of the civil war, fought July 21, 1861, between the Confederates under Beauregard and the Federals under McDowell, in which the latter were routed ; and also of another battle, fought August 29 and 30, 1862, between the Confederates under Lee and the Federals under Pope, in which the latter were again defeated. The battle-ground of the "first Manassas" is 3 or 4 miles from the station, and intersected by the Sudley, Brentsville & Warrenton Turnpike, which crosses at Stone Bridge. The battle-ground of the "second Manassas" was nearly identical with the first, with, however, a *change of sides* by the combatants. At Manassas the Manassas Branch diverges and runs in 63 miles to *Strasburg ;* and from *Warrenton Junction* (48 miles) a branch road runs to *Warrenton.* At *Rappahannock* (58 miles) the train crosses the Rappahannock River. **Culpeper Court-House** (69 miles) was an important military point during the war, the place having been occupied and reoccupied time after time by both armies, between whom numerous engagements occurred in the fields surrounding the village. Culpeper County was famous in Revolutionary times for its company of "Culpeper Minute-Men," in which Chief-Justice Marshall was enrolled and fought, and whose flag bore a picture of a coiled rattlesnake with the motto, "Don't tread on me ! " Of this body of men, John Randolph is reported to have said that "they were summoned in a minute, armed in a minute, marched in a minute, fought in a minute, and vanquished in a minute." Twelve miles beyond Culpeper the train crosses the Rapidan River, which was the line of defense frequently held by the Confederates during the war, and soon reaches *Gordonsville* (95 miles), a busy place at the junction with the Chesapeake and Ohio R. R. Twenty-one miles beyond Gordonsville is **Charlottesville** (*Farish House, Central*), famous as the seat of the University of Virginia and for its proximity to Monticello, the home and tomb of Thomas Jefferson. It is an attractive and well-built town of about 3,000 inhabitants, situated on Moore's Creek, 2 miles above its entrance into Rivanna River. The ** University of Virginia* is situated 1½ mile W. of Charlottesville, is built on moderately elevated ground, and forms a striking feature in a beautiful landscape. It was founded in 1819, and its organization, plan of government, and system of instruction, are due to Thomas Jefferson, who in the inscription prepared by himself for his tomb preferred to be remembered as the "author of the Declaration of Independence and of the statute of Virginia for religious freedom, and father of the University of Virginia." * *Monticello,* once the home and now the burial-place of Jefferson, is about 4 miles W. of Charlottesville. It stands upon an eminence, with many aspen-trees around it, and commands a view of the Blue Ridge for 150 miles on one side, and on the other one of the most extensive and beautiful landscapes in the world. The remains of Jefferson lie in a small family cemetery by the side of the winding road leading to Monticello. Congress has appropriated $5,000 to erect a suitable monument over them, in place of the ruined granite obelisk which now marks the spot. **Lynchburg** (178 miles, *Norvell House, Arlington*) is a city of about 15,000 inhabitants, which derives its importance from the lines of railway which center here, and the extent and character of its tobacco and other manufactures. It is situated on the S. bank of James River, and enjoys an inexhaustible water-power. It occupies a steep acclivity rising gradually from the river-bank, and breaking away into numerous hills, whose terraced walks and ornamental dwellings give a picturesque and romantic appearance to the city. About 20 miles in the background rises the Blue Ridge, together with the Peaks of Otter, which are in full view. In the neighborhood of Lynchburg are vast fields of coal and iron-ore, and the celebrated *Botetourt Iron Works* are not far distant.

Beyond Lynchburg the route is *via* the Atlantic, Mississippi & Ohio R. R. This road passes through the large extent of country known as "Southwestern Virginia," and famous for its wild scenery and inexhaustible mineral resources. It intersects or passes between the parallel ramparts of the great range of the Alleghanies, the backbone of the Atlantic slope of the continent, as the Rocky Mountains are the backbone of the Pacific slope; and scenes full of picturesque grandeur meet the eye of the traveler on every side. At *Liberty* (25 miles from Lynchburg, 203 from Washington) the views are very fine. The Blue Ridge runs across the N. W. horizon, and attains its greatest height in the famous * **Peaks of Otter,** about 7 miles distant. These peaks are isolated from the rest of the range, and, with the exception of some peaks in North Carolina, are the loftiest in the Southern States (4,200 ft. above the plain, 5,307 above the sea). The S. peak is easily ascended, and affords a magnificent view. At *Bonsack's* (225 miles from Washington, 47 from Lynchburg) are the much frequented *Coyner's Springs* (see Route 117). From this point stages run in 30 miles to the wonderful ** **Natural Bridge,** situated in Rockbridge County, Va., at the extremity of a deep chasm in which flows the little stream called Cedar Creek, across the top of which, from brink to brink, there extends an enormous rocky stratum, fashioned into a graceful arch. The bed of the stream is more than 200 ft. below the surface of the plain, and the sides of the chasm, at the bottom of which the water flows, are composed of solid rock maintaining a position almost perpendicular. The middle of the arch is 40 ft. in perpendicular thickness, which toward the sides regularly increases with a graceful curve, as in an artificial structure. It is 60 ft. wide, and its span is almost 90 ft. Across the

20

top of the Bridge passes a public road, and as it is in the same plane with the neighboring country, one may cross it in a coach without being aware of the interesting pass. The most imposing view is from about 60 yards below the bridge, close to the edge of the creek; from

The Natural Bridge.

that position the arch appears thinner, lighter, and loftier. A little above the bridge, on the W. side of the creek, the wall of rock is broken into buttress-like masses, which rise almost perpendicularly to a height of nearly 250 ft., terminating in separate pinnacles which overlook the bridge. On the abutments of the bridge there are many names carved in the rock, of persons who have climbed as high as they dared on the face of the precipice. Highest of all for nearly three-quarters of a century was that of George Washington, who when a youth ascended to a point never before reached, but which was surpassed in 1818 by James Piper, a student in Washington College, who actually climbed from the foot to the top of the rock.

From *Alleghany* (255 miles) stages run in 3 miles to the *Alleghany Springs ;* from *Big Tunnel* (259 miles) a tramway runs to the *Montgomery White Sulphur Springs* (1 mile distant); and from *Christiansburg* (264 miles) stages run to *Yellow Sulphur Springs* (3 miles). All these Springs are described in Route 117. **Bristol** (382 miles, *Virginia House*) is a lively town of about 2,000 inhabitants, situated on the boundary line between Virginia and Tennessee. Here the train takes the track of the E. Tennessee, Virginia & Georgia R. R., which runs S. W. through a highly picturesque portion of East Tennessee. *Greenville* (438 miles) is a pretty village of 1,200 inhabitants, seat of a well-known college. **Knoxville** (512 miles, *Lamar House, Atkin*) is a city of about 12,000 inhabitants, situated at the head of steamboat navigation on the Holston River, 4 miles below the mouth of the French Broad. It is built on a healthy and elevated site, commanding a beautiful view of the river and surrounding country. It is the principal commercial place in E. Tennessee, and has some important manufactures. The *East Tennessee University*, with which is connected the State Agricultural College, is located here; also the *Knoxville University* (Methodist) and the *Freedmen's Normal School* (Presbyterian). The *State Institution for the Deaf and Dumb* is a prominent edifice.

At *Cleveland* (594 miles) the road branches, one line running W. in 30 miles to **Chattanooga** (see route *b*, below), while the present route continues S. W. to **Dalton** (622 miles). Dalton is a mountain-environed town of about 2,000 inhabitants, at the junction of 3 railways. It was the initial point of the famous campaign of 1864, was strongly fortified by Gen. Johnston, and could probably have been held against any direct attack; but the position was flanked by Sherman, and consequently evacuated by the Confederates on May 12, 1864.

The *Selma, Rome & Dalton R. R.* connects with the present route at Dalton and affords another through route to Mobile and New Orleans. It extends S. W. through Georgia and Alabama, and the distance from Dalton to Selma is 236 miles. The principal places on the line are **Rome** (*Rome Hotel*), the most important city of Northern Georgia, with a population of 3,500 ; *Cave Spring,* the seat of the State Asylum for the Deaf and Dumb; *Talladega,* the seat of the Alabama State Asylum for the Deaf and Dumb ; *Shelby Springs,* with valuable mineral waters : *Calera,* at the crossing of the South and North Alabama R. R. ; and **Selma** (*St. James Hotel*), a busy manufacturing city of 8,000 inhabitants, on the right bank of the Alabama River, 95 miles below Montgomery. From Selma the traveler can reach New Orleans *via* Mobile or *via* Meridian, Miss.

From Dalton the route we are describing is *via* Western & Atlanta R. R., which traverses a region interesting as the arena of one of the most obstinate struggles of the civil war—the campaign, namely, between Sherman and Johnston, which culminated in the fall of Atlanta (see p. 451). This campaign began in the vicinity of Chattanooga, and extended directly down the line of the railway to Atlanta. Mementoes of the struggle may be seen by the traveler on the crests of nearly every one of the huge ranges of hills which mark the topography of the country, in the shape of massive breastworks and battlements, which time and the elements are fast obliterating. At *Dalton*, as we have already said, occurred the initial struggle of the campaign. *Resaca* (15 miles beyond Dalton) was the place of the next stand made by John-ston, and was the scene of severe and indecisive fighting between the two armies; it was finally captured by a flank march on the part of Gen. Sherman. Retreating from this point Johnston took a position at *Alatoona* (44 miles below), which was considered impregnable, but it too was successfully flanked and the Confederates forced back to the Chattahooche and Atlanta. The largest town on the line is *Cartersville* (52 miles from Dalton), which has a population of about 3,000. *Marietta* (20 miles from Atlanta) is the most elevated point on the line, has a delightful climate in summer, and is then much resorted to. It con-tains about 2,000 inhabitants, and is the site of a National Cemetery, in which are buried 10,000 Federal soldiers. *Kennesaw Mountain* (2½ miles distant) overlooks a vast extent of country, and played an impor-tant part in the campaign in this vicinity. **Atlanta** (721 miles from Washington) is described on page 451. From Atlanta the route is the same as in Route 111 *a*. (The total distance from Washington to Mo-bile by this route is 1,076 miles; to New Orleans, 1,217 miles.)

b. Via Chattanooga and Meridian.

As far as *Cleveland* (594 miles) this route is the same as the pre-ceding. From Cleveland a branch of the East Tenn., Va. & G. R. R. runs W. in 30 miles to **Chattanooga** (*Reid House*), a city of 7,000 inhabitants, situated on the Tennessee River near where the S. boun-dary of Tennessee touches Alabama and Georgia. Five railroads con-verge here, and the river is navigable to this point by steamboats for 8 months of the year, and by small boats at all times. Chattanooga is the shipping point for most of the surplus productions of East and of a portion of Middle Tennessee, and contains a number of mills and factories. During the civil war Chattanooga was an important strategic point for the operations in Tennessee and Georgia, and played a promi-nent part in most of the campaigns in this region. Above the city the celebrated *** Lookout Mountain** towers to the height of 1,400 ft. It was on this mountain that the battle was fought "above the clouds." The summit of the mountain is reached by a picturesque turnpike road, which leads through a variety of interesting scenes. On the summit stand the large buildings used by the Government during the war as a hospital post for convalescents; they are now occupied in summer by visitors. The views about the mountain are very at-tractive, and few scenes are lovelier than the Valley of the Tennessee as seen from its lofty summit. The points on Lookout best worth visiting are Lake Seclusion, Lulah Falls, Rock City, and the Battle-Field.

From Chattanooga the route is *via* the Alabama & Great Southern R. R. (formerly Alabama & Chattanooga), which runs S. W. across Ala-bama and terminates at Meridian, in the State of Mississippi. Most of the stations on the line are small villages which need not be mentioned. **Tuscaloosa** (198 miles, *Miller's Hotel*) is a city of about 2,500 inhabitants, situated on the left bank of the Black Warrior River, at the head of steamboat navigation. It is the commercial center of a district rich in resources, and has a considerable trade in cotton, wheat, coal, etc. The streets of the city are wide and well shaded. A mile distant are the grounds of the *University of Alabama ;* the buildings, with their contents, were burned in 1865, and have been only partially restored. The *Alabama Insane Hospital*, about a mile beyond the University, has a front of 780 ft., with extensive out-buildings and grounds. The city takes its name from the Indian chief Tuscaloosa ("black warrior"), who was defeated by De Soto in the bloody battle of Malvila, Oct. 18, 1540. From 1826 to 1846 it was the capital of the State. *Eutaw* (233 miles) is a pretty town, capital of Greene County, situated 3 miles W. of the Black Warrior River. The adjacent country is one of the most fertile portions of the State, and Eutaw is surrounded by rich plantations. *York* (268 miles) is at the junction with the Alabama Central R. R., which runs across the State from Selma to Meridian. At *Cuba* (274 miles) the road crosses the boundary line and enters the State of Mississippi, and 21 miles beyond reaches **Meridian**, whose importance is due chiefly to its position at the junction of several railways. It was captured by Gen. Sherman on Feb. 16, 1864, and according to his own account his troops accomplished "the most complete destruction of railways ever beheld." At Meridian the passengers for Mobile take the Mobile & Ohio R. R., which runs S. to Mobile in 135 miles. Those going to New Orleans can go *via* Mobile (see Route 112), or can take the Vicksburg & Meridian R. R., which connects at Jackson with the Chicago, St. Louis & New Orleans R. R. (see Route 115). (The total distance from Washington to Mobile by this route is 1,054 miles; to New Orleans, 1,195 miles).

114. Louisville to Mobile and New Orleans.

By the Louisville & Great Southern R. R. This is one of the great highways of travel and traffic between the Northern and Southern States. At Louisville close connections are made with the various routes, converging there from the North and West (see Routes 71 and 78). Through Palace cars are run without change from New York, Philadelphia, Baltimore, Washington, and St. Louis to Louisville; and from Cincinnati and Louisville to Montgomery, Mobile, and New Orleans. The time from Louisville to Mobile is about 51 hours; to New Orleans, about 56 hours. Distances : to Cave City, 85 miles; to Memphis Junction, 118 (Memphis, 377); to Nashville, 185 ; to Decatur, 308; to Birmingham, 315 ; to Calera, 428 ; to Montgomery, 490 ; to Mobile, 670 ; to New Orleans, 811.

LOUISVILLE is described in Route 72. Leaving Louisville the train runs S. W. across a productive and populous portion of Kentucky, then crosses Tennessee from N. to S., and continues S. through Central Alabama. *Bardstown Junction* (22 miles) is the point whence the Bardstown Branch runs to *Bardstown* (17 miles distant). At *Lebanon Junction* (30 miles) the Knoxville branch diverges. *Mumfordsville* (73 miles) is a pretty village on the right bank of Green River, which is here spanned by a fine bridge. This neighborhood was the scene of

numerous encounters between Generals Buell and Bragg in the campaign of 1862. From *Cave City* (85 miles) stages connecting with the
trains run to the famous **★ ★ Mammoth Cave,** 8 miles distant (fare,
$1). There is a hotel at Cave City, where fair accommodation may be
had, and the *Cave Hotel* is near the cave-entrance. The mouth of the
cave is reached by passing down a wild rocky ravine through a dense
forest; it is an irregular, funnel-shaped opening, from 50 to 100 ft. in
diameter at the top, with steep walls about 50 ft. high. The cave,
which is the largest known, extends about 9 miles; and it is said that
to visit the portions already explored requires from 150 to 200 miles
of travel. This vast interior contains a succession of marvelous
avenues, chambers, domes, abysses, grottoes, lakes, rivers, cataracts,
etc., which for size and wonderful appearance are unsurpassed. The
rocks present numerous forms and shapes of objects in the external
world; while stalactites and stalagmites of gigantic size and fantastic
form abound, though not so brilliant and beautiful as are found in
some other caves. Two remarkable species of animal life are found in
the cave, in the form of an eyeless fish and an eyeless crawfish, which
are nearly white in color. Another species of fish has been found with
eyes but totally blind. Other animals known to exist in the cave are
lizards, frogs, crickets, rats, bats, etc., besides ordinary fish and crawfish washed in from the neighboring Green River. The atmosphere of
the cave is pure and healthful; the temperature, which averages 59°,
is about the same in winter and summer, not being affected by climatic
changes without. To describe the cave in detail would require a volume, and, after all, the visitor would have to entrust himself to the
guides. These give him the choice between the *Short Route* (fee, $2)
and the *Long Route* (fee, $3). They carry lamps and torches, and im-
part all the needful information regarding special localities.

"The stars were all in their places as I walked back to the hotel. I had been 12
hours under ground, in which time I had walked about 24 miles. I had lost a day,
a day with its joyous morning, its fervid noon, its tempest, and its angry sunset of
crimson and gold, but I had gained an age in a strange and hitherto unknown world
—an age of wonderful experience, and an exhaustless store of sublime and lovely
memories. Before taking a final leave of the Mammoth Cave, however, let me
assure those who have followed me through it that no description can do justice to
its sublimity, or present a fair picture of its manifold wonders. It is the greatest
natural curiosity I have ever visited, Niagara not excepted, and he whose expecta-
tions are not satisfied by its marvelous avenues, domes, and starry grottoes, must
either be a fool or a demigod."—BAYARD TAYLOR.

Twenty-nine miles beyond Cave City is **Bowling Green** (114
miles), a thriving town of 5,000 inhabitants, at the head of navigation
on Barren River. At the beginning of the civil war Bowling Green was
regarded as a point of great strategic importance, and was occupied in
Sept., 1861, by a large force of Confederates for the purpose of defending
the approach to Nashville. After the capture of Fort Henry by the Federals (Feb. 6, 1862), the Confederates found themselves outflanked, and
were obliged to evacuate the town. At *Memphis Junction* (118 miles),
the Memphis Line diverges from the main line, and runs, in 259 miles,
to **Memphis** (see p. 492). At *Edgefield Junction* (175 miles) connec-

tion is made with the St. Louis & Southeastern R. R., which forms a short line between St. Louis and points in the Southern States. *Edgefield* (184 miles) is a pretty village on the river just opposite Nashville.

Nashville (*Maxwell House, Scott's Hotel*) is the capital of Tennessee, and the second city of the State in point of population (about 30,000), and is situated on the S. bank of the Cumberland River, 200 miles above its junction with the Ohio. The land on which the city is built is irregular, rising in gradual slopes, with the exception of *Capitol Hill*, which is more abrupt. This eminence is symmetrical, resembling an Indian mound, and overlooks the entire city. Nashville is regularly laid out, with streets crossing each other at right angles, but mostly rather narrow. It is generally well built, and there are numerous imposing public and private buildings. Among the former is the * **Capitol,** situated on Capitol Hill, and constructed inside and out of a beautiful variety of fossiliferous limestone. It is 3 stories high including the basement, and is surmounted by a tower 206 ft. in height. The dimensions of the whole building are 239 by 138 ft.; it was erected in 1845 at a cost of nearly $1,000,000; and it is considered one of the finest public buildings in America. It is approached by 4 avenues, which rise from terrace to terrace by broad marble steps. The * *Court-House* is a large building on the Public Square, with an eight-columned Corinthian portico at each end, and a four-columned portico at each side. The *Market-House*, also on the Public Square, is a handsome structure. The *State Penitentiary* has spacious stone buildings occupying 3 sides of a hollow square enclosed by a massive stone wall, within which are numerous workshops. The *State Institution for the Blind* is located at Nashville, and the *State Hospital for the Insane* is about 6 miles distant. The educational institutions of the city are numerous and important. The *University of Nashville* has about 250 students and a library of 12,000 volumes. The main building is a handsome Gothic edifice of stone. The Medical Department also has a fine building and museum. *Fisk University* was established in 1866 by several Northern gentlemen for the colored youth of the State. The *Tennessee Central College* (Methodist), also for colored people, was established in 1866. The buildings of *Vanderbilt University* (named in honor of the late "Commodore" Vanderbilt, of New York, who gave $500,000 for its establishment) are in course of erection. It is under the control of the Methodist Episcopal Church, South, and is intended to comprise theological, law, medical, literary and scientific departments. The city is lighted with gas, is supplied with water by expensive works, and has several lines of street railway. The railways converging here and the river enable the city to command the trade of an extensive region, and its manufactures are varied and important. *The Hermitage*, the celebrated residence of Andrew Jackson, is 12 miles E. of Nashville.

The Battle of Nashville.—In November, 1864, the Confederate General Hood, having lost Atlanta, placed his army in Sherman's rear and began an invasion of Tennessee. After severe fighting with Gen. Schofield on Nov. 30, he advanced upon Nashville and shut up Gen. Thomas within its fortifications. For two

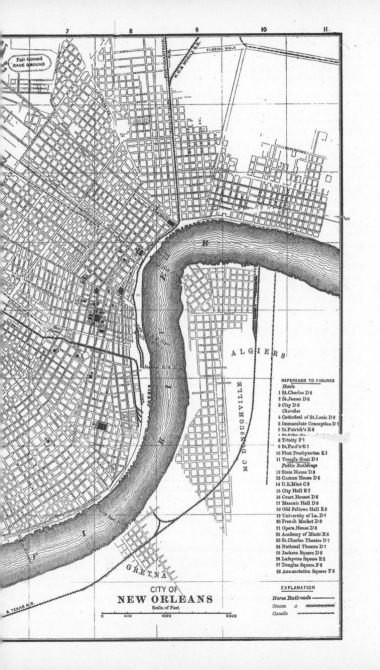

REFERENCE TO FIGURES

Hotels
1 St.Charles D 8
2 St.James D 8
3 City D 8

Churches
4 Cathedral of St.Louis D 8
5 Immaculate Conception D 7
6 St.Patrick's E 8
7 St.John the ... D 8
8 Trinity F 7
9 St.Paul's E 7
10 First Presbyterian E 8
11 Temple Sinai D 7

Public Buildings
12 State House D 8
13 Custom House D 8
14 U.S.Mint C 8
15 City Hall E 8
16 Court House D 8
17 Masonic Hall D 8
18 Odd Fellows Hall E 8
19 University of La. D 7
20 French Market D 8
21 Opera House D 8
22 Academy of Music E 8
23 St.Charles Theatre D 7
24 National Theatre D 7
25 Jackson Square D 8
26 Lafayette Square E 8
27 Douglas Square F 6
28 Annunciation Square F 8

EXPLANATION

Horse Railroads ————
Steam ª |||||||||||||||
Canals ▬▬▬▬

CITY OF
NEW ORLEANS
Scale of Feet

0   400   1000   2000

weeks little was done on either side. When Thomas was fully ready, he suddenly sallied out on Hood, and in a terrible two days' battle drove the Confederate forces out of their intrenchments into headlong flight. The Union cavalry pursued them, the infantry following close behind, and the entire Confederate army, except the rear-guard, which fought bravely to the last, was broken into a rabble of demoralized fugitives, which at last escaped across the Tennessee. For the first time in the war an army was destroyed; and General Sherman, who had been awaiting in Atlanta the issue of Hood's manœuvre, then started on his famous march to the sea.

Between Nashville and Montgomery there is little to attract the tourist's attention. The country traversed offers few picturesque features, and the towns along the line are for the most part unimportant. The largest of them is **Columbia** (48 miles beyond Nashville), a flourishing town of about 3,000 inhabitants, situated on the left bank of Duck River, in the midst of a fertile and productive region. It is the seat of Jackson College, a female Athenæum, a female institute, and a conference college. At *State Line* (281 miles) the train leaves Tennessee and enters Alabama. *Decatur* (308 miles) is a neat village at the junction with the Memphis & Charleston R. R. *Birmingham* (395 miles) is at the crossing of the Alabama Great Southern R. R. (Route 113 *b*), and *Calera* (428 miles) is at the crossing of the Selma, Rome & Dalton R. R. (see p. 459). **Montgomery** (490 miles) has been described on page 452. From Montgomery to Mobile and New Orleans the route is the same as in Route 111 *a*.

115. Chicago and St. Louis to New Orleans.

By the Chicago, St. Louis & New Orleans R. R., known as the "Great Jackson Route." This is one of the main trunk lines between the Northern and Southern States; and Pullman Palace cars are run through without change from Chicago, Cincinnati, Louisville, and St. Louis; and with but one change from New York, Boston, Philadelphia, and Baltimore. Two trains are run daily, and the time from Chicago to New Orleans is about 50 hours; from St. Louis to New Orleans, about 38 hours. Distances: Chicago to Cairo, 365 miles; St. Louis to Cairo, 140 miles; *Cairo* to Milan, 86 miles; to Jackson, Tenn., 109; to Bolivar, 138; to Grand Junction, 156; to Grenada, 256; to Canton, 344; to Jackson, Miss., 368; to Magnolia, 453; to New Orleans, 550.

From Chicago to Cairo this route is *via* the Illinois Central R. R. and has been described in Route 79. From St. Louis the route is *via* the St. Louis & Cairo Short Line, which runs S. E. from St. Louis, and connects at Du Quoin with the Illinois Central R. R. At **Cairo** (see p. 336) the Ohio River is crossed, and the road runs almost due S. across portions of Kentucky and Tennessee and through Central Mississippi. The country traversed is for the most part populous and pleasing, but there are no large cities *en route* and very few important towns. At *Fulton* (44 miles from Cairo) connection is made with the Memphis, Paducah & Northern R. R., and at *Martin's* (55 miles) with the Nashville, Chattanooga & St. Louis R. R. **Milan** (86 miles) is at the crossing of the Memphis Div. of the Louisville & Great Southern R. R., 93 miles from Memphis (see p. 462). The cars from Cincinnati and Louisville going South on the "Great Jackson Route" run through *via* Milan. Twenty-three miles beyond Milan is **Jackson** (*Robinson House*), the largest city in this section of Tennessee, with a population of about 10,000. It is pleasantly situated on the Forked Deer River, in the midst of a fertile region, and has a large and growing trade. There are several manufacturing establishments, including the extensive machine-shops of the Mobile & Ohio R. R., which intersects the present route at this point. Jackson is the seat of the *West Tennessee College,* which is in a prosperous condition, and of a Methodist female institute. *Bolivar* (138 miles) is a handsome and thriving town of about 2,000 inhabitants, situated 1 mile S. of the Hatchee River, which is navigable by steamboats for 6 to 9 months of the year. *Grand Junction* (156 miles) is at the crossing of the Memphis & Charleston R. R. Shortly beyond Grand Junction the train crosses the State line and enters Mississippi, soon reaching the flourishing town of *Holly Springs* (181 miles), which is noted for its educational institutions and the pleasing scenery adjacent. *Grenada* (256 miles) is pleasantly situated on the Yallowbusha River, at the head of steamboat-navigation. It contains a U. S. land-office and several churches. Connection is made here with the Mississippi & Tennessee R. R. *Canton* (344 miles) is a neat and lively village; and 24 miles beyond the train reaches **Jackson** (*Edwards House*), the capital of the State of Mississippi. It is regularly built upon undulating ground on the W. bank of Pearl River, and has about 6,000 inhabitants. The * *State House* is a very handsome edifice erected at a cost of $600,000. The other chief public buildings are the *Executive Mansion*, the *State Lunatic Asylum*, the *State Institutions for the Deaf, Dumb, and Blind*, and the *City Hall*. The *State Penitentiary*, a spacious and handsome edifice, was nearly destroyed during the civil war, but is to be rebuilt. The *State Library* contains 15,000 volumes. Jackson was captured by Gen. Grant on May 14, 1863, after a battle with Gen. Johnston in which the Confederates were defeated. The railroad depots, bridges, arsenals, workshops, storehouses, and many residences were destroyed. Between Jackson and New Orleans there are numerous small towns, but none requiring mention.

116. New Orleans.

Hotels.—The *St. Charles Hotel* ($4.50 a day), bounded by St. Charles, Gravier and Common Sts., is one of the institutions of New Orleans, and one of the largest and finest hotels in the United States. The *St. James Hotel* ($2.50 a day), in Magazine St., between Gravier and Natchez, is a large and well-kept house. The *City Hotel* ($2.50 a day), at the corner of Camp and Common Sts., is much frequented by merchants and planters. All the hotels make considerably lower rates to guests remaining a week or more. Good board may be obtained in all parts of the city at rates ranging from $6 to $20 a week.

Restaurants.—Of restaurants, New Orleans is said to have the best in America; in many of them is still practiced the famous creole *cuisine* of ante-war times. The most noted are *Moreau's*, in Canal St. ; *Victor's*, 38 and 40 Bourbon St.; *John's*, 16 and 18 Bourbon St.: *Antoine's*, 65 St. Louis St.; and *Denechaud's*, 8 Carondelet St. In the French quarter, *cafes* are to be found in nearly every block.

Modes of Conveyance.—The *horse-car* system of New Orleans is perhaps the most complete in the country. Starting from the central avenue—Canal Street—tracks radiate to all parts of the city and suburbs, and passengers are carried to any point within the city limits for 5c. *Omnibuses* attend the arrival of trains and steamers, and convey passengers to the hotels, etc. (fare, 50 cts.). *Carriages* can be found at the stands in front of the St. Charles and other leading hotels. Fare, $2 an hour; $5 for the forenoon or afternoon. The best plan for strangers is to hire a suitable conveyance by the hour and discharge at the end of each trip. *Ferries* connect the city with Algiers, Macdonough, and Gretna, on the opposite side of the river.

Theatres and Amusements.—The French *Opera-House*, cor. Bourbon and Toulouse Sts., has seats for 2,000, and is fitted up in the style of the Théâtre Français, Paris. The *Academy of Music*, in St. Charles St. between Poydras and Commercial Sts., is the usual place for variety performances. The *St. Charles Theatre*, in St. Charles St. between Perdido and Poydras, is handsomely appointed, and has a good company. The *National* (or *Globe*) *Theatre* is at the cor. of Perdido and Baronne Sts., and the *Varieties Theatre* in Canal St. Besides the theatres, there are a score or more of halls in which entertainments of various kinds are given. The principal of these are the *Masonic Hall, Odd-Fellows' Hall, St. Patrick's Hall, Exposition Hall,* and *Grünewald Hall,* in Baronne St. near Canal. *Horse-races* occur at the Fair-Grounds race-track (reached by Shell Road and 3 lines of horse-cars). Besides the regular sources of amusement which it enjoys in common with other cities, New Orleans is noted for its great displays during the holiday and carnival season. Among the many societies which contribute to these displays, the most famous are the *Twelfth-Night Revellers*, who appear on the night of January 6th, and the *Mystick Krewe of Comus*, who appear on the night of *Mardi Gras*, or Shrove-Tuesday. On the same day (Shrove-Tuesday), Rex, King of the Carnival, arrives with a large retinue, takes formal possession of the city for the nonce, and makes a grand display, followed by his staff, courtiers, and attendants, all mounted and dressed in gorgeous Oriental costumes. The processions are followed by receptions, tableaux, and balls, which are largely attended by the *élite* of the city, and by strangers sojourning there, who are generally the recipients of cards of invitation.

Clubs.—There are about twenty clubs in the city, prominent among which are the Boston, the Pickwick, the Shakespeare, and the Jockey Club. The *Jockey Club* has a fine house and beautifully decorated and cultivated grounds near the fair-grounds. The *Shakespeare Club* gives occasional dramatic entertainments which are always largely and fashionably attended. The privileges of these as well as of the *Social Club* are obtained by introduction by a member.

Post-Office.—The Post-Office occupies the basement of the Custom-House, which fronts on Canal St. between Peters and Decatur Sts. It is open from 7 A. M. to 8 P. M. Letters may also be mailed in the lamp-post boxes, whence they are collected at frequent intervals.

NEW ORLEANS, the capital, chief city, and commercial metropolis of Louisiana, is situated on both banks (but chiefly on the left) of the Mississippi River, 100 miles above its mouth, in latitude 29° 57′ N. and longitude 90° W. The older portion of the city is built within a great bend of the river, from which circumstance it derives its familiar *sobriquet* of the " Crescent City." In the progress of its growth upstream, it has now so extended itself as to follow long curves in opposite directions, so that the river-front on the left bank presents an outline somewhat resembling the letter S. The statutory limits of the city embrace an area of nearly 150 square miles, but the actual city covers an area of about 41 square miles. It is built on land gently descending from the river toward a marshy tract in the rear, and from 2 to 4 ft. below the level of the river at high-water mark, which is prevented from overflowing by a vast embankment of earth, called the Levee. This Levee is 15 ft. wide and 14 ft. high, is constructed for a great distance along the river-bank, and forms a delightful promenade.

The site of New Orleans was surveyed in 1717 by De la Tour: it was settled in 1718, but abandoned in consequence of overflows, storms, and sickness; was resettled in 1723, held by the French till 1729, then by the Spanish till 1801, and by the French again till 1803, when, with the province of Louisiana, it was ceded to the

United States. It was incorporated as a city in 1804, and in 1868 was made the capital of the State. The most memorable events in the history of New Orleans are the battle of Jan. 8, 1815, in which the British were defeated by Andrew Jackson, and the capture of the city by Admiral Farragut on April 24, 1862. In 1810, seven years after its cession to the United States, the population of New Orleans was 17,243. In 1850 it had increased to 116,375; in 1860, to 168,675; and in 1870, to 191,418. In 1875 local authorities estimated it at about 210,000.—In the value of its exports and its entire foreign commerce New Orleans ranks next to New York, though several ports surpass it in the value of imports. Not unfrequently from 1,000 to 1,500 steamers and flat-boats may be seen lying at the Levee; and, except in the summer months, its wharves are thronged with hundreds of ships and sailing-craft from all quarters of the globe. New Orleans is the chief cotton mart of the world; and, besides cotton, it sends abroad sugar, rice, tobacco, flour, pork. etc., to the total value in 1874 of $93,715,710. Its imports of coffee, sugar, salt, iron, dry-goods, liquors, etc., amounted in 1874 to $14,583,864. The manufactures of the city are not extensive.

The streets of New Orleans, in width and general appearance, are second to those of no city of its size. As far back as Claiborne St. those running parallel to the river and to each other present an unbroken line from the lower to the upper limits of the city, a distance of about 12 miles. Those at right angles to them run from the Mississippi toward the lake with more regularity than might be expected from the very sinuous course of the river. Many of the streets are well paved and some are shelled; but many are unpaved and consequently scarcely passable in wet weather, while in dry weather they are intolerably dusty. Some of the finest streets of the city are in this condition. **Canal St.** is the main business thoroughfare and promenade, and contains many fine stores and private residences. It is nearly 200 ft. wide, and has a grass-plot 25 ft. wide and bordered with two rows of trees, extending in the center through its whole length. Claiborne, Rampart, St. Charles, and Esplanade Sts. are similarly embellished. *Royal, Rampart*, and *Esplanade Sts.* are the principal promenades of the French quarter.—The favorite drives are out the *Shell Road* to Lake Pontchartrain and over a similar road to Carrollton.

New Orleans is not rich in architecture, but there are a few noteworthy buildings. Chief among these is the * **Custom-House,** which, next to the Capitol at Washington, is the largest building in the United States. This noble structure is built of Quincy granite brought from the Massachusetts quarries. Its main front on Canal St. is 334 ft.; that on Custom-House St., 252 ft.; on Peters St., 310 ft.; and on Decatur St., 297 ft. Its height is 82 ft. The Long Room, or chief business apartment, is 116 by 90 ft., and is lighted by 50 windows. The building was begun in 1848, and is not yet entirely finished. The *Post-Office* occupies the basement of the Custom-House, and is one of the most commodious in the country. The * **State-House** is located in St. Louis St., between Royal and Chartres Sts. Prior to 1874 the building was known as the St. Louis Hotel, and held the same high rank as the St. Charles. The old dining-hall is one of the most beautiful rooms in the country, and the great inner circle of the dome is richly frescoed with allegorical scenes and busts of eminent Americans. The * **U. S. Branch Mint** stands at the cor. of Esplanade and Decatur Sts. It is built of brick, stuccoed in imitation of brown stone, in the Ionic style, and, being 282 ft. long, 180 ft. deep, and 3 stories high, presents an imposing appearance. No coining has been done there since the war, but Congress has taken steps to recommence operations. The window,

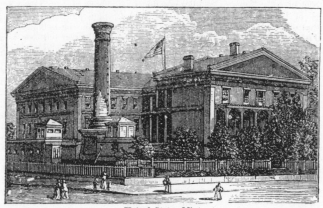

United States Mint.

under the front portico of the main building, from which Mumford was hung by order of General Butler, June 7, 1862, is still pointed out. The *City Hall, at the intersection of St. Charles and Lafayette Sts., is the most artistic of the public buildings of the city. It is of white marble, in the Ionic style, with a wide and high flight of granite steps leading to a beautiful portico supported by 8 columns. The City Library occupies suitable rooms in this building. The *Court-Houses* are on the right and left of the Cathedral, in Jackson Square. They were constructed toward the close of the last century, through the liberality of the founder of the Cathedral, Don Andre Almonaster, and are conspicuous for their quaint style of architecture, which is Tusco-Doric. The *Merchants' Exchange* is a handsome marble structure in Royal St. near Canal. *Masonic Hall*, cor. St. Charles and Perdido Sts., is an imposing edifice, 103 by 100 ft. *Odd-Fellows' Hall* is a massive square structure in Camp St., opposite Lafayette Square. **St. Patrick's Hall,** on the site of the old Odd-Fellows' Hall, is one of the most elegant buildings in the city. Its concert-room seats 3,500 people. *Exposition Hall* is a spacious building in St. Charles St., between Julia and Girod, in which are given floral displays and other exhibitions. The *Mechanics' Institute*, in Dryades St., near Canal, is a commodious building.

The most interesting Church edifice in New Orleans is the old * **Cathedral of St. Louis** (Roman Catholic), which stands in Chartres St., on the E. side of Jackson Square. It has an imposing façade surmounted by a lofty steeple. The foundation was laid in 1792, and the building completed in 1794 by Don Andre Almonaster, perpetual *regidor* of the province. It was altered and enlarged in 1850, from de-

signs by De Louilly. The paintings on the roof of the building are by
Canova and Rossi. The *Church of the Immaculate Conception* (Jesuit),
cor. Baronne and Common Sts., is a striking edifice in the Moorish style.
St. Patrick's (Roman Catholic) is a fine Gothic structure in Camp St.,
N. of Lafayette Square. Its tower, 190 ft. high, was modeled after
that of the famous minster of York, England. The church of *** St.
John the Baptist,** in Dryades St. between Clio and Calliope, is a
very elegant building. The most fashionable Episcopal Churches are
Trinity, cor. Jackson and Coliseum Sts., and **St. Paul's,** cor. Camp
and Gaiennie Sts. The latter is a handsome specimen of the Gothic
style, and has a rich interior. The **First Presbyterian,** fronting on
Lafayette Square, is a fine structure in the Greco-Doric style, much admired for its elegant steeple. The *McGhee Church,* in Carondelet St.
near Lafayette, is the principal of the Methodist Episcopal churches
South. The *Unitarian Church,* cor. St. Charles and Julia Sts., is a
handsome building. The *** Temple Sinai** (Jewish synagogue), in
Carondelet St. near Calliope, is one of the finest places of worship in
the city. Party-colored bricks and pointing give its walls a light, airy
appearance, and it has a handsome portico, flanked by two towers
capped with tinted cupolas. The Gothic windows are filled with beautifully stained glass. One of the most interesting relics of the early
church history of New Orleans is the old *Ursuline Convent* in Condé
St. This quaint and venerable building was erected in 1787, during
the reign of Carlos III., by Don Andre Almonaster. It is now occupied by the bishop, and is known as the " Bishop's Palace."

The **University of Louisiana** is in Common St. near Baronne,
and occupies the entire front of the block. Only two departments,
law and medicine, have been organized, but these are of a very high
order, and are largely attended. *Straight University* is exclusively for
colored students, and gives instruction of good grammar-school grade.
The *** Charity Hospital,** in Common St., is one of the noblest buildings in the city, and one of the most famous institutions of the kind in
the country. It was founded in 1784, has stood on its present site since
1832, and has accommodations for 500 patients. The *Hôtel Dieu*, $\frac{1}{2}$ mile
farther back from the river, is a very fine hospital established by the
Sisters of Charity, and supported entirely by receipts from patients, some
of whom are, nevertheless, beneficiary. It occupies a full square, and
is surrounded by a well-kept garden of shrubbery and flowers. Other
prominent charitable institutions are the *Poydras Female Orphan Asylum*, in Magazine St., the *St. Anna's Widows' Asylum*, the *St. Vincent
Orphan Asylum*, the *Indigent Colored Orphan Asylum*, and the *German Protestant Asylum.* The *Howard Association* is one of the greatest charitable bodies in the world, its special mission being to labor
for the relief of sufferers in epidemics, particularly the yellow fever.

Chief among the pleasure-grounds of the city is *** Jackson Square**
(formerly known as the *Place d'Armes*), covering the center of the
river-front of the old Town Plot, now Second District. It is adorned
with beautiful trees and shrubbery, and shell-strewn paths, and in
the center stands *** Mill's** equestrian statue of General Jackson. The

imposing fronts of the cathedral and courts of justice are seen to great advantage from the river-entrance to the square. *Lafayette Square*, in the First District, bounded by St. Charles and Camp Sts., is another handsome inclosure. The fine marble front of the City Hall, the tapering spire of the Presbyterian Church, and the massive façade of Odd-Fellows' Hall present a striking appearance. In the square is a fine white marble statue of Franklin, by Hiram Powers. In Canal St., between St. Charles and Royal, is a colossal bronze statue of Henry Clay, by Hart. *Douglas Square* is beautifully laid out and well kept. *Annunciation Square* and *Tivoli Circle*, at the head of St. Charles St., are worth a visit. There are some handsome private residences in the neighborhood of the former. The *City Park*, near the N. E. boundary (reached by Canal St. and Ridge Road cars), embraces 150 acres tastefully laid out, but is little frequented.

The *Cemeteries* of New Orleans are noteworthy for their unique arrangement and peculiar modes of interment. From the nature of the soil, which is semi-fluid at a depth of 2 or 3 ft. below the surface, all the tombs are above ground. Some of these are very costly and beautiful structures, of marble, iron, etc.; but the great majority consist of cells, placed one above another, generally to the height of 7 or 8 ft. Each cell is only large enough to receive the coffin, and is hermetically bricked up at its narrow entrance as soon as the funeral rites are over. In most instances a marble tablet, appropriately inscribed, is placed over the brickwork by which the vault (or "oven," as it is called here) is closed. There are 33 cemeteries in and near the city; of these the *Cypress Grove* and *Greenwood*, on the Metairie Ridge, at the N. end of Canal St., are best worth visiting.

The great "sight" of New Orleans, and perhaps the most picturesque to be seen in America, is the *** French Market,** which comprises several buildings on the Levee, near Jackson Square. The best time to visit it is between 8 and 9 o'clock on Sunday morning, or at 6 A. M. on other days. At break of day the gathering commences, and it would seem as if all nations and tongues were represented in the motley crowd which surges in and out until near 10 o'clock. French is the prevailing language, and it will be heard in every variety, from the silvery elegance of the polished creole to the childish jargon of the negroes. The **Levee** affords the visitor one of the most striking and characteristic sights of the Crescent City. For extent and activity it has no equal on the continent. The best points from which to obtain a view of the city and its environs are the roof of the St. Charles Hotel and the tower of St. Patrick's Church.

The most interesting spot in the vicinity of New Orleans is the **Battle-Field,** the scene of General Jackson's great victory over the British, Jan. 8, 1815. It lies 4½ miles S. of Canal St., and may be reached either by carriage along the Levee or by horse-cars. It is washed by the waters of the Mississippi, and extends back about a mile to the cypress-swamps. A marble monument, 70 ft. high and yet unfinished, occupies a suitable site overlooking the ground, and serves to commemorate the victory. A National Cemetery occupies the S. W.

corner of the field.   Between the Battle-Field and the city the *Ursu-line Convent*, an imposing building, 200 ft. long, overlooks the river. *Lake Pontchartrain*, 5 miles N. of the city, is famous for its fish and game.   It is 40 miles long and 24 miles wide.   It is reached by 3 lines of railway with cars drawn by steam, and by drive in carriages on a fine shell-road.   The swamps which lie between the city and the lake are covered with a thick growth of cypress and other trees peculiar to this locality.   *Carrollton*, in the N. suburbs, has many fine public gardens and private residences.   *Algiers*, opposite New Orleans (reached by ferry), has extensive dry-docks and ship-yards.   *Gretna*, on the same side, is a pretty rural spot, abounding in pleasant, shady walks.

117. The Virginia Mineral Springs.

THE most important of the Virginia Springs are either directly on the line of the three great railways which intersect the W. portion of the State—the Baltimore & Ohio, the Chesapeake & Ohio, and the Washington City, Virginia Midland & Great Southern R. R.—or are easily accessible from them by stage.   The most convenient local centers for the tourist are **Staunton** (which is reached *via* the Washington City, Virginia Midland & Great Southern R. R., or *via* the Harper's Ferry & Valley Branch of the Baltimore & Ohio R. R.), and **Lynchburg** (which is reached *via* Route 113 *a*).   Lynchburg is described on page 457.   The greatest number of the springs are reached by stage-connections with points on the Chesapeake & Ohio R. R., between Staunton and the White Sulphur Springs.   Those reached from Lynchburg, however, are much visited, and have the advantage of being situated in a more picturesque country than those farther N.

Hotels, etc.—As a general thing, the hotel, and its cottages, bath-houses, and other buildings, are the only houses in the immediate vicinity of the springs.   The charges at the springs are from $2 to $3 a day ; $30 to $70 per month.   Other expenses are light.   Horses may be hired in the country for $1.50 a day.   At the springs, the charges for horses and vehicles are higher, but very moderate in comparison with the liveries of Northern resorts.   Carriages seating four may usually be hired for $5 a day.   " Let the tourist," says Mr. Pollard, "bring his fishing-rod, and a gun to shoot deer.   A common fault at the springs, and which is perhaps prevalent at all watering-places, is the idle and dawdling life ; but the spas of Virginia have this great and peculiar advantage—that instead of the visitor being compelled to walk or ride on a dusty thoroughfare, or take a paltry stroll on the beach, he may lose himself in a few moments in the neighboring forest, where recreation may be sweetened with perfect solitude, or exercise freshened with the mental excitement that makes it alike pleasant and profitable."

The springs which, owing to the facility with which they are reached, are most resorted to by Northern visitors, are the **Berkeley Springs,** situated in Morgan County, W. Virginia, 2½ miles from *Sir John's Run* on the Baltimore & Ohio R. R. (see p. 286).   The surrounding scenery is highly picturesque, and the spot possesses historic and social associations as connected with Washington, who frequently visited it. From a remote period it has been the resort of large numbers of people from the lower Valley of Virginia and Maryland ; and was a popu-

lar watering-place as far back as 1816, when Paulding visited it and
described it in his "Letters from the South." The waters flow from
five springs at the rate of 2,000 gallons per minute. The temperature
is 74° Fahr. The bathing-pools are very large, and rank with the finest
in Virginia. The water is not remarkable for its curative properties,
and is but slightly impregnated with mineral ingredients, but the bathing is highly invigorating. The main building is a commodious hotel,
in which dancing takes place nightly throughout the season.—**Capon
Springs** is a highly popular resort at the base of the North Mountain,
23 miles from *Winchester*, on the Harper's Ferry Branch of the Baltimore & Ohio R. R. (113 miles from Baltimore), from which it is reached
by stage. The *Mountain House* ($30 to $60 a month) is an excellent
hotel, with several cottages attached, furnishing accommodations for
about 750 guests. Fronting the Mountain House is the bathing establishment, presenting a beautiful colonnade front of 280 ft., with a central building two stories high, 42 by 30 ft., containing parlors, etc., for
the use of bathers. The Capon water contains silicic acid, magnesia,
soda, bromine, iodine, and carbonic-acid gas ; and is recommended for
idiopathic and sympathetic affections of the nervous system, various
forms of dyspepsia, chronic diarrhœa, irritation of the intestinal canal,
and gravel. *Candy's Castle*, the *Tea-Table*, and other curiosities of
the region are accessible from this watering-place.—The **Rawley
Springs** are situated in Rockingham County, 12 miles by stage from
Harrisonburg on the Harper's Ferry & Valley Branch of the Baltimore
& Ohio R. R. (181 miles from Baltimore). The hotel accommodations
are excellent, the grounds are tastefully improved, and the surrounding
scenery is very attractive. The Rawley water is a compound chalybeate ; is alterative and tonic in its effects ; and is held to be remedial
in those chronic diseases which are characterized by low and deficient
vital action.

The most famous and frequented of all the Virginia resorts are the
Greenbrier White Sulphur Springs, situated directly on the line
of the Chesapeake & Ohio R. R., 91 miles W. of Staunton and 227
miles from Richmond. The immediate vicinity of the Springs is very
beautiful. About 50 acres are occupied by the hotels and cottages
and the surrounding lawns and walks, which are admirably kept. The
adjacent scenery is unsurpassed in beauty and picturesqueness. Kate's
Mountain, which recalls some heroic exploits of an Indian maiden of
long ago, is one fine point in the scene southward ; while the Greenbrier Hills lie 2 miles away, toward the W., and the lofty Alleghanies
tower up majestically on the N. and E. It is not known precisely at
what period this spring was discovered. Though the Indians undoubt-
edly knew its virtues, there is no record of its being used by the whites
until 1778. Log-cabins were first erected on the spot in 1784–'86, and
the place began to assume something of its present aspect about 1820.
Since then it has been yearly improved, until it is capable of pleasantly
housing some 1,500 guests. The spring bubbles up from the earth in
the lowest part of the valley, and is covered by a pavilion, formed of
12 Ionic columns, supporting a dome, crowned by a statue of Hygeia.

The principal ingredients of the water are nitrogen gas, oxygen gas, carbonic acid, hydro-sulphuric acid, sulphate of lime and magnesia, and carbonate of lime. Its effect is alterative and stimulant, and it is beneficial in cases of dyspepsia, liver-disease, nervous diseases, cutaneous diseases, rheumatism, and gout.* The position of the White Sulphur is central to nearly all the prominent springs of the region, which may thus be conveniently visited in turn. The Hot Spring is 38 miles distant, on the N.; the Sweet Spring, 17 miles E.; the Salt and the Red Springs, 24 and 41 miles respectively, on the S.; and the Blue Sulphur Spring, 26 miles W. Stages run from the White Sulphur to the **Blue Sulphur Springs,** which are situated in Greenbrier County, in a position of great beauty. The hotel is a brick edifice 180 ft. long, and a canopy rises above the spring in the midst of a beautiful lawn. The water is said to be valuable in chronic hepatitis, jaundice, chronic irritation of the kidneys and bladder, and in diseases of the skin.

The **Old Sweet Springs** are situated in Monroe County and are reached by stage in 9 miles from *Alleghany,* a station on the Chesapeake & Ohio R. R., 86 miles W. of Staunton. This watering-place is said to be the oldest in Virginia, and to have been frequented for its medicinal properties as early as 1764. The water derives a peculiar briskness from the carbonic acid which predominates in it, and is prescribed for all the varieties of dyspepsia, for diarrhœa, dysentery, and general disorder of the system. The springs are situated in a lovely valley, between the Alleghany Mts., which bound the northern prospect, and the Sweet Springs Mountain, rising on the S. The hotel is large, and there are commodious baths for ladies and gentlemen. The **Red Sweet Springs** are situated one mile from the "Old Sweet," and 8 miles from Alleghany Station. The waters are chalybeate and tonic, and the accommodations for visitors ample. The temperature of the water varies from 75° to 79° Fahr., and the three springs discharge 250 gallons per minute.

The **Salt Sulphur Springs** connect by stages with *Fort Spring,* on the Chesapeake & Ohio R. R., 108 miles W. of Staunton. This watering-place is near *Union,* the county-seat of Monroe, about 24 miles from the White Sulphur, and is completely shut in by mountains —Swope's Mountain, Peters's Mountain, and the Alleghanies—the place being near the E. base of the first-named. The springs were discovered in 1805 by Mr. Irwin Benson while boring for salt-water, which he was induced to hope for from the fact that the spot had been a well-known "lick" for deer and buffalo. The hotel and cottages have accommodations for about 400 guests. There are three springs, one of which is styled the "Iodine." The Salt Sulphur water is recommended for chronic affections of the brain; for chronic diseases of the bowels, kidneys, spleen, and bladder; and for neuralgia and the various nervous diseases.

---

* A good guide to the pathological use of the waters of all these springs is Dr. J. J. Moorman's "Mineral Springs of North America."

The **Red Sulphur Springs,** in the S. portion of Monroe County, are 41 miles from the White Sulphur, 17 from the Salt, 32 from the Blue, and 39 from the Sweet. They are reached by stage from *Talcott*, on the Chesapeake & Ohio R. R., 127 miles W. of Staunton. The approach to these springs is beautifully romantic and picturesque. The springs themselves lie in a verdant glen surrounded on all sides by lofty mountains, and the hotels and cottages afford accommodations for about 350 guests. The water of the spring is collected in two white-marble fountains, over which is a tasteful cover. It is clear and cool, with a temperature of 54° Fahr., and is strongly charged with sulphuretted-hydrogen gas, besides containing several of the neutral salts. Its effects are stated to be directly sedative, and indirectly tonic, alterative, diuretic, and diaphoretic ; and it is used with advantage in cases of scrofula, jaundice, chronic dysentery and diarrhœa, dyspepsia, diseases of the uterus, and consumption.

The thermal baths of Bath County are grouped together a short distance N. of the Chesapeake & Ohio R. R., and are unrivaled by any others yet discovered, either in Europe or America. They lie within a short distance of each other, and the visitor may pass from one to another in an hour or two, through magnificent scenery. They are reached by stages from the stations of *Millboro* (39 miles W. of Staunton) and *Covington* (69 miles W. of Staunton). On the stage-ride to the Warm Springs from Millboro, the traveler will be charmed by the magnificent view from the top of Warm Spring Mountain, which he crosses at an elevation of nearly 1,500 ft. above its base (2,250 above the sea). On this route is also seen the curious *Blowing Cave,* situated near the banks of the Cow-Pasture River. The **Warm Springs** were discovered by the Indians, and have long been a popular resort. The water is very abundant, and is used for bathing as well as drinking, chiefly the former. It contains sulphuric, carbonic, silicic, and organic acids, as the first bases, and potash, ammonia, lime, magnesia, protoxide of iron, and alumina, as the second bases. The diseases for which the baths are beneficial are gout, chronic rheumatism, swellings of the joints and glands, paralysis, chronic cutaneous diseases, and calculous disorders. At the lower end of the Warm Spring Valley is the * *Cataract of the Falling Springs,* where a foaming mountain-brook tumbles over a rocky ledge 200 ft. high. The **Hot Springs** are 5 miles S. of the Warm Springs, and 18 from Covington, with which they connect by stages. These are said to be the hottest baths in the world, the temperature reaching 110° Fahr. There are 9 springs, and 9 baths attached, all in the grounds of the hotel. The most marked effect of the free use of these waters is in cases of rheumatism and torpid liver, which are promptly and remarkably relieved. The **Healing Springs** are about 3 miles from the Hot Springs, and connect by stages (15 miles) with Covington. The scenery around this watering-place is extremely agreeable ; there is a fine cascade near, and the Springs buildings make a charming little village, shining pleasantly through the green trees. The waters of this spring are stated to be almost identical in their chemical analysis with the famous Schlagenbad and Ems waters of Germany. Their temperature is uniformly 84° Fahr., and the water is regarded as highly beneficial in cases of scrofula, chronic thrush, obstinate cases of cutaneous disease, neuralgia, rheumatism, ulcers of the lower limbs of long standing, and dyspepsia, in some "hopeless cases" of which it is said to have worked cures. The **Bath Alum Springs** are near the E. base of the Warm Springs Mountains, 5 miles from the Warm Springs, and 10 from Millboro', with which they connect by stages. The waters issue from a slate-stone cliff, and are received into small reservoirs. The springs differ—one of them being a strong chalybeate, with but little alum; another, a milder chalybeate, with more alumina; while the others are alum of different strength, with traces of iron. The waters are decidedly tonic and astringent, and are recommended for scrofula, dyspepsia, eruptive affections, chronic diarrhœa, nervous debility, and in various uterine diseases.

The **Rockbridge Alum Springs** are situated in Rockbridge County. The springs consist of 5 fountains, issuing from beneath irregular slate-stone arches. The hotel and cottages are of brick, and will accommodate about 800 guests. The waters are regarded as highly beneficial in cases of chronic dyspepsia, diarrhœa, scrofula, gastric irritation, and diseases of the skin. The **Rockbridge Baths** are near the Springs just described, and are reached by stage in 9 miles from *Goshen*, on the Chesapeake & Ohio R. R., 32 miles W. of Staunton, and are also reached by stage from Millboro. The springs are within a few feet of the banks of North River, and are surrounded by picturesque scenery. The waters are impregnated with iron, and are strongly charged with carbonic-acid gas. As a tonic bath (adapted to nervous diseases, general debility, especially after the use of alterative mineral waters, and that comprehensive class of cases in which tonic bathing is beneficial) the Rockbridge Baths are highly recommended. *Jordan's Alum Springs* are reached by stage from Millboro. The waters possess qualities similar to those of the other alum springs in this vicinity.

About 300 yards from *Bonsack's* on the Atlantic, Mississippi & Ohio R. R. (see p. 457) are **Coyner's Springs**, a favorite resort with the people of Lynchburg, from which they are only 47 miles distant. The buildings are spacious and comparatively new, and the place has the reputation of being one of the gayest in Virginia. The waters are sulphurous, and, of their class, mild and pleasant. They are recommended in cases of difficult, imperfect, or painful digestion, enfeebled condition of the nervous system, chronic diseases of the bladder or kidneys, salt-rheum, tetters, indolent liver, and in some of the affections peculiar to females.—The **Blue Ridge Springs,** in Botetourt County, directly on the line of the Atlantic, Mississippi & Ohio R. R., have lately become one of the most famous and frequented resorts in Virginia. They are situated near the summit of the Blue Ridge Mountains, 1,300 ft. above the sea, in the midst of delightful scenery, and where the air is exceptionally pure and cool. The hotel is excellent, there are a number of commodious cottages, and the waters have a special reputation for the cure of dyspepsia. From *Alleghany*, on the A., M. & O. R. R. (see p. 459), stages run in three miles to the **Alleghany Springs,** which have long been popular. The large hotel and cottages are situated upon undulating ground, surrounded by wild and picturesque scenery. In the neighborhood (8 miles distant) are the * *Puncheon-Run Falls*, a wonderful series of cascades, where a mountain-brook tumbles for 1,800 ft. down an almost perpendicular ledge. * *Fisher's View* (5 miles from the Springs) is a point on the mountain from which a fine view of the wild and beautiful scenery of the surrounding region may be obtained. The Alleghany water is cathartic, diuretic, and tonic, and is recommended for dyspepsia, depressed biliary secretions, costiveness, scrofula, jaundice, and incipient consumption. From *Big Tunnel*, on the A., M. & O. R. R. (4 miles from Alleghany) a tramway extends 1 mile to the **Montgomery White Sulphur Springs,** located in Montgomery County. The Springs are beautifully situated in the midst of fine scenery, diversified by rippling streams; and the buildings are unusually handsome and substantial, with accommodations for about 1,000 guests. The waters are of two kinds : one a strong sulphur, resembling that of the Greenbrier White Sulphur ; the other a tonic chalybeate. The sulphur is said to be less cathartic and stimulant than other sulphurs, and to act more mildly.—The **Yellow Sulphur Springs** are 5 miles S. W. of the Montgomery White, and 3 miles from *Christiansburg* on the A., M. & O. R. R., with which they connect by stages. This spring is located high up on the E. side of the Alleghany Mountains, and, "in consequence of this elevation, the air is elastic, pure, and invigorating during the hottest days of summer." The water possesses valuable tonic properties, and is delightfully cool, the temperature in the hottest weather remaining at 55°.

The foregoing springs are the most prominent and popular of the "Springs Region." Among other less frequented watering-places are the *Bedford Alum Springs*, W. of Lynchburg, near the Atlantic, Mississippi & Ohio R. R.—The *Grayson White Sulphur Springs*, in Carroll County, near the point where New River passes through the Iron Mountain, and connecting with the A., M. & O. R. R. at Max Meadows.—The *Sharon Alum Springs*, connecting with the A., M. & O. R. R. at Wytheville, 25 miles by stage.—The *Pulaski Alum Springs*, connecting with the A., M. & O. R. R. at Newbern, 10 miles by stage.— *Eggleston's Springs*, near the Salt Pond, a powerful sulphur.—The *Huguenot Springs*, in Pinkerton County, connecting with the Springs Station on the Richmond & Danville R. R., 10 miles by stage.—The *Fauquier White Sulphur Springs*, in Fauquier County, 40 miles from Fredericksburg.—*Jordan's Springs*, in Frederick County, 5 miles from Winchester, and 1½ from Stevenson's Station on the Harper's Ferry & Valley Branch of the Baltimore & Ohio R. R. This is a popular and agreeable summer resort.—The *Shannondale Springs*, in Jefferson County, 5½ miles from Charleston, on the Harper's Ferry & Valley Branch of the B. & O. R. R.—The *Holston Springs*, in Scott County, 28 miles from Bristol, on the A., M. & O. R. R., with which they connect by stage. There are a chalybeate, a white sulphur, a limestone, and a thermal spring here, all within a step or two of each other.

118. Mountain Region of North Carolina, South Carolina, and Georgia.

THE great Appalachian range of mountains, called also the Alleghanies, extends from that part of Canada lying between the New England States and the St. Lawrence River, through the whole length of Vermont, across the W. part of Massachusetts and the middle Atlantic States, to the N. part of Alabama. The White Mts. of New Hampshire and the Adirondack Mts. of New York are really outliers of this range, though separated from it by wide tracts of low elevation. The Catskills form a link of the main range. *Blue Ridge* is the name given to the most eastern of the principal ridges of the chain. It is the continuation S. of the Potomac of the same great ridge which in Pennsylvania and Maryland is known as the South Mountain. It retains the name Blue Ridge till it crosses the James River, from which to the line of North Carolina its continuation is called the Alleghany Mt. Running through North Carolina into Tennessee it again bears the name of the Blue Ridge. The extreme length of the Appalachian range is 1,300 miles; its greatest width (about 100 miles) is in Pennsylvania and Maryland, about midway of its course. In all their extent the Appalachian Mts. are remarkable, not for their great elevation, nor for their striking peaks, nor for any feature that distinguishes one portion of them from the rest; but for a singular uniformity of outline. While varying little in height, the ridges pursue a remarkably straight course, sometimes hardly diverging from a straight line for a distance of 50 or 60 miles, and one ridge succeeding behind another, all continuing the same general course in parallel lines, like successive waves of the sea.

North Carolina.

The mountain region of North Carolina, where the Appalachian system reaches its loftiest altitude, presents scenes of beauty and sublimity unsurpassed by anything E. of the Rocky Mountains. It consists of an elevated table-land, 250 miles long and about 50 broad, encircled by two great mountain-chains (the Blue Ridge on the E. and the Great Smoky on the W.), and traversed by cross-chains that run directly across the country, and from which spurs of greater or lesser height lead off in all directions. Of these transverse ranges there are four: the Black, the Balsam, the Cullowhee, and the Nantahala. Between each lies a region of valleys, formed by the noble rivers and their minor tributaries. The Blue Ridge is the natural barrier, dividing the waters falling into the Atlantic from those of the Mississippi, and its bold and beautiful heights are better known than the grander steeps of the western chain. This W. rampart, known as the Great Smoky, comprises the groups of the Iron, the Unaka, and the Roar Mountains; and from its massiveness of form and general elevation is the master-chain of the whole Alleghany range. Though its highest summits are a few feet lower than the peaks of the Black Mountain, it presents a continuous series of lofty peaks which nearly approach that altitude, its culminating point, *Clingman's Dome*, rising to the height of 6,660 ft.   The most famous of the transverse ranges is that of the Black Mountain, a group of colossal heights, the dominating peak of which—*Mount Mitchell*—is now known to be the loftiest summit E. of the Mississippi.   With its two great branches it is over 20 miles long, and its rugged sides are covered with a wilderness of almost impenetrable forest.   Above a certain elevation, no trees are found save the balsam-fir, from the dark color of which the mountain takes its name. N. of the Black Mountain stand the two famous heights which Prof. Guyot calls "the two great pillars on both sides of the North Gate to the high mountain region of North Carolina."   These are the *Grandfather Mountain* in the Blue Ridge, and *Roan Mountain* in the Smoky. Next to the Black, in the order of transverse chains, comes the Balsam, which in length and general magnitude is chief of the cross-ranges.   It is 50 miles long, and its peaks average 6,000 ft. in height, while, like the Blue Ridge, it divides all waters and is pierced by none. · From its S. extremity two great spurs run out in a northerly direction; one ter-

Asheville.

minates in the *Cold Mountain*, which is over 6,000 ft. high, and the other in the beautiful peak of *Pisgah*, which is one of the most noted landmarks of the region.

The key of the mountain region, and converging point of all the roads W. of the Blue Ridge, is the town of **Asheville** (*Eagle Hotel*), situated in the lovely valley of the French Broad River, 2,250 ft. above the sea, surrounded by an amphitheatre of hills, and commanding one of the finest mountain-views in America. Just above its site the beautiful Swannanoa unites with the French Broad, charming natural parks surround it, and within easy excursion-distance is some of the noblest scenery in the State. The town itself is adorned with many handsome private residences, the hotel accommodations are superior, and there are good churches, schools, banks, and newspapers. There are five routes by which Asheville may be reached from the north, west, and south, and as each of them presents special attractions to tourists by the way, we shall describe them separately.

1st Route.—From Salisbury (see p. 424) *via* Western North Carolina R. R. to Henry's (114 miles), and thence 25 miles by stage. **Morgantown** (*Mountain Hotel*) on this railway, 80 miles from Salisbury, is a popular resort, and well worth the attention of all lovers of mountain-scenery. It is situated on the slopes of the Blue Ridge, 1,100 ft. above the sea, and a very beautiful view may be obtained from any eminence in the vicinity. About 15 miles W. of Morgantown are the *Glen Alpine Springs*, whose waters are of the lithia class, and are said to possess diuretic, tonic, and alterative properties. In this neighborhood the *Hawk's Bill* and *Table Rock* are situated. The latter is a high, bleak rock rising above the top of a mountain to the height of over 200 ft. It can easily be ascended, and upon the summit there is about an acre of rock with a smooth surface. About 25 miles from Morgantown is the grand *** Linnville Gorge,** where the Linnville River bursts through the massive barrier of the Linnville Mountains. Beyond Henry's the stage route penetrates the Blue Ridge through the rugged but picturesque **Swannanoa Gap,** and descends gradually into the elevated basin in which Asheville lies. The latter part of the route lies along the banks of the Swannanoa, loveliest of North Carolina rivers.

2d Route.—From Charlotte (see page 424) *via* the Shelby Div. of the Carolina Central R. R. to Shelby (54 miles), and thence by private conveyance to Asheville (75 miles). Near Shelby are *Wilson's Springs*, somewhat noted as a summer resort. This route lies through the famous *** Hickory-nut Gap,** the scenery of which has been declared by some European travelers to be equal in beauty and grandeur to any pass in the Alps. The entire length of the Gap is about 9 miles, the last 5 being watered by the Rocky Broad River. The gateway of the gorge on the E. side is not more than ½ mile wide, and from this point the road winds upward along a narrow pass, hemmed in on all sides by stately heights. The loftiest bluff is on the south side, and, though 1,500 ft. high, is nearly perpendicular. A stream of water tumbles over one portion of this immense cliff, and falls into an apparently inaccessible pool. From the summit of the Gap there is a most impressive view in all directions.

3d Route.—By stage from Greenville, South Carolina (see p. 451), *via* Saluda Gap, Flat Rock, and Hendersonville, to Asheville (60 miles). This route traverses some of the finest portions of the South Carolina mountain-region (described below), and the entire road lies through the most enchanting and picturesque scenery. **Flat Rock,** once the most frequented of Carolina resorts, has been shorn of its former glories, but the lovely valley still contains some noble mansions, surrounded by beautiful gardens.

4th Route.—By the stage from Greenville, South Carolina (see p. 451), *via* Jones's Gap and Cæsar's Head, to Asheville (about 75 miles). *Cæsar's Head* is a bold and beautiful headland in South Carolina (see p. 481). Beyond Cæsar's Head the route passes near * **Cashier's Valley,** a lofty table-land lying on the side of the Blue Ridge, so near the summit that its elevation above the sea can not be less than 3,500 ft., and hemmed in on all sides by noble peaks, among which *Chimney-top* stands forth conspicuously. On the S. W. edge of the valley is * **Whiteside Mountain,** which is in many respects the most striking peak in North Carolina. Rising to a height of more than 5,000 ft. its S. E. face is an immense precipice of white rock, which, towering up perpendicularly 1,800 ft., is fully 2 miles long, and curved so as to form the arc of a circle. The ascent to the summit can be made partly on horseback and presents no difficulties, and the view is of surpassing grandeur.

"To the N. E., as far as the eye can reach, rise a multitude of sharply defined blue and purple peaks, the valleys between them, vast and filled with frightful ravines, seeming the merest gullies on the earth's surface. Farther off than this line of peaks rise the dim outlines of the Balsam and Smoky ranges. In the distant S. W., looking across into Georgia, we can descry Mount Yonah, lonely and superb, with a cloud-wreath about his brow; 60 miles away, in South Carolina, a flash of sunlight reveals the roofs of the little German settlement of Walhalla; and on the S. E., beyond the precipices and ragged projections, towers up Chimney-Top Mountain, while the Hog-Back bends its ugly form against the sky, and Cold Mountain rises on the left. Turning to the N. we behold Yellow Mountain, with its square sides, and Short-Off. Beyond and beyond, peaks and peaks, and ravines and ravines! It is like looking down on the world from a balloon."—EDWARD KING.

5th Route.—From the north, west, or southwest, Asheville may be reached *via* East Tennessee & Virginia R. R. (Route 113) to Morristown, Tenn.; thence *via* Cumberland Gap & Charleston R. R. to Wolf Creek; and thence by stage (8 miles) to the Warm Springs and up the valley of the French Broad. The Warm Springs and the route thence to Asheville are described further along.

Having reached Asheville (see p. 478), the tourist may spend days or weeks in visiting the many picturesque spots in the vicinity, or in hunting, fishing, or exploring the caves, mines, and Indian mounds. A few miles from the town are some white sulphur springs, from which a variety of lovely views may be had; and 9 miles N. are the so-called *Million Springs*, beautifully situated in a cave between two mountain-ranges, where sulphur and chalybeate waters may be had in abundance. But the excursion which above all others he should not fail to make is that down the * **French Broad River,** the supreme beauty of which has long been famous. Below Asheville the river flows through an ever-deepening gorge, narrow as a Western cañon and inexpressibly grand, until it cuts its way through the Smoky Mountains, and reaches Tennessee. For 36 miles its waters well deserve their musical Cherokee name (Tahkeeostee, "the Racing River"), and the splendor of their ceaseless tumult fascinates both eye and ear. A fine highway follows its banks, and often trespasses upon the stream, as it is crowded by the overhanging cliffs. About 35 miles from Asheville, on the right of the road, is the famous rock *Lover's Leap ;* and just below it, where the left bank widens out into a level plain, the **Warm Springs** (with spacious hotel open all the year) nestle in a beautiful grove of trees. These springs are among the most noted mineral waters in the Southern States, and their virtues have been known for nearly a century. An analysis of the water shows that it contains free carbonic acid, free sulphuretted hydrogen, carbonic acid, and sulphuric acid, in combination with lime, and a trace of magnesia. Though quite palatable as a beverage, it is taken chiefly in the form of baths, for which there are excellent facilities, and is recommended for dyspepsia, liver-complaint, diseases of the kidneys, rheumatism, rheumatic gout, and chronic cutaneous diseases. Five miles below the springs, on the Tennessee boundary, the road passes beneath the bold precipice of the *Painted Rocks,* a titanic mass over 200 ft. high, whose face is marked with red paint, supposed to be Indian pictures. Near by are the *Chimneys,* lofty cliffs, broken at their summits into detached piles of rock bearing the likeness of colossal chimneys, a fancy greatly improved by the fireplace-like recesses at their base.

Among the mountain-ascents that may be readily made from Asheville, those of Mt. Pisgah and Mt. Mitchell will best repay the trouble. *Pisgah* lies to the S., and commands an extensive view over Tennessee, South Carolina, and Georgia, as well as over the greater part of Western North Carolina. The excursion to * **Mt. Mitchell,** including the ascent to the peak and the return to Asheville, can be made in three days, and, though arduous, is entirely free from danger. The summit of Mount Mitchell is the highest in the United States E. of the Mississippi (6,701 ft.), and affords the visitor a view of unsurpassed extent and grandeur. Another attractive mountain-excursion (less often made, however) is to the **Balsam Range,** lying to the W. The route is to *Brevard,* a pleasant village lying in the matchless valley of the Upper French Broad ; and thence along the N. fork of the river into what is called the *Gloucester Settlement.* Here a guide can be secured, and the peaks easily ascended.

South Carolina.

The town of *Greenville* (see p. 451) lies at the threshold of the chief beauties of the South Carolina mountain region, and affords easy access to all the rest. It is beautifully situated on the Reedy River, near its source, at the foot of Saluda Mountain. About 20 miles from Greenville is * **Table Mountain,** one of the most remarkable of the natural wonders of the State, rising 4,300 ft. above the sea, with a long extent on one side of perpendicular cliffs, 1,000 ft. in height. The view of these grand and lofty rock-ledges is exceedingly fine from the quiet glens of the valley below, and not less imposing is the splendid amphitheatre of hill-tops seen from its crown. Among the sights to be seen from Table Mountain is * **Cæsar's Head,** a lofty peak with one side a precipice of great height, just back of which is a large hotel. It is

21

the highest point in the vicinity, and well worth a visit. At the base of Table Mountain, in a romantic glen, are the famous * **Falls of Slicking,** a wonderful series of cascades and rapids. They are situated on the two branches of the Slicking River, of which the right-hand branch is the more picturesque. The **Keowee** is a beautiful mountain-stream in Pickens County, which, with the Tugaloo River, forms the Savannah. The route from Greenville to the valley of Jocasse lies along its banks, amid the most lovely scenery, and the entire region is full of romantic memories of the Cherokee wars. **Jocasse Valley,** near the N. boundary-line, is one of the most charmingly secluded nooks in the State, environed as it is on every side, except that through which the Keowee steals out, by grand mountain-ridges. The great charm of Jocasse is that it is small enough to be seen and enjoyed all at once, as its entire area is not too much for one comfortable picture. It is such a nook as painters delight in. **White Water Cataracts** are an hour's brisk walk N. of Jocasse. Their chief beauty is in their picturesque lines, and in the variety and boldness of the mountain-landscape all around. Adjoining this most attractive region of South Carolina, and easily accessible therefrom, are Tallulah, and Toccoa, and Yonah, and Nacoochee, lying in Georgia and described below.

Falls of Toccoa

Georgia.

The most convenient point from which to visit the mountain region of Georgia is **Clarksville,** a pleasant village in Habersham County, much resorted to in summer by the people of the "Low Country."

It is reached by stage from Toccoa or Mount Airy on the Atlanta & Charlotte Air Line R. R. (see Route 111 *a*); or by stage from Walhalla (on the Greenville & Columbia R. R.) to *Clayton*, which is still nearer the mountains. Fair accommodations for travelers may be had at Clarksville, and also horses or wagons for the exploration of the surrounding country. A few miles from Clarksville is the celebrated *** Toccoa Fall,** where a brook "comes babbling down the mountain's side" and plunges over a precipice 180 ft. high. The *** Cataracts of Tallulah** are 12 miles from Clarksville, by a road of very varied beauty. From Toccoa to Tallulah the cut across is only 5 or 6 miles. There is a comfortable hotel near the edge of the gorges traversed by this wild mountain-stream, and hard by its army of waterfalls. The Tallulah, or *Terrora*, as the Indians more appositely called it, is a small stream, which rushes through a chasm in the Blue Ridge, rending it for several miles. The ravine is 1,000 ft. in depth, and of an equal width. Its walls are gigantic cliffs of dark granite, whose heavy masses, piled upon each other in the wildest confusion, sometimes shoot out, overhanging the yawning gulf. Along the rocky and uneven bed of this deep abyss the Terrora frets and foams with ever-varying course. The wild grandeur of this mountain-gorge, and the variety, number, and magnificence of its cataracts, give it rank with the most imposing waterfall scenery in the Union. The *** Valley of Nacoochee** (or the Evening Star) is a pleasant day's excursion from Clarksville. The valley is said by tradition to have won its name from the story of the hapless love of a beautiful Indian princess, whose scepter once ruled its solitudes; but with or without these associations it will be remembered with pleasure by all whose fortune it may be to see it. *Mt. Yonah* looks down into the quiet heart of Nacoochee, lying at its base; and if the tourist should stay overnight in the valley, he ought to take a peep at the mountain panorama from the summit of Yonah. Another interesting peak in this vicinity is *Mt. Currahee*, which is situated S. of Clarksville, a few miles below the Toccoa Cascade. The *** Falls of the Eastatoia** are about 3 miles from *Clayton*, in Rabun, the extreme N. E. county of Georgia. Clayton may be reached easily from Clarksville, or by a ride of 12 miles from the cataract of Tallulah. The falls lie off the road to the right, in the passage of the Rabun Gap, one of the mountain ways from Georgia into North Carolina; they would be a spot of crowded resort were they in a more thickly peopled country. The scene is a succession of cascades, noble in volume and character, plunging down the ravined flanks of a rugged mountain-height.

Union County, adjoining Habersham on the N. W., is distinguished for natural beauty, and for its objects of antiquarian interest. Among these latter is the *Track Rock*, bearing wonderful impressions of the feet of animals now extinct. *Pilot Mountain*, in Union, is a noble elevation of some 1,200 ft. The *Hiawasse Falls*, on the Hiawasse River, present a series of beautiful cascades, some of them from 60 to 100 ft. in height. The much-visited **Falls of Amicalolah** are in Lumpkin County, 17 miles W. of the village of Dahlonega, near the State road leading to East Tennessee.

119. The Ohio River.

During portions of the summer and in the autumn, when the water is lów, the larger steamboats ascend no farther than Wheeling, and even below this point they pass with difficulty. Those who desire only to see the more interesting portions of the river can take the steamer at *Wheeling* (see p. 289), at *Parkersburg* (see p. 290), at *Huntington*, the W. terminus of the Chesapeake & Ohio R. R., or at *Cincinnati* (see p. 305). Those who wish to see the entire river can take a packet from Pittsburg to Wheeling, whence large and comfortable steamers ply to Cincinnati. From Cincinnati very fine steamers run down the river to Louisville and Cairo.

THE Ohio River is the largest affluent of the Mississippi River from the E., and was known to the early French settlers as *La Belle Rivière*. It is formed by the junction at Pittsburg of the Alleghany and Monongahela Rivers, and has a total length of about 1,000 miles. No other river of equal length has such a uniform, smooth, and placid current. Its average width is about 2,400 ft., and the descent, in its whole course, is about 400 ft. It has no fall, except a rocky rapid of 22¼ ft. descent at Louisville, around which is a ship-canal 2¼ miles long. The course of the Ohio and of all its tributaries is through a region of stratified rocks, little disturbed from the horizontal position in which they were deposited, and nowhere intruded upon by uplifts of the azoic formations, such as in other regions impart grandeur to the scenery. For these reasons the scenery of the Ohio, though often beautiful, is for the most part tame. One interesting feature is the succession of terraces often noticed rising one above another at different elevations. Though they are often 75 ft. or more above the present level of the river, they were evidently formed by fluviatile deposits made in distant periods, when the river flowed at these high levels. Evidence is altogether wanting to fix the date of these periods; but mounds and earthworks constructed on the lower branches of the river fully 2,000 years ago, show that the river must have flowed at its present level at least so far back.

LANDINGS.	Miles.	LANDINGS.	Miles.
Pittsburg, Pa.	0	Covington, Ky.	476
Economy, Pa.	19	Lawrenceburg, Ind.	498
Rochester, Pa	29	Madison, Ind.	567
Wellsville, Ohio	52	Jeffersonville, Ind.	617
Steubenville, Ohio.	71	Louisville, Ky.	618
Wheeling, W. Va.	94	New Albany, Ind.	621
Bellaire, Ohio.	98	Leavenworth, Ind.	680
Newport, Ohio.	151	Hawesville, Ky.	744
Marietta, Ohio.	170	Rockport, Ind.	769
Parkersburg, Ohio.	188	Owensboro, Ky.	778
Racine, Ohio	249	Evansville, Ind.	813
Guyandotte, W. Va.	311	Henderson, Ky.	825
Huntington, W. Va.	316	Mount Vernon, Ind.	851
Ashland, Ky.	319	Shawneetown, Ill.	877
Ironton, Ohio.	327	Elizabethtown, Ill.	907
Greenupsburg, Ky.	337	Smithland, Ky.	945
Portsmouth, Ohio	362	Paducah, Ky.	957
Maysville, Ky.	415	Mound City, Ill.	1,001
Cincinnati, Ohio	476	Cairo, Ill.	1,005

The most important places enumerated in the above list have already been described. *Economy* was settled in 1825 by a German sect called "Harmonists" who hold all property in common. *Beaver* is a busy manufacturing village situated at the mouth of the Beaver River, from which it derives a fine water-power. *Wellsville* is an important wool-shipping point, and contains a number of foundries and machine-shops. Two miles below, near the mouth of Great Yellow Creek, is the locality of the murder of the family of Logan, the Mingo Chief. **Steubenville** (see p. 301). *Wellsburg* is a town of W. Virginia, beautifully situated on the E. bank of the river. **Wheeling** (see p. 289). *Bridgeport*, opposite Wheeling, is connected with it by a magnificent suspension bridge. *Bellaire* is where the Central Ohio Div. of the Baltimore & Ohio R. R. crosses the river (see p. 289). **Marietta** (*Nation Hotel, Brown's*) is a flourishing city of about 7,000 inhabitants, picturesquely, situated at the confluence of the Ohio and Muskingum Rivers. It is the E. terminus of the Marietta & Cincinnati R. R., and the S. terminus of the Marietta, Pittsburg & Cleveland R. R., and has a large trade in petroleum, which is obtained in the vicinity. It is the seat of *Marietta College*, which has four buildings surrounded by ample grounds and a library of 25,000 volumes. On the site of the city is a * group of ancient works which are described by Squier and Davis in their "Ancient Monuments of the Mississippi Valley." *Parkersburg* and *Belpre*, together with the splendid railway bridge uniting them, are described on p. 290. Two miles below Parkersburg is **Blennerhassett's Island,** noted for having been the residence of Herman Blennerhassett, an Irishman of distinction, who improved the island, and built on it a splendid mansion for himself, in 1798. When Aaron Burr was planning his celebrated conspiracy, he induced Blennerhassett to join him, and to embark all his means in the scheme. Although not convicted of treason, Blennerhassett was ruined, his house went to decay, and his beautiful gardens were destroyed. **Pomeroy** (*Remington House*) is the fifth place on the river above Cincinnati in trade and commerce, and has a population of about 7,000. Its prosperity rests mainly on the mines of bituminous coal within its limits and in the immediate vicinity. It is also the center of the salt basin of the Ohio Valley, and there are 26 salt-furnaces within its limits and in the neighborhood, yielding about 6,000,000 bushels a year. At *Point Pleasant*, 14 miles below, the Great Kanawha River empties into the Ohio, and at *Guyandotte* the Big Guyandotte River comes in. *Huntington* is the W. terminus of the Chesapeake & Ohio R. R., which runs to Richmond, Va., in 421 miles. Huntington is an important shipping-point, and the railway connects here with several lines of steamboats. The Big Sandy River, 7 miles below Huntington, is the boundary-line between Kentucky and W. Virginia. **Ironton** is a city of 8,000 inhabitants, built at the foot of lofty hills in the center of the "Hanging Rock" iron-region (embracing a portion of S. Ohio and N. E. Kentucky), of which it is the principal business point. Its iron-trade amounts to about $7,000,000 a year, and it contains a number of blast-furnaces, rolling-mills, machine-shops, etc. *Greenupsburg* is situated at the mouth of

Little Sandy River, and 25 miles below is the prosperous Ohio city of **Portsmouth** (*Briggs House*), beautifully situated at the mouth of the Scioto River, and at the terminus of the Lake Erie & Ohio Canal. It is substantially built and has a population of about 15,000. Being the entrepot of the rich mineral regions of S. Ohio and N. E. Kentucky, it has a large trade, besides numerous iron-furnaces, rolling-mills, foundries, etc. The Scioto Valley is a productive agricultural district. A branch of the Marietta & Cincinnati R. R. terminates at Portsmouth. **Mays-ville** (*Hill House, Central*) is the largest place in N. E. Kentucky and one of the most extensive hemp-markets in the United States. It lies in a bend of the river, and is backed by a range of hills which gives it a very attractive appearance. Its population is about 5,000, and it contains several handsome public buildings. **Cincinnati** (see Route 70).

The view from the steamer when opposite Cincinnati is remarkably fine. On the one hand is the densely populated city, its rows of massive buildings rising tier above tier toward the hill-tops, which, crowned with villas and gardens, form a semicircular background. On the opposite bank rise the beautiful Kentucky hills, at whose feet nestle the twin cities of *Covington* and *Newport*, divided only by the Licking River and connected by a graceful suspension bridge (see p. 313). There are few places of importance on the river between Cincinnati and Louisville, and they are separated by long stretches of virgin woodland and plain. *North Bend* (see p. 317). The Great Miami River, 4 miles below N. Bend, is the boundary between Ohio and Indiana. *Lawrenceburg* and *Aurora* are described on page 317. At *Carrollton*, 74 miles from Cincinnati, is the mouth of the Kentucky River, a navigable stream 200 miles long, noted for its beautiful scenery. **Madison** (*Western Hotel, Central*) is one of the principal cities of Indiana, is beautifully situated and well built, and contains about 12,000 inhabitants. Several pork-packing establishments are located here, the trade in provisions is important, and there are brass and iron foundries, flouring-mills, machine-shops, etc. Madison is the terminus of one branch of the Jeffersonville, Madison & Indianapolis R. R. The approach to **Louisville** (see Route 72) is very fine, affording an impressive view of the city and of *Jeffersonville* on the opposite bank. The river is here about a mile wide, and is crossed by one of the finest bridges in the United States (see p. 317). The falls of the Ohio just below Louisville descend 23 ft. in 2 miles, and to avoid this obstruction a canal $2\frac{1}{2}$ miles long has been constructed around them.

Besides **New Albany** (see p. 317) the only important cities between Louisville and Cairo are Evansville, Ind., and Paducah, Ky. **Evansville** (*St. George Hotel, Sherwood House*) is the principal shipping-point for the grain and pork of S. W. Indiana, and its manufactures are important. It is the terminus of two railroads, and of the Wabash & Erie Canal, which extends 462 miles to Toledo (see p. 275). The city contains a handsome *Court-House, City Hall, U. S. Marine Hospital,* an *Opera House,* and upward of 30 churches. The population is about 25,000, and coal and iron ore are found in the vicinity. *Shawneetown* is a prosperous village. **Paducah** (*Richmond House*) is a city of about 12,000 inhabitants, on the S. bank just below the mouth of the Tennessee River. It is the shipping-point of the surrounding country, the chief productions of which are tobacco, pork, and grain, and contains several tobacco and other factories. The Paducah & Elizabethtown R. R. begins here and runs to Elizabethtown on the Louisville & Great Southern R. R. (see Route 114). **Cairo** is situated at the confluence of the Ohio and Mississippi Rivers, and has been described on page 336.

120. The Mississippi River.

The tour of the Mississippi River is usually made in two distinct stages : From St. Paul or Minneapolis to St. Louis, or *vice versa ;* and from St. Louis to New Orleans, or *vice versa.* A daily line of commodious and comfortable side-wheel passenger packets plies between Minneapolis and St. Paul and St. Louis. The steamers plying between St. Louis and New Orleans are large and fine. That portion of the river above St. Louis is known as the Upper Mississippi; that below St. Louis as the Lower Mississippi.

THE Mississippi River, " Father of Waters," rises in Minnesota, on the dividing ridge between the waters which flow into Hudson's Bay and those flowing into the Gulf of Mexico, and so near the source of the Red River of the North that in times of freshet their waters have been known to commingle. It is, at its source, 3,160 miles from its mouth, a rivulet flowing from a small pool fed by springs. Thence it flows through a number of pools or ponds, each larger than the preceding one, until it expands into Itasca Lake, whence it emerges as a stream of some size, and soon becomes a river. It first flows N. through Cass, Sandy, and other lakes, and then, turning toward the S., rolls downward to the Gulf of Mexico, passing over more than 18 degrees of latitude. Between the source and the Falls of St. Anthony are many rapids and waterfalls, but the only one of any magnitude is the Pecagama Rapids, 685 miles above St. Anthony. From these rapids down to the St. Anthony Falls, the river is navigable, and much of the scenery is very beautiful. The Falls of St. Anthony form an insuperable barrier to navigation, and here the St. Louis steamers stop. From St. Paul to Dubuque the river flows between abrupt and lofty bluffs, distant from each other from 2 to 6 miles, and rising from 100 to 600 ft., the valley or bottom being very beautiful, filled with islands, and intersected in every direction by tributaries of the Mississippi, and by the various channels and " sloughs " of the river itself. The bluffs are principally of limestone ; they are almost uniformly vertical and rugged, and nearly destitute of vegetation, except at the base and summit. The limestone is generally of grayish white, but is stained and streaked until it is of every hue, from that of iron-rust to that of the white cliffs of St. Paul. There are grandeur and sublimity in every mile of this portion of the river ; but it becomes monotonous after a time, the eye becoming surfeited with too much beauty. Below Dubuque, the valley continues to preserve the same general characteristics, but the bluffs are lower and more like hills, and the scenery, though still beautiful, is tamer. Below Alton it begins to assume more the appearance of the "Lower River" (as the portion below St. Louis is called) ; and the waters, turbid and muddy, roll on a mighty torrent between banks often low, flat, and sandy, and the vegetation continually more and more tropical in its nature.

Principal Landings on the Mississippi River.

LANDINGS.	Miles.	LANDINGS.	Miles.
Minneapolis, Minn	0	Louisiana, Mo	691
St. Paul, Minn	14	Mouth of Illinois River	762
Hastings, Minn	46	Alton, Ill	780
Prescott, Wis	49	Mouth of Missouri River	785
Red Wing, Minn	79	St. Louis, Mo	805
Winona, Minn	160	Cape Girardeau, Mo	955
La Crosse, Wis	194	Cairo, Ill	1,005
Lansing, Iowa	239	Columbus, Ky	1,025
Prairie du Chien, Wis	269	New Madrid, Mo	1,080
MacGregor, Iowa	272	Memphis, Tenn	1,255
Dunleith, Ill	335	Helena, Ark	1,345
Dubuque, Iowa	335	White River, Ark	1,425
Galena, Ill	355	Napoleon, Ark	1,445
Fulton, Ill	413	Young's Point, La	1,655
Clinton, Iowa	415	Vicksburg, Miss	1,665
Davenport, Iowa	458	Natchez, Miss	1,785
Rock Island, Ill	458	Red River, La	1,855
Muscatine, Iowa	488	Bayou Sara, La	1,895
Burlington, Iowa	550	Port Hudson, La	1,905
Nauvoo, Ill	582	Baton Rouge, La	1,925
Keokuk, Iowa	597	Plaquemine, La	1,955
Quincy, Ill	641	Donaldsonville, La	1,975
Hannibal, Mo	661	New Orleans, La	2,055

Between St. Paul and *Hastings* there are half a dozen small villages, one of them being somewhat noticeable on account of its name, *Red Rock*, which was given by the Indians, who worshiped a large rock at this point, which they painted red, and called Wacon, or Spirit Rock. *Point Douglas* is the last point of Minnesota on the E. bank of the river, as the *St. Croix River*, which empties here, marks the boundary-line of Wisconsin, between which State and Minnesota the Mississippi now forms the boundary-line for many miles. *Red Wing* (see p. 342) is situated at the head of *** Lake Pepin,** an expansion of the river, about 30 miles long, and 3 miles in average width. By many this is considered the most beautiful portion of the Mississippi. The bluffs on either side present peculiar characteristics, which are found in such perfection nowhere else ; grim castles seem only to want sentries to be perfect, and all the fantastic forms into which the action of the weather can transform limestone cliffs are to be seen. The forests reach to the river-bank, and the water is so beautifully clear that fish may be seen many feet below the surface. Just below Red Wing is *Barn Bluff*, a well-known landmark, 200 ft. high. *Frontenac* lies in the center of the lake-region, and is a favorite resort in summer on account of its fine scenery, and the hunting, bathing, fishing, and sailing, which it affords (see p. 342). *** Maiden Rock,** 3 miles below Frontenac, is a promontory 409 ft. high, near the lower end of the lake, on the E. side. Its name is derived from an incident which is reported to have happened about the commencement of the present century. A young Dakota maiden, named Winona, loved a young hunter; but her parents wished her to marry a warrior of the Wabashaw tribe, to which they belonged, and tried to compel her to accede to their wishes. On the day before that appointed for the marriage she went to the verge of this precipice, and commenced chanting her death-song. Her relatives and friends seeing her on the brink of destruction called to her that they would yield to her wishes; but she did not believe them, and before any one could reach her she leaped over the precipice, and was dashed to pieces on the rocks below. *Reed's Landing* is at the foot of Lake Pepin, where the river again contracts, and is opposite the mouth of the *Chippewa River*, a navigable lumbering-stream.

Near *Fountain City* (48 miles below Lake Pepin) is the famous * **Chimney Rock,** and between this point and Winona there are 12 miles of remarkably fine scenery, in which are seen bluffs conical in form and covered with verdure, others with precipitous fronts worn by the weather into most fantastic shapes, the river lake-like, and almost filled with islands. **Winona** is described on p. 341. Below Winona the scenery continues bold and striking, and 20 miles down is * **Trempealeau Island** (sometimes called *Mountain Island*), a rocky island, 300 to 500 ft. in height, and one of the most noted landmarks on the Upper Mississippi. There is a winding path up Trempealeau, and the view from the summit is exquisite. **La Crosse** (see p. 341). All this portion of the river from La Crosse to Dubuque is delightful, from the great variety of the scenery, the wooded hills, and the exquisitely pure character of the water, which is clear and limpid as that of Lake Leman. The bluffs alternate from massive, densely wooded hills to long walls of limestone, which front precipitously on the river, and assume all manner of quaint, fantastic, and striking shapes. Rivers and rivulets come in at intervals, and the rapid succession of the towns indicates a more thickly settled region. *Prairie du Chien* has already been described on p. 343. Just above Dubuque one of the landmarks of the pilots of the upper river is pointed out—* **Eagle Rock,** a splendid bluff, 500 ft. high. **Dubuque** (*Julien House, Lorimer*), the largest city of Iowa, containing about 35,000 inhabitants, is built partly upon a terrace, 20 ft. above the river, and partly upon the bluffs, which rise 200 ft. The lower or business portion is regularly laid out and compactly built, while in the upper portion the streets rise picturesquely one above another. Among the public buildings worthy of notice are the *U. S. Building,* of marble, 3 stories high, and costing over $200,000; the *Central Market,* and the 4 ward school-houses. The Methodist Episcopal, one of the Presbyterian, the Universalist, the Congregational, and St. Mary's (German Catholic) Churches, and the Cathedral, are imposing structures, the last 3 being surmounted by lofty spires. Dubuque is the commercial center of the great lead-region of Iowa, N. W. Illinois, and S. W. Wisconsin, some of the mines being within the city limits. Two important railways converge here, and the shipping business is immense.

Below Dubuque the character of the scenery changes, and, though

still pleasing, is decidedly tamer. The most noteworthy feature of
this portion of the river is the number of important towns and cities
that stand on either bank. Twenty miles below Dubuque is the mouth
of the Fevre River, 6 miles up which is **Galena,** an important city of
about 10,000 inhabitants, on the N. Div. of the Illinois Central R. R.
(see Route 79). **Fulton** on the E. bank and **Clinton** on the W.
bank, with the great bridge which crosses the river at this point, are
described on page 347. *Le Clair* (25 miles below Clinton) is at the
head of the * *Upper Rapids,* which extend for 15 miles to Rock Island.
The descent of the rapids is exciting, but seldom dangerous. The
cities of **Rock Island** and **Davenport,** on opposite sides of the
river, the magnificent * bridge connecting them, and the extensive U.
S. arsenals on Rock Island, are described in Route 84. *Muscatine* is a
flourishing Iowa city of about 10,000 inhabitants, situated on a rocky
bluff at the apex of the Great Bend of the Mississippi. It is the shipping-point of an extensive and fertile country, and its lumber-business
is large. **Burlington** (see p. 352). *Nauvoo City* was founded by the
Mormons in 1840, and contained about 15,000 inhabitants at the time
of their expulsion in 1846 by the neighboring people. It is now a
place of small importance. *Montrose* is at the head of the "Lower
Rapids," which extend for 12 miles to Keokuk and greatly obstruct
navigation. **Keokuk** (*Patterson House*) is a city of 15,000 inhabitants, situated at the foot of the Rapids. It is built partly at the base
and partly on the summit of a bluff 150 ft. high, and has broad regular streets with many handsome houses. It is the terminus of 7 railroads, has an extensive and growing trade, and has flouring-mills, iron-
foundries, etc. Four miles below Keokuk the Des Moines River, the
boundary between Iowa and Missouri, enters the Mississippi. **Quincy**
(*Tremont House*) is one of the largest cities of Illinois, with a population of about 35,000. It is picturesquely situated on a limestone
bluff 125 ft. above the river, and is regularly laid out and well built,
containing many substantial business blocks and handsome residences.
The streets are lighted with gas, and the principal ones are traversed
by horse-cars. There are 4 small parks and several cemeteries; and
about 2 miles from the center of the city are well-appointed Fair-
Grounds comprising about 80 acres. Eight lines of railway center at
Quincy, and the trade of the city is extensive. The Hannibal & St.
Joseph R. R. crosses the river here on a splendid bridge. Twenty
miles below Quincy is the flourishing city of **Hannibal** (*Planters'
House*), with a population of about 15,000, important manufactures
(including foundries and car-works, flour- and saw-mills, tobacco-fac-
tories and pork-packing houses), and an extensive trade in tobacco,
pork, flour, and other produce. After St. Louis, Hannibal is the greatest lumber-market W. of the Mississippi, and there are numerous spacious lumber-yards. It is one of the northern termini of the Missouri,
Kansas & Texas R. R. (see Route 95 *a*), and several other important
railways converge here. **Alton** (see p. 338). Three miles below Alton
is the * **Meeting of the Waters** of the Missouri and Mississippi
Rivers. This has been pronounced one of the most impressive views

of river scenery in the country. The Missouri nominally empties into the Mississippi, but it is really the Mississippi that empties, as any one can see who ever looks upon the scene. **St. Louis** is fully described in Route 76.

The scenery of that portion of the river below St. Louis is very different from that above. " The prevailing character of the Lower Mississippi," says a recent traveler, " is that of solemn gloom." The dreary solitude, and often the absence of all living objects save the huge alligators, which float past apparently asleep on the drift-wood, and an occasional vulture attracted by its impure prey on the surface of the waters ; the trees, with a long and melancholy drapery of pendent moss fluttering in the wind ; and the gigantic river, rolling onward the vast volume of its dark and turbid waters through the wilderness, form the leading features of one of the most dismal yet impressive landscapes on which the eye of man ever rested. Every now and then a stop is made at a small landing, or at the towns and villages that cluster along the banks ; and the clamor of lading and unlading causes a momentary excitement that subsides at once as the steamer resumes her course.

About 125 miles below St. Louis the mouth of the Ohio River is reached (see Route 119), and a somewhat prolonged stay is made at **Cairo** (see p. 336). Cairo is connected by ferry with **Columbus, Ky.,** which lies on the river 18 miles below. Columbus is situated on the slope of a high bluff commanding the river for about 5 miles, and at the outbreak of the Civil War was strongly fortified by the Confederates, who regarded it as the northern key to the mouth of the Mississippi. They collected in the town and its vicinity an army of 30,000 men, but after the fall of Forts Henry and Donelson, in February, 1862, it was promptly evacuated. *Island No.* 10 (51 miles below Columbus) was the scene of a terrific bombardment by the Mississippi River fleet, extending from March 16 to April 17, 1862, in which the Federals were completely successful. The canal which was cut to assist in the investment of the island, and the remains of some of the earthworks, can still be seen in passing the island. Ten miles below, in Missouri, is *New Madrid*, which was captured at the same time as Island No. 10, both places having formed parts of one position, and mutually dependent upon each other. This was the first battle of the war in which the superiority of gunboats to stationary batteries was clearly demonstrated. New Madrid was settled in 1780, and was the scene of a great earthquake in 1811.

From Columbus to Memphis the river skirts the bluffs of the E. or Kentucky shore, having on its W. the broad, alluvial lands of Missouri and Arkansas. A number of small towns dot either bank, and at intervals spots are pointed out which events of the Civil War have rendered interesting. Conspicuous among these is *Fort Pillow* (148 miles below Columbus), situated on the first Chickasaw Bluff. It was evacuated by the Confederates on June 4, 1862 ; but on April 12, 1864, was the scene of the shameful butchery by the troops under General Forrest, known in history as the Fort Pillow massacre, concerning which the testimony is conflicting, and probably exaggerated, on both sides. Below Fort Pillow a journey of about 100 miles, along desolate and almost uninhabited shores, brings the voyager to **Memphis** (*Peabody Hotel, Gastins*), the chief city of Tennessee, and the largest on the Mississippi between St. Louis and New Orleans. It is situated on the fourth Chickasaw Bluff, 450 miles below St. Louis, and 800 above New Orleans, and has a population of about 65,000. The city presents a striking appearance as seen from the water, with its esplanade several hundred feet in width, sweeping along the bluff, and covered with large warehouses. The streets are broad and regular, and lined with handsome buildings; and many of the residences on the avenues leading from the river are surrounded with beautiful lawns. The city extends over 3 square miles. In the center there is a handsome park, filled with trees, and containing a bust of Andrew Jackson. The principal of the six cemeteries is *Elmwood*, on the S. E. border of the city. Memphis has an immense railroad and steamboat traffic, a vast cotton trade, and numerous manufactures. There are a *U. S. Custom-House*, two theatres seating respectively 800 and 1,000 persons, fine churches and charitable institutions, excellent public and private schools, and a library with 9,000 volumes. Memphis was captured by the Federals early in the war (June 6, 1862), and was never afterward held by the Confederates.

A short distance below Memphis the Mississippi turns toward the W., and crosses its valley to meet the waters of the Arkansas and White Rivers. The latter enters the Mississippi 161 miles below Memphis, and the former about 15 miles farther down. The Arkansas River is 2,000 miles in length, for 800 of which it is navigable by steamers. It rises in the Rocky Mountains, and, next to the Missouri, is the largest tributary of the Mississippi. The town of *Napoleon* lies at its mouth. Near this point commences the great cotton-growing region, and the banks of the river are an almost continuous succession of plantations. Fifty miles below begins the growth of the Spanish moss, which, covering the trees with its dark and somber drapery, forms one of the most notable features of the river scenery. Having received the waters of the two affluents above mentioned, the Mississippi again crosses its valley to meet the Yazoo near Vicksburg, creating the immense Yazoo reservoir on the E. bank, extending from the vicinity of Memphis to Vicksburg, and the valleys and swamps of the Macon and Tensas on the W. side. **Vicksburg** (*Pacific House, Washington Hotel*) is situated on the Walnut Hills, which extend for about 2 miles along the river, rising to the height of 500 ft., and displaying the finest scenery of the Lower Mississippi. It is a well-built city of 15,000 inhabitants, the largest between New Orleans and Memphis, and about equidistant from both. As at Memphis, the view of the city from the water is in the highest degree picturesque and animated, and the pleasing impression is confirmed by a closer examination of the town. Vicksburg was founded in 1836 by a planter named Vick, members of whose family are still living there. As the chief commercial mart on this portion of the river, it has long been a place of some note, but it is more widely known as the scene of one of the most obstinate and decisive struggles of the Civil War. After the loss successively of Columbus, Memphis, and New Orleans, the Confederates made here their last and most desperate stand for the control of the great river. The place was surrounded by vast fortifications, the hills crowned with batteries, and a large army under General Pemberton placed in it as a garrison. Its capture by General Grant after a protracted siege (July 4, 1863) "broke the backbone of the Confederacy, and cut it in twain." Above Vicksburg, at the point where Sherman made his entrance from the "Valley of Death," is the largest national cemetery in the country, containing the remains of nearly 16,000 soldiers.

From Vicksburg to Baton Rouge the river hugs the E. bluffs, with Mississippi on one side and Louisiana on the other. *Grand Gulf*, in Mississippi, is a pretty little town 60 miles below Vicksburg, lying upon some picturesque hills overhanging the river; and **Natchez,** 60 miles nearer New Orleans, is built mostly upon a high bluff, 200 ft. above the level of the stream. That portion of the city lying on the narrow strip of land between the foot of the hill and the river is called "Natchez-under-the-Hill," and, though containing some important business houses, can make no claim to beauty. It communicates by broad and well-graded roads with the upper town, called "Natchez-on-the-Hill," which is beautifully shaded, and contains many handsome residences and other buildings. The houses are principally of brick, and the residences are adorned with gardens. The brow of the bluff along the whole front of the city is occupied by a park. The principal buildings are the *Court-House*, in a public square shaded with trees, the *Masonic Temple*, the *Catholic Cathedral*, with a spire 128 ft. high, the Episcopal Church, and the Presbyterian Church. On the bluff adjoining the city there is a *National Cemetery*, tastefully laid out and decorated.

Natchez was founded by D'Iberville, a Frenchman, in 1700, and is replete with historic associations. Here once lived and flourished the noblest tribe of Indians on the continent, and from that tribe it takes its name. Their pathetic story is festooned with the flowers of poetry and romance. Their ceremonies and creed were not unlike those of the Fire-worshipers of Persia. Their priests kept the fire continually burning upon the altar in their Temple of the Sun, and the tradition is that they got the fire from heaven. Just before the advent of the white man, it is said, the fire accidently went out, and that was one reason why they became disheartened in their struggles with the pale-faces. The last remnant of the race were still existing a few years ago in Texas, and they still gloried in their paternity. It is probable that the first explorer of the Lower Mississippi River, the unfortunate La Salle, landed at this spot on his downward trip to the sea. It is a disputed point as to where was the location of the first fort. Some say it lay back of the town, while others say it was established at Ellis's Cliffs. In 1713, Bienville established a fort and trading-post at this spot. The second, Fort Rosalie, or rather the broken profile of it, is still visible. It is gradually sinking, by the earth being undermined by subterranean springs, and in a few years not a vestige of it will be left. Any one now standing at the landing can see the different strata of earth distinctly marked, showing the depth of the artificial earthworks.

The former capital of Louisiana, **Baton Rouge,** is pleasantly situated on the last bluff that is seen in descending the Mississippi. The site is 30 to 40 ft. above the highest overflow of the river. The bluff rises by a gentle and gradual swell, and the town, as seen from the water, rising regularly and beautifully from the banks, with its singularly shaped French and Spanish houses, and its queer squares, looks like a finely painted landscape. From Baton Rouge to New Orleans " the coast," as it is called, is lined with plantations. Every spot susceptible of cultivation is transformed into a beautiful garden, containing specimens of all those choice fruits and flowers which flourish only in tropical climes. From the deck of the steamer the traveler overlooks a kaleidoscopic succession of the most exquisite land and water views; and when, at last, the steamer rounds the great bend of the river, and he sees the " Crescent City" spread out before him, and knows that his long journey is ended, he will probably experience a feeling of regret. **New Orleans** is fully described in Route 116.

Those who, taking an ocean steamer, pursue the journey below New Orleans, traverse a portion of the river not less interesting if less attractive than that left behind. Very soon after leaving the city the phenomena of a " delta-country" become conspicuous, and one can fairly witness the eternal and ever-varying conflict between land and sea. The thick forest vegetation disappears, giving place to isolated and stunted trees; the river-banks grow less and less defined, and finally lose themselves in what appears to be an interminable marsh; and through this marsh the " passes" furnish channels to the Gulf, which are discernible only by the practiced eyes of the pilots. The " delta" protrudes into the Gulf of Mexico far beyond the general coast-line, and is slowly but imperceptibly advancing by the shoaling caused by the deposition of the sediment brought down by the river. It is impossible, however, for the inexperienced traveler to say where land ends and sea begins; and before he is aware of having reached the " mouth " of the river, he is far out on the Gulf of Mexico, where a muddy surface-current is the only relic of the mighty " Father of Waters."

INDEX.

INDEX.

INDEX.

INDEX.

Salem, Ind., 334.
Salem, Ogn., 383.
Salem, Ohio, 284.
Salisbury, N. C., 424, 479.
Salt Lake City, U. T., 357.
San Antonio, Tex., 398.
San Bernardino, Cal., 380.
San Diego, Cal., 379.
Sandoval, Ill., 318.
Sandusky, Ohio, 401, 290.
Sanford, Fla., 442.
San Francisco, Cal., 364.
San José, Cal., 376.
San Luis Park, Col., 395.
San Mateo, Fla., 441.
San Rafael, Cal., 375.
Santa Barbara, Cal., 378.
Santa Clara, Cal., 377.
Santa Cruz, Cal., 376.
Savannah, Ga., 431, 429.
Schenectady, N. Y., 267.
Sedalia, Mo., 384, 395.
Selma, Ala., 459.
Seymour, Ind., 318.
Shasta Mt., Cal., 382.
Shawangunk Mts., 277.
Shelby, Ohio, 299.
Shelby Springs, Ala., 459.
Sherman, Tex., 396, 400.
Sherman, Wy., 356.
Shohola, N. Y., 277.
Sidney, Neb., 355.
Sidney, Ohio, 319.
Silver Island, 409.
Silver Spring, Fla., 444.
Silverton, Col., 391.
Sing Sing, N. Y., 266.
Sioux City, Io., 336.
Sir John's Run, W. Va., 286.
Sloatsburg, N. Y., 277.
South Bend, Ind., 276.
South Park, Col., 394.
South Vallejo, Cal., 377.
Sparta, Ga., 452.
Sparta, Wis., 341.
Spartanburg, S. C., 451.
Springfield, Ill., 337, 334.
Springfield, Ohio, 299, 305.
SPRINGS:
  Alleghany, Va., 475, 459.
  Bath Alum, Va., 475.
  Bedford Alum, Va., 476.
  Berkeley, Va., 471.
  Blue, Fla., 442.
  Blue Ridge, Va., 475.
  Blue Sulphur, Va., 473.
  Campbell's Soda, Cal., 382.
  Capon, Va., 472.
  Coyner's, Va., 475, 457.
  Eggleston's, Va., 476.
  Fauquier Wht. Sul., 476.
  Geyser, Cal., 378.

SPRINGS:
  Glen Alpine, N. C., 479.
  Glenn, S. C., 451.
  Grayson White Su phur., Va., 476.
  Greenbrier White Sulphur., 472.
  Green Cove, Fla., 441.
  Green Sulphur, Fla., 442.
  Harbin's, Cal., 378.
  Healing, Va., 474.
  Holston, Va., 476.
  Hot, Ark., 399.
  Hot, Va., 474.
  Hot Sulphur, Cal., 379.
  Hot Sulphur, Col., 394.
  Huguenot, Va., 476.
  Idaho, Col., 392.
  Jordan's, Va., 476.
  Jordan's Alum, Va., 475.
  Limestone, S. C., 451.
  Manitou, Col., 388.
  Montgomery White Sulphur, 476.
  Napa Soda, Cal., 377.
  New Holland, Ga., 451.
  Old Sweet, Va., 473.
  Pacific Congress, 377.
  Paso-Robles, Cal., 380.
  Porter, Ga., 451.
  Pulaski Alum, Va., 476.
  Rawley, Va., 472.
  Red Sulphur, Va., 474.
  Red Sweet, Va., 473.
  Rockbridge Alum, Va., 475.
  St. Catherine's, Can., 267.
  Salt Sulphur, Va., 473.
  Shannondale, Va., 476.
  Sharon Alum, Va., 476.
  Silver, Fla., 444.
  Suwanee, Fla., 435.
  Wakulla, Fla., 448.
  Warm, N. C., 481.
  Warm, Va., 474.
  White Mountain Hot, Mon., 412.
  White Sulphur, Cal., 378.
  Wilson's, N. C., 479.
  Yellow Sul., Va., 476.
Staunton, Va., 471.
Sterling, Ill., 347.
Sterling, Kan., 387.
Steubenville, Ohio, 301, 485.
Stockton, Cal., 368.
Strasburg, Va., 456.
Sufferns Station, N. J., 277.
Summerville, Ga., 431.
Summerville, S. C., 425.
Summit, Cal., 361.
Superior Lake, 405.
Suspension Bridge, N. Y., 267.
Susquehanna, Pa., 277.

Swannanoa Gap, N. C., 479.
Syracuse, N. Y., 267.

Table Rock, N. C., 479.
Tahoe Lake, Cal., 360.
Talladega, Ala., 459.
Tallahassee, Fla., 447.
Tamaroa, Ill., 335.
Tampa, Fla., 449.
Tappan Zee, 266.
Tarrytown, N. Y., 266.
Terre Haute, Ind., 321, 323.
Texarkana, Tex., 400.
Thomasville, Ga., 434.
Thunder Bay, 403.
Titusville, Fla., 445.
Toccoa, Ga., 451.
Tocoi, Fla., 441.
Toledo, Ohio, 275, 322.
Tolono, Ill., 335.
Topeka, Kan., 385, 386.
Trempealeau Island, 489.
Trenton, N. J., 281.
Truckee, Cal., 361.
Tuolumne Grove of Big Trees, Cal., 370.
Turner's, N. Y., 277.
Tuscaloosa, Ala., 461.
Tusten, N. Y., 277.
Twelve Apostles' Islands, 408.
Tyrone, Pa., 282.

Union, 319.
Urbana, Ohio, 304, 322.
Ute Pass, Col., 388.
Utica, N. Y., 267.

Vandalia, Ill., 323.
Venango, Pa., 278.
Vicksburg, Miss., 492.
Vincennes, Ind., 318.
Vinita, Ind. Ter., 396.
Virginia City, Mon., 409.
Virginia City, Nev., 360.
Volcano, W. Va., 290.
Volusia, Fla., 442.

Wabasha, Minn., 342.
Waco, Tex., 396.
Wadsworth, Nev., 360.
Wagon-Wheel Gap, Col., 391.
Wakulla Springs, Fla., 448.
Waldo, Fla., 446.
Wallula, Ogn., 384.
Wanatah, Ind., 280, 333.
Warm Springs, N. C., 481.
Warrenton, Ga., 452.
Warrenton, Va., 456.
Warsaw, Ind., 280.
Washington, D. C., 285.
Waukegan, Ill., 339.
Waukesha, Wis., 342.

INDEX.

APPLETONS' GUIDE-BOOKS.

APPLETONS' GUIDE-BOOKS now include comprehensively almost everything that the traveler in any part of the civilized world requires. The full list is as follows:

Appletons' European Guide-book. Containing Maps of the Various Political Divisions, and Plans of the Principal Cities. Being a Complete Guide to the Continent of Europe, Egypt, Algeria, and the Holy Land. In two volumes, morocco. Price, $5.00.

Appletons' General Guide to the United States and Canada. With a Railroad Map of the United States and Canada, and Thirteen Sectional Maps, and Plans (with References) of Fourteen of the Principal Cities. Illustrated. This work is compiled on the plan of the famous BAEDEKER HAND-BOOKS of Europe. COMPLETE IN ONE VOLUME. 500 pages, 16mo, pocket form, bound in roan, price, $2.50; or separately, as follows:

THE NEW ENGLAND AND MIDDLE STATES AND CANADA. One vol., 264 pages, 16mo, bound in cloth, $1.25.

THE WESTERN AND SOUTHERN STATES. One vol., 234 pages, 16mo, bound in cloth, $1.25.

Appletons' Hand-book of Summer Resorts. Illustrated. Large 12mo. Paper cover, 50 cents; cloth, 75 cents.

Appletons' Railway Guide. Paper cover, 25 cents. Published monthly. Revised and corrected to date.

Appletons' Dictionary of New York and Vicinity. A Guide on a New Plan; being an alphabetically arranged Index to all Places, Societies, Institutions, Amusements, and innumerable matters upon which information is daily needed. With Maps of New York and Vicinity. Square 12mo. Paper, 30 cents; cloth, 50 cents.

New York Illustrated. With 102 Illustrations and a Map of the City. The illustrations and text fully delineating the Elevated Railway system, Post-Office, and other Public Buildings, Churches, Street Scenes, Suburbs, etc., etc. 4to. Paper cover, price, 60 cents.

Scenery of the Pacific Railways and Colorado. With Maps, and 71 Illustrations. Paper cover, 75 cents; cloth, $1.25.

The Hudson Illustrated. With 60 Engravings on Wood by J. D. WOODWARD. 4to. Paper cover, price, 50 cents.

Appletons' Hand-book of American Cities. Large 12mo. Illustrated. Paper cover, 50 cents; cloth, 75 cents.

Appletons' Hand-book of Winter Resorts. For Tourists and Invalids. With 47 Illustrations. Paper cover, 50 cents; cloth, 75 cents.

D. APPLETON & CO., PUBLISHERS, 1, 3, & 5 BOND STREET, NEW YORK.

APPLETONS'

Dictionary of New York

AND VICINITY.

A Guide on a New Plan; being an alphabetically arranged Index to all Places, Societies, Institutions, Amusements, and innumerable matters upon which information is daily needed.

SOME OF THE PRINCIPAL TITLES IN THIS VOLUME ARE AS FOLLOWS:

ACADEMIES,	CONEY ISLAND,	OYSTERS,
AMUSEMENTS,	CROTON WATER,	PICNIC-GROUNDS,
APARTMENT-HOUSES,	CUSTOM-HOUSE,	PIERS AND DOCKS,
ARCHITECTURAL FEATURES,	DRIVES,	POPULATION,
ART-GALLERIES,	FERRIES,	POST-OFFICE,
ART-SCHOOLS,	GAS,	PRISONS,
AUCTIONS,	HACK-FARES,	RAILWAYS,
BANKS,	HOLIDAYS,	RESTAURANTS,
BENEVOLENT SOCIETIES,	HOSPITALS,	SIGHT-SEEING,
BIRD AND DOG FANCIERS,	HOTELS,	STATUES,
BOARDING-HOUSES,	LAW COURTS,	STEAMBOATS,
BOATING,	LIBRARIES,	STREET-CLEANING,
BROOKLYN,	LONG BRANCH,	STREETS,
BUREAUS,	MARKETS,	STUDIOS,
CEMETERIES,	MUSEUMS,	THEATRES,
CENTRAL PARK,	NATIONAL GUARD,	TURF,
CHURCHES,	NEWSPAPERS,	YACHTING,
COLLEGES,	NURSES,	And many others.

WITH MAPS OF NEW YORK AND VICINITY.

Square 12mo. Paper cover. Price, 30 cents.

D. APPLETON & CO., Publishers, 1, 3, & 5 Bond St., New York.

UNITED STATES HOTEL, BOSTON.

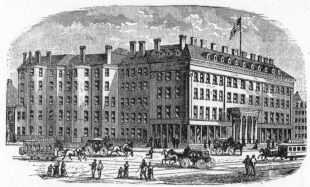

Directly opposite the Boston and Albany, and
Only One Block from the Old Colony and Fall River Lines,
Three Blocks only from the New York and New England
and Providence and Stonington Stations,

And connecting directly by Horse-Cars, every 5 minutes, with all the NORTHERN AND EASTERN RAILROADS AND STEAMBOATS, giving Guests every possible facility and convenience of rapid and economical transfer from all points.

☞ **UNEQUALED BY ANY HOTEL IN BOSTON.**

Isaac N. Andrews, Manager.   TILLY HAYNES, Proprietor.

AMERICAN

HOUSE,

BOSTON.

This Hotel, which in spaciousness, convenience of arrangement, and liberality of appointments, is unequaled in the city, is *centrally located*, and has an established reputation for the *uniform excellence* of its table, the *cleanliness and comfort of its rooms*, and careful attention to details so essential in a FIRST-CLASS HOTEL.

$2.50, $3.00, and $3.50 per Day.

LEWIS RICE & SON.

CATSKILL MOUNTAIN HOUSE.

1824.   **57th SEASON.**   **1880.**

Situated on the Catskill Mountains, *eight miles west of the Hudson River, and twelve miles from the Village of Catskill, N. Y.* Elevation, 2,700 feet. Commands a view of 10,000 square miles of the Valley of the Hudson. Accommodates 400 guests. Open June 1st to October 1st. Send for circular. Regular line of stages and carriages from Catskill Landing.

Address   CATSKILL MOUNTAIN HOUSE CO., CATSKILL, N. Y.

THE WEST POINT HOTEL,

AT WEST POINT, NEW YORK.

THE ONLY HOTEL ON THE POST.

ALBERT H. CRANEY.

THE GREAT

SALINE

APERIENT.

TARRANT'S
EFFERVESCENT SELTZER APERIENT

For THIRTY YEARS has received the favorable recommendation of the Public, and been

Used and prescribed by the First Physicians in the Land

AS THE

BEST REMEDY KNOWN

FOR

Sick-Headache, Nervous Headache, Dyspepsia, Sour Stomach, Bilious Headache, Dizziness, Costiveness, Loss of Appetite, Gout, Indigestion, Torpidity of the Liver, Gravel, Rheumatic Affections, Piles, Heartburn, Sea-Sickness, Bilious Attacks, Fevers, etc., etc.

For Travelers by Sea and Land, for Females in Delicate Health, for Persons of Sedentary Habits, for Physicians in charge of Hospitals, for Soldiers, for Sailors, for Masters of Vessels, especially all going to Hot Climates, the

SELTZER APERIENT IS AN INVALUABLE COMPANION.

SUFFERERS FROM LATE SUPPERS, SUFFERERS FROM ABUSE OF LIQUORS, SUFFERERS FROM EXCESSES OF ANY KIND, WILL FIND IN THE

Seltzer Aperient a Cooling, Refreshing, and Invigorating Draught.

It is in the form of a Powder, carefully put up in bottles, to keep in any climate, and merely requires water poured upon it to produce a delightful effervescent beverage.

Manufactured only by

TARRANT & CO.

278 Greenwich St.,

Cor. Warren, NEW YORK,

And for sale by Druggists generally.

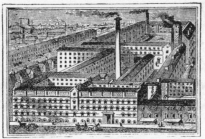

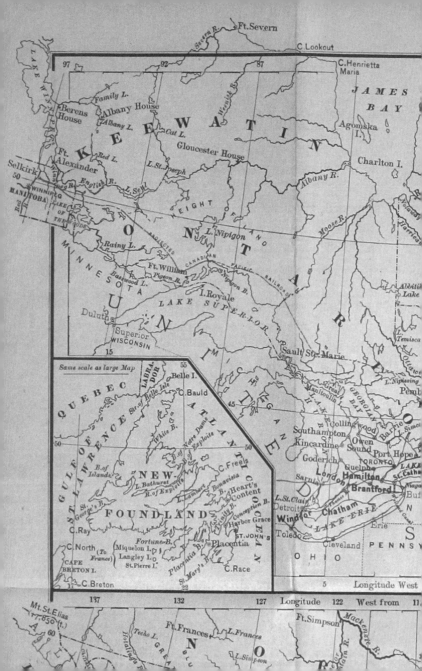

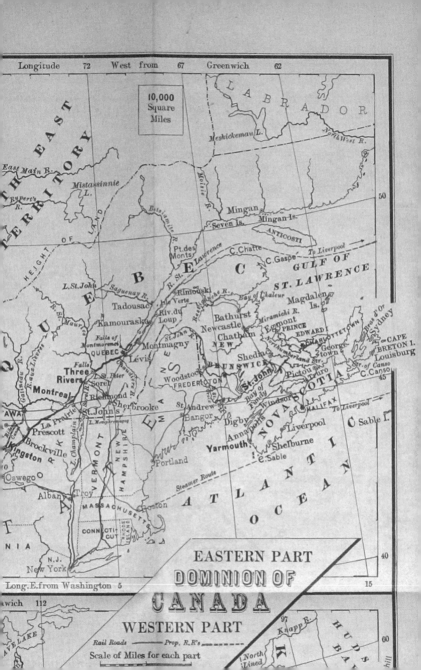

EASTERN PART
DOMINION OF
CANADA
WESTERN PART

Rail Roads ——— *Prop. R.R's* ————

Scale of Miles for each part

100   200

MASSACHUSETTS
Boston
CONNECTICUT
N.J.
New York

Long. E. from Washington 5   15

40

ich 112

HUDSON BAY

KEEWATIN

Knapp R.

North Lined Lake

Seal R.

Button's Bay

Ft. Churchill

C. Churchill

Churchill R.

Ft. York

Nelson R.

Split L.

Nelson L.

Moose R.

Jack L.

Norway House

Jack L.

Family L.

Berens House

LAKE WINNIPEG

Lake St. Martin

Ft. Alexander

Winnipeg R.

Ft. Chippewyan
ATHABASCA LAKE
Ft. Fond du Lac

WOLLASTON LAKE

DEER LAKE

Deer Lake House

La Loche Portage

Ft. Mithy

Buffalo L.

Missinippi or English R.

INDIAN LAKE

W E S T

B R I T I S H

Athabasca R.

ASSINIBOINES & CHIPPEWYANS

St. Paul

Victoria

Ft. Pitt

North Saskatchewan R.

Ft. Edmonton

Edmonton

CANADIAN

Battle R.

BATTLEFORD

PACIFIC RAILROAD

Buffalo L.

STONE INDIANS

Red Deer R.

Arrow R.

BLACKFEET

Red Deer R.

South Saskatchewan R.

Bow R.

Head

PIEGAN INDIANS

Nest Pass

Belly R.

Ft. Hamilton

Boundary Pass

Milk R.

Pass

M E O N T A N A

CYPRESS HILLS

WOOD MT.

Cumberland House

Saskatchewan R.

Ft. à la Corne

Ft. Carleton

Red Deer R.

PORCUPINE MTS.

L. La Rouge

Pine L.

Moose L.

Cedar L.

Ft. Pelly

Winnipegoosis Lake

Manitoba Lake

TOUCHWOOD HILLS

Long L.

Qu'appelle R.

Assiniboine R.

Ft. Ellice

CREE INDIANS

Chaplin Lakes

Souris R.

Portage la Prairie

WINNIPEG

Selkirk

Garry

MANITOBA

Dufferin

Emerson

Pembina R.

Pembina

U N I T E D   S T A T E S

DAKOTA

Missouri R.

shington   35   30   25

60

55

50

97

TON & CO., 1879.

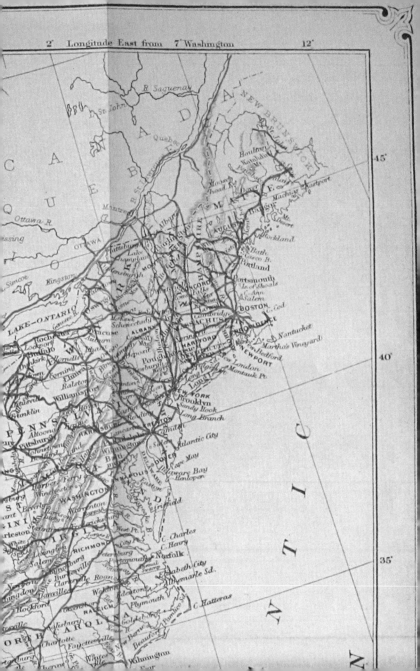

45°

40°

35°

R. Saguenay

St. John

CANADA

NEW BRUNSWICK

Quebec

Ottawa R.

OTTAWA

Kingston

LAKE—ONTARIO

Rochester

Lockport
Buffalo
Dunkirk

Cornell
Elmira
Ralston

Williamsport

PENNSYLVANIA
Altoona
Pittsburgh
Johnstown

VIRGINIA

WASHINGTON
Warrenton

RICHMOND
Petersburg
Norfolk

Portsmouth
Elizabeth City
Albemarle Sd.
Plymouth

RALEIGH
Goldsboro
Pamlico
C. Hatteras
Beaufort

CAROLINA
Charlotte
Fayetteville

Wilmington

MAINE
Houlton

Bangor
Machias
Eastport

AUGUSTA
Rockland
Bath
Casco B.
Portland
Portsmouth
Salem
BOSTON C. Cod
Cambridge
MASSACHUSETTS
Nantucket
Martha's Vineyard
New Bedford
NEWPORT
New London
Montauk Pt.
HARTFORD
Poughkeepsie
Long Island

NEW YORK
Brooklyn
Sandy Hook
Long Branch

Trenton
Atlantic City
Cape May
Delaware Bay
Henlopen

DELAWARE
MARYLAND

C. Charles
C. Henry

CONCORD
NEW HAMPSHIRE
VERMONT
Lake Champlain
Plattsburgh

Montreal
Albany
Schenectady
Syracuse
Auburn

ATLANTIC

OCEAN

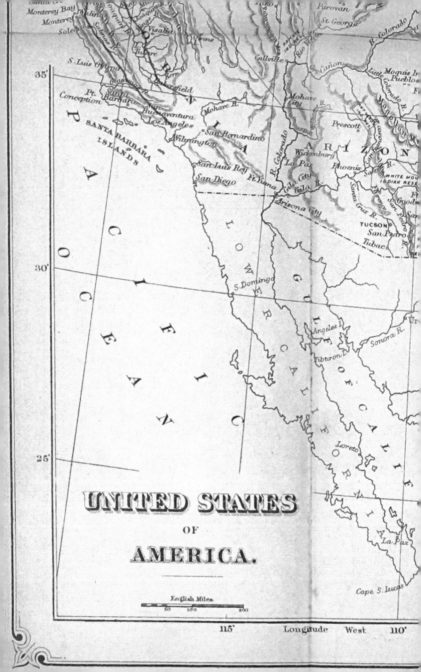

UNITED STATES

OF

AMERICA.

English Miles
50   100   200